Juvenile Justice

Ninth Edition

Juvenile Justice

A Guide to Theory, Policy, and Practice

Ninth Edition

Steven M. Cox
Western Illinois University

Jennifer M. Allen
University of North Georgia

Robert D. Hanser
University of Louisiana at Monroe

John J. Conrad

Los Angeles | London | New Delhi
Singapore | Washington DC | Melbourne

FOR INFORMATION:

SAGE Publications, Inc.
2455 Teller Road
Thousand Oaks, California 91320
E-mail: order@sagepub.com

SAGE Publications Ltd.
1 Oliver's Yard
55 City Road
London EC1Y 1SP
United Kingdom

SAGE Publications India Pvt. Ltd.
B 1/I 1 Mohan Cooperative Industrial Area
Mathura Road, New Delhi 110 044
India

SAGE Publications Asia-Pacific Pte. Ltd.
3 Church Street
#10-04 Samsung Hub
Singapore 049483

Acquisitions Editor: Jessica Miller
Editorial Assistant: Jennifer Rubio
Content Development Editor: Laura Kirkhuff
Production Editor: Tracy Buyan
Copy Editor: Mark Bast
Typesetter: C&M Digitals (P) Ltd.
Proofreader: Tricia Currie-Knight
Indexer: Michael Ferreira
Cover Designer: Candice Harman
Marketing Manager: Amy Lammers

Printed in the United States of America

Library of Congress Cataloging-in-Publication Data

Names: Cox, Steven M., author.

Title: Juvenile justice : a guide to theory, policy, and practice / Steven M. Cox, [and three others].

Description: Ninth edition. | Thousand Oaks : SAGE, [2018] | Includes bibliographical references and index.

Identifiers: LCCN 2017018236 | ISBN 9781506349008 (pbk. : alk. paper)

Subjects: LCSH: Juvenile justice, Administration of—United States.

Classification: LCC HV9104 .C63 2018 | DDC 364.360973—dc23
LC record available at https://lccn.loc.gov/2017018236

This book is printed on acid-free paper.

19 20 21 10 9 8 7 6 5 4

Contents

Detailed Contents

Preface

Since we wrote the first version of this text almost 40 years ago, the juvenile justice system has undergone dramatic and nearly constant change. The pace of this change has been rapid, and the changes have sometimes been confusing. For some time, those who believed that the system "coddled" juveniles were successful in convincing legislators in a variety of jurisdictions that juveniles who committed serious offenses should be treated as adults. More recently, those who believe that treatment and education are better alternatives for most juveniles with problems have established restorative justice programs and other intermediate sanctions as alternatives, or additions, to official processing. Use of the death penalty for juveniles under the age of 18 has been eliminated, although violent crime committed by juveniles, which had declined for a decade beginning in the mid-1990s, remains an issue, and concern with juvenile gangs persists. In addition, increased concerns in the development of school-based programs, victimization on school property, bullying, cyberbullying, and police bias have been pushed to the forefront of issues facing juveniles. New programs promising to be more effective and efficient have been initiated, and older programs have largely disappeared. There has been an increased reliance on evidence-based practices, and demands for accountability for juvenile justice programs have increased with a focus on performance evaluation measures. Globalization has emerged as an issue in juvenile justice in the past several years with the focus on gang activity and child protection (e.g., illegal immigration and sex trafficking) along and across international borders. What sense, if any, can we make of these changes, and what are their implications for policy and practice in juvenile justice?

As both practitioners in the juvenile justice network and instructors in criminology, criminal justice, and sociology courses, we have time and again heard, "That's great in theory, but what about in practice?" We remain convinced that a basic understanding of the interrelationships among notions of causation, procedural requirements, and professional practices is a must if one is to understand, let alone practice in, the juvenile justice system.

With these concerns in mind, we have attempted to write a text that is reader-friendly and comprehensive yet concise. As we revised the text for this new edition, these concerns remain. We have expanded discussions, added contemporary material and examples, and updated reference and legal materials throughout the text. In addition, we have continued to make use of materials and resources available through the Internet.

Approach

In this text, we integrate juvenile law, theories of causation, and procedural requirements while examining their interrelationships. We have attempted to make our treatment of these issues both relevant and comprehensible to those who are actively employed in the juvenile justice network, to those who desire to become so employed, and to those whose interest in juvenile justice is more or less academic. We address the juvenile justice system as a composite of interacting individuals whose everyday decisions have very real consequences for others involved in the network. The day-to-day practical aspects of the system are discussed in terms of theoretical considerations and procedural requirements.

- This approach allows us to examine the interrelationships among practitioners, offenders, victims, witnesses, and others involved with delinquency, abuse, neglect, and other varieties of behavior under the jurisdiction of the juvenile court.

- The roles of practitioners in the system are discussed in relationship to one another and with respect to discretion, politics, and societal concerns. Thus, the police, juvenile probation officers, and social service agents all have roles to play in providing services for juveniles with problems. Unless each contributes, the system is likely to be ineffective in dealing with these problems.

- The law, of course, plays a key role in juvenile justice, and we have attempted to present the most recent and important changes in juvenile law based on an overview of a number of states.

- What we know about theories of behavior should dictate the procedures and treatments employed in dealing with juveniles. To ignore theory is to ignore possible explanations for behavior, and treatment is likely to be ineffective if explanations of behavior are lacking. Thus, we spend time discussing theories of behavior and their importance in juvenile justice.

In the following pages, we define technical terms clearly where they are presented, and we have included numerous practical examples—which we call In Practice boxes—in an attempt to present readers with a basic understanding of both the theoretical and practical aspects of the juvenile justice system. These real-world In Practice boxes are designed to help students connect theory and practice and to focus on a number of critical issues.

The Ninth Edition

In this edition you will find numerous substantive changes:

- New chapter opening "What Would You Do?" scenarios that help students get into the mindset of a practitioner

- "Questions to Consider" in chapter boxed features to help students make the connection between the material presented and the chapter content

- New legislation and court rulings related to juveniles

- Expanded coverage of critical topics in juvenile justice such as the school-to-prison pipeline, drug use, firearm homicide, social media usage, solitary confinement, bullying, cyberbullying, day reporting centers, specialty courts, restorative justice programs, and LGBTQ youth

- Nearly half of the In Practice features have been updated with new examples to demonstrate what it's like to work in juvenile justice today

- Updated references

- Coverage of current concerns and recent trends in juvenile justice

- Expanded discussion of theory, including biosocial and neurological theories, sometimes referred to as neurocriminology

- Discussion of recent changes in juvenile codes from a variety of states

- Expanded discussion of gangs, including females in gangs

- Discussion of juvenile justice from an international perspective

- An updated view of the future of juvenile justice

Pedagogical Aids

To enhance learning, we have included the following:

- New What Would You Do scenarios that serve as an introduction at the beginning of each chapter

- In Practice boxes to help students see the practical applications of what they are reading

- Career Opportunity boxes

- Lists of key terms and end-of-chapter summaries to help students prepare for exams

- End-of-chapter Critical Thinking Questions to encourage students to go beyond memorization of terms and concepts in their learning

- Suggested Readings lists for students who are interested in reading more information on the topics discussed in the respective chapters

- A glossary of terms commonly used in juvenile justice, as well as in this textbook, to assist students in learning the "language" of the system

Digital Resources

Additional ancillary materials further support and enhance the learning goals of *Juvenile Justice*.

SAGE edge offers a robust online environment featuring an impressive array of tools and resources for review, study, and further exploration, keeping both instructors and students on the cutting edge of teaching and learning. Learn more at edge.sagepub.com/coxjj9e.

Instructor Teaching Site

SAGE edge for Instructors supports your teaching by making it easy to integrate quality content and create a rich learning environment for students. A password-protected site, available at edge.sagepub.com/coxjj9e, features resources designed to help instructors plan and teach their courses. These resources include an extensive test bank, chapter-specific PowerPoint presentations, lecture notes, sample syllabi for semester and quarter courses, class activities, video and web resources, SAGE journal articles, and answers to the "Questions to Consider" in chapter boxed features.

Student Study Site

SAGE edge for Students provides a personalized approach to help you accomplish your coursework goals in an easy-to-use learning environment. An open-access student study site is available at edge.sagepub.com/coxjj9e. This site provides access to video and web resources, and SAGE journal articles, as well as several study tools including eFlashcards, web quizzes, web exercises, and state supplements.

Acknowledgments

Over the years, contributions to the book have come from many people. We provide continued thanks to William P. McCamey, Giri Raj Gupta, Dennis C. Bliss, Terry Campbell, Robert J. Fischer, and Courtney Cox for their encouragement and assistance. Additionally, with this edition, Jennifer Allen and Robert Hanser would like to acknowledge and express our sincerest thanks to John J. Conrad, who will be forever remembered as a founding author for the book, and Steven M. Cox, who decided not to write in this edition but has been a mentor and friend for many years. Without the two of them the book would not have been possible. Jennifer and Rob are forever grateful.

We also thank the following reviewers of the manuscript for their many helpful suggestions:

Heather Y. Bersot, Department of Criminal Justice and Criminology, University of North Carolina at Charlotte

E. A. Brockett, Texas State University

Rita Hayes, Public Safety & Human Services, College of Southern Nevada

Lindsey Livingston Runell, Kutztown University, Department of Criminal Justice

Arthur G. Vasquez, University of Texas at Arlington

Lacey N. Wallace, Penn State Altoona

Juvenile Justice in Historical Perspective

1

On completion of this chapter, students should be able to do the following:

- Understand the history of juvenile justice in the United States
- Understand contemporary challenges to the juvenile justice system
- Discuss the controversy between due process and informality in juvenile justice
- Recognize discrepancies between the ideal and real juvenile justice systems
- Recount some of the reforms occurring in the juvenile justice system

WHAT WOULD YOU DO?

On a warm summer night at approximately 8:30 p.m., Matt, a 12-year-old, and Bo, an 11-year-old, entered a mobile home on an overgrown lot that they thought was abandoned. Once inside, the two boys rummaged through the drawers and closets in the home, working their way from the kitchen to the back bedroom. In the back bedroom, they were shocked to find a disabled man lying on the bed. He was missing the bottom half of both legs and was asleep. Before the boys could turn and leave the room he woke up and began shouting at them. He said he was going to shoot them and call the police. He produced a gun and aimed it at Matt. Matt lunged at the man and started wrestling the gun from his hands. Bo also jumped on top of the man and started hitting and kicking him.

After several minutes of punching and kicking, the boys stopped to find the man bloody and nonresponsive. Matt and Bo panicked and left the trailer. The man, who had become disabled during a military tour in Afghanistan, was found the next day by his daughter and was transported to a medical center. He is not expected to live. The police took Matt and Bo into custody a week after the incident based on eyewitness testimony that they were seen in the area at the time of the assault. Both are claiming the assault was self-defense, although they admit to breaking into and entering the home. Nothing was missing from the home as a result of the break-in, and only a few minor damages were recorded to the home (e.g., broken door lock, broken items in a closet).

(Continued)

The juvenile justice network in the United States grew out of, and remains embroiled in, controversy. More than a century after the creation of the first family court in Illinois (1899), the debate continues as to the goals to be pursued and the procedures to be employed within the network, and a considerable gap between theory and practice remains. During the early part of the 21st century, concern over delinquency in general, and violent delinquents in particular, grew while confidence in the juvenile justice system was eroding as indicated by increasing demands for accountability on the part of system participants. In fact, as the 21st century began, Bilchik (1999a) indicated, "The reduction of juvenile crime, violence, and victimization constitutes one of the most crucial challenges of the new millennium" (p. 1). As the public continues to challenge the system and to question practices, such as confidentiality, it appears that numerous jurisdictions in the United States are reviewing the basic operations of juvenile justice and the effectiveness of system reforms.

The juvenile court is supposed to provide due process protections along with care, treatment, and rehabilitation for juveniles while protecting society. Violence committed by juveniles, which some suggest occurs in cycles (Johnson, 2006), has attracted nationwide attention and raised a host of questions concerning the juvenile court, even though such violence has actually declined significantly during the past decade. Can a court designed to protect and care for juveniles deal successfully with those who, seemingly without reason, kill their peers and parents? Is the juvenile justice network too "soft" in its dealings with such juveniles? Is the "get-tough" approach adopted over the past two decades what is needed to deal with violent adolescents? Was the juvenile court really designed to deal with the types of offenders we see today?

Although due process for juveniles (discussed in detail later but consisting of things such as the right to counsel and the right to remain silent), protection of society, and rehabilitation of youthful offenders remain elusive goals, frustration and dissatisfaction among those who work in the juvenile justice system, as well as among those who assess its effectiveness, remain the reality. Some observers have called for an end to juvenile justice as a separate system in the United States. Others maintain that the juvenile court and associated agencies and programs have a good deal to offer juveniles in trouble. Here are two examples of the latter position:

How times have changed for the Texas juvenile justice system. Five years ago the number of youths locked up in state-run detention centers was about 4,700. Since then, the number has dropped steadily. Now, it's less than 1,500. "We've come a long way," said Benet Magnuson, policy attorney at the advocacy group Texas Criminal Justice Coalition. "Thanks to a series of reforms, we've taken many kids out of state-run facilities and keep them closer to their homes where they are helped or rehabilitated." (Rangel, 2012, p. 1)

Juvenile justice is transforming throughout America. Though there is a long road ahead to reform these systems into effective, rehabilitative programs that no longer make children worse, there is great promise in jurisdictions across the country, that are changing how they work with youth. (Muhammad, 2012, p. 1)

The Juvenile Court Building, at Ewing and Halsted in Chicago in 1907, is shown. As noted in this chapter, the first family court in the United States was in Cook County, Illinois.

During the 1990s, fear of juvenile crime led the public to demand that legislators enact increasingly severe penalties for young offenders. Fanton (2006), in discussing the juvenile justice network in Illinois, concluded that "by the end of the 20th century the line between the Illinois juvenile justice and criminal justice systems was hopelessly blurred, reflecting a national trend" (p. A5). As Snyder and Sickmund (2006) pointed out, however, America's youth face a constantly changing set of problems and barriers to successful lives. As a result, juvenile justice practitioners are constantly challenged to develop enlightened policies and programs based on facts, not fears. With this in mind, Brown (2012) noted that over the past decade, juvenile crime rates have actually declined, and she found that state legislatures are reexamining and frequently revising juvenile justice policies and approaches. Sickmund and Puzzanchera (2014) noted similar findings with juvenile arrest rates falling proportionately more than adult arrest rates from 2001 to 2010, across most offenses. As a result of falling crime rates, the National District Attorneys Association (2016) stated in the 3rd edition of their *National Prosecution Standards* that the transfer of cases to criminal court should be reserved for the most serious, violent, and chronic offenders. They also found that states are responding to Supreme Court rulings on life imprisonment, the death penalty, and other issues.

The question remains: Can what actually occurs and what ideally should occur in the juvenile justice system be made more consistent? What can be done to bring about such consistency? What are the consequences of a lack of consistency? A brief look at the history of juvenile justice and a detailed look at the system as it currently operates should help us answer these questions.

Juvenile Justice Historically

The distinction between youthful and adult offenders coincides with the beginning of recorded history. Some 4,000 years ago, the Code of Hammurabi (2270 BC) discussed runaways, children who disowned their parents, and sons who cursed their fathers. Approximately 2,000 years ago, both Roman civil law and later canon (church) law made distinctions between juveniles and adults based on the notion of age of responsibility. In ancient Jewish law, the Talmud specified conditions under which immaturity was to be considered in imposing punishment. There was no corporal punishment prior to puberty, which was considered to be the age of 12 years for females and 13 years for males. No capital punishment was to be imposed for those under 20 years of age. Similar leniency was found among Muslims, where children under the age of 17 years were typically exempt from the death penalty (Bernard, 1992).

By the 5th century BC, codification of Roman law resulted in the Twelve Tables, which made it clear that children were criminally responsible for violations of law and were to be dealt with by the criminal justice system (Nyquist, 1960). Punishment for some offenses, however, was less severe for children than for adults. For example, theft of crops by night was a capital offense for adults, but offenders under the age of puberty were only to be flogged. Adults caught in the act of theft were subject to flogging and enslavement to the victims, but children received only corporal punishment at the discretion of a magistrate and were required to make restitution (Ludwig, 1955). Originally, only those children who were incapable of speech were spared under Roman law, but eventually immunity was afforded to all children under the age of 7 as the law came to reflect an increasing recognition of the stages of life. Children came to be classified as *infans*, *proximus infantia*, and *proximus pubertati*. In general, infants were not held criminally responsible, but those approaching puberty who knew the difference between right and wrong were held accountable. In the 5th century AD, the age of *infantia* was fixed at 7 years, and children under that age were exempt from criminal liability. The legal age of puberty was fixed at 14 years for boys and 12 years for girls, and older children were held criminally liable. For children age 7 through puberty, liability was based on the capacity to understand the difference between right and wrong (Bernard, 1992).

Roman and canon law undoubtedly influenced early Anglo-Saxon common law (law based on custom or use), which emerged in England during the 11th and 12th centuries. For our purposes, the distinctions made between adult and juvenile offenders in England at this time are most significant. Under common law, children under the age of 7 were presumed to be incapable of forming criminal intent and, therefore, were not subject to criminal sanctions. Children ages 7 to 14 years were not subject to criminal sanctions unless it could be demonstrated that they had formed criminal intent, understood the consequences of their actions, and could distinguish right from wrong (Blackstone, 1803, pp. 22–24). Children over the age of 14 were treated much the same as adults.

The question of when and under what circumstances children are capable of forming criminal intent (*mens rea*, or "guilty mind") remains a point of contention in juvenile justice proceedings today. For an adult to commit criminal homicide, for instance, it must be shown not only that the adult took the life of another human without justification but also that he or she *intended* to take the life of that individual. One may take the life of another accidentally (without intending to do so), and such an act is not regarded as criminal homicide. In other words, it takes more than the commission of an illegal act to produce a crime. Intent is also required (and, in fact, in some cases it is assumed as a result of the seriousness of the act, e.g., felony murder statutes).

But at what age is a child capable of understanding the differences between right and wrong or of comprehending the consequences of his or her acts before they occur? For example, most of us would not regard a 4-year-old who pocketed some money found at a neighbor's house as a criminal because we are confident that the child cannot understand the consequences of this act. But what about an 8- or 9- or 12-year-old?

Another important step in the history of juvenile justice occurred during the 15th century when chancery, or equity, courts were created by the king of England. Chancery courts, under the guidance of the king's chancellor, were created to consider petitions of those who were in need of special aid or intervention, such as women and children left in need of protection and aid by reason of divorce, death of a spouse, or abandonment, and to grant relief to such persons. Through the chancery courts, the king exercised the right of *parens patriae* ("parent of the country") by enabling these courts to act *in loco parentis* ("in the place of parents") to provide necessary services for the benefit of women and children (Bynum & Thompson, 1992). In other words, the king, as ruler of his country, was to assume responsibility for all of those under his rule, to provide parental care for children who had no parents, and to assist women who required aid for any of the reasons just mentioned. Although chancery courts did not normally deal with youthful offenders, they did deal with dependent or neglected children, as do juvenile courts in the United States today. The principle of parens patriae later became central to the development of the juvenile court in America and today generally refers to the fact that the state (government) has ultimate parental authority over juveniles in need of protection or guidance. In certain cases, then, the state may act in loco parentis and make decisions concerning the best interests of children. This includes removing children from the home of their parents when circumstances warrant.

In 1562, Parliament passed the Statute of Artificers, which stated that children of paupers could be involuntarily separated from their parents and apprenticed to others (Rendleman, 1974, p. 77). Similarly, the Poor Relief Act of 1601 provided for involuntary separation of children from impoverished parents, and these children were then placed in bondage to local residents as apprentices. Both statutes were based on the belief that the state has a primary interest in the welfare of children and the right to ensure such welfare. At the same time, a system known as the City Custom of Apprentices operated in London. The system was established to settle disputes involving apprentices who were unruly or abused by their masters in an attempt to punish the appropriate parties. When an apprentice was found to be at fault and required confinement, he or she was segregated from adult offenders. Those in charge of the City Custom of Apprentices attempted to settle disputes in a confidential fashion so that the juveniles involved were not subjected to public shame or stigma (Sanders, 1974, pp. 46–47).

Throughout the 1600s and most of the 1700s, juvenile offenders in England were sent to adult prisons—although they were at times kept separate from adult offenders. The Hospital of St. Michael's, the first institution for the treatment of juvenile offenders, was established in Rome in 1704 by Pope Clement XI. The stated purpose of the hospital was to correct and instruct unruly juveniles so that they might become useful citizens (Griffin & Griffin, 1978, p. 7).

The first private separate institution for youthful offenders in England was established by Robert Young in 1788. The goal of this institution was "to educate and instruct in some useful trade or occupation the children of convicts or such other infant poor as [were] engaged in a vagrant and criminal course of life" (Sanders, 1974, p. 48).

During the early 1800s, changes in the criminal code that would have allowed English magistrates to hear cases of youthful offenders without the necessity of long delays were recommended. In addition, dependent or neglected children were to be appointed legal guardians who were to aid the children through care and education (Sanders, 1974, p. 49). These changes were rejected by the House of Lords due to the opposition to the magistrates becoming "judges, juries, and executioners" and due to suspicion concerning the recommended confidentiality of the proceedings, which would have excluded the public and the press (pp. 50–51).

Meanwhile in the United States, dissatisfaction with the way young offenders were being handled was increasing. As early as 1825, the Society for the Prevention of Juvenile Delinquency advocated separating juvenile and adult offenders (Snyder & Sickmund, 1999). Up to this point, youthful offenders had been generally subjected to the same penalties as adults, and little or no attempt was made to separate juveniles from adults in jails or prisons. This caused a good deal of concern among reformers who feared that criminal attitudes and knowledge would be passed from the adults to the juveniles. Another concern centered on the possibility of brutality directed by the adults toward juveniles. Although many juveniles were being imprisoned, few appeared to benefit from the experience. Others simply appealed to the sympathy of jurors to escape the consequences of their acts entirely. With no alternative to imprisonment, juries and juvenile justice officials were inclined to respond emotionally and sympathetically to the plight of children, often causing them to overlook juvenile misdeeds or render lenient verdicts (Dorne & Gewerth, 1998, p. 4).

In 1818, a New York City committee on pauperism gave the term *juvenile delinquency* its first public recognition by referring to it as a major cause of pauperism (Drowns & Hess, 1990, p. 9). As a result of this increasing recognition of the problem of delinquency, several institutions for juveniles were established from 1824 to 1828. These institutions were oriented toward education and treatment rather than punishment, although whippings, long periods of silence, and loss of rewards were used to punish the uncooperative. In addition, strict regimentation and a strong work ethic philosophy were common.

Under the concept of in loco parentis, institutional custodians acted as parental substitutes with far-reaching powers over their charges. In doing so, the house of refuge became common, as a charitable effort to provide shelter and safety to destitute youth. For example, the staff members of the New York House of Refuge, established in 1825, were able to bind out wards as apprentices, although the consent of the child involved was required. Whether such consent was voluntary is questionable given that the alternatives were likely unpleasant. The New York House of Refuge was soon followed by others in Boston and Philadelphia (Abadinsky & Winfree, 1992).

"By the mid-1800s, houses of refuge were enthusiastically declared a great success. Managers even advertised their houses in magazines for youth. Managers took great pride in seemingly turning total misfits into productive, hard-working members of society" (Simonsen & Gordon, 1982, p. 23). However, these claims of success were not undisputed, and by 1850 it was widely recognized that houses of refuge were largely failures when it came to rehabilitating delinquents and had become much like prisons. Simonsen and Gordon (1982) stated, "In 1849 the New York City police chief publicly warned that the numbers of vicious and vagrant youth were increasing and that something must be done. And done it was. America moved from a time of houses of refuge into a time of preventive agencies and reform schools" (p. 23).

In Illinois, the Chicago Reform School Act was passed in 1855, followed in 1879 by the establishment of industrial schools for dependent children. These schools were not unanimously approved, as indicated by the fact that in 1870 the Illinois Supreme Court declared unconstitutional the commitment of a child to the Chicago Reform School as a restraint

World History Archive / Alamy Stock Photo

Founded in 1843 in Hampstead Road, Birmingham, and known as the Brook-Street Ragged and Industrial School, this was an early reform school.

on liberty without proof of crime and without conviction for an offense (*People ex rel. O'Connell v. Turner*, 1870). In 1888, the provisions of the Illinois Industrial School Act were also held to be unconstitutional, although the courts had ruled previously (1882) that the state had the right, under parens patriae, to "divest a child of liberty" by sending him or her to an industrial school if no other "lawful protector" could be found (*Petition of Ferrier*, 1882). In spite of good intentions, the new reform schools, existing in both England and the United States by the 1850s, were not effective in reducing the incidence of delinquency. Despite early enthusiasm among reformers, there was little evidence that rehabilitation was being accomplished. Piscotta's (1982) investigation of the effects of the 19th-century parens patriae doctrine led him to conclude that, although inmates sometimes benefited from their incarceration and reformatories were not complete failures in achieving their objectives (whatever those were), the available evidence showed that the state was not a benevolent parent. In short, there was significant disparity between the promise and practice of parens patriae.

> Discipline was seldom "parental" in nature; inmate workers were exploited under the contract labor system, religious instruction was often disguised proselytization, and the indenture system generally failed to provide inmates with a home in the country. The frequency of escapes, assaults, incendiary incidents, and homosexual relations suggests that the children were not separated from the corrupting influence of improper associates. (Piscotta, 1982, pp. 424–425)

The failures of reform schools increased interest in the legality of the proceedings that allowed juveniles to be placed in such institutions. During the last half of the 19th century, there were a number of court challenges concerning the legality of failure to provide due process for youthful offenders. Some indicated that due process was required before incarceration (imprisonment) could occur, and others argued that due process was unnecessary because the intent of the proceedings was not punishment but rather treatment. In other words, juveniles were presumably being processed by the courts in their own "best interests."

During the post–Civil War period, an era of humanitarian concern emerged, focusing on children laboring in sweatshops, coal mines, and factories. These children, and others who were abandoned, orphaned, or viewed as criminally responsible, were a cause of alarm to reformist "child savers." The child-savers movement, which emerged in the United States in the 19th century, included philanthropists, middle-class reformers, and professionals who exhibited a genuine concern for the welfare of children and who stressed the value of rehabilitation and prevention through education and training. In the 20th century, these reformers continued to seek ways to mitigate the roots of delinquency and were largely responsible for the creation of the first juvenile court in the United States. During the late 1800s, several states (Massachusetts in 1874 and New York in 1892) passed laws providing for separate trials for juveniles, but the first juvenile or family court did not appear until 1899 in Cook County, Illinois. "The delinquent child had ceased to be a criminal and had the status of a child in need of care, protection, and discipline directed toward rehabilitation" (Cavan, 1969, p. 362).

The Progressive Era in the United States from 1900 to 1918 was a time of extensive social reform. Reforms included the growth of the women's suffrage movement, the campaign against child labor, and the fight for the 8-hour workday, among others. Concurrent with this era and extending was the era of socialized juvenile justice in the United States (Faust & Brantingham, 1974). During this era, children were considered not as miniature adults but rather as persons with less than fully developed morality and cognition (Snyder & Sickmund, 1999). Emphasis on the legal rights of the juvenile declined, and emphasis on determining how and why the juvenile came to the attention of the authorities and how best to treat and rehabilitate the juvenile became primary. The focus was clearly on offenders rather than the offenses they committed. Prevention and removal of the juvenile from undesirable social situations were the major concerns of the court. Faust and Brantingham (1974) noted the following:

The blindfold was, therefore, purposefully removed from the eyes of "justice" so that the total picture of the child's past experiences and existing circumstances could be judicially perceived and weighed against the projected outcomes of alternative courses of legal intervention. (p. 145)

By incorporating the doctrine of parens patriae, the juvenile court was to act in the best interests of children through the use of noncriminal proceedings. The basic philosophy contained in the first juvenile court act reinforced the right of the state to act in loco parentis in cases involving children who had violated the law or were neglected, dependent, or otherwise in need of intervention or supervision. This philosophy changed the nature of the relationship between juveniles and the state by recognizing that juveniles were not simply miniature adults but rather children who could perhaps be served best through education and treatment. By 1917, juvenile court legislation had been passed in all but three states, and by 1932, there were more than 600 independent juvenile courts in the United States. By 1945, all states had passed legislation creating separate juvenile courts.

It seems likely that the developers of the juvenile justice network in the United States intended legal intervention to be provided under the rules of civil law rather than criminal law. Clearly, they intended legal proceedings to be as informal as possible given that only through suspending the prohibition against hearsay and relying on the preponderance of evidence could the "total picture" of the juvenile be developed. The juvenile court exercised considerable discretion in dealing with the problems of youth and moved further and further from the ideas of legality, corrections, and punishment and toward the ideas of prevention, treatment, and rehabilitation. This movement was, however, not unopposed. There were those who felt that the notion of informality was greatly abused and that any semblance of legality had been lost. The trial-and-error methods often employed during this era made guinea pigs out of juveniles who were placed in rehabilitation programs, which were often based on inadequately tested sociological and psychological theories (Faust & Brantingham, 1974, p. 149).

Nonetheless, in 1955, the U.S. Supreme Court reaffirmed the desirability of the informal procedures employed in juvenile courts. In deciding not to hear the *Holmes* case, the Court stated that because juvenile courts are not criminal courts, the constitutional rights guaranteed to accused adults do not apply to juveniles (*In re Holmes*, 1955).

Then, in the *Kent* case of 1961, 16-year-old Morris Kent Jr. was charged with rape and robbery. Kent confessed, and the judge waived his case to criminal court based on what he verbally described as a "full investigation." Kent was found guilty and sentenced to 30 to 90 years in prison. His lawyer argued that the waiver was invalid, but appellate courts rejected the argument. He then appealed to the U.S. Supreme Court, arguing that the judge had not made a complete investigation and that Kent was denied his constitutional rights because he was a juvenile. The Court ruled that the waiver was invalid and that Kent was entitled to a hearing that included the essentials of due process or fair treatment required by the Fourteenth Amendment. In other words, Kent or his counsel should have had access to all records involved in making the decision to waive the case, and

Life in the reform schools of the 19th century was not easy.

the judge should have provided written reasons for the waiver. Although the decision involved only District of Columbia courts, its implications were far-reaching by referring to the fact that juveniles might be receiving the worst of both worlds—less legal protection than adults and less treatment and rehabilitation than that promised by the juvenile courts (*Kent v. United States*, 1966).

In 1967, forces opposing the extreme informality of the juvenile court won a major victory when the U.S. Supreme Court handed down a decision in the case of Gerald Gault, a juvenile from Arizona. The extreme license taken by members of the juvenile justice network became abundantly clear in the *Gault* case. Gault, while a 15-year-old in 1964, was accused of making an obscene phone call to a neighbor who identified him. The neighbor did not appear at the adjudicatory hearing, and it was never demonstrated that Gault had, in fact, made the obscene comments. Still, Gault was sentenced to spend the remainder of his minority in a training school. Neither Gault nor his parents were notified properly of the charges against the juvenile. They were not made aware of their right to counsel, their right to confront and cross-examine witnesses, their right to remain silent, their right to a transcript of the proceedings, or their right to appeal. The Court ruled that in hearings that may result in institutional commitment, juveniles have all of these rights (*In re Gault*, 1967). The Supreme Court's decision in this case left little doubt that juvenile offenders are as entitled to the protection of constitutional guarantees as their adult counterparts, with the exception of participation in a public jury trial. In this case and in the *Kent* case, the Court raised serious questions about the concept of parens patriae, or the right of the state to informally determine the best interests of juveniles. In addition, the Court noted that the handling of both Gault and Kent raised serious issues of Fourteenth Amendment (due process) violations. The free reign of socialized juvenile justice had come to an end, at least in theory.

During the years that followed, the U.S. Supreme Court continued the trend toward requiring due process rights for juveniles. In 1970, in the *Winship* case, the Court decided that in juvenile court proceedings involving delinquency, the standard of proof for conviction should be the same as that for adults in criminal court—proof beyond a reasonable doubt (*In re Winship*, 1970). In the case of *Breed v. Jones* (1975), the Court decided that trying a juvenile who had previously been adjudicated delinquent in juvenile court for the same crime as an adult in criminal court violates the double jeopardy clause of the Fifth Amendment when the adjudication involves violation of a criminal statute. The Court did not, however, go so far as to guarantee juveniles all of the same rights as adults. In 1971, in the case of *McKeiver v. Pennsylvania*, the Court held that the due process clause of the Fourteenth Amendment did not require jury trials in juvenile court. Nonetheless, some states have extended this right to juveniles through state law.

In March 2005, in the case of *Roper v. Simmons*, the U.S. Supreme Court reversed a 1989 precedent and struck down the death penalty for crimes committed by people under the age of 18. Christopher Simmons started talking about wanting to murder someone when he was 17 years old. On more than one occasion, he discussed with friends a plan to commit a burglary, tie up the victim, and push him or her from a bridge. Based on the specified plan, he and a younger friend broke into the home of Shirley Crook. They bound and blindfolded her and then drove her to a state park, where they tied her hands and feet with electrical wire, covered her whole face with duct tape, walked her to a railroad trestle, and threw her into the river. Crook drowned as a result of the juveniles' actions. Simmons later bragged about the murder, and the crime was not difficult to solve. On being taken into custody, he confessed, and the guilt phase of the trial in Missouri state court was uncontested (Bradley, 2006). The U.S. Supreme Court held that "evolving standards of decency" govern the prohibition of cruel and unusual punishment and found that "capital punishment must be limited to those offenders who commit a narrow category of the most serious crimes and whose extreme culpability makes them the most deserving of execution" (Death Penalty Information Center, n.d.). The Court further found that there is a scientific consensus that teenagers have "an underdeveloped sense of responsibility" and that, therefore, it is unreasonable to classify them among the most culpable offenders: "From a moral standpoint, it would be misguided to equate the failings of a minor with those of an adult, for a greater possibility exists that a minor's character deficiencies will be reformed." (Death Penalty Information Center, n.d.). In addition, the Court concluded that it would be extremely difficult for jurors to distinguish between juveniles whose crimes reflect immaturity and those whose crimes reflect "irreparable corruption" (Bradley, 2006). Finally, the Court pointed out that only seven countries in the world have executed juveniles since 1990, and even those countries now disallow the juvenile death penalty. Thus, the United States was the only country to still permit it. The pros and cons of this decision are discussed in Chapter 10.

The U.S. Supreme Court also determined in *Graham v. Florida* (2010) that it is unconstitutionally cruel and unusual punishment to lock up teenagers for life without any chance of parole for nonhomicidal crimes. The Supreme Court went on to strike down mandatory life sentences without the possibility of parole for juvenile offenders in *Jackson v. Hobbs* (2011) and reaffirmed this decision in *Miller v. Alabama* (2012). Most recently, in *Montgomery v. Louisiana* (2016) the Supreme Court held that its previous ruling in *Miller v. Alabama* should be applied retroactively. This decision potentially affected up to 2,300 cases nationwide. States have responded to these rulings by allowing individuals who were sentenced as juveniles to life without parole new sentencing hearings based on certain criteria (California Senate Bill 9, 2012); by commuting sentences (Iowa); and by providing for a presentencing hearing discussing aggravating and mitigating circumstances in front of a judge before a life sentence without parole can be determined (South Dakota Senate Bill 39, 2013), among other actions in other states (Sickmund & Puzzanchera, 2014). Suffice it to say that these rulings have furthered the considerable controversy that has characterized the juvenile justice network since its inception.

Continuing Dilemmas in Juvenile Justice

Several important points need to be made concerning the contemporary juvenile justice network. First, most of the issues that led to the debates over juvenile justice were evident by the 1850s, although the violent nature of some juvenile crimes, like the one discussed in the What Would You Do? box, over the past quarter century has raised serious questions about the juvenile court's ability to handle such cases. The issue of protection and treatment rather than punishment had been clearly raised under the 15th-century chancery court system in England. The issues of criminal responsibility and separate facilities for youthful offenders were apparent in the City Custom of Apprentices in 17th-century England and again in the development of reform schools in England and the United States during the 19th century.

Second, attempts were made to develop and reform the juvenile justice network along with other changes that occurred during the 18th, 19th, and early 20th centuries. Immigration, industrialization, and urbanization had changed the face of American society. Parents working long hours left children with little supervision, child labor was an important part of economic life, and child labor laws were routinely disregarded. At the same time, however, treatment of the mentally ill was undergoing humanitarian reforms as the result of efforts by Phillipe Pinel in France and Dorothea Dix and others in the United States. The Poor Law Amendment Act had been passed in England in 1834, providing relief and medical services for the poor and needy. Later in the same century, Jane Addams sought reform for the poor in the United States. Thus, the latter part of the 18th century and all of the 19th century may be viewed as a period of transition toward humanitarianism in many areas of social life, including the reform of the juvenile justice network. It is important to note that during the second decade of the 21st century the issue of juvenile justice reform has once again become a focal point. Recent legislative trends attempt once again to distinguish juveniles from adult offenders, restore the jurisdiction of the juvenile court, and seek to adopt scientific screening and assessment tools to aid in decision making and identifying the needs of juvenile offenders. Current legislative actions attempt to increase due process protections for juveniles, reform detention policies, and address racial disparities. The U.S. Supreme Court has also played a role in recent reforms in *Roper v. Simmons* (2005), *Graham v. Florida* (2010), *Jackson v. Hobbs* (2011), *Miller v. Alabama* (2012), and *Montgomery v. Louisiana* (2016), as previously mentioned.

Third, the bases for most of the accepted attempts at explaining causes of delinquency and treating delinquents were apparent by the end of the 19th century. We discuss these attempts at explanation and treatment later in the book. At this point, it is important to note that those concerned with juvenile offenders had, by the early part of the 20th century, clearly indicated the potentially harmful effects of public exposure and were aware that association with adult offenders in prisons and jails could lead to careers in crime.

Fourth, the *Gault* decision obviated the existence of two major, and more or less competing, groups of juvenile justice practitioners and scholars. One group favors the informal, unofficial, treatment-oriented approach, referred to as a casework or therapeutic approach; the other group favors a more formal, more official, more constitutional approach, referred to as a formalistic or legalistic approach. The *Gault* decision made it clear that the legalists were on firm ground, but it did not deny the legitimacy of the casework approach. Rather, it indicated that the casework approach may be employed but only within a constitutional framework. For example, a child might be adjudicated delinquent (by proving his or her guilt beyond a reasonable doubt) but ordered to participate in psychological counseling (as a result of a presentence investigation that disclosed psychological problems).

All of these issues are very much alive today. Caseworkers continue to argue that more formal proceedings result in greater stigmatization of juveniles, possibly resulting in more negative self-concepts and eventually in careers as adult offenders. Legalists contend that innocent juveniles may be found delinquent if formal procedures are not followed and that ensuring constitutional rights does not necessarily result in greater stigmatization, even if juveniles are found to be delinquent.

Similarly, the debate over treatment versus punishment continues. On the one hand, status offenders (those committing acts that would not be violations if they were committed by adults) have been removed from the category of delinquency, in part as a result of the passage of the Juvenile Justice and Delinquency Prevention Act of 1974 (Snyder & Sickmund, 1999). Whereas severe punishments for certain violent offenses were enacted in the 1980s and 1990s and waivers to adult court for such offenses were made easier, the U.S. Supreme Court's decisions in *Roper v. Simmons*, *Graham v. Florida*, *Jackson v. Hobbs*, *Miller v. Alabama*, and *Montgomery v. Louisiana* have denied the possibility of the ultimate punishment—death—and lifetime incarceration terms for those who do not commit homicide. The perceived increase in the number of violent offenses perpetrated by juveniles led many to ponder whether the juvenile court, originally established to protect and treat juveniles, is adequate to the task of dealing with modern-day offenders. Simultaneously, the concepts of restorative justice, which involves an attempt to make victims whole through interaction with and restitution by their offenders, and juvenile detention alternatives, which reduce reliance on secure confinements, have become popular in juvenile justice (see Chapter 10). These approaches emphasize treatment philosophies as opposed to the "get-tough" philosophy so popular during recent years. Both of these approaches lead observers to believe that if the juvenile court survives, major changes in its underlying philosophy are likely to occur (Cohn, 2004; Ellis & Sowers, 2001; Schwartz, Weiner, & Enosh, 1998). As noted in In Practice 1.1, youth cannot be treated in the same vein as adults. Treatment and rehabilitation have to be considered when youth are involved.

Rethinking Juvenile Justice

Finally, the issue of responsibility for delinquent acts continues to surface. For a number of years, the trend was to hold younger and younger juveniles accountable for their offenses, to exclude certain offenses from the jurisdiction of the juvenile court, and to establish mandatory or automatic waiver provisions for certain offenses. That this trend is currently in question is evident from the article contained in In Practice 1.1.

There are a number of practical implications of the various dilemmas that characterize the juvenile justice system. Juvenile codes in many states were changed during the 1990s to reflect expanded eligibility

IN PRACTICE 1.1

10-YEAR-OLD MURDER DEFENDANT SHOWS FAILURE OF U.S. JUVENILE JUSTICE SYSTEM. WHILE HIS ALLEGED CRIME IS THE BRUTAL MURDER OF A 90-YEAR-OLD WOMAN, SHOULD A 10-YEAR-OLD SPEND THE REST OF [HIS] LIFE IN PRISON FOR IT?

If Pennsylvania had set out to intentionally highlight the glaring defects in the U.S. juvenile justice system, it couldn't have picked a better case than one initiated this week in rural Wayne County.

On Monday, prosecutors there charged a ten-year-old boy as an adult for the murder of an elderly woman under the care of his grandfather—making him one of the youngest Americans ever to face a criminal homicide conviction.

According to an affidavit provided by the Wayne County District Attorney's office, Tristen Kurilla, a fifth-grader who celebrated his tenth birthday in July, confessed to beating 90-year-old Helen Novak with his fists and choking her with a cane after she yelled at him to leave her room. Novak died shortly after the assault. On Monday, Kurilla was arraigned on charges of criminal homicide and aggravated assault. He is currently being held without bail in a segregated area of Wayne County Correctional Facility away from other inmates.

By mid-week the story had made the rounds of the national media—with headlines in a number of major outlets focusing on the age of the defendant and the callous brutality of his crime. But youth advocates tell *The Daily Beast* that the details of the case are secondary to what it says about the lengths the U.S. still has to go in its treatment of juvenile offenders.

"There is no other country in the world that would treat a child as an adult," said Robert Schwartz, co-founder and executive director of the Juvenile Law Center (JLC) in Philadelphia. "Social science has taught us that kids who are this young are not criminals in the same way that adults are. He has to be held accountable, yes, but in a developmentally appropriate way."

Like many other ill-conceived criminal justice policies, the push to begin trying juveniles in adult court began in the 1990s, as state legislatures enacted a series of "get-tough" laws in response to a perceived epidemic of youth crime. Congress got into the act in 1998, passing a series of measures that tied federal grant money to the passage of state laws requiring defendants over the age of 14 charged with serious offenses be adjudicated as adults, according to the Sentencing Project.

"Pretty much every legislature changed their juvenile laws to push more kids into the adult system," said Marsha Levick, JLC's deputy director and chief counsel.

Source: Moraff, C. (2014, October 18). 10-year-old murder defendant shows failure of U.S. juvenile justice system. Used with permission of The Daily Beast Copyright © 2017. All rights reserved.

Questions to Consider

1. True or False: The *Roper v. Simmons* ruling allowed youth to be sentenced to the death penalty in adult court but not in juvenile court.

2. Multiple Choice: The push to try juveniles who committed serious offenses in adult court began in the

   a. 1970s

   b. 1980s

   c. 1990s

   d. Early 2000s

3. If waivers are used in juvenile court, are we, as a society, giving up on youth?

for criminal court processing and adult correctional sanctions. All states now allow juveniles to be tried as adults under certain circumstances. According to Benekos and Merlo (2008), Brown (2012), and others, the impact of policies from the 1990s resulting in the adultification of juveniles through the use of punitive and exclusionary sanctions continues in spite of declining juvenile crime rates. At the same time, however, there are signs of more enlightened approaches on the horizon as attempts to reduce criminalization of juveniles are occurring in an increasing number of jurisdictions. These two conflicting approaches illustrate the continuing ambiguity in the juvenile justice system.

Because the juvenile justice system does not exist in a vacuum, laws dealing with juveniles change with changing political climates—whether or not such changes are logical or supported by evidence. Further, new and modified theories emerge as we attempt to better understand and deal with juveniles in the justice system. Thus, the cycle of juvenile justice is constantly in motion. Disputes between those who represent competing camps are common and difficult to resolve. Finally, the discrepancy between the ideal (theory) and practice (reality) remains considerable. What should be done to, with, and for juveniles and what is possible based on the available resources and political climate may be quite different things. Just over a decade ago, Bilchik (1999b) asked the following:

> As a society that strives to raise productive, healthy, and safe children, how can we be certain that our responses to juvenile crime are effective? Do we know if our efforts at delinquency prevention and intervention are really making a difference in the lives of youth and their families and in their communities? How can we strengthen and better target our delinquency and crime prevention strategies? Can we modify these strategies as needed to respond to the ever-changing needs of our nation's youth? (p. iii)

At the beginning of the second decade of the 21st century, the Coordinating Council on Juvenile Justice and Delinquency Prevention approved a 2010 work plan that identified priority issues for interagency collaboration in the coming year. The four issues the council plans to focus on—(1) education and at-risk youth, (2) tribal youth and juvenile justice, (3) juvenile reentry, and (4) racial and/or ethnic disparities in the juvenile justice system and related systems—suggest that many of the questions raised at the end of the 20th century have yet to be answered (OJJDP News at a Glance, 2010). A further attempt to answer such questions is the movement toward accountability of the juvenile justice system. Mears and Butts (2008) indicated the following:

> The juvenile justice system has been transformed in recent years with a range of policies designed to hold youth accountable, but how does society hold this system accountable? Calls for governmental accountability are common, yet few jurisdictions can provide comprehensive information about the basic operations of juvenile justice and the effectiveness of system reforms. Most elements of the juvenile justice system operate on faith—managers and policy makers have to assume that their programs are based on sound evidence and that reform efforts are fully implemented with fidelity to their designs. (p. 264)

Mears and Butts (2008) concluded the following:

> Policy makers and the public increasingly expect government accountability, yet the gap between ideals and actual practice remains large. The situation is especially pronounced in juvenile justice, where little is known about the system's everyday activities and the implementation of numerous reforms enacted over the past 25 years. Given the growing demands for accountability, the substantial costs of juvenile justice, the potential for harm to victims and communities, and, not least, the risk of failing to improve the life outcomes of young offenders, systematic implementation of performance monitoring in juvenile justice is essential. (p. 280)

Summary

Although the belief that juveniles should be dealt with in a justice system different from that of adults is not new, serious questions are now being raised about the ability of the juvenile justice system to deal successfully with contemporary offenders. The debate continues concerning whether to get increasingly tough on youthful offenders or to retain the more treatment- or rehabilitation-centered approach of the traditional juvenile court. The belief that the state has both the right and responsibility to act on behalf of juveniles was the key element of juvenile justice in 12th-century England and remains central to the juvenile justice system in the United States today.

Age of responsibility and the ability to form criminal intent have also been, and remain, important issues in juvenile justice. The concepts of parens patriae and in loco parentis remain cornerstones of contemporary juvenile justice, although not without challenge. Those who favor a more formal approach to juvenile justice continue to debate those who are oriented toward more informal procedures, although decisions in the *Kent*, *Gault*, and *Winship* cases made it clear, in theory at least, that juveniles charged with delinquency have most of the same rights as adults.

Although some (e.g., Hirschi & Gottfredson, 1993) have argued that the juvenile court rests on faulty assumptions, it appears that the goals of the original juvenile court (1899) are still being pursued (OJJDP News at a Glance, 2010). It remains apparent that the political climate of the time is extremely influential in dictating changing, and sometimes contradictory, responses to juvenile delinquency, as indicated by Benekos and Merlo (2008). Further, accountability for policies, programs, and results in the juvenile justice system through implementation of performance measures is increasingly being demanded by observers of the network (Mears & Butts, 2008).

KEY TERMS

age of responsibility 3	*Holmes* case 8	*Miller v. Alabama* 10
Breed v. Jones 9	house of refuge 6	*Montgomery v. Louisiana* 10
chancery courts 4	*in loco parentis* 5	*parens patriae* 5
child-savers movement 7	*Jackson v. Hobbs* 10	Progressive Era 7
common law 4	*Kent* case 8	reform schools 7
era of socialized juvenile justice 7	legalistic approach 11	*Roper v. Simmons* 9
Gault case 9	*McKeiver v. Pennsylvania* 9	therapeutic approach 11
Graham v. Florida 10	*mens rea* 4	*Winship* case 9

Critical Thinking Questions

1. What do the terms *parens patriae* and *in loco parentis* mean? Why are these terms important in understanding the current juvenile justice network?

2. Discuss your approach to juvenile offenders and juvenile sentencing. Is it therapeutic or legalistic? Why?

3. What is the significance of each of the following Court decisions?

   a. *Kent*

   b. *Gault*

   c. *Winship*

   d. *Roper v. Simmons*

   e. *Jackson v. Hobbs* and *Miller v. Alabama*

   f. *Graham v. Florida*

4. Discuss when waivers to adult court are most appropriate (if at all). What do you think the long-term effects of waivers are on youth, juvenile court, and the adult correctional system?

Suggested Readings

Benekos, P. J., & Merlo, A. V. (2008). Juvenile justice: The legacy of punitive policy. *Youth Violence and Juvenile Justice, 6*(8), 28–46.

Bishop, D. (2004). Injustice and irrationality in contemporary youth policy. *Criminology and Public Policy, 3*, 633–644.

Brown, S. A. (2012, June). Trends in juvenile justice state legislation 2001–2011. *National Conference of State Legislatures.* Retrieved from www.ncsl.org/documents/cj/TrendsInJuvenileJustice.pdf

Cohen, M., & Piquero, A. (2009). New evidence on the monetary value of saving a high risk youth. *Journal of Quantitative Criminology, 25*(1), 25–49.

Cohn, A. W. (2004). Planning for the future of juvenile justice. *Federal Probation, 68*(3), 39–44.

Graham v. Florida, 08-7412 (2010).

Jackson v. Hobbs, 132 S. Ct. 548 (2011).

Lindner, C. (2004, Spring). A century of revolutionary changes in the United States court systems. *Perspectives, 71*(3), 24–29.

Mears, D. P., & Butts, J. A. (2008). Using performance monitoring to improve the accountability, operations, and effectiveness of juvenile justice. *Criminal Justice Policy Review, 19*(3), 264–284.

Models for change: System reform in juvenile justice. (2012). *Justice Reform Program.* John D. and Catherine T. MacArthur Foundation. Retrieved from www.modelsforchange.net/index.html

Montgomery v. Louisiana, 577 U.S. _____ (2016).

National District Attorneys Association. (2016, November 12). *National prosecution standards* (3rd ed.). Retrieved from http://www.ndaa.org/pdf/NDAA%20Juvenile%20Prosecution%20Standards%20Revised%2011%2012%202016%20Final.pdf

OJJDP News at a Glance. (2013, January/February). *Beyond detention.* Retrieved from www.ojjdp.gov/newsletter/240749/sf_2.html

Rosenheim, M. K., Zimring, F. E., Tanenhaus, D. S., & Dohrn, B. (Eds.). (2002). *A century of juvenile justice.* Chicago, IL: University of Chicago Press.

Sickmund, M., & Puzzanchera, C. (Eds.). (2014, December). *Juvenile Offenders and Victims: 2014 National Report.* Pittsburgh, PA: National Center for Juvenile Justice. Retrieved from http://www.ojjdp.gov/ojstatbb/nr2014/downloads/NR2014.pdf

⑤SAGE edge™

Sharpen your skills with SAGE edge at **edge.sagepub.com/coxjj9e**. SAGE edge for students provides a personalized approach to help you accomplish your coursework goals in an easy-to-use learning environment. You'll find action plans, mobile-friendly eFlashcards, and quizzes as well as video and web resources and links to SAGE journal articles to support and expand on the concepts presented in this chapter.

Defining and Measuring Offenses by and Against Juveniles 2

CHAPTER LEARNING OBJECTIVES

On completion of this chapter, students should be able to do the following:

- Understand and discuss the importance of accurately defining and measuring delinquency
- Understand the impact of differences in definitions of delinquency
- Discuss legal and behavioral definitions of delinquency
- Discuss official and unofficial sources of data on delinquency and abuse and the problems associated with each

WHAT WOULD YOU DO?

Tommy could hear his mom sobbing and crying through the thin wooden door in the mobile home. He looked up at his older brother, Robbie, and asked him, "When do you think he will stop?"

Robbie said in a low voice, "Shhh . . . she will apologize and then he will eventually calm down and they will go to the bedroom. After that, it will be okay."

But this time it was different. Both Tommy and Robbie heard a loud yelp that made their blood run cold. Tommy looked under the crack of the door and could see his father's boots moving, apparently kicking his mother in the ribs as she struggled to get away on all fours.

"He's kicking her really bad, Robbie. . . . I'm afraid he might kill Momma this time." Robbie listened to the shrieks and groans of his mother in misery and looked down at his 5-year-old brother.

"Tommy, you gotta stay in here, okay? Don't come out after me, and don't get between me and Dad. I don't wanna hurt you by accident, okay?"

"But . . ." Tommy tried to argue, but Robbie quickly put a hand over the child's mouth.

"We can't argue about this. There's no time. . . . You don't want Momma to die, do you?"

Tommy shook his head no.

"Then you do as I tell you, until the coast is clear, okay?"

"Okay," said Tommy.

"Promise!" demanded Robbie.

"I promise," said Tommy.

In a flash, Robbie went to the back of the room and reached up high in the closet to pull out a .22 Winchester rifle that his grandfather had given him for squirrel hunting a few years back. The 15-year-old motioned for his little brother to get on the bed against the wall.

"But Robbie . . ." said Tommy.

"Shhh! Be quiet, dammit! Don't go getting scared on me. Just hide behind the bed," said Robbie, heart pounding, sweat already building on his forehead.

Robbie opened the door, held the rifle up against his shoulder, and, with it pointed forward, walked down the cheaply paneled hall of the mobile home, arriving in the living room in five quick long gaits. He stood there, gun pointed at his father, who, for a moment, was surprised but then started grinning.

Robbie's mother, still on the ground in the corner of the living room, said faintly, "Robbie, no."

His father then said, "Yeah, Robbie, why don't you stud up? It's about that time now, huh?" as he moved slowly toward Robbie.

"You stay there or I'll shoot!" said Robbie.

His mother said, "Frank, please leave him alone; he's just worried about me," at which point Frank quickly turned, pointed a finger at her, and said, "You both should be worried. I'm gonna kill both of your asses!"

Frank turned back and faced Robbie. Robbie's hands were sweating and he was shaking a little. He only had this .22, not exactly a powerful gun, and no hollow points at that. Robbie was terrified. If he did not shoot, he knew Frank would likely put him in the hospital, might kill his mom, and might even hurt Tommy as well. If he did shoot, he would need to do so more than once because one shot would not be enough to stop him.

Frank took another step, saying, "You ain't got it in ya! Yer yella, just like your mommaaaa. . . ."

The gun went off. The clip that Robbie had loaded the day before let him fire rounds as fast as he could repetitively pull the trigger. The first shot went right through Frank's right eye; the second went into the front of his neck at an angle, as did the third. The fourth went into his heart. The others missed, for the most part, but Frank was on the ground, heaving.

A few minutes later, the police arrived on the scene of a homicide.

While they took down the information from all parties at the house as well as others who lived in the trailer park, they were compelled to put Robbie in cuffs and take him into booking.

What Would You Do?

1. Judging by the circumstances, would you define this crime as one committed by a juvenile, or should Robbie be waived to adult court? Explain your answer.

2. How would you identify and measure the various crimes committed at this scene?

3. How could victim blaming become a problem in a case such as this?

4. What would you have done if you were in Robbie's position?

One of the major problems confronting those interested in learning more about offenses by and against juveniles involves defining the phenomena. Without specific definitions, accurate measurement is impossible, making development of programs to prevent and control delinquency and offenses against juveniles extremely difficult.

There are two major types of definitions associated with delinquency. Strict legal definitions hold that only those who have been officially labeled by the courts are offenders. Behavioral definitions hold that those whose behavior violates statutes applicable to them are offenders whether or not they are officially labeled. Each of these definitions has its own problems and implications for practitioners and leads to different conclusions about the nature and extent of offenses. For example, using the legal definition, a juvenile who committed a relatively serious offense but was not apprehended would not be classified as delinquent, whereas another juvenile who committed a less serious offense and was caught would be so classified.

Legal Definitions

Changing Definitions

A basic difficulty with legal definitions is that they differ from time to time and from place to place. An act that is delinquent at one time and in one place might not be delinquent at another time or in another place. For example, wearing gang colors or using gang signs may be a violation of city ordinances in some places but not in others. Or the law may change so that an act that was considered delinquent yesterday is not considered delinquent today. For instance, the Illinois Juvenile Court Act of 1899 defined as delinquent any juvenile under the age of 16 who violated a state law or city or village ordinance. By 1907, the definition of delinquency had changed considerably to include incorrigibility, knowingly associating with vicious or immoral companions, absenting oneself from the home without just cause, patronizing poolrooms, wandering about the streets at night, wandering in railroad yards, and engaging in indecent conduct. Definitions of delinquency have changed and expanded over the years. Alabama's current Juvenile Court Act defines a delinquent act as "an act committed by a child that is designated a violation, misdemeanor, or felony offense pursuant to the law of the municipality, county, or state in which the act was committed or pursuant to federal law" (Alabama Code, 208, Title 12, Chapter 15, Section 12:15:102, 2013). The definition continues to exclude 16- and 17-year-olds who violate nonfelony traffic or water safety laws, commit a capital offense, commit crimes classified as Class A felonies in Alabama or that involve using a deadly weapon or cause death or serious physical injury, engage in drug trafficking, and commit serious felonies involving certain authority figures such as teachers and court or law enforcement personnel. As Alabama demonstrates, legal definitions are limited in their applicability to a given time and place because of inconsistencies throughout the states. You will note as we proceed through this text that examples provided are from the Illinois Juvenile Court Act (Illinois Compiled Statutes [ILCS], ch. 705, 2013). Illinois has been a national leader in the field of juvenile justice (Fanton, 2006), and other states such as Missouri and Georgia are providing leadership as well. Although it is impossible to cite all of the statutes from the 50 states in the confines of the text, we have included examples of statutes from other states throughout and strongly encourage you to access online recent court cases and the statutes of the state in which you reside to compare and contrast them with the sample statutes cited in the text. This is important because statutes and court decisions relating to the juvenile justice system are in a constant state of change.

Age Ambiguity

Another problem with legal definitions has been the ambiguity reflected with respect to age (age ambiguity) (as noted in In Practice 2.1). What is the lower age limit for a juvenile to be considered delinquent? At what age are children entitled to the protection of the juvenile court? Although custom has established a lower limit for petitions of delinquency at roughly 7 years of age, some states set the limit higher and a few set it lower. For example, some states have statutes that set the minimum age of juvenile court delinquency jurisdiction. In other states, the minimum age is not specified in statute but is governed by case law or common law. One state sets the minimum age at 6 years, three states set the minimum age at 7 years, one state sets the minimum age at 8 years, and 11 states set the minimum age at 10 years (Sappenfield, 2008).

Thinking with respect to the minimum age at which children should be afforded court protection changed with the emergence of crack cocaine and methamphetamines, both of which may have serious prenatal effects (Wells, 2006). According to Illinois statutes, for example, any infant whose blood, urine, or meconium contains any amount of a controlled substance is defined as neglected (ILCS, ch. 705, art. 2, sec. 405, 2013).

JUVENILE PROSTITUTION, AGE AMBIGUITY, AND DISTINGUISHING VICTIMS FROM OFFENDERS: NEW DEVELOPMENTS IN ASSOCIATED DEFINITIONS AND RESPONSE

During the early months of 2016, police in the state of Wisconsin apprehended a victim of sex trafficking who was 16 years old; she had been trafficked since the age of 13. At the time of her abduction, she was sexually assaulted and, shortly thereafter, manipulated through coercion, threat, and intimidation into prostitution. Through brainwashing, threats followed by make-up periods, and other techniques both overt and subtle, an emotional attachment was developed between the girl and her pimp. He became, in essence, her boyfriend.

Unexpected amid this victimization was that this girl, according to Wisconsin law, was considered a criminal for her acts of prostitution.

As a result of this and other similar cases, lawmakers and various advocacy groups pushed for these laws to change so that individuals in these circumstances would be seen solely as victims and in the future would be shielded from criminal charges.

Social movements like the one in Wisconsin have emerged in a number of states throughout the nation. In fact, this push for social change in how prostitution in general, and underage prostitution in particular, is viewed is so widespread that a term has emerged to describe the proposed legal changes among state legislatures: *safe harbor*. These so-called safe-harbor proposals call for legislation that would prohibit charging any person under 18 years of age with prostitution. Whereas this is the most common form of safe-harbor law, other states have implemented versions that decriminalize minors who are 16 or younger, holding those 17

and older culpable and therefore chargeable for prostitution.

Whereas it would seem, on the face of it, that these laws would get automatic support, this has not been the case. Indeed, many states have encountered opposition to such blanket laws to decriminalize prostitution among underage youth because this would undermine the ability of police to intervene and exert their authority over the youth. In other words, law enforcement needs to have the legal ability to detain the underage prostitute for a period as a means of separating her from her pimp, stepping up efforts to charge the pimp, and to arrange for services for the underage individual in their custody. With no criminal violation from which to operate, the power of the police is much more limited.

Currently, there are about a dozen or so states that have decriminalization statutes in place for minors involved in prostitution (Aslanian, 2016). However, this has proven to be no panacea for this issue because many of these youth involved in prostitution do not see themselves as in need of help. Many come from horrible backgrounds and see their pimps as boyfriends and the other women with whom they work as part of their family. There are a multitude of social, emotional, and economic challenges that keep these youth working in prostitution.

Further, though most states do not yet have safe-harbor laws, this does not necessarily mean that these states simply turn a blind eye to this issue. Rather, many of these states have diversion programs or other forms of alternative assistance available. The line of thought is that whereas

(Continued)

youth may still be charged with prostitution, they will be able to benefit from more solid law enforcement intervention and follow-up assistance that will, at least in theory, be more successful in permanently removing youth from prostitution.

This In Practice brings to light how age ambiguity affects public views of at least one type of crime. Many states provide no distinction between prostitutes under the age of 18 and those over the age of majority. In other states, the bar is set at 16, holding girls 17 and older as guilty of their activity in prostitution.

Further, this In Practice also aligns with what is discussed in the next subsection of this chapter dealing with inaccurate images of offenders and victims. As has been shown, states have typically had a difficult time delineating between those who are victims and those who are offenders with underage prostitution. In some cases, states may view these individuals as one or the other, but in other cases they may view them as both.

The fact that many of these victims will outright lie to law enforcement and/or courthouse officials to protect their pimp and/or defend their lifestyle makes these determinations even more difficult. Simply put, some of these youth do not see themselves as victims and do not want assistance from law enforcement or otherwise. For those youth who come from abusive or neglectful families, the unwillingness to disclose this prior abuse means that individuals may not be recognized as in need of services. In addition, official statistics related to child abuse and neglect will continue to have inaccuracies in the data that could have been otherwise remedied. Finally, the willingness of both youth and the justice system to reframe the view of this activity can contribute to various potential sources of error in official statistical counts. In addition, justice might also be served in a manner that is more appropriate for each actor involved.

Sources: Aslanian (2016); Speckhard (2016).

Questions to Consider

1. True or False: Some youth drawn into prostitution view their pimp as their friend or family member.

2. Multiple Choice: Proposed legal changes among state legislatures regarding underage prostitution have been referred to as what kind of proposals?

   a. Antivictimization

   b. Sexual racketeering reformation

   c. Anti–sexual trafficking

   d. Safe harbor

3. Explain the advantages and disadvantages to the decriminalization of juvenile prostitution statutes.

There is also considerable diversity with respect to the upper age limit in delinquency cases. Three states set the maximum age at 15 years, 10 states set the maximum age at 16 years, and 37 states (and the District of Columbia) set the maximum age at 17 years (Office of Juvenile Justice and Delinquency Prevention [OJJDP], 2013). Some states set higher upper age limits for juveniles who are abused, neglected, dependent, or in need of intervention than for delinquents in an attempt to provide protection for juveniles who are still minors even though they are no longer subject to findings of delinquency. Illinois recently changed its maximum age limit depending on whether the offense committed by the juvenile would be a felony (17 years of age) or a misdemeanor (18 years of age) (ILCS, ch. 705, 405/5 [3], 2013). And in most states, juvenile court authority over a juvenile may extend beyond the upper age of original jurisdiction (frequently to the age of 21).

An example of the confusion resulting from all of these considerations is the Illinois Juvenile Court Act (ILCS, ch. 705, 2013). This act establishes no lower age limit; establishes the 17th birthday as the upper limit at which an adjudication of delinquency for serious offenses may be made while setting the limit at the 18th birthday for misdemeanors; makes it possible to automatically transfer juveniles over the age of 15 years to adult court for certain types of violent offenses; and sets the 18th birthday as the upper age limit for findings of abuse, dependency, neglect, and minors requiring intervention. Adding to the confusion is the distinction made in the Illinois Juvenile

Are race and ethnicity really major factors in delinquency? Official statistics point to higher crime rates among minorities; however, self-report studies claim otherwise.

Court Act between minors (those under 21 years of age) and adults (those 21 years of age and over). This raises questions about the status of persons over the age of 18 but under 21 years. For example, a 19-year-old in Illinois is still a minor (although he or she may vote) but cannot be found delinquent, dependent, neglected, abused, or in need of intervention. Such ambiguities with respect to age make comparisons across jurisdictions difficult.

Inaccurate Images of Offenders and Victims

Yet another difficulty with legal definitions is that they may lead to a highly unrealistic picture of the nature and extent of delinquency, abuse, neglect, and dependency. Because these definitions depend on official adjudication, they lead us to concentrate on only a small portion of those actually involved as offenders and victims. This means that a substantial amount of illegal behavior committed by youth is not detected.

Similar problems arise when considering abuse and neglect because only a small portion of such cases are reported and result in official adjudication. In short, most juvenile offenders and victims never come to the attention of the juvenile court, and a strict legal definition is of little value if we are interested in the actual size of offender and victim populations. It may well be, for example, that females are more involved in delinquent activities than official statistics would lead us to believe. It may be that they are not as likely to be arrested by the police as their male counterparts. Not infrequently, we have seen police officers search male gang members for drugs and/or weapons while failing to search females who are with the gang members. It does not take long for the males involved to decide who should carry drugs and weapons. Similarly, blacks and other minority group members may be overrepresented in official statistics simply because they live in high-crime areas that are heavily policed and, therefore, are more likely to be arrested than those living in less heavily policed areas. For example, of all juveniles (individuals under the age of 18) arrested in 2011 in the nation, 65.7% were white, 32.0% were black, and 2.3% were of other races. Juveniles who were black accounted for 51.4% of juvenile arrests for violent crimes, although black youth accounted for about 16% of the youth population ages 10 to 17. Table 2.1 shows the proportion of arrests for black juveniles in 2011.

Table 2.1 Proportion of Black Juvenile Arrests in 2011

Most Serious Offense	Proportion of Black Juvenile Arrests in 2011
Murder/nonnegligent manslaughter	54.3%
Rape	34.3
Robbery	71.4
Aggravated assault	43.4
Burglary	40.2
Larceny-theft	36.4
Motor vehicle theft	43.6
Weapons carrying/possession	38.1
Drug abuse violation	24.4
Curfew and loitering	44.8

Source: Federal Bureau of Investigation (FBI) (2015). Adapted from Table 43B.

Note: Whether these official statistics accurately reflect levels of black juvenile participation in the crimes listed depends on factors such as disproportionate impact discussed throughout this chapter (see especially the forthcoming section on official statistics) and in Chapters 3 and 8.

A final difficulty with legal definitions also characterizes behavioral definitions and results from the broad scope of behaviors potentially included. Does striking a child on the buttocks with an open hand constitute child abuse? What does *beyond the control of parents* mean? How is *incorrigible* to be defined? What does a "minor requiring authoritative intervention" (MRAI) look like? Although all of these questions may be answered by referring to definitions contained in state statutes, in practice they are certainly open to interpretation by parents, practitioners, and juveniles themselves. It should be noted that the broader the interpretation, the greater the number of victims and offenders.

Behavioral Definitions

In contrast to legal definitions, behavioral definitions focus on juveniles who offend or are victimized even if they are not officially adjudicated. Using a behavioral definition, a juvenile who shoplifts but is not apprehended is still considered delinquent, whereas that juvenile would not be considered delinquent using a legal definition. The same is true of a child who is abused but not officially labeled as abused. If we concentrate on juveniles who are officially labeled, we get a far different picture from that if we include all of those who offend or are victimized. Estimates of the extent of delinquency and abuse based on a legal definition are far lower than those based on a behavioral definition. In addition, the nature of delinquency and abuse appears to be different depending on the definition employed.

We might assume, for example, that the more serious the case, the greater the likelihood of official labeling. If this assumption is correct, relying on official statistics would lead us to believe that the proportion of serious offenses by and against juveniles is much higher than it actually is (using the behavioral definition). Finally, relying on legal definitions (and the official statistics based on such definitions) would lead us to overestimate the proportion of lower-social-class children involved in delinquency and abuse. The reasons for this overestimation are discussed later in this chapter.

In general, we prefer a behavioral definition because it provides a more realistic picture of the extent and nature of offenders and victims. It may be applied across time and jurisdictions because it is broad enough to encompass the age and behavioral categories of different jurisdictions and statutes. In addition, the broader perspective provided may help in the development of more realistic programs for preventing or controlling delinquency.

Police prepare to search juveniles for drugs or weapons.

In spite of its advantages, however, there is one major difficulty with the behavioral definition. Because it includes many juveniles who do not become part of official statistics, we need to rely on unofficial, and sometimes questionable, methods of assessing the extent and nature of unofficial or "hidden" delinquency and abuse.

Official Statistics: Sources and Problems

Official Delinquency Statistics

What do current official statistics on delinquency and abuse indicate? Despite growth in the juvenile population over the past decade, crime and violence by juveniles have declined. As per the most recent data available, arrests for juvenile offenses decreased 9.4% from the 8,730,665 youth arrested in 2014 to the 8,248,709 juveniles arrested in 2015 (FBI, 2016a). Similar trends are evidenced across most offense categories for both male and female and white and minority youth. In fact, children are at a much greater risk of being the victims of violent crime than of being the perpetrators of violent crime. According to the Administration for Children and Families (2014),

1. The national estimates of children who received an investigation or alternative response increased 7.4% from 2010 (3,023,000) to 2014 (3,248,000).

2. The number and rate of victims of maltreatment have fluctuated during the past 5 years. Comparing the national estimate of victims from 2010 (698,000) to 2014 (702,000) shows an increase of around 1%.

3. Three-quarters (75%) of victims were neglected, 17% were physically abused, and 8.3% were sexually abused.

4. For 2014, an estimated 1,580 children died of abuse and neglect at a rate of 2.13 per 100,000 children in the national population.

Numbers of children suffering from abuse and neglect remain high in the United States, with a slight increase that was noted by the Administration for Children and Families (2014) in recent years. Regardless of fluctuation in the rates of child abuse and/or neglect, what is important to understand is that these are underlying antecedents to future aberrant behavior and adjustment problems among youth who experience the abuse. Thus, early interventions have substantial opportunity to lower future delinquency.

During the last 10 years, the population of offenders in residential placement dropped by nearly 44%. However, this decline did not affect all racial/ethnic groups similarly. Indeed, according to the OJJDP (2013),

In 2013, the population of youth held in residential placement for delinquency or status offenses was 40% black, 32% white, and 23% Hispanic. Youth of other races, including those of two or more races, accounted for 5% of youth in residential placement. The race/ethnicity profile of offenders in residential placement shifted substantially from a decade earlier. In 2003, 39% of juvenile offenders in residential placement were white, 38% were black, and 19% were Hispanic. (p. 12)

Where do such varied statistics come from, and how accurate are they likely to be?

Official statistics on delinquency are available at the national level in *Crime in the United States*, published annually by the FBI based on *Uniform Crime Reports* (UCRs). Since 1964, these reports have contained information on arrests of persons under 18 years of age. In addition, since 1974, the reports have included information on police dispositions of juvenile offenders taken into custody as well as urban, suburban, and rural arrest rates. For the year 2014, the FBI claimed that UCRs covered 12,656 law enforcement jurisdictions around the nation, with the most complete reporting from urban areas and the least complete reporting from rural areas (FBI, 2014, p. 1). Although the FBI statistics are the most comprehensive official statistics available, they are not totally accurate for several reasons.

First, because UCRs are based on reports from law enforcement agencies throughout the nation, errors in reporting made by each separate agency become part of national statistics. Sources of error include mistakes in calculating percentages and in placing offenders in appropriate categories. Statistics reported to the FBI are based on "offenses cleared by arrest" and, therefore, say nothing about whether the offenders were actually adjudicated delinquent for the offenses in question.

Assuming that more serious offenses are more likely to lead to arrests (however defined) than are less serious and more typically juvenile offenses, arrest statistics would show a disproportionate number of serious juvenile offenses. These types of cases actually account for only a very small proportion of all delinquent acts. Black and Reiss (1970) found that in urban areas only about 5% of police encounters with juveniles involved alleged felonies. Lundman, Sykes, and Clark (1978) replicated the Black and Reiss study and also found a 5% felony rate, noting that only approximately 15% of all police–juvenile encounters result in arrests, leaving 85% of these encounters that cannot become a part of official police statistics. Empey, Stafford, and Hay (1999) concluded the following:

We have seen that the police traditionally have been inclined to avoid arresting juveniles. Because they have been granted considerable discretion, however, the police continue to counsel and release many of those whom they have arrested, albeit less frequently than in the past. (p. 331)

Myers (2004) noted this:

While official statistics tell the story about the number of juveniles arrested and processed into the system, they only capture a fraction of the contacts that police have with juveniles and only a fraction of the information. Little is known about the rest of the story, about the nature of police juvenile encounters, the factors that shape police responses to juveniles in these encounters, and about those juveniles who have contact with the police and are subsequently released with a reprimand that is something other than a formal police response. (p. 2)

Myers observed that of 654 juvenile suspects involved in police encounters, 84, or 13%, were arrested.

There are a variety of other difficulties with UCR data. If one wants to know the number of juveniles arrested for specific serious offenses during a given period in specific types of locations, UCR data are useful. But if one wants to know something about the actual extent and distribution of delinquency, or about police handling of juveniles involved in less serious offenses, UCR data are of little value because, as just noted, "many juveniles who commit crimes (even serious crimes) never enter the juvenile justice system. Consequently, developing a portrait of juvenile law-violating behavior from official records gives only a partial picture" (OJJDP, 2006). Puzzanchera (2009) noted the following:

> While juvenile arrest rates in part reflect juvenile behavior, many other factors can affect the size of these rates. For example, jurisdictions that arrest a relatively large number of nonresident juveniles would have higher arrest rates than jurisdictions where resident youth behave in an identical manner. Therefore, jurisdictions that are vacation destinations or regional centers for economic activity may have arrest rates that reflect more than the behavior of their resident youth. Other factors that influence the magnitude of arrest rates in a given area include the attitudes of its citizens toward crime, the policies of the jurisdiction's law enforcement agencies, and the policies of other components of the justice system. (p. 11)

In an attempt to combat some of the reporting problems found in UCR data since 1987, the FBI has implemented an incident-based reporting system, a modification of the original UCR reporting system, throughout the United States. In 2014, there were 18,498 law enforcement agencies that contributed data to the National Incident-Based Reporting System (NIBRS).

> Based on 2014 data submissions, 16 states (Arkansas, Colorado, Delaware, Idaho, Iowa, Michigan, Montana, New Hampshire, North Dakota, Rhode Island, South Carolina, South Dakota, Tennessee, Vermont, Virginia, and West Virginia) submit all their data via the NIBRS. Thirty-three state UCR Programs are certified for NIBRS participation. (FBI, 2014)

NIBRS was developed to collect information on each crime occurrence. Under this reporting system, policing agencies report data on offenses known to the police (offenses reported to or observed by the police) instead of only those offenses cleared by arrest, as was done in the original UCR crime reporting process. Of all official statistics, offenses known to the police probably provide the most complete picture of the extent and nature of illegal activity, although there is considerable evidence from victim survey research (discussed later in this chapter) that even these statistics include information on fewer than 50% of the offenses actually committed (Hart & Rennison, 2003, p. 1). According to Langton, Berzofsky, Krebs, and Smiley-McDonald (2012, p. 1), from 2006 to 2010, approximately 52% of violent crime victimizations were not reported to the police.

Criminal justice agencies are allowed to customize the NIBRS to meet agency statistical needs while still meeting the requirements of the UCRs without biasing the data. In addition, crimes that were not discussed in UCRs originally are included in the new reporting system, including terrorism, white-collar crime, children missing due to criminal behaviors, hate crimes, juvenile gang crimes, parental kidnapping, child and adult pornography, driving under the influence, and alcohol-related offenses.

Data at the national level are also available from the National Center for Juvenile Justice, which collects and publishes information on the number of delinquency, neglect, and dependency cases processed by juvenile courts nationwide. In addition, the Office of Juvenile Justice and Delinquency Prevention (OJJDP) in the U.S. Department of Justice maintains and publishes statistics on juveniles. Unfortunately, much of the information available from these two agencies is out of date by the time it is published (2- to 4-year time lags are not uncommon).

There are a variety of sources of official statistics available at local, county, and state levels as well. Many service agencies, such as police departments, children and family services departments, and juvenile and adult court systems, maintain statistics on cases in which they are involved. These statistics are often focused on agency needs and are used to secure funding from local or private sources, the county, the state, and/or the federal government. The statistics may also be used to justify to the community or the media certain dispositions employed by the agencies and to alert the community to specific needs of the agencies.

Official Statistics on Abuse and Neglect

Child abuse and neglect may be defined as "any recent act or failure to act on the part of a parent or caretaker which results in death, serious physical or emotional harm, sexual abuse or exploitation; or an act or failure to act, which presents an imminent risk of serious harm" (Child Abuse Prevention and Treatment Act [CAPTA], 42 U.S.C. §5101, 2010). Official statistics on abused and neglected children are available from a number of sources but are probably even more inaccurate than other crime statistics because of underreporting, as In Practice 2.2 indicates. Part II of the UCR contains data on "offenses against family and children." The National Center on Child Abuse and Neglect, the National Children's Advocacy Center, and the National Resource Center on Child Sexual Abuse (under the auspices of the U.S. Department of Health and Human Services, the American Humane Association, and the National Committee for the Prevention of Cruelty to Children, respectively), as well as the OJJDP, publish data on abuse and neglect of children. Data are also kept and periodically published by departments of children and family services of each state. Throughout the nation in 2014, social service agencies received an estimated 3.6 million referrals that involved the alleged maltreatment of approximately 6.6 million children (Administration for Children and Families, 2014). Among these referrals, 60.7% resulted in investigations or assessments that were substantiated. Thus, in 2014, 2.2 million child protection investigations found at least one child to be a victim of abuse or neglect (Administration for Children and Families, 2014). This does not mean that all cases of maltreatment are reported; in fact, according to the U.S. Department of Health and Human Services (2005), because parents are the perpetrators of maltreatment in approximately 80% of substantiated cases, and because most substantiated maltreatment occurs in private settings, it is likely that the majority of such cases are not reported.

National Crime Victimization Survey

The U.S. Department of Justice (Bureau of Justice Statistics) and the U.S. Bureau of the Census semiannually provide us with official data on crime from the perspective of victims. The National Crime Victimization Survey (NCVS) has been collecting data on personal and household victimization since 1973. Based on a survey of a nationally representative sample of residential addresses, the NCVS is the primary source of information on the characteristics of criminal victimization and on the number and types of crimes not reported to law enforcement authorities. Twice each year, data are obtained from a sample of roughly 49,000 households comprising about 100,000 persons on the frequency, characteristics, and consequences of criminal victimization in the United States (National Crime Victimization Survey Resource Guide, n.d.). When NCVS data are compared with the data from the UCRs, we can make some rough estimates of the extent to which certain types of crime occur but are not reported. For example, for the year 2006, Rand and

Catalano (2007) concluded that about 43% of robberies, 41% of aggravated assaults, 50% of burglaries, and 59% of sex offenses experienced were not reported to the police. According to Baumer and Lauritsen (2009), "In most cases, more than half of the crimes experienced by Americans are not conveyed to law enforcement officials" (p. 33).

The reasons for not reporting crime are diverse (see, for example, In Practice 2.2) and include the following:

Private or personal matters

Nonbelief that the police can do anything about the crime

Fear of reprisal

Too inconvenient

Lack of proof (Baumer & Lauritsen, 2009; Bureau of Justice Statistics, 2005; Kruttschnitt & Carbone-Lopez, 2009)

In addition to the NCVS, the Bureau of Justice Statistics has worked with the Office of Community Oriented Policing Services (COPS) to develop a statistical software program measuring victimization and citizen attitudes on crime. Local policing municipalities participating in community policing programs use the software program in conjunction with telephone surveys of local residents to collect data on crime victimization, attitudes toward the police, and other community issues. The results are used to identify which community programs are needed and where those programs should be located in the community.

IN PRACTICE 2.2

WHY DON'T SOME PEOPLE REPORT CHILD ABUSE AND NEGLECT?

Among the most frequently identified reasons for not reporting are lack of knowledge about child abuse and neglect and lack of familiarity with state reporting laws. Other reasons people don't report include the following:

- Choosing instead to effectively intervene independent of the formal system
- Fearing or being unwilling to get involved
- Fearing that a report will make matters worse
- Being reluctant to risk angering the family
- Being concerned that making a report will negatively impact an existing relationship with the child or others

- Believing that someone else will speak up and do something

Although these feelings are understandable and it can be frightening to respond to suspected child abuse and neglect, the consequences of *not* reporting your worries to child welfare professionals could be seriously detrimental to a child's safety. In some cases, they might even be life threatening. So don't be afraid to call and ask for help. Your call will help child welfare professionals determine the most appropriate response, including whether an assessment or investigation of the situation is needed and what further supports may be beneficial or necessary. A trained set of eyes on the situation may be the best response when other efforts have

(Continued)

(Continued)

failed or the seriousness of a situation requires it. It is not your responsibility to investigate; it is your responsibility to be involved and contact appropriate professionals when you have heightened concerns. The safety of a child is at stake.

Source: American Humane (2008).

Questions to Consider

1. True or False: Persons are expected to wait until they are certain of child abuse before making a report.

2. Multiple Choice: Which of the following is not a reason people give for not reporting abuse or neglect?

a. Believing that someone else will report the incident

b. Being afraid to create friction or a negative relationship with the reported family

c. Wanting to get involved and stop the violence

d. Believing that reporting will make the situation worse for the child

3. Given the concerns that people note about reporting suspected child abuse, how do you think that authorities can increase reporting of likely child abuse?

Although victimization surveys would appear to be a better overall indicator of the extent and nature of crime, delinquency, and abuse, they also have their limitations. As is the case with all self-report measures (see the following section), there are serious questions about the accuracy and specificity of reports by victims. In addition, the surveys do not include interviews with children under the age of 12 and do not include questions about all types of crime (the NCVS focuses primarily on violent offenses). Because of this, incidents of family violence like we encountered in our What Would You Do? exercise at the beginning of this chapter may go undetected until after the circumstance ends in a homicide.

Sources of Error in Official Statistics

Official statistics are collected at several different levels in the juvenile justice network, and each level includes possible sources of error. Table 2.2 indicates some sources of error that may affect official statistics collected at various levels. Each official source has its uses, but generally the sources of error increase as we move up each level in the network.

There are two additional sources of error that may affect all official statistics. First, those who are least able to afford the luxury of private counsel and middle-class standards of living are probably overrepresented throughout all levels. Thus, official statistics might not represent actual differences in delinquency and abuse by social class but rather might represent the ability of middle- and upper-class members to avoid being labeled (for a more thorough discussion, see Elliot & Huizinga, 2006, pp. 149–177; Empey & Stafford, 1991, pp. 315–317; Garrett & Short, 1975; Knudsen, 1992, p. 31). Second, it is important to remember that agencies collect and publish statistics for a variety of administrative purposes (e.g., to justify more personnel and more money). This does not mean that all or even most agencies deliberately manipulate statistics for their own purposes. All statistics are open to interpretation and may be presented in a variety of ways, depending on the intent of the presenters.

Table 2.2 Sources of Error at Specified Levels in the Juvenile Justice System

Data Collected	Sources of Error in Official Statistics
Offenses known to the police	All offenses not detected
	All offenses not reported to or recorded by the police
Offenses cleared by arrests	Errors from Level 1
	All offenses that do not lead to arrests
Offenses leading to prosecution	Errors from Levels 1 and 2
	All offenses that result in arrests but do not lead to prosecution
Offenses leading to adjudication of delinquency	Errors from Levels 1, 2, and 3
	All offenses prosecuted that do not lead to adjudication of delinquency
Offenses leading to incarceration	Errors from Levels 1, 2, 3, and 4
	All offenses leading to adjudication of delinquency but not to incarceration

Unofficial Sources of Data

It is clear that relying on official statistics on delinquency and abuse is like looking at the tip of an iceberg; that is, a substantial proportion of these offenses remain hidden beneath the surface. Although it is certain that much delinquency and maltreatment is not reported to, or recorded by, officials (unofficial sources of data), there is no perfect method for determining just how many of these behaviors remain hidden.

Self-Report Studies

Recognizing that official statistics provide a false dichotomy between those who are officially labeled and those who are not, a number of researchers have focused on comparing the extent and nature of delinquency among institutionalized (labeled) delinquents and noninstitutionalized (nonlabeled) juveniles. Short and Nye (1958) used self-reports of delinquent behavior obtained by distributing questionnaires to both labeled and nonlabeled juveniles. These questionnaires called on respondents to indicate what types of delinquent acts they had committed and the frequency with which such acts had been committed. Short and Nye concluded that delinquency among noninstitutionalized juveniles is extensive and that there is little difference between the extent and nature of delinquent acts committed by noninstitutionalized juveniles and those committed by institutionalized juveniles. In addition, the researchers indicated that official statistics lead us to misbelieve that delinquency is largely a lower-class phenomenon given that few significant differences exist in the incidence of delinquency among upper-, middle-, and lower-class juveniles. Conclusions reached in similar self-report studies by Porterfield (1946), Akers (1964), Voss (1966), and Bynum and Thompson (1992, pp. 78–79) generally agreed with those of Short and Nye (1958). Based on these self-report studies, it is apparent that the vast majority of delinquent acts never become part of official statistics (Conklin, 1998, p. 67). This, of course, parallels information from victim survey research at the adult level.

Additional studies of self-reported delinquency have been conducted by Taylor, McGue, and Iacono (2000); Pagani, Boulerice, and Vitaro (1999); Williams and Dunlop (1999); Farrington and colleagues (2003); and Gover, Jennings, and Tewksbury (2009), indicating that the technique is still in use. Self-report studies,

Two teenagers pass drugs in the street. How much impact do drugs have on delinquent activities?

however, are subject to criticism on the basis that respondents may underreport or overreport delinquency or abuse as a result of either poor recall or deliberate deception. To some extent, this criticism applies to victimization surveys as well even though victims are not asked to incriminate themselves. Mistakes in recalling the date of an incident, the exact nature of the incident, or the characteristics of the parties involved may occur. Or for reasons of their own, victims may choose not to report particular incidents. NCVS interviewers attempt to minimize these problems by asking only about crimes during the prior 6 months and by avoiding questions requiring personal admissions of offenses, but there are still no guarantees of accuracy, and this is certainly the case when asking juveniles to report their own crimes or abuse. Hindelang, Hirschi, and Weis (1981, p. 22), for example, contended that illegal behaviors of seriously delinquent juveniles are underestimated in self-report studies because such juveniles are less likely to answer questions truthfully. Farrington and colleagues (2003), Costanza and Kilburn (2004), and Rennison and Melde (2009) concluded that research based on self-reports sometimes yields different conclusions compared with research based on official records or other research techniques.

Some researchers have included trap questions to detect these deceptions. In 1966, Clark and Tifft used follow-up interviews and a polygraph to assess the accuracy of self-report inventories. They administered a 35-item self-report questionnaire to a group of 45 male college students. The respondents were to report the frequency of each delinquent behavior they had engaged in since entering high school. At a later date, each respondent was asked to reexamine his questionnaire and to correct any mistakes after being told he would be asked to take a polygraph test to determine the accuracy of his responses. Clark and Tifft (1966) found that all respondents made corrections on their original questionnaires (58% at the first opportunity and 42% during the polygraph examination). Three-fourths of all changes increased the frequency of admitted deviancy, all respondents underreported the frequency of their misconduct on at least one item, and 50% overreported on at least one item. With respect to self-reported delinquency, Clark and Tifft (1966) concluded that "those items most frequently used on delinquency scales were found to be rather inaccurate" (p. 523).

There are ways of attempting to improve the accuracy of self-reports. In a study of convicted child molesters, official records concerning the sexually abusive activity of the inmates could be compared with their self-reports of behavior. In some cases, it was also possible to confirm through official records the inmates' claims that they themselves had been abused as children (Rinehart, 1991). Without some corroboration, however, the use of self-reports to determine the extent and nature of either delinquency or child abuse is, at best, risky. Empey and colleagues (1999) concluded, "In short, self-report surveys, like other ways of estimating delinquent behavior, have their limitations. Nonetheless, they are probably the single most accurate source of information on the actual illegal acts of young people" (p. 87). As noted earlier, self-reports of delinquency are more comprehensive than official reports because the former include behaviors not reported, or not otherwise known, to the authorities. At least some research indicates that juveniles are willing to report accurate information about their delinquent acts (Farrington, Loeber, Stouthamer-Loeber, Van Kammen, & Schmidt, 1996). Based on a review of self-reported delinquency studies, Espiritu, Huizinga, Crawford, and Loeber (2001) found that the vast majority of juveniles 12 years or under reported involvement in some form of aggression or violence, but only roughly 5% reported being involved in violence serious enough to be considered a delinquent or criminal offense. Furthermore, the authors noted that self-report rates for major forms of delinquency were nearly the same in 1976 and 1998. Still, van Batenburg-Eddes et al. (2012) assessed the differential validity of self-reported delinquency in adolescents as related to self-reported police contacts and concluded that using only self-reported data to measure delinquency in an ethnically diverse population results in substantial bias. They advise the use of multiple sources to measure the prevalence of delinquency.

Finally, self-report studies of juvenile delinquency have been conducted to examine the relationship between prior victimization of youth and future delinquent behavior. Indeed, this has been examined not only in the United States but in 30 other countries around the globe (Enzmann et al., 2015). In studies such as the one conducted by Enzmann et al. (2015), victimization data are gathered through the use of the International Crime Victim Survey (ICVS), which is the international version of the previously discussed National Crime Victimization Survey (NCVS) that is used in the United States. As can be seen, the basic components of studying juvenile delinquency go beyond the borders of the United States and extend to juvenile issues around the world.

Police Observational Studies

Another method for determining the extent and nature of offenses by and against juveniles is observation of police encounters related to juveniles (police observational studies). Several studies over the years have found that most delinquent acts, even when they become known to the police, do not lead to official action and, thus, do not become a part of official statistics (Black & Reiss, 1970; Piliavin & Briar, 1964; Terry, 1967; Werthman & Piliavin, 1967). These studies indicated that 70% to 85% of encounters between police and juveniles do not lead to arrests and inclusion in official delinquency statistics.

In the summers of 1996 and 1997, trained observers rode with patrol and community officers during their assigned shifts and recorded information on 443 police–juvenile encounters where at least one juvenile was treated by the observed officer as a suspect (Myers, 2004, p. 91). The conclusions from this observational study largely confirm what previous studies on police–juvenile interactions have reported with respect to police use of authority. The police used their authority to formally take juveniles into custody infrequently. Only 13% of suspects were taken into custody for the purpose of charging. Police officers were more likely to arrest juvenile suspects when the problem is of a more serious nature and when juvenile suspects are verbally or behaviorally disrespectful toward police, though being disrespectful increases the probability by only a modest amount. The author concluded (p. 200) that "in resolving issues with juvenile suspects, police are clearly using their discretion and acting both as a social control agent and as a public service provider" (Myers, 2004, pp. 180–200).

The reasons given by the police for dealing informally with juvenile offenders are both numerous and critical to a complete understanding of the juvenile justice network. These reasons are discussed in some detail in Chapter 8. The point is that the number of juveniles who commit delinquent acts but do not become part of official statistics seems to be considerably larger than the number of juveniles who do become part of official statistics. Relying only on official statistics to estimate the extent and nature of delinquency, thus, can be very misleading. Some time ago, Morash (1984) came to the following conclusion:

Youths of certain racial groups and in gang-like peer groups were more often investigated and arrested than other youths. Evidence of the independent influence of subject's race and gang-likeness of peers was not provided by the multivariate analysis, however. Thus, there is some question about whether race and gang qualities have an independent influence on police actions, or whether they are related to police actions because they are correlated with other explanatory variables. The multivariate analysis did provide evidence that the police are prone to arrest males who break the law with peers and who have delinquent peers. Alternatively, they are prone not to investigate females in all-female groups. These tendencies cannot be attributed to the delinquency of the youths or to correlations with other independent variables. There is, then, a convincing demonstration of regular tendencies of the police to investigate and arrest males who have delinquent peers regardless of these youths' involvement in delinquency. (pp. 108–109)

Furthermore, Frazier, Bishop, and Henretta (1992) found that black juveniles were more likely to receive harsher dispositions in areas where the proportion of whites was high, thereby introducing another possible source of bias (relative proportion of whites and blacks in the community) in police statistics. Engel, Sobol, and Worden (2000) found that police action was affected by a state of intoxication when combined with displays of disrespect on the part of the suspect. Overall, however, they concluded, "It appears that police officers expect their authority to be observed equally by all suspects, and do not make distinctions based on race, sex, location, and the seriousness of the situation" (pp. 255–256). Using observational and interview data from two medium-sized cities, Rossler and Terrill (2012) "examined how officers respond to noncoercive citizen requests for service during encounters, and the impact that situational and officer characteristics have on their willingness to comply with requests" (p. 3). The researchers concluded that officers complied with a majority of citizen requests involving respectful citizens, wealthier citizens, and white officers, whereas officers were less likely to comply with requests from younger and older citizens. Rydberg and Terrill (2010, p. 92), based on observations of the police in two medium-sized cities, determined that although higher education showed no influence on the probability of an arrest or search occurring in a police–suspect encounter, college education does appear to significantly reduce the likelihood of force occurring. Clearly, a variety of factors influence the extent to which police officers take official action in encounters and the extent to which they report such encounters.

Bell and Bell (1991) also found that the police often fail to take official action, preferring instead to handle incidents of domestic violence (involving child as well as adult victims) by referring the parties to another agency. Finally, Halter (2010), based on case files from six police agencies in major U.S. cities of youth (almost entirely girls) allegedly involved in prostitution, found that a number of factors determined whether the police considered youth to be victims or offenders. When youth were cooperative, when there were identified exploiters, when the youth had no prior records, and when the youth were reported by a third party as victims, the police more often considered them to be victims. Interestingly, it appeared that the police sometimes used criminal charges as a protective response to detain some of the youth, even though they considered these youth victims. Such youth would then be counted as offenders rather than as victims.

The influence of theories of causation cannot be overlooked when it comes to defining and measuring delinquency and child abuse. Such theories provide guidelines as to where to look for victims and offenders and how to define both categories, thus affecting statistics concerning abuse and delinquency. A fairly recent study by Goodrich, Anderson, and LaMotte (2014) examined both youth and police officer views of one another, citing attribution theory as the underlying perspective to their research. The idea was that prior experience from each group would significantly impact the attributions that they made in the future toward one another. What is interesting about this study is that the number of years that police were on duty did not affect their attitude toward youth. Nor was their sense of feeling confident in working with youth necessarily linked to time in the profession. However, this study did show that officers were keenly aware of the potential impact that they could have on a young person's life and adjusted their reactions accordingly (Goodrich, Anderson, & LaMotte, 2014). Thus, it would appear that attributions toward youth, made by police, are neither seasoned nor jaded by years of service. Rather, most police who work with youth understand the juncture among age, adolescent development, decision making, risk factors, and protective factors that can coalesce into a juvenile–police encounter.

CAREER OPPORTUNITY: CHIEF JUVENILE PROBATION OFFICER

Job description: Supervise juvenile probation officers as they supervise probationers, conduct presentence investigations, and hold preliminary conferences. Coordinate with police, judges, and other juvenile justice practitioners. Supervise probationers if dictated by caseloads.

Employment requirements: A master's degree in social work, criminal justice, corrections, or a related field. Ten years of experience in juvenile justice, with at least 5 years of direct service and casework experience.

Beginning salary: $30,000 to $50,000. Typically good retirement and benefits packages.

Summary

Clearly, there are several potential problems arising from definitional difficulties. First, we need to keep in mind the fact that defining a juvenile as a delinquent is often interpreted as meaning a young criminal. Although some juveniles who commit serious offenses are certainly young criminals, it is important to note that others who commit acts that are illegal solely because of their age, or who are one-time offenders, may also be labeled as young criminals. Yet these offenses (e.g., underage drinking, illegal possession of alcohol, curfew violations) would not have been considered criminal if the juveniles had been adults.

Second, rehabilitation and treatment programs are almost certainly doomed to failure if they are based solely on information obtained from officially labeled abused children and delinquents. Recognition of the wide variety of motives and behaviors that may be involved is essential if such programs are to be successful, particularly with respect to prevention.

Third, labels (e.g., *delinquent, abused child, MRAI*) tell practitioners very little about any particular juvenile. All parties involved would benefit far more from focusing on the specific behaviors that led to the labels.

There is no doubt that a good deal more delinquency and abuse occur than are reported, although the exact amount is very difficult to determine. There are scores of delinquent acts and abused children that are never reported. Although it is tempting to divide the world into those who have committed delinquent acts and those who have not—or those who have been abuse victims and those who have not—this polarizes the categories and overlooks the fact that there are many in the official nondelinquent, nonabused category who actually are delinquent or abused.

It is easy to perceive those who are delinquent or abused as abnormal when, in fact, the only abnormal characteristic of many of these juveniles may be that they were detected and labeled. In most other respects, except for extreme cases, these juveniles may differ little from their cohorts. With respect to delinquency at least, there are reasons to be both optimistic and pessimistic based on this view. If most juveniles engage in behavior similar to that which causes some to be labeled as delinquent, there is reason to believe there is no serious underlying pathology in most delinquents. Some types of delinquency occur as a "normal" part of adolescence. Activities such as underage drinking, curfew violation, and experimentation with sex and marijuana seem to be widespread among adolescents. Although these activities may be undesirable when engaged in by juveniles, they are not abnormal or atypical. Thus, reintegration or maintenance within the community should be facilitated.

Those viewing activities that are widespread among juveniles as atypical or abnormal are faced with essentially two choices. Either they can define the majority of juveniles as delinquent, thereby increasing official delinquency rates, or they can reevaluate the legal codes that make these activities violations and remove such behaviors from the category of delinquent. Clearly, many prefer to ignore the latter option and instead continue to polarize "good" and "bad" juveniles.

To some extent, the same argument holds for abused and neglected juveniles. Although those who are labeled are victims instead of perpetrators (as is the case with delinquents), in many cases they are not so terribly different from their peers either. If, as we suspect, the vast majority of abuse and neglect cases go unreported, many juveniles experience a lot of the same behaviors as do those labeled as abused or neglected. Thus, the way we treat those who are labeled may be crucial in determining the extent of psychological damage done. If we recognize them as victims but also recognize that they are not abnormal, our efforts at reintegration and rehabilitation may be more effective.

Practitioners in the juvenile justice network, particularly juvenile court judges and those involved in prevention and corrections, may have an inaccurate image of delinquents and maltreated juveniles. Discussions with numerous practitioners at these levels indicate that many view the lower-social-class black male as the typical delinquent and the lower-social-class female as the typical victim of maltreatment. Some social science research perpetuates these mistaken impressions by focusing on labeled juveniles, but other research indicates that such juveniles are typical only of those who have been detected and labeled. Prevention programs and dispositional decisions based on erroneous beliefs about the nature and extent of delinquency and maltreatment can hardly be expected to produce positive results.

Both legal and behavioral definitions of delinquency and child maltreatment present problems. Legal definitions assess, more or less accurately, numbers and characteristics of juveniles who become officially labeled. However, use of legal definitions can be misleading with respect to the actual extent and nature of offenses by and against juveniles. Behavioral definitions assess the extent and nature of such activities more accurately but raise serious problems in the area of data collection. How do we identify those juveniles who commit delinquent acts or who are mistreated but not officially detected?

Official statistics reflect only the tip of the iceberg with respect to delinquency and mistreatment and are subject to errors in compilation and reporting. The use of self-report techniques, victim survey research, and police observational studies helps us to better assess the extent of unofficial or hidden delinquency, abuse, and neglect—although each of these methods has weaknesses. Success in preventing and correcting offenses by and against juveniles depends on understanding not only the differences but also the similarities between labeled and nonlabeled juveniles. The role of theory in directing us to look in certain places for delinquency while largely ignoring others is also a critical factor.

Critical Thinking Questions

1. What are the two major types of definitions of *delinquency* and *child maltreatment*? Discuss the strengths and weaknesses of each. How might legal definitions lead to mistaken impressions of delinquents and abused juveniles on behalf of juvenile court personnel?

2. What are the national sources of official statistics on delinquency? On child abuse? Discuss the limitations of these statistics.

3. What is the value of self-report studies? Of victim survey research? What are the weaknesses of these two types of data collection?

4. Compare and contrast the nature and extent of delinquency and child abuse as seen through official statistics on the one hand and self-report, victim survey, and police observational studies on the other.

Suggested Readings

Federal Bureau of Investigation. (2013). *National Incident-Based Reporting System (NIBRS)*. Retrieved from www2.fbi.gov/ucr/faqs.htm

Kruttschnitt, C., & Carbone-Lopez, K. (2009, December). Customer satisfaction: Crime victims' willingness to call the police. *Ideas in American Policing*. Retrieved from www.policefoundation.org/docs/library.html

Myers, S. M. (2004, April). *Police encounters with juvenile suspects: Explaining the use of authority and provision of*

support, final report. Retrieved from www.ncjrs.gov/pdffiles1/nij/grants/205125.pdf

Rennison, C. M., & Melde, C. (2009). Exploring the use of victim surveys to study gang crime: Prospects and possibilities. *Criminal Justice Review, 34,* 489–514.

U.S. Department of Health & Human Services. (2012). *Child maltreatment 2011*. Retrieved from http://www.acf.hhs.gov/sites/default/files/cb/cm11.pdf#page=28

$SAGE edge™

Sharpen your skills with SAGE edge at **edge.sagepub.com/coxjj9e**. SAGE edge for students provides a personalized approach to help you accomplish your coursework goals in an easy-to-use learning environment. You'll find action plans, mobile-friendly eFlashcards, and quizzes as well as video and web resources and links to SAGE journal articles to support and expand on the concepts presented in this chapter.

Characteristics of Juvenile Offenders

3

On completion of this chapter, students should be able to do the following:

- Recognize differences between delinquency profiles based on official statistics and behavioral profiles
- Recognize and discuss the multitude of factors related to delinquency
- Discuss the impact of social factors (e.g., family, schools, social class) on delinquency
- Discuss the effects of physical factors (e.g., gender, age, race) on delinquency

WHAT WOULD YOU DO?

You are a juvenile probation officer for youth referred through the court system. Recently, the Mendez family was referred to you at the time of Isabella's third arrest, this time for drug possession. Isabella is a 15-year-old Latina who lives with her mother, Juanita, and younger brother, Gustavo. Juanita is a single parent whose husband is currently locked up in a medium-security prison for a robbery charge. Gustavo is 12 years old and loves his sister but views her as trouble for her mother. Juanita is upset about her daughter's behavior and because she is afraid of losing custody of her daughter to the state.

Recently, the family was referred to the regional office of the Department of Children and Family Services (DCFS). Because Juanita only speaks Spanish, the family was assigned to a Latina bilingual case worker who made a point to call the family. When she called, she noted that

there was screaming and fighting in the house during the call. The caseworker noted that the mother, Juanita, sounded overwhelmed. When the caseworker tried to arrange a session for the family, Juanita explained that she could not ever get Isabella to attend.

You indicate to Juanita that you plan to visit the home but would like to time it so that Isabella would be there when her mother was also there. Juanita works during the day as a domestic worker in a hotel, and Isabella is seldom home unless it is later at night, if at all. You set the time for about 8:30 p.m. the next evening. When you arrive, you find Ms. Mendez at home alone with Gustavo. Juanita explains that Isabella came to the house for a few brief moments and, without warning, left with her friends, giving no explanation. Juanita indicates that she has no idea when her daughter would be home. Young Gustavo also confirms his mother's story and states that Isabella is always causing problems for his mother. He feels that because she does not want to be with them, she should just go away.

What Would You Do?

1. In today's multicultural society, how important is it to have multilingual abilities in juvenile justice agencies?

2. In your opinion, do you think that because Isabella's father is in prison that this is, perhaps, affecting her current behavior?

3. How likely do you think it is that Isabella's behavior will affect Gustavo's behavior when he is a teenager?

4. Do you believe that Juanita is a responsible parent?

The complex shown in this picture processes juvenile offenders, taking into consideration their various characteristics and their circumstances when determining the outcome for these young offenders.

In any discussion of the general characteristics of juvenile offenders, we must be aware of possible errors in the data and must be cautious concerning the impression presented. In general, profiles of juvenile offenders are drawn from official files based on police contacts, arrests, and/or incarceration. Although these profiles may accurately reflect the characteristics of juveniles who are or will be incarcerated or who have a good chance for an encounter with the justice system, as we saw in Chapter 2, they might not accurately reflect the characteristics of all juveniles who commit offenses.

Studies have established that the number of youthful offenders who formally enter the justice system is small in comparison with the total number of violations committed by juveniles (Langton, Berzofsky, Krebs, & Smiley-McDonald, 2012). Hidden-offender surveys, in which juveniles are asked to anonymously indicate the offenses they have committed, have indicated repeatedly that far more offenses are committed than are reported in official agency reports. In addition, even those juveniles who commit offenses resulting in official encounters are infrequently formally processed through the entire system. The determination of who will officially enter the justice system depends on many variables that are considered by law enforcement and other juvenile justice personnel. It is important to remember that official profiles of youthful offenders might not actually represent those who commit youthful offenses but rather represent only those who enter the system.

It is common practice to use official profiles of juveniles as a basis for development of delinquency prevention programs. Based on the characteristics of known offenders, prevention programs that ignore the characteristics of the hidden and/or unofficial delinquent have been initiated. For example, there is official statistical evidence indicating that the major proportion of delinquents comes from lower socioeconomic families and neighborhoods. The correlates of poverty and low social status include substandard housing, poor sanitation, poor medical care, high unemployment, and exposure to violence (Zahn et al., 2010). It has been suggested that if these conditions were altered, delinquency might be reduced. However, as Harcourt and Ludwig (2006) found out in their study of broken-windows policing, changing the disorder does not necessarily reduce or eliminate criminal behavior. (Recall our comments on middle-class delinquency in Chapter 2.)

The factors causing delinquency seem to be numerous and interwoven in complex ways (Tapia, 2011). Multiple factors must be considered if we are to improve our understanding of delinquency. For example, Mallett (2008), in a study using a random sample of all adjudicated delinquent youths who received probation supervision from the Cuyahoga County (greater Cleveland) Juvenile Court in 2004 and 2005, found that over 57% of delinquent youths on probation supervision had either a mental health disorder or a special education disability. Thornberry, Huizinga, and Loeber (2004) found that drug, school, and mental health problems are strong risk factors for male adolescents' involvement in persistent and serious delinquency, although more than half of persistent serious offenders do not have such problems. Still, more than half of the males studied who did have persistent problems with drugs, school, or mental health were also persistent and serious delinquents. Fewer than half of persistent and serious female delinquents studied had drug, school, or mental health problems, but these problems alone or in combination were not strong risk factors for serious delinquency. However, Zahn and colleagues (2010, p. 11) concluded that "attachment to school has protective effects against delinquency for both genders, although several recent studies find a stronger effect for girls." Mitchell and Shaw (2011) also noted that adolescent offenders have high levels of mental health problems, many of which go undetected and lead to poor outcomes. Most criminologists contend that a number of factors combine to produce delinquency (see In Practice 3.1). Further, at least some research indicates that risk factors for delinquency may be different for boys and girls (Carbone-Lopez, Esbensen, & Brick, 2010; Martin, Golder, Cynthia, & Sawning, 2013; National Girls Institute, 2013; Zahn et al., 2010).

IN PRACTICE 3.1

ENDING RACIAL AND ETHNIC DISPARITIES IN THE JUVENILE JUSTICE SYSTEM

Issues related to racial disparity in the treatment of youth processed through the juvenile justice system are still problematic, despite efforts to eliminate this problem. Evidence that this problem still warrants substantive attention exists when one considers that the Office of Juvenile Justice and Delinquency Prevention (OJJDP) continues to allocate funds for grant-funded projects to address disparity problems in processing youthful offenders in the juvenile justice system. The Smart on Juvenile Justice: Technical Assistance to End Racial and Ethnic Disparities in the Juvenile Justice System is one such project initiated by the OJJDP to do this. The overall goal of this project is to establish, operate, and maintain OJJDP's initiative to end racial and ethnic disparities in the juvenile system, serving as a comprehensive clearinghouse on issues related to eliminating racial and ethnic disparities in juvenile justice and to strategically focusing DMC reduction efforts.

This project supports the Juvenile Justice and Delinquency Prevention Act, which requires participating states to address the disproportionate number of minority youth who come into contact with the juvenile justice system. Disproportionate minority contact (DMC) exists if the rate at which a specific minority group comes into contact with the juvenile justice system significantly differs from the rate of contact for non-Latino Caucasians or other minority groups. Research indicates that various contributing factors cause DMC, including but not limited to implicit bias; racial stereotyping; and laws, policies, and procedures that can have a disparate impact. As a result, racial and ethnic disparities throughout the juvenile justice system can occur.

The OJJDP has found that African American youth are arrested more than twice as often as non-Latino Caucasian youth and are diverted from the juvenile justice system less often than Caucasian youth. Going further, Native American youth are diverted less often and are transferred to adult court at more than 1.5 times the rate of Caucasian youth. National estimates from state data through the OJJDP show that Latino youth are placed in secure detention more than 1.5 times as often as Caucasian youth, with similar rates of transfers to adult court as Native American youth. Data such as these provide clear evidence from valid government sources that there is still work to be done to establish consistency in the justice system's response to our youth who run errant of the law.

Source: Office of Juvenile Justice and Delinquency Prevention (2017).

Questions to Consider

1. True or False: Latino youth, but not Native American youth, are transferred to adult court more frequently than Caucasian youth.

2. Multiple Choice: The OJJDP has found that African American youth are arrested more than _____ as often as non-Latino Caucasian youth:

   a. twice
   b. three times
   c. four times
   d. None of the above

3. What reasons do you think are likely to explain the disproportionate minority contact noted in In Practice 3.1?

Unfortunately, simplistic explanations are often appealing and sometimes lead to prevention and rehabilitation efforts that prove to be of very little value. With this in mind, let us now turn our attention to some of the factors viewed as important determinants of delinquent behavior. It must be emphasized once again that most of the information we have concerning these factors is based on official statistics. For a more accurate portrait of the characteristics of actual juvenile offenders, we must also concentrate on the vast majority of juveniles who commit delinquent acts but are never officially labeled as delinquent.

Social Factors

As they grow up, children are exposed to a number of social factors that may increase their risk for problems such as abusing drugs and engaging in delinquent behavior. Risk factors appear to function in a cumulative fashion—that is, the greater the number of risk factors, the greater the likelihood that youth will engage in delinquent or other risky behavior. There is also evidence that problem behaviors associated with risk factors tend to cluster. For example, delinquency and violence cluster with other problems, such as drug abuse, mental health issues, teen pregnancy, and school misbehavior.

Shown in Chart 3.1 are a number of factors experienced by juveniles as individuals, as family members, in school, among their peers, and in their communities. For further information concerning the indicators of these risks and data sources associated with such indicators, visit the website from which the chart was adapted.

Chart 3.1 Risk Factors for Health and Behavior Problems

Individual

Antisocial behavior and alienation, delinquent beliefs, general delinquency involvement, and/or drug dealing

Gun possession, illegal gun ownership, and/or carrying

Teen parenthood

Favorable attitudes toward drug use and/or early onset of alcohol and other drug (AOD) use

Early onset of aggression and/or violence

Intellectual and/or developmental disabilities

Victimization and exposure to violence

Poor refusal skills

Life stressors

Early sexual involvement

Mental disorder and/or mental health problem

Family

Family history of problem behavior and/or parent criminality

Family management problems and poor parental supervision and/or monitoring

Poor family attachment or bonding

Child victimization and maltreatment

Pattern of high family conflict

Family violence

Having a young mother

Broken home

Sibling antisocial behavior

Family transitions

Parental use of harsh physical punishment and/or erratic discipline practices

Low parent education level and/or illiteracy

Maternal depression

School

Low academic achievement

Negative attitude toward school, low bonding, low school attachment, and/or low commitment to school

Truancy or frequent absences

Suspension

Dropping out of school

Inadequate school climate, poorly organized and functioning schools, and/or negative labeling by teachers

Identified as learning disabled

Frequent school transitions

Peer

Gang involvement and/or gang membership

Peer alcohol, tobacco, and other drug (ATOD) use

Association with delinquent or aggressive peers

Peer rejection

Community

Availability or use of ATOD in neighborhood

Availability of firearms

High-crime neighborhood

Community instability

Low community attachment

Economic deprivation, poverty, and/or residence in a disadvantaged neighborhood

Neighborhood youth in trouble

Feeling unsafe in the neighborhood

Social and physical disorder or disorganized neighborhood

Source: Adapted from youth.gov.

Family

One of the most important factors influencing delinquent behavior is the family setting. It is within the family that the child internalizes those basic beliefs, values, attitudes, and general patterns of behavior that give direction to subsequent behaviors. Because the family is the initial transmitter of the culture (through the socialization process) and greatly shapes the personality characteristics of the child, considerable emphasis has been given to family structure, functions, and processes in delinquency research. Although it is not possible to review all such research here, we concentrate on several areas that have been the focus of attention.

Pixland/Thinkstock

Homelessness and poverty have been linked to delinquent behavior, although not all homeless youth or those living in poverty commit crimes.

A great deal of research focuses on the crucial influence of the family in the formation of behavioral patterns and personality. Contemporary theories attach great importance to the parental role in determining the personality characteristics of children. More than half a century ago, Glueck and Glueck (1950) focused attention on the relationship between family and delinquency, a relationship that has remained in the spotlight ever since (see In Practice 3.2).

Through the Prevent Delinquency Project, that is exactly what volunteers attempt to teach, by meeting with parent/teacher associations, community organizations, and individual parents who seek out our assistance.

Source: Prevent Delinquency Project (n.d.).
© Carl A. Bartol.

Questions to Consider

1. True or False: Most juvenile sanctions would not be needed with youth if their parents knew what to do early on when raising their child.

2. Multiple Choice: About _____ of boys ages 12 to 15 who have been classified as bullies have at least one criminal conviction by the time they reach age 24.

   a. 40%

   b. 50%

   c. 60%

   d. 70%

3. What are some of the interventions mentioned that can be used to reform juvenile offenders who are on community supervision?

To young children, home and family are the basic sources of information about life. Thus, many researchers and theorists have focused on the types of values, attitudes, and beliefs maintained and passed on by the family over generations. Interest has focused on the types of behavior and attitudes transmitted to children through the socialization process resulting in a predisposition toward delinquent behavior. For example, the New Jersey Parents' Caucus (2013) said the following:

The NJPC Parents' Empowerment Academy is a comprehensive training and education program that enables parents of children with emotional and behavioral challenges to appropriately and collaboratively negotiate with government agencies and other system partners . . . [and] professionals and providers in the child-serving arena to strengthen their knowledge of family engagement and provides practical tools and strategies which they can implement in their local organizations. (n.p.)

The primary objectives of the academy include the opportunity for parents to

1. Enhance their skills

2. Provide valuable input toward the development and implementation of services for their children

3. Build their capacity to serve as keepers for the vision of "effective and timely services for children with emotional and behavioral challenges"

4. Empower other parents through the use of education, advocacy, and supportive services

5. Better serve their local communities

The primary objectives of the academy include the opportunity for professionals and providers to

1. Explore engagement strategies and barriers, history and principles of family involvement, and specific strategies for high-risk families

2. Develop additional skills focused on building consensus and collaboration with parents and family members, the critical elements of family engagement, the impact of community in family engagement, family-specific strategies, and recruitment and retention

Further support for this argument comes from Worthen (2012), who found that both parent–child bonding and friend relationships affect delinquency and that these relationships differ by both gender and stage of adolescence. And, using data from a sample of 18,512 students in Grades 6, 8, 10, and 12, Fagan, Van Horn, Antaramian, and Hawkins (2011, p. 150) found the following:

Across grades, parents treated girls and boys differently, but neither sex received preferential treatment for all practices assessed, and younger children reported more positive parenting than older students. Family factors were significantly related to delinquency and drug use for both sexes and for all grades. Their findings suggest that "complexities in parent/child interactions that must be taken into account when investigating the causes of adolescent offending and when planning strategies to prevent the development of problem behaviors." (p. 150)

Considerable research indicates a relationship between delinquency and the marital happiness of the children's parents. Official delinquency seems to occur disproportionately among juveniles in unhappy homes marked by marital discord, lack of family communication, unaffectionate parents, high stress and tension, and a general lack of parental cohesiveness and solidarity (Davidson, 1990; Fleener, 1999; Gorman-Smith, Tolan, & Loeber, 1998; Wright & Cullen, 2001). In unhappy familial environments, it is not unusual to find that parents derive little sense of satisfaction from their child-rearing experiences. Genuine concern and interest are seldom expressed except on an erratic and convenient basis at the whim of the parents. Also typical of this familial climate are inconsistent guidance and discipline marked by laxity and a tendency to use children against the other parent (Simons, Simons, Burt, Brody, & Cutrona, 2005). It is not surprising to find poor self-images, personality problems, and conduct problems in children of such families. Families are primary venues for identity disruption, loss, and inner turmoil. The effects of troublesome family circumstances such as separation or divorce, illness, and death are well known and might be summarized by the concept *family trouble* (Francis, 2012). If there is any validity to the adage "chip off the old block," it should not be surprising to find children in unpleasant family circumstances internalizing the types of attitudes, values, beliefs, and modes of behavior demonstrated by their parents.

It seems that in contemporary society, the family home has in many cases been replaced by a house where a related group of individuals reside, change clothes, and occasionally eat. It is somewhat ironic that we often continue to focus on broken homes (homes disrupted through divorce, separation, or desertion) as a major cause of delinquency rather than on unbroken homes where relationships are marked by familial disharmony and disorganization. There is no doubt that the stability and continuity of a family may be shaken when the home is broken by the loss of a parent through death, desertion, long separation, or divorce. At a minimum, one half of the potential socializing and control team is separated from the family. The belief that one-parent families produce more delinquents is supported both by official statistics and by numerous studies. Canter (1982), for example, indicated the following:

Youths from broken homes reported significantly more delinquent behavior than youths from intact homes. The general finding of greater male involvement in delinquency was unchanged when the focus was restricted to children from broken homes. Boys from broken homes reported more delinquent behavior than did girls from broken homes. (p. 164)

Canter concluded, "This finding gives credence to the proposition that broken homes reduce parental supervision, which in turn may increase involvement in delinquency, particularly among males" (p. 164). In the Pittsburgh Youth Study, Browning and Loeber (1999) found that the demographic variable most strongly related to delinquency was having a broken family. According to the Forum on Child and Family Statistics (2006), when children live with two parents who are married to each other, they tend to have more favorable life course outcomes.

There is also, however, some evidence that there may be more social organization and cohesion, guidance, and control in happy one-parent families than in two-parent families marked by discord. It may be that the broken family is not as important a determinant of delinquency as are the events leading to the broken home. Disruption, disorganization, and tension, which may lead to a broken family or may prevail in a family staying intact "for the children's sake," may be more important causative factors of delinquency than the actual breakup (Browning & Loeber, 1999; Emery, 1982; Stern, 1964; Texas Youth Commission, 2004). According to Rebellon (2002), broken homes are strongly associated with a range of delinquent behaviors, including minor status offenses and more severe property or violent offenses. According to Brown (2004), adolescents in single-parent families are significantly more delinquent than their counterparts residing with two biological, married parents. Further, "Seven of the eight studies that used nationally representative data, for example, found that children in single-parent or other non-intact family structures were at greater risk of committing criminal or delinquent acts" (Americans for Divorce Reform, 2005). However, as just noted, several factors, including divorce or separation, recent remarriage, gender of parent, and the long-term presence of a stepparent, appear to be related to different types of delinquency.

Not all authorities agree that broken homes have a major influence on delinquency. Wells and Rankin (1991), reviewing the relationship between broken homes and delinquency, concluded that there is some impact of broken homes on delinquency, although it appears to be moderately weak, especially for serious crime. Bumphus and Anderson (1999) concluded that traditional measures of family structure relate more to criminal patterns of Caucasians than to those of African Americans. Rebellon (2002) found that single parenthood per se does not appear to be associated with delinquency; rather, certain types of changes in family composition appear to be related to delinquency. Schroeder, Osgood, and Oghia (2010), using data from the National Youth Study, determined that the process of family dissolution is not associated with concurrent increases in delinquency.

Demuth and Brown (2004), using data from the 1995 National Longitudinal Survey of Adolescent Health, extended prior research investigating the effects of growing up in two-parent versus single-mother families by also examining delinquency in single-father families. The results indicate that juveniles in single-parent families are significantly more delinquent than their counterparts residing with two biological married parents. However, the authors found that family processes fully account for the higher levels of delinquency exhibited by adolescents from single-father versus single-mother families.

In 2011, 69 percent of children ages 0–17 lived with two parents (65 percent with 2 married parents), 27 percent with one parent, and 4 percent with no parents. Among children living with neither parent, more than half lived with a grandparent. Seven percent of all children ages 0–17 lived with a parent who was in a cohabiting union. A cohabiting union could involve one parent and their cohabiting partner or two cohabiting parents. . . . The percentage of children with at least one parent working year round, full time fell to 71 percent in 2010, down from 72 percent in 2009 and the lowest since 1993. . . . Only 41 percent of children in families maintained by a single mother had a parent who worked year round, full time in 2010, down from 44 percent in 2009. Black, non-Hispanic children and Hispanic children were less likely than White, non-Hispanic children to have a parent working year round, full time. About 61 percent of Hispanic children and 53 percent of Black, non-Hispanic children lived in families with secure parental employment in 2010, compared with 79 percent of White, non-Hispanic children. (Forum on Child and Family Statistics, 2012, pp. 4, 7)

The American family unit has changed considerably during the past 50 years. Large and extended families, composed of various relatives living close together, at one time provided mutual aid, comfort, and protection. Today, the family is smaller and has relinquished many of its socialization functions to specialized organizations and agencies that exert a great amount of influence in the education, training, care, guidance, and protection of children. This often results in normative conflict for children who find their attitudes differing from the views and standards of their parents. These changes may bring more economic wealth to the family, but they may make it more difficult for parents to give constructive guidance and protection to their children. In addition, the rise of "mixed families," in which each parent brings children of his or her own into the family setting, may result in conflicts among the children or between one parent and the children of the other parent.

Over the years, there has been considerable interest in children with working parents who have come to be known as latchkey children. This term generally describes school-age children who return home from school to an empty house. Estimates indicate that there are 5 to 16 million children left unsupervised after school (Alston, 2013). These children are often left to fend for themselves before going to school in the morning, after school in the afternoon, and on school holidays when parents are working or otherwise occupied. This has resulted in older (but still rather young) children being required to care for younger siblings during these periods and is also a factor in the increasing number of children found in video arcades, in shopping malls, on the Internet, and in other areas without adult supervision at a relatively young age. Although the majority of latchkey children appear to survive relatively unscathed, some become involved in illegal or marginally legal activity without their parents' knowledge (Alston, 2013; Coohey, 1998; Flannery, Williams, & Vazsonyi, 1999; Vander Ven, Cullen, Carrozza, & Wright, 2001; Vandivere, Tout, Capizzano, & Zaslow, 2003).

Problems with children occur in families of all races and social classes.

There is little doubt that family structure is related to delinquency in a variety of ways. However, relying on official statistics to assess the extent of that relationship may be misleading. It may be that the police, probation officers, and judges are more likely to deal officially with juveniles from broken homes than to deal officially with juveniles from more "ideal" family backgrounds. Several authorities, including Fenwick (1982) and Simonsen (1991), have concluded that the decision to drop charges against a juvenile depends, first, on the seriousness of the offense and the juvenile's prior record and, second, on the juvenile's family ties. "Youths are likely to be released if they are affiliated with a conventional domestic network" (Fenwick, 1982, p. 450). When parents can be easily contacted by the police and are willing to cooperate with the police, the likelihood is much greater (especially when the offense is minor) that a juvenile will be warned and released to his or her parents (Bynum & Thompson, 1999, p. 364; FindLaw, 2008; Kirk, 2009). Fader, Harris, Jones, and Poulin (2001) concluded that, in Philadelphia at least, juvenile court decision makers appear to give extra weight to child and family functioning factors in deciding on dispositions for first-time offenders.

It often appears that the difference between placing juveniles in institutions and allowing them to remain in the family setting depends more on whether the family is intact than on the quality of life within the family. Concentrating on the broken family as the major or only cause of delinquency fails to take into account the vast number of juveniles from broken homes who do not become delinquent as well as the vast number of juveniles from intact families who do become delinquent (Krisberg, 2005, p. 73).

Education

Schools, education, and families are very much interdependent and play a major role in shaping the future of children. In our society, education is recognized as one of the most important paths to success. The educational system occupies an important position and has taken over many functions formerly performed by the family. The total social well-being of children, including health, recreation, morality, and academic advancement, is a concern of educators. Some of the lofty objectives espoused by various educational commissions were summarized by Schafer and Polk (1967) more than a quarter century ago:

> All children and youth must be given those skills, attitudes, and values that will enable them to perform adult activities and meet adult obligations. Public education must ensure the maximum development of general knowledge, intellectual competence, psychological stability, social skills, and social awareness so that each new generation will be enlightened, individually strong, yet socially and civically responsible. (p. 224)

The child is expected by his or her parents, and by society, to succeed in life, but the child from a poor family, where values and opportunities differ from those of white middle-class America, encounters many difficulties early in school. Studies indicate that students from middle-class family backgrounds are more likely to have internalized the values of competitiveness, politeness, and deferred gratification that are likely to lead to success in the public schools (Braun, 1976). Braun (1976) also found that teachers' expectations were influenced by physical attractiveness, socioeconomic status, race, gender, name, and older siblings. Lower expectations existed for children who came from lower socioeconomic backgrounds, belonged to minority groups, and had older siblings who had been unsuccessful in school. Alwin and Thornton (1984) found that the socioeconomic status of the family was related to academic success both during early childhood and during adolescence. Blair, Blair, and Madamba (1999) found that social class–based characteristics were the best predictors of educational performance among minority students. Hayes (2008) and Kreager, Rulison, and Moody (2011) noted that a number of factors can affect a teacher's expectations of students and student behavior, including race, gender, class, and personality.

Numerous studies show that although some difficulties may be partially attributable to early experience in the family and neighborhood, others are created by the educational system itself (see In Practice 3.3). The label of *low achiever*, *slow learner*, or *learning disabled* may be attached shortly after, and sometimes even before, entering the first grade based on the performance of other family members who preceded the child in school. Teachers may expect little academic success as a result. Identification as a slow learner often sets into motion a series of reactions by the student, his or her peers, and the school itself that may lead to negative attitudes, frustrations, and eventually a climate where school becomes a highly unsatisfactory and bitter experience. Kelley (1977) found that early labeling in the school setting had a lasting impact on children's educational careers and that such labeling occurred with respect to children with both very great and very limited academic potential.

IN PRACTICE 3.3

GOODWILL LAUNCHES PROGRAM TO HELP YOUTH

Goodwill Industries of Central Illinois is combining its commitment to vocational development with a new passion for helping youth.

GoodGuides youth mentoring program officially began Monday. The program funding came from the U.S. Department of Justice through the American Reinvestment and Recovery Act.

Fifty-six Goodwill agencies nationwide are sharing the two-year, $19 million grant. The central Illinois agency's share of the grant money is about $300,000.

"The neat thing is, the program has a vocational focus, which fits in with Goodwill," said Elizabeth McCombs, GoodGuides program manager.

GoodGuides is actively looking for youth participants and professional adults to serve as mentors.

"It would be nice if we had two lines of people out there—students in one and volunteers in the other," said Bill Bontemps, director of vocational services. "But that's not going to happen."

Instead, Goodwill is seeking partnerships with other community programs and faith-based organizations, which can refer youth in need to the new program.

GoodGuides is similar to Big Brothers/Big Sisters. But whereas that program stops accepting youth at age 12, that's when GoodGuides starts. At-risk youth ages 12 to 17 in Peoria, Tazewell and Woodford counties are eligible.

"At risk can mean a lot of things—academic failure, dropping out of school, delinquency," McCombs said. "It can be teen pregnancy. At risk is an all-encompassing thing."

Participants may have experienced those issues or simply be on a path to experience them. For example, a student considering dropping out of high school, with guidance from a mentor, may choose to stay in school.

"We're just beginning to get them thinking about a career," McCombs said. "If their career entails more schooling, that's where we go. If their career entails specific vocational training or certification, we prepare them for that to enter the workforce. The end goal is to give them the positive influence to become more productive citizens."

Volunteer professionals will be asked to commit to four hours a month for at least a year. About 60 adults are needed, with the goal of serving 100 youth.

Mentoring will be done in three ways: Peer to peer, adult to youth and in groups with an adult leader.

"If someone's not comfortable doing one-on-one mentoring, they can do group mentoring," McCombs said.

There's also a family strengthening component, so others in the youth's family may get access to training or services, if needed.

Volunteers must pass a drug screening and thorough background check, plus a check of their driving records if they will be driving youth. Each volunteer will be interviewed as well. Volunteers who pass all components will be trained a minimum of six hours. A support group for volunteers will allow them to share strategies and seek advice from other mentors.

Every four to six weeks, GoodGuides will sponsor an activity for all participants. That might be a picnic or a hockey game.

GoodGuides will employ some of the training opportunities already in place for adults at Goodwill, such as computer and personal finance training.

Mentors will be asked to tailor their career advice to the youth's interests. If a student wants to be a veterinarian, they may be paired with a veterinarian or have a mentor who arranges for them to meet a veterinarian. The mentors will be expected to share their struggles and the paths they took to get where they are today.

"We want to put youth with someone who is what they want to be," McCombs said.

"Someone who's relatable. It kind of gives them hope."

Mentoring has been shown to help youth improve all aspects of their lives.

"Maybe sometimes the mentor might assist them with tutoring. A lot of time, when a youth has a positive influence and they have that attention and support, they become more motivated," McCombs said. "They do better in school. They behave more positively."

Source: Towery (2010). Reprinted with permission of the *Peoria Journal Star*.

Questions to Consider

1. True or False: The GoodGuides program is designed to help youth ages 12 and up, the point in age where Big Brothers/Big Sisters ceases to take participants.

2. Multiple Choice: The GoodGuides program is associated with which well-known nonprofit agency?

   a. The American Red Cross

   b. FEMA

   c. March of Dimes

   d. Goodwill Industries

3. What characteristics might make an individual a good mentor for youth?

Kvaraceus (1945) believed that although school might not directly cause delinquency, it might present conditions that foster delinquent behavior. When aspirations for success in the educational system are blocked, the student's self-assessment, assessment of the value of education, and assessment of the school's role in his or her life may progressively deteriorate. Hawkins and Lishner (1987) indicated that low cognitive ability, poor early academic performance, low attachment to school, low commitment to academic pursuits, and association with delinquent peers appear to contribute to delinquency. Unless the student is old enough to drop out of this highly frustrating experience, the only recourse may be to seek others within the school who find themselves in the same circumstances.

Thornberry, Moore, and Christenson (1985) noted that dropping out of school was positively related to delinquency and later crime over both the long and short terms. Although the presence of others who share the frustrating experience of the educational system may be a satisfactory alternative to dropping out of school, the collective alienation may lead to delinquent behavior. Rodney and Mupier (1999) found that being suspended from school, being expelled from school, and being held back in school increased the likelihood of being in juvenile detention among adolescent African American males. Lotz and Lee (1999) found that negative school experiences are significant predictors of delinquent behavior among white teenagers. Jarjoura (1996) found that dropping out of school is more likely to be associated with greater involvement in delinquency for middle-class youth than for lower-class youth.

Most theorists agree that negative experiences in school act as powerful forces that help to project juveniles into delinquency. Achievement and self-esteem will be satisfied in the peer group or gang. In many ways, the school contributes to delinquency by failing to provide a meaningful curriculum to lower-class youth in terms of future employment opportunities. There is a growing recognition by many juveniles of the fact that satisfying educational requirements is no guarantee of occupational success (Monk-Turner, 1990). More than a quarter century ago, Polk and Schafer (1972) noted that the role of the school was rarely acknowledged as producing these unfavorable conditions. Instead of recognizing and attacking deficiencies in the learning structure of the schools, educational authorities place the blame on "delinquent youth" and thus further alienate them from school. In summarizing, Polk and Schafer listed the following as unfavorable experiences:

(1) Lower socioeconomic–class children enter the formal educational process with a competitive disadvantage due to their social backgrounds; (2) the physical condition and educational climate of a school located in working class areas may not be conducive for the learning process; (3) youths may be labeled early and placed in ability groups where expectations have been reduced; and (4) curriculum and recognition of achievement revolve around the "college bound youth" and not the youth who intends to culminate his educational pursuit by graduating from high school. (p. 189)

Yablonsky and Haskell (1988), Battistich and Hom (1997), Yogan (2000), and Kowaleski-Jones (2000) all have discussed how school experiences may be related to delinquency. First, if a child experiences failure at school every day, he or she not only learns little but also becomes frustrated and unhappy. Curricula that do not promise a reasonable opportunity for every child to experience success in some area may, therefore, contribute to delinquency. Second, teaching without relating the subject matter to the needs and aspirations of the student leaves him or her with serious questions regarding the subject matter's relevancy. Third, for many lower-class children, school is a prison or a "babysitting" operation where they just pass time. They find little or no activity designed to give pleasure or indicate an interest in their abilities. Fourth, the impersonal school atmosphere, devoid of close relationships, may contribute toward the child seeking relationships in peer groups or gangs outside of the educational setting. In a similar vein, Polk (1984) contended that the number of marginal juveniles is growing and agreed that this is so not only because less successful students have unpleasant school experiences but also because their future occupational aspirations are severely limited.

In 1981, Zimmerman, Rich, Keilitz, and Broder investigated the relationship between learning disabilities and delinquency. They concluded that "proportionately more adjudicated delinquent children than public school children were learning disabled," although self-report data indicated no significant differences in the incidence of delinquent activity. They hypothesized that "the greater proportion of learning-disabled youth among adjudicated juvenile delinquents may be accounted for by differences in the way such children are treated within the juvenile justice system, rather than by differences in their delinquent behavior" (Zimmerman et al., 1981, p. 1). In keeping with this hypothesis, Harris, Baltodano, Bal, Jolivette, and Malcahy (2009) found evidence that juveniles with disabilities are overrepresented in correctional facilities.

In another study, Smykla and Willis (1981) found that 62% of the children under the jurisdiction of the juvenile court they studied were either learning disabled or mentally challenged. They concluded the following:

The findings of this study are in agreement with previous incidence studies that have demonstrated a correlation between juvenile delinquency and mental retardation. These results also forcefully demonstrate the need for special education strategies to be included in any program of delinquency prevention and control. (p. 225)

Hume (2010) has asked us to do the following:

Imagine what it must be like for a young person with learning disabilities to be apprehended and questioned by the police. Your fear and nervousness make your impairment more acute, and you do a poor job in answering the questions. Looking guilty (maybe because of your disability not actual guilt) you end up in front of a judge. Even more anxious and scared, you continue to have difficulty in processing verbal questions, sequencing events, mustering demand language and controlling your impulses. Odds are that no one will ask you if you have a disability, or understand what a learning disability is, even if you tell them. (p. 1)

Perhaps the best summation of the relationship between learning disabilities and delinquency is that provided by the National Center on Education, Disability, and Juvenile Justice (2007):

Educational disability does not cause delinquency, but learning and behavioral disorders place youth at greater risk for involvement with the juvenile courts and for incarceration. School failure, poorly developed social skills, and inadequate school and community supports are associated with the over-representation of youth with disabilities at all stages of the juvenile justice system. (p. 1)

The alienation that some students feel toward school and education demands our attention. Rebellion, retreatism, and delinquency may be responses to the false promises of education or simply responses to being "turned off" again in an environment where this has occurred too frequently. Without question, curriculum and caliber of instruction need to be relevant for all children. Social and academic skill remediation may be one means of preventing learning-disabled children from becoming involved in delinquency (Raskind, 2010; Winters, 1997). Beyond these primary educational concerns, the school may currently be the only institution where humanism and concern for the individual are expressed in an otherwise bleak environment. Even this onetime sanctuary is under attack by gang members involved with drugs and guns. In some cases, the question is not whether a child can learn in school but rather whether he or she can get to school and back home alive. Armed security guards, barred windows, and metal detectors have given many schools the appearance of being the prisons that some children have always found them to be. Despite these concerns, the percentage of youth ages 12 to 18 who feared attack at school, or on the way to and from school, fell by half from 1995 to 2001, from 12% in 1995 to 6% in 2001.

By 2013, it was found that only about 4.9% of Latino students, 4.6% of African American students, and 2.6% of Caucasian students still were in fear of an attack at school or on their way home from school (Child Trends DataBank, 2013). What is clear from these percentages is that the overall fear of victimization in school or on the way home from school had greatly declined since the 1990s. Further, the variation observed during the 1990s between these groups (in 1995 about 20.9% of Latino students, 20.3% of African American students, and 8.6% of Caucasian students expressed similar fears) had been significantly reduced during this time (see Figure 3.1).

Figure 3.1 Percentage of Students Ages 12 to 18 Who Feared Attack at School or on the Way to and From School, Selected Years, 1995–2013

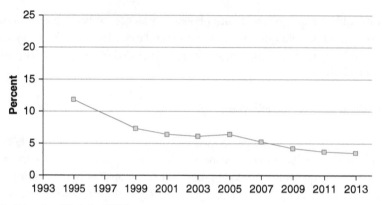

Source: National Center for Educational Statistics (2015).

Fear of attack at school or on the way to and from school may cause some students to miss days of school and may negatively affect academic performance. Fear at school can create an unhealthy school environment, affect students' participation in class, and lead to more negative behaviors among students (Child Trends DataBank, 2013). Furthermore, students in lower grades are more likely to fear for their safety at school and on the way to and from school than are students in higher grades. Six percent of 6th-grade students had such fears, compared with 3% of 11th-grade students in 2009 (Child Trends DataBank, 2013).

In another survey of American schoolchildren, it was found that improvements in school safety have occurred over the past two decades. In 1995, 10% of students reported being victims of at least one crime at school, whereas 4% of students reported at least one victimization crime at school in 2005. Seven percent reported being victims of theft in 1995, and 3% reported theft in 2005. Three percent of students reported being victims of violent crime in 1995, and 1% reported being victims of violent crime in 2005. In both 1995 and 2005, less than 1% of students reported a serious violent crime (Bauer, Guerino, Nolle, Tang, & Chandler, 2008, p. 4). The violent crime victimization rate declined from 48 per 1,000 students in 1992 to 28 per 1,000 students in 2003. The Centers for Disease Control and Prevention (2013) perhaps provided the best and clearest statement on violence at school when it said that "school associated violent deaths are rare" (p. 1). Despite the decrease, violence, theft, bullying, drugs, and weapons are still widespread in some schools, and events of the past few years have raised national concern about school safety. In 2011, over 5% of students in Grades 9 through 12 reported carrying a gun, knife, or club on school property on one or more days in the previous 30 days.

In recent years, school shootings have led to juveniles experiencing increased fears at school, on their way to school, and on their way home from school.

BananaStock/Thinkstock

Further, over 7% reported being threatened or injured with a weapon on school property one or more times in the past 12 months (Centers for Disease Control and Prevention, 2013). A chronology of some of the most serious events leading to this concern follows (includes only events occurring in the United States in Grades 1 through 12 from 2005 through 2012, beginning with the most recent).

December 14, 2012: Adam Lanza, 20, killed 20 children and six others at Sandy Hook Elementary School (Newtown, Connecticut).

March 6, 2012: A 28-year-old teacher at Episcopal High School (Jacksonville, Florida) returned to the campus after being fired and then shot and killed the headmistress.

February 27, 2012: At Chardon High School (Chardon, Ohio), a former classmate opened fire, killing three students and injuring six.

February 10, 2012: A 14-year-old student shot himself in front of 70 fellow students in Walpole, New Hampshire.

January 5, 2011: Two people opened fire during a Worthing High School (Houston, Texas) powder-puff football game. One former student died. Five other people were injured.

January 5, 2011: Two people were killed and two more injured in a shooting at Millard South High School in Omaha, Nebraska.

February 5, 2010: A ninth grader was shot and killed by another student at Discovery Middle School in Madison, Alabama.

November 12, 2008: A 15-year-old female student was shot and killed by a classmate at Dillard High School in Fort Lauderdale.

February 12, 2008: A 14-year-old boy shot a student at E. O. Green Junior High School (Oxnard, California), causing the 15-year-old victim to be brain-dead.

February 11, 2008: A 17-year-old student at Mitchell High School (Memphis, Tennessee) shot and wounded a classmate in gym class.

October 10, 2007: Asa H. Coon, a 14-year-old student at a Cleveland high school, shot and injured two students and two teachers before he shot and killed himself. The victims' injuries were not life threatening.

January 3, 2007: Douglas Chanthabouly, 18, shot fellow student Samnang Kok, 17, in the hallway of Henry Foss High School (Tacoma, Washington).

October 3, 2006: Charles Carl Roberts, 32, took 10 girls hostage in an Amish school in Nickel Mines, Pennsylvania, killing five of them before killing himself.

September 29, 2006: Eric Hainstock, 15, took two guns into his Cazenovia, Wisconsin, school and fatally shot the principal before being captured and arrested.

September 27, 2006: Duane Morrison, 53, took six girls hostage at Platte Canyon High School in Bailey, Colorado, molesting them and holding them for hours before fatally shooting one girl and then himself.

August 24, 2006: Christopher Williams, 27, went to Essex Elementary School in Vermont, and when he could not find his ex-girlfriend, a teacher, he shot and killed one teacher and wounded another. Earlier, he had killed the ex-girlfriend's mother. He attempted suicide but survived and was arrested.

November 8, 2005: Assistant principal Ken Bruce was killed and two other administrators were seriously wounded when Kenny Bartley, a 15-year-old student, opened fire in a Jacksboro, Tennessee, high school.

March 21, 2005: Jeff Weise, 16, shot to death his grandfather and his grandfather's girlfriend and then went to his high school in Red Lake, Minnesota, where he killed a security guard, a teacher, and five students and also wounded seven others before killing himself. (Information Please Database, n.d.)

Responses to these incidents of school violence have been varied, and the violent acts themselves have led to a national debate over control. Among the suggested responses to such violence are target hardening (e.g., locking down schools, using metal detectors, installing bars and safety closets), placing armed security or police personnel in schools, training and arming teachers and/or school administrators, placing bans on certain types of weapons, and improving or expanding background checks for those purchasing weapons. The extent to which any of these actions might reduce gun violence in schools is subject to heated debate.

It is difficult to determine the impact of these events on the students actually involved, on bystanders, and on those who become aware of the events through the national media, but there is little doubt that the impact is considerable. In addition to the school shootings just chronicled, there have been numerous shootings at colleges and universities in the United States during the same period.

The impact of school bullying also deserves our attention. Whether through the use of the Internet or through the use of physical threats or attacks, bullying has become a major focal point in recent years. "Defined as a repeated behavior intended to cause harm to another with one party having more power . . . bullying has increased among students and adults over recent years" (Arnold & Rockinson-Szapkiw, 2012, p. 68). As Moon, Hwang, and McCluskey (2011) indicated, "A growing number of studies indicate the ubiquity of school bullying: It is a global concern, regardless of cultural differences" (p. 849). And there appear to be gender differences related to bullying, with boys being more likely to practice or experience physical aggression and violence and girls being more likely to cyberbully and employ forms of bullying designed to destroy peer relationships or lower self-esteem (Arnold & Rockinson-Szapkiw, 2012, p. 68). Some such acts of bullying have allegedly led to suicides of bullying victims.

Research by Brown, Aalsma, and Ott (2013) indicates that protecting youth from bullying at school is not easy. Based on a small sample of parents, the researchers identified three parent stages in attempting to deal with bullying: (1) discovering, (2) reporting, and (3) living with the aftermath.

> In the discovery stage, parents reported giving advice in hopes of protecting their youth. As parents noticed negative psychosocial symptoms in their youth escalate, they shifted their focus to reporting the bullying to school officials. All but one parent experienced ongoing resistance from school officials in fully engaging the bullying problem. In the aftermath, 10 of the 11 parents were left with two choices: remove their youth from the school or let the victimization continue. (p. 494)

Although school officials have attempted to address bullying using a number of approaches, little is known about what specific intervention strategies are most successful in the school setting. Ayers, Wagaman, Geiger, Bermudez-Parsai, & Hedberg (2012) examined school-based disciplinary interventions using data from a sample of 1,221 students in Grades K through 12 who received an office disciplinary referral for bullying. They concluded that only parent–teacher conferences and loss of privileges were significant in reducing the rate of the reoccurrence of bullying and aggressive behaviors. More than 45 states have also enacted legislation that addresses bullying behaviors in the school and in cyberspace (U.S. Department of Education, 2010). The state of Georgia, for example, requires all schools to provide character education curriculums that include the following:

Focus on the students' development of the following character traits: courage, patriotism, citizenship, honesty, fairness, respect for others, kindness, cooperation, self-respect, self-control, courtesy, compassion, tolerance, diligence, generosity, punctuality, cleanliness, cheerfulness, school pride, respect for the environment, respect for the creator, patience, creativity, sportsmanship, loyalty, perseverance, and virtue. Such program shall also address, by the start of the 1999–2000 school year, methods of discouraging bullying and violent acts against fellow students. Local boards shall implement such a program in all grade levels at the beginning of the 2000–2001 school year and shall provide opportunities for parental involvement in establishing expected outcomes of the character education program. (O.C.G.A. § 20-2-145 [2012])

The authors suggest that school personnel and legislators might develop strategies that deter the reoccurrence of bullying by identifying key factors that impact students, similar to what Georgia is attempting to accomplish (Ayers et al., 2012, p. 539).

Social Class

During the 1950s and 1960s, a number of studies emerged focusing on the relationship between social class and delinquency (Cloward & Ohlin, 1960; Cohen, 1955; Merton, 1955; Miller, 1958). These studies indicated that socioeconomic status was a major contributing factor in delinquency. According to further research, the actual relationship between social class and delinquency may be that social class is important in determining whether a particular juvenile becomes part of the official statistics, not in determining whether a juvenile will actually commit a delinquent act (Dentler & Monroe, 1961; Short & Nye, 1958; Tittle, Villemez, & Smith, 1978). Most studies of self-reported delinquency have shown little or no difference by social class in the actual commission of delinquent acts. Morash and Chesney-Lind (1991), however, did find evidence that lower-class youth report more delinquency, and Elliott and Ageton (1980) found that lower-class juveniles may be more likely to commit serious offenses. Ackerman (1998) also concluded that crime is a function of poverty, at least in smaller communities, and Onifade, Petersen, Bynum, and Davidson (2011) suggested that the risk of delinquency and its relationship to recidivism is moderated by neighborhood socioeconomic ecology.

Some research indicates that middle-class youth are involved in delinquency to a far greater extent than was suspected previously. Scott and Vaz (1963), for example, found that middle-class delinquents adhere to specific patterns of activities, standards of conduct, and values different from their parents. Young people a generation ago had more in common with their parents, including attitudes and outlook on life. However, today's middle-class youth are securely entrenched in a youth culture

Although more males than females are arrested for delinquency, the number of female delinquents has increased significantly during recent years.

© David Young-Wolff/Getty Images

that is often apart from, or in conflict with, the dominant adult culture. Within the youth culture, juveniles are open to the influence of their peers and generally conform to whatever behavior patterns prevail. Scott and Vaz identified partying, joyriding, drinking, gambling, and various types of sexual behavior as dominant forms of conduct within the middle-class youth culture. By participating in and conforming to the youth culture, status and social success are achieved through peer approval. Scott and Vaz argued that the bulk of middle-class delinquency occurs in the course of customary nondelinquent activities but moves to the realm of delinquency as the result of a need to "be different" or "start something new." Wooden and Blazak (2001) noted that these trends continue at the present time: "In the 1990s research began revealing what those who had survived the 1980s already knew: The safe cocoon of middle-class youth was eroding" (pp. 4–5).

In *Youth Crisis: Growing Up in a High-Risk Society*, Davis (1999) pointed out that adolescence is a period of transition from childhood to adulthood. Each of the institutions of this transition (e.g., the family, education, employment) is in a state of turmoil, causing adolescents to be in a state of crisis.

Accessibility to social objects for participating in the youth culture is an important part of delinquent behavior. Social objects, such as cars, the latest styles, alcoholic beverages, and drugs, are frequently part of middle-class delinquency. Peer recognition for male middle-class youth may be a reason for senseless acts of destruction of property. Acts of vandalism in which one's bravery can be displayed for peer approval are somewhat different from the violent behavior often seen in lower-class youth, who may demonstrate their bravery by gang fights or shootings, muggings, robbery, and other crimes against people. Wooden and Blazak (2001) indicated that suburban youth are often told to act like adults but are not given the privileges of adulthood, forcing them into a subculture characterized by delinquency-producing focal concerns (p. 19). Some end up in trouble-oriented male groups, and they sometimes get involved in violent crime to conform to group norms. More typically, those in middle-class coed groups get involved in petty theft and drug use.

Although most evidence indicates that juveniles from all social classes may become delinquent (Elrod & Ryder, 2005, p. 61), the subculture theorists maintain that many delinquents grow up in lower-class slum areas. According to Cloward and Ohlin (1960), the type of delinquency exhibited depends in part on the type of slum in which juveniles grow up. The slum that produces professional criminals is characterized by the close-knit lives and activities of the people in the community. Constant exposure to delinquent and criminal processes coupled with an admiration of criminals provides the model and impetus for future delinquency and criminality. Cloward and Ohlin described this as a criminal subculture in which juveniles are encouraged and supported by well-established conventional and criminal institutions. Going one step further, Miller (1958), in his study of lower- and middle-class norms, values, and behavioral expectations, concluded that a delinquent subculture is inherent in lower-class standards and goals. The desirability of the achievement of status through toughness and smartness, as well as the concepts of trouble, excitement, fate, and autonomy, is interpreted differently depending on one's socioeconomic status. Miller concluded that by adhering to lower-class norms, pressure toward delinquency is inevitable and is rewarded and respected in the lower-class value system. Lawbreaking is not in and of itself a deliberate rejection of middle-class values, but it automatically violates certain moral and legal standards of the middle class. Miller believed that lower-class youth who become delinquent are primarily conforming to traditions and values held by their families, peers, and neighbors. As indicated earlier, Wooden and Blazak (2001) used this same approach to describe middle-class delinquency during the 21st century, and most recently, Siegel (2011) suggested that the maturation process is combined with opportunities to build social networks. These social networks are nurtured along by parents, teachers, family members, and other adults, and allow children to forge relationships that provide opportunities for educational and employment success. Children in lower socioeconomic classes are not able to build the same social networks; thus, they "simply do not have the means that bestow advantages on peers whose families are better off financially. They are disadvantaged educationally because of the schools they attend and the activities in which they can participate. Not surprisingly, then, poor children are less likely to graduate from high school and are more likely to become poor adults" (Siegel, 2011, p. 73).

In summarizing the findings with respect to the relationship between social class and delinquency, Johnson (1980) concluded that some conceptualizations of social class may have been inappropriate and that a more appropriate distinction is the one between the underclass and the earning class. His results suggest, however, that even given this distinction, there is no reason to expect that social class will emerge as a "major correlate of delinquent behavior, no matter how it is measured" (p. 86). Current evidence presented by Wooden and Blazak (2001) seems to indicate that this may well be the case, as does the paucity of current research in this area.

Still, the concept of the underclass (the extremely poor population that has been abandoned in the inner city as a result of the exodus of the middle class) seems to attract continuing attention (Bursik & Grasmick, 1995; Jarjoura, Triplett, & Brinker, 2002). As the more affluent withdraw from inner-city communities, they also tend to withdraw political support for public spending designed to benefit those communities. They do not want to pay taxes for schools they do not use, and they are not likely to use them because they find those left behind too frightening to be around (Ehrenreich, 1990). Those left behind are largely excluded, on a permanent basis, from the primary labor market and mainstream occupations. Economically motivated delinquency is one way of coping with this disenfranchisement to maintain a short-term cash flow. Because many children growing up in these circumstances see no relationship between attaining an education and future employment, they tend to drop out of school prior to graduation. Some then become involved in theft as a way of meeting economic needs, often as members of gangs that may become institutionalized in underclass neighborhoods (Bursik & Grasmick, 1995, p. 122).

Perhaps Chambliss (1973) summed up the impact of social class on delinquency best some years ago when he concluded that the results of some delinquents' activities are seen as less serious than others as the result of class in American society:

No representative of the upper class drew up the operations chart for the police which led them to look in the ghettoes and on street corners—which led them to see the demeanor of lower class youth as troublesome and that of upper middle class youth as tolerable. Rather, the procedures simply developed from experience—experience with irate and influential upper middle class parents insisting that their son's vandalism was simply a prank and his drunkenness only a momentary "sowing of wild oats"— experience with cooperative or indifferent, powerless lower class parents who acquiesced to the law's definition of their son's behavior. (p. 30)

Gangs

The influence of juvenile gangs is so important and has received so much attention in the recent past that we have devoted a separate chapter (Chapter 12) to the subject. In this section, we simply note that gangs are an important factor in the development of delinquent behavior not only in inner-city areas but also increasingly in suburban and rural areas.

Drugs

Although drugs clearly have physical effects on those who use them, drug use is also a social act. We have more to say about drug use later in the book, but for now a brief discussion of the topic is in order.

In 2004, juvenile courts in the United States handled an estimated 193,700 delinquency cases in which a drug offense was the most serious charge. Between 1991 and 2004, the number of cases involving drug offenses that juvenile courts handled more than doubled. Drug offense cases accounted for 12% of the delinquency caseload in 2004, compared with 7% in 1985. (Stahl, 2008a, p. 1)

Our society is characterized by high rates of drug use and abuse, and it should not be surprising to find such use and abuse among juveniles. However, it would appear that this drug use is declining in popularity. Consider that, according to the National Institute on Drug Abuse (2016),

5.4 percent of 8th graders, 9.8 percent of 10th graders, and 14.3 percent of 12th graders used illicit drugs (excluding marijuana) during the past year. When compared to peak rates that were observed 15 years prior, it can be seen that the rate of illicit drug use went down for each age group. Further, daily use of marijuana declined among 8th (from 1.1 to 0.7 percent) and 10th (from 3.6 to 2.5 percent) graders and, though remaining the same among 12th graders (6.0 percent), it did not increase as witnessed during the past few years prior. (p. 1)

Simultaneously, the following is true:

Alcohol use among teens remains at low levels of use. In 2016, 17.6 percent of 8th graders, 38.3 percent of 10th graders, and 55.6 percent of 12th graders reported getting drunk in the past year, continuing a long-term trend of low alcohol use among youth in the 8th grade and above. Further, low levels of daily alcohol use by 8th and 10th graders continued, with a significant decline in daily use by 12th graders (from 2.5 to 1.3 percent, in 2016). In 2016, binge drinking (defined as 5 or more drinks in a row in the past 2 weeks) among 8th graders declined to around 3.4 percent. (p. 1)

One should keep in mind that these statistics apply to students still in school and do not include data from those who have dropped out of school. A 1985 study by Fagan and Pabon (1990) found that 54% of dropouts reported using illicit drugs during the past year, as compared with 30% of students.

The following are data presented by the U.S. Substance Abuse and Mental Health Services Administration (2013):

"The fact that nearly one in seven students drops out of high school has enormous public health implications for our nation," SAMHSA Administrator Pamela Hyde said in an agency news release. "Dropouts are at increased risk of substance abuse, which is particularly troubling given that they are also at greater risk of poverty, not having health insurance, and other health problems. We have to do everything we can to keep youth in school so they can go on to lead healthy, productive lives, free from substance abuse."

The study revealed high school seniors (typically between 16 and 18 years of age) who dropped out of school were more than twice as likely to be smokers—or have smoked in the past month—than students who stayed in school. The study also found that more than 31 percent of seniors who didn't receive their diploma used drugs, compared with about 18 percent of students who had finished high school. (p. 1)

The researchers also noted that about 27% of high school dropouts smoked marijuana, whereas close to one in every 10 abused prescription drugs. Meanwhile, only about 15% of those who completed high school used marijuana, and just 5% abused prescription drugs. Dropouts were also more likely to drink; the study showed that nearly 42% of seniors who didn't finish high school drank, and about a third engaged in binge drinking.

Watson (2004) indicated that research over the past 20 years has established the correlation of substance abuse to juvenile delinquency. There has, of course, been a good deal written about the relationship between illegal drug use and crime. This has been particularly true since the mid-1980s when crack, a cocaine-based stimulant drug, first appeared. As Inciardi, Horowitz, and Pottieger (1993) noted, "Cocaine is the drug of primary concern in examining drug/crime relationships among adolescents today. It is a powerful drug widely available at a cheap price per dose, but its extreme addictiveness can rapidly increase the need for more money" (p. 48). Today, this concern has been replaced in many areas by a concern with the abuse of prescription narcotics and methamphetamines, which, like cocaine, produce a feeling of euphoria. A meth high can last more than 12 hours, and heavy use can lead to psychotic behavior (paranoia and hallucinations) as well as to serious physical ailments. Some evidence suggests that chronic meth users tend to be more violent than heavy cocaine users (Parsons, 1998, p. 4). Abuse of prescription stimulants, opioids, and depressants can result in similar affects to methamphetamines with increased risks of poor judgment and physiological issues (National Institute on Drug Abuse, 2013).

There is also considerable interest in the relationship between illegal drugs and gangs. For example, it was reported that gang members accounted for 86% of serious delinquent acts, 69% of violent delinquent acts, and 70% of drug sales in Rochester, New York (Cohn, 1999a). Possession, sale, manufacture, and distribution of any of a number of illegal drugs are, in themselves, crimes. Purchase and consumption of some legal drugs, such as alcohol and tobacco, by juveniles are also illegal. Juveniles who violate statutes relating to these offenses may be labeled as delinquent or status offenders. Equally important, however, are other illegal acts often engaged in by drug users to support their drug habits. Such offenses are known to include theft, burglary, robbery, and prostitution, among others. It is also possible that use of certain drugs, such as cocaine and its derivatives and amphetamines, is related to the commission of violent crimes, although the exact nature of the relationship between drug abuse and crime is controversial. Some maintain that delinquents are more likely to use drugs than are nondelinquents—that is, drug use follows rather than precedes delinquency—whereas others argue the opposite (Bjerregaard, 2010; Dawkins, 1997; Thornton, Voight, & Doerner, 1987; Williams, Ayers, & Abbott, 1999). Whatever the nature of the relationship between drug abuse and delinquency, the two are intimately intertwined for some delinquents, whereas drug abuse is not a factor for others. Why some juveniles become drug abusers and others in similar environments avoid such involvement is the subject of a great deal of research. The single most important determinant of drug abuse appears to be the interpersonal relationships in which the juvenile is involved—particularly interpersonal relationships with peers. Drug abuse is a social phenomenon that occurs in social networks accepting, tolerating, and/or encouraging such behavior. Although the available evidence suggests that peer influence is most important, there is also evidence to indicate that juveniles whose parents are involved in drug abuse are more likely to abuse drugs than are juveniles whose parents are not involved in drug abuse. Furthermore, behavior of parents and peers appears to be more important in drug abuse than do the values and beliefs espoused (Schinke & Gilchrist, 1984; Williams et al., 1999).

There is no way of knowing how many juveniles suffering from school-, parent-, or peer-related depression and/or the general ambiguity surrounding adolescence turn to drugs as a means of escape, but the prevalence of teen suicide, combined with information obtained from self-reports of juveniles, indicates that the numbers are large. Although juvenile involvement with drugs in general apparently declined during the 1980s, it now appears that the trend has been reversed. There is little doubt that such involvement remains a major problem, particularly in light of gang-related drug operations. When gangs invade and take over a community, drugs are sold openly in junior and senior high schools, on street corners, and in shopping centers. The same is true of methamphetamines that are manufactured easily and sold inexpensively (Bartollas, 1993, p. 341; Scaramella, 2000).

Howell and Decker (1999) and Bjerregaard (2010) suggested that the relationship among gangs, drugs, and violence is complex. Pharmacological effects of drugs can lead to violence, and the high cost of drug use often causes users to support continued use with violent crimes. It is clear that violence is common among gang members, but the exact nature of the relationship among gangs, drugs, and violence is still being investigated (Bjerregaard, 2010).

Physical Factors

In addition to social factors, a number of physical factors are often employed to characterize juvenile delinquents. The physical factors most commonly discussed are age, gender, and race.

Age

For purposes of discussing official statistics concerning persons under the age of 18 years, we should note that little official action is taken with respect to delinquency under the age of 10 years. Rather than considering the entire age range from birth to 18 years, we are basically reviewing statistics covering an age range from 10 to 18 years. Keep in mind also our earlier observations (Chapter 2) concerning the problems inherent in the use of official statistics as we review the data provided by the FBI.

As Table 3.1 indicates, crimes committed by persons under 18 years of age (the maximum age for delinquency in a number of states) declined by 8.4% from 2014 to 2015. However, murder and nonnegligent manslaughter arrests increased by about 6.8%, as did rape arrests by 6.7%, whereas robbery arrests decreased by about 2% and aggravated assault arrests decreased by about 5% among those under 18 years of age.

Table 3.1 also includes statistics on less serious offenses. Considering these offenses, gambling arrests decreased by roughly 8.2% among those under 18 years of age, and weapons-related offenses decreased by 4.8%. As you can see in Table 3.1, total offenses among those under 15 years of age declined by more than 8% from 2014 to 2015.

As illustrated in Table 3.2, the total number of persons under the age of 18 years arrested for all crimes decreased by 36%, the number of persons in this category arrested for murder and nonnegligent manslaughter decreased almost 8.5%, and the number arrested for robbery decreased by 24.2% from 2011 to 2015. The number of arrests for auto theft remained about the same. Among offenses other than index crimes, carrying or possessing weapons (29% decrease), drug abuse violations (31.5% decrease), gambling (52.4% decrease), driving under the influence (36.8% decrease), drunkenness (36.8% decrease), and vandalism (37.4% decrease), among others, showed significant changes among those under 18 years of age.

It is sometimes interesting to compare short-term trends, such as those in Table 3.2, with trends over the longer term. Ten-year arrest trends (2006–2015) in Table 3.3 show a significant decrease in total crime rates among those under 18 years of age (56.1%) and also show decreases in both violent crimes (47.7%) and property crimes (49.1%).

Table 3.1 Current Year Over Previous Year Arrest Trends Totals, 2014 to 2015

Offense charged	Number of persons arrested											
	Total all ages			Under 15 years of age			Under 18 years of age			18 years of age and over		
	2014	2015	Percent change	2014	2015	Percent change	2014	2015	Percent change	2014	2015	Percent change
TOTAL[1]	7,967,934	7,689,755	−3.5	197,475	180,987	−8.3	709,317	649,970	−8.4	7,258,617	7,039,785	−3.0
Murder and nonnegligent manslaughter	7,044	7,519	+6.7	41	47	+14.6	488	521	+6.8	6,556	6,998	+6.7
Rape[2]	14,991	15,934	+6.3	939	991	+5.5	2,356	2,515	+6.7	12,635	13,419	+6.2
Robbery	64,612	66,138	+2.4	2,533	2,348	−7.3	12,597	12,347	−2.0	52,015	53,791	+3.4
Aggravated assault	269,114	271,650	+0.9	7,033	6,667	−5.2	21,579	20,503	−5.0	247,535	251,147	+1.5
Burglary	171,437	156,419	−8.8	8,052	7,543	−6.3	28,386	25,527	−10.1	143,051	130,892	−8.5
Larceny-theft	891,541	838,874	−5.9	35,758	31,006	−13.3	126,889	113,114	−10.9	764,652	725,760	−5.1
Motor vehicle theft	47,027	53,315	+13.4	1,917	2,055	+7.2	8,182	9,236	+12.9	38,845	44,079	+13.5
Arson	6,802	6,064	−10.8	1,330	1,143	−14.1	2,282	1,897	−16.9	4,520	4,167	−7.8
Violent crime[3]	355,761	361,241	+1.5	10,546	10,053	−4.7	37,020	35,886	−3.1	318,741	325,355	+2.1
Property crime[3]	1,116,807	1,054,672	−5.6	47,057	41,747	−11.3	165,739	149,774	−9.6	951,068	904,898	−4.9
Other assaults	775,729	768,114	−1.0	37,723	35,954	−4.7	97,993	94,079	−4.0	677,736	674,035	−0.5
Forgery and counterfeiting	40,838	39,918	−2.3	111	92	−17.1	844	752	−10.9	39,994	39,166	−2.1
Fraud	101,126	94,201	−6.8	606	583	−3.8	3,138	2,977	−5.1	97,988	91,224	−6.9
Embezzlement	11,837	11,657	−1.5	21	25	+19.0	330	436	+32.1	11,507	11,221	−2.5
Stolen property; buying, receiving, possessing	64,555	63,702	−1.3	1,663	1,628	−2.1	7,333	7,407	+1.0	57,222	56,295	−1.6
Vandalism	140,863	138,415	−1.7	12,765	11,870	−7.0	32,429	30,534	−5.8	108,434	107,881	−0.5
Weapons; carrying, possessing, etc.	97,809	101,895	+4.2	4,685	4,262	−9.0	13,994	13,317	−4.8	83,815	88,578	+5.7

(Continued)

61

Table 3.1 (Continued)

| Offense charged | Number of persons arrested | | | | | | | | | | | |
| | Total all ages | | | Under 15 years of age | | | Under 18 years of age | | | 18 years of age and over | | |
	2014	2015	Percent change	2014	2015	Percent change	2014	2015	Percent change	2014	2015	Percent change
Prostitution and commercialized vice	32,767	29,274	−10.7	68	48	−29.4	533	426	−20.1	32,234	28,848	−10.5
Sex offenses (except rape and prostitution)	38,930	37,123	−4.6	3,303	3,038	−8.0	6,786	6,390	−5.8	32,144	30,733	−4.4
Drug abuse violations	1,102,280	1,058,297	−4.0	13,510	11,222	−16.9	79,504	69,964	−12.0	1,022,776	988,333	−3.4
Gambling	2,686	2,580	−3.9	44	33	−25.0	244	224	−8.2	2,442	2,356	−3.5
Offenses against the family and children	70,042	68,628	−2.0	914	877	−4.0	2,513	2,384	−5.1	67,529	66,244	−1.9
Driving under the influence	819,396	783,473	−4.4	121	108	−10.7	4,999	4,753	−4.9	814,397	778,720	−4.4
Liquor laws	231,142	193,643	−16.2	3,641	3,316	−8.9	38,408	31,549	−17.9	192,734	162,094	−15.9
Drunkenness	314,519	289,734	−7.9	586	499	−14.8	4,949	4,026	−18.7	309,570	285,708	−7.7
Disorderly conduct	298,631	272,809	−8.6	21,239	20,005	−5.8	55,145	50,888	−7.7	243,486	221,921	−8.9
Vagrancy	20,254	18,856	−6.9	165	205	+24.2	707	792	+12.0	19,547	18,064	−7.6
All other offenses (except traffic)	2,306,755	2,278,685	−1.2	32,180	29,528	−8.2	131,502	120,574	−8.3	2,175,253	2,158,111	−0.8
Suspicion	750	836	+11.5	58	48	−17.2	164	135	−17.7	586	701	+19.6
Curfew and loitering law violations	25,207	22,838	−9.4	6,527	5,894	−9.7	25,207	22,838	−9.4	—		

Source: Adapted from FBI (2016b).

[1] Does not include suspicion.

[2] The rape figures in this table are aggregate totals of the data submitted based on both the legacy and revised Uniform Crime Reporting definitions.

[3] Violent crimes are offenses of murder and nonnegligent manslaughter, rape, robbery, and aggravated assault. Property crimes are offenses of burglary, larceny-theft, motor vehicle theft, and arson.

Table 3.2 Five-Year Arrest Trends Totals, 2011 to 2015

Offense charged	Total all ages			Under 18 years of age			18 years of age and over		
	2011	2015	Percent change	2011	2015	Percent change	2011	2015	Percent change
TOTAL[1]	8,225,888	7,213,389	-12.3	991,398	634,718	-36.0	7,234,490	6,578,671	-9.1
Murder and nonnegligent manslaughter	6,968	7,005	+0.5	539	493	-8.5	6,429	6,512	+1.3
Rape[2]	13,168	15,126	–	1,917	2,401	–	11,251	12,725	–
Robbery	67,650	60,085	-11.2	15,037	11,404	-24.2	52,613	48,681	-7.5
Aggravated assault	259,015	246,238	-4.9	26,421	19,008	-28.1	232,594	227,230	-2.3
Burglary	197,756	145,163	-26.6	41,018	23,887	-41.8	156,738	121,276	-22.6
Larceny-theft	855,183	799,643	-6.5	175,433	109,356	-37.7	679,750	690,287	+1.6
Motor vehicle theft	44,336	50,447	+13.8	9,581	9,624	+0.4	34,755	40,823	+17.5
Arson	7,876	6,133	-22.1	3,352	1,914	-42.9	4,524	4,219	-6.7
Violent crime[3]	346,801	328,454	-5.3	43,914	33,306	-24.2	302,887	295,148	-2.6
Property crime[3]	1,105,151	1,001,386	-9.4	229,384	144,781	-36.9	875,767	856,605	-2.2
Other assaults	827,577	727,435	-12.1	127,310	89,835	-29.4	700,267	637,600	-8.9
Forgery and counterfeiting	46,264	36,642	-20.8	1,065	694	-34.8	45,199	35,948	-20.5
Fraud	110,363	90,590	-17.9	3,583	3,246	-9.4	106,780	87,344	-18.2
Embezzlement	10,931	11,011	+0.7	301	426	+41.5	10,630	10,585	-0.4
Stolen property; buying, receiving, possessing	63,792	59,223	-7.2	9,127	6,715	-26.4	54,665	52,508	-3.9
Vandalism	160,380	130,154	-18.8	46,688	29,227	-37.4	113,692	100,927	-11.2
Weapons; carrying, possessing, etc.	99,115	95,803	-3.3	18,665	13,078	-29.9	80,450	82,725	+2.8
Prostitution and commercialized vice	26,777	19,797	-26.1	461	292	-36.7	26,316	19,505	-25.9
Sex offenses (except rape and prostitution)	44,870	34,420	-23.3	8,482	6,048	-28.7	36,388	28,372	-22.0
Drug abuse violations	1,020,875	1,016,402	-0.4	101,191	69,355	-31.5	919,684	947,047	+3.0
Gambling	4,929	3,055	-38.0	618	294	-52.4	4,311	2,761	-36.0
Offenses against the family and children	76,387	65,357	-14.4	2,378	2,335	-1.8	74,009	63,022	-14.8
Driving under the influence	825,909	676,560	-18.1	7,013	4,432	-36.8	818,896	672,128	-17.9
Liquor laws	323,529	181,462	-43.9	63,622	30,876	-51.5	259,907	150,586	-42.1
Drunkenness	361,587	268,115	-25.9	8,185	3,836	-53.1	353,402	264,279	-25.2
Disorderly conduct	382,589	264,528	-30.9	91,752	49,315	-46.3	290,837	215,213	-26.0
Vagrancy	14,587	15,495	+6.2	641	648	+1.1	13,946	14,847	+6.5
All other offenses (except traffic)	2,325,288	2,157,131	-7.2	178,831	115,610	-35.4	2,146,457	2,041,521	-4.9
Suspicion	732	573	-21.7	78	132	+69.2	654	441	-32.6
Curfew and loitering law violations	48,187	30,369	-37.0	48,187	30,369	-37.0			

Source: Adapted from FBI (2016c).

[1] Does not include suspicion.

[2] The 2011 rape figures are based on the legacy definition, and the 2015 rape figures are based on both the legacy and revised Uniform Crime Reporting definitions. For this reason, a percent change is not provided.

[3] Violent crimes are offenses of murder and nonnegligent manslaughter, rape, robbery, and aggravated assault. Property crimes are aggregate totals based on both the legacy and revised Uniform Crime Reporting definitions. For this reason, a percent change is not provided. Violent crimes are offenses of burglary, larceny-theft, motor vehicle theft, and arson.

Table 3.3 Ten-Year Arrest Trends by Sex, 2006–2015

Offense charged	Male						Female					
	Total			Under 18			Total			Under 18		
	2006	2015	Percent change	2006	2015	Percent change	2006	2015	Percent change	2006	2015	Percent change
TOTAL[1]	6,605,457	4,913,199	-25.6	922,499	405,325	-56.1	2,070,999	1,826,164	-11.8	357,696	173,213	-51.6
Murder and nonnegligent manslaughter	6,292	5,463	-13.2	612	394	-35.6	812	738	-9.1	30	27	-10.0
Rape[2]	13,932	13,536	–	2,071	2,154	–	188	409	–	40	85	–
Robbery	60,460	46,060	-23.8	16,413	8,658	-47.2	7,977	7,943	-0.4	1,788	1,095	-38.8
Aggravated assault	216,482	179,138	-17.3	27,741	13,273	-52.2	55,258	52,690	-4.6	8,243	4,444	-46.1
Burglary	159,767	110,416	-30.9	45,896	19,254	-58.0	28,355	26,049	-8.1	6,057	2,802	-53.7
Larceny-theft	418,187	424,952	+1.6	106,506	60,365	-43.3	261,103	328,713	+25.9	74,117	41,533	-44.0
Motor vehicle theft	59,234	36,177	-38.9	14,361	6,029	-58.0	13,416	10,286	-23.3	3,290	1,518	-53.9
Arson	8,738	4,633	-47.0	4,538	1,536	-66.2	1,707	1,104	-35.3	685	275	-59.9
Violent crime[3]	297,166	244,197	-17.8	46,837	24,479	-47.7	64,235	61,780	-3.8	10,101	5,651	-44.1
Property crime[3]	645,926	576,178	-10.8	171,301	87,184	-49.1	304,581	366,152	+20.2	84,149	46,128	-45.2
Other assaults	592,204	486,355	-17.9	101,366	52,882	-47.8	199,974	192,182	-3.9	51,030	30,807	-39.6
Forgery and counterfeiting	41,028	22,493	-45.2	1,513	470	-68.9	27,291	12,418	-54.5	775	162	-79.1
Fraud	99,184	52,967	-46.6	3,297	1,811	-45.1	82,679	33,517	-59.5	1,793	965	-46.2
Embezzlement	6,101	4,850	-20.5	517	220	-57.4	6,907	5,073	-26.6	432	171	-60.4
Stolen property; buying, receiving, possessing	63,904	45,331	-29.1	11,930	5,514	-53.8	15,173	12,587	-17.0	2,102	1,086	-48.3
Vandalism	158,590	97,844	-38.3	66,281	23,174	-65.0	31,277	26,214	-16.2	9,921	4,619	-53.4
Weapons; carrying, possessing, etc.	105,054	78,496	–	25,051	10,331	-58.8	9,050	7,947	-12.2	2,656	1,283	-51.7

Offense charged	Male Total			Male Under 18			Female Total			Female Under 18		
	2006	2015	Percent change	2006	2015	Percent change	2006	2015	Percent change	2006	2015	Percent change
Prostitution and commercialized vice	11,754	7,103	−39.6	182	85	−53.3	21,648	10,560	−51.2	551	184	−66.6
Sex offenses (except rape and prostitution)	47,168	29,862	−36.7	9,029	4,914	−45.6	3,488	2,494	−28.5	919	729	−20.7
Drug abuse violations	865,257	715,904	−17.3	93,508	49,170	−47.4	212,899	212,218	−0.3	19,624	13,865	−29.3
Gambling	2,366	1,272	−46.2	279	121	−56.6	441	385	−12.7	13	12	−7.7
Offenses against the family and children	60,217	41,552	−31.0	2,070	1,379	−33.4	19,351	16,825	−13.1	1,278	829	−35.1
Driving under the influence	738,512	508,633	−31.1	9,943	3,251	−67.3	187,306	167,327	−10.7	3,004	1,043	−65.3
Liquor laws	294,825	123,435	−58.1	60,064	17,707	−70.5	113,686	50,795	−55.3	34,665	11,823	−65.9
Drunkenness	310,500	202,628	−34.7	8,281	2,503	−69.8	57,771	48,796	−15.5	2,812	1,025	−63.5
Disorderly conduct	308,923	171,960	−44.3	87,098	29,356	−66.3	113,264	68,763	−39.3	42,850	16,303	−62.0
Vagrancy	13,876	11,847	−14.6	2,390	457	−80.9	4,230	3,170	−25.1	1,085	141	−87.0
All other offenses (except traffic)	1,902,249	1,477,329	−22.3	180,909	77,354	−57.2	575,732	520,470	−9.6	67,920	29,896	−56.0
Suspicion	869	384	−55.8	157	95	−39.5	256	96	−62.5	46	32	−30.4
Curfew and loitering law violations	40,653	12,963	−68.1	40,653	12,963	−68.1	20,016	6,491	−67.6	20,016	6,491	−67.6

Source: Adapted from FBI (2016d).

[1] Does not include suspicion.

[2] The 2006 rape figures are based on the legacy definition, and the 2015 rape figures are aggregate totals based on both the legacy and revised Uniform Crime Reporting definitions. For this reason, a percent change is not provided.

[3] Violent crimes are offenses of murder and nonnegligent manslaughter, rape, robbery, and aggravated assault. Property crimes are offenses of burglary, larceny-theft, motor vehicle theft, and arson.

Gender

As indicated in Table 3.4, total crime in the under-18-years-of-age category declined over the 5-year period from 2011 to 2015 by 36% among males and by 35.9% among females. Murder and nonnegligent manslaughter (6.1%) and robbery (25.3%) among males decreased significantly. Murder and nonnegligent manslaughter decreased significantly among females (33%), and robbery also decreased by 13% during the same period. Aggravated assault decreased among males (28.8%) and females (25.7%). Overall, violent crime decreased among males and females under the age of 18 years (roughly 30% for each group). Property crime decreased for males (24.5%) and for females (22.7%). Weapons offenses decreased among both males and females, as did gambling. Whereas vagrancy went down for males, it increased for females under 18 years of age by 29.6%. Prostitution-related offenses also decreased among both males and females under 18 years of age over the 5-year period in question.

Historically, we have observed three to four arrests of juvenile males for every arrest of a juvenile female. During the period from 2011 to 2015, this ratio changed considerably so that juvenile females now account for roughly 41% of arrests of those under 18 years of age (see Table 3.4). The total number of arrests of males and females under age 18 decreased by about 31% and 19%, respectively.

Females have often been overlooked by those interested in juvenile justice (Chesney-Lind, 1999; OJJDP, 1998), and indeed, many of their survival mechanisms (e.g., running away when confronted with abusers) have been criminalized. The juvenile justice network has not always acted in the best interests of female juveniles because it often ignores their unique problems (Cobbina, Like-Haislip, & Miller, 2010; Dennis, 2012; Holsinger, 2000; Martin et al., 2013; National Girls Institute, 2013). Still, there are a number of girls involved in delinquent behavior and others as victims of abuse, and it may well be that we need to develop treatment methods that address their specific problems. For example, a study conducted by Ellis, O'Hara, and Sowers (1999) found that troubled female adolescents have a profile distinctly different from that of males. The female group was characterized as abused, self-harmful, and social, whereas the male group was seen as aggressive, destructive, and asocial. The authors concluded that different treatment modalities (more supportive and more comprehensive in nature) may need to be developed to treat troubled female adolescents. Johnson (1998) maintained that the increasing number of delinquent females can be addressed only by a multiagency approach based on nationwide and systemwide cooperation. Peters and Peters's (1998) findings seem to provide support for Johnson's proposal. They concluded that violent offending by females is the result of a complex web of victimization, substance abuse, economic conditions, and dysfunctional families, and this would seem to suggest the need for a multiagency response. To research this and other issues and to provide a sound foundation for implementation of strategies designed to prevent girls' delinquency, the OJJDP convened its Girls Study Group in 2004 (Zahn et al., 2010).

It is fairly common for girls fleeing from abusive parents to be labeled as runaways. Krisberg (2005; see also Zahn et al., 2010, p. 3) concluded, "Research on young women who enter the juvenile justice system suggests that they often have histories of physical and sexual abuse. Girls in the juvenile justice system have severe problems with substance abuse and mental health issues" (p. 123). If they are dealt with simply by being placed on probation, the underlying causes of the problems they confront are unlikely to be addressed. To deal with these causes, counseling may be needed for all parties involved, school authorities may need to be informed if truancy is involved, and further action in adult court may be necessary. If, as often happens, a girl's family moves from place to place, the process may begin all over because there is no transfer of information or records from one agency or place to another. According to Krisberg, "There are very few juvenile justice programs that are specifically designed for young women. Gender-responsive programs and policies are urgently needed" (p. 123). The conclusion that female delinquents may benefit from

Table 3.4 Five-Year Arrest Trends by Sex, 2011 to 2015

Offense charged	Male						Female					
	Total			Under 18			Total			Under 18		
	2011	2015	Percent change	2011	2015	Percent change	2011	2015	Percent change	2011	2015	Percent change
TOTAL[1]	**6,088,595**	**5,259,673**	**-13.6**	**700,443**	**448,078**	**-36.0**	**2,137,293**	**1,953,716**	**-8.6**	**290,955**	**186,640**	**-35.9**
Murder and nonnegligent manslaughter	6,143	6,195	+0.8	491	461	-6.1	825	810	-1.8	48	32	-33.3
Rape[2]	13,007	14,667	–	1,872	2,303	–	161	459	–	45	98	–
Robbery	59,300	51,513	-13.1	13,651	10,198	-25.3	8,350	8,572	+2.7	1,386	1,206	-13.0
Aggravated assault	200,997	189,945	-5.5	20,057	14,280	-28.8	58,018	56,293	-3.0	6,364	4,728	-25.7
Burglary	165,578	117,307	-29.2	35,931	20,564	-42.8	32,178	27,856	-13.4	5,087	3,323	34.7
Larceny-theft	483,506	453,042	-6.3	98,996	65,070	-34.3	371,677	346,601	-6.7	76,437	44,286	42.1
Motor vehicle theft	36,406	39,750	+9.2	8,029	7,866	-2.0	7,930	10,697	+34.9	1,552	1,758	+13.3
Arson	6,497	4,924	-24.2	2,873	1,610	-44.0	1,379	1,209	-12.3	479	304	-36.5
Violent crime[3]	279,447	262,320	-6.1	36,071	27,242	-24.5	67,354	66,134	-1.8	7,843	6,064	22.7
Property crime[3]	691,987	615,023	-11.1	145,829	95,110	-34.8	413,164	386,363	-6.5	83,555	49,671	40.6
Other assaults	601,228	523,074	-13.0	82,291	57,093	-30.6	226,349	204,361	-9.7	45,019	32,742	27.3
Forgery and counterfeiting	28,751	23,598	-17.9	759	509	-32.9	17,513	13,044	-25.5	306	185	39.5
Fraud	64,431	55,618	-13.7	2,348	2,160	-8.0	45,932	34,972	-23.9	1,235	1,086	12.1
Embezzlement	5,508	5,436	-1.3	183	244	+33.3	5,423	5,575	+2.8	118	182	+54.2
Stolen property; buying, receiving, possessing	50,724	46,335	-8.7	7,550	5,614	-25.6	13,068	12,888	-1.4	1,577	1,101	-30.2
Vandalism	129,917	102,401	-21.2	39,722	24,312	-38.8	30,463	27,753	-8.9	6,966	4,915	29.4
Weapons; carrying, possessing, etc.	90,934	87,083	-4.2	16,739	11,666	-30.3	8,181	8,720	+6.6	1,926	1,412	26.7

(Continued)

67

Table 3.4 (Continued)

Offense charged	Male						Female					
	Total			Under 18			Total			Under 18		
	2011	2015	Percent change	2011	2015	Percent change	2011	2015	Percent change	2011	2015	Percent change
Prostitution and commercialized vice	8,922	7,945	−11.0	129	98	−24.0	17,855	11,852	−33.6	332	194	41.6
Sex offenses (except rape and prostitution)	41,586	31,775	−23.6	7,563	5,272	−30.3	3,284	2,645	−19.5	919	776	15.6
Drug abuse violations	816,249	785,537	−3.8	84,160	54,534	−35.2	204,626	230,865	+12.8	17,031	14,821	13.0
Gambling	4,383	2,445	−44.2	573	264	−53.9	546	610	+11.7	45	30	33.3
Offenses against the family and children	57,203	46,809	−18.2	1,467	1,448	−1.3	19,184	18,548	−3.3	911	887	2.6
Driving under the influence	621,125	505,968	−18.5	5,192	3,336	−35.7	204,784	170,592	−16.7	1,821	1,096	39.8
Liquor laws	225,595	128,074	−43.2	38,110	18,478	−51.5	97,934	53,388	−45.5	25,512	12,398	51.4
Drunkenness	294,364	215,650	−26.7	5,994	2,734	−54.4	67,223	52,465	−22.0	2,191	1,102	49.7
Disorderly conduct	275,904	189,745	−31.2	60,256	32,008	−46.9	106,685	74,783	−29.9	31,496	17,307	45.1
Vagrancy	11,904	12,198	+2.5	533	508	−4.7	2,683	3,297	+22.9	108	140	+29.6
All other offenses (except traffic)	1,754,766	1,590,807	−9.3	131,307	83,616	−36.3	570,522	566,324	−0.7	47,524	31,994	−32.7
Suspicion	569	457	−19.7	52	99	+90.4	163	116	−28.8	26	33	+26.9
Curfew and loitering law violations	33,667	21,832	−35.2	33,667	21,832	−35.2	14,520	8,537	−41.2	14,520	8,537	−41.2

Source: Adapted from FBI (2016e).

[1] Does not include suspicion.

[2] The 2011 rape figures are based on the legacy definition, and the 2015 rape figures are aggregate totals based on both the legacy and revised Uniform Crime Reporting definitions. For this reason, a percent change is not provided.

[3] Violent crimes are offenses of murder and nonnegligent manslaughter, rape, robbery, and aggravated assault. Property crimes are offenses of burglary, larceny-theft, motor vehicle theft, and arson.

gender-directed programs is supported by Zahn and colleagues (2010, p. 12), who found the following eight factors significantly correlated with girls' delinquency:

1. Negative and critical mothers
2. Harsh discipline
3. Inconsistent discipline
4. Family conflict
5. Frequent family moves
6. Multiple caregivers
7. Longer periods of time with a single parent
8. Growing up in socioeconomically disadvantaged families

While some of these factors are significantly related to male delinquency as well, the lack of prevention, diversion, and treatment programs for girls involved in the juvenile justice network is well documented and requires attention (Cobbina et al., 2010; Dennis, 2012; Martin et al., 2013; National Girls Institute, 2013).

Race

The disproportionate minority contact (DMC) mandate was included in the reauthorization of the Juvenile Justice and Delinquency Prevention Act in 1988. The mandate required states to assess the extent of DMC and to develop strategies to achieve equal treatment of youth within the juvenile justice system. Some authorities argue that DMC is the result of racial bias within the juvenile justice system. The Federal Advisory Committee on Juvenile Justice (2010) said the following:

Research on disproportionate minority contact illustrates how the inequity often begins long before a youth enters the juvenile justice system. It can begin in early childhood when minority youth disproportionately enter the child welfare system, where they are put into foster care faster and stay there longer than other children. The inequity is further exacerbated in the education system, where minority children are more likely to be excluded from school and referred to the court by school officials or law enforcement. The disparity continues once minority youth enter the juvenile justice system, where they are treated differently by law enforcement and throughout the legal process. (p. 2)

Leiber, Bishop, and Chamlin (2011) analyzed data from one juvenile court (note the very small sample size) to determine whether the predictors of juvenile justice decision making before and after the mandate changed, especially in terms of race. They found that the factors impacting decision making, for the most part, did not change in significance or relative impact when considering case outcomes. In other words, the impact of race (among other factors) remained the same after the DMC mandate, at least in the juvenile court in question.

Official statistics on race are subject to a number of errors, as pointed out in Chapter 2. Any index of nonwhite arrests may be inflated as a result of discriminatory practices among criminal justice personnel (Armour & Hammond, 2009, p. 5; Federal Advisory Committee on Juvenile Justice, 2010; National Center for Juvenile Justice, 2014). For example, the presence of a black youth under "suspicious circumstances" may result in an official arrest even though the police officer knows the charge(s) will be dismissed. The National Center for Juvenile Justice (2014) found that black juveniles receive harsher dispositions from the justice system when they live in areas with high proportions of whites (i.e., where they are true numerical minority group members). Hanser and Gomila (2015) found that juvenile justice outcomes were influenced by race at every stage of the juvenile system, including adjudication. Joiner (2005) found that blacks were charged with more offenses more often than were whites and that whites received no charges more often than did blacks. The National Center for Juvenile Justice (2014) found partial support for their hypothesis that African Americans charged with drug offenses would be treated more harshly in jurisdictions characterized by economic and racial inequality and adherence to beliefs in racial differences than in jurisdictions without such characteristics. Hanser and Gomila (2015) pointed out that young black males are more likely to be labeled as slow learners or mentally challenged, to have learning difficulties in school, to lag behind their peers in basic educational competencies or skills, and to drop out of school at an early age. Juvenile black males are also more likely to be institutionalized or placed in foster care. In fact, Huizinga, Thornberry, Knight, and Lovegrove (2007) noted that "disproportionate minority contact (DMC), which we define as contact at any point within the juvenile justice system, is evident at all decision points" (p. 1). And Rodriguez (2010) concluded, "Despite federal and state legislation aimed at producing equitable treatment of youth in the juvenile court system, studies continue to find that race and ethnicity play a significant role in juvenile court outcomes" (p. 391). His own analysis of over 23,000 youth processed in Arizona found that black, Latino, and American Indian youth were treated more severely in juvenile court outcomes than their white counterparts.

Many minority group members live in lower-class neighborhoods in large urban centers where the greatest concentration of law enforcement officers exists. Because arrest statistics are more complete for large cities, we must take into account the sizable proportion of blacks found in these cities rather than the 13% statistic derived from calculating the proportion of blacks in our society. It is these same arrest statistics that lead many to believe that any overrepresentation of black and other minority juveniles in these statistics reflects racial inequities in the juvenile and criminal justice networks. For example, in Illinois, "African Americans comprised 18 percent of the state's youth population but 57 percent of youth arrested; Latino youth are nearly twice as likely as whites to be detained" (Black, 2010, p. 1). Analysis of official arrest statistics of persons under the age of 18 years has traditionally shown a disproportionate number of African Americans. Data presented in Table 3.5 show that African Americans accounted for 33.9% of all arrests of individuals under 18 in 2015. African Americans accounted for 50.8% of reported arrests for violent crime and 37.7% of the arrests for property crimes in the under-18-years-of-age category. American Indians or Alaskan Natives and Asian or Pacific Islanders accounted for very small portions of all crimes, as can be seen in Table 3.5.

With respect to specific crimes, African Americans under the age of 18 years accounted for well over half (60.1%) of the arrests for murder and nonnegligent manslaughter, more than two-thirds (68.6%) of the arrests for robbery, 41.4% of aggravated assaults, 41.6% of burglaries and 47.7% of auto thefts, and 60.4% of the arrests for prostitution-related offenses. They also accounted for some 75% of all arrests for gambling. Based on population parameters, African Americans under the age of 18 years account for a disproportionate amount of the juvenile violations committed, particularly those that are more serious in nature.

As indicated previously, social–environmental factors have an important impact on delinquency rates and perhaps especially on official delinquency rates. Race and ethnicity as causes of delinquency are complicated by social class (Hanser & Gomila, 2015; Huizinga et al., 2007; National Center for Juvenile Justice, 2014). A disproportionate number of blacks are found in the lower socioeconomic class with all of the correlates conducive to high delinquency. Unless these conditions are changed, each generation caught in this environment not only inherits the same conditions that created high crime and delinquency rates for its parents but also transmits them to the next generation. It is interesting to note that, according to research,

Table 3.5 Juvenile Arrests by Race and Ethnicity Under the Age of 18, 2015

Offense charged	Arrests under 18 — Race						Percent distribution[1]						Arrests under 18 — Ethnicity			Percent distribution[1]		
	Total	White	Black or African American	American Indian or Alaska Native	Asian	Native Hawaiian or Other Pacific Islander	Total	White	Black or African American	American Indian or Alaska Native	Asian	Native Hawaiian or Other Pacific Islander	Total[2]	Hispanic or Latino	Not Hispanic or Latino	Total	Hispanic or Latino	Not Hispanic or Latino
TOTAL	702,957	442,364	238,542	11,999	7,392	2,660	100.0	62.9	33.9	1.7	1.1	0.4	545,870	124,563	421,307	100.0	22.8	77.2
Murder and nonnegligent manslaughter	601	234	361	5	1	0	100.0	38.9	60.1	0.8	0.2	0.0	463	118	345	100.0	25.5	74.5
Rape[3]	2,715	1,802	835	42	26	10	100.0	66.4	30.8	1.5	1.0	0.4	1,975	397	1,578	100.0	20.1	79.9
Robbery	14,142	4,190	9,702	60	100	90	100.0	29.6	68.6	0.4	0.7	0.6	11,733	2,520	9,213	100.0	21.5	78.5
Aggravated assault	21,865	12,180	9,061	333	222	69	100.0	55.7	41.4	1.5	1.0	0.3	17,845	4,597	13,248	100.0	25.8	74.2
Burglary	27,344	15,287	11,373	344	262	78	100.0	55.9	41.6	1.3	1.0	0.3	22,536	5,688	16,848	100.0	25.2	74.8
Larceny-theft	119,712	72,434	43,232	1,751	1,815	480	100.0	60.5	36.1	1.5	1.5	0.4	92,529	19,125	73,404	100.0	20.7	79.3
Motor vehicle theft	11,111	5,535	5,296	176	71	33	100.0	49.8	47.7	1.6	0.6	0.3	8,056	2,124	5,932	100.0	26.4	73.6
Arson	2,067	1,517	469	58	17	6	100.0	73.4	22.7	2.8	0.8	0.3	1,701	326	1,375	100.0	19.2	80.8
Violent crime[4]	39,323	18,406	19,959	440	349	169	100.0	46.8	50.8	1.1	0.9	0.4	32,016	7,632	24,384	100.0	23.8	76.2
Property crime[4]	160,234	94,773	60,370	2,329	2,165	597	100.0	59.1	37.7	1.5	1.4	0.4	124,822	27,263	97,559	100.0	21.8	78.2
Other assaults	100,264	58,646	39,133	1,332	772	381	100.0	58.5	39.0	1.3	0.8	0.4	78,816	16,974	61,842	100.0	21.5	78.5
Forgery and counterfeiting	786	481	291	6	6	2	100.0	61.2	37.0	0.8	0.8	0.3	644	147	497	100.0	22.8	77.2
Fraud	3,425	1,730	1,583	60	47	5	100.0	50.5	46.2	1.8	1.4	0.1	2,710	364	2,346	100.0	13.4	86.6
Embezzlement	443	256	175	5	6	1	100.0	57.8	39.5	1.1	1.4	0.2	368	65	303	100.0	17.7	82.3
Stolen property; buying, receiving, possessing	7,941	3,442	4,322	72	88	17	100.0	43.3	54.4	0.9	1.1	0.2	6,370	1,341	5,029	100.0	21.1	78.9
Vandalism	31,840	22,359	8,562	508	308	103	100.0	70.2	26.9	1.6	1.0	0.3	26,635	5,890	20,745	100.0	22.1	77.9
Weapons; carrying, possessing, etc.	14,687	8,308	5,994	135	215	35	100.0	56.6	40.8	0.9	1.5	0.2	11,500	3,589	7,911	100.0	31.2	68.8

(Continued)

Table 3.5 (Continued)

Offense charged	Arrests under 18 — Race						Percent distribution[1]						Arrests under 18 — Ethnicity			Percent distribution[1]		
	Total	White	Black or African American	American Indian or Alaska Native	Asian	Native Hawaiian or Other Pacific Islander	Total	White	Black or African American	American Indian or Alaska Native	Asian	Native Hawaiian or Other Pacific Islander	Total[2]	Hispanic or Latino	Not Hispanic or Latino	Total	Hispanic or Latino	Not Hispanic or Latino
Prostitution and commercialized vice	442	162	267	2	6	5	100.0	36.7	60.4	0.5	1.4	1.1	377	53	324	100.0	14.1	85.9
Sex offenses (except rape and prostitution)	6,632	4,739	1,697	73	83	40	100.0	71.5	25.6	1.1	1.3	0.6	4,949	1,179	3,770	100.0	23.8	76.2
Drug abuse violations	75,461	56,617	16,419	1,347	836	242	100.0	75.0	21.8	1.8	1.1	0.3	60,323	17,506	42,817	100.0	29.0	71.0
Gambling	355	77	267	6	5	0	100.0	21.7	75.2	1.7	1.4	0.0	208	34	174	100.0	16.3	83.7
Offenses against the family and children	2,597	1,656	784	135	22	0	100.0	63.8	30.2	5.2	0.8	0.0	1,769	314	1,455	100.0	17.8	82.2
Driving under the influence	4,993	4,430	295	177	73	18	100.0	88.7	5.9	3.5	1.5	0.4	3,861	928	2,933	100.0	24.0	76.0
Liquor laws	32,663	28,684	2,184	1,326	386	83	100.0	87.8	6.7	4.1	1.2	0.3	25,066	4,114	20,952	100.0	16.4	83.6
Drunkenness	4,209	3,495	386	271	47	10	100.0	83.0	9.2	6.4	1.1	0.2	3,943	1,618	2,325	100.0	41.0	59.0
Disorderly conduct	54,686	30,061	23,100	1,058	367	100	100.0	55.0	42.2	1.9	0.7	0.2	37,696	6,793	30,903	100.0	18.0	82.0
Vagrancy	820	472	313	26	9	0	100.0	57.6	38.2	3.2	1.1	0.0	573	209	364	100.0	36.5	63.5
All other offenses (except traffic)	127,312	85,689	37,354	2,284	1,250	735	100.0	67.3	29.3	1.8	1.0	0.6	94,047	22,576	71,471	100.0	24.0	76.0
Suspicion	144	99	34	11	0	0	100.0	68.8	23.6	7.6	0.0	0.0	52	4	48	100.0	7.7	92.3
Curfew and loitering law violations	33,700	17,782	15,053	396	352	117	100.0	52.8	44.7	1.2	1.0	0.3	29,125	5,970	23,155	100.0	20.5	79.5

Source: Adapted from FBI (2016f).

[1] Because of rounding, the percentages may not add to 100.0.

[2] The ethnicity totals are representative of those agencies that provided ethnicity breakdowns. Not all agencies provide ethnicity data; therefore, the race and ethnicity totals will not equal.

[3] The rape figures in this table are aggregate totals of the data submitted based on both the legacy and revised Uniform Crime Reporting definitions.

[4] Violent crimes are offenses of murder and nonnegligent manslaughter, rape, robbery, and aggravated assault. Property crimes are offenses of burglary, larceny-theft, motor vehicle theft, and arson.

when ethnic or racial groups leave high crime and delinquency areas, they tend to take on the crime rate of the specific part of the community to which they move. It should also be noted that there are differential crime and delinquency rates among black neighborhoods, giving further credibility to the influence of the social–environmental approach to explaining high crime and delinquency rates (Armour & Hammond, 2009, p. 4). It is unlikely that any single factor can be used to explain the disproportionate number of black juveniles involved in some type of delinquency. The most plausible explanations currently center on environmental and socioeconomic factors characteristic of ghetto areas (National Center for Juvenile Justice, 2014). Violence and a belief that planning and thrift are not realistic possibilities may be transmitted across generations. This transmission is cultural, not genetic, and may account in part for high rates of violent crime and gambling (luck as an alternative to planning).

Whatever the reasons, it is quite clear that black juveniles are overrepresented in delinquency statistics—especially with respect to violent offenses—and that inner-city black neighborhoods are among the most dangerous places in America to live. Because most black offenders commit their offenses in black neighborhoods against black victims, these neighborhoods are often characterized by violence, and children living in them grow up as observers and/or victims of violence. Such violence undoubtedly takes a toll on children's ability to do well in school, to develop a sense of trust and respect for others, and to develop and adopt nonviolent alternatives. The same concerns exist for members of other racial and ethnic groups growing up under similar conditions.

Krisberg (2005) summed up the current state of knowledge concerning the impact of the characteristics of juvenile offenders as follows:

If you are feeling confused and getting a mild headache after considering these complexities, you are probably getting the right messages. Terms such as *race*, *ethnicity*, and *social class* are used imprecisely and sometimes interchangeably. This is a big problem that is embedded in the existing data and research. There is no simple solution to this conceptual quagmire except to recognize that it exists and frustrates both good research and sound public policy discussions on this topic. (pp. 83–84)

CAREER OPPORTUNITY: CRIMINALIST

Job description: Includes positions of laboratory technicians who examine evidence such as fingerprints and documents. Use chemistry, biology, and forensic science techniques to examine and classify or identify blood, body fluid, DNA, fiber, and fingerprint evidence that may be of value in solving criminal cases. Often on call, work in dangerous locations and in proximity to dead bodies and chemical and biological hazards. Sometimes testify in court as to evidentiary matters.

Employment requirements: At least a 4-year degree in chemistry, biology, physics, or forensic science. In some agencies, applicant must be a sworn police officer and must complete entry-level requirements for that position before moving to forensics. In other jurisdictions, civilians are hired as criminalists.

Beginning salary: Between $30,000 and $40,000. Benefits vary widely depending on jurisdiction and whether the position requires a sworn officer.

Summary

Official profiles of juvenile offenders reflect only the characteristics of those who have been apprehended and officially processed. Although they tell little or nothing about the characteristics of all juveniles who actually commit delinquent acts, they are useful in dealing with juveniles who have been officially processed. These official statistics currently lead us to some discomforting conclusions about the nature of delinquency in America as it relates to social and physical factors.

It might not be the broken home itself that leads to delinquency; instead, it may be the quality of life within the family in terms of consistency of discipline, level of tension, and ease of communication. Therefore, in some instances, it may be better to remove children from intact families that do not provide a suitable environment than to maintain the integrity of the families. In addition, it might not be necessary to automatically place juveniles from broken homes into institutions, foster homes, and so forth provided that the quality of life within the broken homes is good.

We perhaps need to rethink our position on the "ideal" family consisting of two biological parents and their children. This family no longer exists for most American children. For many children, the family of reality consists of a single mother who is head of the household or a biological parent and stepparent. Although many one-parent families experience varying degrees of delinquency and abuse or neglect, children in many others are valued, protected, and raised in circumstances designed to give them a chance at success in life.

Because education is an important determinant of occupational success in our society and because occupational success is an important determinant of life satisfaction, it is important that we attempt to minimize the number of juveniles who are "pushed out" of the educational system. Both juvenile justice practitioners and school officials need to pursue programs that minimize the number of juveniles who drop out. It may be that we are currently asking too much of educators when we require them not only to provide academic and vocational information but also to promote psychological and social well-being, moral development, and a sense of direction for juveniles (formerly provided basically by the family). At the current time, however, if educators fail to provide for these concerns, the juvenile often has nowhere else to turn except his or her peers, who may be experiencing similar problems. One result of this alienation from both the family and the educational system is the development of delinquent behavior patterns. Another may be direct attacks on school personnel or fellow students. Though schools in the United States remain relatively safe havens for students, there is no denying the impact of bullying (both physical and cyber) on students and the school environment. There are indications that schools have gone too far in zero-tolerance policies in some cases, although in others, bullying has not been taken seriously, and it is imperative that programs to prevent bullying through early identification and intervention are made available to school administrators, teachers, and parents. Programs aimed directly at youth may also be effective. Although school shootings are rare occurrences, they undoubtedly cause extreme concern among the students, youth, and parents involved. Further, they attract national media attention and thereby involve many, if not most, Americans on some level. It may never be possible to totally prevent such tragedies, but steps like target hardening; improved security; and training for schoolteachers, administrators, and students are widely regarded as necessary. We have concentrated our interest and research activities on delinquency and abuse and neglect of the lower social class and have generally ignored the existence of these problems in the middle and upper classes. The importance of lower-class delinquency cannot be ignored, but we must also realize that the problem may be equally widespread, although perhaps in different forms, in the middle and upper classes. We can no longer afford the luxury of viewing delinquency as only a problem of lower-class neighborhoods in urban areas. The delinquency also exists in what are commonly considered to be "quiet middle-class suburban areas" and in many rural areas as well. Because motivations and types of offenses committed by middle-class delinquents may differ from those of their lower-class counterparts, new techniques and approaches for dealing with these problems may be required.

If those working with children can develop more effective ways of promoting good relationships between juveniles and their families and of making the importance of a relevant education clear to juveniles, involvement in gang activities may be lessened. At the current time, however, understanding the importance of peer group pressure and the demands of the gang on the individual juvenile is extremely important in understanding drug abuse and related activities. If gangs could be used to promote legitimate concerns rather than illegitimate concerns, one of the major sources of support for certain types of delinquent activities (e.g., vandalism, drug abuse) could be weakened considerably. Reasonable alternatives to current gang activities need to be developed and promoted.

Finally, there is no denying that black juveniles are disproportionately involved in official delinquency. Although there are still those who argue racial connections to such delinquency, the evidence that such behavior is a result of family, school, and neighborhood conditions and perhaps the actions of juvenile justice practitioners rather than genetics is overwhelming. Whatever the reasons for the high rates of delinquency—and especially violent offenses—in black neighborhoods, it behooves us all to address this issue with as many resources as possible in the interests of those living in both high-crime areas and the larger society.

None of the factors discussed in this chapter can be considered a direct cause of delinquency. It is important to remember that official statistics reflect only a small proportion of all delinquent activities. We use them because they are one of the most consistent sources of data available, but we must always keep in mind their limitations. Profiles based on the characteristics discussed in this chapter are valuable to the extent that they alert us to a number of problem areas that must be addressed if we are to make progress in the battle against delinquency.

Attempts to improve the quality of family life and the relevancy of education and attempts to change discriminatory practices in terms of social class, race, and gender are needed badly. Improvements in these areas will go a long way toward reducing the frequency of certain types of delinquent activity.

KEY TERMS

broken homes 44	dropouts 58	socialization process 41
bullying 54	latchkey children 46	socioeconomic status 47
crack 59	learning disabled 48	underclass 57
criminal subculture 56	methamphetamines 59	youth culture 55
disproportionate minority contact (DMC) 69	social factors 39	

Critical Thinking Questions

1. What is the relationship between profiles of delinquents based on official statistics and the actual extent of delinquency?

2. Discuss the relationships among the family, the educational system, drugs, and delinquency.

3. Discuss some of the possible reasons for the overrepresentation of black juveniles in official delinquency statistics. What could be done to decrease the proportion of young blacks involved in delinquency?

4. Discuss DMC and its consequences.

5. How do an area of the city, race, and social class combine to affect delinquency?

6. Is delinquency basically a lower-class phenomenon? If so, why should those in the middle and upper classes be concerned about it?

7. Discuss the methamphetamine crisis. How does it differ from other drug-related crises we have faced in the past? What do you think can be done to deal with this crisis?

Suggested Readings

Alston, F. K. (2013). *Latch key children.* New York, NY: NYU Study Center. Retrieved from www.education.com/reference/article/Ref_Latch_Key_Children/?page=2

Bishop, D. M., Leiber, M., & Johnson, J. (2010). Contexts of decision making in the juvenile justice system: An organizational approach to understanding minority overrepresentation. *Youth Violence & Juvenile Justice, 8*(3), 213–233.

Bjerregaard, B. (2010). Gang membership and drug involvement: Untangling the complex relationship. *Crime and Delinquency, 56*(1), 3–34.

Brown, J. R., Aalsma, M. C., & Ott, M. A. (2013). The experiences of parents who report youth bullying victimization to school officials. *Journal of Interpersonal Violence, 28*(3), 494–518.

Carter, P. L. (2003). "Black" cultural capital, status positioning, and schooling conflicts for low-income African American youth. *Social Problems, 50,* 136–155.

Centers for Disease Control and Prevention. (2013). *Fact sheet: Understanding school violence.* Atlanta, GA: Author. Retrieved from www.cdc.gov/violenceprevention/pdf/schoolviolence_factsheet-a.pdf

De Coster, S., Heimer, K., & Wittrock, S. M. (2006). Neighborhood disadvantage, social capital, street context, and youth violence. *Sociological Quarterly, 17,* 723–753.

Demuth, S., & Brown, S. L. (2004). Family structure, family processes, and adolescent delinquency: The significance of parental absence versus parental gender. *Journal of Research in Crime and Delinquency, 41,* 58–81.

Deutsch, A., Crockett, L., Wolff, J., & Russell, S. (2012). Parent and peer pathways to adolescent delinquency: Variations by ethnicity and neighborhood context. *Journal of Youth & Adolescence, 41*(8), 1078–1094.

Forum on Child and Family Statistics. (2012). *America's children in brief: Key national indicators of well-being, 2012.* Retrieved from www.childstats.gov/pdf/ac2012/ac_12.pdf

Francis, A. A. (2012). The dynamics of family trouble: Middle-class parents whose children have problems. *Journal of Contemporary Ethnography, 41*(4), 371–401.

Ginwright, S. A. (2002). Classed out: The challenges of social class in black community change. *Social Problems, 49,* 544–562.

Hanser, R. D., & Gomila, M. D. (2015). *Multiculturalism and the criminal justice system.* Upper Saddle River, NJ: Pearson.

Hayes, L. (2008). Teachers' expectations affect kids' grades, student-teacher relationships. *EduGuide.* Retrieved from www.eduguide.org

Huizinga, D., Thornberry, T., Knight, K., & Lovegrove, P. (2007, September). *Disproportionate minority contact in the juvenile justice system: A study of differential minority arrest/referral to court in three cities.* Washington, DC: Office of Juvenile Justice and Delinquency Prevention. Retrieved from www.ojjdp.ncjrs.gov/dmc

Hume, R. (2010). *Learning disabilities and the juvenile justice system.* Lansing, MI: Learning Disabilities Association of Michigan. Retrieved from www.ldaofmichigan.org/articles/ld.jj.htm

Joiner, C. T. (2005). An examination of racial profiling data in a large metropolitan area. *Professional Issues in Criminal Justice, 1*(2), 1–14.

Leiber, M., Bishop, D., & Chamlin, M. B. (2011). Juvenile justice decision-making before and after the implementation of the disproportionate minority contact (DMC) mandate. *JQ: Justice Quarterly, 28*(3), 460–492.

Mallett, C. (2008). The disconnect between youths with mental health and special education disabilities and juvenile court outcomes. *Corrections Compendium, 33*(5), 1–7.

McNulty, T. L., & Bellair, P. E. (2003). Explaining racial and ethnic differences in adolescent violence: Structural disadvantage, family well-being, and social capital. *Justice Quarterly, 20,* 1–31.

Mitchell, P., & Shaw, J. (2011). Factors affecting the recognition of mental health problems among adolescent offenders in custody. *Journal of Forensic Psychiatry & Psychology, 22*(3), 381–394.

National Center for Juvenile Justice. (2014). *Juvenile Offenders and Victims: 2014 National Report.* Washington, DC: Office of Juvenile Justice and Delinquency Prevention.

National Institute on Drug Abuse. (2013). *Facts on drugs: Prescription drugs.* Retrieved from http://teens.drugabuse.gov/drug-facts/prescription-drugs

National Institute on Drug Abuse. (2016). *Monitoring the future survey: High school and youth trends.* Bethesda, MD: NIDA. Retrieved from https://www.drugabuse.gov/publications/

drugfacts/monitoring-future-survey-high-school-youth-trends

Office of Juvenile Justice and Delinquency Prevention. (2010). *How OJJDP is forming partnerships and finding solutions: Annual report.* Washington, DC: Office of Justice Programs, U.S. Department of Justice. Retrieved from www.ojjdp.gov/pubs/237051.pdf

Raskind, M. (2010). *Research trends: Is there a link between LD and juvenile delinquency?* San Francisco, CA: Great Schools. Retrieved from www.greatschools.org/LD/managing/link-between-ld-and-juvenile-delinquency.gs?content=932

Schroeder, R. D., Osgood, A. K., & Oghia, M. J. (2010). Family transitions and juvenile delinquency. *Sociological Inquiry, 80*(4), 579–604.

Seigel, J. A. (2011). *Disrupted childhoods: Children of women in prison.* New Brunswick, NJ: Rutgers University Press.

U.S. Substance Abuse and Mental Health Services Administration. (2013, February 14). *Drug, alcohol abuse more likely among high school dropouts.* Rockville, MD: U.S. Substance Abuse and Mental Health Services Administration. Retrieved from www.healthfinder.gov/News/Article.aspx?id=673547

Weerman, F. M., & Hoeve, M. (2012). Peers and delinquency among girls and boys: Are sex differences in delinquency explained by peer factors? *European Journal of Criminology, 9*(4), 228–244.

Zahn, M. A., Agnew, R., Fishbein, D., Miller, S., Winn, D.-M., Dakoff, G., . . . Chesney-Lind, M. (2010, April). *Causes and correlates of girls' delinquency. Girls study group: Understanding and responding to girls' delinquency.* Washington, DC: Office of Juvenile Justice and Delinquency Prevention. Retrieved from www.ncjrs.gov/pdffiles1/ojjdp/226358.pdf

$SAGE edge™

Sharpen your skills with SAGE edge at **edge.sagepub.com/coxjj9e**. SAGE edge for students provides a personalized approach to help you accomplish your coursework goals in an easy-to-use learning environment. You'll find action plans, mobile-friendly eFlashcards, and quizzes as well as video and web resources and links to SAGE journal articles to support and expand on the concepts presented in this chapter.

Theories of Causation

4

On completion of this chapter, students should be able to do the following:

- Recognize the requirements for a good theory
- Understand and discuss the strengths and limitations of various theories
- Recognize and discuss the importance of the relationship between theory and practice
- Evaluate research relating to theories of causation

WHAT WOULD YOU DO?

Chuck is a 16-year-old male who has had numerous encounters with law enforcement. He is currently on juvenile probation and is in an alternative school. Chuck has had a long history of attention-deficit/hyperactivity disorder and was diagnosed with conduct disorder in his early childhood. He is presently in counseling for bullying, anger management, and substance abuse (he consumes methamphetamine as well as ecstasy from time to time). Further, Chuck's parents, both divorced and remarried, have brought him to your office because even they feel that the requirements of his probation are not stringent enough. In short, they want you, his probation officer, to do something about Chuck. In fact, you get the idea that they want to get rid of him.

Chuck has constantly been in trouble at school and in the community. He surrounds himself with a number of younger youth who look up to his acts of violence and intimidation. Chuck is also fond of taking risks, such as jumping in the street to force cars to veer aside while he throws eggs at the windshield to blind the driver.

Chuck also loves to fight and bully others. He gets mad easily, and when he does, he becomes a real "loose cannon," hurling verbal insults and often simply attacking people who "piss him off."

Chuck is likewise a skilled liar. He lies to everyone about his whereabouts and is difficult to locate. He is fond of going from house to house and friend to friend. When he gets caught for something, even if the person actually *sees* him do it, he will vehemently deny his involvement.

He stays out late despite his parents' directions and breaks the city ordinance curfew for juveniles. In fact, two nights ago Chuck was reportedly out in a neighborhood at 2 a.m. with some other youth, drinking beer and beating mailboxes with an aluminum bat. One of the girls who was with the group told him that he was immature and he should stop. Chuck called her a number of inappropriate names and then threw a brick at her; luckily, he missed.

When Chuck was 10 years old, he was diagnosed with conduct disorder. He exhibited acts of cruelty toward pets and other animals from time to time, and he seemed indifferent to the pain they suffered. In fact, he indicated a bizarre and morbid fascination with their death. At the age of 13, Chuck reportedly tried to coerce one of his cousins into sexual intercourse but was stopped just before the act could be committed.

Chuck's parents are not naive about Chuck's behavioral problems. In fact, they are very worried because he is now 16 and they feel as if they have completely failed as parents. Chuck has been on probation with you for nearly 3 months without incident. However, his parents claim that he threatens kids in the neighborhood and gets one of his friends to do his dirty work, all so he does not get caught fighting. You look to Chuck, and he just says that his parents are out to get him.

What Would You Do?

1. What do you think, if anything, can be done to prevent Chuck from committing further acts of delinquency?

2. What might be some of the causal factors to Chuck's behavior?

L et us now examine some of the theories that have been developed in an attempt to explain offenses by and against juveniles. For example, one theory proposes that child abuse and neglect are important causal factors in delinquency. In fact, numerous studies over the past 50 years have suggested links between delinquency and child abuse and neglect (Ford, Chapman, Mack, & Pearson, 2006). Scudder, Blount, Heide, and Silverman (1993) noted that the results of their research "suggest that children who break the law, especially through acts of violence, often have a history of maltreatment as children" (p. 321). The results of their research indicate further that "a child abused at a young age is at higher risk for subsequent delinquent behaviors than a nonabused child" (p. 321). Siegel (2011) found that as many as 10 million children are exposed to domestic violence in their homes annually (see also Onyskiw, 2003). Other researchers have arrived at similar conclusions (Siegel & Williams, 2003). Hunter, Figueredo, and Malamuth (2010) found a relationship between exposure to violence and nonsexual delinquency, and Way and Urbaniak (2008) found that adolescents engaging in sexually offensive behaviors with prior delinquent behaviors were older and had higher rates of documented childhood maltreatment. In addition, Schaffner (2007) noted that "young women adjudicated delinquent in juvenile court report suffering inordinate amounts of emotional, physical, and sexual trauma in early childhood and adolescence" (p. 1229). Ryan, Williams, and Courtney (2013) thus indicated the following:

Victims of child abuse and neglect are at an increased risk of involvement with the juvenile justice and adult correctional systems. . . . Neglect likely plays a critical role in continued offending as parental monitoring, parental rejection and family relationships are instrumental in explaining juvenile conduct problems. (p. 454)

Their study sought to determine whether neglect is associated with recidivism for moderate- and high-risk juvenile offenders in Washington State. Using official records from child protection, they identified juvenile offenders with a history of child neglect and juvenile offenders with an ongoing case of neglect. Ryan et al. (2013) concluded the following:

Adolescents with an ongoing case of neglect were significantly more likely to continue offending as compared with youth with no official history of neglect. These findings remain even after controlling for a wide range of family, peer, academic, mental health, and substance abuse covariates. (p. 454)

Based on these findings, it appears empirical evidence leads to the conclusions that abuse and neglect are factors in delinquency and recidivism. Yet, is the empirical research conclusive? It is one thing to argue that many delinquents have been abused or neglected (almost certainly true) and another to determine whether most abused or neglected youth become delinquent (an empirical question). As we shall see, scientific theory requires more than empirical evidence based on a conceptual scheme. In this case, if many delinquents have been subjected to abuse or neglect, does it logically follow that most youth who are abused or neglected become delinquent? If not, we need to determine what other factors play a role in the relationship (as Ryan et al. [2013] attempted to do). Abuse and neglect is discussed in more detail in Chapter 5.

Scientific Theory

Although dozens of conceptual schemes have been proposed in attempts to specify the causes of crime and delinquency, only a few of the more prominent attempts are discussed here.

A scientific theory may be defined as a set of two or more related, empirically testable assertions (statements of alleged facts or relationships among facts about a particular phenomenon [Fitzgerald & Cox, 2002, p. 47]). Although this definition may sound complex, it is really quite simple if we look at it one part at a time. A testable assertion or proposition is simply a statement of a relationship between two or more variables. In an acceptable theory, these assertions or propositions are related in a logical manner so that some other assertions or propositions can be derived (deduced) from others. Here is an example:

Proposition 1: All delinquents are victims of child abuse and/or neglect.

Proposition 2: Harry is a delinquent.

Proposition 3: Harry is a victim of child abuse and/or neglect.

In this case, Proposition 3 is derived from Propositions 1 and 2; that is, Proposition 3 is said to be explained by Propositions 1 and 2 and is logically correct. Our definition of a theory, however, requires that at least some of the propositions be empirically testable. To be acceptable, then, a theory must be logically correct and must accurately describe events in the real world. Suppose that Harry is not, in fact, a victim of child abuse and/or neglect. Clearly, our explanation of delinquency is erroneous, and our theory must be revised or rejected.

Although conceptual schemes that suggest relationships between variables but do not meet our requirements for theory may be useful stepping-stones in describing delinquency or abuse, only a logically correct and empirically accurate theory will enable us to explain these phenomena. Explanation is central to preventing or controlling delinquency

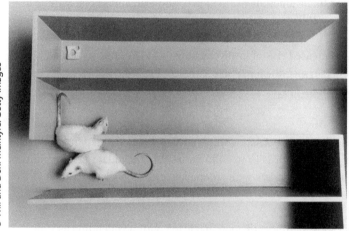

© Will and Deni McIntyre/Getty Images

Behaviorists believe that many of the principles learned in the study of animal behavior can be applied to humans.

and abuse. All policy and practice in juvenile justice is shaped, intentionally or not, by theory. For example, "get-tough" policies are an offshoot of classical theory and hedonism; policies relying on individual or group therapy are based in psychological or social psychological theory; and policies stressing neighborhood improvement, better education, and job opportunities are based on sociological theories.

As we discuss some theories and conceptual schemes, you may find it useful to assess the extent to which they meet the requirements of our definition and the extent to which they are useful in helping us to understand offenses by and against juveniles. Klofas and Stojkovic (1995) indicated the following:

> Our ideas about crime—what it means and why it happens—have varied considerably over the past several hundred years. We have changed from (1) viewing crime as the work of the devil to (2) describing it as the rational choice of free-willed economic calculators to (3) explaining it as the involuntary causal effects of biological, mental, and environmental conditions, and then back to (2). (p. 37)

Assessing the state of criminological theory toward the end of the 20th century, Bernard (1990) concluded that not much progress had been made during the prior 20 years in weeding out theories that cannot be supported or in verifying other theories. We hope that we have made progress during the past 20 years, but efforts to develop and empirically test theories remain sporadic. If a trend with respect to theories of juvenile delinquency can be identified, it would appear to be an emphasis on multidimensional, multidisciplinary theories based on the recognition that one-dimensional theories are unlikely to provide explanations for the wide range of delinquent behaviors observed (see, for example, Cruz & Cruz, 2007; Wood & Alleyne, 2010).

Our intent in this chapter is simply to familiarize you with some of the numerous conceptual schemes and to note some of the strengths and weaknesses of these schemes. For those who desire more detailed information about specific theories, the Suggested Readings list at the end of the chapter should prove to be useful.

Some Early Theories

Demonology

Early attempts to explain various forms of deviant behavior (e.g., crime, delinquency, mental illness) focused on demon or spirit possession (demonology). Individuals who violated societal norms were thought to be possessed by some evil spirit that forced them to commit evil deeds through the exercise of mysterious supernatural power (Moyer, 2001, p. 13). Deviant behavior, then, was viewed not as a product of free will but rather as determined by forces beyond the control of the individual; thus, the demonological theory of deviance is referred to as a deterministic approach. To cure or control deviant behavior, a variety of techniques were employed to drive the evil spirits from the mind and/or body of the perceived deviant.

One process that was employed was trephining, which consisted of drilling holes in the skulls of those perceived as deviants to allow the evil spirits to escape. Various rites of exorcism, including beating and burning, were practiced to make the body of the perceived deviant such an uncomfortable place to reside that the evil spirits would leave or to make the deviant confess his or her association with evil spirits. As might be expected, such torture of the body often resulted in death or permanent disability to the individual who was allegedly possessed. In addition, either confession or failure to confess could be taken as evidence of possession. Tortured sufficiently, many individuals undoubtedly confessed simply to prevent further torture. Those who persisted in claiming innocence were often thought to be so completely under the control of evil spirits that they could not tell the truth. Needless to say, the consequences for both categories of accused were frequently very unpleasant.

Many observers believe that belief in spirit possession as a cause of deviance is rare today, but our analysis of news articles over the past few years has turned up numerous articles on ritual abuse of children by persons or groups claiming to have been instructed by deities, typically God or Satan, to commit the acts in question (Bishop, 2010; Charton, 2001; "In This Church," 2001; "NYC Mom Arrested," 2006; Stearns & Garcia, 2001). As Klofas and Stojkovic (1995, p. 39) noted, supernatural bases for crime have not been totally rejected, although they have been largely supplanted by more scientific explanations.

Perhaps demonology as an explanation of deviance persists because, in some respects, attempts to deal with deviance thought to be caused by spirits are logical if the basic premise is accepted as true; that is, if one believes that spirit possession causes deviance, it makes sense to drive the spirits away if possible. As is the case with all theories of deviance, this one implies a method of cure or control. Although such an explanation of deviance seems simplistic to criminologists today, it cannot be scientifically disproved and is still clearly accepted as valid by significant numbers of people in a substantial number of countries. Precisely because it cannot be scientifically tested, however, this attempt to explain deviant behavior is of little value from a theoretical perspective.

Classical Theory

During the last half of the 18th century, the classical school of criminology (classical theory, often referred to as a freewill approach) emerged in Italy and England in the works of Cesare Beccaria and Jeremy Bentham, respectively. This approach to explaining and controlling crime was based on the belief that humans exercise free will and that human behavior results from rationally calculating rewards and costs in terms of pleasure and pain. In other words, before an individual commits a specific act, he or she determines whether the consequences of the act will be pleasurable or painful. Presumably, acts that have painful consequences will be avoided. To control crime, then, society simply needed to make the punishment for violators outweigh the benefits of their illegal actions. Thus, penalties became increasingly more severe as offenses became increasingly more serious. Under classical theory, threat of punishment is considered to be a deterrent to criminals who rationally calculate the consequences of their illegal actions.

By the early 1800s, Beccaria's approach had been modified in recognition of the fact that not all individuals were capable of rationally calculating rewards and costs. The modified approach, generally referred to as the neoclassical approach, called for the mitigation of punishment for the insane and juveniles (Conklin, 1998, p. 41; Moyer, 2001, p. 27). By definition, the insane were not capable of rational calculation, and juveniles (up to a certain age at least) were thought to be less responsible than adults.

It is important to understand the classical approach because its propositions (punishment deters crime, the punishment should fit the crime, and juveniles and the insane should be treated differently from sane adults) are basic to our current criminal and juvenile justice system.

Rational Choice Theory

The rational choice theory or postclassical theory of the 20th century also involves the notion that before people commit crimes, they rationally consider the risks and rewards. A burglar noting no lights on and no police presence at an expensive mansion over several nights might rationally conclude that the risk is relatively low and the potential rewards are worth pursuing and, therefore, may commit the crime. According to the rational choice model, focusing on the development of rational thought and the application of scientific laws, as well as using empirical research, might help the state to develop policies that better control crime and deviance and thereby improve quality of life (Bohm, 2001, p. 15; Bouffard, 2007; Lanier & Henry, 1998, p. 72; S. T. Reid, 2006, pp. 77–78).

This view, that delinquents exercise free will and rationally calculate the consequences of their behavior, fits well with the conservative ideology and the get-tough approach to delinquency. If delinquency is a product of free will and not predetermined by social conditions, the delinquent may best be deterred by the threat of punishment rather than by the promise of treatment. Gang members who go into the drug business with the clear intent of making a profit by outwitting both their competitors and law enforcement officials may be described as using rational choice theory.

Deterrence Theory

Deterrence theory is another extension of the classical approach. It focuses on the relationship between punishment and misbehavior at both the individual and group levels. Specific deterrence refers to preventing a given individual from committing further crimes, whereas general deterrence refers to the effect that punishing one wrongdoer has on preventing others from committing offenses. When we attempt to measure the extent of deterrence, we are actually measuring perceived deterrence—what individuals believe will happen to them (Will they be caught? Will they be punished? Will the punishment be severe?) if they commit offenses. Most authorities appear to agree that the deterrent effects of punishment are greater if the punishment is swift and certain. It appears that the deterrent effect of severe punishment is moderated by celerity (swiftness) and certainty (S. T. Reid, 2006, pp. 74–78). With respect to delinquents, we might ask whether the increasingly severe punishments suggested by get-tough policies are likely to have significant impact on juveniles who do not believe they will be apprehended for their delinquent acts or who do not believe they will be punished if apprehended. The effect of criminal experience on risk perceptions plays a critical role in deterrence theory. One assumption is that offenders will update their risk perceptions over time in response to the signals they receive during their offending experiences. Anwar and Loughgran (2011) found that an individual who commits a crime and is arrested will increase his or her perceived probability of being caught by 6.3% compared with if he had not been arrested. Based on their crime-specific analysis, they conclude that risk perception updating, and thus potentially deterrence, may be partially crime specific.

Kaufman (2010) said the following:

The data from longitudinal studies on this question [concerning the deterrent effects of arrest] are robust and consistent. More than a dozen studies found that people who have been arrested are at least as likely to be arrested in the future as those who have not. Thus, rather than being a deterrent, arrest resulted in similar or higher rates of later offending. (p. 27)

Yet another concern with respect to deterrence theory has to do with the fact that in some instances, those about to commit delinquent acts do not consider the possibility of being apprehended or punished (e.g., those under the influence of intoxicants, those who strike out in a passionate or angry state of mind).

Routine Activities Theory

Routine activities theory is yet another extension of the belief that rational thought and sanctions largely determine criminal behavior. According to this approach, crime is simply a function of people's everyday behavior. One's presence in certain types of places, frequented by motivated offenders, makes him or her a suitable target and, in the absence of capable guardians, is likely to lead to crime (Conklin, 1998, p. 319; Cote, 2002, p. 286; Groff, 2007, p. 75; Lanier & Henry, 1998, p. 82). Plass and Carmody (2005) studied the effect of engaging in risky activities on the violent victimization experiences of delinquent and nondelinquent juveniles. Their results showed that there are some modest differences in the effects of routinely engaging in risky behaviors and the likelihood of violent victimization. Other research has shown that juveniles who socialize with peers in unstructured and unsupervised settings are more likely to engage in deviant behavior. Augustyn and McGloin (2013, p. 117) investigated whether the strength of the relationship between how juveniles use their time and different forms of deviance varies for males and females. They hypothesized that "unstructured and unsupervised socializing with peers would be a significantly stronger risk for predatory delinquency (i.e., violent and property crime) for male adolescents than for females, whereas it will be an equivalent risk across gender for substance use" (p. 117). Their research supported this hypothesis. Similarly, Bossler, Holt, and May (2012) noted that online harassment is especially prevalent among middle and high school populations who frequently use technology as a means to communicate with others. Using a routine activities framework, the researchers used a survey to explore the online harassment experiences of middle and high school students. They concluded "that online harassment victimization increased when juveniles maintain [routine activities including] social network sites, associate with peers who harass online, and post sensitive information online" (p. 500).

There is also research that supports the existence of "hot spots," or areas in which crimes occur repeatedly over time (Buerger, Cohn, & Petrosino, 2000; Sherman & Weisburd, 1995). In other cases, however, victims' absence may be critical to the crime in question (e.g., burglary is easier if no one is home). Schreck and Fisher (2004) indicated that the routine activities perspective suggests that exposure to delinquent peers will enhance risk. Their analysis indicated that family and peer context variables correspond with a higher risk of violent victimization among teenagers, net controls for unstructured and unsupervised activities and demographic characteristics. However, conceptualizing and measuring variables associated with routine activities theory is critical to determining the validity of the theory (Groff, 2007, 2008; Spano & Freilich, 2009; Spano, Freilich, & Bolland, 2008).

For a variety of reasons, the classical approach to controlling crime has never been very successful. Although there seems to be some logic to the approach, the premise that the threat of punishment deters crime, at least as currently employed, is inaccurate. There are a variety of possible sources of error in this premise. First, it may be that humans do not always rationally calculate rewards and costs. An individual committing what we commonly refer to as a "crime of passion" (as in the case of the murder of a spouse caught in an adulterous act or excessive corporal punishment of a child in a moment of anger) might not stop to think about the consequences. If this individual does not stop to make such calculations, the threat of punishment (no matter how severe) will not affect that person's behavior. Second, an individual may calculate rewards and costs in a way that appears rational to him or her (but perhaps not to society) and may decide that certain illegal acts are worth whatever punishment he or she will receive if apprehended (as in the case of a starving person stealing food). Finally, the individual may rationally calculate rewards and costs but have no fear of punishment because he or she believes that the chances of apprehension are slight (as in the case of many juveniles involved with alcohol and minor vandalism). If the individual believes that he or she will not be apprehended for his or her illegal acts, the threat of punishment has little meaning. In addition, the individual may believe that even if he or she is caught, punishment will not be administered (as in the cases of juveniles who are aware that most juvenile cases never go to court and of parents who abuse their children in the name of discipline).

For whatever reasons, the classical approach to explaining and controlling crime has not been shown to be successful. It would appear that whatever possibility of success this approach has rests with delivering punishment relatively immediately and with a great deal of certainty. Because our society largely continues to rely on the classical approach, and because neither immediacy of punishment nor certainty of apprehension exists, it is not surprising that we are unsuccessful in our attempts to control crime and delinquency.

In spite of the fact that severe punishment does not appear to lead to desirable behavior, many child abusers obviously believe that such punishment will lead to improved behavior on behalf of their children. Thus, when a child fails to meet the expectations of abusive parents, whether in the area of toilet training, eating habits, schoolwork, or showing proper deference to the parents, emotional and/or physical abuse results. This often leads to lowered self-esteem on behalf of the child, whose performance then suffers even more, leading to more severe punishment on the part of the parents and so forth. This cycle of violence, once begun, is difficult to break, and there is at least some evidence that the abused child may later abuse his or her own children in the same ways (Knudsen, 1992, pp. 61–63).

The Positivist School

The positivist school of criminology emerged during the second half of the 19th century. Cesare Lombroso is recognized as the founder of the positivist school and also as the father of modern criminology. Lombroso, with other positivists such as Raffaele Garofalo and Enrico Ferri, believed that criminals should be studied scientifically and emphasized determinism as opposed to free will (classical school) as the basis of criminal behavior. Although a number of positivists believed that heredity is the determining factor in criminality, others believed that the environment determined, in large measure, whether an individual became a criminal.

The positivists emphasized the need for empirical research in criminology, and some stressed the importance of environment as a causal factor in crime. Although their methodology was unsophisticated by modern standards, their contributions to the development of modern criminology are undeniable. Lombroso may also be considered, earlier in his career at least, as one of the founders of the biological school of criminology.

Biological Theories

Biological theories of delinquency were initially based on the assumption that delinquency (criminality) is inherited. Over the past century, the approach has tended to emphasize more the belief that offenders differ from nonoffenders in some physiological way (Conklin, 1998, p. 146). This approach has offered a number of explanations of delinquency, ranging from glandular malfunctions to learning disabilities, to racial heritage, to nutrition. Rafter (2004) noted that today biological explanations are again gaining credibility and are joining forces with sociological explanations in ways that may make them partners in explaining crime and delinquency. She advised (and we agree) students of crime and delinquency to become familiar with the biological tradition that includes physiognomists, phrenologists, Lombroso, Goddard, Hooton, the Gluecks, and Sheldon, among others. By studying where these forerunners of contemporary biological theories came from, we can determine how they developed, what they contributed, and where they went astray. As we examine some of these explanations, keep in mind our definition of an acceptable theory.

Cesare Lombroso's "Born Criminal" Theory

Lombroso (1835–1909) became known for the theory of the "born criminal." As a result of his research, he became convinced at one point in his career that criminals were atavists, or throwbacks, to more primitive beings.

Boyer/Roger Viollet/Getty Images

Cesare Lombroso is recognized as one of the founding fathers of criminology.

According to Lombroso, these born criminals could be recognized by a series of external features such as receding foreheads, enormous development of their jaws, and large or handle-shaped ears. These external traits were thought to be related to personality types characterized by laziness, moral insensitivity, and absence of guilt feelings.

Individuals with a number of these criminal features or anomalies were thought to be incapable of resisting the impulse to commit crimes except under very favorable circumstances. Many of Lombroso's assumptions can be traced to the influence of Darwinism (which provided a means of ranking animals as more or less primitive) at the end of the 19th century and to the influence of phrenology (the study of the shape of the skull) and physiognomy (the study of facial features) as they related to deviance (Conklin, 1998, pp. 146–147; S. T. Reid, 2006, pp. 62–63).

Later in his career, Lombroso modified his approach by recognizing the importance of social factors, but his emphasis on biological causes encouraged many other researchers to seek such causes. Lombroso remains important today largely because of his attempts to explain crime scientifically rather than as a result of his particular theories.

Other Biological Theories

Following Lombroso, there have been a number of attempts over the years to find biological or genetic causes for crime and delinquency. Identical-twin studies were conducted based on the belief that if genetics determines criminality, when one twin is criminal, the other will also be criminal. In general, these studies provide evidence that genetic structure is not the sole cause of crime given that none of them indicate that 100% of the twins studied were identical with respect to criminal behavior. Research on the relationship between genetics and crime in twins continues nonetheless. The results of twin studies conducted over the past 75 years do seem to indicate that there may be a genetic factor in delinquency, but the exact nature of the relationship remains undetermined (Fishbein, 1990).

The next logical step in studying the relationship between heredity and crime involved studies of children adopted at an early age who had little or no contact with biological parents. Would the offense rates and types of the children more closely resemble those of the adoptive parents or the biological parents? Evidence suggests a hereditary link, but it is very difficult to separate the effects of heredity and environment (Bohm, 2001, pp. 36–41). Jones and Jones (2000) concluded that the similar behavior of the twins they studied might have more to do with the contagious nature of antisocial behavior than with heredity. They noted that the more antisocial behavior present in a family or community in which boys grew up, the greater the risk that boys will be affected. Unnever, Cullen, and Pratt (2003) studied the relationships among attention-deficit/hyperactivity disorder (ADHD), parenting, and delinquency and concluded that the effects of ADHD on delinquency are affected by low self-control. Wright and Beaver (2005) noted that genetic research has demonstrated that ADHD and other deficits in the frontostriatal system of the brain are related to heredity. Their research tested whether the role of parents in creating low self-control was important once genetic influences are taken into account. Based on a sample of twins, they found that parenting activities demonstrate a weak and inconsistent effect. These authors concluded that researchers have often failed to address genetic influences in parenting studies.

Richard Dugdale made the Jukes family a famous test case for inherited criminality during the late 1800s when he demonstrated that over generations this family had been characterized by criminality. Dugdale (1888) believed that crime and heredity were related, but his own admission that over the years the family had established a reputation for deviant behavior points to the possibility that other factors (e.g., learning and labeling) might be of equal or greater importance in explaining his observations.

Other researchers, including Kretschmer (1925), Sheldon (1949), and Glueck and Glueck (1950), turned to studies of the relationship between somatotypes (body types) and delinquency or criminality. Causes of delinquency and body type were thought by Sheldon to be biologically determined, for example, and selective breeding was suggested as a solution to delinquency. The Gluecks continued the body type tradition of explaining delinquency but included in their analysis a variety of other factors as well. The basic conclusion of the Gluecks' work with respect to body type and crime is that a majority of delinquents are muscular as opposed to thin or obese. One possible explanation for this conclusion, which does not require any assumptions about biological determination, is that juveniles who are not particularly physically fit recognize this fact and, therefore, consciously tend to avoid at least those delinquent activities that might require strength and fitness. In addition, measurements of body type are rather subjective, and the data presented by the body typists do not account for different individuals with the same body type being delinquent, on the one hand, and nondelinquent, on the other.

Over time, emphasis in the biological school has shifted. Studies examining the relationships among learning disabilities, chromosomes, chemical imbalances, and delinquency have emerged. We have already discussed some of the literature on the relationship between learning disabilities and delinquency in Chapter 3. Here we simply state that many learning disabilities, as typically conceived, are psychosocial (as opposed to biological) in nature. Others are more clearly organic in nature, and there is some evidence that brain dysfunctions and neurological defects are more common among violent individuals than among the general population. Such individuals seem to have defects in the frontal and temporal lobes of the brain, and these may lead to loss of self-control. Other dysfunctions include dyslexia (the failure to attain language skills appropriate to intellectual level), aphasia (problems with verbal communication and understanding), and attention-deficit disorder (manifested in hyperactivity and inattentiveness). Satterfield (1987) found that children who are hyperactive are several times more likely to be arrested during adolescence than are children without the disorder. None of these disorders, at this point, have been shown to be directly causally related to delinquency. In fact, Satterfield found that arrest rates for hyperactive children were affected by social class, with those from the lower social class being more likely to be arrested. In addition, many children with learning disabilities adapt and find ways to overcome the handicap. Perlmutter (1987) suggested that there is little middle ground and indicated that those who are not able to overcome the disability appear to be at risk for developing emotional and behavioral difficulties as adolescents. Fishbein (1990) summarized the relationship between learning disabilities and delinquency by stating that low IQ and/or learning disabilities are not inherently determinants of delinquency. However, without proper intervention, juveniles may become frustrated in attempting to pursue mainstream goals without the skills to achieve them and eventually succumb to delinquent behavior.

During the 1960s, a number of researchers explored the relationship between the presence of an extra Y chromosome in some males and subsequent criminal behavior. Mednick and Christiansen (1977) found that roughly 42% of the XYY chromosome cases identified in Denmark had criminal histories, compared with only 9% of the XY population. Research is still being conducted on the possible relationship between chromosomes and criminality, although little if any work has been done specifically on the relationship between delinquency and chromosomes.

It is safe to say that a direct relationship between chromosome structure and criminality has not been scientifically established and that many of the studies conducted to date are characterized by serious methodological problems.

Jeffery (1978, 1996), Booth and Osgood (1993), and Denno (1994) viewed behavior as the product of interaction between a physical environment and a physical organism and believed that contemporary criminology should represent a merger of biology, psychology, and sociology. The basis for this argument, biosocial criminology, is that most contemporary criminologists believe that criminal or delinquent behavior is learned but neglect the fact that learning involves physical (biochemical) changes in the brain. These researchers contend that although criminality is not inherited, the biochemical preparedness for such behavior is present in the brain and will, given a particular type of environment, produce criminal behavior (Fishbein, 1990; Nichols, 2004; Turkheimer, 1998; Walsh, 2000).

More recent studies on the relationship among genetics, the environment, and delinquency have yielded interesting results. For example, one attempt to link molecular genetic variants to adolescent delinquency identifies three genetic predictors of serious and violent delinquency that gain predictive precision when considered together with social influences, such as family, friends, and school processes (Guo, Roettger, & Cai, 2008). The authors noted that social influences such as family, friends, and school seem to impact the expression of specific genetic variants to influence delinquency, and they concluded that understanding both the socioeconomic–cultural components and the genetic components of delinquency is crucial (see In Practice 4.1).

IN PRACTICE 4.1

STUDY FINDS GENETIC LINK TO VIOLENCE, DELINQUENCY

(Reuters)—Three genes may play a strong role in determining why some young men raised in rough neighborhoods or deprived families become violent criminals, while others do not, U.S. researchers reported on Monday.

One gene called MAOA that played an especially strong role has been shown in other studies to affect antisocial behavior—and it was disturbingly common, the team at the University of North Carolina reported.

People with a particular variation of the MAOA gene called 2R were very prone to criminal and delinquent behavior, said sociology professor Guang Guo, who led the study.

"I don't want to say it is a crime gene, but 1 percent of people have it and scored very high in violence and delinquency," Guo said in a telephone interview.

His team, which studied only boys, used data from the National Longitudinal Study of Adolescent Health, a U.S. nationally representative sample of about 20,000 adolescents in grades 7 to 12. The young men in the study are interviewed in person regularly, and some give blood samples.

Guo's team constructed a "serious delinquency scale" based on some of the questions the youngsters answered.

"Nonviolent delinquency includes stealing amounts larger or smaller than $50, breaking and entering, and selling drugs," they wrote in the August issue of the *American Sociological Review*.

"Violent delinquency includes serious physical fighting that resulted in injuries needing medical treatment, use of weapons to get something from someone, involvement in physical fighting between groups, shooting or stabbing someone, deliberately damaging property, and pulling a knife or gun on someone."

Genes Plus Environment

They found specific variations in three genes—the monoamine oxidase A (MAOA) gene, the dopamine transporter 1 (DAT1) gene and the dopamine D2 receptor (DRD2) gene—were associated with bad behavior, but only when the boys suffered some other stress, such as family issues, low popularity and failing school.

MAOA regulates several message-carrying chemicals called neurotransmitters that are important in aggression, emotion and cognition such as serotonin, dopamine and norepinephrine.

The links were very specific.

The effect of repeating a grade depended on whether a boy had a certain mutation in MAOA called a 2 repeat, they found.

And a certain mutation in DRD2 seemed to set off a young man if he did not have regular meals with his family.

"But if people with the same gene have a parent who has regular meals with them, then the risk is gone," Guo said.

"Having a family meal is probably a proxy for parental involvement," he added. "It suggests that parenting is very important."

He said vulnerable children might benefit from having surrogates of some sort if their parents are unavailable.

"These results, which are among the first that link molecular genetic variants to delinquency, significantly expand our understanding of delinquent and violent behavior, and they highlight the need to simultaneously consider their social and genetic origins," the researchers said.

Guo said it was far too early to explore whether drugs might be developed to protect a young man. He also was unsure if criminals might use a "genetic defense" in court.

"In some courts (the judge might) think they maybe will commit the same crime again and again, and this would make the court less willing to let them out," he said.

Source: Study Finds Genetic Link to Violence, Delinquency. Author/Editor: Fox, M. Volume/Issue: 2008, July 14. *Reuters.* http://www.reuters.com/article/idUSN1444872420080714.

Questions to Consider

1. True or False: Because genes have been found to be important to determining violent behavior and delinquency, the environment is not considered to be very important.

2. Multiple Choice: The author contends that the link between genetic variations and crime could be used for what in the future?

   a. Criminal prosecutions
   b. Criminal defenses
   c. Insurance policies
   d. None of the above

3. In your opinion, are there potential ethical issues associated with Guang Guo's comment suggesting that drugs might be developed to prevent youth from being potentially crime prone?

There have been numerous other attempts to explain both delinquency and crime in terms of biology, genetics, and biochemistry. As early as 1939, Ernest Hooton wrote of the consequences of biological causes of crime for rehabilitation and control of offenders. According to Hooton (1939), if criminality is inherited, the solutions to crime lie in isolation and/or sterilization of offenders to prevent them from remaining active in the genetic pool of a society. A third alternative is extermination (which Hooton opposed), and a fourth is the practice of eugenics (Rafter, 2004). At various times, European societies have isolated (e.g., Devil's Island, the Colonies), sterilized, and exterminated offenders. Experiments with eugenics are certainly possible but raise serious ethical and moral issues. The extent to which genetic engineering becomes acceptable as a means of dealing with a wide variety of social problems will likely determine its use in controlling criminality if genetic deficiencies or abnormalities are shown to be causes of crime and delinquency (see In Practice 4.1). Biological and psychological theorists have worked together in recent years to identify treatment approaches that include dietary intervention, psychopharmacology, neurofeedback, and electrical stimulation of the brain (Farah & Raine, 2011). Recent developments that have made it possible to create human genetic blueprints, hailed as one of the greatest scientific contributions of the 21st century, make it likely that if there is a genetic link to crime, it will be discovered (Friend, 2000). Thus, for example, Yun, Cheong, and Walsh (2011) noted that criminologists have long maintained that delinquent peer group formation is largely a function of family–environmental variables but have ignored self-selected peer groups based on genetic proclivities. The results of their research provide some evidence of genetic underpinnings of delinquent peer group formation. Further, Beaver, Gibson, DeLisi, Vaughn, and Wright (2012) found that environmental and genetic factors work interactively and often moderate the effects of the other as indicated in their research, which demonstrated that antisocial outcomes appear to be affected by gene–environment interactions between certain genes and neighborhood disadvantage. Finally, Vaske, Boisvert, and Wright (2012) noted that research has shown a significant association between violent victimization and criminal behavior. Their research focused on genetically mediated processes to determine whether they contribute to both violent victimization and criminal behavior. Using twin data from the National Longitudinal Study of Adolescent Health, they examined whether genetic and/or environmental factors explain the correlation between violent victimization and criminal behavior in adolescence and early adulthood. Their results indicate that genetic factors explain roughly 40% of the covariance between violent victimization and delinquency in adolescence and 20% of the correlation between violent victimization and criminal behavior in early adulthood.

Biosocial/Neurological Theory

This section focuses on biological theories on the brain and nervous system, specifically. In some circles, this has been referred to as neurocriminology. Neurocriminology is based on the idea that criminal behavior is only partially explained by social issues and that physiological factors, particularly neurological factors, play a more important role in determining criminality (Raine, 2014). This approach to studying criminal behavior has come in vogue during the past 15 to 20 years due to innovations and advances in the field of neuroscience.

Research on cerebral deficiencies shows that persons who exhibit antisocial or criminal behavior tend to have structural neural anomalies. These abnormal structure may affect brain functioning on a general level or may be restricted to specific regions of the brain that regulate emotional reactions and/or analytical reasoning. One example of structural deficiencies in the brain that have been studied is when there are a low number of neurons in the prefrontal cortex. A meta-analysis based on the collective findings of a dozen brain-scanning studies of offenders found that there is a higher-than-average likelihood of structural impairment in the prefrontal cortex of the brain for participants (Yang & Raine, 2009). Other studies have found that problematic officers, such as those diagnosed with antisocial personality disorder, tend to have impaired amygdalae, an area of the brain that regulates emotional response (Pardin, Raine, Erickson, & Loeber, 2014).

Adrian Raine (2014), in his book *The Anatomy of Violence: The Biological Roots of Crime*, describes the story of Michael Oft, a man who, up until he turned 40 years old, had no prior history of criminal or deviant behavior. It was noted that, after he turned 40, Oft's behavior began to change rapidly. He started going to massage parlors, was found with child pornography, sexually abused his stepdaughter, and was ultimately convicted on charges of child molestation. While incarcerated, Oft was in a sex offender treatment program but, during his stay there, continued to solicit both staff and other programmers for sex acts. Eventually, neurologists conducted a brain scan and found a growing tumor in his brain that was pressing on the prefrontal areas of his brain, the areas where higher-order decision making (i.e., right from wrong) are made. Doctors removed the tumor through surgery, and, overnight, Oft's behavior, emotions, and sexual arousal patterns returned to normal. However, a few months after the surgery, Oft was found again with child pornography. When neurologists again scanned Oft's brain, they found that the tumor had partially grown back. A second surgery to remove the remaining tumorous tissue resulted in a full recovery for Oft, whose behavior has remained stable and appropriate since that time. What is unique about the case of Michael Oft is that there is specific evidence of a direct link between neurological problems and criminality, on two occasions rather than simply one. In other words, these results were essentially replicated, making these findings quite convincing. This as well as many other examples provided by Raine (2014) demonstrate how neurocriminology has explained undesired behavior among much of the criminal population with empirically sound specificity. As scientific advances continue, support for neurological approaches in explaining criminality continue to gain support.

Psychological Theories

The human mind has long been considered a source of abnormal behavior and, therefore, crime (Lanier & Henry, 1998, p. 113). Early varieties of psychological theories of delinquency and crime focused on lack of intelligence and/or personality disturbances as major causal factors. Several of the early pioneers in the psychological school were convinced that biological factors played a major role in determining intelligence; therefore, they could be considered proponents of both schools of thought. Goddard's (1914) studies of the Kallikak family and the intellectual abilities of reformatory inmates, for instance, led him to conclude that feeblemindedness, which he believed to be inherited, was an important contributing factor in criminality. He suggested that "eliminating" a large proportion of mental defectives would reduce the number of criminals and other deviants in society. Similarly, Goring (1913) focused on defective intelligence and psychological characteristics as basic causes of crime in his attempt to refute Lombroso and the other positivists. As we indicated previously, research concerning the relationship between defective intelligence, IQ, or learning disabilities and delinquency continues. Problems concerning the reliability and validity of IQ tests and personality inventories, as well as other methodological shortcomings, continue to plague such research, and the psychological school as a whole has taken other directions. Still, many believe that those who commit heinous crimes must be emotionally disturbed—different from the rest of us in some identifiable way.

Sigmund Freud's Psychoanalytic Approach

Sigmund Freud, born in 1856, spent most of his life in Vienna, Austria. He is regarded as the founder of the psychoanalytic approach to explaining behavior that relies heavily on the techniques of introspection (looking inside one's self) and retrospection (reviewing past events). Freud's theories were introduced in the United States during the early 1900s. Freud divided personality into three separate components: (1) the id, (2) ego, and (3) superego. The function of the id, according to Freud, is to provide for the discharge of energy that permits the individual to seek pleasure and reduce tension. The id is also said to be the seat of instincts in humans and not thought to be governed by reason. The ego is said to be the part of the personality that controls and governs the id and the superego by making rational adjustments to real-life situations. For example, the ego might prevent the id from causing the individual to seek immediate gratification of his or her desires by deferring gratification to a later time. The development of the ego is said to be a product of interaction between the individual's personality and the environment and is thought to be affected by heredity as well. The superego is viewed as the moral branch of the personality and may be equated roughly with the concept of conscience. Both the ego and the superego are thought to develop out of the individual's interactions with his or her environment, whereas the id is said to be a product of evolution.

In general, deviance is viewed as the product of an uncontrollable id, a faulty ego, or an underdeveloped superego or some combination of the three. Therefore, those who commit a criminal or delinquent act do so as the result of a personality disturbance. To correct or control this behavior, the causes of the personality disturbance are located primarily through introspection and retrospection, with a particular emphasis on childhood experiences, and then are eliminated through therapy.

Freud is one of the most important figures (if not the most important figure) in the history of psychology. There are, no doubt, many cases where psychoanalytic techniques prove to be effective in therapeutic treatment. As a system for explaining the causes of deviance, however, Freudian psychology has several shortcomings. First, the existence of the id, ego, and superego cannot be demonstrated empirically. Second, instincts, which Freud viewed as the driving forces in the id, are thought by many behavioral scientists to be extremely rare or nonexistent in humans. Third, there seems to be faulty logic among practitioners using Freud's system. They accept the premise that those who commit deviant acts must be experiencing personality disturbances; that is, they employ circular reasoning rather than logical deduction (Akers, 1994, p. 85; Lanier & Henry, 1998, p. 117). In response to the question, How do you know X has a disturbed personality? they might answer, Because he committed a deviant act, he must have been experiencing a personality disturbance. Such a response is more a statement of faith than a matter of fact. Currently, it is safe to say that the psychoanalytic approach is of very little value in explaining crime and delinquency (or any other form of deviance, for that matter). Nonetheless, the Freudian approach has remained popular in much of the Western world, and Freud has had many disciples who have applied his techniques directly to delinquency.

Among those who emphasized the psychoanalytic perspective were Healy and Bronner (1936), who believed that the delinquent was a product of a personality disturbance resulting from thwarted desires and deprivations that led to frustration and a weak superego. Healy and Bronner interviewed numerous juvenile offenders and came to the conclusion that 90% of them were emotionally disturbed. Adler (1931), Halleck (1971), and Fox and Levin (1994) concluded that those who are frustrated, believe the world is against them, and feel inferior may turn to crime as a compensatory means of expressing their autonomy.

Others, using a variety of personality inventories (e.g., the Minnesota Multiphasic Personality Inventory [MMPI], the California Personality Inventory [CPI]), have concluded that such inventories do appear to discriminate between delinquents and nondelinquents, but the reasons for such discrimination are not at all clear-cut and neither are the numerous definitions of "abnormal" personality employed (Bohm, 2001, pp. 56–57). Akers and Sellers (2004) concluded, "The research using personality inventories and other methods of measuring personality characteristics has not been able to produce findings to support personality variables as major causes of criminal and delinquent behavior" (p. 47). More recently, Nederlof, van der Ham, Dingemans, and Oei (2010), in a study of 142 Dutch male delinquents, found that personality dimensions do not appear to be related to offense type or severity.

Psychopathology

One of the terms most commonly employed to describe certain types of criminals and delinquents is psychopath. Typically, the term is used to describe aggressive criminals who act impulsively with no apparent reason. Sutherland and Cressey (1978) indicated that some 55 descriptive terms are consistently linked with the concept of psychopathy (sociopathy or antisocial personality). Bohm (2001) listed 16 characteristics ranging from "unreliability" to "fantastic and uninviting behavior" to "failure to follow any life plan" (p. 54). Attempts have been made to clarify the concept of psychopathology, but such attempts have helped little in understanding the relationship between psychopathology and criminality because criminality is typically included in the symptomatic basis for psychopathology. In other words, the two conditions are often perceived as being one and the same.

Although the concept of psychopathology is generally considered to be too vague and ambiguous to distinguish psychopaths from nonpsychopaths, there have been attempts to operationalize the concept in more meaningful fashion. Gough (1948, 1960) conceptualized psychopathy as the inability to take the role of the other (the inability to identify with others). The scales he developed to measure role-taking ability generally result in lower scores for offenders than for nonoffenders. Whether such differences could have been detected before the offenders committed offenses is another matter.

Research in this area continues. Martens (1999) reported a case in which psychopathy appeared to have been cured as a result of therapeutic psychosocial influences and life events. In this case, the individual began a career in delinquency at 15 years of age and went on to commit offenses, including fraud, theft, rape, and assaults, until 26 years of age. Following life-changing events and therapy, the individual had remained crime-free for more than 20 years and appeared to be leading a "normal" life.

Poythrees, Edens, and Lilienfeld (1998) administered the Psychopathic Personality Inventory (PPI), a self-report measure of psychopathic personality features, and the Psychopathy Checklist–Revised (PCL–R) to youthful offender prison inmates. They found that the PPI could be used to accurately predict PCL–R classifications of psychopath and nonpsychopath, raising the possibility that the PPI could be used for clinical purposes to detect psychopathic personalities.

Lynam (1998) hypothesized that there is a developmental relationship between adult psychopathy and children with symptoms of hyperactivity, impulsivity, attention problems, and conduct problems (HIA-CP). Using a large sample of adolescent boys, Lynam found that boys who were hyperactive and impulsive, with attention disorders and conduct problems, scored high on a measure of psychopathic personality. These boys were the most antisocial, were the most disinhibited, and tended to be the most neuropsychologically impaired of the groups studied. Further support for the relationship between adolescent behavior patterns of this type and adult psychopathy comes from Gresham, MacMillan, and Bocian (1998), who found marked differences between third- and fourth-grade students with HIA-CP and other students on peer measures of rejection and friendship and teachers' ratings of social skills. The notion of the "fledgling psychopath" appears to emerge from these recent studies.

Additional attempts to explore the relationship between psychopathology and delinquency include those by Ireland, Smith, and Thornberry (2002), who focused on the theory of developmental psychopathology. The basis for this theory is that development is age-graded and hierarchical in nature; for example, a child must acquire a certain set of skills before subsequent appropriate development can occur. If these skills are not developed, subsequent age-appropriate development may not occur, and this may persist into adulthood. The authors explore whether maltreatment in early childhood or in later childhood interrupt the development of age-specific skills leading to inappropriate conduct. Unlike some other researchers, these authors found that childhood-limited maltreatment is not a risk factor for either occasional or frequent offending, whereas maltreatment in adolescence and persistent maltreatment both pose significant risks to adolescent behavioral development.

Akers (1994, p. 87) concluded, based on the research available at the time, that the term *psychopath* appears to be so broad that it could be applied to anyone who violates the law. After reviewing attempts to relate psychopathy to child abuse, Knudsen (1992) concluded that there is little evidence of such a relationship. Wolfe (1985) also found no relationship between underlying personality attributes and child abuse beyond general descriptions of stress-related complaints and displeasure in the parenting role. Walsh, MacMillan, and Jamieson (2002) concluded that the exact nature of the relationship between psychopathology and child abuse remains unclear. That conclusion appears to be accurate in the second decade of the 21st century as well. Most importantly, attempts to discover the nature of relationships, if any, between psychopathology and delinquency and abuse continue.

Further research on the relationship between psychopathology and delinquency and abuse is ongoing (see, for example, DeLisi, Wright, & Vaughn [2010]; Verschuere, Candel, Reenen, & Korebrits [2012]; and Wareham & Boots [2012]). Researchers are also focusing on symptom-based treatment approaches with those diagnosed with psychopathology to see if deviant behaviors can be deterred. At present, there is no conclusive evidence that behavioral treatment for psychopathy works (Farah & Raine, 2011). On the one hand, it may turn out that behavior patterns involving hyperactivity, impulsivity, and inattention, combined with conduct problems, are forerunners of psychopathology. On the other hand, most children exhibit one or more of these behaviors periodically but do not turn out to be psychopaths.

Behaviorism and Learning Theory

During the latter 19th century, a number of psychologists became increasingly concerned about weaknesses in the theory and techniques developed by Freud and his followers and those of the biological school emphasizing heredity. Tarde, by contrast, thought that crime was learned by normal people in the process of interacting in specific environments (Bohm, 2001, p. 82). He and others called for a change in focus from genetics and the internal workings of the mind to observable behavior. Although the major work on this learning theory model as it relates to delinquency has been done by sociologists and is discussed under that topic, the psychological underpinnings are discussed here.

As indicated previously, behaviorists called for a change of techniques from the subjective speculative approach based on introspection and retrospection to a more empirical objective approach based on observing and measuring behavior. Perhaps the most important individual in the behaviorist tradition was B. F. Skinner, who directed his attention toward the relationship between a particular stimulus and a given response and to the learning processes involved in connecting the two. Skinner (1953) viewed human social behavior as a set of learned responses to specific stimuli. Criminal and delinquent behaviors are viewed as varieties of human social behavior, learned in the same way as other social behaviors. Through the process of conditioning (rewarding for appropriate behavior and/or punishing for inappropriate behavior), any type of social behavior can be taught (see In Practice 4.2). Therefore, when an individual behaves in a delinquent manner (exhibits an inappropriate response in a given situation), his or her behavior can be modified using conditioning. To control and rehabilitate delinquents, then, the therapist employs behavior modification techniques to extinguish inappropriate behavior and replace it with appropriate behavior.

IN PRACTICE 4.2

BEHAVIOR MODIFICATION—CHILD BEHAVIOR PROBLEMS— OUT OF CONTROL TEENS—BEHAVIOR MODIFICATION SCHOOLS

How do parents effect change in their out of control teen?

Behavior Modification is part of a behavioral tradition developed by Pavlov in the early part of the twentieth century. This therapy was adapted by John Watson in 1920 and eventually translated into behavior therapy by researchers and clinicians such as B. F. Skinner and Hans Eysenck in the 1950s. These approaches were later incorporated with cognitive behavior therapy as developed by researchers such as Donald Meichenbaum.

Today, there are many branches and schools of thought with varying terminology as regards Behavior Modification therapy. Generally however, Behavior Modification therapy as we know it today is defined as the use of rewards or punishments to reduce or eliminate problematic behavior, and can teach new responses to an individual in response to environmental stimuli. It is also defined as a "therapy that seeks to extinguish or inhibit abnormal or maladaptive behavior by reinforcing desired behavior and extinguishing undesired behavior."

The goal of a program of behavior modification is to change and adjust behavior that is inappropriate or undesirable in some way. When embarking on a program of behavior modification with a teen or child, it is important that the undesirable behavior be isolated and observed. With this observation comes awareness of the behavior on the part of the parent and/or teacher, and also on the part of the individual whose behavior is being modified. And with this awareness also comes the greater goal of understanding the cause and effect of the behaviors, thus helping to effect change.

In many cases, some form of behavior modification along with cognitive therapy and medication therapy are the preferred methods of treatment for disorders such as ADD, ADHD and Conduct Disorders. Behavior modification and cognitive therapy are also commonly used in the treatment for disorders such as Eating Disorders and Substance Abuse, Mood, and Anxiety Disorders.

Behavior modification therapy is based on the concepts of observable antecedents (events that occur before a behavior is apparent), observable behavior, and consequences (the events that occur after the behavior occurs). A behavioral modification program to affect behavioral change consists of a series of stages. An inappropriate behavior is observed, identified, targeted, and stopped. Meanwhile, a new, appropriate behavior must be identified, developed, strengthened, and maintained.

Two types of reinforcers are used to strengthen positive behavior. The use of pleasant rewards to reinforce a positive behavior to help effect change is called positive reinforcement. Negative reinforcement strengthens a behavior because

a negative condition is stopped or avoided as a consequence of the behavior. Two other reinforcers are identified as those that weaken negative behavior. One is called extinction, where a particular behavior is weakened by the consequence of not experiencing a positive condition or stopping a negative condition, and the other is called punishment, when a particular behavior is weakened by the consequence of experiencing a negative condition.

To stop an inappropriate child behavior, first the behavior must be observed. It is helpful to chart the behavior: what events precede the behavior, what time of day it is observed, etc., to understand the pattern of the behavior. It's important to at first focus on just one or two offending behavior patterns. Once a behavior pattern is recognized and its pattern charted and understood, a system of reinforcements and consequences can then be constructed.

An example of a positive reinforcement used immediately after appropriate behavior can be as simple as offering praise immediately after the behavior occurs. Extinction can be used when the behavior can be seen and measured, and an example of this would be to ignore the child's whining behavior. This can be particularly effective if the parent has given in to whining demands in the past. However, when inappropriate behavior is ignored, then another, more appropriate behavior, must be reinforced.

An example of negative reinforcement is when a child is allowed to skip a required chore if homework is finished by a certain time. A simple example of punishment is when a child is reprimanded or criticized for the inappropriate behavior.

In order to teach and develop new behaviors, successive steps can be reinforced until the final, appropriate behavior is achieved. Based on the observed behavioral patterns, another behavioral method for success is to teach cueing: arranging for the child to receive a cue for correct behavior prior to the expected action can reinforce the child for the appropriate behavior and for

(Continued)

(Continued)

recognizing the cue even before the child has a chance to perform the inappropriate behavior.

The key to a successful program of child behavior modification is consistency. And a key piece of behavior modification that parents and teachers can perform is to present their own behavior and reactions in a positive way, so that children can learn and model successful behavior.

References

Mental Health Glossary, C. J. Newton, MA, Learning Specialist (July 1996).

WordNet, Princeton University, Princeton University Cognitive Science Lab.

Maricopa Community College Center for Learning and Instruction, 2004.

Utah Students at Risk, Utah State University, 2004.

Source: National Youth Network (2010). *Behavior modification - child behavior problems - out of control teens - behavior modification school.* Available online at http://www.nationalyouth .com/behaviormodification.html. Reprinted with permission.

Questions to Consider

1. True or False: When getting rid of an undesirable behavior, plans must be made to replace it by reinforcing another behavior that is desired. Otherwise, behavior modification is less likely to succeed.

2. Multiple Choice: Using an alarm clock to wake up is an example of _____ because the alarm is undesirable and waking up to turn off the alarm reinforces one's waking up so that one can eliminate the undesirable stimulus.

   a. positive reinforcement

   b. negative reinforcement

   c. punishment

   d. extinction

3. What is the key to effective child behavior modification, and why is this so important?

Although behaviorists do not seek to explain the ultimate causes of social behavior except in the sense that they are learned, their approach holds considerably more promise for understanding and controlling delinquent behavior than does the psychoanalytic approach. The behaviorist approach forces us to focus on the specific problem behavior and to recognize that it is learned, so it can—hypothetically at least—be unlearned (S. T. Reid, 2006, p. 106). With this focus, we are dealing with observable behavior that can be measured, counted, and perhaps modified. Success in modifying behavior in the laboratory has been noted (Echeburua, Fernandez-Montalvo, & Baez, 2000; Krasner & Ullman, 1965; Martin & Peas, 1978; Paul, Marx, & Orsillo, 1999). The extent to which this success can be transferred to the world outside the laboratory remains an empirical question (Florsheim, Shotorbani, & Guest-Warnick, 2000; Ross & McKay, 1978; Shelton, Barkley, & Crosswait, 2000). Think about the difficulties of transferring desirable behavior from the laboratory to the street in the following hypothetical case.

Joe Foul Up, a juvenile, is repeatedly apprehended for fighting. Finally, he is turned over to a therapist who, over a period of several weeks, eliminates the undesirable behavior by punishing Joe (e.g., with electric shock) when he begins to exhibit the undesirable behavior and by rewarding him when he exhibits appropriate alternative behavior. After therapy ends, Joe's behavior has been modified, and he returns home to his old neighborhood and his old street gang. When Joe refuses to fight, the gang thinks that it is appropriate to punish him by calling him a coward and excluding him from gang activities. When he does fight, they reward him by treating him like a hero. What are the chances that the behavior modification that occurred in the laboratory will continue to exist?

In spite of the odds, there is recent evidence that at least one form of behavioral therapy does have an impact on recidivism among both juveniles and adults (Clark, 2011). Cognitive behavioral therapy (CBT) suggests that once individuals become conscious of their own thoughts and behaviors and the attitudes, beliefs, and values underlying those thoughts and behaviors (with the assistance of trained therapists), they can make positive changes in both. Lipsey (2009) and Landenberger and Lipsey (2005) found that such therapy can be effective with a variety of types of problems (e.g., drug abuse, juvenile offenders, prisoners) in institutions and the community. Bahr, Masters, and Taylor (2012) found that participants in CBT, therapeutic communities, and drug courts had lower rates of drug use and crime than comparable individuals who did not receive treatment. Gleacher et al. (2011) noted the adoption and implementation of a statewide training program in CBT for youth in New York. Christensen, Pallister, Smale, Hickie, and Calear (2010) studied the use of CBT programs among adolescents who left or dropped out of school and found that these programs consistently lowered symptoms or prevented depression or anxiety.

B. F. Skinner believed that social behaviors can be taught through the process of conditioning (rewarding desired behavior and/or punishing undesirable behavior).

There are a variety of offshoots of CBT. For example, mindfulness-based cognitive therapy (MBCTC) is a form of group psychotherapy for children ages 9 to 13 years old, which was developed specifically to increase social–emotional resiliency through the enhancement of mindful attention (Semple, Lee, Rosa, & Miller, 2010). Researchers found that participants who completed the program showed fewer attention problems than waitlisted controls and those improvements were maintained at 3 months following the intervention. Semple et al. (2010) concluded that "MBCT-C is a promising intervention for attention and behavior problems, and may reduce childhood anxiety symptoms" (p. 218).

Redondo, Martínez-Catena, and Andrés-Pueyo (2012) reported that several treatment evaluations have highlighted the effectiveness of cognitive behavioral programs with both youth and adult offenders. They studied interventions based on six therapeutic components (self-control, cognitive restructuring, problem solving, social skills/assertiveness, values/empathy, and relapse prevention) among a group of juvenile offenders. Their results show that the program was somewhat effective in improving participants' social skills and self-esteem and in reducing their aggressiveness. However, they determined that the intervention had no positive influence on empathy, cognitive distortions, or impulsiveness. Their results "are in line with those of many other correctional studies, in which the treatment applied had a significant but partial effect on participants" (Redondo et al., 2012, p. 159).

Reviewing over 500 studies, Landenberger and Lipsey (2005) found that interventions based on cognitive behavior skill-building were the most effective form of intervention studied in reducing recidivism even among high-risk offenders. These authors note that more research is needed to determine the impact of CBT under differing conditions. Such research is ongoing, and CBT appears to offer some promise as a means of intervention into adolescent problems at least in some circumstances.

Sociological Theories

There have been a number of different sociological theories of delinquency causation, some dealing with social class and/or family differences (Cloward & Ohlin, 1960; Cohen, 1955; Miller, 1958; Quinney, 1975), some dealing with blocked educational and occupational goals (Merton, 1938), some dealing with neighborhood and peers (Miller, 1958; Shaw & McKay, 1942; Thrasher, 1927), and some dealing with the effects of official labeling (Becker, 1963). Most of these theories share the notion that delinquent behavior is the product of social interaction rather than the result of heredity or personality disturbance. For sociologists, delinquency must be understood in social context. Thus, we must consider time, place, audience, and nature of the behavior involved when studying delinquency.

Anomie and Strain Theory

Beginning in the 1930s in the United States, a number of theorists focused on a systems model to explain crime and delinquency. Adapting Durkheim's anomie theory (a breakdown of social norms or the dissociation of the individual from a general sense of morality of the times), Merton (1938) focused on the discrepancy between societal goals and the legitimate means of attaining those goals. He argued that strain is placed on those who wish to pursue societal goals but lack the legitimate means of doing so (strain theory). According to Merton, people adapt to this strain in different ways; some attempt to play the game, some retreat (and may become addicts and outcasts), some develop innovative responses (including the illegitimate responses of crime and delinquency), and some rebel (another potential source of crime).

During the 1950s, Cohen (1955) adapted Merton's theory in an attempt to explain juvenile gangs. He argued that lower-class juveniles experience the strain of being unsuccessful in middle-class terms, especially in the school setting. Because many lower-class youth find success in school difficult to achieve, they reject middle-class values and seek to gain status by engaging in behaviors contrary to middle-class standards. Thus, they establish their own anti-middle-class value system and, through mutual recruitment, form delinquent gangs. Miller (1958) disagreed with Cohen's theory that lower-class youth act in terms of inverted middle-class values; instead, Miller focused on what he called the "focal concerns" (toughness, trouble, smartness, fate, autonomy, and excitement) of the lower social class as the sources of delinquent behavior.

Sykes and Matza (1957) argued in their theory of delinquency and drift that firm commitment to subcultural values was not necessarily a precursor of delinquent behavior (unlike the view of Cohen, Miller, and others). Sykes and Matza viewed delinquency as being based on an extension of defenses to crimes in the form of justifications for deviant behavior that are accepted by delinquents but not necessarily by the legal system or larger society. These defenses were called techniques of neutralization and included (1) the denial of responsibility (for the consequences of delinquent actions), (2) the denial of injury (to the victim or larger society), (3) the denial of a victim (the victim "had it coming"), (4) condemnation of the condemners (as hypocrites or spiteful people), and (5) an appeal to higher loyalties (e.g., to the gang). Using these techniques, juveniles drift in and out of the delinquent subculture over time.

Cloward and Ohlin (1960) extended anomie, or strain theory, by focusing on the differential opportunities that exist among juveniles. If an illegitimate opportunity structure is readily available, they argued, juveniles who are experiencing strain or anomie are attracted to that structure and are likely to become involved in delinquent activities.

In 1985, Agnew again revised strain theory. He discussed three types of strain that may produce deviant behavior. The first is the individual's failure to achieve goals, the second involves loss of a source of stability (e.g., death of a loved one), and the third occurs when the individual is confronted by negative stimuli (e.g., lack of success in school). Furthermore, Agnew (1985) suggested that, rather than pursuing specific goals, many people are simply interested in being treated justly based on their own efforts and resources. People who do not perceive themselves to be treated fairly experience strain, according to Agnew. Reactions to this perception of unfair treatment may lead to crime and delinquency. Later, Agnew (2001) argued that criminal victimization might be among the most consequential strains experienced by adolescents and, therefore, might be an important cause of delinquency. Subsequently, Hay and Evans (2006) examined predictions from general strain theory about the effects of victimization on later involvement in delinquency. They concluded that violent victimization significantly predicted later involvement in delinquency, even when controlling for the individual's earlier involvement in delinquency, and that the effects of victimization were slightly greater for juveniles with weak emotional attachment to their parents and significantly greater for those low in self-control.

Using a sample of homeless street youth, Baron (2004) examined how specific forms of strain, including emotional abuse, physical abuse, sexual abuse, homelessness, being a victim of robbery, being a victim of violence, being a victim of theft, relative deprivation, monetary dissatisfaction, and unemployment, are related to crime and drug use. He also explored how strain is conditioned by deviant peers, deviant attitudes, external attributions, self-esteem, and self-efficacy. He concluded that all 10 types of strain examined can lead to criminal behavior either as main effects or when interacting with conditioning variables.

Hay and Evans (2006) examined the stressful effects of being violently victimized on later delinquency. Consistent with strain theory, the authors found that being a victim of violence increased a youth's subsequent delinquency and that the effects of such victimization on delinquency were somewhat mediated by the youth's feelings of anger. As feelings of anger increased so did involvement in delinquency. When anger was controlled, the direct effects of victimization on delinquency were reduced and the youth's level of self-control was related to coping with victimization in that youth who were impulsive and demonstrated low self-control had more difficulty in coping.

Hollist, Hughes, and Schaible (2009), focusing on parent–child problems as a source of strain leading to delinquency, found a significant association between maltreatment and delinquency. Their findings supported strain theory in that they found negative emotions to be important intervening mechanisms in this relationship. However, contrary to the tenets of strain theory, they noted that the direct effects of the negative emotions were equally, if not more, important for involvement in delinquency than the direct effect of maltreatment.

Partial support for general strain theory was reported by Tsunokai and Kposowa (2009), who found that Asian youth who responded to school-related stress with anger and frustration were more likely to commit future delinquent acts. At the same time, however, the study failed to show a significant relationship among strain, negative effect, and gang involvement among Asian youth. The hypothesis that stress produced by generational conflict would increase gang involvement and delinquency was not supported. Instead, results showed that youth involved in such conflict were less likely to engage in future delinquent acts. The researchers hypothesize that this may be a result of the nature and structure of family relationships among Asian Americans. Huck, Lee, Bowen, Spraitz, & Bowers (2012) used a young-adult sample of university students to complete a

comprehensive analysis of the main tenets of general strain theory with the specific inclusion of conditioning variables such as self-esteem, self-efficacy, and delinquent peers, and expansion of the traditional measures of affective states, coping strategies, and types of deviant and criminal behaviors. (p. 25)

The authors report general support for the theory, though some traditional measures of strain such as perceptions of success and fairness appeared not to be related to crime and deviance, while more subjective measures of stress did show a relationship with crime and deviance.

Using data from a national sample of adolescents, Jackson (2012) examined how the effects of general strain on offending vary by level of physical development. Results suggest that advanced pubertal development may increase the effects of general strain on delinquent outcomes and that these effects may differ by gender. In other words, advanced pubertal development may result in increased strain, which may lead to delinquent behavior, and the impact may be different for males than for females. Jackson noted, "Determining the accuracy and predictors of self-reported drug use is important for researchers who examine drug-related issues and for criminal justice professionals so that they are better able to provide proper treatment referrals for those in the criminal justice system" (p. 292).

As Ryan (2012, p. 16) indicated, only some strained individuals become involved in delinquency. It is therefore important to determine the conditions under which strain results in deviance. The goal of this research was to examine the conditioning effects of exposure to delinquent friends or peer pressure on the relationship between strain and delinquency. Some theorists (Agnew, 1992, 2001, 2007) have argued that a criminogenic environment will increase the effect of strain on delinquency; others (Warr, 1993) have indicated that other correlates of delinquency lose their influence when adolescents are enmeshed in a network of delinquent peers. Ryan's (2012) research found "a preponderance of evidence supporting the latter position. Peer pressure and having friends that commit delinquency tend to reduce the direct effect of strain on serious delinquency, as well as reducing the indirect effects of strain on negative emotions and negative emotions on serious delinquency" (p. 16).

In their national study of 413 children and adolescents in which they examined the influence of negative life experiences (strain) on antisocial behavior, Higgins, Piquero, and Piquero (2011) found that peer rejection and delinquency were not strongly related overall but that high peer rejection was related to high delinquency among males but not among females.

As is the case with many of the other theories discussed in this chapter, the impact of strain/anomie theory on delinquency remains subject to controversy, but research continues. According to Higgins et al. (2011), "The development of general strain theory (GST) has led to a renewed focus on the influence of negative life experiences on antisocial behavior" and "a number of studies have generated an impressive array of support for the theory" (p. 1272).

Ecological/Social Disorganization Approach

The ecological/social disorganization approach to explaining crime and delinquency was developed during the 1930s and 1940s and is one of the oldest interest areas of American criminologists. This approach focuses on the geographic distribution of delinquency. Shaw and McKay (1942), and later others, found that crime and delinquency rates were not distributed equally within cities. They mapped the areas marked by high crime and delinquency rates along with the socioeconomic problems of those areas. Using Burgess's (1952) concentric-zone theory of city growth, the ecological/social disorganization studies generally found that zones of transition between residential and industrial neighborhoods consistently had the highest rates of crime and delinquency. These zones are characterized by physical deterioration and are located adjacent to the business district of the central city. The neighborhoods in this zone are marked by deteriorating buildings and substandard housing with accompanying overcrowdedness, lack of sanitation, and generally poor health and safety conditions. In addition, the area is marked by a transient population, high unemployment rates,

Sociologists often look at environmental factors and their relationship to delinquent behavior.

poverty, broken homes, and a high adult crime rate. In short, the area is characterized by a general lack of social stability and cohesion or social disorganization.

Wilks (1967) best summarized early ecological/social disorganization studies and their findings on the distribution of delinquency. Her conclusions were as follows:

1. Rates of delinquency and crime vary widely in different neighborhoods and within a city or town.

2. The highest crime and delinquency rates generally occur in the low-rent areas located near the center of the city, and the rates decrease with increasing distance from the city center.

3. High-delinquency-rate areas tend to maintain their rates over time, although the population composition of the area may change radically within the same period.

4. Areas that have high rates of truancy also have high rates of juvenile court cases and high rates of male delinquency and usually have high rates of female delinquency. The differences in area rates reflect differences in community background. High-rate areas are characterized by things such as physical deterioration and declining population.

5. The delinquency rates for particular nationality and ethnic groups show the same general tendency as the entire population; namely, they are high in the central area of the city and low as the groups move toward the outskirts of the city.

6. Delinquents living in areas with high delinquency rates are the most likely to become recidivists and are likely to appear in court several times more often than are those living in areas with low delinquency rates.

7. In summary, delinquency and crime follow the pattern of social and physical structures of the city, with concentration occurring in disorganized, deteriorated areas.

According to Wilks (1967), to predict delinquency using the ecological/social disorganization approach, it is necessary to be aware of the existing social structure, social processes, and population composition, as well as the area's position within the large urban societal complex, because these variables all affect the distribution of delinquency. In general, this approach found that family and neighborhood stability were lacking and that the street environment was the prevailing determinant of behavior. If delinquent behavior is learned behavior, this learning would be maximized in environments such as those in transitional zones. In transitional zones, those agencies or institutions that traditionally produce stability, cohesion, and organization have often been replaced by the street environment of adult criminals and delinquent gangs.

Investigations into the impact of ecology on crime and delinquency continue. For example, Browning et al. (2010) explored relationships between commercial and residential density and violent crime in urban neighborhoods. Their findings indicated the following:

> [At] low levels, increasing commercial and residential density is positively associated with homicide and aggravated assault. Beyond a threshold, however, increasing commercial and residential density serves to reduce the likelihood of both outcomes. In contrast, the association between commercial and residential density and robbery rates is positive and linear. (p. 329)

And Bottrell, Armstrong, and France (2010) found that ecological forces of different types affect the lives of young people and their relationship to criminality.

Socia and Stamatel (2012), in a study of registered sex offenders (RSOs) in Chicago, found that they "were concentrated in neighborhoods that had higher levels of social disorganization and lower levels of collective efficacy, offered greater anonymity, and were near other neighborhoods with high concentrations of RSOs" (p. 565). Furthermore, they discovered that "while social control mechanisms mediated some of the effects of structural disorganization, the neighborhoods where RSOs were likely to live did not exhibit characteristics that would support the informal social control of such offenders" (p. 565).

The ecological/social disorganization approach to explaining delinquency has been challenged on the grounds that using only one variable to explain delinquency is not likely to lead to success. In Lander's (1970) study of Baltimore, for example, he found anomie, or normlessness, to be a more appropriate explanation of delinquency rates than socioeconomic area. Nonetheless, follow-up studies by Shaw and McKay (1969) in other American cities (Boston, Philadelphia, and Cleveland) support their contention that official delinquency rates decrease from the central city out to the suburbs. Similarly, Lyerly and Skipper (1981) found that significantly less delinquent activity was reported by rural youth than by urban youth in their study of juveniles in detention. Stark (1987) concluded that certain geographic areas (those characterized by high population density, poverty, transience, dilapidation) attract deviant people who drive out those who are not so deviant, and these places then become "deviant places" with high crime rates and weak social control. Gibson (2012), noting that low self-control increases the likelihood of violent victimization, examined this association across neighborhoods that differed in concentrated disadvantages. Gibson's conclusion was that low self-control's influence in the most disadvantaged neighborhoods dissipates, although it is amplified for those living in the least disadvantaged neighborhoods. Alternatively, Steenbeek, Völker, Flap, and Oort (2012) found a possible alternative to the deviant places argument. Examining traditional explanations of disorder (e.g., poverty, residential mobility, and ethnic heterogeneity), they found a positive relationship between business presence and neighborhood disorder. According to the authors, this suggests that the presence of neighborhood businesses could rival the effects of social disorganization theory.

Whatever the cause, the fact remains that high official delinquency rates are found in certain areas or types of areas where serious and repetitive misconduct not only is common but also appears to have become traditional and more or less acceptable (Lowencamp, Cullen, & Pratt, 2003). There is a real danger here, however, of drawing false conclusions based on what has been called the ecological fallacy. This term refers to false conclusions drawn from analyzing data at one level (e.g., the group level) and applying those conclusions at another level (e.g., the individual level). In short, group crime rates tell us nothing about whether a particular individual is likely to become involved in crime (Bohm, 2001, p. 71). In spite of these criticisms, Moyer (2001) found that "one can find the early development of the interactionist perspective, control theory, and conflict theory in their works" (p. 118).

Edwin Sutherland's Differential Association Theory

Sutherland (1939) developed what is known as the theory of differential association. Sutherland's approach combines some of the principles of behaviorism (or learning theory) with the notion that learning takes place in interaction within social groups. For Sutherland, the primary group (family or gang) is the focal point of learning social behavior, including deviant behavior. In this context, individuals learn how to define different situations as appropriate for law-abiding or law-violating behavior. Therefore, seeing an unattended newsstand might be defined as a situation appropriate to the theft of a newspaper by some passersby but not by others. The way a given individual defines a particular situation depends on that individual's prior life experiences. An individual who has a balance of definitions favorable to law-violating behavior in a given situation is likely to commit a law-violating act. The impact of learned definitions on the individual depends on how early in life the definitions were learned (priority), how frequently the definitions are reinforced (frequency), the period over which such definitions are reinforced (duration), and the importance of the definition to the individual (intensity) (Sutherland, Cressey, & Luckenbill, 1992, pp. 88–90).

Sutherland's approach has the advantage of discussing both deviant and normal social behavior as learned phenomena. The approach also indicates that the primary group is crucial in the learning process. In addition, Sutherland suggested some important variables to be considered in determining whether behavior will be criminal or noncriminal in given situations. Finally, Sutherland suggested that it is not differential association with criminal and noncriminal types that determines the individual's behavior; rather, it is differential association with, or exposure to, definitions favorable or unfavorable to law-violating behavior. A study of Korean youth by Moon, Hwang, and McCluskey (2011) found general support for differential association theory in explaining the etiology (causes or origins) of bullying. Miller (2010), in a study of peer influence among Mexican American youth, also found support for differential association and notes that association with delinquent peer groups is one of the best predictors of delinquent behavior.

The learning theory and differential association approaches have been used to try to explain child abuse and neglect as well as delinquency. According to these approaches, abusive parents learned abusive behavior when they were abused as children. Thus, child abuse is said to be an intergenerational phenomenon. Kaufman and Zigler (1987, p. 190), after reviewing self-report data, concluded that the rate of abuse by individuals with a history of abuse is 6 times higher than that in the general population. This finding supports the belief that abusive behavior is learned in primary groups that define it as acceptable behavior (as Sutherland suggested is the case with other forms of deviance). However, other researchers have criticized Kaufman and Zigler and have failed to find a relationship between being abused and abusing. Knudsen (1992, p. 63) also concluded that the cycle of violence appears to be a minor factor in explaining child abuse. Still, as we indicated earlier, there is evidence to the contrary. Scudder and colleagues (1993, p. 321) concluded that children who break the law often have a history of maltreatment as children. These researchers and Siegel and Williams (2003) indicated that a child abused at a young age is at higher risk for subsequent delinquent behaviors than is a nonabused child.

There are a number of criticisms of Sutherland's approach. It is clearly difficult to operationalize the terms *favorable to* and *unfavorable to*. There are serious problems with trying to measure the variable intensity. How many exposures to definitions favorable to law violation are required before definitions unfavorable to law violation are outweighed and the individual commits the illegal act? These and other weaknesses have been pointed out over the years by critics of differential association. Nonetheless, there is a certain logic to Sutherland's approach. Some of the propositions are empirically testable, and the description of the learning process seems to be relatively accurate. Sutherland's approach has sensitized us to an approach to understanding crime and delinquency that has been built on by other theorists and researchers (Akers, 1998; Burgess & Akers, 1968; Curran & Renzetti, 1994; Glaser, 1960).

One attempt to improve on Sutherland's theory was made by Glaser (1978). Glaser referred to his theory as the theory of differential anticipation, which, in his view, combines differential association and control theory and is compatible with biological and personality theories. Differential anticipation theory assumes that a person will try to commit a crime wherever and whenever the expectations of gratification from it—as a result of social bonds, differential learning, and perceptions of opportunity—exceed the unfavorable anticipations from these sources (pp. 126–127). In short, expectations determine conduct, and expectations are determined by social bonds, differential learning, and perceived opportunities. Burgess and Akers (1968) also expanded on the learning theory approach developing differential association–differential reinforcement theory. Akers (1985, 1992) later referred to his theoretical approach as social learning theory. This theory holds that social sanctions of engaging in (deviant) behavior may be perceived differently by different individuals. However, so long as these sanctions are perceived as more rewarding than alternative behavior, the deviant behavior will be repeated under similar circumstances. Progression into sustained deviant behavior is promoted to the extent that reinforcement, exposure to deviant models, and definitions are not offset by negative sanctions and definitions. These theories are eclectic in the sense that they extend Sutherland while being compatible with most of the approaches we have discussed and with labeling theory, to which we now turn our attention.

Labeling Theory

A number of social scientists have contributed to what might be called the labeling theory school of crime or delinquency causation. Becker (1963) discussed the process of labeling deviants as outsiders. Erikson (1962) pointed out the importance of what he called the labeling "ceremony" for deviants. These authors and others shifted the focus of attention from the individual deviant (e.g., delinquent, criminal, mentally ill) to the reaction of the audience observing and labeling the behavior as deviant. As we have indicated repeatedly, it is clear that many individuals commit deviant acts, but only some are dealt with officially. The time at which the act occurs, the place where it occurs, and the people who observe the act all are important in determining whether official action will be taken. Thus, the juvenile using heroin in the privacy of his gang's hangout in front of other gang members is not subject to official action. If, however, he used heroin in a public place in the presence of a police officer who was observing his behavior, official action would be likely.

From the labeling theorist's point of view, then, society's reaction to deviant behavior is crucially important in understanding who becomes labeled as deviant. Erikson (1962) discussed the ceremony that deviants typically go through once the decision to take official action has been made. First, the alleged deviant is apprehended (arrested or taken into custody). Second, the individual is confronted, generally at a trial or hearing. Third, the individual is judged (a verdict, disposition, or decision is rendered). Finally, the individual is placed (imprisoned, committed to an institution, or put back into society on probation). The result is that the individual is officially labeled as deviant.

One of the consequences of labeling in our society is that, once labeled, the individual may never be able to redeem himself or herself in the eyes of society. Therefore, John Q. Convict does not become John Q. Citizen on release from prison. Instead, he becomes John Q. Ex-Convict. Having been labeled may make it extremely difficult for the rehabilitated deviant to find employment and establish successful family ties. The more difficult it becomes for the rehabilitated deviant to succeed in the larger society, the greater the chances that he or she will return to old associates and old ways. Of course, these are often the very associates and ways that led the individual to become officially labeled in the first place. Thus, the individual may be more or less forced to continue his or her career in deviance, partially as a result of the labeling itself.

Research by Blankenship and Singh (1976) indicated that a juvenile's prior career of delinquent behavior (the extent to which he or she has been officially labeled previously) is indeed an important determinant of official action. These authors, as well as Covington (1984), pointed out that labeling comes in different forms (e.g., legalistic vs. peer group) and has different consequences for different types of offenders (e.g., whites vs. blacks). If we could assume that society never makes a mistake in attaching the label of deviant and that rehabilitation programs never succeed, we might regard the consequences of labeling as somewhat less alarming. As we have already seen in Chapters 2 and 3, the assumption that society never makes a mistake is unwarranted. We see later that there is at least some hope that rehabilitation programs do succeed. If the result of official labeling forces the labeled individual back into a deviant career, in the case of juveniles at least, we are accomplishing exactly the opposite of what we intended when we created a separate juvenile justice system designed to protect, educate, and treat juveniles rather than to punish them. One of the consequences of negative societal reaction to the label of delinquent may be the changing of the delinquent's self-concept, so the individual, like society, begins to think about himself or herself in negative terms. Possibilities for rehabilitation may be lessened as a result.

An interesting contribution to labeling theory was made by Braithwaite (1989). He discussed what he referred to as "disintegrative shaming" (negative stigmatization) and noted that it is destructive of social identities because it morally condemns and isolates people but involves no attempt to reintegrate the shamed people at some later time. He contrasts this harmful approach to stigmatization with "reintegrative shaming" in which there is an attempt to reconnect the stigmatized person to the larger society.

A 2006 study by Bernburg, Krohn, and Rivera found that teens processed by the juvenile justice system were more likely than teens who had not been processed to become gang members or to be part of a delinquent network. According to the authors, official labeling as a delinquent plays a significant role in the maintenance and stability of delinquency. They concluded that intervention may in some cases increase associations with deviant peers by placing youth in the company of other delinquent youth.

Lopes et al. (2012) examined the following:

Direct and indirect effects of police intervention in the lives of adolescents who were followed into their 30s. The authors found that early police intervention is indirectly related to drug use at the ages of 29 to 31, as well as unemployment and welfare receipt. Given that such effects were found some 15 years after the labeling event, on criminal and noncriminal outcomes, and after controlling for intraindividual factors, the authors conclude that the labeling perspective is still relevant within a developmental framework. (p. 456)

Murray, Loeber, and Pardini (2012) studied the impact of parental incarceration on children in terms of the development of youth theft, marijuana use, and poor academic performance and concluded that "labeling and stigma processes might be particularly important for understanding the consequences of parental incarceration for children" (p. 255). Siegel (2011) also pointed to the importance of stigma for children whose parents, especially if it's the mother, are incarcerated. The child's anxiety and life disruption combined with the child's perceived need to hide the whereabouts of the parent from others can lead to acting-out behaviors. Although the child has not necessarily been directly involved in delinquent activity, the child may feel marked as different.

The labeling approach accurately describes how individuals become labeled, why some maintain deviant careers, and some of the possible consequences of labeling (Krisberg, 2005, p. 184). It does not deal with the issue of why some individuals initially commit acts that lead them to be labeled; rather, it deals only with what is referred to as secondary deviance. In addition, those who support the approach often lose sight of the fact that the individual is in some way responsible for the actions that are viewed as unacceptable; that is, social audiences do not appear to attach negative labels haphazardly. They are responding to some stimulus presented by the individual committing a crime for which he or she must accept some responsibility (unless we return to a completely deterministic concept of deviance). Finally, as McAra and McVie (2010) indicated, attempting to identify at-risk children early in life (whether as victims or offenders) "is not an exact science and runs the risk of labeling and stigmatizing" (p. 179).

Despite some weaknesses, the labeling approach contributes significantly to our understanding of deviance. Through this approach, deviance is viewed as a product of social interaction in which the actions of both the deviant and his or her audience must be considered.

Conflict, Radical, Critical, and Marxist Theories

Conflict, radical, critical, and Marxist theories focus on political and economic systems and on class relations in these systems as they relate to crime.

Chambliss (1984) described conflict theories of crime as focusing on whole political and economic systems and on class relations in those systems. Conflict theorists argue that conflict is inherent in all societies, not just capitalist societies, and focus on conflict resulting from gender, race, ethnicity, power, and other relationships. Conflict results from competition for power among many groups. Those who are successful in this competition define criminality at any given time. Thus, criminal behavior is viewed not as universal or inherent but rather as situational and definitional. This view does not account for individual acts of criminality occurring outside of the group context but serves basically to alert us to the social factors that may be related to criminality. Why, for example, did we, for years, pass laws with severe sanctions for use of marijuana but deal with tobacco use among teens much less harshly? Is it because the tobacco lobby is powerful and able to convince legislators that tobacco use among juveniles should, at most, be regulated but not outlawed?

The Marxist approach to criminology and delinquency finds the causes of such phenomena in the repression of the lower social classes by the "ruling class." In short, laws are passed and enforced by those who monopolize power against those who are powerless (e.g., the poor and minorities). The causal roots of crime are assumed, by many proponents of this approach, to be inherent in the social structure of capitalistic societies. Crime control policies are developed and implemented by those who have power (e.g., own the means of production, have wealth), and these policies serve to criminalize those who threaten the status quo (Beirne & Quinney, 1982; Chambliss & Mandoff, 1976; Platt, 1977; Quinney, 1970, 1974; Turk, 1969; Vold, 1958). Labeling the discontented as criminals and delinquents allows the ruling class to call on law enforcement officials to deal with such individuals without needing to grant legitimacy to their discontent. Although there are a number of variations on the theme as discussed here, these are the essential components of most radical or critical explanations of delinquency and crime.

Radical criminology became relatively popular in the United States during the 1970s and 1980s, but its popularity has declined over the years and some of its most important spokespersons have abandoned this approach, at least in part, as an explanation of crime and delinquency. Little empirical research that supports the radical/critical approach has been done (Moyer, 2001, p. 238).

However, a study reported in 2011 sought to test the conflict theory of Sellin, which proposes that crime is often a product of culture conflict between the values and norms of a certain subculture in a given society and those of the general culture (Einat & Herzog, 2011, p. 1072). In this case, Einat and Herzog sought to determine whether youths constitute a social subculture with accompanying values, norms, and stances toward the criminal law that may be quite different from the values and norms of adults (who determine the content of the criminal law). To determine whether such differences exist, the authors used a crime seriousness study, in which adult and teenage respondents were asked to evaluate the seriousness of various criminal offenses committed by adolescents. Significant differences were found "between the seriousness and punishment values given by the adult and juvenile respondents to violent offenses (high) and self-use of illegal drugs (low), with adult respondents providing significantly higher seriousness values and punishment options for them" (p. 1072). Their results provide some support for conflict theory in that those of different age groups appear to be in conflict over both seriousness and punishment options for at least some offenses. Thus, although researchers have often found that delinquency appears to be rather uniformly distributed across social classes, contrary to the teachings of the Marxist approach, it may well be that generational conflict plays some role in determining perceptions of crime and punishment.

Still, the conflict approach fails to recognize that the legal order serves the purpose of maintaining the system in all known types of societies, including those that claim to be Marxist, communist, or socialist (Cox, 1975). As Klockars (1979) noted, "The leading figures of American Marxist criminology have not raised the details of Gulag or Cuban solutions to the problems of crime in America, nor have they seriously examined such solutions in states which legitimate them" (p. 477). Bohm (2001) added, "Today, it probably makes little sense to speak of capitalist and socialist societies anyway, because no pure societies of either type exist. (They probably never did.)" (p. 119).

Feminism

Feminism as an approach to studying crime and delinquency focuses on women's experiences, typically in the areas of victimization, gender differences in crime, and differential treatment of women by the justice network. Some feminists focus on equal rights and equal participation for women, some focus on the ills of capitalist society, and others focus on the issue of patriarchal oppression (in the form of male control over sex, money, and power) that has resulted in second-class citizenship for women in our society. Traditional criminology has certainly largely ignored female crime, raising the issue of whether any of the theories of crime apply directly to women. Furthermore, there are clearly differences in the extent and nature of crime by gender, and there is a question as to whether current theories can explain these differences (Cobbina, Like-Haislip, & Miller, 2010; Daly & Chesney-Lind, 1988; Naffine, 1996; Martin, Golder, Cynthia, & Sawning, 2013; National Girls Institute, 2013). Nonetheless, the focus on gender as a major determinant of delinquent and criminal behavior has traditionally been questioned because there appeared to be limited empirical support for the approach (Akers, 1994, p. 177; Bohm, 2001, p. 122).

However, more than two decades ago, Chesney-Lind (1989) examined the prevalence of female delinquency focusing on girls' aggression and violence. Chesney-Lind argued that analysis of the data indicated that changes in arrests of girls for certain violent offenses reflected changes in the policing of girls' aggression (including the arrest of girls for minor forms of family violence) rather than actual changes in their behavior.

Cobbina et al. (2010) found that "despite persistent gender gaps in the use of violence, recent research suggests that young women use violence more often than commonly believed" and also found their violence is tied to concerns about status and respect (as is the case with young men) (p. 596). Creaney (2012, p. 111) determined that girls tend to be drawn into the system for welfare rather than crime-related matters and that policy and practice in juvenile justice appears to negate girls' gender-specific needs. Creaney concluded that "youth justice policy and practice must be re-developed in favor of incorporating gender-specific, child and young person centred practices" (p. 111).

Martin et al. (2013, p. 27) noted that women are the fastest growing segment of the criminal justice population and that efforts to reduce women's involvement in the criminal justice system and the negative consequences associated with such involvement are urgently needed. The authors went on to identify three major factors contributing to women's involvement in the criminal justice system: (1) victimization, (2) mental disorders, and (3) substance use.

According to the National Girls Institute (2013), gender-responsive theories argue that there are three such theories: (1) the feminist pathways; (2) relational–cultural; and (3) intersectionality theories, which focus on gender-specific considerations dealing with how girls' behaviors and responses lead to their justice system involvement. The feminist pathways theory proposes unique factors associated with female delinquency, including the following:

- Having higher rates of substance use, abuse or victimization, depression, and anxiety

- Experiencing distinct personal and social effects (family and peers, high-risk sexual behaviors)

- Dating older partners

- Self-harming

Feminist pathways theory stresses that events during childhood lead to risk factors for female delinquency and crime. The differences in risk factors create different pathways that lead to the justice system. Thus, females' pathways typically include "histories of personal abuse, mental illness tied to early life experiences, substance abuse and addiction, economic and social marginality, [and] homelessness" (National Girls Institute, 2013, p. ix).

Proponents of relational–cultural theory (RCT) focus on psychological problems for females involving disconnections or violations within relationships in families, among personal acquaintances, or in society at large. Thus, in order to understand delinquent behavior among females, it is necessary to focus on relationships that are meaningful to them and on the influences such relationships exert on behavior (Foley, 2008).

The theory of intersectionality proposes that girls share many similar experiences based on gender, but they also experience important differences. Thus, racial or ethnic discrimination may result in the differential treatment of girls of color in the justice system. These girls may be labeled, processed, or treated differently than their white counterparts. Similarly, some research indicates that lesbians and bisexual girls are disproportionately impacted by these sanctions. Each of these theories has implications for practice with girls. Thus, programs consistent with the pathways theory should provide services and treatment for abuse and victimization and associated problems such as substance use. RCT should provide services for abuse and its impact on relationships. Practical implications of intersectionality theory focus on both individual- and system-level issues such as respect for diversity and positive identity development.

Finally, Tzoumakis, Lussier, and Corrado (2012) explored the intergenerational transmission of aggression and antisocial behavior by examining mothers' juvenile delinquency, their pregnancies, and transmission of aggression to their children. Results indicated that mothers who reported being delinquents had children who were more physically aggressive and had an earlier onset of physical aggression, thus demonstrating the "importance of understanding the role and impact of female delinquency and motherhood on the intergenerational transmission of antisocial behavior" (p. 211).

It appears safe to say that research on feminist theories continues and that there appears to be considerable support for the notion that the causes and treatment of delinquency are indeed impacted by gender. For example, women represent a relatively small percentage of known violent offenders, and the percentage decreases as the severity of the crime increases, with one exception (Jordan, Clark, Pritchard, & Charnigo, 2012). In intimate partner homicides, some studies have found that rates of offending by women approach those of men (in the United States, at least). Understanding why this is the case requires a more complete picture of the female offenders and the pathways leading them to intimate partner violence. What are the circumstances under which females kill or seriously assault intimate partners?

Control Theories

Control theories assume that all of us must be held in check or "controlled" if we are to resist the temptation to commit criminal or delinquent acts. The types of systems used to control or check delinquent behavior fall into two categories: (1) personal (internal) and (2) social (external). The containment theory of Reckless (1961, 1967), for instance, emphasizes the importance of both inner controls and external pressures on self-concept. A poor self-concept is thought to increase the chances that a juvenile will turn to delinquency; a positive self-concept is seen as insulating the juvenile from delinquent activities. Negative self-concepts and low self-esteem have also been frequently noted as characteristics of those who abuse or neglect children (Marshall, Cripps, Anderson, & Cortoni, 1999; Shorkey & Armendariz, 1985).

Hirschi's (1969) control theory places more emphasis on social factors (bonds and attachments) than on inner controls. For example, the term *attachment* is used to refer to the feelings one has toward other persons or groups. The stronger one's attachment to nondelinquent others, the less likely one is to engage in delinquency. The same type of argument is applied to commitment (profits associated with conformity vs. losses associated with nonconformity), involvement (in conforming vs. nonconforming activities), and beliefs (in the conventional value system vs. some less conventional value system). Although these four components of control theory may vary independently, Hirschi maintained that in general they vary together. Strong positive ties in each of these four areas minimize the possibility of delinquency, whereas strong negative ties maximize the likelihood of delinquency. Hirschi's formulation has encouraged considerable research, and although there is some empirical evidence to support portions of the control theory approach, this approach leaves unanswered a number of important questions. What is the exact nature of the relationship between self-concept and labeling? How is it that some juveniles who appear to be well insulated from negative attachments and bonds commit delinquent acts? Do such bonds and attachments themselves actually inhibit delinquent behavior, or are the bonds and attachments perceived by law enforcement and criminal justice personnel simply used to determine whether or not to take official action? Are there longitudinal data that support the approach? Attempts to answer some of these questions are ongoing. In a reanalysis of Hirschi's original data, Costello and Vowell (1999) found support for Hirschi's theory. May (1999) found that social control theory had a significant association with juvenile firearms possession in school. But Greenberg's (1999) reanalysis of Hirschi's data found that social control theory has only limited explanatory power.

In 1990, Hirschi collaborated with Michael Gottfredson to develop what they referred to as a "general theory of crime" in which they sought to examine criminal conduct in the more general context of deviant behavior that they regarded as simply one form of behavior, not a distinct category (Gottfredson & Hirschi, 1990). From this perspective, crime and delinquency are viewed as routine behaviors that are poorly planned, not very lucrative, and largely localized geographically. In general, these authors viewed crime as a result of low self-control that results in a desire for immediate gratification. Furthermore, they indicated that the degree of self-control one possesses is determined largely by child-rearing practices.

The general theory developed by Gottfredson and Hirschi (1990) has been criticized on several grounds but has provoked a good deal of empirical research. For example, Piquero, Gomez-Smith, and Langton (2004) used Gottfredson and Hirschi's notion of self-control to examine whether an individual perceives sanctions as fair or unfair and how perceptions of sanctions and low self-control influence the perceived anger that may result from being singled out for sanctioning. Piquero and colleagues also examined the relationship among self-control, perceptions of fairness, and anger. Their results suggest that individuals with low self-control are more likely to perceive sanctions as being unfair and that this combination leads to anger for being singled out for punishment.

Church, Wharton, and Taylor (2009) investigated family stressors, family cohesion, and nonfamilial relationships in an assessment of differential association (discussed earlier in this chapter) and control theories and found that only family stressors had a direct effect on delinquency. They also found that being male was the strongest predictor of delinquency. Overall, these findings appear to provide little support for control theory.

Piquero, Jennings, and Farrington (2010) indicated the following:

Gottfredson and Hirschi's general theory of crime has generated significant controversy and research, such that there now exists a large knowledge base regarding the importance of self-control in regulating antisocial behavior over the life-course. Reviews of this literature indicate that self-control is an important correlate of antisocial activity. (p. 803)

The authors evaluated existing research on the effectiveness of programs designed to improve self-control up to age 10 among children and adolescents and assessed the effects of these programs on self-control and delinquency/crime. Their findings indicated the following:

(1) Self-control programs improve a child/adolescent's self-control, (2) these interventions also reduce delinquency, and (3) the positive effects generally hold across a number of different moderator variables and groupings as well as by outcome source (parent-, teacher-, direct observer-, self-, and clinical report). (p. 803)

Boisvert, Wright, Knopik, and Vaske (2012, p. 477) noted that low self-control has emerged as a consistent and strong predictor of antisocial and delinquent behaviors. They used the twin subsample of the National Longitudinal Study of Adolescent Health to conduct genetic analyses to examine the impact of genetic and environmental contributions to low self-control and offending as well as to their relationship with one another. Results revealed that low self-control and criminal behaviors are influenced by genetic and nonshared environmental factors (those experienced by only one twin) with the effects of shared environmental factors being negligible.

In a study assessing the correlates of self-control and police contact in a sample of Chicago public high school students, the effects of parental attachment or identification, family structure, and peer association on self-control and the effects of parental attachment or identification, family structure, peer association, and self-control on police contact were examined (Flexon, Greenleaf, & Lurigio, 2012). The researchers found the following:

Weak parental attachment/identification and gang affiliation (peer association) predicted low self-control among all students. Among African American youth, only weak maternal attachment/identification predicted low self-control; both weak maternal attachment/identification and gang affiliation predicted low self-control among Latino youth. Gang affiliation predicted police stops (delinquency) among African Americans but not among Latinos. However, both African American and Latino students with lower self-control were more likely to be stopped by the police than those with higher self-control.

While associations with deviant peers are well understood to impact individual development, less is understood about the relationship between friendship quality and delinquency. . . . Social control and self-control theories both premise that delinquents will have largely fractured, weak, and "cold and brittle" friendships. (p. 218)

However, research conducted by Bowman, Krohn, Gibson, and Stogner (2012) found that "delinquents have as intense, or more intense, friendships as non-delinquents. . . . Supplemental analyses demonstrate that the effect of self-control on friendship quality may be reduced when individuals in dyads (groups of two) are [both] delinquent" (p. 1526).

Clearly the impact of control theory and its relationship to delinquent behavior are still being examined.

Integrated Theories

Numerous attempts have been made to combine two or more preexisting theories to provide more comprehensive explanations (integrated theories) of criminal and delinquent behavior. The resulting theories or conceptual schemes are far too numerous to discuss here, but we mention a few of the more prominent attempts. Developmental and life course theory (DLC) attempts to explain how antisocial behavior develops, how different risk factors exist at different stages of life, and the differential effects of life events on antisocial behavior (Farrington, 2003; S. T. Reid, 2006, pp. 195–198). Moffitt (1993, 2006) developed a life course-persistent–adolescence-limited theory that attempts to explain two types of antisocial behavior using biological, psychological, and sociological approaches. According to Moffitt, antisocial behavior either persists across the life course or is limited to adolescence. Those who persist in crime suffer from neuropsychological problems that begin in prenatal development and lead to psychological disorders during childhood that facilitate the delinquent behaviors. Offenders that persist across the life course also grow up in disadvantaged neighborhoods and suffer from inadequate parenting (Moffitt, 1993, 2006). According to Hagan and Parker (1999, p. 259), for example, life course capitalization theory proposes that low intergenerational educational aspirations and educational underachievement is disadvantageous to adolescents and that subsequent adult and parenting problems may well result from this disadvantage. Thus, a parent's educational disinvestment as an adolescent leads to dropping out of school, teen parenthood, unemployment, and marriage and parenting problems, all of which contribute to the intergenerational causation of delinquency among children and adolescents.

Interactional theory represents an attempt to combine social learning, social bonding, and social structural theories (Thornberry, 1987). This theory holds that, like all other human social behavior, delinquency is the result of interactions among individuals and is the result of the learning and exchanges that occur in such interaction. Thus, understanding interaction among juveniles and their parents, siblings, peers, gang members, school personnel, and others is critical. Interaction with gang members, for example, may increase the level of delinquent behavior among new members, but those who leave the gang and interact with others who may be less criminally inclined become less likely to engage in behaviors encouraged by the gang.

Hayes (1997) noted that labeling, differential association, social learning, and social control theory all provide useful information in the delinquency process. None of these theories, however, account for the entire process. Hayes incorporated elements of labeling, differential association, social learning, and social control theories in an attempt to explain both initial and continued delinquency. Using data from the National Youth Survey, Hayes found that the new model showed that weakened social controls increase opportunities for associating with delinquent peers, learning delinquent behaviors, and committing initial delinquent acts. Initial delinquency increases the likelihood of being observed and negatively labeled by parents. These labels, in turn, increase the likelihood of future delinquency (Hayes, 1997, p. 161). The author concluded that these findings support the use of integrated theory in the study of juvenile delinquency.

Other integrated theories that you may wish to examine further include network analysis, control balance theory, and strain and control theories.

Building on more than 25 years of criminological research, Robert Agnew attempts to provide an answer to the question, "Why do criminals offend?" His answer is a concise integrated theory, which he calls a general theory of crime and delinquency. (Zhang, Day, & Cao, 2012, p. 856)

This theory proposes the following:

Delinquency is more likely to occur when constraints against delinquency are low and motivations for delinquency are high. In addition, he argues that constraints and motivations are influenced by variables in five life domains: self, family, school, peer, and work . . . which affect delinquency both directly and indirectly through their effects on motivations for and constraints against crime. (p. 856)

In a limited test of the theory, Zhang et al. (2012) found support for the core proposition of the theory.

As noted, integrated theories represent attempts to improve on our understanding of delinquent behavior and have inspired considerable research. Ultimately, those proposing such theories are searching for commonalities among existing theories that will form the background for a more comprehensive theory. This is important because, as we mentioned at the beginning of this chapter, all criminological theories have implications for criminal justice policy and practice (Akers & Sellers, 2004; Zhang et al., 2012).

CAREER OPPORTUNITY: CRIMINAL JUSTICE PROFESSOR

Job description: Teach courses in the field of criminal justice, criminology, and juvenile justice with respect to causes, consequences, extent, and nature of crime and delinquency, justice system responses, and problems. Conduct research related to these issues.

Employment requirements: At least a master's degree, and preferably a PhD, in criminology, criminal justice, sociology, psychology, law, or a related field.

Beginning salary: Between $55,000 and $75,000. Benefits include tenure (job security) for those who are successful as teachers, as researchers, and in publishing the results of their research. Other benefits include health and life insurance for faculty members and their families as well as solid retirement plans.

Summary

We have provided a brief overview of some of the attempts to explain delinquency. It should be clear at this point that, using our definition of *theory*, few if any of these attempts have resulted in explanations that are scientifically sound. Many have been more or less discarded over time, and others continue to provide leads that need to be pursued. Bridging the gap between theory and practice is crucial to controlling delinquency and to improving the juvenile justice network. The input of practitioners is extremely useful in testing our theoretical statements. The benefits to be reaped, if and when a sound theoretical base is established, are considerable. We can no longer afford to ignore the importance of theory, nor can we continue to rely on commonsense notions of causation that are, as we have seen, very often inaccurate.

Unlike demonology, which has been largely discounted as an explanation of delinquency today, the classical school of criminology remains important as a basis of our current criminal and juvenile justice networks. Public opinion continues to indicate a belief that severe punishment will deter crime and delinquency, and legislatures around the country continue to pass get-tough measures in the hope of meeting public expectations. As a result, there is pressure for more arrests, more convictions, and more severe punishment, none of which seem to have accomplished the desired goal, perhaps because of the lack of certainty and swiftness of punishment. Even capital punishment, which certainly deters the subject, has been shown to have little effect on others, and the procedures currently employed are fraught with difficulties that have led to moratoria in some states.

Biological theories of causation raise some important issues. Although biological factors do not appear to be a direct cause of delinquency, we must remain constantly alert to the possibility that genetics and physiological malfunctions or abnormalities may be important in assessing juveniles' behaviors. For example, a juvenile who has become increasingly aggressive, irrational, and uncooperative with others could conceivably be suffering from brain damage (e.g., tumor, lesion) that causes these symptoms. In cases where physical ailments or the use of intoxicants might be related to delinquency, it is obviously best to provide for appropriate medical intervention.

There is always, of course, the possibility that some emotional or psychological difficulty may be present in a specific delinquent. The evidence in support of personality disturbances as causes of delinquency is ambiguous at best, due in part to measurement and definitional difficulties. Nevertheless, the psychological approach to explaining delinquency remains important because psychotherapy of some type—individual or group therapy or counseling—is often prescribed as treatment within correctional facilities. Whether such treatment is likely to help remains an empirical question, but some successes are reported.

The sociological school views delinquency as a result of social interaction, learned in much the same way as nondelinquent behavior. According to this approach, much of the juvenile justice network makes sense, but some does not. For example, if labeling is an important factor in delinquency, attempts to keep juvenile proceedings confidential make sense. However, it does not make sense, within this theoretical context, to house minor or first-time delinquents in large institutions with more serious delinquents from whom they are likely to learn additional delinquent behaviors. This may account for our failure to rehabilitate many delinquents in such settings. In addition, the sociological approach looks for causes of delinquency in society as well as in the individual. It may be that the only way to significantly reduce delinquency rates is to change some social policies such as those leading to educational and racial discrimination and unemployment. Finally, the sociological approach suggests methods of control and rehabilitation that do not require the death penalty, the practice of eugenics, or complete restructuring of the individual's personality. This approach suggests that positive reinforcement, administered in surroundings where the juvenile lives and by those with whom the juvenile regularly interacts, may provide more positive results than do many techniques currently employed. Although the sociological approach is not a panacea, it does provide a number of leads for future research and treatment that may prove to be beneficial provided that public and agency cooperation can be obtained.

Finally, the search for new and better theories of delinquency continues in attempts to combine the tenets of different theories into more comprehensive theories that do a better job of explaining delinquent behavior. Ultimately, the success or failure of policies and practices in the field of juvenile delinquency is determined by the accuracy of explanations for its existence and persistence.

KEY TERMS

anomalies 86

anomie theory 98

atavists 85

behaviorists 94

biological theories 85

biosocial criminology 88

classical theory 81

cognitive behavioral therapy (CBT) 97

concentric-zone theory 100

conceptual schemes 80

conditioning 94

conflict, radical, critical, and Marxist theories 106

control theories 109

delinquency and drift 98

demonology 81

deterrence theory 83

ecological/social disorganization approach 100

feminism 107

freewill approach 82

id, ego, and superego 92

illegitimate opportunity structure 98

integrated theories 111

labeling theory 104

learning theory 94

neoclassical approach 82

neurocriminology 90

personality inventories 91

phrenology 86

positivist school of criminology 85

postclassical theory 82

psychoanalytic approach 91

psychological theories 91

psychopath 92

rational choice theory 82

routine activities theory 83

scientific theory 80

sociological theories 81

somatotypes 87

strain theory 98

techniques of neutralization 98

theory of differential anticipation 104

theory of differential association 103

trephining 81

XYY chromosome 87

Critical Thinking Questions

1. What is a scientific theory, and why is the development of such theories crucial to our understanding and control of delinquency?

2. What are the strengths and weaknesses of our current juvenile justice network in terms of the learning theory and labeling theory approaches? Discuss some of the reasons why the classical approach to the control of delinquency has been, and continues to be, ineffective. Why do you think the approach has remained popular in spite of its ineffectiveness? What contemporary theories are extensions of the classical approach?

3. What are the major strengths and weaknesses of the psychological approach to understanding and controlling delinquency? What has been Freud's impact on the treatment of delinquency? Does the cognitive behavioral approach appear to hold promise for future explanations of delinquency or suggestions for treatment or prevention?

4. Is there evidence in support of the biological school of delinquency causation? Discuss some of the attempts to demonstrate a relationship between biology and delinquent behavior.

5. What is your overall assessment of the sociological approach to understanding and controlling delinquency? Which of the various attempts in this school do you think does the best job of explaining delinquency? The worst job?

6. What are some of the current issues in the area of juvenile justice or delinquency attracting proponents of feminism? Is there any convincing empirical evidence of gender differences in delinquency or its treatment or prevention?

Suggested Readings

Agnew, R. (2012). Reflection on "A revised strain theory of delinquency." *Social Forces, 91*(1), 33–38.

Augustyn, M., & McGloin, J. (2013). The risk of informal socializing with peers: Considering gender differences across predatory delinquency and substance use. *Justice Quarterly, 30*(1), 117–143.

Bellair, P. E., & Browning, C. R. (2010). Contemporary disorganization research: An assessment and further test of the systemic model of neighborhood crime. *Journal of Research in Crime and Delinquency, 47*(4), 496–521.

Bernburg, J. G., Krohn, M. D., & Rivera, C. J. (2006). Official labeling, criminal embeddedness, and subsequent delinquency: A longitudinal test of labeling theory. *Journal of Research in Crime and Delinquency, 43*(1), 67–88.

Boisvert, D., John, P. W., Knopik, V., & Vaske, J. (2012). Genetic and environmental overlap between low self-control and delinquency. *Journal of Quantitative Criminology, 28*(3), 477–507.

Bottrell, D., Armstrong, D., & France, A. (2010). Young people's relations to crime: Pathways across ecologies. *Youth Justice, 10*(1), 56–72.

Bouffard, J. A. (2007). Predicting differences in the perceived relevance of crime's costs and benefits in a test of rational choice theory. *International Journal of Offender Therapy and Comparative Criminology, 51*(4), 461–485.

Chesney-Lind, M. (1989). Girl's crime and woman's place: Toward a feminist model of female delinquency. *Crime and Delinquency, 35*, 5–29.

Church, W. T., II, Wharton, T., & Taylor, J. K. (2009). Examination of differential association and social control theory: Family systems and delinquency. *Youth Violence and Juvenile Justice, 7*(1), 3–15.

Clark, P. (2011). Preventing future crime with cognitive behavioral therapy. *American Jails, 25*(1), 45–48.

DeLisi, M. M., Wright, J. P., & Vaughn, M. G. (2010). Nature and nurture by definition means both: A response to males. *Journal of Adolescent Research, 25*(1), 24–30.

Donald, N. D. (2012). Child representation in America: Progress report from the National Quality Improvement Center. *Family Law Quarterly, 46*(1), 87–123, 129–137. Retrieved from http://search.proquest.com/docview/1271 860934?accountid=14982

Farah, F., & Raine, A. (2011). Antisocial personality disorders. In W. J. Chambliss (Ed.), *Crime and criminal behavior: Key issues in crime and punishment.* Thousand Oaks, CA: Sage.

Flexon, J. L., Greenleaf, R. G., & Lurigio, A. J. (2012). The effects of self-control, gang membership, and parental attachment/identification on police contacts among Latino and African American youths. *International Journal of Offender Therapy & Comparative Criminology, 56*(2), 218–238.

Gibson, C. L. (2012). An investigation of neighborhood disadvantage, low self-control, and violent victimization among youth. *Youth Violence & Juvenile Justice, 10*(1), 41–63.

Gleacher, A. A., Nadeem, E., Moy, A. J., Whited, A. L., Albano, A. M., Radigan, M., . . . Hoagwood, K. E. (2011). Statewide CBT training for clinicians and supervisors treating youth: The New York state evidence based treatment dissemination center. *Journal of Emotional & Behavioral Disorders, 19*(3), 182–192.

Groff, E. R. (2008). Adding the temporal and spatial aspects of routine activities: A further test of routine activity theory. *Security Journal, 21*(1–2), 95–116.

Guo, G., Roettger, M. E., & Cai, T. C. (2008, August). The integration of genetic propensities into social-control models of delinquency and violence among male youths. *American Sociological Review, 73*, 543–568.

Hollist, D. R., Hughes, L. A., & Schaible, L. M. (2009). Adolescent maltreatment, negative emotion, and delinquency: An assessment of general strain theory and family-based strain. *Journal of Criminal Justice, 37*(4), 379–387.

Jeannot, T. (2010). The enduring significance of the thought of Karl Marx. *International Journal of Social Economics, 37*(3), 214–238.

Lopes, G., Krohn, M. D., Lizotte, A. J., Schmidt, N. M., Vásquez, B., & Bernburg, J. (2012). Labeling and cumulative disadvantage: The impact of formal police intervention on life chances and crime during emerging adulthood. *Crime & Delinquency, 58*(3), 456–488.

Martin, T. H., Golder, S., Cynthia, L. C., & Sawning, S. (2013). Designing programming and interventions for women in the criminal justice system. *American Journal of Criminal Justice, 38*(1), 27–50.

Miller, H. (2010). If your friends jumped off of a bridge, would you do it too? Delinquent peers and susceptibility to peer influence. *Justice Quarterly, 27*(4), 473–491.

Moffitt, T. (2003). Life-course-persistent and adolescence-limited antisocial behavior: A ten-year research review and a research agenda. In B. B. Lahey, T. E. Moffitt, & A. Caspi (Eds.), *Causes of conduct order and juvenile delinquency*. New York, NY: Guilford Press.

Nederlof, E., van der Ham, A., Dingemans, P., & Oei, K. (2010, October). The relation between dimensions of personality and personality pathology and offence type and severity in juvenile delinquents. *Journal of Forensic Psychiatry & Psychology, 21*(5), 711–720.

Onyskiw, J. E. (2003). Domestic violence and children's adjustment: A review of research. In R. A. Geffner, R. S. Igelman, & J. Zellner (Eds.), *The effects of intimate partner violence on children* (pp. 11–45). New York, NY: Haworth Maltreatment & Trauma Press.

Piquero, A. R., Jennings, W. G., & Farrington, D. P. (2010). On the malleability of self-control: Theoretical and policy implications regarding a general theory of crime. *Justice Quarterly, 27*(6), 803–834.

Seipel, C., & Eifler, S. (2010). Opportunities, rational choice, and self-control: On the interaction of person and situation in a general theory of crime. *Crime & Delinquency, 56*(2), 167–197.

Siegel, J. A. (2011). *Disrupted childhoods: Children of women in prison*. New Brunswick, NJ: Rutgers University Press.

Simons, R. L., Man, K. L., Stewart, E. A., Beach, S. R. H., Broday, G. H., Philbert, R. A., & Gibbons, F. X. (2012). Social adversity, genetic variation, street code, and aggression: A genetically informed model of violent behavior. *Youth Violence and Juvenile Justice, 10*, 3–24.

Spano, R., & Freilich, J. (2009). An assessment of the empirical validity and conceptualization of individual level multivariate studies of lifestyle/routine activities theory published from 1995 to 2005. *Journal of Criminal Justice, 37*(3), 305–314.

Spano, R., Freilich, J., & Bolland, J. (2008). Gang membership, gun carrying, and employment: Applying routine activities theory to explain violent victimization among inner city, minority youth living in extreme poverty. *Justice Quarterly, 25*(2), 381–410.

Vachon, D. D., Lynam, D. R., Loeber, R., & Stouthamer-Loeber, M. (2012). Generalizing the nomological network of psychopathy across populations differing on race and conviction status. *Journal of Abnormal Psychology, 121*(1), 263–269.

Verschuere, B., Candel, I., Reenen, L., & Korebrits, A. (2012). Validity of the Modified Child Psychopathy Scale for juvenile justice center residents. *Journal of Psychopathology & Behavioral Assessment, 34*(2), 244–252.

Wareham, J., & Boots, D. (2012). The link between mental health problems and youth violence in adolescence: A multilevel test of *DSM*-oriented problems. *Criminal Justice & Behavior, 39*(8), 1003–1024.

Zavala, E., & Ryan, E. S. (2013). The role of vicarious and anticipated strain on the overlap of violent perpetration and victimization: A test of general strain theory. *American Journal of Criminal Justice, 38*(1), 119–140.

Zhang, Y., Day, G., & Cao, L. (2012). A partial test of Agnew's general theory of crime and delinquency. *Crime & Delinquency, 58*(6), 856–878.

⊛SAGE edge™

Sharpen your skills with SAGE edge at **edge.sagepub.com/coxjj9e**. SAGE edge for students provides a personalized approach to help you accomplish your coursework goals in an easy-to-use learning environment. You'll find action plans, mobile-friendly eFlashcards, and quizzes as well as video and web resources and links to SAGE journal articles to support and expand on the concepts presented in this chapter.

Child Abuse and Neglect

5

On completion of this chapter, students should be able to do the following:

- Discuss domestic violence
- Define and discuss physical abuse of juveniles
- Discuss the importance of mandated reporting
- Define and discuss child neglect
- Discuss the vicious cycle of child abuse
- Enumerate the consequences of psychological or emotional abuse of juveniles
- Define and discuss sexual abuse of juveniles
- Discuss intervention strategies

WHAT WOULD YOU DO?

You meet a colleague at a local buffet restaurant for lunch. The restaurant is just opening, and a line has formed at the entry as people pay to enter. A mother is in line with another adult and a young girl who appears to be about 3 years old. The girl is talking, interrupting the mother's conversation, and moving around in the line and entryway. You notice that the child has stepped out of the line a few times to look at the vending machines with balls, rings, and various trinkets in them. The mother has briskly scolded the child at least twice and has jerked the child back into the line by her arm on at least one occasion. After several minutes in line

the girl started to run around the entryway. The mother yelled "No!" and as the girl returned to her mother, the mother slapped her across the head, knocking the child into the vending machines and onto the ground. The girl's head hit one of the vending machines as she fell. The young girl started crying, stood up, and returned to the mother, who grabbed her by the arm and yanked her into the restaurant seating area. The girl continued to cry, "Oh my nose, oh my nose" for about 5 minutes after her mother smacked her. No one in line offered to assist the girl, and the restaurant clerk acted as though she didn't see the incident.

(Continued)

What Would You Do?

1. Is this child abuse? If yes, why? If no, why not?

2. Do you think it would be appropriate to say something to the mother? The other adult? The restaurant staff? If so, what should be said and by whom?

3. If you work in the criminal justice system, what should be your response to this type of incident? What if you are a teacher?

4. Why do you think the other individuals in line and the restaurant staff refused to assist the child? Or say something to the mother?

A 2009 study by the U.S. Department of Justice exposed that nearly 1 in 10 American children saw a family member assaulted by another family member and more than 25% of children surveyed had been exposed to family violence during their life (Finkelhor, Turner, Ormrod, Hamby, & Kracke, 2009). Research has also shown that "children in the United States are more likely to be exposed to violence and crime than are adults" (Finkelhor, 2008; Finkelhor et al., 2009, p. 2; Hashima & Finkelhor, 1999; Rennison, 2003; Siegel, 2011; Tjaden & Thoennes, 2000). The violence can directly (through physical, emotional, or sexual assaults) or indirectly (the murder or assault of a friend or family member) affect the child, causing lasting physical, mental, and emotional damage (Finkelhor et al., 2009; Margolin & Gordis, 2000). Children exposed to violence may also abuse drugs and alcohol, suffer from depression and other mental health issues, and engage in delinquent behaviors (Finkelhor et al., 2009). Nonetheless, children react to violence in different ways and are often capable of "remarkable resilience" (Finkelhor et al., 2009, p. 2). The concern is with those who don't "bounce back." According to the U.S. Department of Justice (2012),

> Major disruptions of the basic cognitive, emotional, and brain functioning that are essential for optimal development and [violence] leaves children traumatized. When their trauma goes unrecognized and untreated, these children are at significantly greater risk than their peers for aggressive, disruptive behaviors; school failure; posttraumatic stress disorder (PTSD); anxiety and depressive disorders; alcohol and drug abuse; risky sexual behavior; delinquency; and repeated victimization. When left unaddressed, these consequences of violence exposure and the impact of psychological trauma can persist well beyond childhood, affecting adult health and productivity. They also significantly increase the risk that, as adults, these children will engage in violence themselves. (p. 27)

According to Finkelhor et al., (2009), children exposed to violence may be more likely to experience dating violence, additional victimizations, and involvement in the welfare and juvenile justice systems. These children may continue the cycle of violence into the next generation (p. 2). Siegel's (2011, p. 37) study supports this research. Three of the four teen parents she interviewed were raising their children alone and had mothers who would be considered "chronic offenders: they had been arrested numerous times. . . . Throughout the children's lives, two of these mothers spent so much time in and out of jail and on the streets that they were rarely available to take on parenting responsibilities" (Siegel, 2011, p. 37). Additionally, all four of the teenage parents had dropped out of school and found that they had no financial resources or parental support to resume their education. Several of them were living on welfare and relying on other public support services.

Over the past four decades, studies on the family have touched on an aspect that was rarely discussed before—family violence, which is also called domestic and/or intimate partner violence (intentional violence committed, attempted, or threatened by spouses, ex-spouses, common-law spouses, boyfriends or girlfriends past or present, and/or child abuse [Bureau of Justice Statistics, 2005, p. 1]). Hester, Pearson, and Harwin (2000) claim that domestic violence is used by one person to control or dominate another within a relationship or with someone whom they have had a relationship. The family, which had traditionally been viewed as an institution characterized by love, compassion, tenderness, and concern, has been shown to be an institution in which members are at considerable risk due to increasing reported episodes of physical abuse and violence.

The Bureau of Justice Statistics (2005) found that "family violence accounted for 11% of all reported and unreported violence between 1998 and 2002. Females made up the majority of victims (73%) in both fatal and nonfatal attacks with children under the age of 13 being 23% of the murder victims killed by family members" (p. 1). Hamby, Finkelhor, Turner, and Ormrod (2011) reported that

more than 1 in 9 (11 percent) [youth] were exposed to some form of family violence in the past year, including 1 in 15 (6.6 percent) exposed to IPV between parents (or between a parent and that parent's partner). One in four children (26 percent) were exposed to at least one form of family violence during their lifetimes. Most youth exposed to family violence, including 90 percent of those exposed to IPV, saw the violence, as opposed to hearing it or other indirect forms of exposure. Males were more likely to perpetrate incidents that were witnessed than females, with 68 percent of youth witnessing only violence by males. (p. 1)

Table 5.1 demonstrates the exposure of family violence and abuse by age and gender from this study.

Table 5.1 Nationally Representative Percentages of Exposure to Family Violence and Abuse: Past Year and Lifetime

		Gender of Youth		Age of Youth			
	Total	Male	Female	0–5	6–9	10–13	14–17
Item	4,549	2,331	2,219	1,458	1,041	1,037	1,014
Exposure to Intimate Partner Violence (interparental)							
1. Verbal threat							
Past-Year	2.0	2.0	2.0	2.5	2.0	1.1	2.2
Lifetime	6.4	6.4	6.4	5.4	7.6	2.7	10.5***
2. Displaced aggression (broke something, punched wall, or threw things)							
Past-Year	4.9	4.8	5.0	6.7	3.8	2.3	6.2***
Lifetime	15.2	14.2	16.1	11.5	13.7	11.5	25.5***
3. Eyewitness to assault of parent							
Past-Year	2.6	2.4	2.9	3.2	1.6	2.3	3.2
Lifetime	11.7	11.2	12.3	7.1	10.0	11.4	20.6***
4. Pushed							
Past-Year	3.9	3.7	4.0	5.1	2.9	3.4	3.7*
Lifetime	13.7	13.2	14.2	10.5	12.9	11.0	22.0***

(Continued)

Table 5.1 (Continued)

	Total	Gender of Youth		Age of Youth			
		Male	Female	0–5	6–9	10–13	14–17
5. Hit or slapped							
Past-Year	2.4	2.1	2.6	3.6	1.4	1.9	2.1**
Lifetime	10.1	9.9	10.4	8.2	10.5	8.0	14.7***
6. Severe physical (kicked, choked, or beat up)							
Past-Year	1.3	1.2	1.4	1.6	0.8	1.4	1.2
Lifetime	5.3	5,2	5.5	4.6	5.7	4.0	7.3**
Exposure to Other Family Violence							
7. Parental assault of sibling							
Past-Year	1.8	1.7	1.9	1.6	0.9	2.1	2.9**
Lifetime	4.6	4.9	4.3	2.5	2.4	4.4	10.3***
8. Other family violence (Grownup or teen pushed, hit, or beat up another relative)							
Past-Year	3.4	3.1	3.7	3.0	2.3	2.6	5.9,,
Lifetime	7.8	7.4	8.3	4.5	6.9	5.7	15.8***
Aggregate Percentages							
Any exposure to psychological/emotional IPV (1 and 2 above)							
Past-Year	5.7	5.5	6.5	6.5	5.2	3.9	7.7**
Lifetime	16.0	14.7	17.4†	11.8	15.6	11.8	25.4***
Any exposure to physical IPV (3, 4, 5, and 6 above)							
Past-Year	6.6	6.3	7.6	6.6	5.6	7.9	7.8
Lifetime	17.9	16.9	19.0t	11.9	15.5	17.9	27.7***
Any exposure to any family violence (1 through 8 above)							
Past-Year	11.1	10.5	11.7	10.2	9.0	11.4	13.8**
Lifetime	25.6	24.8	26.4	17.2	22.8	24.0	40.3***

Source: Hamby, Finkelhor, Turner, & Ormond (2011).

Notes: Weighted *n*; detail may not add to total due to rounding. Age differences are significant for *$p < .05$; **$p < .01$; ***$p < .001$. Gender differences are significant for †$p < .05$.
IPV = Intimate partner violence.

Violence in the home can lead to child maltreatment and neglect and is a prime example of the exposure to violence discussed in the first paragraph of this chapter. Finkelhor, Turner, Ormrod, Hamby, and Kracke (2009) found in a self-report study of exposure to violence among children ages 17 and younger from January to May 2008 that 1 in 10 children reported "some form of maltreatment (including physical abuse other than sexual assault, psychological or emotional abuse, child neglect, and custodial interference) during the past year," whereas one in five reported exposure to child maltreatment in their lifetimes (p. 6). Age made a difference in reported exposure, with one in six 14- to 17-year-olds reporting maltreatment during the past year and one in three claiming maltreatment in their lifetimes. Hamby et al. (2011) supported these findings in their study. Looking at youth ages 14 to 17, they found that 40.3% reported exposure to at least one form of family violence over their lifetimes, and 27.7% reported exposure to physical IPV. Age also matters in the type of maltreatment and exposure to violence, as noted in Figure 5.1. According to Finkelhor et al. (2009), gender did not matter except in cases of sexual assault (by strangers and known adults), where it was higher for girls than boys. Other research has shown that males experience higher rates of physical assault than girls (Finkelhor et al., 2009; Kilpatrick et al., 2003; Stein et al., 2003; Woodward & Fergusson, 2000), and Hamby et al. (2011) reported that girls were more likely to report exposure to psychological and physical IPV than boys. In addition, the U.S. Department of Health and Human Services (2016) reported that states substantiated an estimated 702,000 cases of child abuse and neglect in the United States in 2014: "Approximately 1,580 of these children died from abuse or neglect" (p. ii). This statistic does not account for those children involved in multiple reports or investigations. The U.S. Department of Health and Human Services (2016) also reported that age, gender, and race affected abuse and neglect statistics—just as Finkelhor et al. (2009) found age mattered. According to the 2016 report, children younger than 3 years were the most vulnerable to maltreatment. In the United States, more than 27.4% of victims were younger than 3 years. Victimization rates were highest for children younger than 1 year, and in general, the rate of victimization decreased with age (U.S. Department of Health and Human Services, 2016, p. 22). Victimization was split between the sexes with 48.9% of boys and 50.7% of girls being victims. Finally, white children had the highest rate of victimization (44%), followed by Hispanic (22.7%) and African American children (21.4%) (U.S. Department of Health and Human Services, 2016, p. 23).

Figure 5.1 Developmental Patterns in Exposure to Violence

Victimization in Infancy

Most common victimizations during this period:

- Assault by a sibling
- Assault with no weapon or injury
- Witnessing family assault

Victimization in the Toddler Years (Ages 2 to 5)

Most common victimizations during this period:

- Assault by a sibling
- Assault with no weapon or injury
- Bullying (physical)
- Witnessing family assault

Victimization in Middle Childhood (Ages 6 to 9)

Peak risk period for:

- Assault by a sibling
- Assault with no weapon or injury
- Bullying (physical)
- Emotional bullying/teasing

Victimization in Preteens and Early Adolescence (Ages 10 to 13)

Peak risk period for:

- Assault with weapon
- Sexual harassment (same rate ages 10 to 17)
- Kidnapping
- Witnessing family assault
- Witnessing intimate partner (interparental) violence

(Continued)

Figure 5.1 (Continued)

Victimization in Later Adolescence (Ages 14 to 17)

Peak risk period for:

    Assault with injury

    Assault by peer (nonsibling)

    Genital assault

    Dating violence

    Sexual victimizations of all types

    Sexual assault

    Sexual harassment (same rate ages 10 to 17)

    Flashing or sexual exposure

    Unwanted online sexual solicitation

    Any maltreatment

    Physical abuse

    Psychological or emotional abuse

    Witnessing community assault

    Exposure to shooting

    School threat of bomb or attack

Source: Finkelhor, Turner, Ormrod, Hamby, & Kracke (2009).

Although the privacy of the home and family has made research on this topic difficult, there is now little doubt that the seeds of violence are frequently sown in this setting or that one cause of violence among juveniles is that of being reared in a violent family.

The privacy of the home and the fear of retaliation or exposure make identifying and helping maltreated juveniles (including abused and neglected juveniles) extremely difficult. And some juvenile court judges who hear cases of suspected child abuse are hesitant to break up the family by removing the child to other circumstances—a trait not difficult to understand in light of the emphasis of most juvenile court acts on preserving the integrity of the family. It may be, however, that preserving the family also preserves child abuse and perpetuates violence on the part of some abused children as they grow into adulthood—not to mention the impact it has on direct and indirect costs related to child abuse and neglect. Gelles and Pearlman (2012) estimated the costs to be enormous—over $80 billion per year. Likewise, the Centers for Disease Control and Prevention (2012) estimates the costs of child abuse and neglect to be over $124 billion annually. Their report that looked at 579,000 confirmed child maltreatment cases included the following costs:

- The estimated average lifetime cost per victim of nonfatal child maltreatment includes
    - $32,648 in childhood health care costs
    - $10,530 in adult medical costs
    - $144,360 in productivity losses
    - $7,728 in child welfare costs
    - $6,747 in criminal justice costs
    - $7,999 in special education costs

- The estimated average lifetime cost per death includes
  - $14,100 in medical costs
  - $1,258,800 in productivity losses

High divorce rates, increasing numbers of stepparents, increasing numbers of children reported as abused, the development of coalitions against domestic violence, and changes in state statutes dealing with domestic violence all indicate that family life is often problematic and sometimes violent. Furthermore, child abuse is typically not a one-time event. Children who have been prior victims of maltreatment are more likely to experience a recurrence than those who have not been prior victims (Finkelhor et al., 2009; U.S. Department of Health and Human Services, 2012).

Nixzmary Brown's body lies in a casket at her wake at the Ortiz Funeral Home in New York on January 16, 2006. The abuse case was another in a string of incidents that forced Mayor Michael Bloomberg to call for investigations and legislative reforms.

Child Maltreatment

In 2014, an estimated 1,580 children died from abuse or neglect, an estimated 1.3% increase from 2010. More than 70% of child fatalities are children younger than 3 years of age (U.S. Department of Health and Human Services, 2016). These deaths are simply the tip of the iceberg. Children who are brain damaged or maimed are less visible but far more frequent. As in recent years, more than 75% of child victims suffer from neglect, 17% suffer from physical abuse, 8.3% suffer from sexual abuse, and 6.8% suffer from some other type of maltreatment such as psychological maltreatment or emotional abuse (U.S. Department of Health and Human Services, 2016).

Because of the seriousness and number of reports of child abuse and neglect, legislatures in all 50 states have enacted child abuse reporting laws. In Illinois, the Abused and Neglected Child Reporting Act (Illinois Compiled Statutes [ILCS], ch. 325, art. 5, sec. 5/1-11 [2010]) not only designates the state agency for investigating reports made under the act but also lists persons mandated to report such acts. In 2015, 48 states, the District of Columbia, American Samoa, Guam, the Northern Mariana Islands, Puerto Rico, and the Virgin Islands had statutes requiring mandated reporting of abuse by designated professionals in the medical, social service, school, and law enforcement fields (with typical mandated reporters including those listed in Figure 5.2) (Child Welfare Information Gateway, 2015).

Civil immunity for persons reporting in good faith as well as waiver of the spousal and physician–patient privilege is typically spelled out in these acts.

In general, child abuse occurs when a child under a specific age (typically 18 years) is maltreated by a parent, another immediate family member, or any person responsible for the child's welfare. Child maltreatment includes physical, sexual, and emotional abuse as well as physical, emotional, and educational neglect and is defined by the Child Abuse Prevention and Treatment Act (CAPTA) (42 U.S.C. §5101 [2010]) as including, at a minimum, the following:

Any recent act or failure to act on the part of a parent or caretaker which results in death, serious physical or emotional harm, sexual abuse or exploitation; or an act or failure to act, which presents an imminent risk of serious harm.

Individual states define the types of abuse and neglect in their statutes and may include more detailed definitions than that provided by CAPTA.

Physical Abuse

Although legal definitions of physical abuse are quite specific, it is important to realize that, in practical terms, what constitutes abuse differs considerably depending on time, place, and audience and that the line between abuse and discipline is often vague. Does spanking a 4-year-old with an open hand on the buttocks constitute child abuse? What if the child is 2 years of age? Suppose that a belt is used instead of the hand? Suppose that the child is struck on the torso instead of the buttocks? On the head? What kind of behavior are we talking about here? Most people in a given society can agree that certain behaviors are unreasonable—kicking, biting, cutting, burning, strangling, shooting, and so on—when it comes to dealing with children. Cases involving these behaviors are relatively clear-cut and, although not problem free, present the lowest degree of difficulty for intervening authorities. It is the more frequent, less clear-cut cases that are most difficult to resolve.

Figure 5.2 Common Mandated Reporters

Mandated Reporters Include the Following:

physicians	teachers
psychiatrists, surgeons	school personnel
residents	educational advocates assigned to a child pursuant to the School Code
interns	truant officers
dentists	directors and staff assistants of day care centers and nursery schools
dental hygienists	child care workers
medical examiners	truant officers
pathologists	probation officers
osteopaths	law enforcement officers
coroners	field personnel of the Departments of Children and Family Services, Public Health, Public Aid Human Services (acting as successor to the Department of Mental Health & Developmental Disabilities Rehabilitation Services, or Public Aid), Corrections and Human Rights
Christian Science practitioners	
chiropractors	
podiatrists	
registered and licensed practical nurses	
emergency medical technicians	
hospital administrators and other personnel involved in the examination, care or treatment of patients	

Source: Illinois Department of Children and Family Services (2009).

Physical abuse can be defined as any physical acts that cause or can cause physical injury to a child (Snyder & Sickmund, 1999). Physical abuse is often a vicious cycle involving parents with unrealistic expectations for their children, perhaps prior experiences as victims of abuse themselves, and often feelings of insecurity. The result is conflict between the two parties or perhaps parentally perceived conflict in the case of infants. For example, the parent wants a young child to eat nicely in the presence of guests. As is often the case with young children, the child does not eat, plays with his food, and eventually ends up wearing a good deal of it. The parent may regard this as a direct reflection of her child-rearing abilities and may discipline the unruly child as a result. The extent of discipline depends on the extent of anger and frustration present in the parent, the level of parenting skills involved, the age of the child, the nature of the audience, and so on. With older children who have clearly defined goals in the interactive process, the conflict may be more intentional, for example, when an adolescent chooses to go out with friends rather than respect her parents' wishes to stay home and clean her room. In the negotiations that follow, physical abuse is one of several options available to the parent and is more likely under certain circumstances. These circumstances often exist in situations where a teenage single parent attempts to raise a child (or children) in conditions bordering on poverty. The young parent might not have learned how to care for an infant, might not know what realistic expectations are for the child, and might be frustrated by needing to raise a dependent child alone, thereby reducing his or her own life chances. If the child fails to meet the expectations that the parent has established (or that have been mutually established in the case of older children), disappointment results. When this is expressed by the parent, it may lead to lower self-esteem on behalf of the child and then to underachievement and further failure to meet parental expectations. The parent, disappointed and fearing that he or she may be perceived as a failure, responds with emotional and/or physical abuse, and the cycle may begin again (Administration for Children and Families, 2008; Crosson-Tower, 1999; Cunningham, 2003; DePaul & Domenech, 2000; DiLillo, Tremblay, & Peterson, 2000; Pears & Capaldi, 2001, Widom & Maxfield, 2001).

It is important to point out that child abuse occurs among all social classes, genders, and racial and ethnic groups. Still, some researchers have found relationships between child abuse and factors such as the age of the mother and socioeconomic, educational, and employment factors as well as the individual characteristics of the child (Brown, Cohen, Johnson, & Salzinger, 1998; Cadzow, Armstrong, & Fraser, 1999; Finkelhor et al., 2009; Paxson & Waldfogel, 1999; Siegel, 2011; U.S. Department of Health and Human Services, 2016). "Parents who experience loneliness, lack social support, and are socially isolated may be more prone to neglecting their children than families who have a strong network of social supports" (Child Welfare Information Gateway, 2006, par. 24).

The American Association for Marriage and Family Therapy (2002) reported that children with disabilities are 4 times more likely to suffer abuse and neglect. According to the Children's Defense Fund (2006), poverty is the largest predictor of child abuse and neglect, although many states do not factor in economic resources when determining if abuse or neglect has occurred. In other words, poverty alone is not a valid reason for intervention by child protective services (CPS). An Arkansas statute, for example, states that a finding of neglect applies "except when the failure or refusal is caused primarily by the financial inability of the person legally responsible" for the child (Arkansas Code Ann.§ 12-12-503 [12][b] [2001]). Twelve other states and the District of Columbia provide exceptions for abuse and neglect based on financial inability to provide for a child (Child Welfare Information Gateway, 2016). Additionally, previous studies have shown that low-income and minority youth are more likely to have witnessed serious violence in their communities (Buka, Stichick, Birdthistle, & Felton, 2001). Only about 1% of upper- and middle-class youth have witnessed a murder, and 9% have witnessed a stabbing (Gladstein, Rusonis, & Heald, 1992; Kracke & Hahn, 2008), but 43% of low-income African American school-aged children have witnessed a murder, and 56% have witnessed a

Physical abuse of children must be taken seriously in the interests of both current and future generations.

stabbing (Fitzpatrick & Boldizar, 1993). In summary, abused and neglected children showed significantly lower levels of academic attainment in adulthood (Perez & Widom, 1994).

Child Neglect

Children experience neglect more than any other form of child maltreatment (U.S. Department of Health and Human Services, 2012, 2016). There is no federal definition of child neglect, but child neglect generally involves an individual under the age of 18 years whose parent, or another person responsible for the child's welfare, abandons the child or does not provide the proper or necessary support; education as required by law; or medical or other remedial care recognized under state law as necessary, including adequate food, shelter, and clothing. There are three types of neglect: (1) physical, (2) emotional, and (3) educational. Physical neglect includes abandonment; expulsion from the home ("throwaway child"); failure to seek medical help for the child; delay in seeking medical care; inadequate supervision; and inadequate food, clothing, and shelter. Emotional neglect includes inadequate nurturing or affection, permitting maladaptive behavior such as illegal drug or alcohol use, and inattention to emotional and developmental needs. Educational neglect happens when a parent or caretaker permits chronic truancy or ignores educational or special needs (Snyder & Sickmund, 1999). Although the impact of neglect may be less obvious than that of abuse, the long-term consequences for the child may be equally harmful (Brown et al., 1998), and families that have been identified by CPS as neglectful are significantly more likely to have a reoccurrence of neglect than those families involved in abuse (Child Welfare Information Gateway, 2006; U.S. Department of Health and Human Services, 2016).

Effects on the neglected child may include emotional, behavioral, and physical developmental delays, the juvenile may drop out of school, medical problems may ensue, and encounters with the juvenile and/or criminal justice system(s) may result.

Emotional Abuse of Children

Emotional abuse occurs in families where the children's opinions do not count or where they are never sought. It occurs in families where the adult members fail to spend quality time with their children and where children's requests are met with responses such as "not right now," "maybe later," "we'll see," and "after a while." This type of abuse occurs in families fighting for economic survival, in families where drugs and their pursuit are more important than children, and in dual-career families where there just never seems to be enough time to do things with the children, where the television or video game is a constant built-in babysitter, and where giving the latest toy or electronic game takes the place of giving time.

Some states include emotional or psychological abuse within the general definition of harm to a child that includes "mental injury." Typical language in these definitions includes "injury to the psychological capacity or emotional stability of the child as evidenced by an observable or substantial change in behavior, emotional response or cognition, or as evidenced by anxiety, depression, withdrawal or aggressive behavior" (Child Welfare Information Gateway, 2009). Although not all states specifically address psychological or emotional abuse in their codes, 33 states, the District of Columbia, Guam, the Northern Mariana Islands, and Puerto Rico do (Child Welfare Information Gateway, 2016). Alaska, Arizona, Arkansas, California, Colorado, Connecticut, Delaware, Florida, Hawaii, Idaho, Iowa, Kansas, Kentucky, Maine, Maryland, Massachusetts, Minnesota, Montana, Nevada, New Hampshire, New York, North Carolina, Ohio, Oregon, Pennsylvania, Rhode Island, South Carolina, South Dakota, Tennessee, Texas, Vermont, Wisconsin, and Wyoming all include definitions of emotional or psychological abuse (Child Welfare Information Gateway, 2009, 2016).

Even with emotional abuse defined in the statute, there is the opportunity for ambiguous definitions that do not apply well in practice and often preclude protective agencies from intervening in suspected emotional abuse cases (Hamarman & Bernet, 2000). Adding to this is the difficulty that exists in proving emotional abuse in court; some protective agencies are slow to react to psychological or emotional abuse accusations, choosing instead to focus resources on what is "seen" (physical injury) and what is morally unacceptable (sexual abuse) (Iwaniec, 2006).

Sexual Abuse of Children

Sexual abuse of a child is "involvement of the child in sexual activity to provide sexual gratification or financial benefit to the perpetrator, including contacts for sexual purposes, prostitution, pornography, or other sexually exploitative activities" (Snyder & Sickmund, 1999, p. 41). Twenty-one states include human trafficking, such as the sex trafficking of children, in their definitions of sexual abuse (Child Welfare Information Gateway, 2016). It usually involves a victim who is too young to understand the act as sexually gratifying and who experiences force or the threat of force prior to, during, or following the act. Under most statutes, it includes incest (sexual relations with family members), criminal sexual abuse, and criminal sexual assault. In general, criminal sexual abuse involves the intentional fondling of the genitals, anus, breasts, or any other part of the body, through the use of force or threat of force of a victim (child) unable to understand the nature of the act, for the purpose of sexual gratification. Criminal sexual assault involves contact with or intrusion into the sex organ, anus, mouth, or other body part by the sex organ of another, or some other object wielded by another, with accompanying force or threat of force or with a victim (child) unable to understand the nature of the act. Some states include sexual exploitation as an element or expanded statutory definition of sexual abuse. This includes allowing the child to engage in pornography or prostitution (Child Welfare Information Gateway, 2009, 2016).

Despite increasing numbers of child maltreatment reports during the 1990s, the percentage of reports that were child sexual abuse allegations decreased. Sexual abuse reports dropped from 16% of all child maltreatment reports in 1986 to an average of 8% of reports from 1996 to 1998 (Office of Juvenile Justice and Delinquency Prevention [OJJDP], 2001). This trend seems to be continuing in the 2000s with sexual abuse being the third highest reported type of abuse behind neglect and physical abuse. In both 2012 and

2016 reports, the U.S. Department of Health and Human Services reported that sexual abuse accounted for roughly 8% of all reported cases of abuse. Older children (12–15) were more likely to experience sexual abuse than younger children (U.S. Department of Health and Human Services, 2016). In most cases, the abuser is an adult male and the victim is a female child, but all other combinations are reported as well (Australian Bureau of Statistics [ABS], 2005; Lamont, 2011; McCloskey & Raphael, 2005; Peter, 2009; U.S. Department of Health and Human Services, 2016). Research has shown that more child sexual abuse offenses are committed by adults who are not in the caregiver role, which is contradictory to research on other forms of abuse (ABS, 2005; U.S. Department of Health and Human Services, 2005).

> Findings from the ABS Personal Safety Survey (2005) indicated that for participants who had experienced sexual abuse before the age of 15, only 13.5% identified that the abuse came from their father/stepfather, 30.2% was perpetrated by other male relative, 16.9% by family friend, 15.6% by acquaintance/neighbour and 15.3% by other known person. (Lamont, 2011, p. 3)

Perhaps as a consequence, it has been reported that girls in the juvenile justice system have high rates of past sexual abuse. Some support for this relationship was indicated in a study by Goodkind, Ng, and Sarri (2006), who found girls who had experienced sexual abuse had more negative mental health, school, substance use, risky sexual behavior, and delinquency outcomes. Whatever the gender of the child victim, when the offender is a parent, the nonoffending spouse is sometimes aware of the sexual abuse but does little to prevent it. For a variety of reasons, the nonoffending spouse may even take the side of the perpetrator, possibly defending the perpetrator's innocence in court.

In some instances, the offender is a pedophile who seeks out children for purposes of sexual gratification. Pedophilia is defined as an "on-going sexual attraction toward pre-pubertal children" (Tenbergen et al., 2015, p. 2). Such individuals may be relatives, friends, or strangers. Only about 50% of people who sexually abuse children are pedophiles (Tenbergen et al., 2015), and not every pedophile has sexually abused children. Although they frequently fail to develop meaningful sexual relationships with adults, pedophiles can be skillful predators when it comes to children. Table 5.2 shows the *DSM-5* definition and identifiers of pedophiles.

Table 5.2 Diagnostic Criteria of a Pedophilic Disorder According to *DSM-5*

DSM-5 Pedophilic Disorder	
Over a period of at least 6 months, recurrent, intense sexually arousing fantasies, sexual urges, or behaviors involving sexual activity with a prepubescent child or children (generally age 13 years or younger)	**Specify if:** Sexually attracted to males Sexually attracted to females Sexually attracted to both
The fantasies, sexual urges, or behaviors cause clinically significant distress or impairment in social, occupational, or other important areas of functioning	**Specify if:** Limited to incest
The person is at least age 16 years and at least 5 years older than the child or children in Criterion A	**Specify type:** Exclusive type (attracted only to children) Nonexclusive type

Source: Reprinted with permission from the *Diagnostic and Statistical Manual of Mental Disorders*, Fifth Edition (Copyright ©2013). American Psychiatric Association. All Rights Reserved.

Detection of child sexual abuse is difficult for a variety of reasons. First and foremost, sexual interaction with children is a very complex phenomenon. A great deal of ambiguity exists about what is and what is not appropriate behavior, especially in the mind of the child. In determining inappropriate behavior, we must ask this question: At what point does touching, fondling, kissing, and stroking become sexual? Cases that might appear clear-cut to an adult are often far less so to a child, particularly when the adult involved is an authority figure (parent) who assures the child that the behavior is okay if it is kept secret. Second, once the child begins to question the appropriateness of the sexual behavior, several difficult alternatives emerge. Does the child tell the nonoffending parent? Will that parent or any other adult believe the child? What will the adult to whom the report is made think of the child? What will happen to the child if the offending adult is arrested or, perhaps worse, confronted but not arrested? How important is the love of the offending adult to the child? Is the child in some way responsible for what has happened? These and other questions make it difficult for the child to disclose sexual behavior considered inappropriate and, therefore, make child sexual abuse difficult to detect. Clearly, many of these questions are related to the possibility of creating conflict within the interactive patterns of the family and a desire to avoid doing so.

Sometimes children do not perceive sexual acts by a member of the family or a family friend as abuse because children might not think that such a person can abuse them. At least two studies have found that the identity of the perpetrator makes a difference in whether sexual abuse is reported, finding that cases involving strangers are more likely to be reported than are those involving adults known to the children (Hanson, Resnick, & Saunders, 1999; Stroud, Martens, & Barker, 2000). Public exposure of such abuse may help to prevent further abuse, yet publicity, medical evaluation, court appearances, interviews by investigators, and unnecessary visibility might not be in the best interests of the children. Very young children do not know that incest is bad or wrong at the same level as do older children and adolescents (Yates & Comerci, 1985). A sense of guilt may develop, be buried in the subconscious of the child, and then surface during later years, often in the teens when the child is approaching adulthood. Acting-out behavior—running away, attempting suicide, engaging in self-mutilation, becoming sexually promiscuous, being on drugs, unhealthy diet-related behaviors, and having a high level of apathy—tends to occur more often among older children (Cyr, McDuff, Wright, Theriault, & Cinq-Mars, 2005; Centers for Disease Control and Prevention, 2016).

Internet Exploitation

No discussion of child abuse today is complete without considering Internet exploitation and its relationship to sexual abuse. Kloess, Beech, and Harkins (2014) reported that there is no agreed upon definition of Internet offending; however, it may include "exchanging child pornography; locating potential victims for sexual abuse; engaging in inappropriate sexual communication; and corresponding with other individuals who have a deviant sexual interest in children" (p. 126). Individuals engaged in Internet offending may use websites, chat rooms, newsgroups, discussion and bulletin boards, and e-mail (Durkin, 1997). As an example, BoyWiki, GirlWiki, and Boys in the Real World are websites that support pedophilia and may validate those individuals with a deviant sexual interest in children (Elliott & Ashfield, 2011; Kloess, Beech, & Harkins, 2014; Lambert & O'Halloran, 2008). To deter these types of websites and those individuals who may be searching for this type of information, the federal government has enacted legislation. "The PROTECT Our Children Act of 2008 requires that the Attorney General develop and implement a National Strategy for Child Exploitation Prevention and Interdiction (National Strategy). The first National Strategy was published in 2010" (U.S. Department of Justice, 2016, par. 1). In 2006, U.S. attorney general Alberto Gonzales noted that "we are in the midst of an epidemic of sexual abuse and exploitation of our children" (U.S. Department of Justice, 2006, par. 2). Unfortunately, he may be correct. According to a report by the Bureau of Justice Statistics (BJS) (2007), during 2006,

> 3,661 suspects were referred to U.S. attorneys for child sex exploitation offenses. Child pornography constituted 69% of referrals, followed by sex abuse (16%) and sex transportation (14%). Child pornography matters accounted for 82% of the growth in sex exploitation matters referred from 1994 to 2006. Sex transportation referrals accounted for 17% and sex abuse accounted for 1% of the growth over this period. (p. 1)

Most of the suspects charged by federal prosecutors were male and white and had attended some college. Further, more than one-half of the defendants had victims under the age of 12, and more than one-third (37%) were sentenced for having a victim in their custody, care, or supervision (BJS, 2007). Table 5.3 provides selected federal statutes on child Internet exploitation.

The Internet provides child sexual predators with a means of communicating and committing online victimization with unsuspecting youth. Figure 5.3 describes sexual online victimization, according to Wolak, Mitchell, and Finkelhor (2006). Because of its anonymity, rapid transmission, and often unsupervised nature, the Internet has become a medium of choice that predators use to contact juveniles and transmit and/or receive child pornography. Cyberspace provides child sexual predators with the opportunity to engage children in exchanges that can lead to personal questions designed to lure children into sexual conversations and sexual contact. It should be noted that not all children who are victimized via the Internet are innocent. Some are curious, rebellious, or troubled adolescents who are seeking sexual information or contact and are easily seduced and manipulated because they fail to fully understand or recognize the possible consequences of their actions (Armagh, 1998).

Table 5.3 Selected Federal Statutes on Child Internet Exploitation

Crime	Federal Statute
Child pornography	18 U.S.C. §§ 2251 & 2251A: Sexual exploitation of children and selling or buying of children 18 U.S.C. §§ 2252 & 2252A & 2252B: Production, distribution, and possession of child pornography 18 U.S.C. § 2260: Production of child pornography for importation into the United States
Sex abuse	18 U.S.C. § 2241: Aggravated sexual abuse 18 U.S.C. § 2242: Sexual abuse 18 U.S.C. § 2243: Sexual abuse of a minor or ward 18 U.S.C. § 2244: Abusive sexual contact
Transportation for illegal sexual activity	18 U.S.C. § 1591: Sex trafficking of children by force, fraud, or coercion 18 U.S.C. § 2422: Coercion and enticement 18 U.S.C. § 2423: Transportation of minors; includes engaging in illicit sexual conduct in foreign countries

Figure 5.3 What Is Online Victimization?

Sexual solicitations and approaches: Requests to engage in sexual activities or sexual talk or give personal sexual information including naked pictures that are unwanted or, whether wanted or not, made by an adult

Aggressive sexual solicitation: Sexual solicitations involving offline contact with the perpetrator through regular mail, by telephone, or in person or attempts or requests for offline contact

Unwanted exposure to sexual material: Without seeking or expecting sexual material, being exposed to pictures of naked people or people having sex when doing online searches, surfing the web, opening e-mail or instant messages, or opening links in e-mail or instant messages

Harassment: Threats or other offensive behavior (not sexual solicitation) sent online to the youth or posted online about the youth for others to see

Distressing incidents: Episodes where youth feel very or extremely upset or afraid as a result of the online contact

Source: Adapted and modified from Internet Crimes Against Children, U.S. Department of Justice, Office of Justice Programs.

Intervention

Child abuse cases have typically been difficult to litigate for several reasons, including the following:

- Establishing the competency and credibility of the child victim or witness

- Questions concerning the admissibility of the child's out-of-court statements

- Questions concerning the applicability of husband–wife, physician–patient, and clergy–penitent privileges

- The use of character witness evidence in the form of either evidence of prior acts of abuse or expert testimony on the "battered child" or "battering parent" syndrome

- The difficulty of the child victim confronting the alleged perpetrator in court

Intervention begins with someone reporting the abuse or suspected abuse, moves into the investigatory stage that typically involves a home visit and interviews with the parties involved, and then moves to risk assessment and a decision concerning what type of action to take. When charges appear to be substantiated, the question of removing the child from the home must be considered, as must the propriety of arresting the suspect(s). Sometimes a medical team becomes involved either as the result of emergency needs on behalf of the child or to attempt to determine whether abuse has occurred. If it is determined that abuse has occurred, the police and the investigator for the child protection agency involved take up the case and present it to the prosecutor for further action. Along the way, educators and mental health professionals often become involved as well in an attempt to ensure the well-being of the child (Crosson-Tower, 1999). Figure 5.4 provides a flowchart of the child welfare system.

Figure 5.4 The Child Welfare System

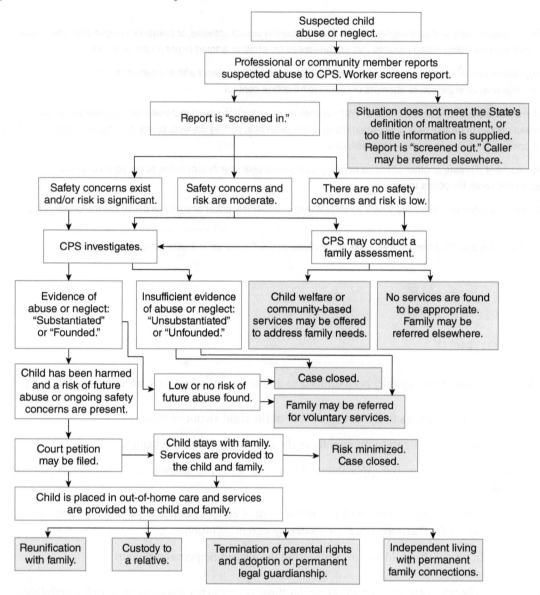

Source: Child Welfare Information Gateway (2013b).

In 1990, the U.S. Supreme Court gave tacit approval to procedures designed to protect the child victim in abuse cases. These procedures include the use of videotaped testimony, testimony by one-way closed-circuit television, and testimony by doctors and other experts in child abuse (Carelli, 1990). In 1992, the U.S. Supreme Court took another step in facilitating the intervention process. In *White v. Illinois* (1992), the Court affirmed the use of hearsay statements in child sexual abuse cases. In this case, the 4-year-old child victim did not testify, but others (her mother, a doctor, a nurse, and a police officer) to whom she had talked about the assault were allowed to testify.

In spite of court decisions and other attempts to improve the way we deal with abused children, a 2010 report to Congress on CPS investigations of abuse and neglect shows that CPS agencies investigate a minority of the cases identified as child maltreatment. Further, whether a case is investigated depends on the referring agency to CPS (e.g., police, schools, mental health services, hospitals), if CPS has sole responsibility for investigating the case (no police or mental health assistance), if CPS has alternative response mechanisms in place in their agency, and whether a report of abuse was combined with an ongoing case or placed as a new case. CPS investigated fewer referrals from schools than any other referring agency. Child Welfare Information Gateway (2016) reported:

> For FFY 2014, three-fifths (62.7 percent) of all reports of alleged child abuse or neglect were made by professionals. The term "professional" means that the person who was the source of the report had contact with the alleged child maltreatment victim as part of their job. The most common professional report sources were legal and law enforcement personnel (18.1 percent), education personnel (17.7 percent), social services staff (11.0 percent), and medical personnel (9.0 percent). Professionals have submitted more than one-half of all reports for the past 5 years. The remaining reports were made by nonprofessionals (18.6 percent), such as friends, neighbors, and relatives, and by unclassified reporters (18.7 percent), a category that includes anonymous and unknown reporters. (p. 2)

More and more police agencies are recognizing the importance of using specially trained investigators to conduct initial interviews with victims of abuse. Many investigations are now carried out jointly between the police and child protective agencies (Heck, 1999). Investigators have been briefed concerning the needs of all of the various agencies involved in such cases, eliminating the need for repeated interviews that sometimes result in conflicting testimony due to fear of the interviews themselves, poor recall, new settings for the interviews, and/or different responses to questions that are worded differently even though they are addressing the same issue.

Special investigative techniques have been used by police in the investigation of a form of child abuse known as Munchausen syndrome by proxy (MSBP). In this form of abuse, the abuser fabricates (or sometimes creates) an illness in the child victim. The child is then taken to a physician, usually by the mother, who knows that hospitalization for tests and observation is likely to be recommended because the symptoms are described as severe but no apparent cause exists. Tests, especially those that may be painful for the child, are welcomed by the apparently concerned parent. In addition, the parent may inject foreign substances (e.g., feces) into the hospitalized child, and there are documented reports of attempts by the parent to suffocate the hospitalized child. Perpetrators have been apprehended with the cooperation of medical staff members and the use of hidden video cameras, and prevention has been accomplished through placing the child in an open ward where medical staff members are in constant attendance. The former alternative is desirable because if the perpetrator is not arrested, she or he may relocate and further injure or kill the child (McMahon, 2002).

States are also realizing the importance of maintaining the family unit while investigating and working with families involved in abuse and neglect. Rather than the child protective agency investigator immediately removing a child suspected of being victimized, states are implementing differential or alternative responses that provide a continuum of services that attempt to work with parents as partners in identifying the needs and stressors of the family and in remedying the causes of the abuse and neglect. In differential or alternative responses, varied efforts to address the abuse and neglect are allowed depending on the type and severity of the alleged maltreatment, the number of previously reported incidents with the same family, the age of the child, and the willingness of parents to participate in services (Kaplan & Merkel-Holguin, 2008).

Examples of an alternative response may include providing one-time cash assistance to families who find themselves in need of extra money, purchasing a refrigerator for a family that cannot afford one even though the children are happy and well-cared for otherwise, or providing a life coach to a family working hard to get out of debt so that they can better provide for the needs of their children. The benefit of differential or alternative responses is that it allows protective services to be involved with the family while deterring abuse and neglect and keeping the child in the home with the mother and/or father and siblings.

In an attempt to curb Internet crimes against children, agencies like the National Center for Missing and Exploited Children are working with local, state, and federal organizations to stop the exploitation of children and locate missing children. Obviously, however, those in the best position to intervene in Internet-related activities are the parents of the children involved. By monitoring the Internet activities of their children, parents can identify and report suspicious contacts and can counsel young users as to the dangers inherent in certain types of websites and contacts.

Other prevention initiatives include child death review teams (consisting of experts with medical, social services, and/or law enforcement backgrounds), established in most states to review suspicious deaths of children, and statutory changes facilitating the prosecution of those involved in child maltreatment (Finkelhor & Ormrod, 2001b, p. 11).

Finally, legal alternatives are available at state and federal levels to prosecute those involved in child maltreatment. There are, for example, a number of federal statutes dealing with child abuse and exploitation (as noted in Table 5.3). To mention just a few others, 18 U.S.C. 1466A (2008) prohibits individuals from producing, receiving, distributing, or possessing any visual depiction of a minor engaged in sexual acts or sexually explicit conduct; 18 U.S.C. 1470 (2008) prohibits the transfer of obscene materials to anyone under the age of 16 through the mail or interstate or foreign commerce; 18 U.S.C. 1591 (2008) prohibits the sex trafficking of children by force, fraud, or coercion; 18 U.S.C. § 2422(b) (2003) prohibits engaging in any type of enticement or coercion of individuals under 18 years of age to engage in prostitution or other criminal sexual activity; and 18 U.S.C. § 2251A(a) (2003) prohibits parents or guardians from selling or transferring custody, or offering to do so, of minors knowing that the minors will be portrayed in a visual depiction of sexually explicit conduct. U.S. Immigration and Customs Enforcement has created a program called Operation Predator that has resulted in the arrest of over 8,000 child predators nationwide and closed several cases under Operation Sunflower, among others.

The Center for Children and Families provides therapeutic services for youth and their families of origin. Family Foundations is a subdivision of the center that provides aftercare services for youth who are released from state custody. Note the Family Justice Center sign farther back in the photo. The Family Justice Center provides services for victims of domestic violence. The two agencies are adjacent to one another and represent the partnering that is emphasized in this text.

Table 5.4 Operation Sunflower Closed Cases

BRUNSWICK, Ga. — On Nov. 15, HSI special agents rescued three abused children and arrested Stephen Keating, 52, of Jesup, Ga. In September, HSI's Cyber Crimes Center received a referral from Interpol after Danish police discovered child abuse material depicting two young girls being sexually abused by an adult male. On Nov. 14, the Cyber Crimes Center identified an Internet service connected to the Jesup residence and referred the case to HSI special agents in Savannah, Ga. HSI was assisted in this investigation by the U.S. Customs and Border Protection (CBP) Office of Field Operations in Savannah, CBP Air and Marine Operations in Jacksonville, Fla., the Georgia Bureau of Investigation, the U.S. Coast Guard Investigative Service and the Liberty County Sheriff's Office.
CLOVIS, Calif. — On Nov. 1, HSI special agents in Fresno, Calif., arrested Samuel Gueydan, 48, of Clovis, for distribution and possession of child pornography. A search of Gueydan's residence revealed that he was in possession of approximately 1.2 million still images, and over 7,000 videos of child pornography, including images known to have been produced in known source countries such as Russia, Thailand and Ukraine. In addition, he owned several hundred printed images of child pornography organized into books and catalogues. Gueydan was indicted by a federal grand jury in the Eastern District of California and has been ordered to home confinement under supervision while awaiting trial. Assisting HSI in the search warrant was the Fresno County Sheriff's Office, Clovis Police Department and California Department of Justice.
COLUMBUS, Ohio — On Nov. 8, HSI special agents in Columbus arrested Mickell E. Close, 31, of Quincy, Ohio, on charges of child pornography production, and rescued three children who Close secretly videotaped in a bathroom in order to create still photos and videos that he used to trade on the Internet for other images of child pornography. HSI was assisted by the Franklin County Internet Crimes Against Children Task Force and the Logan County Sheriff's Office.
DETROIT — On Nov. 27, HSI special agents in Detroit arrested Michael Wioskowski, 54, of Eastpointe, Mich., for possession and receipt of child pornography. He was indicted in the Eastern District of Michigan on the same day. During the execution of the search warrant, special agents discovered hidden video of two underage females using the shower in his residence. Wioskowski was employed as a court security officer in Macomb County and has previously held positions as a reserve police officer in Hamtramck, Mich., and as a security officer.
FRESNO, Calif. — On Nov. 6, HSI special agents in Fresno arrested Bradley Vaine, 26, of Fresno, for distribution and possession of child pornography and rescued a 7-year-old girl who had a severe mental disability. Vaine, a convicted sex offender, was charged Nov. 15 in a two-count federal indictment with possession and receipt of child pornography. He remains in federal custody at this time awaiting the outcome of his case. Additional potential charges are being pursued by the Fresno Police Department, which together with the Fresno County Sheriff's Office and Tulare Police Department, assisted HSI with the case.
HOUSTON — On Nov. 13, HSI special agents in Houston arrested William C. Noonan, 38, of Houston, for production, possession and distribution of child pornography and rescued two children in Dallas. Noonan was indicted in the Southern District of Texas Nov. 8 after a joint investigation with HSI Dallas that revealed he had engaged in the production of child pornography involving children ages 5 and 7. Search warrants executed in this case resulted in the discovery of 235 images of unidentified minor victims and 48 images related to the two victims identified and rescued. Noonan is a registered sex offender.
MYRTLE BEACH, S.C. — On Nov. 8, HSI special agents identified a 6-year-old victim of child pornography and arrested Gerald Roberts, 51, of Pageland, S.C., the man who allegedly victimized her to produce child pornography. HSI's Cyber Crimes Center had initiated a child victim identification effort in October based on images found on Internet websites known to host child pornography. Following an intensive investigation, special agents were able to identify both Roberts and the abused female child. Roberts is being prosecuted by the U.S. Attorney's Office for South Carolina.

(Continued)

Table 5.4 (Continued)

SAN FRANCISCO — On Nov. 8, HSI special agents in San Francisco arrested Michael Lindsay, 53, of San Jose, Calif., a U.S. citizen, for engaging in child sex tourism. Lindsay was arrested as he was boarding a flight from San Francisco International Airport to Manila, Philippines. The arrest was pursuant to an investigation initiated by HSI Manila into allegations of sex tourism activities. On Sept. 4, the subject arrived at the San Francisco International Airport from Manila, where a complaint had been filed by Philippine prosecutors that alleged Lindsay had sexual contact with a 13-year-old girl. HSI continues to search for additional victims as evidence suggests Lindsay may have had sexual contact with additional children.
SPRINGFIELD, Ill. — On Nov. 15, Ann Marie Piper, 48, was sentenced in the Central District of Illinois to 25 years in federal prison and a lifetime of supervised release for her involvement in the production and distribution of child pornography. The images that led to Piper's arrest in Springfield in May 2012 were first discovered by HSI special agents in Oregon in October 2011 in an unrelated case. The images, depicting an adult woman sexually abusing a child, were submitted to the National Center for Missing & Exploited Children (NCMEC). NCMEC examined the files, both abuse and non-abuse material, and discovered clues in one of the non-abuse images that would later lead to the victim's rescue and Piper's arrest: a photo of the two of them by a lake at an outdoor camp site. Clues in the photo led investigators to the site of the photo, a resort in Richville, Minn., and ultimately to Piper in Peoria, Ill.

Source: U.S. Immigration and Customs Enforcement (2012).

Table 5.5 National Child Exploitation Threat Assessment 2010 Key Areas of Focus

Child pornography	• Globalization. Child pornography cases frequently involve offenders or evidence located abroad, which complicates, delays, or thwarts successful investigation and prosecution.
	• Mobile devices. Mobile devices can be used to photograph or film a child being sexually abused, access child pornography stored in remote locations, and stream video of child sexual abuse.
	• Encryption. Readily available, easy-to-use, often built-in encryption thwarts the collection and analysis of critical evidence in child sexual exploitation cases. Even with proper legal process, law enforcement often is unable to obtain the evidence on an encrypted device, allowing an offender to escape justice.
	• The Dark Internet. Networks of technologies and platforms can obfuscate traditional IP addresses and make it highly difficult to identify offenders. This anonymity emboldens users to commit more egregious offenses than are seen on traditional Internet platforms.
	• Offender communities. In closed and highly protected online spaces, online communities dedicated to the sexual abuse of children have proliferated. Handpicked members normalize each other's sexual interest in children and encourage each other to act on their deviant sexual interests.
Sextortion and live-streaming of child sexual abuse	• Evolving threats. Novel methods of child sex abuse, such as sextortion, continue to emerge in the online context.
	• Evolving means of exploitation. Mobile devices have fundamentally changed the way offenders can abuse children. Apps on these devices can be used to target, recruit or groom, and coerce children to engage in sexual activity.
	• Large number of victims, easily targeted. Offenders are adept at tricking and/or coercing children who are online and typically do so in large numbers.

Child sex trafficking	• The impact of the Internet. Websites like Backpage.com have emerged as a primary vehicle for the advertisement of children to engage in prostitution. At the same time, offenders are using social networking sites as a tool to identify and recruit underage victims.
	• Gangs. In addition to, or instead of, the drug trade, gang members have begun to prostitute children as a means to derive revenue.
	• Concentrated spikes in criminal activity. Major public events, such as championship or all-star sporting events or national conferences, can be venues for child sex trafficking such that offenders will transport children to those events to meet the demand.
	• Offender danger. Unlike other child sex offenders, child sex traffickers typically have extensive criminal histories for a variety of violent offenses.
Child sex tourism	• Exploitation of systemic vulnerabilities. U.S. citizens, often with seemingly legitimate reasons for travel, seek sex with children in countries with high levels of poverty, large populations of at-risk youth, legalized prostitution, and/or fewer law enforcement resources.
Sex offender registry violations	• Deliberate evasion. Sex offenders who fail to register are often trying to evade their registration obligations so that they can offend again.

Source: U.S. Department of Justice (2016).

Examples of closed cases from Operation Sunflower are discussed in Table 5.4. The Federal Bureau of Investigation and the National Center for Missing and Exploited Children have also joined forces to target child trafficking. During Operation Cross Country X that ran from October 13 to 16, 2016, 82 minors were rescued and 239 traffickers and their associates were arrested by the FBI. In Practice 5.1 provides news releases from this operation. Further, the National Child Exploitation Threat Assessment 2010 National Strategy identified key areas where efforts to prevent exploitation will focus. Table 5.5 discusses these areas.

It would be inappropriate to conclude our discussion of violence against juveniles without emphasizing the difficulties involved in dealing with them as victims. Effective advocacy for such juveniles is imperative for a variety of reasons. First, as we have seen, they are often ashamed and unable or afraid to tell anyone about their plights. In many cases, even though they are being regularly and severely abused, children will not tell others because of the fear (sometimes instilled by their abusers) that their parents will be taken away from them if they do seek help. For many young children, this prospect is more frightening than their fear of continued abuse. Second, in many cases that do reach the courts, children are unable to testify effectively due to fear and/or inability to express themselves adequately. There are now adequate means available to deal with this problem, but these means are of little value unless they are recognized and used. Third, even when children are able to express themselves adequately, perhaps as a result of the hesitancy to break up families (discussed earlier), judges or children and family services officials might not remove juveniles from their homes. Even where there is evidence of abuse based on the testimony of teachers, caseworkers, and physicians, children have been returned to the homes in which they were being abused. To avoid such occurrences, it is crucial that the rights of child abuse victims be ensured by making certain that the children have proper representation and counseling and that their testimony is taken seriously. A study in Denver revealed that less than 3% of the allegations of sexual abuse made by children were demonstrated to be erroneous. The conclusion of the authors was that erroneous concerns about sexual abuse by children are rare (Oates et al., 2000), yet the fear of an erroneous accusation may keep some children and others from coming forward to authorities when abuse is suspected.

Because state agencies, law enforcement, and the court system cannot ensure that the full range of services are provided to meet the needs of children who are victimized, a number of nongovernmental organizations (NGOs), as nonprofits, have emerged to address these needs. These organizations often use community resources to optimize the opportunities that can be provided for youth. One such organization, the Center for Children and Families, is an example of a nonprofit agency that works to provide a comprehensive set of services. The Center for Children and Families includes a program known as Family Foundations that provides assistance for youth who are released from juvenile detention and are reintegrated with their families. In many cases, these youth have been abused or come from dysfunctional family systems. Family Foundations (2007) provides parenting education to families involved in their program while also working with juveniles who have been abused or neglected.

IN PRACTICE 5.1

FBI ANNOUNCES RESULTS OF OPERATION CROSS COUNTRY X

Child Sex Trafficking Crackdown Spreads to International Stage in 2016

The Federal Bureau of Investigation, along with representatives from the National Center for Missing and Exploited Children (NCMEC) and several international law enforcement partners, today announced that, domestically, 82 minors were rescued and 239 traffickers and their associates were arrested as part of Operation Cross Country X, an international effort focusing on underage human trafficking that ran from October 13 to 16, 2016. FBI Director James Comey and NCMEC Director John Clark announced the results of Operation Cross Country X today at the International Association of Chiefs of Police (IACP) convention in San Diego, California.

This is the 10th iteration of the FBI-led initiative, which took place across the United States and, for the first time, also in several countries around the world. Law enforcement partners from Cambodia, Canada, the Philippines, and Thailand had operations in their respective countries. In Canada, as part of a corresponding effort called Northern Spotlight, authorities recovered 16 children, while in Cambodia, Thailand, and the Philippines, authorities recovered 25 children, including a 2-year-old girl.

"Operation Cross Country aims to shine a spotlight into the darkest corners of our society that seeks to prey on the most vulnerable of our population," said FBI Director Comey. "As part of this effort, we are not only looking to root out those who engage in the trafficking of minors, but through our Office for Victim Assistance, we offer a lifeline to minors to help them escape from a virtual prison no person ever deserves."

Operations took place in a number of locations, including hotels, truck stops, and street corners. Minors recovered during an arrest are engaged with state protective services and victim assistance. Depending on the level of need, a law enforcement officer and, if available, an FBI victim specialist will accompany the survivor to obtain these services.

"Child sex trafficking is a global problem and we must throw every resource we can at combating it," said NCMEC Director John Clark. "All of us at the National Center for Missing and Exploited Children are proud to work side by side with the FBI and their law enforcement partners as we work tirelessly every day to find and rescue child victims and while ensuring that those responsible for this horrible crime are held accountable."

Operation Cross Country X is the largest ever in the history of the initiative, with 55 FBI field offices and 74 Child Exploitation Task Forces representing more than 400 law enforcement organizations taking part in the operation.

In addition, several dozen operations across Canada, and approximately 10 operations took place in six cities across Cambodia, Thailand, and the Philippines.

"The IACP is proud of the work of the FBI and the many agencies that have committed resources to Operation Cross Country," said IACP 1st Vice President Chief Donald W. De Lucca, Doral, Florida Police Department. "Child sex trafficking involves a number of complex crimes requiring law enforcement to collaborate with multiple law enforcement agencies and community partners to identify and respond to child victims, while holding accountable those who are responsible for their exploitation. We are committed to tackling this crime together because no one single agency, no single department, no single squad can attack this problem alone. It is too large, it is too prevalent, and it is too important."

Operation Cross Country X is part of the FBI's Innocence Lost Initiative, which began in 2003 and has yielded more than 6,000 child identifications and locations. For additional information on Operation Cross Country X and the Innocence Lost initiative, please visit fbi.gov.

Examples of stories from various cities that took part in Operation Cross Country X follow.

Milwaukee Division

Through a website advertisement, an undercover agent went to a home where two children, aged 16 and 17, were recovered. The girls indicated they were sisters and were being pimped out by their mother. The girls also informed authorities that their mother was allegedly renting out the girls' brother's room to a man who was a registered sex offender.

Atlanta Division

Authorities arrested two adults (prostitute and pimp) after pursing a lead that appeared to offer the services of juveniles. While there were no juveniles present, the two arrested both had active warrants related to first-degree murder, human trafficking of a child, procuring a minor

for prostitution, racketeering, and possession and transmission of child pornography. The adult prostitute and pimp were subjects out of Orlando. They, along with two other individuals, are alleged to have trafficked two juvenile females (14 and 15 years old), forcing them into prostitution and providing them with drugs. The 14-year-old was later found dead of an overdose.

Detroit Division

Federal and local law enforcement recovered a 17-year-old girl who had been reported from her placement by the state. The girl, who was recovered as part of Cross Country IX last year, was found after investigators saw an ad with her real photo on a website advertising sexual services. An undercover investigator made arrangements to meet the girl and recovered her when she arrived at the hotel. During an interview with investigators, she indicated another juvenile female was located in a vehicle waiting outside. A surveillance team located the second juvenile (also 17 years old) in a vehicle engaged in illicit acts with a male. Both girls admitted to being trafficked by the same female suspect. The two girls lived at home with one of their mothers and the female suspect.

Thailand

The TICAC, a task force composed of the Royal Thai Police and the Police and the Department of Special Investigation, arrested an American in Thailand. The registered sex offender is alleged to have coerced five juvenile Filipino females, ages 14 to 16, to take illicit photos of themselves and send them to him via the Internet. TICAC will continue the investigation, as there may be more victims who have had contact with the American.

Philippines

During operations in the Philippines, local law enforcement recovered two boys, ages five and 11, and one girl from a location being used to house a website-based service. The girl was 2 years old. Authorities arrested five adults who

(Continued)

ran a web-streaming service for individuals who would pay for access to livestreaming sexual abuse, as well as access to the children for purpose of illegal sexual acts. The investigation continues to identify additional suspects.

Source: Federal Bureau of Investigation (2016g).

Questions to Consider

1. True or False: The Federal Bureau of Investigation has completed 16 operations targeting child trafficking and exploitation.

2. Multiple Choice: The youngest victim reported to have been rescued by the operations was how old?

   a. 2 years old

   b. 7 years old

   c. 10 years old

   d. 16 years old

3. Thinking in terms of legal limitations, what challenges might the Federal Bureau of Investigation face in working with international governments to identify trafficked children? Identify at least three challenges.

Several of the theories discussed in Chapter 4 may be used to explain child abuse and neglect. Feminism contends that girls and women are frequently victims not only of violence and aggression but also of the justice system itself. Psychological theories, strain theory, conflict theory, and a variety of other approaches may be used to describe and explain abuse/neglect as well.

If some parents are bent on destroying their own children, it is imperative that the state exercise the right of *parens patriae* to protect such children. Last but not least, the state should proceed as rigorously as possible in the prosecution of abusers, if only to prevent them from abusing their own spouses or children again. Stopping this abuse can prevent victimization that might be repeated in the future. Thus, when we prevent child abuse now, we are likely saving would-be victims for generations to come.

CAREER OPPORTUNITY: FOSTER CARE PLACEMENT SPECIALIST

Job description: These individuals work for state CPS agencies by providing stable family environments for children brought into foster care. They are responsible for visiting foster homes, supervising visits between children and their parent(s), testifying in court about the status of the case, and working with foster children and families involved in foster care. Foster care specialists may also provide travel and transportation for foster children.

Employment requirements: Requires a minimum of a bachelor's degree in a social science with a preference in social work. Most agencies also prefer someone with casework experience and/or who interned at a CPS agency. Experience with children and good organization and communication skills are ideal.

Beginning salary: Salary ranges from $29,000 to $33,000 yearly. Benefits are provided according to the state benefit program, which usually includes health and life insurance, paid vacations and holidays, and retirement programs.

Summary

With respect to violence committed against juveniles, we must be aware that the incidence of such violence is great even by the most conservative estimates. All suspected cases should be treated as serious and given immediate attention so as to protect the juveniles involved, to prevent the juveniles from learning violent behavior that they may duplicate later in life, and to attempt to seek treatment or prosecution of the offenders.

Although family integrity is important, maintaining such integrity in cases of domestic violence or child abuse may be less important than saving lives or limbs (of either children or parents). Most states now have in place legislation that enables the state to protect children from abuse, but many practitioners remain hesitant to take official action that would break up the involved families. One need only read any newspaper with a large circulation to note the sometimes deadly consequences of failure to remove abused children from the homes of abusers. The failure to remove abused children from the homes in which they are abused is sometimes rationalized by pointing to the uncertainty of appropriate foster home or shelter care placement. Although it is true that such placement is sometimes problematic, leaving a child who has been, or is being, physically or sexually abused in the home of the abuser is unconscionable. It requires clear guidelines and good common sense on behalf of those working protective agencies to know when differential or alternative responses are appropriate and when removal of the child from the home is necessary.

Violence against juveniles has received considerable attention over the past two decades. Even though violence committed against juveniles appears to be declining in the United States, it is still considered an epidemic by some. Clearly, child abuse in its various forms is a relatively common occurrence, although it is likely that only a small proportion of abuse cases are reported or discovered. Child abuse is particularly alarming because of the physical and psychological damage done to children, because most research indicates that at least some parents who were abused as children go on to abuse their own children or to become criminals, and because, in spite of numerous programs designed to help prevent or halt child abuse, child abuse is by nature difficult to detect and control.

KEY TERMS

Abused and Neglected Child Reporting Act 123	family violence 118	pedophile 128
child death review teams 134	human trafficking 127	pedophilia 128
child neglect 120	Internet exploitation 129	sexual abuse 123
criminal sexual abuse 127	Internet offending 129	sexual exploitation 127
criminal sexual assault 127	intervention 125	types of neglect 126
emotional or psychological abuse 127	Munchausen syndrome by proxy (MSBP) 133	White v. Illinois 132

Critical Thinking Questions

1. Thinking of the What Would You Do? scenario at the start of the chapter, how might the cycle of violence explain the incident?

2. How much progress have we made in dealing with those who abuse children? In protecting children from abuse? How has the Internet affected our ability to protect children from sexual exploitation?

3. What recommendations would you make to a parent of a teenager with regard to the Internet? How might this parent protect his or her child from online harassment? Or online exploitation?

4. Suppose you are a CPS worker and you receive a report that a single mother is neglecting her two children. Upon an investigation in the home, you find that there are cats and dogs who come in and out of the home freely, animal feces is present on the floor and is not being cleaned up quickly, there are cigarette butts on the floor, and there is a noticeable number of roaches. There is very little furniture, and the two children share a mattress in the bedroom. The children are happy, not abused in another way, and well fed. What is your response to the situation? Would you remove the children from the home? What differential or alternative responses might resolve this case?

Suggested Readings

Administration for Children and Families. (2008). *Child maltreatment 2008*. U.S. Department of Health and Human Services. Retrieved from www.acf.hhs.gov/programs/cb/pubs/cm08/figure3_5.htm

Australian Bureau of Statistics. (2005). *Personal Safety Survey Australia* (Cat No. 4906.0). Canberra, Australia: ABS. Retrieved from http://www.abs.gov.au/AUSSTATS/abs@.nsf/DetailsPage/4906.02005%20(Reissue)

Baum, K. (2005). *Juvenile victimization and offending, 1993–2003*. Washington, DC: U.S. Department of Justice, Office of Justice Programs, Bureau of Justice Statistics.

Bureau of Justice Statistics. (2005). *Family violence statistics: Including statistics on strangers and acquaintances*. Washington, DC: Office of Justice Programs. Retrieved from www.bjs.gov/content/pub/pdf/fvs02.pdf

Bureau of Justice Statistics. (2007). *Federal prosecution of child sexual exploitation offenders, 2006*. Washington, DC: U.S. Department of Justice, Office of Justice Programs, Bureau of Justice Statistics. Retrieved from https://www.bjs.gov/content/pub/pdf/fpcseo06.pdf

Centers for Disease Control and Prevention. (2016). *Sexual violence: Consequences*. Washington, DC: National Center for Injury Prevention and Control. Retrieved from https://www.cdc.gov/violenceprevention/sexualviolence/consequences.html

Child Welfare Information Gateway. (2006). *Child neglect: A guide for prevention, assessment and intervention*. Retrieved from www.childwelfare.gov/pubs/usermanuals/neglect/chaptersix.cfm

Child Welfare Information Gateway. (2009). *Definitions of child abuse and neglect: Summary of state laws*. Retrieved from www.childwelfare.gov/systemwide/laws_policies/statutes/define.cfm

Child Welfare Information Gateway. (2013a). *Child maltreatment 2011: Summary of key findings*. Washington, DC: U.S. Department of Health and Human Services, Children's Bureau. Retrieved from www.childwelfare.gov/pubs/factsheets/canstats.pdf#Page=2&view=What%20Were%20the%20Most%20Common%20Types%20of%20Maltreatment?

Child Welfare Information Gateway. (2013b). *How the child welfare system works*. Washington, DC: U.S. Department of Health and Human Services. Retrieved from www.childwelfare.gov/pubs/factsheets/cpswork.pdf#page=3&view=What%20Happens%20When%20Possible%20Abuse%20or%20Neglect%20Is%20Reported

Durkin, K. F. (1997). Misuse of the Internet by pedophiles: Implications for law enforcement and probation practice. *Federal Probation, 61*, 14–18.

Elliott, I. A., & Ashfield, S. (2011). The use of online technology in the modus operandi of female sex offenders. *Journal of Sexual Aggression, 17*, 1–13.

Finkelhor, D. (2008). *Childhood victimization: Violence, crime, and abuse in the lives of young people*. New York, NY: Oxford University Press.

Finkelhor, D., Turner, H., Ormrod, R., Hamby, S., & Kracke, K. (2009). *Children's exposure to violence: A comprehensive national survey*. Washington, DC: Office of Juvenile Justice and Delinquency Prevention, Office of Justice Programs. Retrieved from www.ncjrs.gov/pdffiles1/ojjdp/227744.pdf

Goldman, J., Salus, M. K., Wolcott, D., & Kennedy, K. Y. (2003). *A coordinated response to child abuse and neglect: The foundation for practice*. Washington, DC: Child Welfare Information Gateway. Retrieved from www.childwelfare.gov/pubs/usermanuals/foundation/foundationf.cfm

Goodkind, S., Ng, I., & Sarri, R. C. (2006). The impact of sexual abuse in the lives of young women involved or at risk of involvement with the juvenile justice system. *Violence Against Women, 12*, 456–477.

Iwaniec, D. (2006). *The emotionally abused and neglected child: Identification, assessment and intervention: A practice handbook* (2nd ed.). New York, NY: Wiley.

Jones, L. M., Mitchell, K. J., & Finkelhor, D. (2012). Trends in youth Internet victimization: Findings from three youth Internet safety surveys 2000–2010. *Journal of Adolescent Health, 50*, 179–186.

Kaplan, C., & Merkel-Holguin, L. (2008). Another look at the national study on differential response in child welfare. *Protecting Children, 23*(1/2), 5–21.

Kracke, K., & Hahn, H. (2008). The nature and extent of childhood exposure to violence: What we know, why we don't know more, and why it matters. *Journal of Emotional Abuse, 8*(1/2), 29–49.

Lamont, A. (2011, February). *Who abuses children?* National Child Protection Clearinghouse. Retrieved from www.aifs.gov.au/nch/pubs/sheets/rs7/rs7.pdf

McCloskey, K., & Raphael, D. (2005). Adult perpetrator gender asymmetries in child sexual assault victim selection: Results from the 2000 National Incident-Based Reporting system. *Journal of Child Sexual Abuse, 14*(4), 1–24.

Pears, K. C., & Capaldi, D. M. (2001). Intergenerational transmission of abuse: A two-generational prospective study of an at-risk sample. *Child Abuse & Neglect, 25*, 1439–1461.

Peter, T. (2009). Exploring taboos: Comparing male- and female-perpetrated child sexual abuse. *Journal of Interpersonal Violence, 24*(7), 1111–1128.

Rennison, C. M. (2003, February). *Intimate partner violence, 1993–2001* (NCJ 197838). Crime Data Brief, Bureau of Justice Statistics. Washington, DC: U.S. Department of Justice. Retrieved from https://www.bjs.gov/content/pub/pdf/ipv01.pdf

Sedlak, A. J., Mettenburg, J., Basena, M., Petta, I., McPherson, K., Greene, A., & Li, S. (2010). *Fourth national incidence study of child abuse and neglect (NIS–4): Report to Congress.* Washington, DC: U.S. Department of Health and Human Services, Administration for Children and Families.

Seigel, J. A. (2011). *Disrupted childhoods: Children of women in prison.* New Brunswick, NJ: Rutgers University Press.

Smart, C. (2000). Reconsidering the recent history of child sexual abuse, 1910–1960. *Journal of Social Policy, 29*(1), 55–71.

Tjaden, P., & Thoennes, N. (2000, November). *Full report of the prevalence, incidence, and consequences of violence against women: Findings from the National Violence Against Women Survey. Research Report* (NCJ 183781). Washington, DC, and Atlanta, GA: U.S. Department of Justice, National Institute of Justice, and U.S. Department of Health and Human Services, Centers for Disease Control and Prevention.

U.S. Department of Health and Human Services. (2012). *Child maltreatment 2011.* Washington, DC: U.S. Department of Health and Human Services, Administration for Children and Families, Children's Bureau. Retrieved from www.acf.hhs.gov/sites/default/files/cb/cm11.pdf#page=57

U.S. Department of Justice. (2012). *Report of the attorney general's national task force on children exposed to violence.* Washington, DC: Office of Juvenile Justice and Delinquency Prevention, Office of Justice Programs, U.S. Department of Justice. Retrieved from https://www.justice.gov/defendingchildhood/cev-rpt-full.pdf

Wolak, J., Mitchell, K., & Finkelhor, D. (2006). *Online victimization of youth: Five years later.* Washington, DC: National Center for Missing & Exploited Children. Retrieved from www.missingkids.com/en_US/publications/NC167.pdf

$SAGE edge™

Sharpen your skills with SAGE edge at **edge.sagepub.com/coxjj9e**. SAGE edge for students provides a personalized approach to help you accomplish your coursework goals in an easy-to-use learning environment. You'll find action plans, mobile-friendly eFlashcards, and quizzes as well as video and web resources and links to SAGE journal articles to support and expand on the concepts presented in this chapter.

Purpose and Scope of Juvenile Court Acts

6

WHAT WOULD YOU DO?

You have a 16-year-old son attending the 10th grade. He is enrolled in a charter school that has rules on behavior as well as academic progress. He has never been a dedicated student, having failed the 2nd grade, but he has maintained a low C average most semesters. His grades this year have been in the D and F range. He isn't willing to repeat work to bring up the scores and has been purposefully violating the rules of the school. For instance, he wears boots when he's not supposed to, wears unauthorized uniform pants, hugs people longer than he should in the hallway, and refuses to sit down in the lunchroom on some occasions. These violations have resulted in numerous in-school suspensions and expulsions and a general dislike of him by teachers and school administrators. For the most part, your son is a loving child. He hasn't broken any laws to your knowledge or skipped school. He is, however, a typical teenager who challenges your authority and has a bad attitude about most things you ask him to do. You've caught him smoking vapor cigarettes, and another mother reported to you that he and her son had tried to buy marijuana. Lately, he has been expelled from school more than he's been present. He's told you that he wants to get his GED so that he can stop going to school and move out of your house. He has also said he will run away if you don't allow him to take the exam for the GRE. He hasn't challenged you in a physical manner yet, but there have been two recent occasions where he refused to back down and approached you in an aggressive way while you were correcting his behavior. When you didn't flinch or back down, he finally moved away and sulked to his room.

Since the inception of the juvenile court in 1899, some critics have argued that the court ought to be abandoned. Some believe that the court is now far removed from the original concepts on which it was based or too limited in scope to be viable today. Others believe that it is currently incapable of meeting the purposes for which it was created. In this chapter, we review the purpose and scope of a variety of juvenile court acts in terms of both constitutional requirements and legislative differences among several states.

Every juvenile court act contains sections that discuss purpose and scope. The purpose statement of a juvenile court act spells out the intent or basic philosophy of the act. The scope of a juvenile court act is indicated by sections dealing with definitions, age, jurisdiction, and waiver. In this chapter, we discuss and refer to the Uniform Juvenile Court Act (National Conference of Commissioners on Uniform State Laws, 1968), which was developed in an attempt to encourage uniformity of purpose, scope, and procedures in the juvenile justice network. (A copy of the act is included in the appendix.) For purposes of comparison, sections of various state juvenile codes are presented and analyzed. Revisions of most states' juvenile court acts are now in accord with the recommendations of the Uniform Juvenile Court Act.

States customize their juvenile court acts to meet their own needs, and revisions occur on a continuous basis. With this in mind, we have used recent statutes from a variety of states to illustrate different points throughout the text, and we encourage those using the text to seek out statutes relating to juvenile justice from states in which they reside or have a special interest. You can use the Internet to find state-specific juvenile court acts.

Purpose

As indicated previously, the first juvenile court act in the United States was passed in Illinois in 1899. By 1945, all U.S. states had juvenile court acts within their statutory enactments or constitutions (Tappan, 1949). Juvenile court acts typically authorize the creation of a juvenile court with the legal power to hear designated kinds of cases such as delinquency, neglect, abuse, and dependency cases as well as other special cases numerated in the acts.

Typically, a juvenile court act establishes both procedural and substantive law relative to juveniles within the court's jurisdiction. Historically, the law was administered in a general atmosphere of rehabilitation and parental concern rather than with punitive overtones. Table 6.1 provides information on purpose clauses found in states' juvenile court acts. Some declare their goals and objectives in exhaustive detail; others mention only the broadest of aims. More than one philosophy can guide a state juvenile court act. Juvenile court proceedings were originally conceptualized as civil, not criminal, proceedings (Davis, 2001, sec. 1.3). As a result of reformers' interests in divorcing the juvenile court from the criminal court in 1899, a separate nomenclature was developed based on the philosophy underlying juvenile courts as opposed to criminal courts. This nomenclature is still followed today in spite of the get-tough approach that has been suggested for serious delinquents.

Table 6.1 Purpose Clauses for Juvenile Court, 2012

State	Balanced and Restorative Justice	Standard Juvenile Court Act	Legislative Guide	Emphasis on Punishment, Deterrence, Accountability, and/or Public Safety	Child Welfare
Number of states	21	20	11	6	5
Alabama	X				
Alaska	X				
Arizona					X
Arkansas		X	X		
California	X	X			
Colorado	X				
Connecticut				X	
Delaware		X			
District of Columbia	X				
Florida	X	X			
Georgia		X			
Hawaii				X	
Idaho	X				
Illinois	X	X			
Indiana	X				
Iowa		X			
Kansas	X				
Kentucky					X
Louisiana		X			
Maine		X	X		
Maryland	X				
Massachusetts		X			X
Michigan		X			
Minnesota	X	X			
Mississippi		X			

State	Balanced and Restorative Justice	Standard Juvenile Court Act	Legislative Guide	Emphasis on Punishment, Deterrence, Accountability, and/or Public Safety	Child Welfare
Missouri		X			
Montana	X		X		
Nebraska	X				
Nevada		X			
New Hampshire			X		
New Jersey	X	X	X		
New Mexico			X		
New York		X			
North Carolina				X	
North Dakota					X
Ohio			X		
Oklahoma	X				
Oregon	X				
Pennsylvania	X				
Rhode Island		X			
South Carolina		X			
South Dakota		X			
Tennessee			X		
Texas			X	X	
Utah				X	
Vermont	X				
Virginia			X		
Washington	X				
West Virginia					X
Wisconsin	X				
Wyoming			X	X	

(Continued)

Table 6.1 (Continued)

- The juvenile court purpose clause in at least 20 states and the District of Columbia incorporates the language of the balanced and restorative justice movement, which advocates that juvenile courts give balanced attention to three primary interests: public safety, individual accountability to victims and the community, and the development in offenders of those skills necessary to live law-abiding and productive lives.

- The purpose clauses in at least 20 states appear to be influenced by the Standard Juvenile Court Act. The purpose of this act, originally issued in 1925 and subsequently revised numerous times, was that "each child coming within the jurisdiction of the court shall receive . . . the care, guidance, and control that will conduce to his welfare and the best interest of the state, and that when he is removed from the control of his parents the court shall secure for him care as nearly as possible equivalent to that which they should have given him."

- Other states use all or most of a more elaborate, multipart purpose clause contained in the *Legislative Guide for Drafting Family and Juvenile Court Acts*, a publication issued by the Children's Bureau in the late 1960s. The legislative guide's opening section declares four purposes: (a) to provide for the care, protection, and wholesome mental and physical development of children involved with the juvenile court; (b) to remove from children committing delinquent acts the consequences of criminal behavior, and to substitute therefore a program of supervision, care, and rehabilitation; (c) to remove a child from the home only when necessary for his welfare or in the interests of public safety; and (d) to assure all parties their constitutional and other legal rights.

- Purpose clauses in 6 states can be loosely characterized as "tough," in that they stress community protection, offender accountability, crime reduction through deterrence, or outright punishment, either predominantly or exclusively.

- Statutory language in 5 states emphasizes the promotion of the welfare and best interests of the juvenile as the sole or primary purpose of the juvenile court system.

Source: Office of Juvenile Justice and Delinquency Prevention (2012).

Comparison of Adult Criminal Justice and Juvenile Justice Systems

As Table 6.2 indicates, we find a petition alleging that the respondent may have committed a delinquent act instead of a complaint charging a defendant with a crime. We find an adjudicatory hearing and a dispositional hearing instead of a criminal trial and a sentencing hearing, respectively. The entire proceeding is initiated by a petition in the interests of the juvenile rather than by an indictment against him or her. The juvenile, therefore, may not be found guilty in juvenile court but may be adjudicated as delinquent. Juvenile court acts are predicated on the basic assumption that all personnel involved in the juvenile justice system act in the best interests of the juvenile. There are, however, differences of opinion concerning how to best ensure the interests of the juvenile. In August 1968, in the hope of bringing some uniformity to legal definitions of delinquency and delinquency proceedings, the National Conference of Commissioners on Uniform State Laws drafted and recommended for enactment in all states a Uniform Juvenile Court Act. This act was approved by the American Bar Association (ABA) at its annual meeting during the same year. Since that time, the Uniform Juvenile Court Act has served as a model for states to follow in developing their own acts.

In essence, Section 1 of the Uniform Juvenile Court Act reaffirms the basic philosophy of all juvenile court acts by stating specifically that the major purpose of the act is "to provide for the care, protection, and wholesome moral, mental, and physical development of children coming within its provisions" (National Conference of Commissioners on Uniform State Laws, 1968, sec. 1). This basic philosophy was first stated in the Cook County Juvenile Court Act of 1899 and has been stated in each state's juvenile court act adopted or revised since then. The philosophy has been controversial because of the questionable ability of the juvenile

Table 6.2 Comparison of Adult Criminal Justice and Juvenile Justice Systems

Adult	Juvenile
Arrest	Taking into custody
Preliminary hearing	Preliminary conference/detention hearing (both optional)
Grand jury/information/indictment	Petition
Arraignment	—
Criminal trial	Adjudicatory hearing
Sentencing hearing	Dispositional hearing
Sentence	Disposition (e.g., probation, incarceration)
Appeal	Appeal

justice system to provide the specified benefits to juveniles. Considerable documentation exists on the deficiencies of the state's ability to provide for the welfare of juveniles. A week seldom passes where a column in a newspaper or an article in a journal or magazine does not relate an instance of neglect by the state in its parental role (see In Practice 6.1). Although the philosophy of providing "care, guidance, and protection" is entrenched in the juvenile justice system, it would appear that a reevaluation of the state's effectiveness in adhering to that philosophy is in order.

IN PRACTICE 6.1

U.S. FAILURE TO PROTECT CHILDREN A "NATIONAL DISGRACE" REPORT SAYS

The federal government's failure to enforce the nation's child protection laws is a "national disgrace" that leaves abused children vulnerable to future harm, according to a three-year study by two child advocacy groups.

The 110-page report released Tuesday identified some of the same failures reported in December by The Associated Press after an eight-month investigation into hundreds of children who died of abuse or neglect in plain view of child protection authorities.

"Our laws are weak. We don't invest in solutions. Federal laws aren't enforced. And courts are turning their backs. This creates a trifecta of inertia and neglect," said Amy Harfeld,

policy director at the Children's Advocacy Institute at the University of San Diego School of Law, which wrote the report with the nonprofit group First Star.

AP's investigation, published Dec. 18, also revealed a system in crisis, hobbled by weak federal oversight, budget constraints, worker shortages and a voluntary data collection system so flawed that nobody can say with accuracy how many children die from abuse or neglect each year.

The AP found that at least 786 children died of abuse and neglect over a six-year span—many of them beaten, starved or left alone to drown— while agencies had good reason to know they

(Continued)

(Continued)

were in danger. That figure represents the most comprehensive statistics publicly available, but the actual number who died even as authorities were investigating their families or providing some form of protective services is likely much higher because antiquated confidentiality laws allow many states to withhold vital information, shrouding their failures.

The federal government estimates an average of about 1,650 children have died annually from abuse or neglect in recent years, whether or not they were known to the child welfare system, but many experts believe the actual number is twice as high. And many more suffer from near-fatal abuse and neglect every year.

"Almost everything that happens to these children is cloaked in endemic secrecy, and most efforts by the media and advocates to provide the public with much needed transparency—which leads to accountability—are thwarted by the very governmental entities and officials who have turned their backs on their official duties to children," the groups said.

Michael Petit, who was appointed by President Barack Obama to serve on the Federal Commission to Eliminate Child Abuse and Neglect Fatalities and serves as adviser to the advocacy group Every Child Matters, said he agreed with what he has read thus far in the report, entitled "Shame on U.S."

"The report is saying what a lot of people have been experiencing," Petit said, who wasn't speaking on the commission's behalf. "I share many of those sentiments that the federal government is not providing the kind of oversight needed."

The Children's Advocacy Institute and First Star fault all three branches of federal government for failing to protect children. The U.S. Department of Health and Human Services is responsible for implementing and enforcing federal child welfare laws and programs, but the agency largely takes a hands-off approach,

allowing states to self-certify that they are in compliance with federal requirements.

"There is no meaningful oversight and the states know it," the report said.

Agency spokeswoman Laura Goulding did not immediately return a call and an email seeking comment on the report Monday. Congress needs to mandate that HHS impose fines, withhold funds or take other punitive actions when states don't follow federal regulations, the report said.

Because HHS and Congress so rarely hold states accountable for their failings, filing a lawsuit is usually the only way private parties can challenge problems within the child welfare system. But lawsuits are time consuming, expensive and often limited in their reach, covering violations in only one state or county rather than widespread systemic failures, the groups said.

"Federal courts have turned their backs on private attempts to enforce federal child welfare law and Congress has shown little interest in advancing the law itself," the report said.

Emily Douglas, a child welfare expert at Bridgewater State University in Bridgewater, Mass., called the report's findings about the judicial branch's shortcomings particularly revealing.

"When something goes wrong, usually you hear that the state child welfare agency is a wreck or that the governor is stepping in to fire someone," Douglas said. "But increasingly judges are going to be on the radar about the important role that they play in determining these kids' safety. Judges are not trained social workers, so are we sure they always know the risk factors when deciding children should be sent back home?"

Source: 2015, January 27. U.S. failure to protect children a "national disgrace," report says. The Associated Press via CBSNews.com.

Other basic themes expressed in the Uniform Juvenile Court Act include protecting juveniles who commit delinquent acts from the taint of criminality and punishment and substituting treatment, training, and rehabilitation; keeping juveniles within their families whenever possible and separating juveniles from their parents only when necessary for their welfare or in the interests of public safety; and providing a simple judicial procedure for executing and enforcing the act through a fair hearing with constitutional and other legal rights recognized and enforced. We now discuss each of these philosophical themes.

Protecting the Juvenile From Stigmatization

For a long time, some states allowed a wide variety of activities to be labeled as delinquent. However, a majority of states have revised their juvenile codes and changed their legal definitions of acts considered delinquent. At issue is the difference between unthinking mischievous misbehavior of a nonserious nature and vicious intentional conduct that endangers life and property. It is difficult to ascertain exactly when mischievous behavior ends and vicious conduct begins because it is often left to individual perception of each. As a result, we sometimes encounter cases where hard-core delinquents have benefited from the treatment or rehabilitation philosophy of the juvenile court to the point where any concept of justice or accountability has been eliminated. The same is true for those who abuse or neglect their children to an extent that raises concern but where it is difficult to determine whether the legal standards required for abuse or neglect have been satisfied. Similarly, we sometimes note that mischievous juveniles are treated as hard-core delinquents. Clearly, rehabilitation and treatment might be helpful to both mischievous offenders and hard-core delinquents as well as to children who are abused or neglected. For mischievous offenders, a variety of rehabilitative or treatment programs have been developed as alternatives to punishment and are more or less effective in community-based agencies.

For delinquents who commit serious offenses, rehabilitative or treatment programs have typically been located in institutions. Some serious juvenile offenders learn how to "play the game" and are able to shift all responsibility for their actions to others or to society and, therefore, escape accountability under the rehabilitative/treatment philosophy. Such offenders and/or their attorneys are able to persuade juvenile court judges, prosecutors, and the police to "give them a break." Others, who are less skilled at playing the game or unable to retain private counsel, may be unable to escape more serious consequences for acts that may be less serious. The dilemma facing reformers of the juvenile court revolves around the obvious: Avoid labeling juveniles who do not deserve the label of delinquent and, at the same time, prevent the juvenile court from becoming so informal that those who are a threat to the community remain at large. This is a much bigger challenge than it might initially appear to be. Juvenile court systems throughout the nation have struggled with this issue historically and at present.

Maintaining the Family Unit

The concept that a child should remain in the family unit whenever possible is another basic element of the Uniform Juvenile Court Act. The child and family are not to be separated unless there is a serious threat to the welfare of the child or society. However, once there is an established necessity for removing the child, the juvenile court must have the power to move swiftly in that direction. Determining exactly when it is necessary to remove the child is not, of course, an easy task. Child protective service (CPS) employees and the juvenile court system are typically very careful not to label acts as child abuse and intervene in family dynamics unless all efforts to maintain the family unit have failed and/or the circumstances are clearly harmful to the child. Careful investigation of the total family environment and its effect on the juvenile is typically required in cases of suspected abuse, neglect, and delinquency. Removal may be permanent or may include an option to return the child if circumstances improve. Careful consideration is given to the family's attitudes toward the child and the past record of relationships among other family members.

Although most of us would agree that it is generally desirable to maintain the family unit, there are certainly circumstances when removal is in the best interests of both the minor and society (see In Practice 6.2). The welfare of the child is clearly jeopardized by keeping him or her in a family where gross neglect, abuse, or acts of criminality occur. The emphasis placed on maintaining the integrity of the family unit at times seems to be taken so seriously by juvenile court judges and other juvenile justice practitioners that they maintain family ties even when removal is clearly the better alternative.

Preserving Constitutional Rights in Juvenile Court Proceedings

The Uniform Juvenile Court Act provides judicial procedures so that all parties are assured of fairness and recognition of legal rights. The early philosophy of informal hearings void of legal procedures and evidentiary standards has a limited place in the modern juvenile justice system. The application of due process standards has not deterred the court from its rehabilitative pursuits. If the issue is delinquency and the act for which the child has been accused is theft, the procedural rules of evidence should support the allegation, and the result would be an adjudication of delinquency. If the evidence does not support the allegation, no adjudication of delinquency should occur. In an informal hearing where there is an absence of established guilt and where an adjudication of delinquency is based on the attitude of the child, the types of peers with whom that child associates, or his or her family's condition, the rights of the juvenile and perhaps other parties have been violated. The philosophy of a fair hearing, where constitutional rights are recognized and enforced and where a high standard of proof for establishing delinquency is strictly imposed, has been generally established in

WOMAN ARRESTED FOR STARVING HER CHILDREN

A Dawsonville woman was arrested early last month for reportedly starving her children and allowing her toddler to wander away from her residence.

The woman, Susan Diane Neeley, 34, was arrested Dec. 8 on three counts of cruelty to children and one count of reckless conduct.

According to Sheriff Jeff Johnson, Neeley is accused of willingly depriving her three children of necessary sustenance to the extent that the children's health and well-being were jeopardized. Johnson said the arrest stemmed from a missing juvenile call that occurred on Dec. 7.

The ages of the children were not released.

Neeley is also accused of allowing her toddler daughter to wander approximately 1 1/2 miles away from the residence, Johnson said.

"The child was out after dark on an evening with a temperature of 52 degrees," Johnson said. "The child's two siblings, who went to search for the toddler, were also missing. All were located at another residence."

When located, the toddler was found soaking wet, apparently from falling into a creek. Neeley was released on a $30,000 bond on Dec. 12.

Source: Dean, A. (2017, January 4). Woman arrested for starving her children. *Dawson County News.*

Questions to Consider

1. True or False: The abuse would not have been discovered if the police had not received a missing child call.

2. Multiple Choice: In this situation, the toddler child would be classified by juvenile court as which of the following?

   a. Delinquent

   b. Abused/neglected

   c. Status offender

   d. Child in need of supervision

3. In your opinion is removal of the child appropriate? Would you remove all children in the home or only the toddler?

---

juvenile court acts since 1967, when the U.S. Supreme Court decided in the *Gault* case (*In re Gault*, 1967) that due process (observing constitutional guarantees and rules of exclusion) was generally required in juvenile court adjudicatory proceedings. Informality is generally accepted in postadjudicatory hearings on disposition of the juvenile and is often permitted in prehearing stages. The adjudicatory hearing for delinquency must, however, be based on establishing beyond a reasonable doubt (with as little doubt as possible) that the allegations are supported by the admissible evidence.

The general purpose of juvenile court acts, then, is to ensure the welfare of juveniles while protecting their constitutional rights in such a way that removal from the family unit is accomplished only for a reasonable cause and in the best interests of the juvenile and society. A review of your state's juvenile court act should reflect these basic goals.

Scope

In addition to the basic themes discussed previously, all juvenile court acts define the ages and subject matter (conduct) within the scope of the court.

Age

Section 2 of the Uniform Juvenile Court Act defines a child as a person who is under the age of 18 years, who is under the age of 21 years but who committed an act of delinquency before reaching the age of 18 years, or who is under the age of 21 years and committed an act of delinquency after becoming 18 years of age but who is transferred to the juvenile court by another court having jurisdiction over him or her (National Conference of Commissioners on Uniform State Laws, 1968, sec. 2).

As stated in Chapter 2, both upper and lower age limits vary among the states (see your state's code). The Uniform Juvenile Court Act establishes the age of 18 as the legal age at which actions of an illegal nature will be considered criminal and the wrongdoer will be considered accountable and responsible as an adult. Prior to the 18th birthday, illegal activities will be considered acts of delinquency, with the wrongdoer processed by the juvenile court in a way that removes the taint of criminality and punishment and substitutes treatment, training, and rehabilitation in its place. The Uniform Juvenile Court Act allows two exceptions regarding the legal jurisdictional age of 18 years. Section 2(1)(iii) states that a person under the age of 21 years who commits an act of delinquency after becoming 18 years of age can be transferred to the juvenile court by another court having jurisdiction and, therefore, would be accorded all of the protection and procedural guidelines of the juvenile court. Section 34 allows for a transfer to other courts of a child under 18 years of age if serious acts of delinquency are alleged and the child was 16 years of age or older at the time of the alleged conduct (National Conference of Commissioners on Uniform State Laws, 1968, sec. 34). There are stringent guidelines to follow before a waiver to adult court jurisdiction may be permitted. Waivers of juvenile jurisdiction are occurring more frequently and are discussed later in this chapter.

In establishing the age of 18 years as the legal break point between childhood and adulthood, almost all states are consistent with the Uniform Juvenile Court Act, as noted in Table 6.3.

Table 6.3 Upper Age of Original Juvenile Court Jurisdiction, 2015

State	Age 15	Age 16	Age 17
Number of States	2	7	42
Alabama			X
Alaska			X
Arizona			X
Arkansas			X
California			X
Colorado			X
Connecticut			X

State	Age 15	Age 16	Age 17
Delaware			X
District of Columbia			X
Florida			X
Georgia		X	
Hawaii			X
Idaho			X
Illinois			X
Indiana			X
Iowa			X
Kansas			X
Kentucky			X
Louisiana		X	
Maine			X
Maryland			X
Massachusetts			X
Michigan		X	
Minnesota			X
Mississippi			X
Missouri		X	
Montana			X
Nebraska			X
Nevada			X
New Hampshire			X
New Jersey			X
New Mexico			X
New York	X		
North Carolina	X		
North Dakota			X
Ohio			X
Oklahoma			X

(Continued)

Table 6.3 (Continued)

State	Age 15	Age 16	Age 17
Oregon			X
Pennsylvania			X
Rhode Island			X
South Carolina		X	
South Dakota			X
Tennessee			X
Texas		X	
Utah			X
Vermont			X
Virginia			X
Washington			X
West Virginia			X
Wisconsin		X	

Note: Table information is as of the end of the 2015 legislative session.

- A juvenile is a youth at or below the upper age of original jurisdiction in a state.

- The upper age of jurisdiction is the oldest age at which a juvenile court has original jurisdiction over an individual for law-violating behavior.

- State statutes define which youth are under the original jurisdiction of the juvenile court. These definitions are based primarily on age criteria. In most states, the juvenile court has original jurisdiction over all youth charged with a criminal law violation who were below the age of 18 at the time of the offense, arrest, or referral to court. Many states have higher upper ages of juvenile court jurisdiction in status offense, abuse, neglect, or dependency matters—often through age 20.

- Many states have statutory exceptions to basic age criteria. The exceptions, related to the youth's age, alleged offense, and/or prior court history, place certain youth under the original jurisdiction of the criminal court. This is known as *statutory exclusion*.

- In some states, a combination of the youth's age, offense, and prior record places the youth under the original jurisdiction of both the juvenile and criminal courts. In these situations where the courts have concurrent jurisdiction, the prosecutor is given the authority to decide which court will initially handle the case. This is known as *concurrent jurisdiction, prosecutor discretion*, or *direct filing*.

- Since 1975 eight states have changed their age criteria. Alabama raised its upper age from 15 to 16 in 1976 and from 16 to 17 in 1977; Wyoming lowered its upper age from 18 to 17 in 1993; New Hampshire and Wisconsin lowered their upper age from 17 to 16 in 1996; Rhode Island lowered its upper age from 17 to 16 and then raised it back to 17 again 4 months later in 2007; Connecticut passed a law in 2007 to raise its upper age from 15 to 17 gradually from 2010 to 2012; Illinois raised its upper age for misdemeanors from 16 to 17 in 2010; Massachusetts raised its upper age from 16 to 17 in 2013; Illinois raised its upper age for most felonies from 16 to 17 in 2014; and New Hampshire raised its upper age from 16 back to 17 in 2015.

Source: Office of Juvenile Justice and Delinquency Prevention (2016).

States may also establish higher age limits in cases of status offenders and abuse, neglect, and dependency—typically through the age of 20 years. In addition, courts may retain jurisdiction after the age of adulthood if the child is serving a disposition in juvenile court. Some states also exclude married or emancipated youth from juvenile court jurisdiction. A total of 36 states allow juvenile court to maintain jurisdiction until the child's 21st birthday in cases where the child is under juvenile court supervision for delinquency at the time of the 18th birthday (OJJDP, 2003) (as noted in Table 6.4). As we have indicated elsewhere, there is no clearly established minimum age set by juvenile courts with respect to their jurisdiction, although 16 states have attempted to identify a limit. In Table 6.5, we see that children as young as 6 years of age are allowed into the juvenile justice system in North Carolina.

Table 6.4 Extended Age of Juvenile Court Jurisdiction, 2015

State	Age 18	Age 19	Age 20	Age 21	Age 22	Age 24	Full Term of Disposition Order
Number of States	**2**	**4**	**36**	**1**	**1**	**4**	**3**
Alabama			X				
Alaska		X					
Arizona*			X				
Arkansas			X				
California						X	
Colorado							X
Connecticut		X					
Delaware			X				
District of Columbia			X				
Florida			X				
Georgia			X				
Hawaii							X
Idaho			X				
Illinois			X				
Indiana			X				
Iowa			X				
Kansas					X		
Kentucky			X				
Louisiana			X				
Maine			X				
Maryland			X				
Massachusetts			X				
Michigan			X				
Minnesota			X				
Mississippi		X					

(Continued)

Table 6.4 (Continued)

State	Age 18	Age 19	Age 20	Age 21	Age 22	Age 24	Full Term of Disposition Order
Missouri			X				
Montana						X	
Nebraska			X				
Nevada**			X				
New Hampshire			X				
New Jersey							X
New Mexico			X				
New York			X				
North Carolina			X				
North Dakota		X					
Ohio			X				
Oklahoma	X						
Oregon						X	
Pennsylvania			X				
Rhode Island			X				
South Carolina			X				
South Dakota			X				
Tennessee			X				
Texas	X						
Utah			X				
Vermont				X			
Virginia			X				
Washington			X				
West Virginia			X				
Wisconsin						X	
Wyoming			X				

Notes: Extended jurisdiction may be restricted to certain offenses or juveniles.

* Arizona statute extends jurisdiction through age 20, but a 1979 state supreme court decision held that juvenile court jurisdiction terminates at age 18.

** The Nevada statute extends jurisdiction until the full term of the disposition order for sex offenders.

Table information is as of the end of the 2015 legislative session.

- Juvenile court authority over a youth for dispositional purposes in delinquency matters may extend beyond the upper age of original jurisdiction.

- Through extended jurisdiction mechanisms, legislatures enable the court to provide sanctions and services for a duration of time that is in the best interests of the juvenile and the public, even for older juveniles who have reached the age at which original juvenile court jurisdiction ends.

- An upper age of 18 means that the juvenile court loses jurisdiction over a child when they turn 19; an upper age of 19 means that a juvenile court loses jurisdiction when a child turns 20; and an upper age of 20 means that a juvenile court loses jurisdiction over a child when they turn 21.

- Extended jurisdiction may be restricted to certain offenses or juveniles (such as violent offenses, habitual offenders, and juveniles under correctional commitment).
- In some states, the juvenile court may actually impose adult correctional sanctions on certain adjudicated delinquents that extend the term of confinement well beyond the upper age of juvenile jurisdiction. Such sentencing options are included in the set of dispositional options known as *blended sentencing*.
- In Alaska, jurisdiction can extend for an additional one-year period if it is in the best interests of the person and the person consents.
- Mississippi law states that juveniles charged with robbery, arson, and drug offenses can remain in the juvenile justice system.

Source: Office of Juvenile Justice and Delinquency Prevention (2016).

Table 6.5 Upper and Lower Age of Juvenile Court Delinquency and Status Offense Jurisdiction, 2015

| State | Delinquency Jurisdiction | | Status Jurisdiction | |
	Lower Age	Upper Age	Lower Age	Upper Age
Alabama	NS	17	NS	17
Alaska	NS	17	NS	17
Arizona	8	17	NS	17
Arkansas	10	17	Birth	17
California	NS	17	NS	17
Colorado	10	17	NS	17
Connecticut	7	17	7	17
Delaware	NS	17	NS	17
District of Columbia	NS	17	NS	17
Florida	NS	17	NS	17
Georgia	NS	16	NS	17
Hawaii	NS	17	NS	17
Idaho	NS	17	NS	17
Illinois	NS	17	NS	17
Indiana	NS	17	NS	17
Iowa	NS	17	NS	17
Kansas	10	17	NS	17
Kentucky	NS	17	NS	17
Louisiana	10	16	NS	17
Maine	NS	17	NS	17
Maryland	7	17	NS	17
Massachusetts	7	17	6	17
Michigan	NS	16	NS	17
Minnesota	10	17	NS	17

(Continued)

Table 6.5 (Continued)

State	Delinquency Jurisdiction		Status Jurisdiction	
	Lower Age	Upper Age	Lower Age	Upper Age
Mississippi	10	17	7	17
Missouri	NS	16	NS	17
Montana	NS	17	NS	17
Nebraska	NS	17	NS	17
Nevada	NS	17	NS	17
New Hampshire	NS	17	NS	17
New Jersey	NS	17	NS	17
New Mexico	NS	17	NS	17
New York	7	15	NS	17
North Carolina	6	15	6	17
North Dakota	7	17	NS	17
Ohio	NS	17	NS	17
Oklahoma	NS	17	NS	17
Oregon	NS	17	NS	17
Pennsylvania	10	17	NS	17
Rhode Island	NS	17	NS	17
South Carolina	NS	16	NS	16
South Dakota	10	17	NS	17
Tennessee	NS	17	NS	17
Texas	10	16	10	16
Utah	NS	17	NS	17
Vermont	10	17	NS	17
Virginia	NS	17	NS	17
Washington*	NS	17	NS	17
West Virginia	NS	17	NS	17
Wisconsin	10	16	NS	17
Wyoming	NS	17	NS	17

Notes: Table information is as of the end of the 2015 legislative session. NS = lower age not specified.

* In Washington the lower age of delinquency jurisdiction is applied through a state juvenile court rule, which references a criminal code provision establishing the age youth are presumed to be incapable of committing crime.

- The upper age of jurisdiction is the oldest age at which a juvenile court has original jurisdiction over an individual for law-violating behavior. An upper age of 15 means that the juvenile court loses jurisdiction over a child when they turn 16; an upper age of 16 means that a juvenile court loses jurisdiction when a child turns 17; and an upper age of 17 means that a juvenile court loses jurisdiction over a child when they turn 18.

- State statutes define which youth are under the original jurisdiction of the juvenile court. These definitions are based primarily on age criteria. In most states, the juvenile court has original jurisdiction over all youth charged with a criminal law violation who were below the age of 18 at the time of the offense, arrest, or referral to court. Some states have higher upper ages of juvenile court jurisdiction in status offense, abuse, neglect, or dependency matters—often through age 20.

- Many states have statutory exceptions to basic age criteria. The exceptions, related to the youth's age, alleged offense, and/or prior court history, place certain youth under the original jurisdiction of the criminal court. This is known as *statutory exclusion*.

- In some states, a combination of the youth's age, offense, and prior record places the youth under the original jurisdiction of both the juvenile and criminal courts. In these situations where the courts have concurrent jurisdiction, the prosecutor is given the authority to decide which court will initially handle the case. This is known as *concurrent jurisdiction, prosecutor discretion,* or *direct filing*.

- Since 1975 eight states have changed their age criteria. Alabama raised its upper age from 15 to 16 in 1976 and from 16 to 17 in 1977; Wyoming lowered its upper age from 18 to 17 in 1993; New Hampshire and Wisconsin lowered their upper age from 17 to 16 in 1996; Rhode Island lowered its upper age from 17 to 16 and then raised it back to 17 again 4 months later in 2007; Connecticut passed a law in 2007 to raise its upper age from 15 to 17 gradually from 2010 to 2012; Illinois raised its upper age for misdemeanors from 16 to 17 in 2010; Massachusetts raised its upper age from 16 to 17 in 2013; Illinois raised its upper age for most felonies from 16 to 17 in 2014; and New Hampshire raised its upper age from 16 back to 17 in 2015.

Source: Office of Juvenile Justice and Delinquency Prevention (2016).

Other states rely on case law or common law in determining the lower age limit. They presume that children under a certain age cannot form *mens rea* and are exempt from prosecution and sentencing (OJJDP, 2003). Just as there have been few clear guidelines for processing youth in matters of delinquency, there have been vague guidelines for determining the age youth may be found to be abused or neglected.

Delinquent Acts

The Uniform Juvenile Court Act clearly limits the definition of delinquency by stating, in essence, that a delinquent act is an act designated as a crime by local ordinance, state law, or federal law. Excluded from acts constituting delinquency are vague activities, such as incorrigibility, ungovernability, habitual disobedience, and other status offenses, which are legal offenses applicable only to children and not to adults. At the time when the Uniform Juvenile Court Act was drafted in 1968, many states legally defined delinquency as encompassing a broad spectrum of behaviors. The proposal by the drafters of the Uniform Juvenile Court Act excluded the broader definition of activities labeled as delinquent and focused only on violations of laws that are applicable to both adults and children. This narrow interpretation was consistent with the legalistic trend occurring during the latter 1960s. By narrowing the legal definition of delinquency, the Uniform Juvenile Court Act did not ignore other types of activities that fall within the court's jurisdiction but placed these activities outside the realm of delinquent acts. A child who is "beyond the control of his parents," "habitually truant from school," or "habitually disobedient, uncontrolled, wayward, incorrigible, indecent, or deports himself or herself as to injure or endanger the morals or health of themself [sic] or others" was at one time considered to be delinquent in some states (Indiana Code Annotated, 31-37-1-1 to 31-37-2-6, 1997). The number of states with such a broad definition of delinquency is decreasing. A major difficulty with including these vague activities within the delinquent behavior category concerns the issue of who defines what is incorrigible, indecent, or habitual misconduct and the nature of the standard used to determine this behavior. These statutory expressions and a number of others like them have invited challenge on the grounds that they are unconstitutionally vague. There are no standardized definitions for *habitual, wayward, incorrigible,* and so on. As a result, such charges in conjunction with delinquency are inevitably challenged in the courts.

It is interesting to note that prior to the development of the Uniform Juvenile Court Act in 1968, several states had already started restricting the definition of delinquency to include only those activities that would be punishable as crimes if committed by adults. For example, in New York under the pre-1962 Children's Court Act, the term *juvenile delinquency* included ungovernability and incorrigibility. However, in 1962, the Joint Legislative Committee on Court Reorganization, which drafted the Family Court Act (New York Sessions Laws, vol. 2, 3428, 3434, McKinney, 1962), developed the concept of a person in need of supervision to cover noncriminal status offenses, and the term *juvenile delinquent* was narrowed to include only persons over 7 and under 16 years of age who commit any act that, if committed by an adult, would constitute a crime. With a more specific definition of delinquency, it was inevitable that due process procedures, rules of evidence, and constitutional rights would emerge as important issues in Supreme Court decisions involving the rights of juveniles in delinquency proceedings. As the states moved toward a more specific definition of delinquency, additional appellate decisions were rendered regarding "due process and fair treatment." The effect of this narrow interpretation of delinquency has been the advent of an adjudicatory process that is more formalized and that ensures and protects the juvenile's procedural and constitutional rights. This trend is clearly consistent with the spirit behind the creation of the Uniform Juvenile Court Act. Some states even list all forms of conduct subject to juvenile court jurisdiction in one general category (Louisiana Law, Children's Code, 2012; Montana Code Annotated, Title 41, 2011; Wisconsin Code, ch. 938, 2011).

Section 2(3) of the Uniform Juvenile Court Act indicates that an adjudicated delinquent is in need of "treatment or rehabilitation." The development of narrower definitions of delinquency and more formalized "due process models" is not intended to cause the juvenile court to abandon rehabilitation and treatment. This philosophy was stated as early as 1909, when it was pointed out that "the goal of the juvenile court is not so much to crush but to develop, not to make the juvenile a criminal but a worthy citizen" (Consolidated Laws of New York Annotated, bk. 29A, art. 7; McKinney, 1975). This initial concept of rehabilitation and treatment has been affirmed in many decisions and is summarized briefly by the Supreme Court case *In re Gault*, where the Court reaffirms the original juvenile court philosophy that "the child is to be 'treated' and 'rehabilitated' and the procedures, from apprehension through institutionalization, are to be 'clinical' rather than 'punitive'" (Faust & Brantingham, 1974, pp. 369–370). It is important to remember that although the juvenile court operates under the "treatment and rehabilitation" concept, the court is also charged with protecting the community against unlawful and violent conduct. To fulfill this obligation, the court may resort to incarceration or imprisonment. This clash between the rehabilitative ideal and the clear, present necessity to protect the community in certain situations has been described as the "schizophrenic nature" of the juvenile court process (Consolidated Laws of New York Annotated, bk. 29A, art. 7; McKinney, 1975).

It is clear that a majority of the states have moved toward a narrower definition of delinquency. Inherent in this trend is the movement toward formalizing the legal procedures and processes afforded to the accused delinquent. The importance of this trend is twofold. First, legal definitions of delinquency have become more standardized and by law require a violation or attempted violation of the criminal code. Second, the process of proving the allegation of delinquency may include only the same types of evidentiary materials that would be admitted if the same charges were levied against an adult. This is a considerable change from past practices in many juvenile courts, where much of the evidentiary material that was introduced to prove an act of delinquency was basically irrelevant material concerning the juvenile's family, peers, school behavior, and other information about his or her environment. The establishment of reasonable proof that the juvenile did violate the law was lost in the process. The case was often weighed and decided on factors other than establishing, beyond a reasonable doubt, that the juvenile committed the act of which he or she had been accused. The juvenile court is a court of law. The juvenile adjudicatory process and the juvenile court must be totally dedicated to working within a legal framework that is conducive to reaching the truth and serving the ends of justice. To do otherwise would result in what is best described in an often-quoted passage of the *Kent* decision where the U.S. Supreme Court Justice Abe Fortas stated, "There is evidence . . . that the child receives the worst of both worlds; that he gets neither the protections accorded to adults nor the solicitous care and regenerative treatment postulated for children" (*Kent v. United States*, 383 U.S. 541, 546, 1966).

Without a doubt, there is a place in the juvenile justice system for consideration of the adjudicated delinquent's family and his or her environment. However, such consideration should be given only *after* an adjudication of delinquency rather than used as the basis for adjudication. For instance, suppose that as an adult you have been accused of "breaking and entering" and that throughout the pretrial process and during the course of the trial nearly all of the evidence and information introduced focuses on your family, your associations, your attitude, and your overall environment. Furthermore, only a minimum amount of court time and effort is devoted to establishing beyond a reasonable doubt that you did in fact violate the law by breaking and entering, and even then most of this evidence is hearsay, not subjected to cross-examination, and based on belief rather than proof. Yet you are convicted. Such cases were fairly common in the juvenile justice system until the *Gault* decision in 1967. The focus on due process to protect the accused juvenile's constitutional rights is as important as determining whether the act was committed by the accused. The legal issue of delinquency must be determined not on the basis of a social investigation describing the minor's environment but rather on the basis of whether the evidence supports or denies the allegation of delinquent acts.

Unruly Children

Section 2(4) of the Uniform Juvenile Court Act defines an unruly child as a child who does the following:

1. While subject to compulsory school attendance is habitually and without justification truant from school
2. Is habitually disobedient of the reasonable and lawful commands of his parent, guardian, or other custodian and is ungovernable
3. Has committed an offense applicable only to a child
4. In any of the foregoing is in need of treatment or rehabilitation

At one time, a majority of states included these activities in the delinquent behavior category, which often resulted in the official label of delinquent and led to the possibility of being incarcerated in a juvenile correctional institution for treatment and rehabilitation. The Uniform Juvenile Court Act recognizes that such activities may require the aid and services provided by the juvenile court but also recognizes that these minors should not be included in the delinquent category. According to Section 32 of the Uniform Juvenile Court Act, unruly children cannot be placed in a correctional institution unless the court finds, after a further hearing, that they are not amenable to treatment or rehabilitation under a previous noncorrectional disposition.

The unruly child is generally characterized by activities that are noncriminal or minor violations of law. Types of offenses, such as curfew violations and running away from home, are referred to as status offenses (acts that are offenses only because of the age of the offender). If the same acts were committed by an adult, they would not be violations of law. A substantial number of states have separated the types of activities described as unruly by the Uniform Juvenile Court Act from delinquency and have placed them in the nondelinquent category of in need of supervision (New York Family Court Act, 712[a]; McKinney, 1999; North Carolina Code, 7b-1501, 2010; Ohio Revised Code § 2151.022, 2011; Texas Family Code, Title 3, Juvenile Justice Code, ch. 51[15], 2011). Table 6.6 describes the various titles used to classify unruly children in U.S. states.

Table 6.6 Status Offender Classification, 2013

State	In Need of Supervision*	Status Offender	In Need of Services**	In Need of Aid, Assistance or Care***	Unruly	No Specific Classification	Other
Number of States	**12**	**11**	**12**	**4**	**3**	**3**	**15**
Alabama	X	X					
Alaska				X			
Arizona							X
Arkansas			X				
California							X
Colorado		X					X
Connecticut			X				
Delaware							X
DC	X						
Florida			X				
Georgia			X				
Hawaii		X					
Idaho		X					
Illinois	X		X				
Indiana							X
Iowa				X			X
Kansas				X			
Kentucky		X					
Louisiana			X				
Maine						X	
Maryland	X						
Massachusetts				X			
Michigan						X	
Minnesota			X				X
Mississippi	X						
Missouri		X					
Montana							X
Nebraska		X					
Nevada	X						
New Hampshire			X				
New Jersey							X
New Mexico			X				
New York	X						
North Carolina							X

State	In Need of Supervision*	Status Offender	In Need of Services**	In Need of Aid, Assistance or Care***	Unruly	No Specific Classification	Other
North Dakota					X		
Ohio					X		
Oklahoma	X						
Oregon							X
Pennsylvania							X
Rhode Island							X
South Carolina		X					
South Dakota	X						
Tennessee					X		
Texas		X					X
Utah						X	
Vermont	X						
Virginia	X	X	X				
Washington			X				X
West Virginia		X					
Wisconsin			X				
Wyoming	X						

Notes: Table information is as of the end of the 2013 legislative session.

* **In need of supervision** includes variations such as child in need of supervision (CHINS) and person in need of supervision (PINS).

** **In need of services** includes variations such as children in need of protection or services, child in need of services (CHINS), family in need of services (FINS), family in need of court-ordered services, family with service needs, and juvenile alleged to be in need of protection or services.

*** **In need of aid, assistance, or care** includes variations such as child in need of aid, child in need of care, child requiring assistance, and families in need of assistance.

- States use many different terms to classify status offenders. Some terms, such as *child in need of services* or *child in need of supervision*, relate to the needs of the juvenile. Other terms, such as *unruly child* or *chronic runaway*, describe the juvenile's behavior.

- While some states have multiple classifications for status offenders depending on the violating behavior or situational factors, such as Washington (at-risk youth, truant, and child in need of services), Virginia (child in need of services, child in need of supervision, and status offender), and Minnesota (juvenile petty offender and children in need of protection or services), most have a single label.

- Truant youth in Illinois are classified as truant minors in need of supervision. Youth who are runaways, ungovernable, or unruly are classified as minors in need of authoritative intervention and are eligible for community-based services.

- In Maine, there is no specific classification for youth who commit status offenses; however, legislation in the Maine Juvenile Code allows a law enforcement officer to take a juvenile runaway into interim care (temporary physical control).

- Youth who are truant or runaway, who violate curfew, or who violate the alcoholic beverage code in Texas are classified as status offenders. The behaviors are referred to as "conduct indicating a need for supervision."

- Some states classify status offenders in the same category as abused and neglected children. For example, in Pennsylvania, youth who commit a status offense are processed as dependent children.

Source: Office of Juvenile Justice and Delinquency Prevention (2014).

Regardless of the title, the importance of the development of this category lies in separating the delinquent from the nonserious violator and in realizing that the behavioral activities included in the unruly child and the child in need of supervision categories are often symptomatic of problems in the juvenile's home life and environment and might not indicate criminal tendencies. The unruly child category allows the juvenile court to be involved with the youth who needs supervision and allows the court flexibility and options short of the label of delinquent. Still, the labels of unruly child and in need of supervision may become terms of disrepute and produce a stigmatizing effect on the juvenile similar to the label of delinquent. As a result, one of the major benefits of the distinction is lost if, and when, an unruly child ends up in court.

To further distinguish the differences between the delinquent and the unruly child, most states have developed different procedural requirements. These requirements allow the civil standard of preponderance of evidence in the adjudicatory hearing for the latter, where the bulk of the evidence, but not necessarily all of it, must support the charges. They also provide for different dispositional options and for different upper ages for the unruly and in need of supervision categories. Again, reviewing your state's juvenile code will provide information on how these issues are addressed in your jurisdiction.

In distinguishing between juveniles whose misconduct is criminal and those whose misconduct is not criminal, it is assumed that the unruly child's behavior may be of a predelinquent nature and that early remedial treatment might prevent the incipient delinquency. However, it may be that the unruly child has more intense emotional and behavioral problems than do some delinquents who commit a single criminal act or a series of minor criminal acts.

The unruly child and in need of supervision categories are generally written without specificity because it is difficult to define and describe all of the noncriminal (delinquent) conduct that could ultimately fall within these categories. The term *habitually* is frequently used to distinguish between isolated incidents and a recurring pattern of incorrigibility, ungovernability, or disobedience. The flagrant repetitive nature of these behaviors often serves as the basis for filing a petition and the justification for pursuing treatment.

It was noted earlier that in some instances the behavior engaged in by the juvenile and alleged in a petition (often filed by the parents) may actually reflect neglect rather than an unruly child. A lack of parental supervision, whether due to unwillingness or inability of the parents, may have created a situation within the family that resulted in the juvenile's behavior. This behavior, although alleged to be unruly in the petition, may have been precipitated by a family crisis resulting in the minor rebelling against the family.

Deprived, Neglected, or Dependent Children

In Section 2(5) of the Uniform Juvenile Court Act, a "deprived" child is defined as a child under the age of 18 years who exemplifies the following:

1. Is without proper parental care or control, subsistence, education as required by law, or other care or control necessary for his physical, mental, or emotional health, or morals, and the deprivation is not due primarily to the lack of financial means of his parents, guardian, or other custodian

2. Has been placed for care or adoption in violation of law

3. Has been abandoned by his parents, guardian, or other custodian

4. Is without a parent, guardian, or legal custodian

A number of jurisdictions use a single classification to describe a child who is without a parent, who has been abandoned or abused, or who is without adequate parental care or supervision. Such a child is variously referred to as a "dependent child" (California Code, Welfare and Institutions Code, art. 6, Dependent Children—jurisdiction, 2010; Georgia Code, Title 19—domestic relations ch. 10—abandonment of spouse or child § 19-10-1, 2010), a "deprived child" (Georgia Code Title 15—Courts, ch. 11—juvenile proceedings, art. 1—juvenile proceedings, part 6—deprivation § 15-11-55, 2010), or a "neglected child" (Illinois Code, ch. 720 criminal offenses, 720, Illinois Compiled Statutes [ILCS] 130/Neglected Children Offense Act, 2010; New Mexico Statutes—sec. 32A-4-2—Definitions, 2006).

Some states separate deprived children into several categories with specific labels. For example, in the state of Georgia, a deprived child means a child who is without proper parental care or control, subsistence, education as required by law, or other care necessary for the child's physical, mental, or emotional health or morals; has been placed for care or adoption in violation of the law; has been abandoned by his or her parents, or other legal custodian; or is without a parent, guardian, or custodian. The Georgia Code excludes from the definition of a deprived child any child who is being treated through spiritual means and prayer in good faith and through recognized church or religious practices (Georgia Code, Title 15—Courts, ch. 11—Juvenile Proceedings, art. 1—Juvenile Proceedings, part 1—General Provisions, § 15-11-2—Definitions, 2010). Within the neglect language of some codes is a special section on abused children who are minors under a given age whose parent or immediate family member, custodian, or any person living in the same family or household, or a paramour of the minor's parent (1) allows the child to be destitute, homeless, or abandoned or dependent on the public for support; (2) habitually begs or is found living in a home with vicious or disreputable persons; (3) is in a home with neglectful and/or cruel, parents, guardians, or caregivers who deprave the child; or (4) any child under the age of 10 years who is found begging, peddling, or selling articles or playing or singing a musical instrument for gain on the street or accompanying someone who is doing so (Illinois Code, ch. 720 Criminal Offenses, 720ILCS 130/Neglected Children Offense Act, 2010).

Frequently, juvenile court acts have a special "dependent child" provision for children under a specified age who have no living parent, have been abandoned, or lack adequate parental care or supervision. Georgia, for example, mentions dependent children as those who have been abandoned by its father or mother when the father or mother does not furnish sufficient food, clothing, or shelter for the needs of the child (O.C.G.A. 1910-1, 2010). Ohio claims a dependent child is one who (1) is homeless or destitute or without adequate parental care, through no fault of the child's parents, guardian, or custodian; (2) lacks adequate parental care by reason of the mental or physical condition of the child's parents, guardian, or custodian; (3) lives in a condition or environment to warrant the state, in the interests of the child, in assuming the child's guardianship; and (4) because the child resides in a household where the parent, guardian, custodian, or other member committed an abusive, neglectful, or dependent act that was the basis for adjudication of a sibling of the child or any other child, and because circumstances surrounding the abuse, neglect, or dependency of the sibling or other child places the current child in danger of abuse, neglect, or dependency (Ohio Rev Code § 2151.04, 2011).

Even though the Uniform Juvenile Court Act specifically disallows "a lack of financial means" as a basis for alleging that a minor is a "deprived child," some states, under circumstances where the deprivation is so extreme that it seriously endangers the well-being of the child, provide for handling these cases under the "neglected child" portion of their juvenile court acts. Deprivation may be considered "gross neglect" if the amount of parental income is sufficient but is misappropriated and jeopardizes the well-being of the children within the family. Appropriate juvenile court remedies are generally available for this type of deprivation. According to Fox (1984), "Where a statutory distinction is made between a neglected child and one who is dependent, the difference generally is a matter of the presence of some parental fault in the former case and its absence in the latter" (p. 58). Regardless of the statutory definitions of the *deprived*, *neglected*, *abused*, and *dependent* child, it is quite clear that the situations described in these statutes exist basically through no fault of the child.

Jurisdiction

The jurisdiction of a court concerns persons, behavior, and relationships over which the court may exercise authority. The word *jurisdiction* also may be used to describe geographical areas or to describe the process through which the juvenile court acquires authority to make orders concerning particular individuals. As Regoli and Hewitt (1994) pointed out, the question of jurisdiction is of basic importance to the juvenile court judge; without jurisdiction over the subject matter and the subject, that judge's court has no power to act. The term *jurisdiction* means "the legal power, right, or authority to hear and determine a cause or causes" (p. 390). Jurisdiction is created and defined in juvenile court acts.

There is a distinction between the juvenile court's inherent jurisdictional powers and its discretion to exercise jurisdiction over a case. For example, the statutory law creating the juvenile court in a state may give that court exclusive jurisdiction in any proceeding involving cases of delinquency, unruly children, dependency, or neglect provided that the respondent is within the age range and geographical area specified by the court. However, unless a petition is duly filed and the respondent receives a copy or summary of the petition as well as adequate notification of when and where the allegations against him or her will be presented and heard, the court has not exercised proper jurisdiction over the case.

In some states, the juvenile court acts have been repealed and broader family court acts have been created, allowing for broader jurisdictional powers over virtually all problems directly involving families (Texas Family Code, 51.02, 2011). Adoptions, divorces, proceedings concerning mentally retarded or mentally ill children, custody and support of children, paternity suits, and certain criminal offenses committed by one family member against another all are within the jurisdiction of some family court acts. It is important to note, however, that for the most part, those adults who abuse or neglect their children are subject to prosecution not in juvenile courts but rather in criminal courts. The children who are abused or neglected may nonetheless be removed from their homes and placed in shelter care or other living arrangements by the juvenile court judge and/or the state department of children and family services.

Age is obviously an important factor in determining jurisdiction in all states. As stated previously, age limits for delinquency vary among the states. The majority of juvenile court acts are silent on the lower age limits at which a child falls within the court's jurisdiction; however, in some states the common-law age of 7 years has been established by statute as the lower age limit for delinquency. Statutes in 16 states define the minimum age for delinquency. In the remaining states, it is technically possible that a child could be adjudicated delinquent from birth. Such adjudication is unlikely given that the juvenile court requires a reasonable degree of capacity such as the ability to understand the act and to know or appreciate its consequences (*In re Register*, 1987; *In re William A.*, 1988).

The unruly child or child in need of supervision has been generally subjected to the same upper age limit for jurisdictional purposes as the delinquent. Because common law does not deal directly with this category, the common-law age of 7 years has not traditionally been recognized as the minimum age for the unruly child.

Determining the upper and lower age limits in delinquency raises difficult questions about responsibility and accountability in the law. For example, a 6-year-old who is fully aware of the wrongfulness of a criminal act and its consequences and still commits the act will be immune from prosecution if the jurisdictional age of 7 years is part of the state's juvenile court act. Another child who is less mature at 7 years may commit the same act while being unaware of its consequences and may need to face juvenile court. The question becomes whether either child is fully and completely responsible for his or her actions.

States differ about whether a juvenile who commits a delinquent act while within the age jurisdiction of the juvenile court, but who is not apprehended until he or she has passed the maximum age of jurisdiction, can be handled as a juvenile. Some states have determined through court decisions or previous statutory enactments that it is the age at the time of the offense, rather than the age at the time of apprehension, that determines jurisdiction. In the Uniform Juvenile Court Act, Section 2(1)(iii) allows a person under 21 years of age who commits an act of delinquency before reaching the age of 18 years to be considered a child and within the juvenile court's jurisdiction for delinquency proceedings.

States differentiate between the upper ages for delinquency and other categories; they believe that a minor might still need the care and protection of the family even though he or she is beyond the age for an adjudication of delinquency. Similarly, the deprived, neglected, abused, or dependent child is generally not subject to a lower age limit because a younger child may have a greater need for the protection of the juvenile court than does an older counterpart. Currently, some states have set one age for all categories included in the juvenile court act, whereas others have different ages for each category. For example, Texas defines a child as a person 10 years of age or over but under 17 years of age and over 17 but under 18 years of age for those alleged or found to have engaged in delinquent conduct or conduct indicating a need for supervision as a result of acts committed before becoming 17 years of age. This child still qualifies for a wardship petition or delinquency petition, respectively, in a Texas Juvenile Court (Texas Family Code, Title 3—Juvenile Justice Code, ch. 51—General Provisions, 2011). Illinois continues to follow different ages for delinquency (up to the 17th birthday) and for a dependent and neglected child (up to the 18th birthday) (Illinois Code, ch. 720—Criminal Offenses, ILCS 130, 2012). Section 2 of the Uniform Juvenile Court Act recommends the establishment of an upper age of 18 for all categories.

Concurrent, Exclusive, and Blended Jurisdiction

The issue of concurrent or exclusive jurisdiction of the juvenile court is generally determined by the legislature and specifically stated in the state's juvenile court act. Section 3 of the Uniform Juvenile Court Act provides the juvenile court with exclusive jurisdiction of certain proceedings listed in that section. In effect, exclusive jurisdiction means that the juvenile court will be the only tribunal legally empowered to proceed and that all other courts are deprived of jurisdiction. In some juvenile court acts, concurrent jurisdiction may be present when certain specified situations exist. For example, certain criminal acts may be concurrently under the jurisdiction of the juvenile court and the criminal court (Tennessee Code Title 37—Juveniles, ch. 1—Juvenile Courts and Proceedings, Part 1—General Provisions, 37-1-104—Concurrent jurisdiction, 2010; Utah Code Title 78A Judiciary and Judicial Administration, ch. 6 Juvenile Court Act of 1996, sec. 104 Concurrent jurisdiction—District court and juvenile court, 2011). Table 6.7 shows how states handle concurrent jurisdiction. The court that acts first may exercise jurisdiction over a case not because the court has exclusive jurisdiction but simply because it exercises its jurisdiction before the other court acts. In some states, juvenile court acts may allow exclusive jurisdiction over adults who play a role in encouraging a minor to violate a law. In other states, this jurisdiction may be concurrent with the adult criminal court. In still other states, the juvenile court may have no jurisdiction over such adults, so exclusive jurisdiction rests with the adult criminal courts. To determine whether the juvenile court has exclusive or concurrent jurisdiction over the subject matter and the subject, it is necessary to refer to the juvenile court act of the state in question. Concurrent jurisdiction is at times awkward, with every state having a statutory scheme for waiving jurisdiction in the best interests of the minor and/or in the best interests of the community.

Some juvenile courts are also using blended sentencing by sharing jurisdiction with adult courts. Blended sentencing allows juvenile and/or adult courts to impose adult sanctions and youth correctional sanctions on certain types of juveniles. In this case, both courts would share jurisdiction of the child. Blended sentencing typically occurs in one of two ways: (1) exclusive or (2) inclusive. In an exclusive model, the judge imposes

Table 6.7 Concurrent Jurisdiction Offense and Minimum Age Criteria, 2015

State	Minimum Age for Concurrent Jurisdiction	Concurrent Jurisdiction Offense and Minimum Age Criteria							
		Any Criminal Offense	Certain Felonies	Capital Crimes	Murder	Certain Person Offenses	Certain Property Offenses	Certain Drug Offenses	Certain Weapon Offenses
Arizona	14		14						
Arkansas	14		14	14	14	14			
California	14		14	14	14	14	14	14	
Colorado	16		16			16			
District of Columbia	16		16		16	16	16		
Florida	NS	16	14	NS	14	14	14		14
Georgia	NS			NS					
Louisiana	15				15	15	15	15	
Michigan	14		14		14	14	14	14	
Montana	12				12	12	16	16	16
Nebraska	NS	NS	14						
Oklahoma	15		15		15	15	15	16	15
Vermont	16	16							
Virginia	14				14	14		14	
Wyoming	13	13	14		14	14	14		

Note: Ages in the minimum age column may not apply to all offense restrictions but represent the youngest possible age at which a juvenile may be judicially waived to criminal court. "NS" indicates that no minimum age is specified.

- Concurrent jurisdiction provisions vary considerably with respect to minimum age and offense criteria.
- All states have provisions for trying certain juveniles as adults in criminal court. This is known as *transfer to criminal court*. There are three basic transfer mechanisms: *judicial waiver, statutory exclusion,* and *concurrent jurisdiction.*
- As of the end of the 2014 legislative session, 14 states and the District of Columbia had concurrent jurisdiction provisions, which give both juvenile and criminal court original jurisdiction in certain cases. Under such provisions, prosecutors have discretion to file eligible cases in either court.
- Often, concurrent jurisdiction is limited to cases involving violent or repeat crimes or offenses involving firearms or other weapons. (Juvenile and criminal courts often share jurisdiction over minor offenses such as traffic, watercraft, or local ordinance violations as well as serious offenses in states where they are not excluded from juvenile court jurisdiction by statute.)
- State appellate courts have taken the view that prosecutor discretion is equivalent to the routine charging decisions made in criminal cases. Thus, prosecutorial transfer is considered an "executive function," which is not subject to judicial review and is not required to meet the due process standards established by the U.S. Supreme Court in *Kent v. United States* (383 U.S. 541, 86 S.Ct. 1045 [1966]).

Source: Office of Juvenile Justice and Delinquency Prevention (2017a).

either a juvenile or an adult sanction that is effective immediately. In an inclusive model, the judge may impose both a juvenile sanction and an adult sanction with the latter being suspended as long as the child has no additional criminal violations. States using blended sentencing laws usually limit their usage by age and offense (as noted in Table 6.8). Research on blended sentencing has shown that youthful offenders who tend to receive blended sentences mirror those youth who are most often transferred to adult court, although

Table 6.8 Juvenile Court Blended Sentencing Offense and Minimum Age Criteria, 2015

State	Minimum Age for Juvenile Court Blended Sentencing	Juvenile Court Blended Sentencing Offense and Minimum Age Criteria							
		Any Criminal Offense	Certain Felonies	Capital Crimes	Murder	Certain Person Offenses	Certain Property Offenses	Certain Drug Offenses	Certain Weapon Offenses
Alaska	16					16			
Arkansas	NS		13	NS	NS	13			14
Colorado	NS		NS			NS			
Connecticut	NS		NS			NS			
Illinois	13		13						
Kansas	12	12							
Massachusetts	14		14			14			14
Michigan	NS	NS	NS		NS	NS	NS	NS	
Minnesota	14		14						
Montana	NS		12		NS	NS	NS	NS	NS
New Mexico	14		14		14	14	14		
Ohio	10		10		10				
Rhode Island	NS		NS						
Texas	NS		NS		NS	NS		NS	

Note: Ages in the minimum age column may not apply to all offense restrictions but represent the youngest possible age at which a juvenile may be judicially waived to criminal court. "NS" indicates that no minimum age is specified.

- As with transfer laws, states' juvenile court blended sentencing provisions are limited by age and offense criteria.
- Blended sentencing laws address the correctional system (juvenile or adult) in which certain offenders of juvenile age will be sanctioned. Such statutes can be placed into two general categories: *juvenile court blended sentencing* and *criminal court blended sentencing*.
- With juvenile court blended sentencing, the juvenile court has the authority to impose adult criminal sanctions on certain juvenile offenders. The majority of such laws authorize the juvenile court to combine a juvenile disposition with a criminal sentence that is suspended. If the youth successfully completes the juvenile disposition, the criminal sanction is not imposed. If, however, the youth does not cooperate or fails in the juvenile sanctioning system, the adult criminal sanction is imposed.
- As of the end of the 2014 legislative session, 14 states had blended sentencing laws that enable juvenile courts to impose criminal sanctions on certain juvenile offenders.
- Although the impact of juvenile blended sentencing laws depends on the specific provisions—which vary by state—in general, juvenile court blended sentencing expands the sanctioning powers of the juvenile court such that juvenile offenders may face the same penalties as adult offenders.

Source: Office of Juvenile Justice and Delinquency Prevention (2017b).

they are younger in age, are considered less of a risk to public safety, and are most amenable to the reform and rehabilitation efforts provided in the juvenile justice system (Cheesman, 2011). A blended sentence provides the youth an incentive to avoid adult court transfer while allowing for more choices in treatment and sentencing for the judge (Sickmund, 2003).

Waiver

As stated previously, statutory provisions in juvenile court acts have given juvenile courts original and exclusive jurisdiction over certain cases if the subject is within the defined jurisdiction. However, juvenile court acts contain provisions for the waiver of the juvenile court's jurisdiction over certain offenses committed by minors of certain ages. Policies regarding waiver of juveniles to the criminal justice system differ from state to state and include discretionary judicial waivers, presumptive waiver laws, and mandatory waivers. Forty-five states have discretionary waiver provisions that allow judges to determine whether the youth should be transferred to adult court jurisdiction. These waivers are not required but are used in instances where the crime is of a very serious nature and/or the youth is a habitual or serious offender. Several states use a process called presumptive waivers, which identify types of crimes in which transfers to adult court are most appropriate. In these cases, the juvenile will meet age limit, offense, and other statutory criteria identified as being appropriate for transfer to adult court. The judge can use the criteria to make a sufficient argument for or against the transfer to adult criminal court. Finally, other states provide for mandatory waivers in cases where the youth meets certain age, offense, and prior record criteria. Mandatory waiver proceedings are initiated in juvenile court where it is confirmed that the youth meets mandatory waiver requirements. The case is then immediately forwarded to the adult criminal court (Adams & Addie, 2011).

The waiver should not be confused with concurrent jurisdiction, where two courts have simultaneous jurisdiction over the subject matter and the subject. *Waiver*, in this case, refers to the process by which a juvenile over whom the juvenile court has original jurisdiction is transferred to adult criminal court. Terminology varies from state to state—some call the process a "certification," "bind-over," or "remand" for criminal prosecution, a "transfer" or "decline" rather than a waiver proceeding (Office of Juvenile Justice and Delinquency Prevention, 1998). Regardless, most authorities agree that the waiver represents a critical stage of the juvenile justice process. At this point, the juvenile may lose the *parens patriae* protection of the juvenile court, including its emphasis on treatment and rehabilitation as opposed to punishment. Once transferred (waived) to the adult criminal justice network, the juvenile is subjected to contact with adult offenders, may obtain a criminal record, and finds himself or herself in a generally vulnerable position. In some states, an automatic waiver of the exclusive jurisdiction of the juvenile court occurs when specific offenses are allegedly committed by a juvenile. For example, in Hawaii, the court may waive jurisdiction and order the following:

> Minor or adult held for criminal proceedings after full investigation and hearing where the person during the person's minority, but on or after the person's sixteenth birthday, is alleged to have committed an act that would constitute a felony if committed by an adult, and the court finds that: (1) There is no evidence the person is committable to an institution for individuals with intellectual disabilities or the mentally ill; (2) The person is not treatable in any available institution or facility within the State designed for the care and treatment of children; or (3) The safety of the community requires that the person be subject to judicial restraint for a period extending beyond the person's minority. (Hawaii Revised Statute § 571-22, 2011)

States have outlined the provisions setting forth the circumstances under which a waiver may be granted. These are quite varied. Most states require that a child be over a certain age and that he or she be charged with a particularly serious offense before jurisdiction may be waived (see Table 6.9). Other states allow the prosecutor to file directly with adult criminal court, whereas others (all but four states: Massachusetts, Nebraska, New Mexico, and New York) provide for juvenile court judge authorization before waiving a case to adult court (Puzzanchera, 2003, p. 1).

Table 6.9 Judicial Waiver Offense and Minimum Age Criteria, 2015

State	Minimum Age for Judicial Waiver	Judicial Waiver Offense and Minimum Age Criteria							
		Any Criminal Offense	Certain Felonies	Capital Crimes	Murder	Certain Person Offenses	Certain Property Offenses	Certain Drug Offenses	Certain Weapon Offenses
Alabama	14	14							
Alaska	NS	NS	NS			NS			
Arizona	NS		NS						
Arkansas	14		14	14	14	14			14
California	14	16	14		14	14	14	14	14
Colorado	12		12		15	12	12		
Connecticut	15		15	15	15	15	15		
Delaware	NS	NS	15		NS	NS	16	16	
District of Columbia	NS	15	15		15	15	15		NS
Florida	14	14							
Georgia	13		15	13		13			
Hawaii	NS		14		NS				
Idaho	NS	14			NS	NS	NS	NS	
Illinois	13	13	15					15	
Indiana	NS		NS		12			16	
Iowa	10	14	10						
Kansas	12	12	12			14		14	
Kentucky	14		14	14					
Louisiana	14				14	14	NS		
Maine	NS		NS		NS	NS	NS		
Maryland	NS	15		NS					
Michigan	14		14						
Minnesota	14		14						
Mississippi	13	13							
Missouri	12		12						
Nebraska	14	16	14						
Nevada	13	16	14		13	16			
New Hampshire	13		15		13	13		15	
New Jersey	14	14	14		14	14	14	14	14
North Carolina	13		13	13					
North Dakota	14	14	14		14	14	14		

(Continued)

Table 6.9 (Continued)

State	Minimum Age for Judicial Waiver	Judicial Waiver Offense and Minimum Age Criteria							
		Any Criminal Offense	Certain Felonies	Capital Crimes	Murder	Certain Person Offenses	Certain Property Offenses	Certain Drug Offenses	Certain Weapon Offenses
Ohio	14		14		14	16	16		
Oklahoma	NS		NS						
Oregon	NS	15	15		NS	NS	15		
Pennsylvania	14		14		14	14			
Rhode Island	NS		16	NS	17	17			
South Carolina	NS	16	14		NS	NS		14	14
South Dakota	NS		NS						
Tennessee	NS	NS							
Texas	14		14	14				14	
Utah	14		14		16	16	16		16
Vermont	10	16	10		10	10	10		
Virginia	14		14		14	14			
Washington	NS	NS							
West Virginia	NS		NS		NS	NS	NS	NS	
Wisconsin	14	15	14		14	14	14	14	
Wyoming	13	13							

Note: Ages in the minimum age column may not apply to all offense restrictions but represent the youngest possible age at which a juvenile may be judicially waived to criminal court. "NS" indicates that no minimum age is specified.

- Most states with judicial waiver provisions specify minimum age and offense criteria to aid the decision to transfer.
- All states have provisions for trying certain juveniles as adults in criminal court. This is known as *transfer to criminal court.* There are three basic transfer mechanisms: *judicial waiver, statutory exclusion,* and *concurrent jurisdiction.*
- Under judicial waiver provisions the juvenile court judge has the authority to waive juvenile court jurisdiction and transfer the case to criminal court.
- Waiver provisions vary in terms of the degree of flexibility allowed. Some waiver provisions are entirely *discretionary.* In other provisions there is a rebuttable *presumption* in favor of waiver, and in others waiver is *mandatory* once the juvenile court judge determines that certain statutory criteria have been met.
- As of the end of the 2014 legislative session, 45 states and the District of Columbia allow juvenile court judges to waive jurisdiction over certain cases and transfer them to criminal court, a practice known as judicial waiver.
- Age and offense criteria are common components of judicial waiver provisions, but other factors come into play as well. For example, most state statutes limit judicial waiver to juveniles who are "no longer amenable to treatment." The specific factors that determine lack of amenability vary, but they typically include the juvenile's offending history and previous dispositional outcomes.
- Many (18) states with judicial waiver provisions establish 14 as the minimum age for waiver, but there is variation across states. The provision in Vermont, for example, permits 10-year-olds to be waived.

Source: Office of Juvenile Justice and Delinquency Prevention (2017c).

For the most part, mandatory waivers are restricted to the more serious offenses and to lesser offenses such as traffic violations. Even in the most serious offenses, a mandatory waiver may occur only if the juvenile involved is over a certain age. For example, in Wisconsin the juvenile must be over the age of 14 years before a waiver is possible, unless there is a statutory exclusion (Wisconsin Code 938.18 Jurisdiction for criminal proceedings for juveniles 14 or older; waiver hearing, 2011). As noted in Table 6.10, other states authorize waivers similarly if the jurisdictional age is established and met and the specific offense is within the statutory allowance for such a waiver. In some states with statutory exclusion provisions, certain types of juvenile cases originate in criminal rather than juvenile court. This can also occur in those states where the age of adulthood is 16 rather than 17 or 18.

Table 6.10 Statutory Exclusion Offense and Minimum Age Criteria, 2015

State	Minimum Age for Statutory Exclusion	Any Criminal Offense	Certain Felonies	Capital Crimes	Murder	Certain Person Offenses	Certain Property Offenses	Certain Drug Offenses	Certain Weapon Offenses
Alabama	16		16	16				16	
Alaska	16		16			16	16	16	16
Arizona	15		15		15	15	15		15
California	14				14	14			
Delaware	15		15						
Florida	NS		NS		16	NS	16	16	
Georgia	13		13		13	13			
Idaho	14				14	14	14	14	
Illinois	13		15		13	15			15
Indiana	16				16	16			16
Iowa	NS	NS	16					16	16
Louisiana	15				15	15			
Maryland	14			14	16	16			16
Massachusetts	14				14				
Minnesota	16				16				
Mississippi	13		13	13					
Montana	17				17	17	17	17	17
Nevada	NS	16	NS		16	NS			
New Mexico	15				15	15			
New York	13				13	13	14		14
Oklahoma	13		13		13	13			
Oregon	15		15		15	15			
Pennsylvania	NS				NS	NS			
South Carolina	16		16						

(Continued)

Table 6.10 (Continued)

State	Statutory Exclusion Offense and Minimum Age Criteria								
	Minimum Age for Statutory Exclusion	Any Criminal Offense	Certain Felonies	Capital Crimes	Murder	Certain Person Offenses	Certain Property Offenses	Certain Drug Offenses	Certain Weapon Offenses
South Dakota	16		16						
Utah	16		16		16	16	16		16
Vermont	14		14		14	14	14		
Washington	16				16	16	16		
Wisconsin	10				10	10			

Notes: Ages in the minimum age column may not apply to all offense restrictions but represent the youngest possible age at which a juvenile may be judicially waived to criminal court. "NS" indicates that no minimum age is specified.

* In Nevada, the exclusion applies to any juvenile with a previous felony adjudication, regardless of the current offense charged, if the current offense involves the use or threatened use of a firearm.

- All states have provisions for trying certain juveniles as adults in criminal court. This is known as *transfer to criminal court.* There are three basic transfer mechanisms: *judicial waiver, statutory exclusion,* and *concurrent jurisdiction.*

- Legislatures "transfer" large numbers of young offenders to criminal court by enacting statutes that exclude certain cases from juvenile court jurisdiction. As of the end of the 2014 legislative session, 29 states had statutory exclusion provisions.

- Under statutory (or legislative) exclusion provisions, State statutes exclude certain serious, violent, or repeat juvenile offenders from juvenile court jurisdiction. In most states, statutory exclusion provisions are limited by age, offense, and/or prior court history criteria.

- The offenses most often excluded are murder, capital crimes in general (offenses punishable by death or life imprisonment), and other serious offenses against persons.

- Some states (14) hold a hearing in juvenile court to determine if there is probable cause to believe the juvenile is of the required age and committed an offense targeted by the provision. Such provisions are referred to as *mandatory waiver* and were previously considered statutory exclusion.

- Minor offenses, such as traffic, watercraft, fish or game, and local ordinance violations, are also often excluded from juvenile court jurisdiction in states where they are not covered by concurrent jurisdiction provisions.

- Although not typically thought of as transfers, large numbers of youth younger than 18 are tried in criminal court in the 10 states where the upper age of juvenile court jurisdiction is set at 15 or 16. More than 2.5 million 16- and 17-year-olds live in these 10 states. If these youth are referred to criminal court at the same rate that 16- and 17-year-olds elsewhere are referred to juvenile court, then a large number of youth younger than 18 face trial in criminal court because they are defined as adults under state laws.

Source: Office of Juvenile Justice and Delinquency Prevention (2017d).

Another type of waiver is the discretionary waiver. A number of states permit waivers of jurisdiction for children over a certain age without regard to the nature of the offense involved. Where the juvenile court finds that the minor is not a fit and proper subject to be dealt with under the juvenile court act and the seriousness of the offense demands that the best interests of society be considered, the juvenile court judge may order criminal proceedings to be instituted against the minor (Bilchik, 1999a, p. 16).

Discretionary determination of waivers may be left to juvenile court judges to decide after a petition for a waiver has been filed and a hearing has been conducted on the advisability of granting the waiver. In general, the criteria used by juvenile court judges to determine the granting or denial of waivers of juveniles to criminal courts are rather vague and, for the most part, quite subjective. As stated previously, if the minor is not a fit and proper subject to be dealt with under the juvenile court, an order instituting criminal proceedings may be rendered by the juvenile court. Factors typically cited by the courts as weighing heavily in the decision to waive jurisdiction include the seriousness of the offense, the age of the juvenile, and the past history of the juvenile. However, some jurisdictions confer on the prosecutor the authority to decide which court (juvenile or criminal) should hear the case. According to Redding (2010), 14 states and the District of Columbia allow prosecutors to file charges in either juvenile or adult court against youth who commit violent offenses. Twenty-five states also have reverse waiver laws where the adult criminal court judge has the discretion to send the youth back to the juvenile court for sentencing purposes (Snyder & Sickmund, 2006).

With respect to waivers, in the *Kent* case, the U.S. Supreme Court ruled that to protect the constitutional rights of the juvenile, the juvenile is entitled to the following:

1. A full hearing on the issue of a waiver
2. The assistance of legal counsel at the hearing
3. Full access to the social records used to determine whether such transfer should be made
4. Statement of the reasons why the juvenile judge decided to waive the juvenile to (adult) criminal court (*Kent v. United States*, 383 U.S. 541, 1966)

In *Kent*, the Court held that a waiver of jurisdiction is a critically important stage in the juvenile process that must be considered in terms of due process and fair treatment as required by the Fourteenth Amendment. Although the *Kent* decision applied only to the District of Columbia, most states that allow waivers have incorporated the waiver procedures of *Kent* into their juvenile court acts. A clear majority of states statutorily guarantee a waiver hearing.

Some states have attempted to establish at least some criteria that would aid the juvenile court judge in making a determination on a motion to waive the juvenile court's jurisdiction. For example, in Illinois the court must consider the following:

1. The seriousness of the alleged offense
2. Whether there is evidence that the alleged offense was committed in an aggressive and premeditated manner
3. The age of the minor
4. The previous delinquency history of the minor
5. The culpability of the minor
6. Whether there are facilities particularly available to the juvenile court for the treatment and rehabilitation of the minor
7. Whether the best interests of the minor and the security of the public may require that the minor continue in custody or under supervision for a period extending beyond his minority
8. Whether the minor possessed a deadly weapon when committing the alleged offense (ILCS, ch. 705, art. V, sec. 405/5-805 [3][b], 2012)

The juvenile court judge, as well as the prosecuting officials, must weigh the consequences of a waiver for the future of the juvenile. The question concerning a waiver of a juvenile to the adult criminal court for prosecution of an offense that might result in a felony record is extremely important due to the lasting effects that a felony record might have. To justify a waiver for criminal prosecution, the juvenile court must agree to accept the more punitive, retributive, and punishment-oriented approach of the adult court. In such cases, the juvenile court judge must act not only in the best interests of the minor but also in the best interests of the community by protecting the community against further unlawful, and perhaps violent, conduct by the juvenile offender. Juvenile court judges, realizing the full effect of a felony record (e.g., in terms of future employment) generally permit a waiver for criminal prosecution only when the offense is so serious that relegating the offense to the realm of delinquency would be unconscionable and would result in a mockery of justice and when the offense is not an isolated act but rather a series of acts showing a trend toward becoming more serious.

Double Jeopardy

The Fifth Amendment states that no person shall be subject to being tried twice for the same offense. Courts in the United States at one time held that the double jeopardy clause did not prohibit a juvenile adjudicated delinquent from subsequently being tried for the same offense in criminal court. In *Breed v. Jones* (421 U.S. 519, 1975), the U.S. Supreme Court unanimously ruled that the Fifth Amendment's prohibition against double jeopardy precludes criminal prosecution of a juvenile subsequent to proceedings in juvenile court involving the same act.

After dealing with scope and purpose, most juvenile court acts go on to describe in detail the procedures to be employed by various components of the juvenile justice system in handling the juvenile. We discuss these procedural requirements in the following chapter.

CAREER OPPORTUNITY: COURT ADMINISTRATOR

Job description: Carries out the nonjudicial functions of the court including the following: management of the jury; court finances; fines collection; case flow management of all civil, criminal, traffic, juvenile, family, and probate matters; and records management. In addition, a court administrator provides a wide range of services to the public, judges, attorneys, agencies, and other members of the judicial branch.

Employment requirements: Must have a 4-year degree. Prior administrative experience may be required.

Beginning salary: Between $20,000 and $40,000 depending on jurisdiction. Benefits vary widely but are typically included.

Summary

A thorough understanding of both the purpose and scope of juvenile court acts is crucial because the intent of the juvenile court acts cannot be carried out without this understanding.

The primary purpose of juvenile court acts is to ensure the welfare of the juvenile within a legal framework while maintaining the family unit and protecting the public. Most of us would agree that this is an admirable goal. At the same time, however, we should be aware of the inherent difficulties involved in achieving this goal. Consider, for example, the police officer who has apprehended a particular juvenile a number of times for increasingly serious offenses. Repeated attempts at enlisting the aid of the juvenile's family in correcting the undesirable behavior have failed. If the officer decides that protection of the public is now of primary importance, the officer may feel compelled to arrest the juvenile even though this action may result in the juvenile being sent to a detention facility. As a result, the family unit is broken up and the welfare of the juvenile has been, to some extent, sacrificed by placing him or her in detention.

Also consider the dilemma of the juvenile court judge who must make the final decision concerning what is in the best interests of both the juvenile and the public. If the judge adheres to the philosophy of the juvenile court, the judge may be tempted to leave the juvenile with his or her family even though the public may suffer. In addition, the judge and prosecutor are faced with the difficult task of making distinctions between unruly and delinquent juveniles. These distinctions are crucial given that different types of treatment, correctional, and rehabilitation programs are available depending on the label attached.

A thorough understanding of the scope of juvenile court acts is equally important. The police officer on the street must be aware of both the age limits and the different categories into which juveniles are separated if the requirements of the juvenile court act are to be met. Prosecutors and judges must be certain that jurisdictional requirements have been met and must understand the consequences of requesting or granting waivers. In short, the purposes of juvenile court acts cannot be achieved without thorough knowledge of the subjects and behaviors dealt with in the scope of such acts.

The purposes of juvenile court acts are, in general, to create courts with the authority to hear designated kinds of cases, to discuss the procedural rules to be used in such cases, and to provide for the best interests of juveniles while at the same time protecting the interests of the family and society. Unfortunately, it is not always possible to achieve all of these purposes in any one case. For example, it might be in the best interests of society to send a particular juvenile to a correctional facility, but this action is not likely to be in the best interests of the juvenile.

Sections in juvenile court acts dealing with scope generally include information on age requirements, geographical requirements, types of behaviors covered by the acts, and waivers.

The Uniform Juvenile Court Act requires legal accountability, narrows the definition of delinquency (excludes status offenses), and attempts to ensure the best interests of juveniles while maintaining the family unit and protecting the public.

In 1967, the President's Commission on Law Enforcement and Administration of Justice recommended that serious thought be given to completely eliminating from juvenile court jurisdiction children who commit noncriminal acts or status offenses. Consistent with this recommendation, two national commissions (the ABA's [1977] Standards Project and the Twentieth Century Fund Task Force on Sentencing Policy Toward Youthful Offenders [1987]) proposed the elimination of juvenile court jurisdiction over status offenders, and most states have followed this recommendation.

KEY TERMS

adjudicatory hearing   148

automatic waiver   172

beyond a reasonable doubt   153

blended sentencing   169

concurrent jurisdiction   169

delinquency, neglect, abuse, and dependency cases   145

discretionary waiver   172

dispositional hearing   148

double jeopardy   178

due process   153

exclusive jurisdiction   168

in need of supervision   162

petition   148

purpose statement of a juvenile court act   145

scope of a juvenile court act   145

standard of preponderance of evidence   166

status offenses   161

Uniform Juvenile Court Act   145

unruly children   163

Critical Thinking Questions

1. In addition to protecting the community from youthful offenders, what are the three major purposes or goals of juvenile court acts?

2. How and why did the Uniform Juvenile Court Act (see appendix) come into existence? Has this act had much impact on the various state juvenile court acts? Give some examples to support your answer.

3. In what situation would the juvenile court use concurrent jurisdiction? Suppose that a 10-year-old is chronically running away from home. When taken into custody, the child makes claims of sexual abuse at home. Would this juvenile case be heard in adult or juvenile court? Is this an unruly child or a child who is abused/neglected or dependent? How do you make the distinction? What are likely alternatives for this child's care and custody? What are treatment alternatives?

4. What types of crimes are most suitable for waivers to adult court? Should waivers be mandated by the state legislators or be discretionary for prosecutors and judges? Why?

Suggested Readings

Adams, B., & Addie, S. (2011). *Delinquency cases waived to criminal court, 2008* (OJJDP Fact Sheet). Washington, DC: U.S. Department of Justice, Office of Juvenile Justice and Delinquency Prevention. Retrieved from www.ojjdp.gov/pubs/236481.pdf

Cheesman, F. (2011). *A decade of NCSC research on blended sentencing of juvenile offenders: What have we learned about "who gets a second chance?"* Washington, DC: National Center for State Courts. Retrieved from www.ncsc.org/sitecore/content/microsites/future-trends-2011/home/Special-Programs/4-4-Blended-Sentencing-of-Juvenile-Offenders.aspx

Davis, S. M. (2006). *Rights of juveniles: The juvenile justice system* (2nd ed.). Eagan, MN: Thomson/West.

National Council of Juvenile and Family Court Judges. (2005). *Juvenile delinquency guidelines: Improving court practice in juvenile delinquency cases.* Washington, DC: U.S. Department of Justice, Office of Juvenile Justice and Delinquency Prevention.

Office of Juvenile Justice and Delinquency Prevention. (2000). *OJJDP research report.* Washington, DC: U.S. Department of Justice, Office of Juvenile Justice and Delinquency Prevention. Retrieved from www.ncjrs.gov/pdffiles1/ojjdp/186732.pdf

Office of Juvenile Justice and Delinquency Prevention. (2012, December 17). *Statistical briefing book.* Retrieved from www.ojjdp.gov/ojstatbb/structure_process/qa04113.asp?qaDate=2011

Office of Juvenile Justice and Delinquency Prevention. (2015, October 1). *Statistical briefing book.* Retrieved from http://www.ojjdp.gov/ojstatbb/structure_process/qa04112.asp?qaDate=2014

Palmer, E. A. (2000). Weary of juvenile justice logjam, members move provisions separately (Aimee's Law). *CQ Weekly, 58*(29), 1727–1728.

Puzzanchera, C. M. (2000). *Delinquency cases waived to criminal court, 1988–1997.* OJJDP Fact Sheet. Washington, DC: U.S. Department of Justice.

Redding, R. E. (2010, June). *Juvenile transfer laws: An effective deterrent to delinquency?* Washington, DC: Office of Juvenile Justice. Retrieved from www.ncjrs.gov/pdffiles1/ojjdp/220595.pdf

Sickmund, M. (2003). *Juvenile offenders and victims: National report series bulletin.* Washington, DC: U.S. Department of Justice, Office of Juvenile Justice and Delinquency Prevention. Retrieved from www.ncjrs.gov/html/ojjdp/195420/contents.html

Snyder, H. N., & Sickmund, M. (2006). *Juvenile offenders and victims: 2006 national report.* Washington, DC: U.S. Department of Justice, Office of Justice Programs, Office of Juvenile Justice and Delinquency Prevention.

Stevenson, C. S., Larson, C. S., Carter, L., Gomby, D. S., Terman, D. L., & Behrman, R. E. (2013). The juvenile court: Analysis and recommendations. *The Future of Children.* Retrieved from www.princeton.edu/futureofchildren/publications/journals/article/index.xml?journalid=55&articleid=310&sectionid=2054

Juvenile Justice Procedures

7

CHAPTER LEARNING OBJECTIVES

On completion of this chapter, students should be able to do the following:

- Understand and discuss juvenile court procedures
- Discuss the rights of juveniles at various stages, from taking into custody through appeals
- Understand requirements for bail, notification, and filing of petitions
- Discuss procedures involved in detaining juveniles

WHAT WOULD YOU DO?

It is Friday night and you are in bed. Your 13-year-old daughter is spending the night with a friend. The two girls told you they were going to a movie and back to her friend's home. Her friend's older sister, who is 18, is going to drive them to and from the movie. At approximately 2:15 a.m. you get a phone call. The caller identifies herself as Lisa Strom, an employee of the Forten County Detention Center. She says that your daughter has been taken into custody for curfew violation, possession of alcohol by a minor, peace disturbance, and assaulting a police officer. Ms. Strom informs you that your daughter will be held in detention pending a review of her case by a juvenile intake officer. This review will take place within the next 24 hours and you will receive another phone call once the juvenile intake officer decides to hold or release the child. She states that you are allowed to visit your daughter once within the next 24 hours and informs you that visitation is allowed between 6:00 p.m. and 8:00 p.m. that day. The only question you can think to ask is if your daughter is okay. Ms. Strom says your daughter is going through the intake process and is in good health. You hang up the phone wide awake and wondering what to do next.

What Would You Do?

1. Would your daughter be classified as a status offender or a delinquent, according to the charges?

2. What would be your next course of action? Would you contact a lawyer, wait for the phone call from the juvenile intake officer, visit your daughter during visiting hours, or do something else?

3. If you were the juvenile intake officer, would you continue to detain this child or release her to her parents pending court?

Juvenile court acts discuss not only the purposes and scope of the juvenile justice system but also the procedure the juvenile courts are to follow. Proceedings concerning juveniles officially begin with the filing of a petition alleging that a juvenile is delinquent, dependent, neglected, abused, in need of supervision, or in need of authoritative intervention. Most juvenile court acts, however, also discuss the unofficial or diversionary activities available as remedies prior to the filing of a petition such as a stationhouse adjustment and a preliminary conference. A stationhouse adjustment occurs when a police officer negotiates a settlement with a juvenile, often with his or her parents, without taking further official action (a full discussion of stationhouse adjustments follows in Chapter 8). A preliminary conference is a voluntary meeting arranged by a juvenile probation officer with the victim, the juvenile, and typically the juvenile's parents or guardian in an attempt to negotiate a settlement without taking further official action. Juvenile court acts clearly indicate those persons who are eligible to file a petition. For example, in Illinois any adult person (21 years of age or over), agency, or association by its representative may file a petition, or the court on its own motion may direct the filing through the state's attorney of a petition in respect to a minor under the act (Illinois Compiled Statutes [ILCS], ch. 705, art. 1, sec. 405/1-3, 2012). Tennessee's statute says, "The petition may be made by any person, including a law enforcement officer, who has knowledge of the facts alleged or is informed and believes that they are true" (Tennessee Code Annotated, § 37-1-119, 2012).

Although it is true that a petition may be filed by any eligible person by going directly to the prosecutor (state's attorney or district attorney), a large proportion of petitions are filed following police action or by

©Kevin Beebe/Photo Library/Getty Images

Are stationhouse adjustments more common for juveniles of some ages, races, and gender than others?

social service agencies dealing with minors by either juvenile court personnel or prosecuting attorneys. To understand the step-by-step procedures involved in processing juveniles, we discuss the typical sequence of events occurring after the police take a juvenile into custody. We rely heavily on the procedures given in the Uniform Juvenile Court Act and the Illinois Juvenile Court Act, which closely resemble similar acts in many states. Although a general discussion of juvenile justice procedures is given, some states differ with respect to specific requirements. You should consult the juvenile court act or code relevant to your state for exact procedural requirements.

Rights of Juveniles

Regardless of the particular jurisdiction, juveniles in the United States have been (since the 1967 *Gault* decision) guaranteed a number of basic rights at the adjudicatory stage. Thus, a juvenile who is alleged to be delinquent has the following rights (*In re Gault*, 1967):

1. The right to notice of the charges and time to prepare for the case
2. The right to counsel
3. The right to confront and cross-examine witnesses
4. The right to remain silent in court

As a direct result of the *Gault* decision, the constitutional guarantees of the Fifth Amendment and Sixth Amendment are applicable to states through the Fourteenth Amendment and not only apply to delinquency matters but also have been extended to some cases involving the need for supervision or intervention. The question remaining after the *Gault* decision concerned the extent to which its mandate logically extended to other stages of the juvenile justice process, particularly the police investigatory process. Both the *Gault* and *Kent* decisions (*Kent v. United States*, 1966) have been interpreted to require the application of the Fourth Amendment and the exclusionary rule to the juvenile justice process. The most difficult issue has revolved around the juvenile's competency to waive his or her rights under Miranda. In general, the courts have relied on a totality of circumstances approach in determining the validity of the waiver. Circumstances considered include the age, competency, and educational level of the juvenile; his or her ability to understand the nature of the charges; and the methods used in, and length of, the interrogation (Davis, 2001, sec. 3.13, pp. 3-86–3-90).

The Uniform Juvenile Court Act (National Conference of Commissioners on Uniform State Laws, 1968, sec. 26) provides that all parties to juvenile court proceedings are entitled to representation by counsel. Many jurisdictions currently provide for representation by counsel in neglect, abuse, and dependency proceedings, extending the *Gault* decision to such cases (Montana Code Annotated, 41-3-425, 2015; 32A-1-1; NMSA, 1978). In a neglect and/or abuse case, legal counsel for the minor may be the state's attorney, who represents the state that has a duty to protect the child. The court may also appoint a guardian ad litem for a juvenile if the juvenile has no parent or guardian appearing on his or her behalf or if the parent's or guardian's interests conflict with those of the juvenile—as is often the case in abuse and neglect cases. Some states allow for both the prosecuting attorney and the guardian ad litem, with the guardian ad litem presenting a separate case based on evidence he or she believes to demonstrate the best interest of the child (Missouri Revised Statutes, 211.462, 2015).

The protection afforded by the Fourth Amendment against illegal search and seizure extends to juveniles. All courts that have specifically considered the issue of the applicability of the Fourth Amendment to the juvenile justice process have found it to be applicable, or more correctly, no court has found it to be inapplicable (Davis, 2001, 3–17; Montana Code Annotated, 41-5-1415, 2015). The Uniform Juvenile Court Act (National Conference of Commissioners on Uniform State Laws, 1968, sec. 27[b]) states that evidence seized illegally will not be admitted over objection. Similarly, a valid confession made by a juvenile out of court is, in the words of the Uniform Juvenile Court Act, "insufficient to support an adjudication of delinquency unless it is corroborated in whole or in part by other evidence." This extends some protection to juveniles not normally accorded to adults. In addition, the Uniform Juvenile Court Act (sec. 27[a]) recommends that a party be entitled to introduce evidence and otherwise be heard in his or her own behalf and to cross-examine adverse witnesses. Furthermore, a juvenile accused of a delinquent act need not be a witness against, or otherwise incriminate, himself or herself. A majority of juvenile court acts do not spell out a detailed code of evidence. However, most do specify whether the rules permit only competent, material, and relevant evidence and whether the rules of evidence that apply in criminal or civil cases are applicable in juvenile cases. A number of states provide that the rules of evidence applicable in criminal cases apply in delinquency proceedings and that the rules of evidence applicable in civil cases apply in other proceedings (i.e., neglect, dependency, and in-need-of-supervision cases). In Georgia, for example, the standard of proof in dependency cases is clear and convincing evidence, whereas in delinquency cases the standard of proof is beyond a reasonable doubt (Georgia Criminal and Traffic Law Manual, 2014, 15-11-180 and 15-11-581).

The Children's Bureau of the U.S. Department of Health and Human Services recommended many years ago that, unless a child is advised by counsel, the statements of the child made while in the custody of the police or probation officers, including statements made during a preliminary inquiry, predisposition study, or consent decree, should not be used against the child prior to the determination of the petition's allegations in a delinquency or in need of supervision/intervention case or in a criminal proceeding prior to conviction (Children's Bureau, 1969, sec. 26). In abuse and neglect cases, however, the courts have eased restrictions on the admission of statements made in the totality of circumstances, witness testimony, and so on (see Chapter 5).

It should be noted that some rights guaranteed to adults are not guaranteed to juveniles in most jurisdictions. As a result of the *McKeiver* decision (*McKeiver v. Pennsylvania*, 1971), juveniles are not generally guaranteed the right to a trial by jury or a public trial. The U.S. Supreme Court, in deciding *McKeiver*, indicated that a jury was not necessary for fact-finding purposes and left the issue of trial by jury up to the individual states. Although the majority of jurisdictions provide for hearings without juries, some provide for jury trials by statute (which specify certain criminal acts that are eligible for jury trials and when a youth may request a jury trial) or judicial decision (Colorado Revised Statutes, 19-2-107, 2002; Massachusetts General Laws Annotated, ch. 119, sec. 55A, 2016; Montana Code Annotated, 41-5-1502 [1], 2015; Texas Family Code Annotated, 54.03 [c], 2007; West Virginia Code Annotated, 49-5-6, 2012). In addition, the *McKeiver* decision left open the question of whether juvenile court proceedings are necessarily adversarial in nature and left on the states the burden of establishing that a separate justice system for juveniles represents a useful alternative to criminal processing.

Bail

The issue of bail (release from custody pending trial after payment of a court-ordered sum) for juveniles is controversial. Some jurisdictions permit bail, whereas others do not on the grounds that the juvenile has not been charged with a crime and, therefore, is not entitled to bail. Because of special release provisions for juveniles (to the custody of parents or a guardian), bail has not been a question of paramount concern in terms of litigation. A number of states forbid the use of bail with respect to juveniles (Hawaii Revised Statutes, 571-32 [h], 2015; Missouri Revised Statutes, 211.061, 2015), several states authorize release on bail at the discretion of a judge (Connecticut General Statutes Annotated, sec. 46b-133b, 2012; Nebraska Revised Statutes, 43-253 [5], 2012), and some states allow the same right to bail enjoyed by adults (Colorado Revised Statutes 19-2-509, 2012; Georgia Code, 15-11-47 (d), 2010).

Finally, most jurisdictions require that official records kept on juveniles be maintained in separate and confidential files. These may be opened only by court order or following stringent guidelines established by state statutes (Missouri Revised Statutes, 211.321, 2015). As an example, Arkansas states very specifically which juvenile records are open for review, for example:

(1) Adoption records, including any part of a dependency-neglect record that includes adoption records, shall be closed and confidential as provided in the Revised Uniform Adoption Act, 9-9-201 et seq.; (2) Records of delinquency adjudications for which a juvenile could have been tried as an adult shall be made available to prosecuting attorneys for use at sentencing if the juvenile is subsequently tried as an adult or to determine if the juvenile should be tried as an adult; and (3) Records of delinquency adjudications for a juvenile adjudicated delinquent for any felony or a Class A misdemeanor wherein violence or a weapon was involved shall be made available to the Arkansas Crime Information Center; and (b) (1) (A) Records of delinquency adjudications for which a juvenile could have been tried as an adult shall be kept for ten (10) years after the last adjudication of delinquency or the date of a plea of guilty or nolo contendere or a finding of guilt as an adult. (Arkansas Code 9-27-309, 2010)

Taking Into Custody

The Uniform Juvenile Court Act (National Conference of Commissioners on Uniform State Laws, 1968) states the following:

> A child may be taken into custody pursuant to an order of the court under that Act, or pursuant to the laws of arrest; or by a law enforcement officer if there are reasonable grounds to believe that the child is suffering from illness or injury or is in immediate danger from his surroundings and that his removal is necessary; or by a law enforcement officer if there are reasonable grounds to believe that the child has run away from his parents or guardian. (sec. 13)

The broad jurisdictional scope of the juvenile courts generally provides that any juvenile can be taken into custody (detained) without a warrant if the law enforcement officer reasonably believes the juvenile to be delinquent, in need of supervision, dependent, abused, or neglected as defined within that state's juvenile court act. However, some states have recognized that removing a juvenile from home before there has been any trial is a power to be used on a limited basis. For truancy, disobedience, and even neglect, the legal

A series of court decisions and some constitutional amendments help to protect the rights of juveniles taken into custody.

process should begin with a summons unless there is "imminent danger" involved and unless waiting for the court's permission would result in unnecessary and dangerous delay. In Illinois, a law enforcement officer may, without a warrant, take into temporary custody a minor whom the officer, with reasonable cause, believes to be delinquent and requiring authoritative intervention, dependent, abused, or neglected as defined within that state's juvenile court act (ILCS, ch. 705, sec. 405/2-5, 3-4, 4-4, 5-401, 2011). In addition, the officer may take into custody any juvenile who has been adjudged a ward of the court and has escaped from any commitment ordered by the court. Alabama, for example, states a child can be taken into custody "by a law enforcement officer having reasonable grounds to believe that the child has run away from a detention, residential, shelter or other care facility" (Alabama Code § 12-15-56, 2015). The officer may also take into custody any juvenile who is found on any street or in any public place suffering from any sickness or injury requiring care, medical treatment, or hospitalization. The Alabama juvenile code also states the following:

> By a law enforcement officer having reasonable grounds to believe that the child is suffering from illness or injury or is in immediate danger from the child's surroundings and that the child's immediate removal from such surroundings is necessary for the protection of the health and safety of such child. (Alabama Code § 12-15-56, 2015)

The taking into temporary custody under the Uniform Juvenile Court Act does not constitute an official arrest. Although statutes in various states provide that taking into custody is not deemed an arrest, this is somewhat a legal fiction given that the juvenile is often held in involuntary custody. In light of recent court decisions, when delinquency is the alleged reason for taking into custody, law enforcement officers must adhere to appropriate constitutional guidelines. For categories other than delinquency, the *parens patriae* concern for protecting minors from dangerous surroundings will suffice constitutionally as reasonable grounds for taking minors into custody when it is not abused by law enforcement officers.

Interrogation

While in custody, the juvenile has rights similar to those of an adult with respect to interrogation. To determine whether a confession or statement was given freely and voluntarily, the totality of circumstances surrounding the giving of the statement is to be considered. Even prior to *Gault*, the U.S. Supreme Court in *Haley v. Ohio* (1948) and *Gallegos v. Colorado* (1969) used the voluntariness test to determine the admissibility of statements made by juveniles to the police. If the police desire to question a juvenile concerning a delinquent act,

---

IN PRACTICE 7.1

DEFENSE: POLICE NEVER READ RIGHTS TO TEEN SUSPECT IN MERCER CO. MURDER

MERCER COUNTY, Ky. (WKYT) - 16-year-old Trenton Easterling went before a judge inside the Mercer County Courthouse Monday morning.

Monday's hearing in the case involved a request to suppress evidence. Easterling's defense attorneys called into question if the Miranda rights were read to Easterling before he spoke with detectives.

Sgt. Swavey of the Mercer County's Sheriff's Office was one of three officers to take the stand on Monday. He testified that on April 14th officers visited the school to speak with students and staff about the death investigation of Tristan Cole. Easterling was one of those students with which the police wanted to speak.

His mother, Melissa Easterling, said in court that police called her to the school. She went on to say she was then asked by officers to come down with Trenton to the Police Department for questioning. Trenton was taken to the police department in a squad car but was not arrested.

Officers say, Trenton, along with his mother and grandfather, went into a room once arriving at the police department. Officers also say that Trenton's mother was asked to step out of the room so they could explain the Miranda rights to her. They said she could be present with Trenton while in the room and stop the interview at any time.

Trenton's mother agreed to proceed, but after 30 minutes of questioning, stopped the interview. Police recorded that interview, but the defense says since Miranda rights were never read to Trenton specifically, it should not be used in court.

According to police, officers never read Miranda rights to Trenton, and no one ever signed a waiver.

We spoke with the father of Tristan who says he was not happy with what he heard in court:

"I don't know what to say. I'm not too happy what went by in court today. I mean somebody did not do their job, and maybe it will come out good, or maybe it will come out bad. I mean that was a mistake that was made that shouldn't of been made. That's all I'm going to say," Cole's father, Gary Devine told WKYT.

A judge set a competency hearing for Easterling for December 13th.

Source: Defense: Police never read rights to teen suspect in Mercer Co. murder (2016).

the juvenile should be given the Miranda warning and should be clearly told that a decision to remain silent will not be taken as an indication of guilt. This can be problematic, as seen in In Practice 7.1, when police or others are not aware of the policies, procedures, and requirements with regard to juveniles. Many police administrators, prosecutors, and juvenile court judges believe that it is best not to question the juvenile unless his or her parents or a counselor are present. In Colorado, for example, "no statement or admission of a child made as a result of interrogation by law enforcement officials . . . shall be admissible . . . unless a parent, guardian, or custodian was present . . . and the child was advised of his right to counsel and to remain silent" (Colorado Revised Statutes Annotated, 19-2-511 [1], 2009). Any confession obtained without these safeguards might be considered invalid on grounds that the juvenile did not understand his or her rights or was frightened. The Uniform Juvenile Court Act (sec. 27[b]) contains similar provisions.

Juveniles taken into custody may be either detained or released to the custody of their parents or guardian. Most model juvenile court acts and the Uniform Juvenile Court Act (sec. 15) dictate that the police make an "immediate" and "reasonable" attempt to notify the juvenile's parents or guardian of his or her custody. The maximum length of time considered to be immediate is usually established by statute. The definition of *reasonable* usually includes attempts to phone and/or visit the residence of the juvenile's parents, place of employment, and any other known "haunts." In Oregon, as an example, the statute states the following:

> The person taking the youth into custody shall notify the youth's parent, guardian or other person responsible for the youth. The notice shall inform the parent, guardian or other person of the action taken and the time and place of the hearing. (Oregon Juvenile Code 419C.097, 2015)

Detention Hearing

In the What Would You Do? scenario at the beginning of the chapter, an intake officer would likely decide to hold or release the child and another phone call would be placed to the child's parent informing her of the decision. If a juvenile is not released to his or her parents soon after being taken into custody, most states require that a detention hearing (a court hearing to determine whether detention is required) be held within a specified period. Sufficient notification must, of course, be given to all parties concerned before the proceeding. Section 17 of the Uniform Juvenile Court Act indicates that if a juvenile is brought before the court or delivered to a detention or shelter care facility, the intake or other authorized officer of the court will immediately begin an investigation and release the juvenile unless it appears that further detention or shelter care is warranted or required. If the juvenile is not released within 72 hours after being placed in detention, an informal detention hearing is held to determine whether further detention is warranted or required. Reasonable notice of the hearing must be given to the juvenile and to the parents or guardian. In addition, notification of the right to counsel and of the juvenile's right to remain silent regarding any allegations of delinquency or unruly conduct must also be given by the court to the respondents. States vary with respect to the criteria used to determine the need for further detention, but they usually focus on the need to ensure the protection of society and the juvenile and on the possibility of the juvenile fleeing the jurisdiction. For example, in Illinois, after a minor has been delivered to the place designated by the court, the following must occur:

> The intake personnel shall immediately investigate the circumstances of the minor and the facts surrounding his being taken into custody. The minor shall be immediately released to the custody of his parents unless the intake officer finds that further detention is a matter of immediate and urgent necessity for the protection of the minor, or of the person or property of another, or that he is likely to flee the jurisdiction of the court. (ILCS, ch. 705, sec. 5-501 [2], 2011)

Detention can be authorized by the intake officer (generally a designated juvenile police officer or the juvenile probation officer) for up to 36 hours, at which time the minor is either released to his or her parents or brought before the court for a detention hearing. Failure to file a petition or to bring the juvenile before the court within 40 hours will result in a release from detention (ILCS, ch. 705, sec. 405/5-415, 2011). Some states use 24-hour, 48-hour, and 72-hour standards for release, filing of the petition, and the detention hearing. Weekends and holidays do not typically count in the statutory requirements. In West Virginia, the juvenile code states,

The referee, judge or magistrate shall hear testimony concerning the circumstances for taking the juvenile into custody and the possible need for detention in accordance with section two, article five-a of this chapter. The sole mandatory issue at the detention hearing is whether the juvenile should be detained pending further court proceedings. The court shall, if the health, safety and welfare of the juvenile will not be endangered thereby, release the juvenile on recognizance to his or her parents, custodians or an appropriate agency; however, if warranted, the court may require bail, except that bail may be denied in any case where bail could be denied if the accused were an adult. (West Virginia Code, ch. 49, art. 5, §49-5-8a, 2009)

For a sample temporary custody order, see Figure 7.1.

Figure 7.1 Temporary Custody Hearing Order

SS:

IN THE COURT OF THE 9th JUDICIAL CIRCUIT McDONOUGH COUNTY, ILLINOIS

NO.

IN THE INTEREST OF: Ex Parte ☐

_____   Without Prejudice ☐

Minor(s)

TEMPORARY CUSTODY HEARING ORDER

(705) ILCS 405/2-10

THIS CAUSE coming to be heard upon the motion of _____ for _____.

The Court having jurisdiction over the matter and parties, and being fully advised in the premises.

THE COURT FINDS:

1. The minor's

Mother received	☐ notice	☐ no notice and was	☐ present	☐ not present
Father received	☐ notice	☐ no notice and was	☐ present	☐ not present
Guardian/custodian/ relative received	☐ notice	☐ no notice and was	☐ present	☐ not present

2. Probable cause

   ☐ A. does not exist that the minor is (abused/neglected/dependent); or

   ☐ B. does exist that the minor is (abused/neglected/dependent)

The basis of the finding is:

_____

_____

_____

3. Immediate and urgent necessity
   ☐ A. does not exist to support removal of the minor from the home; or
   ☐ B. does exist to support the removal of the minor from the home and remaining in the home is contrary to the child's welfare, safety, or best interest.

The basis of the finding is:

_____

_____

_____

4. Reasonable efforts
   ☐ A. have been made but have not eliminated the immediate and urgent necessity to remove the child (children) from the home; or
   ☐ B. reasonably be made at this time, for good cause, prevent or eliminate the necessity of removal of the minor(s) from the home; or
   ☐ C. have been made and have eliminated the immediate and urgent necessity to remove the child (children) from the home.
   ☐ D. have not been made.

The basis of the finding is:

_____

_____

_____

5. Consistent with the health, safety and best interest of the minor
   ☐ A. the minor shall be released to the parent; or
   ☐ B. the minor shall be placed in shelter care.

Case #_____

IT IS ORDERED:
   ☐ A. The petition is dismissed.
   ☐ B. Consistent with the health, safety, and best interests of the minor, the minor shall (be returned to/remain) in the custody of the (mother/father/parents/guardian/custodian/responsible relative).
   ☐ C. Consistent with the health, safety, and best interests of the minor, the minor shall be removed from the home; and
      (1) Temporary custody of the minor is granted to

(Continued)

Figure 7.1 (Continued)

☐ (A) private custodian/guardian _____ whose relationship to the minor is

_____.

☐ (B) DCFS Guardianship Administrator with the right to place the minor.

(2) The temporary custodian is authorized to consent to

☐ (A) ordinary and routine medical care AND major medical care* on behalf of the minor (temporary custody with the right to consent to major medical care).

☐ (B) only ordinary and routine medical care on behalf of the minor (temporary custody without the right to consent to major medical care).

*Major medical care is defined as those medical procedures which are not administered or performed on a routine basis and which involve hospitalization, surgery, or use of anesthesia (e.g., appendectomies, blood transfusion, psychiatric hospitalization).

☐ (C)

_____

_____

☐ (D) A 405/2-25 or 405/2-20 Order of Protection entered this date is incorporated herein against

_____

_____

☐ (E) DCFS shall investigate the need for services in the following areas:

_____

_____

☐ (F) If there is a finding of no reasonable efforts under paragraph 4 above, DCFS shall make all reasonable efforts to ameliorate the causes contributing to the finding of probable cause or the immediate and urgent necessity which led to the removal of this child from the home.
These efforts shall include

_____

_____

☐ (G) CFS shall prepare and file with the court on or before _____, 20 _____, a 45 day Case Plan pursuant to 705 ILCS 405/2-10.1.

☐ (H) The Order on Visiting entered this date or on subsequent dates is incorporated herein by reference.

☐ (I) A Social Investigation shall be filed by _____, 20 _____.

☐ (J) The next hearing is set on _____, 20_____, at _____a.m./p.m. for

A substantial number of juvenile cases are "unofficially adjusted" by law enforcement personnel at the initial encounters as well as at the stationhouse. Among those juveniles who are turned over to the court's intake personnel, a substantial number are disposed of at the intake stage and at the detention hearings. In many instances, the intake personnel, the minor and his or her family, and the injured party are able to informally adjust the differences or problems that caused the minor to be taken into custody. This is often encouraged in state juvenile codes. This occurs in Tennessee, for example:

Before or after a petition is filed, the probation officer or other officer of the court designated by it, subject to its direction, may give counsel and advice to the parties with a view to an informal adjustment if it appears: (1) The admitted facts bring the case within the jurisdiction of the court; (2) Counsel and advice without an adjudication would be in the best interest of the public and the child; and (3) The child and the child's parents, guardian or other custodian consent thereto with knowledge that consent is not obligatory. (Tennessee Code Annotated, § 37-1-110, 2012)

Only the most serious cases of delinquency, cases of unruly behavior, and cases involving serious abuse or neglect result in processing through the entire juvenile justice system. There are both legal and ethical questions about unofficial dispositions at the intake stage and the assumption of guilt that often leads to some prescribed treatment program. Although most practitioners make it clear that participation in informal dispositions is voluntary and that following advice or referrals is not mandatory, there may still be some official pressure perceived by the juvenile or the juvenile's parents that violates the presumption of innocence.

Detention or Shelter Care

The following takes place in accordance with the Uniform Juvenile Court Act (National Conference of Commissioners on Uniform State Laws, 1968):

A child taken into custody shall not be detained or placed in shelter care prior to the hearing on the petition unless such detention is required to protect the person or property of others or of the child or because the child may abscond [flee] or be removed from the jurisdiction of the court or because he has no parent or guardian who is able to provide supervision and to return him to the court when required or an order for detention or shelter care has been made by the court pursuant to this Act. (sec. 14)

The absence of any of these conditions must result in the child's release to his or her parents or guardian with their promise to bring the child before the court as requested (sec. 15[1]). Failure to bring the child before the court will result in the issuance of a warrant directing that the child be taken into custody and brought before the court (sec. 15[b]).

The Uniform Juvenile Court Act (National Conference of Commissioners on Uniform State Laws, 1968) requires that the "person taking a child into custody, with all reasonable speed and without first taking the child elsewhere, shall release the child to his parents or guardian . . . unless detention or shelter care is warranted or required" (sec. 15[a][1]). This section of the Uniform Juvenile Court Act is designed to reduce the number of children in detention by specifying criteria that would "require and warrant" further detention.

If reasonable cause for detention cannot be established, the juvenile should be released to his or her parents. In practice, and according to most juvenile court acts, the juvenile is taken to a police or juvenile facility, at which time the parents or guardian are contacted. However, the Uniform Juvenile Court Act implies that the juvenile should be taken immediately to his or her parents or guardian unless detention appears to be warranted. This policy spares the juvenile the experience of being held in the most depressing and intimidating of all custodial facilities—the jail or police lockup.

In some states, if the juvenile is not released to his or her parents or guardian, the juvenile must be taken without unnecessary delay to the court or to a place designated by the court to receive juveniles (ILCS, ch. 705, sec. 405/5-405, 2011; Missouri Revised Statutes, 211.151, 2015). The Uniform Juvenile Court Act does allow detention in a local jail if, and only if, a detention home or center for delinquent children is unavailable (sec. 16[a][4]). If the juvenile is confined in a jail, detention must be in a room separate and removed from the rooms for adults. This required separation from confined adults is commonly found in statutes and extends to cell, room, and yard and sometimes even to any sight or sound. Hawaii allows for the following standard with regard to separation of sight and sound in its juvenile court act:

> The department of human services through the office of youth services shall certify police station cellblocks and community correctional centers that provide sight and sound separation between children and adults in secure custody. Only cellblocks and centers certified under this subsection shall be authorized to detain juveniles pursuant to section 571-32(d). The office of youth services may develop sight and sound separation standards, issue certifications, monitor and inspect facilities for compliance, cite facilities for violations, withdraw certifications, and require certified facilities to submit such data and information as requested. In addition, the office of youth services may monitor and inspect all cellblocks and centers for compliance with section 571-32(d). (Hawaii Revised Statutes, 571-32 [k], 2015)

In all categories other than delinquency, the child is normally taken to a designated shelter care facility, meaning a "physically unrestricted facility," according to the Uniform Juvenile Court Act (sec. 2[6]). The procedures for contacting the parents or guardian and the criteria used to maintain custody in such a facility are the same as for the delinquent child. Shelter care facilities are generally licensed by the state and designated by the juvenile court to receive children who do not require the physically restrictive surroundings of a jail or juvenile detention center (typically, this includes those children believed to be abused or neglected or status offenders).

Maximum time limits for detention are set forth in the various juvenile court acts so that a juvenile will not be detained for lengthy periods without a review by the courts. In some cases, the issue of bail may arise (see discussion earlier in this chapter).

Once the juvenile has been taken into custody and either released to his or her parents or guardian or, with just cause, placed in a detention facility, an officer of the court may attempt to settle the case without a court hearing by arranging for a preliminary conference.

Preliminary Conference

The Uniform Juvenile Court Act (sec. 10) includes a provision that allows a probation officer or other officer designated by the court to hold a preliminary conference so as to give counsel or advice with a view toward an informal adjustment without filing a petition (mentioned earlier in the chapter). This preliminary conference is in order only if the admitted facts bring the case within the jurisdiction of the court and if such an informal adjustment, without an adjudication, is in the best interests of the public and the child. The conference is to be held only with the consent of the juvenile's parents or guardian. However, such a conference is not obligatory (sec. 10[a]). As mentioned earlier, a similar provision is found in the Tennessee juvenile code as well as the Illinois Juvenile Court Act, which states the following:

> The court may authorize the probation officer to confer in a preliminary conference with any person seeking to file a petition . . . concerning the advisability of filing the petition, with a view to adjusting suitable cases without the filing of a petition. (ILCS, ch. 705, sec. 405/5-305, 2011)

If agreement between the parties can be reached at the preliminary conference, no further official action may be necessary. If judicial action seems necessary, the probation officer may recommend the filing of a petition. However, if the injured party demands that a petition be filed, that demand must be satisfied. Although the preliminary conference or *informal* adjustment may be of value in diverting cases that could be better settled outside of juvenile court, it has been subject to criticism as a method of engaging in legal coercion without trial (Tappan, 1949, pp. 310–311). In general, information or evidence presented at the preliminary conference is not admissible at any later stage in the juvenile court proceedings.

Petition

As indicated earlier, juvenile court proceedings begin with the filing of a petition naming the juvenile in question and alleging that this juvenile is delinquent, dependent, abused, neglected, or a minor in need of intervention/supervision. A copy of a sample petition is shown in Figure 7.2. Although states vary regarding who is eligible to file a petition, similarities do exist concerning the content of petitions and the initiation of follow-through activities as a result of the petition. In some states, a preliminary inquiry may be conducted by juvenile court personnel to determine whether the best interests of the child or the public will require that a petition be filed. In other states, this inquiry is accomplished after the petition has been filed and may result in the petition being dismissed by the court if the alleged facts are not supported. Regardless of whether the inquiry is conducted before or after the filing of a petition, a common stipulation is one in which a court authorizes a person to endorse the petition as being in the best interests of the public and the child. The Uniform Juvenile Court Act (National Conference of Commissioners on Uniform State Laws, 1968) specifies that "a petition may be made by any person who has knowledge of the facts alleged or is informed and believes that they are true" (sec. 20). The act also states that "the petition shall not be filed unless the court or designated person has determined and endorsed upon the petition that the filing is in the best interest of the child and the public" (sec. 19). It should be noted that the signing of a petition and the authority to file the petition may be separate and distinct acts. This has led to some confusion. Some states require designated court personnel to sign the petition to establish some sufficiency of the allegations at the outset.

Figure 7.2 Petition for Adjudication of Wardship

In the Circuit Court for the Ninth Judicial Circuit, McDonough County, Illinois

IN THE INTEREST OF: (   )

PETITION FOR ADJUDICATION OF WARDSHIP

I, _____, State's Attorney, on oath state on information and belief:

1. That _____ is a male/female minor, born on _____, who resides or may be found at _____, McDonough County, Illinois.

2. The names and residence addresses of the minor's parents are:

   _____

   _____

   The minor and the persons named in this paragraph are designated respondents.

3. That the minor is delinquent by reason of the following:

   _____

   _____

4. The minor is/is not in detention custody.

5. It is in the best interests of the minor and the public that the minor be adjudged a ward of the Court. I ask that the minor be adjudged a ward of the Court and for other relief under the Juvenile Court Act.

I have read the aforesaid Petition for Adjudication of Wardship and do hereby swear that the facts contained herein are true and correct to the best of my knowledge and belief.

_____

Assistant State's Attorney

Subscribed and sworn to before me this _____ day of _____, 2018

_____

Notary Public

Assistant State's Attorney

McDonough County

McDonough County Courthouse

Macomb, Illinois 61455

The contents of the petition are governed by statutory requirements in each juvenile court act. The petition may be filed on "information and belief" rather than on verified facts necessary for an adjudicatory hearing. The petition is generally prefaced with the words "in the interests of." The petition continues by giving the name and age of the child and frequently giving the names and addresses of the parents. It typically indicates whether the minor is currently in detention. Also included in the petition is the statement of facts that bring the child within the jurisdiction of the juvenile court. This particular requirement has been a troublesome area because questions are often raised about whether sufficient facts have been stated and about the specificity of the charges. According to the Uniform Juvenile Court Act (sec. 21[1]), the petition must also contain allegations that relate to the child's need of treatment or rehabilitation if delinquency or unruly conduct is alleged. Once the petition has been filled out, it is filed with the prosecutor, who then decides whether to prosecute. If the prosecutor decides to go ahead with the case, proper notice must be given to all concerned parties.

Notification

In establishing a notification requirement (all interested parties are given official notice of time, places, and changes), the U.S. Supreme Court in *Gault* set forth two conditions that must be met: (1) timeliness and (2) adequacy. Although petitions might not need to meet all the legal requirements of an indictment, they do need to describe the alleged misconduct with some particularity so that all parties involved are clear as to the nature of the charges involved. Delinquency petitions, for example, must contain sufficient factual details to inform the juvenile of the nature of the offense leading to allegation of delinquency and must be sufficient to enable the accused to prepare a defense to the charges.

Once a petition has been filed, the court will issue a summons to all concerned adult parties informing them of the time, date, and place of the adjudicatory hearing and of the right of all parties to counsel. In addition, many states direct a separate summons to the child who is over a certain age and is within a designated category such as delinquent or unruly child. A copy of the petition will accompany the summons unless the summons is served "by publication" (printed in a newspaper of reasonable circulation). States vary regarding the length of time required between the serving of the summons and the actual proceedings. However, in accordance with the *Gault* decision, a reasonable amount of time should be allowed to provide the parties with sufficient time to prepare. Unnecessary and long delays should be avoided, particularly in those cases where a child is held in detention or shelter care. For example, Illinois allows at least 3 days before appearance when the summons is personally served to the parties, 5 days when notification is by certified mail, and 10 days when notification is by publication. If it becomes necessary to change dates, notice of the new dates must be given, by certified mail or other reasonable means, to each respondent served with a summons (ILCS, ch. 705, sec. 405/5-525, 2011). Further, Texas law states the following:

> If a person to be served with a summons is in this state and can be found, the summons shall be served upon him personally at least two days before the day of the adjudication hearing. If he is in this state and cannot be found, but his address is known or can with reasonable diligence be ascertained, the summons may be served on him by mailing a copy by registered or certified mail, return receipt requested, at least five days before the day of the hearing. If he is outside this state but he can be found or his address is known, or his whereabouts or address can with reasonable diligence be ascertained, service of the summons may be made either by delivering a copy to him personally or mailing a copy to him by registered or certified mail, return receipt requested, at least five days before the day of the hearing. (Texas Family Code Annotated, 53.07 [a], 2007)

Illinois law, Texas law, and the Uniform Juvenile Court Act (sec. 23[a, b]) provisions on service of summons are similar. The Uniform Juvenile Court Act allows at least 24 hours before the hearing when the summons is personally served and 5 days when certified mail or publication is used.

Service of the summons may be made by any person authorized by the court—usually a county sheriff, coroner, or juvenile probation officer. If the information received by the court indicates that the juvenile needs to be placed in detention or shelter care, the court may endorse on the summons an order that the child should be taken into immediate custody and taken to the place of detention or shelter care designated by the court.

Following the filing of the petition and proper notification, the adjudicatory hearing is held. In delinquency cases, this is the juvenile court's equivalent of an adult criminal trial.

Adjudicatory Hearing

The adjudicatory hearing is a fact-finding hearing to determine whether the allegations in the petition are valid. In delinquency cases, it is the rough equivalent of a criminal trial. In cases of dependency, neglect, or authoritative intervention, the adjudicatory hearing more closely resembles a civil trial. Although the U.S. Supreme Court has extended the legalistic principle of due process to the juvenile justice system, not all rights accorded under the Constitution and its amendments have been incorporated into the juvenile system. For example, in 1971 the Court held that juveniles had no constitutional right to a jury trial because the juvenile proceeding had not yet been held to be a criminal prosecution within the meaning and reach of the Sixth Amendment (*McKeiver v. Pennsylvania*, 1971). The Court reiterated that the due process standard of "fundamental fairness" should be applied to juvenile court proceedings. However, the Court further stated that it was unwilling to "remake the juvenile proceeding into a full adversary process." As indicated previously, some states do currently allow trial by jury. However, most cases are tried by a juvenile judge. The Uniform Juvenile Court Act (sec. 24[a]) recommends that hearings be conducted by the court without a jury. The Supreme Court was clear in its holding that when the state undertakes to prove a child delinquent for committing a criminal act, it must do so beyond a reasonable doubt (*In re Winship*, 1970). The Uniform Juvenile Court Act not only advocates this standard of proof for the delinquency issue but also extends this standard to the unruly category (sec. 29[b]). Some states have adopted this recommended standard (New York Family Court Act, 342.2 [2], 2010; North Dakota Century Code, 27-20-29 [2], 2007; Texas Family Code Annotated, 54.03 [f], 2007). The standard applicable to categories such as deprived, abused or neglected, and dependent is usually the civil standard of preponderance of evidence or clear and convincing evidence. For example, the Uniform Juvenile Court Act (sec. 29[c]) requires "beyond a reasonable doubt" to determine delinquency but allows the civil standard of "clear and convincing evidence" to determine whether the adjudicated delinquent is in need of treatment or rehabilitation. In general, of course, it is more difficult to establish guilt beyond a reasonable doubt (no reasonable doubt in the mind of the judge) than to determine fault based on a preponderance of evidence.

The adjudicatory hearing is generally, but not always, closed to the public. Because of intense pressures to get tough on juvenile crime and to hold the juvenile court more accountable, some states have authorized open hearings in selected criminal cases (Georgia Code, 15-11-78, 2010; Texas Family Code Annotated, 54.08 [a], 2007); however, the judge can close the court to public access if he or she believes it is in the best interest of the child to do so. Colorado, as an example, states the following:

The general public shall not be excluded from hearings held under this article unless the court determines that it is in the best interest of the juvenile or of the community to exclude the general public, and, in such event, the court shall admit only such persons as have an interest in the case or work of the court, including persons whom the district attorney, the juvenile, or his or her parents or guardian wish to be present. (Colorado Revised Statutes, 19-2-110, 2012)

Although the Sixth Amendment declares that "in all criminal prosecutions, the accused shall enjoy the right to a speedy and public trial," juvenile court acts prohibit these public hearings on the grounds that opening such hearings would be detrimental to the child. Although the application of the "public trial" concept of the Sixth Amendment has not been adopted in most juvenile court acts, other due process provisions of the amendment have been incorporated into juvenile court acts as a result of the *Gault* decision. The Uniform Juvenile Court Act (sec. 24[d]) states that the general public shall be excluded except for parties, counsel, witnesses, and other persons requested by a party and approved by the court as having an interest in the case or in the work of the court. Those persons having an interest in the work of the court include members of the bar and press who may be admitted on the condition that they will refrain from divulging any information that could identify the child or family involved.

As discussed previously, the due process concept of "speedy trial" contained in the Sixth Amendment has been incorporated into juvenile court acts. Specific time frames are contained in most acts designating the length of time between custody, detention, adjudicatory, and disposition hearings. Requests for delay are entertained by the juvenile court whenever reasonable and justifiable motions are submitted. Unfortunately, it has been common in some jurisdictions for juvenile court judges to ignore the time limits established by the statute, so a speedy trial might not result. Some judges appear to ignore the statutory requirement of an adjudicatory hearing within 30 days of the time the petition is filed (without detention) even when there is no motion for a continuance by defense counsel (Butts, 1997; Schwartz, Weiner, & Enosh, 1999). Although this practice has been overturned in the New York Court of Appeals (*In re George T.*, 2002), on occasion a juvenile might not be brought before the court for an adjudicatory hearing for as long as 6 months—a clear violation of the statutory requirement. It is possible, of course, for defense counsel to move for dismissal or to appeal, but very seldom are such actions taken. When motions to dismiss based on procedural irregularities are made, they are almost routinely overruled. Once again, the gap between theory and practice comes to light.

According to the Uniform Juvenile Court Act (sec. 29), after hearing the evidence on the petition, the court will make and file its findings about whether the child is deprived, delinquent, abused, neglected, or unruly as alleged in the petition. If the evidence does not support the allegation, the petition will be dismissed, and the child will be discharged from any detention or other restrictions. If the court finds that the allegation is supported by evidence using the appropriate standard of proof for that hearing, the court may proceed immediately or hold an additional hearing to hear evidence and decide whether the child is in need of treatment or rehabilitation. In the absence of evidence to the contrary, the finding of delinquency where felonious acts were committed is sufficient to sustain a finding that the child is in need of treatment or rehabilitation. However, even though the court may find that the child is within the alleged criteria of the petition, it might not find that the child is in need of treatment or rehabilitation. The court may then dismiss the proceeding and discharge the child from any detention or other restrictions (sec. 29[a, b]).

It should also be noted that juvenile court judges in many states may decide prior to or in the early stages of the adjudicatory hearing to "continue the case under supervision." An example of an order for continuance under supervision is shown in Figure 7.3. This usually means that the judge postpones adjudication and specifies a period during which the judge (through court officers) will observe the juvenile. If the juvenile has no further difficulties during the specified period, the petition will be dismissed. If the juvenile does get into trouble again, the judge will proceed with the original adjudicatory hearing.

Continuance under supervision may benefit the juvenile by allowing him or her to escape adjudication as delinquent. It is generally used by juvenile court judges for precisely this purpose. However, if the juvenile did not commit the alleged delinquent act, he or she may be unjustly subjected to court surveillance. If the juvenile's parents or counselor object to the procedure and request the judge to proceed with the adjudicatory hearing, the judge must, in most jurisdictions, comply with those wishes.

In the adjudicatory hearing, the Uniform Juvenile Court Act and the juvenile court acts of many states separate the issues of establishing whether the child is within the defined category and whether the state should

Figure 7.3 Continuance Under Supervision Form

IN THE CIRCUIT COURT FOR THE NINTH JUDICIAL CIRCUIT, McDONOUGH COUNTY, ILLINOIS

IN THE INTEREST OF: (   )

a MINOR.

CONTINUANCE UNDER SUPERVISION

(Before Adjudication)

This cause coming before the Court on the Motion of the Petitioner for an Order of Continuance Under Supervision (Before Adjudication) pursuant to Chapter 705, Act 405, Section 5-19 of the Illinois Compiled Statutes. And the Court having been fully advised in the premises and there being no objection made in Open Court by the minor, his counsel, parents, guardian, or responsible relative, the Court finds that the Petition has been proved by stipulation of the parties in the manner and form as alleged in the Petition for Adjudication of Wardship signed and sworn on _____, 2018.

NOW THEREFORE IT IS ORDERED that this matter is continued until _____, at _____ p.m. The minor shall be subject to the following conditions during the period of said continuance:

1. That the minor shall not violate any criminal statute or city ordinance of any jurisdiction;

2. That the minor shall not possess a firearm or any other dangerous weapon;

3. That the minor shall not leave the State of Illinois without written permission of the State's Attorney's Office and the Probation Officer;

4. That the minor shall attend school while it is in session without any absences unless excused by the school; shall abide by all school rules; and shall cooperate with school officials;

5. That the minor shall report to the Juvenile Probation Officer as directed by the officer and shall permit the officer to visit him at any time or place, with or without prior notice, and he shall at all times abide by the directives of the Probation Officer;

6. That the minor shall notify the Probation Officer within twenty-four (24) hours of a change of address or of any arrest or traffic ticket;

7. That the minor shall follow his parents' rules of supervision;

8. That the minor shall write a letter of apology to _____ apologizing for his actions;

9. That the minor shall pay probation fees in the amount of $ _____;

10. That the minor shall consent to having his photograph taken by the Probation Officer to be placed in the Probation file;

11. That the minor shall participate in and successfully complete the LIFT Program if accepted into said program;

12. That the minor shall obtain a mental health evaluation at the Fulton/McDonough County Community Mental Health Center and shall successfully complete all recommendations of said evaluation;

DATED: _____   _____

                                                                                            Judge

exercise wardship or further custody. The determination of further custody or wardship is usually made on the basis of what type of treatment or rehabilitation the court believes is necessary.

The term *ward of the court* means simply that the court, as an agency of the state, has found it necessary to exercise its role of *in loco parentis*. The decisions that are normally made by the parents are now made by a representative of the court, usually the juvenile probation officer in consultation with the juvenile court judge. As indicated in the Uniform Juvenile Court Act (sec. 29[c, d]), the determination for continued custody for treatment or rehabilitation purposes may be made as part of the adjudicatory hearing or in a separate hearing. The court, in determining wardship, will receive both oral and written evidence and will use this evidence to the extent of its probative value even though such evidence might not have been admissible in the adjudicatory hearing. The standard of clear and convincing evidence is recommended by the Uniform Juvenile Court Act (sec. 29[c]) in determining wardship. The Uniform Juvenile Court Act (sec. 29[e]) also permits a continuance of hearings for a reasonable period to receive reports and other evidence bearing on the disposition or the need of treatment or rehabilitation. The child may be continued in detention or released from detention and placed under the supervision of the court during the period of continuance. Priority in wardship or dispositional hearings will always be given to those children who are in detention or have been removed from their homes pending a final dispositional order.

To avoid giving a child a record, it has become a common practice in some jurisdictions for juvenile courts to place a child under probation supervision without reaching any formal finding. This practice may be engaged in without filing any formal petition. Placing children under probation supervision should not be confused with continuances granted by the court to complete investigations for wardship or disposition proceedings. Although "unofficial probation or supervision" may help to divert less serious cases from adjudication and thus avoid stigmatizing the child involved, it has been subject to much criticism as the result of disregarding due process requirements.

Social Background Investigation, Social Summary Report, Presentence Investigation, or Predisposition Investigation

After a determination in the adjudicatory hearing that the allegations in the petition have been established and that wardship is necessary, a dispositional hearing is set to determine final disposition of the case. There are differences among the states as to whether the dispositional hearing must be separated from the adjudicatory hearing (ILCS, ch. 705, sec. 405/2-22 [1], 2011; Texas Family Code Annotated, 54.04 [1], 2007). In some states, the two hearings are separate because different procedures and rights are involved. For example, in some states in an adjudicatory hearing on delinquency, the standard of proof and the rules of evidence in the nature of criminal proceedings are applicable; however, the civil rules of evidence and standard of proof are applicable to adjudicatory hearings on neglect, dependent, abuse, and minors requiring authoritative intervention (in need of supervision) cases (ILCS, ch. 705, sec. 405/2-18[1], 2011; Iowa Code Annotated, 232.47 [5], 2009). Yet in the Illinois dispositional hearing for all categories, all evidence helpful in determining the disposition, including oral and written reports, may be admitted and relied on to the extent of its probative value even though it might not be relevant for the purposes of the adjudicatory hearing (ILCS, ch. 705, sec. 405/5-22, 2011). Similar wording and evidentiary concepts are contained in the Uniform Juvenile Court Act's (sec. 29[d]) references to determination of whether the adjudicated child requires treatment and rehabilitation and to the dispositional stage of the case.

Between the adjudicatory hearing and the dispositional hearing, the court's staff members (usually probation officers) are engaged in obtaining information useful in aiding the court to determine final disposition of a case. This information is obtained through social background investigations and is premised on the belief that individualized justice is a major function of the juvenile court. Social background investigations, also known as social summary reports or predisposition investigations in some states, typically include information about the child, the child's parents, school, work, and general peer relations as well as other environmental factors. This information is gathered through interviews with relevant persons in the community and is compiled in report form to aid the judge in making a dispositional decision. The probative value of some information collected is questionable and can certainly be challenged in the dispositional hearing. Some juvenile judges delegate the court's staff to make recommendations and to justify the elimination of some options or alternatives from consideration. Unfortunately, social background investigations have been used by some courts prior to the adjudicatory hearings, and this can result in an adjudication of delinquency without proving that the accused juvenile committed the acts of delinquency alleged in the petition. As a result of the *Kent* decision (*Kent v. United States*, 1966), counsel for the juvenile has been extended the right to review the contents of staff social background investigations used in waiver hearings because there is no irrefutable presumption of accuracy attached to staff reports. This principle has been extended by most juvenile court acts to legal counsel representing the child in dispositional hearings.

Dispositional Hearing

Whereas the adjudicatory hearing determines whether the allegations are supported by the evidence, the dispositional hearing is concerned only with what alternatives are available to meet the needs of the juvenile. In fact, some states specify by statute that the rules of evidence do not apply during dispositional proceedings (ILCS, 705 sec. 405/2-22 [1], 2011; Iowa Code Annotated, 232.50 [3], 2009). Dispositional alternatives are clearly stated in each state's juvenile court act, although states may differ in the dispositional alternatives available to juveniles in the separate categories (i.e., delinquency, dependency, abused/neglected). An option available for the deprived child might not be available for the delinquent child. According to the Uniform Juvenile Court Act (sec. 30), the deprived child may remain with his or her parents, subject to conditions imposed by the court, including supervision by the court. Also according to Section 30, the deprived child may be temporarily transferred legally to any of the following:

(i) any individual . . . found by the court to be qualified to receive and care for the child;

(ii) an agency or other private organization licensed or otherwise authorized by the law to receive and provide care for the child;

(iii) the Child Welfare Department of the [county] [state] [or other public agency authorized by law to receive and provide care for the child]; or

(iv) an individual in another state with or without supervision.

For the delinquent child, the Uniform Juvenile Court Act (sec. 31) states that the court may make any disposition best suited to the juvenile's treatment, rehabilitation, and welfare, including the following:

1. any order authorized by Section 30 for the disposition of a "deprived child";

2. probation under the supervision of the probation officer . . . under conditions and limitations the court prescribes;

3. placing the child in an institution, camp, or other facility for delinquent children operated under the direction of the court [or other local public authority]; or

4. committing the child to [designate the state department to which commitments of delinquent children are made or, if there is no department, the appropriate state institution for delinquent children].

According to the Uniform Juvenile Court Act (sec. 32), the unruly child may be disposed of by the court in any authorized disposition allowable for the delinquent except commitment to the state correctional agency. However, if the unruly child is found to be not amenable to treatment under the disposition, the court, after another hearing, may make any disposition otherwise authorized for the delinquent.

A general trend occurring in juvenile court acts is to refrain from committing all categories of youth, other than delinquents, to juvenile correctional institutions unless the unruly or in-need-of-supervision child warrants such action after other alternatives have failed. Commitment to an institution is generally regarded as a last resort.

Most juvenile court acts also provide for transferring a juvenile demonstrating mental challenges or mental illness to the appropriate authority within the state. A similar section is included in the Uniform Juvenile Court Act (sec. 35). With the advent of a multiplicity of community treatment programs and child guidance centers, many of the current dispositions contain conditions for attendance at these centers. Dispositions of probation or suspended sentence often require compulsory attendance at a community-based treatment or rehabilitation program. Violation of these conditions may result in revocation of probation or a suspended sentence. This is accomplished through a revocation hearing. Most states now specify the maximum amount of time for confinement of a juvenile. Extensions of the original disposition generally require another hearing with all rights accorded in the original dispositional hearing. The court may, under some circumstances, terminate its dispositional order prior to the expiration date if it appears that the purpose of the order has been accomplished. Juvenile court acts generally terminate all orders affecting the juvenile on reaching the age of majority in those states. This termination results in discharging the juvenile from further obligation or control. If the disposition is probation, both the conditions of probation and its duration are spelled out by the court. For copies of dispositional and sentencing court orders, see Figures 7.4 and 7.5.

Figure 7.4 Dispositional Order

IN THE CIRCUIT FOR THE NINTH JUDICIAL CIRCUIT, McDONOUGH COUNTY, ILLINOIS

IN THE INTEREST OF: (   )

both MINORS.

DISPOSITIONAL ORDER

This cause coming to be heard for the purposes of a Dispositional

Hearing, _____, Assistant State's Attorney for McDonough County present, with _____ of the Illinois Department of Children and Family Services; Guardian ad Litem present for the minor(s), _____; Attorney present with respondent father, _____; and Attorney present with respondent mother, _____.

(Continued)

Figure 7.4 (Continued)

The Court, having received the evidence and heard the arguments of counsel, having jurisdiction and being fully advised in the premises FINDS:

1. That it is in the best interests of the minors that Guardianship shall be granted to the Guardianship Administrator of the Illinois Department of Children and Family Services.

IT IS HEREBY ORDERED:

1. That Guardianship of the children shall be granted to the Guardianship Administrator of the Illinois Department of Children and Family Services, with the Department having the right to consent to medical and dental care and the right to place;

2. That _____ shall successfully complete the _____ program, individual counseling, and all other services as outlined in the client service plan;

3. That _____ shall successfully complete counseling, participate in Victim Services programs, secure and maintain safe and appropriate housing, and complete all other services as outlined in the client service plan;

4. That _____ shall adhere to his/her safety plan regarding contact between _____ and the minor(s), _____;

5. That _____ shall cooperate with the Illinois Department of Children and Family Services, shall comply with the client service plan, and correct the conditions which led to the Department's involvement or shall risk loss of custody and possible termination of parental rights;

6. That the Permanency Goal shall be _____;

7. That _____ shall comply with all early childhood education service for _____;

8. That a Status Hearing shall be held on _____, at _____ a.m./p.m.

DATED: _____   _____
                                                 Judge

Figure 7.5 Sentencing Order

STATE OF ILLINOIS IN THE CIRCUIT COURT FOR THE NINTH JUDICIAL CIRCUIT COUNTY OF McDONOUGH

CASE NO. _____ JD _____

IN THE INTEREST OF:

a MINOR.

Date of hearing:

Parties present for hearing:

Assistant State's Attorney:

Minor: Attorney for Minor:

Mother: Attorney for Mother:

Father: Attorney for Father:

SENTENCING ORDER

THIS MATTER comes before the Court for hearing on the date noted above with the parties indicated being present. The parties have been advised of the nature of the proceedings as well as their rights and the dispositional alternatives available to the Court. The minor admits the allegations of Count I _____ of the Petition filed _____. The Court makes the following FINDINGS:

___ 1. The Court has jurisdiction of the subject matter.

___ 2. The Court has jurisdiction of the parties.

___ 3. The admission by the minor is knowingly and voluntarily made.

___ 4. The minor has signed an Admission form.

___ 5. There is a factual basis for the admission by the minor.

___ 6. The parties have agreed to a sentencing recommendation with regard to this matter.

THEREFORE, it is the ORDER OF THIS Court that the request of the parties for an immediate sentencing hearing is GRANTED:

THIS MATTER then proceeds to sentencing hearing. Both parties waive the preparation of a social investigation. The agreement of the parties is heard. The Court makes the following FINDINGS:

1. The agreement of the parties is in the best interests of the minor.
2. The agreement of the parties should be affirmed and incorporated in the Sentencing Order of this Court.

THEREFORE, it is the ORDER of this Court that:

1. The minor is adjudicated to be a delinquent minor.

2. The minor is made a Ward of this Court.

3. The minor is placed on probation pursuant to 705 ILCS 405/5-23 for a period of _____.

4. This probation is conditioned upon the following terms and conditions:

_____ The respondent minor shall obey his/her parents' rules of supervision; and

_____ The respondent minor shall attend school regularly and put forth his or her best efforts; and

_____ The respondent minor shall maintain a 9:00 p.m. to 7:00 a.m. curfew unless he or she is accompanied by a parent or responsible adult. Discretion shall be left to the Juvenile Probation Officer to adjust the respondent minor's curfew; and

_____ The respondent minor shall not possess any firearm or other dangerous weapon; and

_____ The respondent minor and parents shall cooperate with the Juvenile Probation Officer in any and all programs deemed to be in the minor's best interest; and

(Continued)

Figure 7.5 (Continued)

_____ The respondent minor shall meet with the Juvenile Probation Officer as directed; and

_____ The respondent minor shall notify the Juvenile Probation Officer within twenty-four (24) hours of a change in address; and

_____ The respondent minor shall reside in McDonough County unless authorized to reside elsewhere by the Probation Officer, the State's Attorney's Office and the Court; and

_____ The respondent minor shall not leave the State of Illinois without the approval of the Probation Officer, the State's Attorney's Office, and the Court; and

_____ The respondent minor shall obey all federal, state, and local laws; and

_____ The respondent minor shall obtain a Drug and Alcohol evaluation and follow any and all recommendations of the evaluator; and

_____ The respondent minor shall obtain a Mental Health evaluation and follow any and all recommendations of the evaluator; and

_____ The respondent minor shall refrain from having in his or her body the presence of any illicit drug prohibited by the Cannabis Control Act or the Illinois Controlled Substance Act, unless prescribed by a physician. Furthermore, if the Juvenile Probation Officer receives any report of illicit drug or alcohol use by the minor, the minor shall submit to random drug screens to determine the presence of any illicit drug. The minor shall be responsible for all related costs to the drug screens; and

_____ The respondent minor shall pay $ ___ in restitution to the McDonough County Circuit Clerk's Office for the benefit of the victim in this case; and

_____ The respondent minor shall draft a letter of apology to ___. The letter shall be approved and sent by the Probation Officer. The minor shall continue to revise the letter until the Probation Officer is satisfied with the content of the letter; and

_____ Other terms and conditions shall be:

THIS ORDER MAY BE MODIFIED BY THE COURT.

Entered this _____ day of _____, 2018.

_____

Judge

CAREER OPPORTUNITY: MAGISTRATE

Job description: Determine whether probable cause exists when the police make arrests. Determine whether, and ensure that, defendants have been properly advised of their rights. Decide whether to detain defendants. Supervise preliminary hearings, hold trials, and sentence offenders.

Employment requirements: Must have a law degree and be admitted to the bar.

Beginning salary: Varies widely depending on jurisdiction. Benefits also vary widely.

Summary

It is essential that those involved in the juvenile justice network be completely familiar with the appropriate procedures for dealing with juveniles and with the rules governing other members of the juvenile justice system. This awareness helps to ensure that the interests of juveniles will be protected within the guidelines established by society. Otherwise, juveniles' rights may be violated, practitioners may be put in a position where they cannot take appropriate actions, and society might not be protected as a result of ignorance of proper procedures.

For example, a police officer may take a juvenile into custody for a serious delinquent act (e.g., robbery). The officer may, on interrogation, obtain a confession from the juvenile. It may be impossible for the state's attorney to prosecute if the police officer failed to warn the juvenile of his or her rights according to Miranda, if a reasonable attempt to contact the juvenile's parents was not made, if the juvenile was frightened into confessing when his or her parents or legal representative were not present, or if the evidence in the case was obtained illegally. Of course, there will be no adjudication by the judge, and rehabilitation or corrections personnel will have no chance to rehabilitate, correct, or protect through detention. In the long run, then, neither the best interests of society nor those of the juvenile will be served.

Every state has a juvenile court act spelling out appropriate procedures for dealing with juveniles from the initial apprehension through final disposition. In looking at several juvenile court acts, we have seen that there are many uniformities in these acts as well as many points of disagreement. Uniformities are often the result of U.S. Supreme Court decisions, whereas differences often result from legislative efforts in the individual states. It is crucial, therefore, for all juvenile justice practitioners to become familiar with the juvenile court act under which they operate so that the best interests of juveniles, other practitioners, and society may be served to the maximum extent possible.

KEY TERMS

bail   184

clear and convincing evidence   196

continuance under supervision   197

detention   187

detention hearing   187

Fourth Amendment   183

guardian ad litem   183

interrogation   183

notification   195

preliminary conference   182

shelter care   187

Sixth Amendment   183

social background investigations   200

stationhouse adjustment   182

taking into custody   185

totality of circumstances   183

Critical Thinking Questions

1. What are the constitutional rights guaranteed to adults in our society that are not always guaranteed to juveniles in juvenile court proceedings? What is the rationale for depriving juveniles of these rights?

2. What are the strengths and weaknesses of informal adjustments, unofficial probation, and continuance under supervision?

3. Discuss the pros and cons of confidentiality of juvenile court records and of allowing public access to juvenile court.

4. Consider the What Would You Do? scenario at the beginning of the chapter and answer the following questions:

a. At what point in the process was your daughter when you received the phone call from the county detention center?

b. Was there an opportunity for your daughter to be released prior to court? If so, what factors might influence this decision? Who would make this decision? What role would you play in this decision? What about the past behaviors of your daughter?

c. If your daughter proceeded to a detention hearing, what factors would the judge consider in determining to hold or release your daughter?

d. Assuming that a petition is filed, what are the juvenile court's obligations with respect to the parties in the proceedings?

Suggested Readings

32A-1-1 NMSA (1978).

Alabama Code § 12-15-56 (2015).

Arkansas Code § 9-27-309 (2010).

Colorado Revised Statutes, 19-2-110 (1997).

Colorado Revised Statutes, 19-2-509 (2012).

Davis, S. M. (2006). *Rights of juveniles: The juvenile justice system* (2nd ed.). Eagan, MN: Thomson/West.

Fagan, J. (2005, September). Adolescents, maturity, and the law. *American Prospect, 16*, A5–A7.

Georgia Code, 15-11-47 (d) (2010).

Georgia Code Annotated (2009).

Georgia Criminal and Traffic Law Manual. (2014). *Juvenile Code*. Charlottesville, VA: LexisNexis.

Hawaii Revised Statutes, 571-32 (h) (2015).

Illinois Compiled Statutes, ch. 705, sec. 5-501 (2) (2011).

In the matter of George T. (2002). *New York Law School Law Review, 47*(2/3). Retrieved from www.nyls.edu

Massachusetts General Laws Annotated, ch. 119, sec. 55A (2016).

Missouri Revised Statutes, ch. 11, sec. 211.061 (2015).

Missouri Revised Statutes, ch. 11, sec. 211.321 (2015).

Missouri Revised Statutes, ch. 11, sec. 211.462 (2015).

Montana Code Annotated, 41-3-425 (2015).

Montana Code Annotated, 41-5-1502 (1) (2015).

Myers, W. (2006). *Roper v. Simmons*: The collision of national consensus and proportionality review. *Journal of Criminal Law and Criminology, 96*, 947–994.

National Council of Juvenile and Family Court Judges. (2005). *Juvenile delinquency guidelines: Improving court practice in juvenile delinquency cases.* Washington, DC: U.S. Department of Justice, Office of Juvenile Justice and Delinquency Prevention.

Nebraska Revised Statutes, 43-253 (5) (2012).

New York Family Court Act, 342.2 (2) (2010).

Oregon Juvenile Code, 419C.097 (2015).

Tennessee Code Annotated, § 37-1-110 (2012).

Tennessee Code Annotated, § 37-1-119 (2012).

Texas Family Code Annotated, 54.03 (c) (2007).

Texas Family Code Annotated (2009).

West Virginia Code Annotated, 49-5-6 (2012).

SAGE edge™

Juveniles and the Police

8

CHAPTER LEARNING OBJECTIVES

On completion of this chapter, students should be able to do the following:

- Discuss the importance of police discretion in juvenile justice
- Compare and contrast unofficial and official police procedures in dealing with juveniles
- Discuss the importance of training police officers to deal with juveniles
- Describe police–school liaison programs
- Discuss the impact of community policing on the relationships among the police, school authorities, and juveniles

---

WHAT WOULD YOU DO?

It was Monday at 2:15 p.m., and Officer Jones stood in front of a group of 11th-grade high-schoolers during a time of the day when most of the youth were focused on school letting out. This was a large high school in an inner-city neighborhood of a major metropolitan area. Officer Jones was there to discuss the potential benefits of joining the municipal police.

There were about 25 students in the class. Most were ethnic minorities, predominately African American and Latino American. Officer Jones was African American.

When he concluded his discussion of the potential incentives to being a police officer with his agency, he closed with the following statement:

"In reality, becoming a police officer should be to become a *peace officer*, to serve and protect the community as a whole."

One of the students then asked, "So, since might makes right, I guess that peace is kept by tasing or shooting people if they don't mind, right?"

Another student chimed in and said, "Yeah, like Chaz's older cousin who was just walking back from his night classes and the cops got him mixed up with another dude. Chaz's cousin was afraid and tried to keep walking and they tased his ass so bad he still has nerve problems."

Officer Jones noted that "there is no doubt about it, there are some embarrassing incidents where officers do not use good judgment."

One of the students cut in and said, "Well, all I know is that you are a black officer, a sell-out, because you gotta know how our communities get treated, and you go along with it anyway. I bet they just give you crumbs where you work, give you the crappy jobs and all, like talking with us."

(Continued)

Officer Jones thought about it . . . he had talked with his wife just the night before about his disappointment over not being promoted recently during an organizational selection process. He also did not always feel that his agency understood the minority community, the means by which they could hire and retain more minorities (which was a goal of the agency), and he also felt that some decisions were sometimes biased.

Sometimes, he felt the same unfairness that these youth expressed. He thought to himself and realized that, in order to remain professional in the remainder of his presentation, he would need to lie about what he thought. To do otherwise would make his agency look bad and would give the kids bogus advice. He looked at the clock . . . there were still 20 minutes left in class. For a few seconds, he wondered what he might say or do.

What Would You Do?

1. In your opinion, do youth of today look favorably on being a police officer?

2. What do you think Officer Jones should tell the kids in the classroom?

3. What do you think might work to improve relationships between minority youth and the police?

One of the first specializations in police departments following World War II was the juvenile bureau. Juvenile bureaus grew in number during the 1940s, 1950s, and 1960s until virtually all police departments of all sizes had them by the 1970s (Mays & Winfree, 2000, pp. 61–62). Historically, the police are the first representatives of the juvenile justice network to encounter delinquent, dependent, and abused or neglected children. The importance of the police in the juvenile justice system is considerable for this very reason. If the police decide not to take into custody or arrest a particular juvenile, none of the rest of the official legal machinery can go into operation. In fact, although the police often decide not to take official action when dealing with juveniles (22% of all juveniles arrested in 2009 were handled within the police department and then released), roughly 83% of all cases referred to juvenile court in 2009 were referred by the police (Office of Juvenile Justice and Delinquency Prevention [OJJDP], 2012).

Police Discretion in Encounters With Juveniles

Many of the situations law enforcement officers encounter in the field are riddled by conundrums or fall into a gray area. Not every scenario is dictated by a strict policy or follows the rule of law to the letter. . . . In any interaction between police and citizens, there will always be an area where the police are going to exercise discretion. . . . They are not bound by law to arrest everyone they believe may have committed a crime. (Hernandez, 2011)

It is well established that a considerable amount of police discretion (individual judgment concerning the type of action to take) is exercised in handling juveniles. Although the exercise of discretion is a necessary and normal part of police work, the potential for abuse exists because there is no way to routinely review this practice. Police officers are sometimes inconsistent in the decision-making process because of frequent ambiguity with respect to whether any formal rule of law applies in a specific case as well as a variety of other factors.

Are police officers' decisions concerning whether to take official action with respect to juveniles influenced by the demeanor of the juvenile involved?

Myers (2004) pointed out the following:

It is the nature of police work itself that in most cases allows individual patrol officers to decide how they will handle both the incidents brought to their attention, as well as those discovered independently as they work the street. In light of this discretion, one should be concerned with how police make decisions involving juveniles as it is an important decision. (p. 2)

There are, of course, a number of cues to which most police officers respond in making decisions about whether to take official action against a particular juvenile. These cues include the following:

1. The wishes of the complainant
2. The nature of the violation
3. The race, attitude, and gender of the offender
4. Knowledge about prior police contacts with the juvenile in question
5. The perceived ability and willingness of the juvenile's parents to cooperate in solving the problem
6. The setting or location (private or public) in which the encounter occurs (Black & Reiss, 1970; Mays & Winfree, 2000; Piliavin & Briar, 1964; Regoli & Hewitt, 1994; Werthman & Piliavin, 1967)
7. Adolescents who are out late at night
8. The age of the police officer (Allen, 2005)
9. Laws, statutes, and ordinances (Myers, 2004)

In general, the wishes of the complainant and the nature of the offense weigh heavily on police officers' decisions to arrest. If the offense is serious (e.g., a violent robbery), the police are generally expected by their department and by the public to arrest, and under most circumstances they do so. There is some evidence, however, that the police might not arrest, even for a serious offense, if the complainant does not wish to pursue the matter (Davis, 1975; Kelling, 1999). If the offense is minor and the complainant does not desire to pursue the matter, the police will often handle the case unofficially (Allen, 2005). Again, in the case of a minor offense, the police will often intervene on behalf of the juvenile to persuade the complainant not to take official action. It should be noted, however, that in most jurisdictions the police cannot prevent a complainant from filing a petition if he or she insists.

Historically, research has shown that juveniles who show proper respect for the police have few if any known prior police contacts, and are perceived as having cooperative parents, are more likely to be dealt with unofficially than are those who show little respect, have a long history of encounters with the police, and are perceived as having uncooperative parents (Allen, 2005; Black & Reiss, 1970). Most authorities agree that those juveniles who are most likely to have a "police record of arrest are those who conform to police preconceptions about delinquent types, who are perceived as a threat to others, and who are most visible to the police" (Morash, 1984, p. 110). Morash (1984) indicated that she found a "convincing demonstration of regular tendencies of the police to investigate and arrest males who have delinquent peers regardless of these youths' involvement in delinquency" (p. 110). Moyer (1981), while indicating that gender and race are not critical factors in the police decision-making process with respect to adults, indicated that the nature of the offense and the demeanor of the offender when confronting the police are important in determining the type of action taken by the police (Allen, 2005; Walker, Spohn, & DeLone, 2004). Biases on behalf of the police may lead to more informal adjustments for certain types of juveniles. This is largely a matter of speculation given that records of such dispositions have not been routinely kept, although there is currently a trend to formalize such dispositions. It is clear, however, that based on their perceptions of a number of cues, police officers make decisions as to whether official action is in order or whether a particular juvenile can be dealt with unofficially (Sutphen, Kurtz, & Giddings, 1993; Walker et al., 2004).

Research on the relationship between the police and juveniles was sparse during the 1970s and 1980s. However, research by Engel, Sobol, and Worden (2000) on 24 police departments in three metropolitan areas indicated that in most situations "officers do not treat hostile adults and juveniles, males and females, and blacks and whites differently" (p. 256), as was speculated by Klinger (1996, p. 76). The authors found that the police are likely to take official action in cases where there are disrespectful suspects who are intoxicated by use of alcohol or other drugs and in circumstances where disrespect is demonstrated in front of other officers. The effects of demeanor, then, were not contingent on suspects' personal characteristics, at least in this study.

In contrast, Sealock and Simpson (1998), in analyzing data collected from a 1958 Philadelphia birth cohort, found that race, gender, and socioeconomic status significantly affect the arrest decision. They also noted that within gender categories, officers consider the seriousness of the offense and the number of prior police contacts in making arrest decisions. Similarly, Walker and colleagues (2004) contended that age, race, and gender have been found to be significant variables with arrest decisions. However, the authors provided an extensive analysis of public racial perceptions of police officers, showing that Latino Americans have a view less favorable than that of Caucasian Americans but that this is not as negative a view as tends to exist among the African American population. These researchers pointed out that these negative attitudes—and behavior that belies these negative attitudes—can be the actual reason that racial variables appear to be significant. Walker and colleagues (2004) noted that "individuals who are less respectful or more hostile are more likely to be arrested" and that "African Americans were more likely to be arrested" (p. 332). They concluded that the hostility that is transmitted during these encounters results in higher arrest rates. Pollock, Oliver, and

Menard (2012) examined a national sample of individuals with respect to socioeconomic variables, offending behavior, and prior police contact as predictors of self-reported police contact (questioning or arrest) over a period of 24 years and concluded that police contact is predominately predicted by sex, delinquent peers, and offending behavior. These authors also concluded that several of the variables commonly discussed in police contact literature, including race, are not predictors of police contact at the national level in the United States. However, Benekos, Merlo, and Puzzanchera (2011) examined trends in juvenile violent offending over a 20-year period and focused specifically on the race of the offender. They found that aggregate data indicated a disproportionate representation of black youth in the juvenile justice system but noted it is difficult to determine the role that race plays in specific violent offenses. When focusing on murder, aggravated assault, and robbery, the authors believe that a more complete picture of youthful offending and system responses emerges, and they indicate that data clearly demonstrate disproportionate handling of black juvenile offenders (p. 132). Despite some disagreement among researchers concerning the role of race in police juvenile encounters, in minority communities where police–community relations have typically been impaired, it is perhaps to be expected that citizens will have a negative and distrustful view of the police. This is particularly true among juvenile offenders who have been exposed to the effects of negative encounters (Shusta, Levine, Wong, Olson, & Harris, 2015). Further, according to Watkins and Maume (2012), research on juveniles' attitudes toward the police has indicated that youths generally hold less favorable opinions of the police than do adults. They noted, however, that the concept of police is not explicitly defined in most such research (meaning it's not clear if they are referring to school resource officers [SROs], patrol or beat officers on the street, or something else)—thus making it difficult to interpret the findings of the research. Whatever the case, it is clear that the police must be sensitive to this issue—when and where feasible—to prevent encounters from escalating (Shusta et al., 2015). This is a particularly relevant point if one is concerned with citizen perceptions of the police agency and if one hopes to build a genuine rapport and/or connection with juveniles from diverse backgrounds (Shusta et al., 2015).

Bazemore and Senjo (1997), looking at the relationship of police and juveniles from the community policing viewpoint, analyzed data collected from field research and ethnographic interviews over a 10-month period. Among the community police officers they studied, they found a distinctive style of interaction with young people, different attitudes toward juveniles, and unique views of the appropriate role of officers in response to youth crime. The authors concluded that the officers' efforts to enhance prevention, creative diversion, and advocacy provide at least partial support for the belief that community policing can lead to positive outcomes.

Although the exact nature of the relationships among personal characteristics, demeanor, and police decisions remains unclear, it is likely that all of these factors and others continue to play a role in police–juvenile encounters (Hurst, 2007). On numerous occasions, for example, we have seen police officers respond differently to male and female juveniles. As we pointed out in Chapter 3, it appears that male officers seldom search ("pat down") juvenile females even in circumstances where the juveniles are likely to be carrying drugs and/or weapons for their male companions (Hurst, McDermott, & Thomas, 2005). Wooden and Blazak (2001) discussed the emergence of the "mall rat" as a type of delinquent, noting that petty theft is the most frequent crime committed by these juveniles and that females are as likely to be caught as are males, although the latter are more likely to be arrested (pp. 32–33).

Perhaps Myers (2004) best summarized the complexities involved in police discretion as it relates to juveniles:

> More sophisticated analysis shows that when controlling for offense seriousness, evidence strength, suspects' race, and victim preference, suspects who fail the attitude test are more likely to be arrested; thus it is suspect demeanor driving police outcomes, not suspect race. Even when controlling for

demeanor, race effects are sometimes still significant (i.e., they reach statistical significance) and minorities are more likely to be arrested, but it is more often the case that the race effects drop out. (p. 6; see also Pope & Snyder, 2003)

Although there has been increased attention during recent years to juvenile perceptions of the police, few studies have focused specifically on the attitudes of young girls (Hurst et al., 2005). In response to the lack of research that examines the perceptions of police held by juvenile girls, Hurst and colleagues (2005) conducted a study in Ohio and examined one key determinant that tends to be relevant to many young females—the fear of victimization. Their research found generally low support for police—particularly when respondents expressed more concern with potential victimization (Hurst et al., 2005). It is interesting to point out that although girls in this survey did find police to be helpful in service roles (e.g., providing aid when a car breaks down, helping persons who are sick or disabled), they did not view the police as effective in general law enforcement functions (e.g., curbing drug activity, preventing violence). Overall, therefore, it was determined that girls tended to have little trust or support for the police (Hurst et al., 2005). Girls may actually benefit more from other agencies such as transitional-living programs and counseling programs (see In Practice 8.1).

IN PRACTICE 8.1

BRAINSTORMING FOR SOLUTIONS: THE OJJDP POLICE AND YOUTH ENGAGEMENT ROUNDTABLE

On April 27–28, 2016, the Office of Juvenile Justice and Delinquency Prevention (OJJDP) convened a police and youth engagement roundtable that brought together 15 youth and 14 law enforcement executives to discuss the current climate of police-youth relations. The purpose of the roundtable, titled "Supporting the Role of Law Enforcement in Juvenile Justice Reform," was to identify ways to support, sustain, and expand youth and law enforcement engagement.

Lessons from the roundtable will be used to develop a Juvenile Justice Leadership Institute planned as part of a cooperative agreement with the International Association of Chiefs of Police (IACP) and the OJJDP.

IACP partnered with the Coalition for Juvenile Justice to make sure that a diverse group of youth advisors were part of the discussion. The roundtable was preceded by a full day of police- and youth-focused training to allow for a better understanding of resources and programs related to the audience. Sessions provided an overview of—

- The Juvenile Justice and Delinquency Prevention Act
- The developmental approach
- Collaborative problem-solving
- Trauma-informed responses
- Children exposed to violence

The roundtable provided an opportunity for youth to share their personal experiences, offering a unique perspective from those who have been directly impacted by the justice system and highlighting their opinions about how to improve interactions with law enforcement. Listening to youth's experiences across multiple juvenile justice systems can help law enforcement improve its ability to address juvenile victimization, delinquency, and crime, and build trust between law enforcement agencies and the people they protect and serve.

Assistant Attorney General of the Office of Justice Programs Karol V. Mason provided opening remarks. "It's wonderful that we have all of you in this room to talk about ways we can work together to improve the safety of our communities," she said. "If we can give our young people the services and support they need; intervene early in situations where they are exposed to violence and trauma; and keep them in school and connected to their families, communities, and faith-based and neighborhood organizations, we are far more likely to keep them out of the justice system and on the path to healthy, productive lives—and we'll be better able to ensure public safety."

OJJDP has worked diligently to strengthen the voice of America's youth so it can be heard by the law enforcement community. OJJDP will continue to work with law enforcement to ensure that the youth perspective is a part of its decision making as well as an integral part of the solutions law enforcement embraces to build trust within communities and effectively realize juvenile justice reform.

Source: Listenbee (2016).

Questions to Consider

1. True or False: By listening to youth on the roundtable, it is hoped that the process will help law enforcement to build trust with youth and improve its ability to address juvenile victimization, delinquency, and crime.

2. Multiple Choice: During the meeting between the IACP and the Coalition for Juvenile Justice, which of the following topics were discussed?

   a. The developmental approach

   b. Collaborative problem solving

   c. Trauma-informed responses

   d. All of the above

3. In your opinion, explain why trauma-informed response was included as one of the areas of focus for law enforcement who deal with juveniles.

A variety of researchers have found significantly different attitudes toward police when examined by race (Hurst et al., 2005; Penn, 2016). As in previously discussed research, researchers have found that African American girls expressed much more negative perceptions of the police than did Caucasian girls. In fact, African American youth consistently had poorer outlooks than did Caucasian youth on measures related to attitude for liking the police, trusting the police, or being satisfied with the police (Hurst et al., 2005; Penn, 2016). Researchers have consistently found that race is a significant predictor of attitudes toward the police (Hurst et al., 2005; Penn, 2016). Researchers have pointed toward differences in racial socialization, the analysis of social situations in terms of relationship power between African Americans and Caucasians, and other psychological and sociological factors. From this and similar to what was observed in the What Would You Do? opening for this chapter, it is clear that many of the attitudes toward police are part and parcel of racial socialization, particularly in communities that already have poor police–community relations (Hurst et al., 2005; Penn, 2016). This, again, points to the need for police training in diversity and cultural differences with juveniles, just as would be expected with the adult population (Broaddus et al., 2013; Hurst et al., 2005; Shusta et al., 2015).

In inner-city neighborhoods, police beat officers often arrive at a kind of "working peace" with groups of young black males hanging out on street corners (Anderson, 1990). They may allow juveniles to get away with certain minor violations for which they could take official action so as to "keep the peace." The police face a dilemma in such neighborhoods. On the one hand, the police are accused of overpolicing in black neighborhoods; on the other hand, they are accused of failing to provide sufficient protection (Shusta et al., 2015; Walker et al., 2004). Complaints concerning the former are typically voiced by young black males who are often stopped, frisked, and questioned on the streets; complaints concerning the latter often arise when the police fail to act against street corner juveniles or in domestic violence situations where the police do not make arrests (Walker et al., 2004).

According to Joiner (2005), race makes a difference at all stages of the juvenile justice process but may be most important at the initial point of contact with the police. He maintained that minority representation throughout the juvenile justice network would drop if the police used arrest as a last rather than as a first resort. This is also the contention of other experts who study minority citizens' perceptions of the police and/or cross-cultural training needs for police officers (Hanser & Gomila, 2015; Shusta et al., 2015; Walker et al., 2004).

Unofficial Procedures

As Piliavin and Briar (1964) pointed out, police officers who encounter juveniles involved in delinquent activities have a number of alternatives available for handling such juveniles. Basically, police officers may simply release the juvenile in question, release the juvenile and submit to the juvenile probation office or the police department a "juvenile card" briefly describing the encounter, reprimand the juvenile and release him or her, take the juvenile into custody to make a stationhouse adjustment, or arrest the juvenile and request that the state attorney file a petition in juvenile court. Only the last two alternatives involve official action. Each of the other alternatives may occur either on the street or in a police facility. The informal adjustment is commonly referred to as street corner adjustment or stationhouse adjustment. A typical street corner adjustment might occur when the police have been notified by a homeowner that a group of juveniles have congregated on his or her property and have refused to leave when asked to do so. Because the offense is not serious, and because the homeowner is likely to be satisfied once the juveniles have left, the officer may simply tell the juveniles to leave and not return. If, for some reason, the police officer is not satisfied that the orders to move on and not return will be obeyed, the officer may take the juveniles to the police station and request that the juveniles' parents meet with them there. If an agreement can be reached among the juveniles and their parents that the event leading to the complaint will not recur, the officer may release the juveniles to the custody of the parents. In Illinois, for example, this may be considered a formal stationhouse adjustment, and the minor and parent, guardian, or legal custodian must agree in writing to the adjustment and must be advised of the consequences of violation of any term of the agreement (Illinois Compiled Statutes [ILCS], ch. 705, sec. 405/5-301 [2]a, 2013). Further, a minor arrested for any offense or a violation of a condition of previous station adjustment may receive an informal station adjustment for that arrest (ILCS, ch. 705, sec. 405/5-301 [1], 2013). A stationhouse adjustment in Illinois results in a record being kept either by the police department or with the juvenile probation office for offenses that would be a felony if committed by an adult and may be maintained if the offense would be a misdemeanor.

Informal adjustments such as these usually cause little controversy so long as all parties (complainant, police, parents, and juveniles) are reasonably satisfied. In fact, some states have attempted to formalize the stationhouse adjustment process by spelling out exactly what the police officer's alternatives are in such adjustments (ILCS, 705, 405/5-301, 2013; New Jersey Office of the Attorney General, 2005). For example, in Illinois a police officer may, with the consent of the minor and his or her guardian, require the minor to perform public or community service or make restitution for damages. Although police officers often see solutions of this type as being better for the juvenile than official processing, some serious objections have been raised by parents, the courts, and sometimes the juveniles involved.

Suppose that a juvenile was allegedly involved in vandalism where he or she spray painted some derogatory comments on the front of a school building. Also suppose that, as a condition of not taking official action, a police officer instructs the juvenile to spend every night after school cleaning the paint off the school building with paint remover and brushes that are provided at the expense of the juvenile or his or her parents.

Contacts between the police and juveniles occur frequently and help to shape the perceptions each group has of the other.

Finally, suppose that the juvenile persists in maintaining his or her innocence. The implications of this type of "treatment without trial" should be relatively clear. First, it has not been demonstrated that the juvenile did commit the delinquent act in question; that is, the juvenile has not been adjudicated delinquent in a court of law. Second, because it has not been demonstrated that the juvenile committed the vandalism, there is no legal basis for punishment. Third, even if the juvenile did, in fact, commit the offense, the police generally have no legal authority to impose punishment on alleged offenders unless, of course, such offenders voluntarily agree to the punishment. But how voluntary is such agreement?

Although many police officers who employ informal adjustments realize that their actions might not be strictly legal, they justify the use of informal adjustments on the basis that the juvenile and/or parent (guardian) entered into it voluntarily. These officers reason that because the treatment or punishment is not mandatory and is in the juvenile's best interests, there does not need to be prior adjudication of delinquency or finding of guilt. Many of these officers fail to recognize that the extent to which their "suggested" treatment or punishment programs are voluntary is highly questionable. The threat of taking official action, if unofficial suggestions are not acceptable to the offenders involved, largely removes any element of voluntarism and is coercive. In cases of this type (which are not atypical), the juvenile may be upset about being punished for an act that he or she did not commit, the parents may be upset because their child did not receive a fair trial, and the juvenile court judge may be upset because the functions of the court have been usurped (taken over) by the police. Of course, not all stationhouse adjustments are negative. Some can be very successful in resolving minor instances of delinquency through proper referral to competent counselors by officers skilled in accurately assessing the needs of the juveniles (see, e.g., In Practice 8.2).

YOUTH ASSESSMENT MODEL: ASSESSMENT, REFERRAL, AND DIVERSION

The Miami-Dade, Florida, Schools Police Department (MDSPD) has participated in dozens of diversion models over the past decade in an attempt to reduce juvenile arrests and provide needed services. The department was determined to create an effective program and to change the process for handling youth challenges. In order to accomplish this change, a partnership which included the Florida Department of Juvenile Justice, the Miami-Dade County Juvenile Services Department, the Miami-Dade Criminal Mental Health Project, the Miami-Dade School Board, and the Miami-Dade Schools Police Department was formed.

Utilizing appropriate tools and interventions, psychosocial issues of at-risk youth were identified so that suitable treatment plans and referrals could be developed in order to reduce the number of juvenile arrests. The model begins with a law enforcement contact with a juvenile and includes the following steps.

Step 1. The officer assesses regular police issues such as the safety of the area and the medical status of the youth.

Step 2. The officer completes a mental health assessment preferably based upon training and certification in Crisis Intervention Team training.

Step 3. If the youth is in crisis or is under the influence of illegal alcohol or drugs, the youth is treated under the Baker Act or taken into protective custody per the Marchman Act in lieu of arrest unless the case involves a violent act with injuries or a sexual act.

Step 4. Mobile Crisis Units are called to handle issues that cannot be addressed by the police due to time constraints or policy.

Step 5. If the incident involves an arrestable offense, the officers are instructed on alternatives to this arrest pursuant to state law and through local juvenile state attorney's office agreements, or the youth is civil cited. The Civil Citation Program allows for the diversion of misdemeanor arrests, and, once an assigned program is completed, the arrest is nullified, giving the youth a chance at a fresh start without a criminal record.

Step 6. The officer takes steps to access pertinent information on the youth so that decision making is meeting the best interests of the youth and community.

Step 7. A prevention referral form is completed and faxed to the Juvenile Services Department's Prevention Initiative, which is designed for any youth 17 years of age and younger who may be experiencing behavior and family difficulties, as well as those at risk of being arrested. "The program includes referrals that address issues such as anger management, disruptive behavior, family issues, drug experimentation, substance abuse, poor academic performance, school attendance and truancy, disciplinary problems, runaways, mental health issues, and negative peer association."

Step 8. The school district and school police take steps to ensure that all gaps in possible services are filled and that the youth and family receive what is needed to avoid negative future contact with law enforcement.

Use of the model is intended to:

- create partnerships within the community, school, and corrections functions of a county;
- train police officers in the full assessment of juveniles before making arrest decisions; and
- reduce arrests, lower recidivism, and provide much-needed quality services to youths and families.

Source: Adapted from Gerald Kitchell, "Youth Assessment Model: Assessment, Referral and Diversion," *The Police Chief* 80 (March 2013): 46–47.

With respect to abused or neglected children, police options are technically more restricted and require more training and expertise (see Figure 8.1). As mandated reporters (those required to report suspected cases of abuse to the state), police are often required to report suspected incidents of child abuse or neglect to the state department of children and family services even though they might not have enough evidence to arrest the suspected abusers. Investigators from the children and family services unit are typically required to contact the parties involved within 72 hours of the time of notification. If the investigators are convinced that neglect or abuse is occurring, or if the original investigating officer is convinced it is occurring, the child may be taken into protective custody until further hearings can be held. It is the responsibility of the local law enforcement department to develop the procedures to handle abuse and neglect situations, to ensure that law enforcement officials are properly trained in identifying cases of abuse or neglect, to objectively investigate abuse or neglect cases, and to interview victims and perpetrators of abuse or neglect. Many major law enforcement agencies have staff specifically assigned to investigate crimes against children. Separation of the investigative and protective services allows law enforcement officers to address enforcement aspects pertaining to the alleged crime, and child protective investigators have the responsibility for interviewing, investigating, and managing abuse or neglect cases (Reaume, 2009). Finkelhor and Ormrod (2001a) noted the following:

> When parents assault or molest their children, it is conventionally thought of as child abuse and, therefore, a child welfare problem. However, these acts are also crimes, and a substantial portion of child abuse cases are investigated and adjudicated by the criminal justice system. Some cases are referred to law enforcement agencies by child welfare investigators, while others are reported directly to law enforcement by victims, families, and other concerned individuals. (p. 1)

As noted in Chapter 5, caregivers are often the perpetrators of abuse and neglect and other violent crimes.

The major concerns of police officers when dealing with abused or neglected children are, of course, the safety and well-being of the minors involved. Still, there are officers who, for a variety of reasons, prefer not to take formal action in cases that they conclude do not involve serious abuse or neglect.

Figure 8.1 Considerations for Child Abuse Investigations

When you receive the referral

- Identify personal or professional biases with child abuse cases. Develop the ability to desensitize yourself to those issues and maintain an objective stance.
- Know the department guidelines and state statutes.
- Know what resources are available in the community (e.g., therapy, victim compensation), and provide this information to the child's family.
- Introduce yourself, your role, and the focus and objective of the investigation.
- Ensure that the best treatment will be provided for the protection of the child.
- Interview the child alone, focusing on corroborative evidence.
- Do not rule out the possibility of child abuse with a domestic dispute complaint. Talk with the children at the scene.

Getting information for the preliminary report

- Inquire about the history of the abusive situation. Dates are important to set the time line for when the abuse may have occurred.
- Cover the elements of the crime necessary for the report. Inquire about the instrument of abuse or other items on the scene.
- Do not discount children's statements about who is abusing them, where and how the abuse is occurring, or what types of acts occurred.
- Save opinions for the end of the report, and provide supportive facts. Highlight the atmosphere of disclosure and the mood and demeanor of participants in the complaint.

Preserving the crime scene

- Treat the scene as a crime scene (even if abuse has occurred in the past) and not as the site of a social problem.
- Secure the instrument of abuse or other corroborative evidence that the child identifies at the scene.
- Photograph the scene, and, when appropriate, include any injuries to the child.
- Rephotograph injuries needed to capture any changes in appearance.

Follow-up investigation

- Be supportive and optimistic to the child and the family.
- Arrange for a medical examination and transportation to the hospital. Collect items for a change of clothes if needed.
- Make use of appropriate investigative techniques.
- Be sure that the child and family have been linked to support services or therapy.
- Be sure that the family knows how to reach a detective to disclose further information.

During the court phase

- Visit the court with the child to familiarize him or her with the courtroom setting and atmosphere before the first hearing. This role may be assumed by the prosecutor or, in some jurisdictions, by victim/witness services.

- Prepare courtroom exhibits (e.g., pictures, displays, sketches) to support the child's testimony.
- File all evidence in accordance with state and court policy.
- Unless they are suspects, update the family about the status and progress of the investigation and stay in touch with them throughout the court process. Depending on the case, officers should be cautious about the type and amount of information provided to the family because they may share the information with others.
- Provide court results and case closure information to the child and the family.
- Follow up with the probation department for preparation of the presentence report and victim impact statement(s).

Source: Office of Justice Programs. (1997, May). *Law enforcement response to child abuse.* Washington, DC: Office of Juvenile Justice and Delinquency Prevention.

Rarely are abusive and neglectful parents arrested. Exceptions exist when the injury to the child is extremely severe or obviously sadistically inflicted, when a crime has been committed, when the parents present a danger to others, or when arrest is the only way to preserve the peace. (Tower, 1993, p. 275)

Official action is more likely to occur today because of mandated reporting laws. Still, even though they are mandated reporters, officers sometimes hesitate to take official action. This is sometimes the case because police officers are concerned about the possibility of false allegations or of being used by one party involved in a hostile divorce or separation to cause trouble for the other party through implanting false allegations in the mind of the child or by falsely reporting abuse or neglect (Goldstein & Tyler, 1998; OJJDP, 2001).

As noted in Chapter 2, it is estimated that a substantial amount of all police–juvenile contacts are resolved informally (Black & Reiss, 1970; Mays & Winfree, 2000; Myers, 2004). The proportion of child abuse or neglect cases handled unofficially is unknown but is probably considerable. Here is an example:

Columbus [Ohio] police investigated 2,295 reports of rape (a crime that requires penetration) or gross sexual imposition (fondling) with children as victims in 2010 and 2011. Of the 1,285 cases in which detectives think that a crime occurred, 19 percent resulted in an arrest or a referral to a grand jury. After eight years of supervising child-sexual-abuse investigations, [Sgt] Kaeppner still finds the number and nature of the cases alarming. "It's distasteful and it's prevalent," he said. "And for the kids who are victimized, it stays with them their entire lives." (Futty, 2012)

Police officers who use informal dispositions often see such dispositions as more desirable than official processing, which is certain to leave the offender with a record and may lead to detention for some time. Most police officers agree that neither juvenile records nor attempts to rehabilitate juveniles who are detained are beneficial to juveniles. The latter holds true for child abusers as well, although when the abuse is severe, officers are typically more than willing to take official action (Willis & Welles, 1988). When police officers act informally, they often sincerely believe they are doing so in the best interests of the parties involved. This may be the case if we assume that all of the persons apprehended did commit a delinquent or criminal act and if we assume that treatment and rehabilitation are of little or no value. However, if we recognize that sometimes the police do make mistakes, that some juveniles and some parents do need and might benefit from treatment of some type, that the police have no mandate to impose punishment or treatment, and that the juvenile court judge often has no way of knowing how many times a particular juvenile or abusive parent has been dealt with informally, the problems inherent in informal adjustments become very apparent (Portwood, Grady, & Dutton, 2000; Walker, 2007).

Official Procedures

The official procedures to be followed when processing juveniles are clearly spelled out in juvenile court acts. It is important to note that police procedures for juvenile offenders differ from adult procedures in most jurisdictions. As a rule, these procedures are tailored specifically toward implementing the juvenile court philosophy of treatment, protection, and rehabilitation rather than punishment. As a result, to carry out proper procedures, specialized training is necessary. It has been our observation that many officers in most jurisdictions believe that being assigned as a juvenile officer is not particularly desirable. We have heard juvenile officers referred to as "kiddie cops" and seen distinctions made between "real" police officers and "juvenile" officers. These traditional police attitudes have slowed the development of a professional corps of juvenile officers. Nonetheless, being an effective juvenile police officer requires more skill than being a good patrol officer. In addition to learning the basics of policing, the juvenile officer is required to learn a great deal about the special requirements of juvenile law, about the nature of adolescence, about the nature of parent–child relationships, and about the social service agencies (public and private) to which juveniles may be referred for assistance (National Children's Advocacy Center, 2010; OJJDP, 2001; Tower, 1993, p. 275). These skills are not easy to acquire, and those who have mastered them should take pride in their accomplishments. In addition, police organizations should reward those who possess and actively employ these skills in terms of both salary and promotional opportunities.

Although the development of effective juvenile officers and juvenile bureaus is highly desirable, most initial contacts between juveniles and the police involve patrol officers. It would appear logical to provide at least minimal training in the area of juvenile law for all patrol personnel to safeguard the rights of juveniles and to ensure proper legal processing by the police. It does little good, either for the juvenile or for the prosecutor's case, to have a competent juvenile officer if the initial encounter between the juvenile or abusive parent and the police has been mishandled (Listenbee et al., 2012; National Children's Advocacy Center, 2010; OJJDP, 2001).

Police officers who are involved in the official processing of juveniles need to be aware that all of the guarantees in terms of self-incrimination and searches and seizures characteristic of adult proceedings also hold for juveniles. In addition, juveniles are, in most jurisdictions, extended even further protection by law. Thus, the police are required to notify a juvenile's parents about their child's whereabouts and are required to release the juvenile to his or her parents unless good cause exists for detention. Detention in a lockup routinely used for adult offenders is often illegal, and the police must, in these cases, make special arrangements to transport and detain juveniles if further detention is necessary. In Texas, for example, juveniles must be separated by sight and sound from adults detained in the same building (Texas Family Code, sec. 51.12, 2012). Similarly, police records concerning juveniles must, in most jurisdictions, be kept separate from adult records and are more or less confidential (see Chapter 7). Although fingerprints and photographs of juvenile offenders may be taken, there are often restrictions placed on their use; that is, they may not be transmitted to other law enforcement agencies without a court order in many jurisdictions. However, some states permit individuals with a legitimate interest in the workings of the court (such as researchers), or a particular case, to gain access to juvenile records (see, e.g., Missouri Revised Statutes, ch. 211, sec. 211.321, 2012). At least some courts have held that a juvenile charged with a delinquent act has a right to counsel prior to placement in a police lineup—at least under certain circumstances (see, e.g., *1 No. 18, The People & C., Respondent, v. Ricky Mitchell, Appellant*, 2004, NY Int. 49). There is also some concern that a juvenile's waiver of his or her right to remain silent during interrogation without a parent or lawyer present is of questionable value (Dorne & Gewerth, 1998, p. 34; Feld, 2006; Illinois Juvenile Justice Commission, 2012). As a result, police officers may delay interrogation until either a parent and/or an attorney is present. Should they decide to conduct an interrogation absent the parents, Feld (2006) has pointed out that "the Supreme Court does not require any special procedural safeguards when police interrogate youths and use the adult standard—'knowing, intelligent, and voluntary under the totality of the circumstances'—to gauge the validity of juveniles' waivers of Miranda rights" (p. 219).

In many jurisdictions, police officers who have been designated juvenile officers have the task of ensuring that juveniles are properly handled. These juvenile officers are, presumably, specially trained in juvenile law and procedures.

Training and Competence of Juvenile Officers

For roughly the past 75 years, there have been repeated calls for professionalization of the police through increased education and training (Shusta et al., 2015). The number of 2- and 4-year college programs in criminal justice and law enforcement has increased dramatically during the past four decades, as has the number of special institutes, seminars, and workshops dealing with special police problems. Because juvenile cases present special problems for the police, one might expect considerable emphasis on training for juvenile officers. Indeed, the number of police officers qualified by training to serve in juvenile bureaus has increased dramatically over the years—especially in large metropolitan departments. In these departments, promotion within the juvenile bureau is possible, and both male and female officers deal with juvenile offenders and victims. The possibilities of promotion and recognition for a job well done provide incentive and rewards for those choosing to pursue a career in juvenile law enforcement.

The situation of juvenile officers in smaller cities has also improved. More jurisdictions require compliance with laws mandating special training for juvenile officers, although personnel shortages and reduced financial resources sometimes make both training and specific assignment to purely juvenile matters difficult. There are still many smaller police departments with no female officers, so male officers must deal with juveniles of both genders (Shusta et al., 2015). Some rural departments have no officers specifically trained to deal with juveniles, and others, to conform to statutory requirements, simply select and designate an officer—often one who has no prior training in juvenile matters, as juvenile officer. Considering the fact that juvenile officers are frequently expected to speak to civic-action groups about juvenile problems, run junior police programs, visit schools and preschools, form working relationships with personnel of other agencies, and investigate cases of abused and missing children, this lack of training is a very serious matter. Police departments with 10 or fewer sworn officers still face difficulties in providing adequately trained officers for 24-hour-a-day service. When these departments do train and appoint officers to handle juvenile offenders, they can seldom afford to relieve these officers of other duties. This, in effect, makes it impossible for the appointed officers to become specialized in juvenile matters. This also eliminates the possibility of developing a stable juvenile bureau and of advancing one's career as a juvenile officer. One result of these difficulties is that officers have little incentive to volunteer for service in juvenile bureaus. Consequently, juvenile officers are frequently appointed on the basis of a perceived affinity for "getting along" with juveniles. Unfortunately, this affinity is not a substitute for proper training, although it may appear to be to police administrators who regard handling juvenile offenses as something less than real police work.

It is essential that police departments train officers to handle juvenile cases. In Illinois, for example, a juvenile police officer is defined by statute as the following:

> A sworn police officer who has completed a Basic Recruit Training Course, has been assigned to the position of juvenile officer by his or her chief law enforcement officer, and has completed the necessary juvenile officers training as described by the Illinois Law Enforcement Training Standards Board or, in the case of a State police officer, juvenile officer training approved by the Director of the Department of State Police. (ILCS, ch. 705, sec. 405/1-3 [17], 2013)

Professional associations of juvenile police dedicated to training, information sharing, and developing relationships with others in the juvenile justice network exist in a number of states including New York, Ohio, Louisiana, Minnesota, Wisconsin, Michigan, North Carolina, Illinois, and Missouri.

It is worth noting here that the training of juvenile police officers (and other police officers in juvenile matters) is an ongoing process because the demands they face are constantly changing. For example, the use of social media on the Internet by both juveniles and adults for illegitimate purposes has become a major issue in recent years. Here is an example:

> Juvenile sexting is increasing in frequency. A recent study found that 20 percent of teenagers (22 percent of girls and 18 percent of boys) sent naked or seminude images of themselves or posted them online. Another survey indicated that nearly one in six teens between the ages of 12 and 17 who own cell phones have received naked or nearly nude pictures via text message from someone they know. Law enforcement officers and prosecutors face increased pressure to handle these cases as effectively as possible. (Bowker & Sullivan, 2010, p. 1)

Further, cyberbullying has received increasing attention as a result of highly publicized suicides related to this form of bullying. Cyberbullying is a distinct type of bullying in which the victim is targeted online or through the use of text messages using cell phones (BullyingStatistics.com, 2009, p. 1; OJJDP, 2011b, p. 1). According to BullyingStatistics.com (2009), "There have been cases where cyber bullying has led to severe depression, self harm and even suicide." One such case receiving national attention involved Megan Taylor Meier, a teenager who committed suicide by hanging 3 weeks before her 14th birthday. A year later, an investigation into her suicide attributed the act to cyberbullying through a social networking website. An indictment of the mother of the alleged bully followed, but she was acquitted (Zetter, 2009). Police investigators and juvenile officers conduct undercover investigations on the Internet in an attempt to prevent such bullying and to arrest those who prey on victims through cyberspace. Common types of undercover investigations involve police officers posing online as minors and undercover investigations of child pornography. Investigators also pose as adults having access to minors to sell or wanting to purchase sex with a minor. The efficacy of various types of investigations remains to be determined (Mitchell, Wolak, Finkelhor, & Jones, 2012). Wells, Mitchell, and Ji (2012) examined the role of the Internet in juvenile prostitution cases using information from a national sample of law enforcement agencies. They found that in comparison to non-Internet juvenile prostitution cases, Internet juvenile prostitution cases involved younger juveniles, and police were more likely to treat juveniles as victims rather than offenders. If police officers are to keep up with the variety of ever-changing types of crime occurring on the Internet, continued education and training will be required.

Police–School Resource Officer and Liaison Programs

Over the past four decades, police departments and schools have worked together to develop programs to help prevent delinquency and improve relationships between juveniles and the police (Brown, 2006; Ervin & Swilaski, 2004; OJJDP, 2006). These programs involve more than simply providing security through police presence in the schools. Rather, the programs attempt to foster a more personal relationship between juveniles and the police by using police officers in counseling settings, by improving communications between the police and school officials, and by increasing student knowledge of the law and the consequences of violations (Brown, 2006; Ervin & Swilaski, 2004; OJJDP, 2006).

One early police–school consultant program was developed in Flint, Michigan, in 1958. Police–school liaison officers (PSLOs; often referred to as resource officers) are located in schools and serve as sources of information and counselors for students. They are often funded, at least in part, by school districts even though they work for police agencies. Evaluations of these programs have consistently concluded that police officers assigned have difficulty in being both an authority figure as well as a counselor or confidant. Multiple program evaluations have shown similar results in Tucson, Arizona; Montgomery, Alabama; Woodburn, Oregon; and Tampa, Florida, to mention just a few. As a result of recent school shootings in various locales across the United States, there has been a call for more armed police officers in schools for security reasons. Although armed officers do provide protection for students, recent research by the Justice Policy Institute (JPI) (2012) suggests that SROs have little impact on reducing school-based crime. Still, there is little doubt that school-based officers can and do provide valuable services. For instance, SROs or D.A.R.E. (Drug Abuse Resistance Education) officers become familiar with the layout of the campus and can thus respond immediately to the area in which a critical situation exists. They can also be involved in training school staff concerning appropriate responses during crises, and they serve as visible evidence of police presence to those contemplating violence in the school (Quinn, 2012).

Assigned officers, acting as additional resource persons in the school setting, have generally been evaluated positively by school officials, although not always by students (Brown, 2006). These programs have proliferated based on these evaluations and the belief that the closer the relationship between police and juveniles in nonthreatening situations (those other than investigatory or crime intervention), the better in terms of improving the image of the police, uncovering information concerning abuse and neglect, and decreasing delinquency (Brown, 2006; Gandhi, Murphy-Graham, Anthony, Chrismer, & Weiss, 2007).

In some cases, PSLOs assist with classroom lessons on topics such as bullying, Internet safety, laws involving dating and relationships, and drug and alcohol use consistent with the D.A.R.E. program (City of Wichita Police Department, 2010; Michigan State Police, 2009; Oshkosh, Wisconsin, Police Department, 2010).

D.A.R.E. programs, in which police officers teach children how to avoid use of illicit drugs, are widespread in the United States and abroad (Gandhi et al., 2007). A number of schools and police agencies throughout the country are now involved with such programs, and they appear to have at least some positive effects on officers, juveniles, and school authorities—particularly when the officers involved have received special training to prepare them for their assignments (Brown, 2006; Martin, Schulze, & Valdez, 1988). Even though some research shows that D.A.R.E. is ineffective at preventing drug use among those who have gone through the program (Aniskievicz & Wysong, 1990; Berman & Fox, 2009; Drug Policy Alliance, 2010; Ennett, Tobler, Ringwalt, & Flewelling, 1994; Gandhi et al., 2007), the program may still improve understanding and relationships between juveniles and the police officers involved. This alone is thought to be a beneficial outcome given that such positive experiences can reduce the likelihood that juveniles will engage in delinquent behavior. This is much more likely to be true if educators ensure that the material is developmentally appropriate so as to be positively received by peer groups at various age ranges. In addition, it has been found that juveniles are more receptive to an emphasis on short-term negative social consequences as opposed to physiological consequences. As mentioned earlier in this chapter, it is important to consider race, gender, and cross-cultural effects when educating on the topic of drugs, thereby necessitating that programs or curricula be culturally sensitive (Goldberg, 2003). In response to research reports indicating that D.A.R.E. failed to achieve many of its goals, a new D.A.R.E. program has been developed.

An independent, federally-funded cost effectiveness study evaluating prevention programs reported that *"keepin' it REAL"* was ranked among the top 3 overall with a cost benefit of $28 in benefits for every $1 spent. . . . The multicultural keepin' it REAL curriculum has proven effective in reducing adolescent alcohol, marijuana, and tobacco use in 7th and 8th grade students. . . . The core of the program is the REAL strategies for resisting drug offers: Refuse, Explain, Avoid, and Leave. By highlighting these four methods of communicating, the program helps kids understand the risks of drugs, teaches them to make good decisions and resist the temptation to use drugs. (D.A.R.E., 2012, p. 1)

Another program, GREAT (Gang Resistance Education and Awareness Training), is described as the following:

An evidence-based and effective gang and violence prevention program built around school-based, law enforcement officer-instructed classroom curricula . . . intended as an immunization against delinquency, youth violence, and gang membership for children in the years immediately before the prime ages for introduction into gangs and delinquent behavior. (GREAT, 2013, p. 1)

Not surprisingly, it has been subject to criticisms similar to those concerning the D.A.R.E. program (Palumbo & Ferguson, 1995). There is little doubt that GREAT programs are very popular throughout the United States (Hanser & Gomila, 2015; Valdez, 2005). Similar to D.A.R.E. programs, these gang resistance programs train police officers to conduct comprehensive antigang education programs for children who are not yet in high school (Hanser & Gomila, 2015; Valdez, 2005). Since its inception in 1991, over 10,000 law enforcement officers have been certified as GREAT instructors and more than 5 million students have graduated from the GREAT program (National Institute of Justice, 2010). As with D.A.R.E. programs, there is a need for such programs to be appropriate for the age range of the peer group. Valdez (2005) noted that one way to overcome this challenge is to provide student training and allow the students to share in the formal leadership roles that the educator and/or police presenter might have. This empowers the students and likewise provides for more internalization of the anti-gang (and anti-drug) values that are being transmitted (Valdez, 2005). According to the National Institute of Justice (NIJ) (2010), a 5-year longitudinal evaluation of the GREAT program showed that students who had completed the training had lower levels of victimization, more negative views about gangs, more favorable attitudes about police, a reduction in risk-seeking behaviors, and increased association with peers involved in prosocial activities. Currently the program is used in North America, including the United States, Canada, Belize, Guatemala, El Salvador, Honduras, Nicaragua, Costa Rica, and Panama (GREAT, 2013).

Mark Perlstein/The LIFE Images Collection/Getty Images

Oklahoma City police officer Terry Yeakey talks with young students about D.A.R.E. in school.

FAR EAST EL PASO SCHOOL BEATING BRINGS CALL FOR ANTI-BULLYING AID

"After a bullying attack left a 13-year-old student bruised and battered this week, a local civil rights group is demanding that the Socorro Independent School District improve its bullying awareness and prevention programs."

According to sources a female student was attacked at school and the beating she suffered was so violent that she became unconscious and needed medical attention.

In a letter to the Socorro district, the Paso Del Norte Civil Rights Project says it wants a full and open investigation, implementation of measures to prevent future bullying incidents, and training with students and staff to promote awareness of bullying.

"We decided to become involved because the violence and brutality of it (the beating) was so jarring," said lawyer Jed Untereker, who represents the Paso Del Norte Civil Rights Project. "And the fact that someone could be put in the hospital from an attack that occurs on school grounds is very disturbing."

Untereker said bullying appears to be an ongoing problem at the middle school.

On Thursday, another student in the El Paso Independent School District was injured in a fight while walking home from school.

The district does have an anti-bullying program, the Olweus Bullying Prevention Program, in which students can report bullying online.

The school district is working to be proactive and not reactive and is working with the El Paso Police Department on bullying cases. School officials said they were taking measures to prevent further bullying incidents.

Source: Adapted from Hinojosa (2013).

Questions to Consider

1. True or False: In the bullying example provided, the person harmed was female.

2. Multiple Choice: In response to bullying, the El Paso Independent School District has taken measures to be which of the following?

   a. Proactive

   b. Reactive

   c. Better aligned to partner with the El Paso Police Department on bullying cases

   d. All of the above

3. List some ideas that could help prevent bullying in the future.

Although they may or may not directly involve police officers, antibullying programs (also discussed in Chapter 3) deserve at least a brief mention here in conjunction with school-oriented programs. An evaluation of 44 antibullying programs showed that school-based antibullying programs are effective in reducing bullying perpetration and victimization (being bullied) by 17% to 20% (Farrington & Ttofi, 2009). The Olweus Bullying Prevention Program appears to be effective in reducing the incidence of bullying and improving attitudes toward school and academic achievement in middle- and upper-class areas, but the effectiveness of the program has not yet been tested in low-income schools (Hong, 2009). (See In Practice 8.3.)

The Olweus Bullying Prevention Program (pronounced *Ol-VEY-us*; the *E* sounds like a long *A*) is a comprehensive, schoolwide program designed and evaluated for use in elementary, middle, or junior high schools. The program's goals are to reduce and prevent bullying problems among schoolchildren and to improve peer relations at school. The program has been found to reduce bullying among children, improve the social climate of classrooms, and reduce related antisocial behaviors, such as vandalism and truancy. Schools are also gathering data about the program's implementation at the high school level. The program has been implemented in more than a dozen countries around the world and in thousands of schools in the United States (Clemson University, 2013).

From the examples just discussed, it is clear that there are various, more or less successful, means of addressing drugs, gangs, and other issues that might face juveniles while in and out of public schools. For an interesting evaluation of a police–school resource or liaison program, see In Practice 8.4.

IN PRACTICE 8.4

AN EVALUATION OF CAPE BRETON REGIONAL POLICE SERVICE'S COMMUNITY LIAISON OFFICER PROGRAM IN CAPE BRETON VICTORIA REGION SCHOOLS

Overall, the interview and survey results indicate that the CLOP [community liaison officer program] has as yet unrealized potential. On the positive side, the officers and the police chief demonstrated an acute awareness of the difficulties facing young people; they were empathetic, enthusiastic about the opportunities the program provides for helping youth; they received satisfaction from their interactions with youth; and they perceived significant support from all stakeholders. There were also some challenges noted. Officers felt some role strain from conflicting demands and lack of peer interaction, and from insufficient resources. And importantly, there were concerns from both the officers and the police chief that the CLOP remained somewhat misunderstood and that schools with officers present tended to be stigmatized. However, there were significant satisfaction and improved relationships with youth.

On the negative side, the concern expressed that the CLOP may be devolving into a disciplinary, rather than proactive, program may be well-founded. Students perceived the major role of their on-site officer to be that of a kind disciplinarian who would go where the problems necessitated police intervention. In essence, the students viewed their officers as friendly and significantly more respectful to them than other (off-site) officers, but as police officers nonetheless. This perception was reflected in the survey findings that help was most frequently sought from friends or teachers.

The survey data indicated that the presence of an officer at the school may not be as predictive of student behaviors and sense of safety as other school variables. If the CLOP was itself making a significant difference, then we would expect the pattern of findings to be similar at the two schools with the program, and different from the schools without it. Further research is needed here to examine the contributions of structural factors such as school size and location, and functioning factors such as disciplinary policies, student involvement, and overall ethos. It is interesting to note here that school D (no CLO) students reported a significantly higher sense of community than the other schools as well as the lowest use of situational control strategies.

Students' concerns may be of use in guiding further interventions. Students emphasized the need for more caring and involved teachers, and for more fair school rules that are consistently enforced. Students also emphasized the need to feel respected, to be listened to, and to have a voice in the school. The community liaison officers appear to be filling this need to some extent, but students need to feel respected by educators as well. Students identified their greatest vulnerability to victimization as being during lunch hour on school grounds. Their response is to try to stay in groups of friends. School staff and CLOs may be able to target their intervention efforts to this issue.

The evaluation data described in this report indicate the CLOP suffers similar difficulties to other school police liaison programs in three areas. First, the officers, although enjoying the school placement overall, did have some challenges posed by role conflict. Second, there was evidence of the perennial problem of insufficient resources.

Third, the students in this study, as reported in earlier evaluation data, see their officer as atypical. It is important to emphasize here, however, that unlike students in other studies, there was no derision behind this perception. Students in this study unambiguously perceived their officer to be much friendlier and respectful to young people than other officers and in no way inferior to "real cops."

Finally, it is particularly noteworthy that, unlike in previous evaluation studies, there was evidence here of a very successful and viable relationship among the school board, school personnel and the officers and police department. There was no evidence of the commonly reported power struggles and no evidence of credibility problems. The Cape Breton-Victoria Regional School District and the Cape Breton Regional Police provide an excellent model of a successful partnership.

Source: McKay, Covell, & McNeil (2006). Reprinted with permission.

Questions to Consider

1. True or False: In the CLOP study, officers reported challenges posed by role conflicts in their duties.

2. Multiple Choice: According to the information provided, the primary factor in predicting student behavior was which of the following?

   a. The presence of an officer at school

   b. The school size and location

   c. Disciplinary policies, student involvement, and overall ethos

   d. All of the above

   e. None of the above

3. Identify and discuss some of the findings from the evaluation data of this report.

Community-Oriented Policing and Juveniles

Community-oriented policing refers to a strategy that relies on identification of problems by police and members of the community they serve and shared ownership of law enforcement and order-maintenance duties (Hanser & Gomila, 2015; Glensor, Correia, & Peak, 2000; Shusta et al., 2015; Walters, 1993; Webber, 1991). Although community-oriented policing is a general police strategy, it certainly has applications in police work with juveniles given that it requires joint community–police identification of, and efforts to solve, problems (Shusta et al., 2015). Thus, police officers and school, probation, civic action, neighborhood, and political groups work together to find solutions to problems rather than asking the police to handle incidents as and after they occur (Brown, 2006; Hanser & Gomila, 2015). One example of programs of this type, sponsored by the Department of Justice, is Youth-Focused Community Policing (YFCP). These programs provide information-sharing activities that promote proactive partnerships among the police, juveniles, and community agencies cooperating to identify and address juvenile problems in a manner consistent with community policing philosophy. In 2011, the International Association of Chiefs of Police (IACP) (2011) launched a website providing information and resources for YFCP programs. One example of the types of programs included is the Tallahassee Police Athletic League, Inc. (TAL PAL), which is a juvenile crime prevention program operated by the Tallahassee Police Department and a board of directors. The goal of TAL PAL is to team young persons, ages 7 to 17, with police officers and other caring individuals within the community. This is accomplished through recreation and educational programs in order to foster long-term, positive relationships through mentorship (City of Tallahassee, 2013).

Still other programs have been introduced to improve the relationship between schools and the police concerning juvenile offenders. One example is SHOCAP (Serious Habitual Offender Comprehensive Action Program). SHOCAP does the following—at least in Alachua County, Florida:

> [It] is designed to help monitor juveniles in Alachua County that have been charged and convicted of any law violations that meet the program criteria. Juveniles who qualify for this program are selected by a panel of people in law enforcement, juvenile justice, counseling agencies, public housing, state attorney's office, and the public defender's office. This program monitors 30 juveniles at a time, and works on deterring them from committing a law violation as well as maintaining attendance in school. Juveniles in this program that violate probation sanctions can be arrested at the time of the violation whereas juveniles not on SHOCAP but on probation can only have a violation of probation filed with the court and the juvenile's probation officer. (Alachua County Sheriff's Office, 2012, p. 1)

Using multidisciplinary interagency case management and information sharing, the SHOCAP model is intended to help the agencies involved make informed decisions about juveniles who repeatedly engage in delinquent acts. It is hoped that the sharing of such information on a need-to-know basis will result in better coordination of efforts to intervene and deal appropriately with repeat offenders.

Police and Juvenile Court

The police are the primary source of referral to juvenile court, and juvenile court judges rely heavily on the police for background information concerning juveniles who come before them. Because the police and the court may have different goals with respect to juveniles (e.g., control vs. treatment), this might not always be in the best interests of juveniles. On the one hand, the juvenile court may become overly concerned with control; on the other hand, the police officer who believes that the court is unfair to the police or too lenient with offenders may fail to report cases to the court because, in his or her opinion, nothing will be gained by official referral. Further, there is at least some evidence that "heavy-handed tactics" during interviews and interrogations by the police may produce false evidence, especially when the individuals being questioned are particularly vulnerable, such as juveniles or those who are intellectually disabled or mentally ill (Thompson, 2012). In some cases, the police may attempt to resolve the case at hand by themselves, and this, as we pointed out earlier, may or may not be in the best interests of the juvenile involved. In short, whether a particular juvenile is referred to juvenile court depends in part on the police officer's attitude toward the court.

Finally, it is important to note that theories of causation play a role in the nature of police–juvenile encounters. To the extent that race and ethnicity play a role in such encounters, one may consider the biological and genetic theories that suggest they influence police behavior in a latent fashion. As the police attempt to intervene early in juvenile misbehavior, learning theories, deterrence theories, and behavior modification theories may play a role (e.g., if the behavior can be modified early, it may not lead to continuing careers in crime). To the extent that certain youth become labeled (e.g., gang members, bullies, drug addicts), police officers may react differently in encounters with them. And theories based on social class and differential association may also be tied to police encounters with juveniles in terms of allocation of police resources and decisions concerning whether to take official action. The exact nature and extent of the influence of each theory on police–juvenile encounters is difficult, if not impossible, to determine, but actions are most often based on the way in which we understand the world around us and theories play an important role in organizing perceptions.

CAREER OPPORTUNITY: MUNICIPAL POLICE OFFICER

Job description: Enforce laws and maintain order. Patrol the community, control traffic, make arrests, prevent crime, investigate criminal activity, and work with the public and representatives of other agencies to improve the quality of life in the community.

Employment requirements: Must be a U.S. citizen, have a valid driver's license, and be at least 20 years old at the time of application. Must not have any felony convictions. Must be able to pass physical, written, medical, polygraph, psychological, and background investigations. Must possess good communication skills. Must be a high school graduate, but preference is frequently given to those with 2- or 4-year degrees. Appointment contingent on completion of basic training.

Beginning salary: Salary typically ranges between $25,000 and $55,000 depending on jurisdiction; average is roughly $52,000. Additional benefits package (insurance, vacation, sick leave, and pension).

Note: To become a juvenile police officer, an applicant typically needs to serve as a patrol officer first and then may be required to participate in special training to be certified as a juvenile officer.

Future: Employment of police officers and detectives is expected to increase about as fast as the average for all occupations through 2018.

Source: Bureau of Labor Statistics (2011).

Summary

To implement proper juvenile procedures and benefit from theoretical notions concerning prevention, causes, and correction of delinquent behavior and child abuse and neglect, juvenile officers must first know proper procedures and understand theories of causation. Because both types of knowledge are specialized, it is imperative that juvenile officers receive special training in these areas. This specialized training is advantageous for the police department, juveniles, the justice network, the social service network, and the community. The police department benefits in terms of creating a more professional image and in terms of efficiency because mistakes in processing should be reduced. Juveniles benefit in that trained personnel can better carry out the intent of juvenile court acts that were developed to protect the best interests of juveniles. The justice system benefits from the proper initial processing of juveniles and abusive adults who are to be processed further (e.g., prosecuted) in that system. Finally, the community and social service network benefit from decisions made by police officers who are properly trained. In return for these benefits, it is essential to reward juvenile officers who perform well through recognition and promotional opportunities.

The majority of police–juvenile contacts result in unofficial dispositions in the form of street corner or stationhouse adjustments. It is important that decisions concerning proper disposition of juvenile cases by police officers be based on a thorough knowledge of procedural requirements and the problems of juveniles and abusive or neglectful adults. When trained, competent officers make such decisions, the imposition of punishment by the officers handling cases unofficially is reduced, and the rights of all parties are better protected. In cases that require official disposition, further processing is facilitated by proper initial processing. To ensure that police officers handle juvenile cases properly, specialized training programs need to be developed and used, and incentives for good performance by juvenile officers need to be provided. Technological advances, such as the development of social media and the Internet, demand that police personnel view training as an ongoing process if they are to prevent and apprehend predators who approach victims through cyberspace. Finally, the more we understand about the theories providing the foundations for police actions when dealing with juveniles, the better we will be able to understand such actions.

KEY TERMS

D.A.R.E. (Drug Abuse Resistance Education)   223

GREAT (Gang Resistance Education and Awareness Training)   224

mandated reporters   217

official procedures   220

Olweus Bullying Prevention Program   225

overpolicing   213

police discretion   208

police–school liaison officers (PSLOs)   222

SHOCAP (Serious Habitual Offender Comprehensive Action Program)   228

street corner adjustment   214

Youth-Focused Community Policing (YFCP)   227

Critical Thinking Questions

1. List and discuss some of the cues frequently used by police officers in deciding whether to handle a case officially or unofficially. What are some of the dangers in relying on these cues from the point of view of the juvenile offender? From the point of view of the victim of abuse or neglect?

2. Joe, a 13-year-old white male, has just been apprehended by a police officer for stealing a bicycle. Joe admits taking the bicycle but says that he only intended to go for a joyride and was going to return the bicycle later in the day. Joe has no prior police contacts of which the officer is aware. The bicycle has been missing for only an hour and is unharmed. The owner of the bicycle is undecided about whether to proceed officially. Discuss the various options available to the police officer in handling this case. What options do you consider to be most appropriate and why?

3. Why do you think that juvenile officers handle the majority of contacts with juveniles unofficially even when they could clearly proceed officially? Why are police officers often hesitant to take official action in cases involving abuse or neglect even though they are mandated reporters? What are some of the advantages and disadvantages of unofficial dispositions to both juveniles and society?

4. Locate the website for the Department of Justice and see what information you can obtain on the YFCP program. Is there a recent evaluation of the program? If so, what conclusions can you draw about the program based on the evaluation?

5. In your opinion, how can bullying in person and over the Internet best be handled? How effective are the police in dealing with these issues as they relate to juveniles?

Suggested Readings

Allen, T. T. (2005). Taking a juvenile into custody: Situational factors that influence police officers' decisions. *Journal of Sociology and Social Welfare, 32*, 121–129.

Berman, G., & Fox, A. (2009). *Lessons from the battle over D.A.R.E.: The complicated relationship between research and practice.*

Washington, DC: Center for Court Innovation. Retrieved from www.ojp.usdoj.gov/BJA/pdf/CCI_DARE.pdf

Broaddus, E. T., Scott, K. E., Gonsalves, L. M., Parrish, C., Rhodes, E. L., Donovan, S. E., & Winch, P. J. (2013). Building connections between officers and Baltimore city youth: Key components of a police–youth teambuilding program. *Journal of Juvenile Justice, 3*(1), 1–4. Retrieved from http://www.journalofjuvjustice.org/JOJJ0301/article04.htm

City of Tallahassee. (2009). *Juvenile programs.* Retrieved from www.talgov.com

City of Wichita. (2010). *Police-school liaison program.* Retrieved from www.wichita.gov/CityOffices/Police/Schools/SchoolLiaison

Clemson University. (2009). *Olweus Bullying Prevention Program (OBPP).* Retrieved from www.clemson.edu/olweus

Engel, R. S., Sobol, J. J., & Worden, R. E. (2000). Further exploration of the demeanor hypothesis: The interaction effects of suspects' characteristics and demeanor on police behavior. *Justice Quarterly, 17,* 235–258.

Farrington, D. P., & Ttofi, M. M. (2009, October). *School-based programs to reduce bullying and victimization.* Retrieved from www.ncjrs.gov/pdffiles1/nij/grants/229377.pdf

Feld, B. C. (2013). Real interrogation: What actually happens when cops question kids. *Law & Society Review, 47*(1), 1–36.

Finkelhor, D., & Ormrod, R. (2001). Child abuse reported to the police. *Juvenile Justice Bulletin.* Retrieved from www.ncjrs.gov/html/ojjdp/jjbul2001_5_1/contents.html

Gandhi, A. G., Murphy-Graham, E., Anthony, P., Chrismer, S. S., & Weiss, C. H. (2007). The devil is in the details: Examining the evidence for "proven" school-based drug abuse prevention programs. *Evaluation Review, 31,* 43–74.

GREAT. (2013). *GREAT Program.* Retrieved from www.great-online.org

Hanser, R. D., & Gomila, M. N. (2015). *Multiculturalism and the criminal justice system.* Upper Saddle River, NJ: Pearson.

Hong, J. S. (2009). Feasibility of the Olweus Bullying Prevention Programs in low-income schools. *Journal of School Violence, 8*(1), 81–97.

Hurst, Y. G. (2007). Juvenile attitudes toward the police: An examination of rural youth. *Criminal Justice Review, 32*(2), 121–141.

Hurst, Y. G., Frank, J., & Browning, S. L. (2000). The attitudes of juveniles toward the police: A comparison of black and white youth. *Policing: An International Journal of Police Strategies and Management, 23,* 37–53.

Hurst, Y. G., McDermott, M. J., & Thomas, D. L. (2005). The attitudes of girls toward the police: Differences by race. *Policing: An International Journal of Police Strategies and Management, 28,* 578–594.

International Association of Chiefs of Police. (2012). The IACP partners with the MacArthur Foundation to address juvenile justice issues. *Police Chief, 79*(4), 110.

Joiner, C. T. (2005). An examination of racial profiling data in a large metropolitan area. *Professional issues in Criminal Justice, 1*(2), 1–14.

Listenbee, R. L., Jr., Torre, J., Boyle, G., Cooper, S. W., Deer, S., Durfee, D. T., . . . Taguba, A. (2012, December 12). *Report of the attorney general's national task force on children exposed to violence.* Retrieved from www.justice.gov/defendingchildhood/cev-rpt-full.pdf

Lundman, R. L., Sykes, E. G., & Clark, J. P. (1978). Police control of juveniles: A replication. *Journal of Research in Crime and Delinquency, 15,* 74–91.

Michigan State Police. (2009). *MSP T.E.A.M. School Liaison Program.* Retrieved from www.michigan.gov/msp/0,1607,7-123-1589_1711_40754-10270—,00.html

National Children's Advocacy Center. (2010). *Law enforcement's initial response to child sexual abuse: Guidelines for patrol officers.* Retrieved from www.nationalcac.org/professionals/index.php?option=com_content&task=view&id=40&Itemid=60

Office of Juvenile Justice and Delinquency Prevention. (2001). *Law enforcement response to child abuse: Portable guide to investigating child abuse.* Retrieved from www.ncjrs.gov/pdffiles/162425.pdf

Oshkosh, Wisconsin, Police Department. (2010). *Police school liaison officers.* Retrieved from www.oshkoshpd.com/administrative.htm

Penn, B. E. (2016). *Responding to strained minority youth and police relations: Policing by TOTALS.* Houston, TX: Teen and Police Service Academy.

Piliavin, I., & Briar, S. (1964). Police encounters with juveniles. *American Journal of Sociology, 70,* 206–214.

Pope, C. E., & Snyder, H. N. (2003, April). Race as a factor in juvenile arrests. *Juvenile Justice Bulletin.* Retrieved from www.ncjrs.gov/pdffiles1/ojjdp/189180.pdf

Shusta, R. M., Levine, D. R., Wong, H. Z., Olson, A. T., & Harris, P. R. (2015). *Multicultural law enforcement: Strategies for peacekeeping in a diverse society* (6th ed.) Upper Saddle River, NJ: Pearson.

Walker, S., Spohn, C., & DeLone, M. (2004). *The color of justice: Race, ethnicity, and crime in America* (3rd ed.). Belmont, CA: Wadsworth/Thomson Learning.

$SAGE edge™

Sharpen your skills with SAGE edge at **edge.sagepub.com/coxjj9e**. SAGE edge for students provides a personalized approach to help you accomplish your coursework goals in an easy-to-use learning environment. You'll find action plans, mobile-friendly eFlashcards, and quizzes as well as video and web resources and links to SAGE journal articles to support and expand on the concepts presented in this chapter.

Key Figures in Juvenile Court Proceedings

9

On completion of this chapter, students should be able to do the following:

- Explain the roles of the prosecutor, defense counsel, judge, and probation officer in juvenile court
- Discuss differences between private and state-appointed defense counsel
- Discuss conflicting views of the relationship between the prosecutor and defense counsel
- Explain plea bargaining
- Discuss the roles of child and family services and court-appointed advocates in juvenile court proceedings

WHAT WOULD YOU DO?

Bill has been a juvenile probation officer for over 11 years. On his caseload is a 15-year-old teen by the name of Malik who lives in an area of the city where the school system and surrounding community is infested with gang activity and drug selling. He comes from a challenged family life for his father is in prison and his mother works two jobs so she can scrape up enough to make it from month to month. He has two older brothers and several cousins who are members of an area gang, and his sister is currently dating a gang banger. Malik also has a younger brother and sister, ages 10 and 8, whom he takes care of when they come home from school.

Bill does not really see any way out for Malik and, from the looks of it, has determined that it is only by luck that Malik has not yet been brought into the gang family. Bill recalls talking with Malik's mother, KiKi, who did not know how she could continue to keep him from rubbing

shoulders with gang members. Bill remembers the conversation:

Bill: "You know, KiKi, it is just a matter of time until he is bangin' with the rest of them . . . the only thing that will prevent this is if he does not stay in this area . . . even then, he could still join some other set in another area of this or some other city."

KiKi: "I know, but I don't have anywhere to go and we cannot afford to move. I don't have the money to move and start all over."

Bill: "I don't know what kind of assistance there might be . . . what if you placed him some place where he would have structure and be away from all the gang influence?"

KiKi: "I really just don't know what to do . . . if I have him placed in a residential facility, he will hate me for it. But there ain't nothing but bad news here, and I can't get him to stay home when I am at work at night. . . . I don't know what to do."

Bill thought about that conversation that happened just 3 days ago and then thought about Malik's upcoming court date. Malik was caught smoking "purple" or "purp," as it is sometimes called. As everyone on the streets knows, purp is a highly potent form of cannabis, not the typical "reggie" or regular pot that most people smoke. In addition, Malik was found "hanging out" or loitering around a business well after the store had closed. Bill, of course, thinks that it was Malik's intent to case the store and, perhaps, break in.

Currently, Malik is doing well enough in school. He also appears to have some latent potential that is going untapped. Malik is surrounded by a number of negative and high-risk circumstances and does not have enough protective factors to keep him within a safe zone of behavior.

Bill thinks that Malik needs to be removed from the home to a more stable environment and has talked to the county child and family services agency about this. Bill has also talked with a supervisor of the Court-Appointed Special Advocate (CASA) program just to see about support that might be available for Malik.

Bill will need to make a recommendation to the judge to either have Malik placed in a residential facility for a few months to get him away from the noxious environmental influences or to allow Malik to continue staying with his mother, who cares about Malik but is not able to keep him in compliance with his community supervision requirements.

What complicates Bill's decision is that the judge who presides over this case is more of a "lawgiver" rather than a "parent figure" with juveniles. Bill knows that to move Malik will leave nobody at home to take care of his younger brother and sister. Then again, he tells himself that he cannot allow Malik to stay at home to fulfill day care needs after school for his mother. Further, this would also overlook potential treatment options within the community.

Bill considers the reasonableness of any recommendations that he might provide, while the state's child protection services agency attorney considers various options that can be requested of the judge. Meanwhile, Bill weighs both potential recommendations.

What Would You Do?

1. Do you think Bill should recommend that Malik be sent to a residential home or be given more intensive probation and treatment programming while staying at home?

2. Should Bill attempt to find assistance for Malik's mother, KiKi?

One of the alternatives available to the police in dealing with juvenile offenders or adults who commit offenses against children involves official action through the juvenile justice network or, in the case of adult perpetrators, the adult justice network. Once the decision to take official action has been made, juvenile court personnel become involved in the case. We use the term *juvenile court personnel* in a broad sense to include the prosecutor, defense counsel, judge, juvenile probation officer, and (in abuse and neglect cases) representatives from the department of children and family services (also known as child protective services, or CPS).

Prosecutor

The final decision about whether a juvenile will be dealt with in juvenile court rests with the prosecutor. Regardless of the source of the referral (e.g., police officer, teacher, parent), the prosecutor may decide not to take the case to court and, for all practical purposes, no further official action may be taken on the case in question. The prosecutor, then, exercises an enormous amount of discretion in the juvenile (and adult) justice system (Stuckey, Roberson, & Wallace, 2004). Although the police officer may "open the gate" to the juvenile justice system, the prosecutor may close that gate. The prosecutor may do this without accounting for his or her reasons to anyone else in the system (except, of course, to the voters who elect the prosecutor to office, with the next election often occurring long after the case in question has been dismissed).

Clearly, there are some circumstances under which the prosecutor would be foolish to proceed with court action. For example, lack of evidence, lack of probable cause, or lack of due process may make it virtually impossible to prosecute a case successfully. There are, however, a number of somewhat less legitimate reasons for failure to prosecute. There have been instances where prosecutors have failed to take cases to court for political or personal reasons (e.g., when the juvenile in question is the son or daughter of a powerful and influential citizen) or because the caseload of the prosecutor includes an important or serious case in which successful prosecution will result in favorable publicity. As a result, the prosecutor may screen out or dismiss a number of "less serious" cases such as burglary and assault (Neubauer & Fradella, 2013). In short, the prosecutor is the key figure in the justice system and is recognized as such by both defendants and defense counsel (Ellis & Sowers, 2001, p. 40; Laub & MacMurray, 1987; Mays & Winfree, 2000).

During recent years, however, the prosecutor has lost some discretion historically afforded to him or her because of discretionary controls enacted within state legislation. These controls have been designed to decrease the amount of discretion a prosecutor has in determining whether a case remains in the jurisdiction of the juvenile court or is waived to adult court. In Illinois, for example, it is mandated that the prosecutor request to transfer a juvenile to adult court if the child is 15 years of age or over, commits an act that is a forcible felony, and has previously been adjudicated delinquent or committed the act in conjunction with gang-based activity (Illinois Compiled Statutes [ILCS], ch. 705, sec. 405/5-805, 1999). There are also presumptive transfers that deal with violence involving firearms and other clearly stated legislative policies on when prosecutors may use their discretion to transfer juveniles to adult criminal court. The discretionary controls have not been designed to take away from the prosecutor's role in court or to undermine the duties placed on the prosecutor but rather are in place to ensure that the prosecutor is not abusing the position and power given to him or her by the court system. The discretionary controls are also a political response to the public's recent outcries against juvenile violence. Despite the discretionary controls, prosecutors are still key figures in the juvenile court system (Backstrom & Walker, 2006; Neubauer & Fradella, 2013; Viljoen, Klaver, & Roesch, 2005).

The prosecutor's key role in the American juvenile justice system has emerged slowly over time. Initially, the prosecutor or state's attorney was seen as both unnecessary and harmful in juvenile court proceedings that were supposedly nonadversarial proceedings "on behalf of the juvenile" (U.S. Department of Justice, 1973). The Gault (In re Gault, 1967) decision, along with the decisions in Kent (Kent v. United States, 1966) and Winship (In re Winship, 1970), brought about a number of changes in juvenile court proceedings. Among these changes was a growing recognition of the need for legally trained individuals to represent both the state and the juvenile (and, in some instances, the juvenile's parents) at all stages of juvenile justice proceedings. The need resulted from increased emphasis on procedural requirements and the adversarial nature of the proceedings.

Today the prosecutor is a key figure in juvenile justice because he or she determines whether a case will go to court, most waiver decisions, the nature of the petition, and (to a large extent) the disposition of the case after adjudication (the judge seldom imposes more severe punishment than is recommended by the prosecutor). Siegel & Welsh (2007) noted that it is likely that the prosecutor will continue to play a primary role in the juvenile justice system due to the constitutional safeguards provided to youthful offenders and to the publicity associated with juvenile crime.

In addition, there is a tendency on the part of some prosecutors to impose unofficial probation. The prosecutor indicates that he or she has a prosecutable case but also indicates that prosecution will be withheld if the suspect in question agrees to behave according to certain guidelines. These are often the same guidelines handed down by probation officers subsequent to an adjudication of delinquent, abused, or neglected. This amounts to a form of continuance under supervision without proving the charges in court and may result from an admission of the facts by the minor or a lack of objection to this procedure by the minor, his or her parents, and legal counsel. In essence, this procedure provides an alternative to official adjudication as a delinquent and is regarded as beneficial in that sense. However, although the use of unofficial probation is clearly beneficial to the prosecutor because it eliminates the need to prepare a case for court and may be beneficial for the juvenile court by reducing the number of official cases, unofficial probation has the same potential disadvantages as do informal adjustments by the police. In short, unofficial probation imposed by the prosecutor amounts to punishment without trial, and the voluntary nature

Courtesy of the authors

The building above has multiple courtrooms where juvenile cases are routinely heard. This building includes a detention facility where youth are housed.

of this probation is highly questionable. Informal agreements may also work to the disadvantage of juveniles who are suspected of being abused or neglected and who are allowed to remain in their homes as a result of such agreements.

However, Backstrom and Walker (2006) noted that the role of juvenile prosecutors, while still being that of a gatekeeper, requires much more than this in order to address the complexity of juvenile crime today. They noted that greater expertise is essential if prosecutors are to address violent crimes committed by juveniles, new laws dealing with victims' rights, the transfer of youth to adult court, as well as the expanded jurisdiction of the juvenile court. According to Backstrom and Walker (2006), "Today's juvenile prosecutor must not only serve as an advocate for justice, for the victim, and for community values, he or she must also serve as a negotiator and dispositional advisor in juvenile cases" (p. 965). It is important to understand that, whereas juvenile prosecutors do hold the key position in determining if a case will be heard in juvenile court, these court professionals do see different types of crimes and different youth on a routine basis; it becomes clear to them that not all juvenile offenders are the same. Indeed, just as our What Would You Do? feature demonstrated with Bill (the probation officer) and Malik, the probationer, there are a number of factors that may aggravate or mitigate a case. Even the prosecutors of these crimes realize this and, during plea bargaining, these prosecutors may modify their original charges to reflect these circumstances.

Regardless of the specific parameters of each case and the offenders involved, the attorney for the state (prosecutor) participates in every proceeding of every stage of every case that is under the jurisdiction of the family court, whenever the state has an interest. Figure 9.1 provides an overview of the process by which prosecutors may determine if a juvenile case will be formally charged within the juvenile court system.

Defense Counsel

The Institute of Justice Administration (IJA) and the American Bar Association (ABA) (1980a) described the responsibility of the legal profession to the juvenile court in Standard 2.3 of *Standards Relating to Counsel for Private Parties*. The IJA and ABA stated that legal representation should be provided in all proceedings arising from, or related to, a delinquency or in need of supervision action—including mental competency, transfer, postdisposition, probation revocation and classification, institutional transfer, and disciplinary or other administrative proceedings related to the treatment process—that may substantially affect the juvenile's custody, status, or course of treatment.

Figure 9.1 Steps and Timelines for Engaging the Formal Juvenile Court System

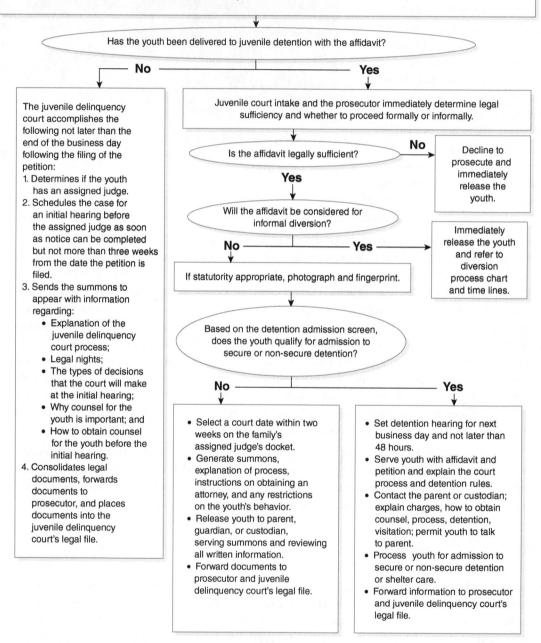

Juvenile court proceedings involving delinquency and abuse are adversarial in nature in spite of the intent of the early developers of juvenile court philosophy. It is for this reason that the role of defense counsel (the attorney representing the defendant) has become increasingly important. Today, in most jurisdictions, all juveniles named in petitions are represented by counsel. In Illinois, for example, no proceeding under the state's juvenile court act may be initiated unless the juvenile is represented by counsel (ILCS, ch. 705, sec. 405/1–5, 1999). In many cases, the juvenile's parents also have legal representation. In some cases, a guardian ad litem may be appointed by the court. The guardian ad litem is a person appointed by the court as a third party to protect the interests of the child both in court and while placed in social services (Davidson, 1981). In general, the guardian ad litem is used in abuse, neglect, and dependency cases where the minor is in need of representation because of immaturity (Sedlak, Doueck, Lyons, & Wells, 2005; Siegel & Welsh, 2007).

There are two basic categories of defense counsel: (1) private counsel and (2) court-appointed counsel. Private counselors are sometimes retained or appointed to represent the interests of juveniles in court. Frequently, however, juveniles are represented by court-appointed counsel (attorneys or public defenders). The former are typically drawn from a roster of practicing attorneys in the jurisdiction, whereas the latter are full-time salaried employees. Both are paid by the county or state (or by both) to represent defendants who do not have the money to retain private counsel. For many young lawyers interested in criminal law, the position of public defender represents a stepping-stone (Neubauer & Fradella, 2013). In most areas, the public defender is paid a relatively low salary, but the position guarantees a minimal income that can be supplemented by private practice (Stuckey et al., 2004). For example, the most recent information available on defense systems for the indigent found that the average cost per case to state and local government for indigent defense was $5.37 per capita, ranging from a low of $0.11 per case in West Virginia to a high of $11.23 per case in Alaska (Barlow, 2000, p. 374).

In addition to the low personal pay, many public defender programs are inadequately funded (National Juvenile Defense Center, 2016; Wice, 2005). This makes the job of public defenders even more difficult because, in addition to being underpaid personally, they must work with fewer agency resources at their disposal (Wice, 2005). This low pay and inadequate agency funding have led to a reputation of providing low-quality representation (Neubauer & Fradella, 2013; Wice, 2005) that is further compounded by the fact that, understandably, many public defenders have short job tenures. These factors have contributed to a public image of ineptness that has become a virtual stigma for persons working in the role of public defender (Botch, 2006; Wice, 2005).

As a rule, public defender caseloads are heavy, investigative resources are limited, and many clients are, by their own admission, guilty or delinquent (Barlow, 2000; Stuckey et al., 2004). The public defender, therefore, spends a great deal of time negotiating pleas and often very little time talking with clients. In fact, sometimes a public defender in juvenile court will indicate to the judge that he or she is ready to proceed and then ask someone in the courtroom which of the several juveniles present is the client. As a result, public defenders often enjoy a less-than-favorable image among their clients (Barlow, 2000, pp. 377–379).

Some public defenders seem to have little interest in using every possible strategy to defend their clients (Botch, 2006; "Too Poor," 1998; Wice, 2005). On occasion, prosecutors and juvenile court judges make legal errors to which public defenders raise no objections. Appeals initiated by public defenders in cases tried in juvenile court are relatively rare even when the chances of successful appeals seem to be good. There are also public defenders who pursue their clients' interests with all possible vigor, but on the whole it appears that juveniles who have private counsel often fare better in juvenile court than do those who are represented by public defenders. There is little doubt that the office of public defender is frequently underfunded and that such underfunding is a major factor in most of the criticisms leveled at the office.

In response to the insufficient nature of the public defender system that is used in juvenile courts, the National Juvenile Defender Center (2016) has provided a series of recommendations. The NJDC notes that specific attention should be given to establishing a productive and realistic means for beginning lawyers to establish opportunities that might make juvenile defense a viable career choice. In particular, the NJDC recommends the following:

1. Support the expansion of public and private law school clinical and experiential learning.
2. Engage historically black colleges and universities, Latino serving institutions of higher education, and Native American colleges and universities.
3. Establish dedicated juvenile defense committees in bar associations.
4. Expand legal incubator programs to promote juvenile defense.

Although these recommendations might seem a bit unusual, the NJDC (2016) provides numerous examples of how these recommendations might work and/or how they have already been implemented in certain areas of the nation. The key point to noting the work of the NJDC is to showcase that the challenges associated with gaining defense counsel for juveniles are well known and understood by scholars, practitioners, and organizations associated with the court system. Unfortunately, the means by which these issues can be remedied are, perhaps, much more difficult to discern.

Whether defense counsel is private or public, his or her duties remain essentially the same. These duties are to see that the client is properly represented at all stages of the system, that the client's rights are not violated, and that the client's case is presented in the most favorable light possible regardless of the client's involvement in delinquent or criminal activity (Pollock, 1994, pp. 145–152). To accomplish these goals, the defense counsel is expected to battle the prosecutor, at least in theory, in adversarial proceedings. However, the quality of representation afforded is not guaranteed. The public defender's office is frequently understaffed, and private counsel is often too expensive to be considered an option. As Siegel and Senna (1994) noted, "Representation should be upgraded in all areas of the juvenile court system" (p. 557).

Relationship Between the Prosecutor and Defense Counsel: Adversarial or Cooperative?

In theory, adversarial proceedings result when the "champion" of the defendant (defense counsel) and the "champion" of the state (prosecutor) do "battle" in open court, where the "truth" is determined and "justice" is the result. In practice, the situation is quite often different due to considerations of time and money on behalf of both the state and the defendant (Stuckey et al., 2004).

The ideal of adversarial proceedings is perhaps most closely realized when a well-known private defense attorney does battle with the prosecutor. The *O. J. Simpson* case of the 1990s is an excellent example (Bugliosi, 1997). Prominent defense attorneys often have competent investigative staffs and considerable resources in terms of time and money to devote to a case. Thus, the balance of power between the state and the defendant may be nearly even. This is generally not the case when defense counsel is a public defender who is often paid less than the prosecutor, often has less experience than the prosecutor, and generally has more limited access to an investigative staff than the prosecutor. For a variety of reasons, then, both defense counsel and the prosecutor may find it easier to negotiate a particular case rather than to fight it out in court because court cases are costly in terms of both time and money. The vast majority of adult criminal cases in the United States are settled by plea bargaining. A substantial proportion of delinquency and abuse and neglect cases are disposed of in this way as well. In fact, it has been suggested that justice in the United States is not the result of the adversarial system but rather the result of a cooperative network of routine interactions among defense counsel, the prosecutor, the defendant, and (in many instances) the judge (Barlow, 2000, p. 349; Blumberg, 1967; Sudnow, 1965).

In plea bargaining, both the prosecutor and defense counsel hope to gain through compromise (Neubauer & Fradella, 2013; Viljoen et al., 2005). The prosecutor wants the defendant to plead guilty—if not to the original charge, then to some less serious offense. Defense counsel seeks to get the best deal possible for his or her client, and this may range from an outright dismissal to a plea of guilty to some offense less serious than the original charge (Neubauer & Fradella, 2013). The nature of the compromise depends on conditions such as the strength of the prosecutor's case and the seriousness of the offense. Most often, the two counselors arrive at what both consider a "just" compromise, which is then presented to the defendant to accept or reject (Siegel, Welsh, & Senna, 2003). As a rule, the punishment to be recommended by the prosecutor is also negotiated. Thus, the nature of the charges, the plea, and the punishment are negotiated and agreed on before the defendant actually enters the courtroom. The adversarial system, in its ideal form at least, has been circumvented (Edwards, 2005; Stuckey et al., 2004). Perhaps a hypothetical example will help to clarify the nature and consequences of plea bargaining.

Consider Joe, a house burglar, who is seen breaking into a house. The break-in is reported to the police, who apprehend Joe in the house with a watch and some expensive jewelry belonging to the homeowner. The police decide to take official action. Because Joe is over 13 years of age and the offense is fairly serious, the prosecutor threatens to prosecute Joe as an adult in adult court. She also indicates that she intends to seek a prison sentence for Joe. Joe's attorney, realizing that the prosecutor has a strong case, knows that he cannot get Joe's case dismissed. He argues with the prosecutor that this is Joe's first appearance before the juvenile court and that Joe is, after all, a juvenile. After some discussion, the prosecutor agrees to prosecute Joe in juvenile court provided that the allegation of delinquency is not contested. Joe's attorney agrees provided that the prosecutor recommends only a short stay in a private detention facility in the community. Joe's attorney then presents the deal to Joe and perhaps to Joe's parents, indicating that it is the best he can do and recommending that Joe accept because he could be found guilty and sentenced to prison if he is tried in adult court. Joe accepts and the bargain is concluded. The case has been settled in the attorney's offices. All that remains is to make it official during the formal court appearance. Most judges will concur with the negotiated plea.

The benefits of plea bargaining to the prosecutor, defense counsel, and the juvenile court are clear. The prosecutor is successful in prosecuting a case (she obtains an adjudication of delinquency), defense counsel has reduced the charges and penalty against his client, and all parties have saved time and money by not contesting the case in court. The juvenile may benefit as well given that he might have been convicted of burglary in adult court (if the judge had accepted the prosecutor's motion to change jurisdiction) and ended up in prison with a felony record. The dangers of plea bargaining, however, should not be overlooked. First, there is always the possibility that the motion to change jurisdiction might have been denied. Second, Joe might have been found not guilty even if he had been tried in adult court or might have been found not delinquent if his case had been heard in juvenile court. Third, because negotiations most often occur in secret, there is a danger that the constitutional rights of the defendant might not be stringently upheld. For example, Joe did not have the chance to confront and cross-examine his accusers. Finally, the juvenile court judge is little more than a figurehead, left only to sanction the bargain, in cases settled by plea bargaining. The juvenile court judge has the responsibility to see that the hearings are conducted in the best interests of both the juvenile and society and has the responsibility to ensure due process. Neither of these can be guaranteed in cases involving plea bargaining. A final concern in all plea bargaining processes, whether adult or juvenile, is that the victim seldom feels good about the bargain.

Juvenile Court Judge

Theoretically, the juvenile court judge is the most powerful and central figure in the juvenile justice system, although he or she does not always exercise this power (Edwards, 2005). Noting that this is *theoretically* the case in the courthouse underlies the fact that there are many actors who are involved within the courtroom work group that processes a juvenile case (Edwards, 2005; Neubauer & Fradella, 2013). This courtroom work group tends to develop a sense of shared informal norms and understandings, with a strong organizational emphasis being placed on effective case processing (Neubauer & Fradella, 2013; Viljoen et al., 2005). Indeed, there will be the typical members of the adult courtroom work group; however, the juvenile court will also typically rely heavily on professional judgments of nonlawyers in assessing both the background of the juvenile and other circumstances such as the quality of family supervision (Hanser, 2007a; Viljoen et al., 2005). In many cases, the input of various mental health workers may weigh heavily in the judge's decision (Hanser, 2007a; Viljoen et al., 2005).

In the end, however, it is the juvenile court judge who decides whether a juvenile will be adjudicated delinquent, abused, in need of intervention, dependent, or neglected. Because there is no jury in most instances, the decision of the judge is final unless an appeal overturns the judge's decision. In addition, the judge makes the final determination about the disposition of the juvenile (Stahl, 2008b). Therefore, the juvenile court judge decides matters of law, matters of fact, and the immediate futures of those who come before the bench (see Figure 9.2 for an overview of the adjudication hearing process). Juvenile judges likewise tend to have a wide degree of discretion when fulfilling their role (Leiber & Fox, 2005; Neubauer & Fradella, 2013). Despite this flexibility, assignment to the juvenile court is often not considered to be a highly desired position among many judges, and many may seek rotation as a means of advancing their judicial careers (Stuckey et al., 2004).

In many states, hearing officers known as referees or commissioners are appointed to assist juvenile court judges (see In Practice 9.1 and 9.2). These hearing officers typically submit recommendations that must be certified by a judge before they have the effect of law (Roberts, 1989, p. 114). Within the confines of legislative mandates, juvenile judges rule on pretrial motions involving issues such as arrest, search and seizure, interrogation, and lineup identification. They make decisions about the continued detention of children prior to hearings, and they make decisions about plea bargaining agreements and informal adjustments (Siegel et al., 2003; Stahl, 2008b). They hold bench hearings, rule on appropriateness of conduct, and settle questions concerning evidence and procedure. They guide the questioning of witnesses. They decide on treatment for juveniles. They preside over waiver hearings, and they handle appeals where allowed by statute (Siegel & Welsh, 2007; Stahl, 2008b).

Although judges in some jurisdictions are assigned to juvenile court on a full-time basis, there are also many juvenile court judges who serve on a part-time basis. The latter are circuit judges who perform judicial functions in civil, criminal, probate, and other divisions of the court and are occasionally assigned to juvenile

Figure 9.2 Steps and Timelines for the Trial/Adjudication Hearing Process

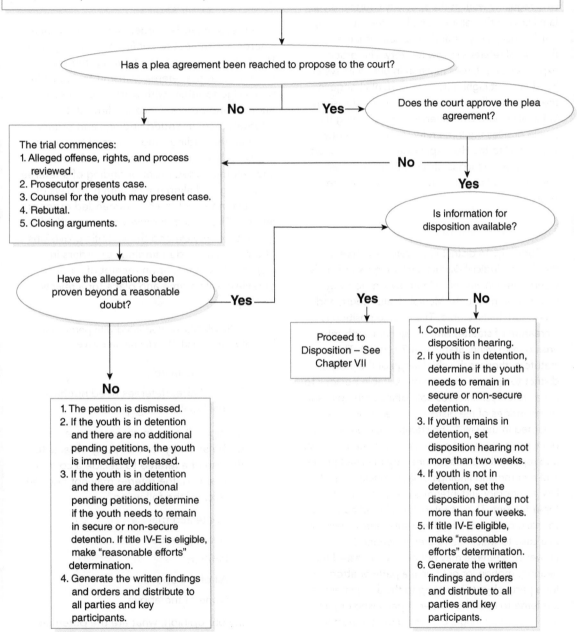

PRIOR PROCESS STEPS: (1) The petition has been filed, determined legally sufficient, and handled formally; (2) Counsel has been appointed; (3) An initial or detention hearing has been held and the youth has entered a plea of deny; (4) Discovery and pre-trial issues were covered at the initial or detention hearing or subsequent hearing if necessary; (5) The youth may be placed in secure or non-secure detention (in which case the trial is set within two weeks of the detention hearing) or the youth is not detained (in which case the trial is set not later than four weeks from the initial hearing); and, (6) Both counsel and prosecutor have prepared for the trial, determined whether a plea agreement will be proposed, and if not, have subpoenaed witnesses to testify.

Has a plea agreement been reached to propose to the court?

No — Yes→

Does the court approve the plea agreement?

The trial commences:
1. Alleged offense, rights, and process reviewed.
2. Prosecutor presents case.
3. Counsel for the youth may present case.
4. Rebuttal.
5. Closing arguments.

No

Yes

Is information for disposition available?

Have the allegations been proven beyond a reasonable doubt?

Yes

Yes — No

Proceed to Disposition – See Chapter VII

No

1. The petition is dismissed.
2. If the youth is in detention and there are no additional pending petitions, the youth is immediately released.
3. If the youth is in detention and there are additional pending petitions, determine if the youth needs to remain in secure or non-secure detention. If title IV-E is eligible, make "reasonable efforts" determination.
4. Generate the written findings and orders and distribute to all parties and key participants.

1. Continue for disposition hearing.
2. If youth is in detention, determine if the youth needs to remain in secure or non-secure detention.
3. If youth remains in detention, set disposition hearing not more than two weeks.
4. If youth is not in detention, set the disposition hearing not more than four weeks.
5. If title IV-E eligible, make "reasonable efforts" determination.
6. Generate the written findings and orders and distribute to all parties and key participants.

Source: National Council of Juvenile and Family Court Judges (2005).

THE ROLE OF REFEREES IN DISTRICT COURT

Hearing and resolving thousands of cases a year, referees play a key role in the administration of justice in Hennepin County District Court. Lawyers who regularly work in the specialty courts are very familiar with the referees and how they function, but for many lawyers and the public at large, the role of referees is new territory. This article explains how referees function in our court system. In addition, it highlights an important change in the law regarding the review of referee decisions in Family Court. One sidebar accompanying this article profiles the three referees most recently appointed to the Hennepin County District Court, while another reacquaints us with the 13 other referees who have already been serving in the court.

The Referee Position

Currently, 16 district court referees serve in the Fourth Judicial District, including six in Family Court, three in Juvenile Court, two in Housing Court, four in Probate/Mental Health Court, and one Court Trials referee. The referee position is a creature of statute, with the general authority arising from Minn. Stat. § 484.70 (2004). The statute authorizes the chief judge of the judicial district to appoint one or more suitable persons to act as referees. Referees hold office at the pleasure of the judges of the district court and must be "learned in the law." The statute enumerates the duties and powers of a referee. A referee is to hear and report all matters assigned by the chief judge and recommend findings of fact, conclusions of law, temporary and interim orders, and final orders for judgment. Thus, a referee has broad authority to make both procedural and substantive decisions in a case to which the referee is assigned. However, a referee may not hear a contested trial, hearing, motion, or petition if a party or attorney for a party objects in writing to the assignment of a referee to hear the matter. A party who objects to a referee hearing a contested matter must serve and file the objection within 10 days of notice of the assignment of the referee but not later

than the commencement of any hearing before a referee.

Referee Decisions

All recommended orders and findings of a referee are subject to confirmation by a judge. Upon the conclusion of a hearing, the statute requires that the referee transmit the court file to a judge together with written recommended findings and orders. Once confirmed, the referee's recommended findings and orders become the findings and orders of the court. In general, a party may seek judicial review of any recommended order or finding of a referee by serving and filing notice within 10 days of effective notice of the recommended order or finding. The notice of review must specify the grounds for review and the specific provisions of the recommended findings or orders in dispute. The court, upon receipt of a notice of review, sets a time and place for a review hearing.

Source: Chawla (2006). Reprinted with permission from the author and *The Hennepin Lawyer*.

Questions to Consider

1. True or False: Referees need not have formal legal training, per se.

2. Multiple Choice: In cases where a party or the attorney for that party objects to the use of a referee to decide a court proceeding, the referee may not engage in which of the following?

   a. Contested trial

   b. Hearing motion

   c. Petition

   d. All of the above

   e. None of the above

3. In your opinion, what are the potential advantages to using referees in juvenile court? What about potential pitfalls?

court. It is difficult for such judges to become specialists in juvenile court proceedings, and some are not as well versed in juvenile law as they could be, although many perform well.

Juvenile court judges may be placed along a continuum ranging from those who see themselves largely as parent figures to those who are concerned mainly about the juvenile court as a legal institution. The "parent figure" judge is often genuinely concerned about the total well-being of juveniles who appear before the court. He or she is likely to overlook some of the formalities of due process in an attempt to serve as a parent figure who both supports and disciplines juveniles. This judge's primary concern is serving what he or she perceives as the best interests of the juveniles who appear in court, based on the assumption that they must have problems even though they might not have committed the specific acts that led to the filing of the petitions or been victims of abuse or neglect in the specific instances in question (Ford, Chapman, Mack, & Pearson, 2006). Often these judges talk to the juveniles and/or parents involved in an attempt to obtain expressions of remorse or regret (Edwards, 2005; Ford et al., 2006; Viljoen et al., 2005). Once these expressions are given, the acts involved can often be "forgiven," and attention centers on how to best help the juveniles to avoid future trouble or victimization. If these expressions of remorse or regret are not given, the judge frequently resorts to a role as disciplinarian, sometimes overlooking the facts in the case.

There is a tendency among parent-figure judges to continue juvenile cases under supervision for various lengths of time. These judges apparently assume that an adjudication of delinquency, abuse, neglect, or minor requiring authoritative intervention (MRAI) is less desirable than using the threat of adjudication in an attempt to induce acceptable behavior. Although most juvenile court acts provide for judicial continuance, this action can be carried to the extreme in situations where the case against the juvenile, parent, or guardian is weak and the continuance period is long. These continuances amount to punishment without trial much as informal adjustments and unofficial probation do. It is also not unlikely that during this period the child will be caught for another offense and may be brought to court again. This creates a revolving-door effect.

At the other end of the continuum is the "lawgiver" judge, who is concerned primarily that all procedural requirements are fulfilled. This type of judge has less interest in the total personality of the juvenile than in the evidence of the case at hand. The lawgiver judge dismisses cases that the prosecutor cannot prove beyond a reasonable doubt (or, in abuse and neglect cases, cannot demonstrate a preponderance of evidence for) and does not believe that it is his or her duty to prescribe treatment for juveniles who have not committed the offenses of which they have been accused or who cannot be shown to have been victims of abuse or neglect. The dispositions of the lawgiver judge are based on statutory requirements more than on the personal characteristics of the parties involved (see In Practice 9.2).

Most juvenile court judges fall somewhere between the two extremes, reflecting the lack of consensus about the proper role of the juvenile court discussed in Chapter 1. Most judges make a sincere effort to maximize legal safeguards for juveniles while attempting to act in the best interests of both the juveniles and society (National Council of Juvenile and Family Court Judges, 2005). They ensure that legal counsel is available, they try to arrive at objective decisions during adjudicatory hearings, and they try to ensure that the disposition of each case takes into account the needs of the juvenile involved. Tower (1993) described the efforts of the juvenile court judge in abuse and neglect cases as follows:

> Deprived of the support of a jury (in most cases), the judge must base the final decision on the report of the investigator, on what has been heard in the courtroom, on the judge's own experience, and often on the assumption of what will be best for all concerned. (p. 293)

THE ROLE OF JUDGES IN JUVENILE DRUG COURT

The judge's involvement in and supervision of youth participation in the juvenile drug court is essential. Frequent court hearings provide an open forum where everyone involved in a case can gather to share information, discuss issues, and reach consensus on the next step(s) toward a youth's successful rehabilitation and completion of the juvenile drug court program. Hearings also provide leadership and team building opportunities for juvenile drug court staff.

As they conduct judicial reviews, judges need to take into account the delicate nature of adolescent behavior and consider what setting will provide the most positive atmosphere for the discussion of sensitive issues. Although statutes and court rules dictate the conduct of review hearings, in most jurisdictions hearings may be either *open* (in the presence of all drug court participants, their families, and others involved with their cases) or *closed* (only in the presence of the drug court team), or they may be open but with some exceptions. For most cases, an open hearing is appropriate, but the unique circumstances of some cases may warrant an adjustment to the open court procedure. For example, to avoid conflicts between a parent and youth during an open court session, it may be necessary for the case manager to report sensitive issues during a staff meeting.

One of the hallmarks of the juvenile drug court—in contrast to adult courts or other juvenile courts—is the personal relationship between each youth and the judge. Often, the judge is the only constant in the youth's life, providing the structure and support that are *otherwise absent*. *In loco parentis* has a special meaning in this context: Judges need to demonstrate interest in each youth's accomplishments and sensitivity to his or her unique issues.

Source: Bureau of Justice Assistance (BJA) (2003).

Questions to Consider

1. True or False: In juvenile drug courts, there is usually a personal relationship between each youngster and the judge.

2. Multiple Choice: In most jurisdictions hearings may be which of the following?

   a. Open

   b. Closed

   c. Open, with some exceptions

   d. All of the above

   e. None of the above

3. In your opinion, what are some distinct differences between a juvenile drug court judge and most other roles of judges?

Tower (1993) concluded the following:

Since people's motivations are never predictable, the juvenile court judge realizes there is no assurance that a child will be safe when returned home or happy in placement. Using only best judgment and the hope that it is correct, the judge renders the decision. (p. 293)

In a study of serious child maltreatment cases brought before the Boston Juvenile Court in 1994, Bishop, Murphy, and Hicks (2000) concluded that despite some improvements during the past decade, "the system still fails to promptly find permanent placements for seriously maltreated children" (p. 610). In attempting to arrive at an acceptable disposition, the juvenile court judge frequently relies heavily on the recommendations of the juvenile probation officer, as discussed in the What Would You Do? exercise at the beginning of this chapter. In some cases, alternative forms of processing and punishment may be given with juvenile offenders. For example, consider In Practice 9.3, which discusses the use of a teen court in Phoenix, Arizona. Though this type of processing may sound soft in approach, persons who go through teen court seem to indicate that their peers hold them accountable and provide serious consequences for delinquent behavior.

IN PRACTICE 9.3

TEENS DEAL OUT JUSTICE THEIR WAY IN MARYVALE

Crystal Dorosky was the first teenager to appear in the Maryvale Teen Court when it opened its doors in west Phoenix last week.

At this court, defendant Dorosky's attorney was younger than she is. The prosecutor was not old enough to vote. The four-member jury had not graduated from high school. And the court clerk plays guitar in a budding rock band called Third Right Turn.

The only adult was Maryvale Justice of the Peace, Maryvale Precinct, Judge Hercules Dellas, who oversaw the proceedings.

The jury ordered Dorosky, 17, to do 10 hours of community service as her punishment for possessing alcohol at a New Year's Eve party in December. A traditional juvenile court judge might have issued a series of trips to a probation officer, a monetary fine, or community service and a potential record for the same offense.

Dorosky believes the sentence was steep. Her court-appointed attorney, Diane Villafana, a Maryvale High School student, had asked for eight hours of community service. Then again, Dorosky can't imagine being judged by an adult in a traditional juvenile court.

"I think a teen jury knows how it is to be a kid in this day and age. We like to party, and we like to be with friends," Dorosky said. "Maybe if the jury were adults, they would have given me a harsher consequence."

Maryvale Teen Court is the most recent addition to the Maricopa County Teen Court Youth Diversion Program. The others are in Phoenix, Tempe, Fountain Hills, Glendale, and Gilbert. To make the court a reality in Maryvale, Judge Dellas asked Phoenix Union High School District's Maryvale High for help, and a high school business law class served as prosecutors, legal counsel, and jurors.

Students take responsibility for their mistakes and understand the consequences. On the flip side, they gain experience "serving as a juror or as a courtroom participant," Dellas said.

Maryvale Teen Court is expected to hear two to eight cases per session once a month during the school year.

Teen Court is designed after a traditional adult courtroom. It benefits students who are younger than 17 whose offenses range from alcohol possession, [to] theft valued at less than $250, [to] disorderly conduct.

With a probation officer's approval and a parent's permission, a teen's case could end up in Teen Court. A child also accepts responsibility for the offenses before making an appearance at Teen Court, where a jury delivers the punishment with a deadline. Students must complete the orders within two months after the hearing. If a teen fails to comply, the case is returned to the juvenile probation officer for action. If a defendant successfully meets all of the requirements, his or her case is closed without a criminal record.

The success rate of Teen Court impressed Maricopa County Supervisor Mary Rose Wilcox, who asked Dellas to add the program to his schedule. Dellas agreed.

Studies show that a high percentage of teens sentenced at Teen Court complete the jury's orders, Wilcox said. At least 92 percent

(Continued)

(Continued)

of juveniles who complete Teen Court are not referred to Juvenile Court within a year, she said.

Maryvale Teen Court, at 4622 W. Indian School Road, also is closer to home for teens than a trip to Juvenile Justice Courts at Durango.

"When peers judge peers, you get a whole different outcome," Wilcox said. "The hardest critics are your peers. It also exposes them to the court's legal system. They don't want to be on one side of the table but be a lawyer and prosecutor."

Tom Camp, who teaches business law at Maryvale High, watched his 13 students become prosecutors, jurors, legal counsel, court bailiff, and clerk.

"They were scared," he said. "I guess what made them nervous were the people. When kids are held accountable, it makes them very nervous. That is kids in general. They do not like to be held responsible."

Derek Penne, 16, said he was so nervous as a Teen Court clerk that he mispronounced the judge's name. He introduced a Judge George to the audience and corrected himself.

The Maryvale teen isn't aspiring to be a lawyer, at least for now. He is exerting his energy studying music and playing guitar for the Third Left Turn band. "It was nerve-racking because there were too many people watching," Penne said.

Questions to Consider

1. True or False: The Maryvale Teen Court is part of a youth diversion program.

2. Multiple Choice: According to the information provided, at least _____ of juveniles who complete teen court are not referred to juvenile court within a year.

   a. 32%

   b. 52%

   c. 72%

   d. 92%

   e. None of the above

3. What potential drawbacks, if any, might exist when using a teen court?

Juvenile Probation Officer

Probation is the oldest and most widely used disposition, with more than 18,000 juvenile probation officers in the United States (Torbet, 1996). Probation is a disposition by the juvenile court in which the minor is placed and maintained in the community under the supervision of a duly authorized officer of the court, the juvenile probation officer. "Probation may be used at the 'front-end' of the juvenile justice system for the first-time, low-risk offenders or at the 'back-end' as an alternative to institutional confinement for more serious offenders" (p. 1). Either way, it allows the minor to remain with the family or a foster family under conditions prescribed by the court to ensure acceptable behavior in a community setting.

The juvenile probation officer is a key figure at all levels of the juvenile justice system (Siegel et al., 2003). He or she may arrange a preliminary conference between interested parties that may result in an out-of-court settlement between an alleged delinquent and the injured party or between parties in cases of abuse or neglect. After an adjudicatory hearing, the juvenile probation officer is often charged with conducting a social background investigation (Neubauer & Fradella, 2013; Siegel et al., 2003). This investigation will be used to help the judge make a dispositional decision. Probation officers are also charged with supervising those juveniles who are placed on probation and released into the community and with supervising parents deemed to have committed neglect or abuse (Ford et al., 2006; Goodkind, Ng, & Sarri, 2006; Siegel et al., 2003).

Courtesy of the authors

Deputies Henry and Turpin of the Ouachita Parish Sheriff's Office work as truancy officers. They provide reports to the juvenile court and work in tandem with juvenile probation officers to ensure that youth attend school on a routine basis.

Probation officers have the power to request a revocation of probation if violations of the conditions of probation occur.

The duties of chief probation officers generally include assignment of cases and supervision of subordinates (Stuckey et al., 2004). Chief probation officers may or may not handle cases themselves, depending on available staff. In addition, they normally serve as a liaison between judges and other department heads. The better the rapport they are able to establish with the juvenile court judge, and the more effective they are in transmitting information to subordinates, other juvenile justice practitioners, and the judge, the better the opportunity to serve the interests of juveniles and the community.

The role of juvenile probation officers is an ambiguous one. Indeed, the What Would You Do? exercise at the beginning of this chapter demonstrates some of the challenging circumstances that juvenile probation officers face. They are officers of the court who occasionally must act as authority figures and disciplinarians. At the same time, they are charged with helping juveniles in trouble by attempting to keep the juveniles out of court, by recommending the most beneficial dispositions, by protecting juveniles from abusive parents while counseling those parents, and by being available to help probationers solve problems encountered during their probationary periods. If they are to be effective in their role as helping professionals, they must encourage open interaction and trust among the juveniles and parents or guardians they encounter (Gardner, Rodriguez, & Zatz, 2004; Parker-Jimenez, 1997). If they seem too authoritarian, they may receive little cooperation. If they become too friendly, they may find it difficult to take disciplinary steps when necessary.

Juvenile probation officers may find that they are integral in coordinating a variety of services for juveniles. A range of skills, services, and resources are often brokered by juvenile probation officers to aid juveniles in reintegrating into the community and improving their ability to meet the conditions of their probation (Champion, 2002; Hanser, 2007a; Siegel et al., 2003). Juvenile probation officers may coordinate a number of services such as mental health counseling, drug and alcohol counseling, academic achievement, vocational and employment training, alternative education programs, Big Brothers Big Sisters programs, and foster parent or grandparent programs (Champion, 2002; Hanser, 2007a).

As a result of the ambiguous role requirements, several different types of juvenile probation officers exist. Some think of themselves largely as law enforcement officers whose basic function is to detect violations of probation. Others see themselves as juvenile advocates whose basic function is to ensure that the rights of juveniles are not violated by the police or potential petitioners. Still others view themselves basically as social workers whose function is to facilitate treatment and rehabilitation. Hanser (2010) noted that none of these approaches are ideal. Rather, each has

Officer Mark Miller is a juvenile probation officer with the Office for Youth Development in Louisiana. Juvenile probation officers have a key role in the juvenile system throughout the state of Louisiana and in other states.

its time and place, depending on the circumstances. Therefore, the most effective juvenile probation officers exercise all of these options at different times under differing circumstances. However, it should be pointed out that the balancing of these different orientations in supervision can lead to a sense of role identity confusion (Hanser, 2010). This is a primary source of burnout among community supervision officers, including those assigned to juvenile offenders (Hanser, 2010). Role identity confusion occurs when officers are unclear about the expectations placed on them when they attempt to balance the competing interests of their "policing" role and their "reform"-oriented role (Hanser, 2010).

Perhaps the most difficult task for most juvenile probation officers is the supervision of probationers. Many have excessive caseloads and have little actual contact with their clients other than short weekly or monthly meetings (Hanser, 2010). High caseloads have been defined as 50 or more juvenile offenders, with caseloads actually going as high as 300 juveniles or more in some jurisdictions (Champion, 2002). Obviously, not a great deal of counseling or supervision can occur under these circumstances. When field contacts are made with probationers, probation officers are often considerably concerned about further stigmatizing their clients. Parents who have problems with their children sometimes try to use juvenile probation officers' official position to frighten the children into compliance with their demands. As a result of these difficulties, most juvenile probation officers, in discussing probation conditions with their clients, make it clear that they are available to discuss whatever problems probationers believe are significant. Some juvenile probation officers using this technique allow clients to choose the time and place for conferences to minimize stigmatization.

Juvenile probation officers must also work daily to overcome several issues, including job safety, rising caseloads, a lack of resources, and feelings of failure (Champion, 2002). In a study by the Office of Juvenile Justice and Delinquency Prevention (OJJDP) in 1996, it was reported that more than one-third of juvenile probation officers had been assaulted on the job and that 42% stated they were usually or always concerned about their personal safety while working (Torbet, 1996). In response to these concerns, some jurisdictions have implemented intensive supervision and school-based programs into local schools. Along with safety concerns, rising caseloads have also become a problem for juvenile probation officers. Respondents to the 1996 OJJDP survey stated that their caseloads ranged between two and more than 200, with the typical caseload at roughly 41 probationers. It was also reported that probation caseloads are involving more violent juveniles than in previous years. However, the number of resources available to juvenile probation officers has not increased with the number of probationers. Juvenile probation officers are still limited in the types of placements available to probationers and in the amount of funding they can receive from the jurisdiction for treatment of juveniles on their caseloads. This often means that juvenile probation officers must be creative in their approach to their probationers' treatments and rehabilitative efforts. In the same 1996 OJJDP survey, it was reported that "although [juvenile probation officers] chose this line of work 'to help kids,' their greatest sources of frustration are an inability to impact the lives of youth, the attitudes of probationers and their families, and difficulties in identifying successes" (p. 1).

Technological innovations such as electronic monitoring are of some help to probation officers in supervising their clients. These supervision tools often work to augment the supervision of juveniles who are processed through juvenile intensive supervision programs (JISPs), which typically accommodate violent and/or repeat youthful offenders (Champion, 2002; Hanser, 2007a). Recently, the Florida Department of Corrections began a pilot project using the global positioning system (GPS) to track the movements and locations of probationers, warn prior victims if necessary, and determine whether probationers are in "off-limits" locations (Mercer, Brooks, & Bryant, 2000).

Children and Family Services Personnel

Although personnel from departments of children and family services (or CPS) do not actually work for the juvenile courts, they play major roles in investigation, presentation of evidence, and dispositional recommendations in abuse and neglect cases. Typically when law enforcement officers believe they have discovered a case of abuse or neglect, they are required to report the case to children and family services. Departments of children and family services usually maintain a central register of abuse and neglect cases. On receiving a report of suspected or confirmed abuse or neglect, personnel from the child protective agency begin an investigation of the allegation (Sedlak et al., 2005). In emergency cases, such investigations are to be conducted immediately, in theory at least. In other cases, investigators are normally required to conduct an investigation within a specified time period, typically 24 to 72 hours. Such an investigation normally involves interviews with the alleged victim and offender and an evaluation of risk factors in the child's environment. Where appropriate, the child may be removed from the home to safeguard his or her welfare.

If the allegations of abuse or neglect are found to be true, caseworkers from children and family services are involved in assisting the children involved in court proceedings and in formulating plans to provide services or treatment to both the children and the families involved (Sedlak et al., 2005). In cases where abuse or neglect occurs in institutional settings, the institutions involved, if allowed to remain open, are monitored by children and family services.

Ms. Denna McGrew, assistant director (on the left), and Ms. Lynda Gavioli, executive director (on the right), of the Children's Coalition for Northeast Louisiana, routinely work with court personnel regarding youth welfare and delinquency issues.

Other children services personnel may come from a conglomerate of agencies that pool together into what may be referred to as a coalition. Increasingly, federal and state funders are requiring organizations to develop collective bodies that address various social issues. This is true within the field of substance abuse, domestic violence, children's services, sexual assault, mental health, and offender reentry. The idea is that communities can offer better overall services if their agencies (both state and nonprofit) and organizations work in tandem with one another. Thus, collaborative groups of agencies that include local, state, and nonprofit entities are becoming more common, and this even means that issues related to juvenile delinquency are addressed by these networks, both in and out of the courtroom. One example is the Children's Coalition of Northeast Louisiana, which is involved with service delivery for children of abuse and teens who commit delinquency throughout their service region. This coalition works in tandem with the local district attorney's office, judges who preside over juvenile cases, juvenile probation officers, and various persons from youth-oriented social services.

Court-Appointed Special Advocates

A Court-Appointed Special Advocate (CASA) works closely with departments of children and family services on abuse and neglect cases (Center for Children and Families, 2012). CASA volunteers are trained citizen volunteers who are appointed by the court to give advice in the best interests of children who are victims of abuse or neglect. The volunteers are ordinary people, usually without legal expertise, who care about what happens to children who have been victimized by abusive or neglectful parents. The juvenile court rarely appoints CASAs in delinquency cases (this may happen only if the delinquent child has an extensive history of abuse or neglect that may be influencing his or her delinquent behavior).

In jurisdictions with CASA programs, CASA volunteers are assigned to one case at a time by the juvenile court judge. They are responsible for researching the background of the case, reviewing court documents, and interviewing everyone involved in the case, including the child. CASA volunteers also prepare a report for the court discussing what they believe is in the best interests of the child based on the evidence they have reviewed (Center for Children and Families, 2012). The judge may use this report when deciding on a disposition for the child. Once the judge has decided on the case, the CASA volunteers continue monitoring the case to ensure that the child and/or family receive the services ordered by the court.

Training and Competence of Juvenile Court Personnel

If the goals of the juvenile justice system are to be achieved, the system needs to be staffed by well-trained, competent practitioners. Unfortunately, a number of circumstances have prevented total success in this area. Prosecutors and defense attorneys who handle juvenile court cases generally have little to gain by large investments of time and money. Few defense attorneys have gained national renown as the result of their efforts in juvenile court. Few prosecutors can count on being reelected on the basis of successful prosecutions in juvenile court. In addition, in many locales the juvenile court is regarded as something less than a real court of law where technical proficiency in law is necessary. Prosecutors often assign inexperienced assistants to handle juvenile court cases, and few defense attorneys specialize in the practice of juvenile law. As a result, many cases presented in juvenile court are poorly prepared by both sides. Some prosecutors are not thoroughly familiar with the juvenile code governing their jurisdiction. Similarly, defense attorneys will at times accept hearsay evidence, fail to present witnesses for the defense, and fail to object to procedural violations that might result in the dismissal of the petitions concerning their clients. In short, although the frequency of legal representation for both the state and defense has increased considerably during the past decade, the quality of such representation often leaves something to be desired.

Many judges handle juvenile cases as a part-time assignment. Although many clearly have the best interests of juveniles at heart, far too many show the same unfamiliarity with juvenile codes that characterizes many attorneys appearing before them. In fact, as we have observed, some appear to disregard juvenile codes altogether and rule their jurisdictions as dictators whose decisions on the bench are law.

A particularly disturbing example of judicial lack of familiarity with juvenile law was a case in which a part-time juvenile court judge sentenced a 14-year-old truant (MRAI) to the department of corrections. This clearly violates the juvenile code prohibiting status offenders from being transferred to that department. Intervention by the prosecutor and probation officer prevented this illegal act, which otherwise might have gone unchallenged until the department of corrections refused to accept the juvenile.

It should not be too much to ask that attorneys and judges practicing in juvenile court read and become familiar with applicable juvenile codes. If they do not, none of the constitutional guarantees or court decisions regarding due process in juvenile cases will have any impact. Treating juvenile court cases as if they did not involve the real practice of law has made practice before the juvenile court unattractive to many lawyers and judges and will continue to do so in the future. Fortunately, there is some evidence that a corps of better-informed sincere lawyers and judges is beginning to emerge. To encourage the growth of such a corps, proper recognition and rewards must be forthcoming.

Many jurisdictions require a bachelor's degree for employment in probation and social service positions, and a number of practitioners in these positions have master's degrees. The typical juvenile probation officer, for example, is a college-educated white male earning between $20,000 and $39,000 annually with a caseload of 41 juveniles (Torbet, 1996, p. 1). The OJJDP (1996) reported that more than three-quarters of all probation officers responding to their survey earned less than $40,000 a year, and 30% of these did not receive yearly pay increases. In some states, probation officers' salaries, typically paid by the county, are subsidized by state funds in an attempt to alleviate this problem (Torbet, 1996, p. 2).

In *Standards for the Administration of Juvenile Justice*, published by the IJA and the ABA (1980b), various sections address the issue of training for juvenile court personnel. For example, one recommendation states the following:

> Family court judges should be provided with preservice training on the law and procedures governing subject matter by the family (juvenile) court, the causes of delinquency and family conflict, [and] a thorough understanding of agencies responsible for intake and protective services. In addition, inservice education programs should be provided to judges to assure they are aware of changes in law, policy, and programs. (sec. 1.4220)

Other recommendations (secs. 1.423, 1.424, and 1.425) address similar issues of preservice and in-service training in juvenile matters with prosecutors, public defenders, and other court personnel and their staffs. Today there is a good deal of in-service training available to juvenile justice court personnel. The National Council of Juvenile and Family Court Judges, for example, sponsors training programs for court personnel on a continuing basis and publishes the *Juvenile and Family Court Journal* to keep practitioners informed of the latest happenings in juvenile justice.

CAREER OPPORTUNITY: YOUTH SERVICES COORDINATOR

Job description: Responsible for coordinating the treatment and rehabilitation services of juvenile offenders. Provide for the assessment, classification, procurement, coordination, and evaluation of services for juvenile offenders incarcerated in state correctional and residential facilities. Required to work with families, governmental agencies, local courts, schools, and service agencies to create and provide comprehensive treatment programs for troubled youth. May provide counseling to youth.

Employment requirements: Usually required to have 1 year of professional experience in the juvenile justice field. Required to have knowledge, experience, and an understanding of group and individual counseling, interactional strategies, and child development and behavior. College education needed in the areas of criminal justice, psychology, sociology, social work, education, and other closely related fields. Must complete an oral interview process before being hired.

Beginning salary: Benefits are provided by the state and include health and life insurance, paid vacations and holidays, and retirement plans. Salaries vary depending on the geographical location of the position but can range from $26,000 to $38,000.

Summary

Key figures in juvenile court proceedings include attorneys for the state and for the defendant, the judge, representatives from the department of children and family services, and the probation officer. Although the frequency of legal representation in juvenile court is increasing, the quality of this representation needs to be improved. The practice of juvenile law must be taken more seriously if we do not want to deal with juveniles who repeat their offenses and eventually come before adult courts.

Competent lawyers and judges need to be rewarded for their performances in juvenile court proceedings. Whenever possible, juvenile court judges should be assigned exclusively to juvenile court for a time. Judges who combine the best elements of the parent figure and lawgiver roles are a definite asset to the juvenile justice system. Probation officers and department of children and family services personnel are crucial if a juvenile justice philosophy is to be implemented. Their services to the court and to juveniles with problems complement the roles of the other juvenile court personnel. Although the overall quality of juvenile court personnel is improving, there is still considerable variance. Continued emphasis on training and competence at all levels is essential.

KEY TERMS

children and family services 233	electronic monitoring 249	preservice and in-service training 251
court-appointed counsel 237	juvenile court judges 237	private counsel 237
Court-Appointed Special Advocate (CASA) 250	juvenile probation officer 246	prosecutor or state's attorney 234
	"lawgiver" judge 243	role identity confusion 248
defense counsel 237	"parent figure" judge 243	unofficial probation 234

Critical Thinking Questions

1. Discuss the roles of the prosecutor and defense counsel in juvenile court. Why is the presence of legal representatives for both sides crucial in contemporary juvenile court? Discuss the relationship between the prosecutor and defense counsel.

2. Why is the judge such a powerful figure in juvenile court? What are the advantages and disadvantages of the judge as lawgiver and parent figure? How well trained are juvenile court judges?

3. In what sense is the role of juvenile probation officer ambiguous? What are the consequences of this ambiguity? How important is the probation officer in juvenile court proceedings?

4. What role do representatives from the department of children and family services play in juvenile court proceedings? Why are CASAs important in juvenile court proceedings?

Suggested Readings

Backstrom, J. C., & Walker, G. L. (2006). The role of the prosecutor in juvenile justice: Advocacy in the courtroom and leadership in the community. *William Mitchell Law Review, 32*(3), 964–988.

Berlow, A. (2000, June 5). Requiem for a public defender. *American Prospect, 11*, 28–32.

Bishop, S. J., Murphy, M. J., & Hicks, R. (2000). What progress has been made in meeting the needs of seriously maltreated children? The course of 200 cases through the Boston Juvenile Court. *Child Abuse and Neglect, 24*, 599–610.

Bridges, G. S., & Steen, S. (1998). Racial disparities in official assessments of juveniles: Attributional stereotypes as mediating mechanisms. *American Sociological Review, 63*, 554–570.

Fox, R. W., Kanitz, H. M., & Folger, W. A. (1991). Basic counseling skills training program for juvenile court workers. *Journal of Addictions and Offender Counseling, 11*(2), 34–41.

Gahr, E. (2001, June). Judging juveniles. *American Enterprise, 12*(4), 26–28.

National Juvenile Defender Center. (2016). *Defend children: A blueprint for effective juvenile defender services.* Washington, DC: National Juvenile Defender Center.

Payne, J. W. (1999, January). Our children's destiny. *Trial, 35*, 83–85.

Reddington, F. P., & Kreisel, B. W. (2000). Training juvenile probation officers: National trends and patterns. *Federal Probation, 64*(2), 28–32.

Rubin, H. T. (1980). The emerging prosecutor dominance of the juvenile court intake process. *Crime & Delinquency, 6*, 229–318.

Rush, J. P. (1992). Juvenile probation officer cynicism. *American Journal of Criminal Justice, 16*(2), 1–16.

Siegel, L. J., Welsh, B. C., & Senna, J. J. (2003). *Juvenile delinquency: Theory, practice, and law* (8th ed.). Belmont, CA: Wadsworth/Thomson Learning.

Too poor to be defended [Editorial]. (1998, April 9). *The Economist*, 21–22.

Torbet, P. M. (1996). *Juvenile probation: The workhorse of the juvenile justice system.* Washington, DC: Office of Juvenile Justice and Delinquency Prevention.

Viljoen, J. L., Klaver, J., & Roesch, R. (2005). Legal decisions of preadolescent and adolescent defendants: Predictors of confessions, pleas, communication with attorneys, and appeals. *Law and Human Behavior, 29*, 253–277.

Prevention and Diversion Programs

10

On completion of this chapter, students should be able to do the following:

- Discuss the advantages and disadvantages of prevention and diversion programs
- Describe three major types of prevention
- List and discuss several specific prevention and diversion programs
- Discuss the concept of restorative justice
- Describe some specialty or therapeutic courts and their role in the prevention of juvenile crime
- Critique prevention and diversion programs

WHAT WOULD YOU DO?

You are the on-call officer at the juvenile probation office this week. A mother calls in one morning and says that she's been having problems with her son, who is 13. She claims that he's lying about where he's going, where he's been, and who he is with. He is smoking cigarettes (and possibly marijuana), he's skipped school twice in the last couple of months, and he's leaving the house even when told not to do so. The mother states that she's tried grounding him and other types of punishments, just short of physical punishment, to no avail. She's also taken his cellphone, computer, and other electronics away. Last night, she thinks he got into her purse and took $20.00 before storming out of the house. He didn't come home until almost 3:00 a.m. She questioned him this morning about his whereabouts and the money. He told her he was at a friend's but wouldn't identify the friend and claimed he didn't take the $20.00. The mother knows she has $20.00 missing from her wallet. She doesn't want to call the police and report him because she doesn't want him to get arrested or go to jail. She is afraid that this behavior will continue if she doesn't do something. Exasperated, she says she's at her rope's end. The call to you is her last resort.

Questions to Consider

1. True or False: This child would be considered a status offender if brought before the juvenile court.

2. Multiple Choice: A potential diversion program for this child might include which of the following?

   a. Anger management classes
   b. Sex offender treatment
   c. Shoplifting diversion
   d. None of the above

3. What advice would you provide to the mother after hearing her story, if she continues to call the police and report the theft?

In 2010, McCollister, French, and Fang estimated the direct and indirect costs associated with adult and juvenile crime in the United States in 2007 at over $15 billion. This likely has not changed with the increase in technology crimes adding to the costs and estimated to reach billions of dollars in loss per year (Federal Bureau of Investigation, n.d.). Greenwood (2008) speculated that the cost of apprehending, prosecuting, incarcerating, and treating delinquents has become the fastest growing part of state budgets in the United States, with billions of dollars spent annually. Although a number of these attempts prove to be more or less successful with some offenders, the results are not particularly impressive on the whole. It would seem logical, therefore, to explore the possibilities of concentrating resources on programs that might provide better returns. Although this trend may be changing slightly with the use of specialty/therapeutic courts, many authorities have come to believe that most of our money is spent at the wrong end of the juvenile justice process—on treatment after the crime has been committed instead of on prevention to stop a crime from ever occurring.

In most cases, we wait until a juvenile comes into official contact with the system before an attempt is made to modify the behavior that has, by the time contact becomes official, been more or less ingrained. Our legal system generally prevents intervention by justice authorities without probable cause, and we would have it no other way. Still, this makes it more difficult for corrections personnel, or personnel in related agencies, to modify offensive behavior after the fact either by intervening prior to adjudication (preadjudication intervention) or by intervening after the juvenile has been adjudicated (postadjudication intervention). A 2003 study by the Office of Juvenile Justice and Delinquency Prevention (OJJDP) (p. 9) pointed out that the earlier intervention can be introduced, the better the opportunity to change the behavior. Greenwood (2008) and others (Farrington & Welsh, 2007; Sherman et al., 1997) supported this approach, noting that most adult offenders begin their criminal careers as juveniles. It makes sense then that if we prevent juvenile offending, we can prevent the beginning of adult criminal offending as well as reduce juvenile drug use and dependency, school dropouts, and long-term financial costs for taxpayers and victims (Greenwood, 2008; McCollister

Wilderness camps are popular alternatives to incarceration. Youth at wilderness camps participate in a variety of activities such as hiking, swimming, and mountain climbing, as well as therapy and rehabilitation programs.

et al., 2010). For example, consider the difficulty of trying to rehabilitate a juvenile addicted to heroin. By the time the juvenile is addicted, apprehended, and processed, he or she has probably developed problems in the family, problems in school, and delinquent habits oriented toward ensuring his or her supply of heroin (e.g., burglary, mugging, pushing drugs). To rehabilitate the juvenile, we need to deal with all of these problems. If, however, we had effective programs to detect and help resolve problems that are likely to lead to heroin use—known as prevention—the necessity for solving all of these complicated and related problems would be eliminated. Suppose that we found the juvenile in question to be dissatisfied with traditional education but interested in pursuing a specific vocation, like welding or drafting. Suppose that we were to provide an alternative education that enabled the juvenile to pursue that vocation and heightened his or her interest in success within the system. We might, then, prevent the juvenile from dropping out of school, joining a heroin-abusing gang, and developing the undesirable behavior patterns just mentioned. Consequently, it would seem reasonable to bring as many resources as possible to bear so as to *prevent* the offender from engaging in illegal behavior in the first place (predelinquent intervention) or to try to *divert* the juvenile, as early as possible, when he or she does encounter the justice system (Lundman, 1993).

Prevention

There are three major types of prevention programs. Primary prevention is directed at preventing illegal acts among the juvenile population as a whole before they occur by alleviating social conditions related to the offenders. Secondary prevention seeks to identify juveniles who appear to be at high risk for delinquency and/or abuse and to intervene in their lives early. Tertiary prevention attempts to prevent further illegal acts among offenders once such acts have been committed (OJJDP, 2000). None of these programs are a cure-all, and there are a number of difficulties in attempting to develop and operate such programs (Mays & Winfree, 2000, p. 324). For example, there should be a good match between the program concept, host organization, and the targeted juvenile if the program is to change behavior or have an effect on the youth (Lipsey, Wilson, & Cothern, 2000).

During the 1930s, several projects addressed the issue of delinquency prevention. The Chicago Area Project involved churches, social clubs, and community committees that sponsored recreation programs for juveniles; addressed problems associated with law enforcement, health services, and education; targeted local gangs; and helped to reintegrate juveniles who had been adjudicated delinquent. In spite of these efforts, no solid evidence that delinquency was prevented or reduced resulted from the project (Lundman, 1993).

During the late 1960s, the President's Commission on Law Enforcement and Administration of Justice (1967) recommended the establishment of alternatives to the juvenile justice system. According to the report, service agencies capable of dealing with certain categories of juveniles should have these juveniles diverted to them. The report further recommended the following:

1. The formal sanctioning system and pronouncement of delinquency should be used only as a last resort.
2. Instead of the formal system, dispositional alternatives to adjudication must be developed for dealing with juveniles, including agencies to provide and coordinate services and procedures to achieve necessary control without unnecessary stigma. Alternatives already available, such as those related to court intake, should be more fully exploited.
3. The range of conduct for which court intervention is authorized should be narrowed, with greater emphasis on consensual and informal means of meeting the problems of difficult children. (President's Commission on Law Enforcement and Administration of Justice, 1967, pp. 19–25)

During the early 1970s, the National Advisory Commission on Criminal Justice Standards and Goals (1973) stated that "the highest attention must be given to preventing juvenile delinquency, minimizing the involvement of young offenders in the juvenile and criminal justice system, and reintegrating them into the community" (p. 36). The commission further recommended minimizing the involvement of the offender in the system. This does not mean that we should coddle the offender. It recognizes that the further the offender penetrates into the system, the more difficult it becomes to divert him or her from a criminal career. Minimizing a child's involvement with the juvenile justice system does not mean abandoning the use of confinement for certain individuals or failing to protect victims of abuse or neglect. Until more effective means of treatment are found, chronic and dangerous delinquents should be incarcerated to protect society, and abused children must be made wards of the court and removed from unsafe conditions. However, the juvenile justice system must search for beneficial programs outside institutions for juveniles who do not need confinement or sheltered care. As discussed in Chapter 7, most state juvenile court acts make this clear in their discussions of the goals of juvenile court.

Both labeling and learning theories stress the desirability of prevention rather than correction. The basic premise of labeling theory is that juveniles find it difficult to escape the stigmatization of being known as delinquents or abuse victims. Once labeled, juveniles are often forced out of normal interaction patterns and into associations with others who have been labeled. From this perspective, the agencies of the juvenile justice system that are established to correct delinquent behavior often contribute to its occurrence even as they try to cope with it. Learning theory holds that individuals engage in delinquent behavior because they experience an overabundance of interactions, associations, and reinforcements with definitions favorable to delinquency. Therefore, if agencies cast potential or first-time delinquents into interaction with more experienced delinquents, the process of learning delinquent behavior is enhanced greatly. Alternatively, concentration on the problems of youth that tend to lead to delinquent behavior and abuse or neglect not only may result in preventing some juveniles from becoming involved in progressively more serious offenses but also might allow the justice network to concentrate efforts on hard-core delinquents and abusers whose labels and stigmatization have been earned.

Because delinquency and abuse or neglect are complex problems, no single program is likely to emerge as being effective in preventing all such behaviors. Delinquency prevention, for example, involves many variables, and no one program is likely to be foolproof. Inherent in the multifaceted problems of delinquency and child abuse prevention is the fact that these behaviors have roots in the basic social conditions of our society. Increasing urbanization with accompanying problems of poverty, inferior education, poor housing, health and sanitary problems, and unemployment are but a few social conditions that seem to be related to delinquency and abuse or neglect. Therefore, we should focus our attention on these problems if preventive efforts are to have a chance of success (Johnson, 1998; Kowaleski-Jones, 2000; Lane & Turner, 1999; Liddle & Hogue, 2000; Thornberry, Huizinga, & Loeber, 2004; Yoshikawa, 1994). Although a number of programs are important for the prevention of delinquency and child abuse, we would be remiss if we focused only on programs directed specifically at preventing such behaviors and ignored these underlying conditions. Large-scale social change directed at the areas just discussed is clearly an important preventive measure and would enable more people to achieve culturally approved goals without needing to resort to illegal means.

In June 1970, a group was invited by the Youth Development and Delinquency Prevention Administration of the Department of Health, Education, and Welfare to meet in Scituate, Massachusetts, to consider the problem of youth development and delinquency prevention. The document produced at that meeting stated the following:

We believe that our social institutions [e.g., school, family, church] are programmed in such a way as to deny large numbers of young people socially acceptable, responsible, and personally gratifying roles. These institutions should seek ways of becoming more responsible to youth needs. (Youth Development and Delinquency Prevention Administration, 1971, p. 2)

The group further stated that any strategy for youth development and delinquency prevention should give priority to "programs which assist institutions to change in ways that provide young people with socially acceptable, responsible, personally gratifying roles and assist young people to assume such roles" (p. 2).

It follows from this premise that the development of viable strategies for the prevention and reduction of delinquency and abuse or neglect rests on the identification, assessment, and alteration of those features of institutional functioning that impede development of juveniles—particularly those whose social situations make them most prone to developing delinquent careers, becoming victims of abusive behavior, or participating in collective forms of withdrawal and deviancy. This approach does not deny the occurrence of individual deviance, but it does assert that in many cases the deviance is traceable to the damaging experiences of juveniles in institutional encounters.

Katkin, Hyman, and Kramer (1976) pointed the following out some time ago:

It is social institutions in the broader community—families, churches, schools, social welfare agencies, etc.—which have the primary mandate to control and care for young people who commit delinquent acts. It is only when individuals or institutions in the community fail to divert (or decide not to divert) that the formal processes of the juvenile justice system are called into action. (p. 404)

In this respect, Yoshikawa (1994) found that comprehensive family support combined with early childhood education may well be successful in bringing about long-term prevention. Similarly, Johnson (1998) noted that the actions of parents and teachers may reduce juvenile crime more effectively than do those of the police. Lane and Turner (1999) discussed the importance of interagency cooperation in preventing delinquency, and Liddle and Hogue (2000) found that family-based intervention in the form of the multidimensional family prevention model can help to build resilient family ties and strong connections with prosocial agencies among adolescents. Kowaleski-Jones (2000) found that residential stability and schools perceived as high quality by mothers were factors related to preventing juveniles from getting into trouble. Mihalic, Fagan, Irwin, Ballard, and Elliot (2004) stated that limiting opportunities for bullying and other school victimization reduces delinquency in schools (and perhaps in communities as well). Roman, Kane, Baer, and Turner (2009) found that neighborhoods with more local organizations nearby had lower rates of aggravated assault.

During the past 15 years or so, the OJJDP has evaluated model programs that identify exemplary, effective, and promising programs in preventing or reducing juvenile offending. As suggested in the previous paragraph, the research is most supportive of programs in schools and in the community, prior to residential placement of the offender. According to the OJJDP (2012), programs focused on gender-specific issues, academics, job training, and conflict resolution are promising in preventing delinquency. Greenwood (2008) has also found that nurse home visits reduced instances of child abuse and neglect and subsequent births for mothers who were young and/or unmarried; preschool education for at-risk youth and other programs offered in educational settings prevented child abuse and neglect as well as delinquent and status-offending behaviors, such as smoking and the use of alcohol; and programs in the community that emphasized family interactions were successful. For youth on probation, both Greenwood (2008) and the OJJDP (2012) recommend programs like cognitive behavioral therapy (CBT), family counseling, and drug and alcohol therapy as well as mentoring, tutoring, and interpersonal skills and parenting training (Greenwood, 2008). With regard to youth placed in institutions, Greenwood (2008, p. 199) and the OJJDP (2012) have found that programs that focused "on dynamic and changeable risk factors—low skills, substance abuse, defiant behavior, relationships with delinquent peers"; those that tailored themselves to individual client needs using evidence-based methods; and those that focused on higher-risk youth with the most room to improve or the greatest consequences to suffer were most successful. "Generally, programs that focus on specific skills such as behavior management, interpersonal skills training, family counseling, group counseling, or individual counseling have all demonstrated positive effects in institutional settings" (Greenwood, 2008, p. 200). The OJJDP even recommends the use of day reporting centers (DRCs) and group homes to treat those who need residential supervision. Even though this offers a baseline for promising and/or proven prevention or diversion strategies, the juvenile justice system cannot do it alone. Unfortunately, the responsibility for dealing with juveniles who have problems has been placed too frequently solely on juvenile justice practitioners. The public has been more than willing to place the blame for failures in preventing delinquency and abuse or neglect on these practitioners and has been quick to criticize their efforts. These practitioners are often faced with the task of attempting to modify undesirable behavior that has become habitual and deep-rooted and that a variety of other agencies have failed to modify. In addition, the period available for rehabilitation is usually short. As noted in Greenwood's (2008) study, other social institutions play a vital role in crime prevention and are significant to the overall lowering of delinquency and abuse/neglect. The OJJDP (2012) suggested wraparound services in almost all of their approaches to prevention and diversion. This includes a comprehensive combination of individual and social services that support the child and his or her family in order to keep the delinquent youth at home and out of institutions whenever possible. In our society, there are a number of agencies with which juveniles come into contact earlier, more consistently, and with less stigmatization than the juvenile justice system. Some of these agencies or institutions are functionally related to the juvenile justice system and are, thus, able to build on the goals of crime prevention. The term functionally related agencies is used to describe those agencies having goals similar to those of the juvenile justice system—improving the quality of life for juveniles by preventing offensive behavior, providing opportunities for success, and correcting undesirable behavior. However, it is not always the case that functionally related agencies work in conjunction with the juvenile justice system. When this does not occur, delinquency prevention is undermined.

Diversion Programs

One form of prevention is diversion, which has carried many different, and sometimes conflicting, meanings. Diversion is often used to describe prejuvenile justice, as well as postjuvenile justice, activities. Some diversion programs are designed to suspend or terminate juvenile justice processing of juveniles in favor of release or referral to alternate services—known as secondary diversion. Secondary diversion programs may include formal or informal processing by the police, perhaps through stationhouse adjustments, or limiting the youth's penetration into the justice system by expunging records or using restorative justice programs. On the other hand, other diversionary activities involve referrals to programs outside of the justice system prior to juveniles entering the system—often referred to as pure diversion programs. In this case the youth may be channeled to a noncourt institution such as an afterschool outreach program or community service. Most diversion programs occur after an arrest so they involve both a justice and a service component (Dembo, Wareham, & Schmeidler, 2005).

Past research on diversion programs has shown positive results (Dembo et al., 2005). Those programs that provide direct services have reported less penetration into the justice system by youth (Roberts, 1989) and lowered recidivism rates (Baron, Feeney, & Thornton, 1973; Bohnstedt, 1978; McCord, Widom, & Crowell, 2001; Palmer, Bohnstedt, & Lewis, 1978) when compared to youth processed through the juvenile court system. Diversion programming has also shown a reduction in costs related to juvenile justice (Baron et al., 1973). McCord et al. (2001) have reported that diversion programs providing intensive in-home family intervention have consistently shown positive results. Vincent, Guy, and Grisso (2013) reported that diversion from the formal system is the best choice because youth involved in even minor juvenile justice sanctions were twice as likely to reoffend than those who were diverted.

Diversion programming is not without pitfalls. It sometimes permits intervention into juveniles' lives and their families with little or no formal processes and inadequate safeguards of individual liberties. One of the major concerns with diversion programs is that they result in net widening or bringing to the attention of juvenile authorities children who otherwise would not be labeled, thereby increasing rather than decreasing stigmatization. A second issue relates to the coordinating of diversion programs and the agencies sponsoring them. The problem is one of territorial jealousy, which refers to a belief commonly held by agency personnel that attempts to coordinate efforts are actually attempts to invade the territory they have staked out for themselves. Agency staff members have a tendency to view themselves as experts in their particular field, to resent suggestions for change made by outsiders, and to fear that they will be found to be lacking in competence. As a result, these staff members tend to keep agency operations secret and reject attempts by personnel from other agencies to provide services or suggest improvements. Changes in policy and an increased focus on get-tough philosophies have also shifted attention and funding away from diversion programs. As a result, more youth are being referred to juvenile court, processed and committed to institutions (Dembo et al., 2005; Greenwood, Model, Rydell, & Chiesa, 1998; Puzzanchera et al., 2000), and fewer resources or youth are available for diversion services. Those agencies that are able to secure funding may be even more territorial than they were in the past for fear of losing the funding and the clientele.

The consequences of territorial jealousy can be extremely serious for both juveniles and taxpayers. Duplication of services is a costly enterprise in a time of budgetary cutbacks and financial restraints; however, denial of available services to juveniles with problems can be disastrous. Lack of cooperation, understanding, and confidence among agency personnel greatly hampers attempts to provide for the welfare of juveniles.

Examples of Prevention and Diversion Programs

In Chapter 3, the importance of school personnel in shaping the behavior of children was discussed. No other institution in our society, with the possible exception of the family, has as much opportunity to observe, mold, and modify youthful behavior as does the school. The importance of education as a stepping-stone to future opportunities for success cannot be stressed too much. In today's economy, education is vital to employment and future earnings. Take a look at the Bureau of Labor Statistics chart that follows in Figure 10.1. In 2016, those without high school diplomas had an 8.0% unemployment rate, whereas someone with a high school diploma or GED had only a 5.4% unemployment rate and earned approximately $185.00 more a week when working. The provision of meaningful educational opportunities for children who have been labeled as delinquent or in need of supervision is of great importance in attempts to keep these children in society as productive future workers and in keeping them involved in the school environment.

Although it was once possible, and fairly common, for educators to deal with "problem youth" by pushing them out of the educational system, recent court decisions indicate that all children have the right to an education. Therefore, children who have been found delinquent and status offenders can no longer be dismissed from school legally without due process. School counselors who formerly concerned themselves with academic and career counseling, advising, and scheduling also face the reality of coping with behavioral and emotional problems. It is hoped that teachers who in the past simply passed juveniles with such problems on to their colleagues by refusing to fail problem youth (giving them social promotion) will begin to seek other more desirable alternatives. Illinois, for example, has created the Regional Safe Schools program, which

Figure 10.1 Education Matters

Earnings and unemployment rates by educational attainment, 2016

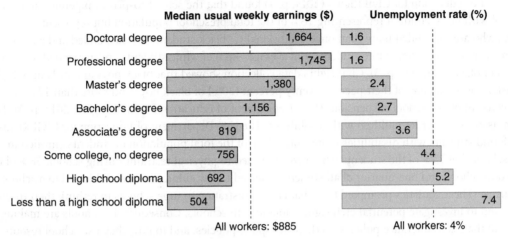

	Median usual weekly earnings ($)	Unemployment rate (%)
Doctoral degree	1,664	1.6
Professional degree	1,745	1.6
Master's degree	1,380	2.4
Bachelor's degree	1,156	2.7
Associate's degree	819	3.6
Some college, no degree	756	4.4
High school diploma	692	5.2
Less than a high school diploma	504	7.4

All workers: $885   All workers: 4%

Source: U.S. Bureau of Labor Statistics, Current Population Survey. (2017, April). *Employment projections.* Available from https://www.bls.gov/emp/ep_chart_001.htm.

Note: Data are for persons age 25 and over. Earnings are for full-time wage and salary workers.

targets 6th through 12th graders. This program allows children who were traditionally expelled or suspended to transfer into an alternative learning environment to continue with academic work, counseling, community service, and vocational activities. The primary focus of the program is academic instruction, although the staff also deal with social and emotional needs, "such as behavior modification training, life skills training, and counseling" (Illinois State Board of Education, 2012). In 2012, the program serviced over 4,500 students who would have traditionally been suspended or expelled from school permanently. The program's notable outcomes included the facts that 77.3% of high school students earned academic credits, incidents of behavior problems for which the students were referred to the program (i.e., drugs, fighting, weapons) were reduced for 76% of the students, and 53.2% of Grade 12 students graduated from high school (Illinois State Board of Education, 2012, p. 9).

In north Georgia there is another program that focuses on youth who drop out (or are pushed out) of high school for a variety of reasons but want to complete a high school education. This program is offered as a night school for youth from 15 to 21 years of age where students can complete their high school degree, repeat courses that they may have failed in the traditional school, and/or continue getting high school credits so they can transfer back to a traditional state high school. This program has seen an increase in graduation rates from 89 in 2005 to over 315 in the 2015–2016 school year (Mountain Education Center High School, 2017). The program is completely voluntary and demonstrates that, if given the choice and opportunity, young people will make the effort to complete high school and conform to customary social norms. It is clear that educational personnel and programming play an important role in preventing and correcting delinquent behavior by providing appropriate referrals and instruction.

Schools, juvenile courts, and police departments have worked together in recent years to reduce the school-to-prison pipeline, a term used to describe children who have trouble at school (i.e., out-of-school suspensions) ending up in the juvenile justice system. The school-to-prison pipeline encourages police presence at schools, physical restraints, and automatic suspensions and out-of-class time. Additionally, when combined with zero-tolerance policies, minority children and children with disabilities are more often than others pushed out of the classroom and into the criminal justice system by arrests for nonviolent acts such as disorderly conduct, willful defiance, and insubordination (Elias, n.d.; Nelson & Lind, 2015). The U.S. Department of Education for Civil Rights (2014, p. 1) found that the school-to-prison pipeline can begin in preschool with black children representing 18% of the total preschool population but representing 43% of students who are suspended more than once. Additionally, "black students are suspended and expelled at a rate three times greater than white students. On average, 4.6% of white students are suspended, compared to 16.4% of black students" (p. 3). Civil rights data collection showed that black boys and girls have higher suspension rates than any of their peers: "Twenty percent (20%) of black boys and more than 12% of black girls receive an out-of-school suspension" (U.S. Department of Education for Civil Rights, 2014, p. 3). The problem is even greater for children with disabilities. The U.S. Department of Education for Civil Rights (2014) found students with disabilities represented 12% of the total population of students enrolled in public schools but 75% of the students who were subjected to physical restraint during school, 58% of those secluded in school, and one-quarter of all students referred to law enforcement or subjected to a school-based arrest. These statistics prompted the Obama administration to urge schools to rethink their discipline policies and to investigate potential civil rights violations in schools. Consequently, schools are making changes to their zero-tolerance policies, to their discipline policies, and to how they use school resource officers. Clayton County, Georgia, for example, made an agreement with the police force and school district to restrict the school cases where police made an arrest. The results have included a high school graduation increase of 24% from 2004 to 2010. Broward County, Florida, schools decided to handle their own disciplinary actions when nonviolent misdemeanants were involved, and the Chicago public schools have been attempting to reduce the number of suspensions for children younger than second grade, among other approaches (Nelson & Lind, 2015).

School Programs

Along with the changes mentioned, there are numerous school programs designed to prevent juveniles from engaging in delinquent activities or to divert them from such activities once they become involved. In Chapter 8, we mentioned the police officer school resource or liaison programs. To prevent the distraction of delinquency activities from the educational environment, school districts such as that in Camdenton City, Missouri, have hired police officers to handle the public safety issues on campus. In 2007, school resource officers (SROs) in Camdenton met with 1,500 students and discussed safety-related issues, prepared a new safety plan for the high school, and used cameras to decrease campus crime and for investigations. They also handled 178 incidents of violence on campus in that year. Officers met with numerous kids on the dangers of drug and alcohol use and did drug sweeps through the school district (City of Camdenton Police Department, 2007). This program is not uncommon, with SROs being a mainstay in most schools in the United States since the school shootings of the 1990s (Garry, 1996). As noted, efforts to refine what types of behaviors SROs handle in schools are currently underway and changes to their roles in schools may be forthcoming.

As noted in Chapter 8, another program presented in the schools by police officers is the D.A.R.E. (Drug Abuse Resistance Education) program. Originally developed in California in 1983, the program spread rapidly to other states. The goal of the semester-long program aimed at fifth and sixth graders is to equip juveniles with the skills to resist peer pressure to use drugs. Trained police officers present the program as a part of the regular school curriculum in an attempt to provide accurate information about drugs and alcohol, teach students decision-making skills, help students to resist peer pressure, and provide alternatives to drug abuse.

Unfortunately, research has shown that participation in the D.A.R.E. program during elementary school has no effect on later alcohol use, cigarette smoking, or marijuana use in the 12th grade, although it may deter a small amount of the use of illegal and more deviant drugs such as inhalants, cocaine, and LSD among teenage males (Dukes, Stein, & Ullman, 1997). Other research has shown that the impact of D.A.R.E. on drug-related behavior of children who have been through the program is minimal (Cauchon, 1993; Walker, 1998, p. 275). After reviewing various studies on D.A.R.E. programs during the 1990s, Kanof (2003, p. 2) reported that D.A.R.E. had no statistically significant effect on long-term drug use. Proponents argue, perhaps with some justification, that at a minimum the program introduces police officers and children to one another as real people at an early age and that the effects of classroom interaction may have beneficial outcomes for both.

In response to the criticisms of the D.A.R.E. program, a new research-based curriculum that focused on prevention science and drug use was created and implemented in 2001. The University of Akron and the D.A.R.E. program combined to execute the curriculum in six U.S. cities (Carnevale Associates, 2006). The new program targets children in seventh grade with a 10-week curriculum and provides another short program to those same children as they enter the ninth grade. "To date, University of Akron researchers have preliminary results that the Take Charge of Your Life program may be effective in reaching those adolescents who are at elevated risk for substance abuse" (p. 4). These results seem promising, although the study has had a number of methodological problems (e.g., Hurricane Katrina causing the closure of some test schools, declining rates of drug use in the general population, implementation of similar programs in the schools). Additionally, a Minnesota study from 1999 to 2001 used an enhanced D.A.R.E. Plus curriculum with 6,237 seventh graders. The curriculum relied more heavily than the traditional approach on peer-led classroom instruction, parent involvement and education, adult community action teams (CATs), and youth planned and facilitated activities (Perry et al., 2003). The researchers found significant differences among males in the D.A.R.E. Plus program as compared to those in the traditional program or in no program at all. The findings show that seventh-grade boys in the D.A.R.E. Plus schools were less likely than those in the control schools to show increases in alcohol use, tobacco use, multidrug use, and victimization in past year and past month measures. The only effect recorded for females was a tendency to report fewer cases of ever having been drunk. There were no other differences in girls in the D.A.R.E. Plus program versus girls in the traditional program or in no program at all (Perry et al., 2003). D.A.R.E. has also implemented a curriculum that focuses on prescription drugs and over-the-counter medications. In a 2008 study of this curriculum, Darnell and Emshoff found that of the 381 fifth, seventh, and ninth graders that participated in the curriculum, there were statistically significant differences in the following:

1. Fifth graders understood the definition of a medicine, the distinction between Rx and OTC medicines, that Rx drugs are prescribed for use by only one person, that there is proper disposal of Rx drugs, and accurate measurement of dosages

2. Seventh graders understood the distinction between Rx and OTC medicines, that Rx drugs are prescribed for use by only one person, how to carefully read drug facts labels, and that the abuse of Rx and OTC is as dangerous as other drugs

3. Ninth graders understood that people use Rx and OTC drugs to get high, that it is unsafe to share Rx and OTC drugs, it is harmful to abuse OTC drugs, it is illegal to use Rx drugs not prescribed for you, the negative health effects of Rx and OTC abuse, the risk of addiction to Rx drugs, and refusal of an offer to use Rx and OTC drugs

This appears promising even as the overall funding for the D.A.R.E. program has decreased as policy focus has shifted with both national and state legislators, and some D.A.R.E. programs have ceased existence in schools over the last 8 to 10 years. D.A.R.E. proponents are hopeful that states will again adopt D.A.R.E. programs in schools since medical and recreational marijuana has become legal in some states and efforts to curb use among youth in those states is more important than ever. In Colorado, a state known for early adoption of recreational and medical marijuana legalization, youth marijuana use rates in the past 2 years (2013–2014) since legalization have increased more than 20% compared to the 2-year average use rate prior to legalization (2011–2012) (Rocky Mountain High Intensity Drug Trafficking Area, 2016). Additionally, Colorado youth ranked #1 in the nation for past-month marijuana use in 2013–2014 and had a use rate 74% higher than the national average (Rocky Mountain High Intensity Drug Trafficking Area, 2016). If this is not enough cause for concern, there may be some evidence that marijuana distributors in Colorado are marketing to youth, as noted in In Practice 10.1.

IN PRACTICE 10.1

DRUG INFORMATION BRIEF: MARIJUANA PIXY STIX

Hyoung Chang/The Denver Post via Getty Images

Details

This powdered, edible sugar substance has a high THC content, can be discreetly consumed, and the packaging can appeal to a younger audience. Marijuana infused Pixy Stix are similar to the original candy product in size, packaging, and appearance. In Colorado, they were originally called Wizzie Stix, made by We Be Infused and are now called Stixx, made by At Home Baked. Each stick contains 50mg THC and 25mg CBD, although an individual dose is listed at 10mg. They come in two different formulas: A.M. for Morning/Day use and P.M. for "relaxation and sleep aid." Consumption can be very discreet in that they easily fit into a pocket or purse. They are available throughout Colorado in various dispensaries and prices range from around $6 to $22 per stick. Also, a similar product is now available in some Washington dispensaries called Legit Sticks.

Significance

Use rate among youth in Colorado is a major concern and this product may be very appealing to them. Also, Stixx were a part of an edibles recall from At Home Baked in July of 2014 because an ingredient in the edibles, bubble hash—a concentrated form of THC—was prepared using a dirty washing machine. Further, forty minutes after consuming half a tube, a new user to marijuana self-reported he "could barely speak, felt sick to his stomach, couldn't see, had a raging headache, felt extreme nausea" and essentially "knocked out of reality."

Source: Rocky Mountain High Intensity Drug Trafficking Area. (2015). *Drug information brief: Marijuana Pixy Stix.* Retrieved from http://www.dare.org/wp-content/uploads/2015/01/Marijuana-Drug-Info-Brief-Pixy-Stix011215.pdf.

Questions for Consideration

1. True or False: Pixy Stix are only appealing to adults, and these are clearly being marketed to an adult population.

2. Multiple Choice: Students in schools may be able to hide Stixx or Wizzles in which of the following?

   a. Bookbags

   b. Computer bags

   c. Coat pockets

   d. All of the above

3. As a school resource officer, what action would you take with a youth who tells you he feels "knocked out of reality"?

Yet another program involving police and school cooperation is the GREAT (Gang Resistance Education and Awareness Training) program. Unlike D.A.R.E., the GREAT program is a 13-week curriculum offered in middle schools, elementary schools, during the summer, and to families (GREAT, 2013). Its focus is on reducing the number of children joining gangs. It is taught by uniformed police officers and has been evaluated. Esbensen and Osgood (1999) found that students who participated in the program were less likely to join gangs and had an increase in gang-related knowledge. They also held higher prosocial attitudes and had fewer delinquent associations than those students who had not participated in the program (Esbensen & Osgood, 1999). In 2004, Esbensen also found that students who had completed the program gained more education on the "consequences of gang involvement, and they develop[ed] favorable attitudes toward the police. . . . However, the program did not reduce gang membership or future delinquent behavior" (p. 4). In 2012, Esbensen again studied the GREAT program with Peterson, Taylor, and Osgood. They reported that results 1 year post-GREAT program showed a 39% reduction in odds of gang joining among students who received the program compared to those who did not and an average of 24% reduction in odds of gang joining across the 4 years postprogram (p. 5). Ramsey, Rust, and Sobel (2003) found little change in their analysis of participant attitudes from the GREAT program.

Other approaches used by schools include antibullying programs, mentoring programs, Promoting Alternative Thinking Strategies (PATHS), truancy reduction programs, and alternative education programs. Nansel, Overpeck, Haynie, Ruan, and Scheidt (2003) reported that bullying victimization affects approximately 15% to 20% of the American student population. It is important to note though that even those students not directly bullied may be affected by the bullying incident (Adams & Connor, 2008, p. 212). Beale and Hall (2007) claimed that in bullying there is a perpetrator, a victim, and a bystander. This assertion is supported by Silvernail (2000), who found that 88% of students in the fourth through eighth grades had

Denver Juvenile Probation officer Deborah Garcia-Sandoval works with Johnson Elementary students during a GREAT (Gang Resistance Education and Training) class in March 2015.

observed bullying at school even though only 20% of 9th to 12th graders report experiencing bullying in school (Centers for Disease Control and Prevention, 2011). The 2014 Bullying in U.S. Schools Status Report found that 14% of students included in the sample reported being bullied, whereas 5% reported bullying others. Additionally, bullying decreases with increasing grade level. "While 22 percent of third graders report being bullied two to three times a month or more, by eighth grade this decreases to 15 percent, and by twelfth grade to 7 percent. On the other hand, the percentage of students who report bullying others is more stable over grade levels, remaining between 4 and 6 percent between third and twelfth grade" (Luxenburg, Limber, & Olweus, 2015, p. 5). These findings confirm that the increased attention and research on bullying is warranted. To combat this issue, the Olweus Bullying Prevention Program, implemented primarily by school staff members, involves school-based intervention for the reduction of bullying. Research has shown that the program results in significant reductions in reports of students being bullied or bullying others and of antisocial behaviors. It also shows improvements in the overall "social climate" of the school (American Psychological Association, 2004, par. 11). The OJJDP (2011a) also suggests the following strategies for schools to deter bullying: mentoring programs, opportunities for community service, addressing the transition between elementary and middle school, and the introduction of intervention and prevention programs early in the school career.

Another area of concern in bullying is cyberbullying. As we move to quickly embrace the Internet and other communication devices, we open the door for those with cruel intentions to more easily attack us in our homes and in our private lives. Cyberbullying is a form of bullying that relies on technological programs such as e-mail; instant messaging; websites; and chat or bash boards to intimidate, shame, and inflict "unwarranted hurt and embarrassment on its unsuspecting victims" (Beale & Hall, 2007, p. 9). Data available on cyberbullying show an increase in recent years. Hinduja and Patchin found that 32% of boys and more than 36% of girls reported being victims of cyberbullying in an online survey of 1,378 adolescent Internet users in 2008. Of these, 18% of the boys and 16% of the girls also reported acting as perpetrators of cyberbullying. In nationally representative surveys of 10- to 17-year-olds, twice as many children and youth indicated that they had been victims and perpetrators of online harassment in 2005 compared with data from 1999 and 2000 (Wolak, Mitchell, & Finkelhor, 2006). Research has also shown that 18% of 3,700 middle school children surveyed in the United States had been victims of cyberbullying (Chu, 2005). In another study, Shariff and Johnny (2007) reported the following:

> In Britain, the National Children's Home and Tesco Mobile (2002), found that approximately 16 per cent of British children and adolescents reported receiving threatening text messages or being bullied over the Internet; one in four young people between the ages of eleven and nineteen were threatened via personal cell phones or personal computers; and, approximately 29 percent of those surveyed had not reported the cyber-bullying. Forty-two percent had confided to a friend and 32 percent had reported to parents. Moreover, caregivers' knowledge of cyber-bullying was disclosed as minimal. The survey found that 56 percent of parents surveyed were not concerned about their children being bullied electronically and many were in denial as to the impact of such behavior. Nineteen percent believed such incidents were rare. (p. 313)

Research on cyberbullying has led to some interesting insights. For example, 18% of students in Grades 6 through 8 indicated they had been cyberbullied at least once, and 6% said it had happened to them two or more times. Further, some 11% of students in Grades 6 through 8 said they had recently cyberbullied another person, and 2% said they had done it two or more times (Kowalski et al., 2005). According to Ybarra and Mitchell (2004), 19% of regular Internet users ages 10 to 17 reported being involved in online aggression—15% had been aggressors, and 7% had been targets. Further, 3% identified themselves as both aggressors and targets. A study by Kowalski and colleagues (2005) found that girls were about twice as likely as boys to be victims and perpetrators of cyberbullying. Wolak et al. (2006) found the most common way that middle and high school children and youth reported being cyberbullied was through instant messaging. "As with traditional bullying, cyber bullying seems to increase through the elementary school years, peak during middle school years, and decline in high school" (Beale & Hall, 2007, p. 9). The 2014 U.S. Bullying in Schools Status Report suggested that, even though there has been much media and research attention on cyberbullying, cyberbullying actually was the least common reported form of bullying among their sample, 4% for boys and 6% for girls (Luxenburg et al., 2015). Although still a serious problem, it may well be that cyberbullying is exaggerated in the media.

Research in cyberbullying constantly suggests that parents turn to school authorities and Internet providers for help when cyberbullying occurs (Beale & Hall, 2007; WiredKids, 2005). Perhaps this is because most cyberbullying statutes have relied on schools to enforce bullying policies. In Delaware, for example, the School Bullying Prevention Act passed in 2007 calls for school administrators to take action against technologically based actions that occur off campus. Idaho's 2006 law also allows schools to suspend students for disrupting school by bullying on campus or through communication devices ("State Action on Cyberbullying," 2008). The lines between enforcement and cyberbullying may continue to blur, but the evidence is clear that schools are viewed by the legislatures to bear some responsibility in deterring bullying through the use of technology. Regardless of how states choose to handle bullying and cyberbullying, it is important that they address the issue because students who are bullied, who bully, and who both bully and are bullied are twice as likely than other students to dislike school. This number increases with rising grade levels, with students involved in bullying having the potential to have a negative school experience and drop out of school prior to graduation (Luxenburg et al., 2015).

Big Brothers Big Sisters of America provides adult mentoring programs for children. They have two essential programs—(1) community mentoring and (2) school-based mentoring. The community-based program is the traditional program where community members spend a few hours a month with a child in a one-on-one relationship doing something they both enjoy. The school-based program is one-to-one mentoring that takes place a few hours a month in the school environment. This can include homework help, reading, or class discussions but may also include involvement in lunch or physical education activities. Big Brothers Big Sisters also sponsors a Bigs in Blue program for at-risk youth to be mentored by police officers. Research has shown that children with mentors are 46% less likely to initiate drug use, 27% less likely to initiate alcohol use, and 52% less likely to be truant. They are more confident in their school performance and have better relationships with their families (Herrera, Grossman, Kauh, & McMaken, 2011; Tierney, Grossman, & Resch, 1995).

The PATHS curriculum is primarily school based but also includes activities for parents. It is aimed at promoting emotional and social competencies by acknowledging that children may experience and react to strong emotions long before they can verbalize their feelings effectively. In 1- and 2-year follow-up matched studies of youth in the PATHS program and youth not exposed to the PATHS program, researchers have found that teachers reported reduced instances of aggressive behavior, reduced behavioral and conduct problems, reduced depression and sadness among students with special needs, decreased frustration levels, and increased self-control and vocabulary among students exposed to the PATHS curriculum (Arda & Ocak, 2012; Riggs, Greenberg, Kusché, & Pentz, 2006).

As pointed out in In Practice 10.2, truancy can lead to criminal behavior. Research also indicates that students who become truant often eventually drop out of school completely (OJJDP, 1996, p. 49). Schools and the police have become more actively involved in reducing truancy, in some cases working in collaboration with specialized truancy courts. In Milwaukee, local police officers pick up truants and take them for counseling while the school works with parents to support regular school attendance. The prosecuting attorney can get involved when efforts fail. In a community in California, the police issue citations for truants and return students to school for meetings with school officials and the student's parents. In Connecticut, a truancy court is used to identify why the student is missing school and to work to resolve the issues. In other areas of the country, probation officers and civil court fines are used to reduce missed school days (OJJDP, 1996). Research on truancy courts has been mixed. One study in 2010 found the following:

The [truancy court] was most successful in increasing attendance for students with severe truancy, but had limited impact on students with moderate truancy, and no impact on mild truancy. The intervention did not result in improved school attachment or grade point averages, nor did it significantly reduce discipline offenses. Furthermore, the aftercare intervention, consisting of regular meetings with an authority figure (e.g., a juvenile officer), was only effective at maintaining truancy court attendance gains for students with severe truancy at baseline, although it was associated with a substantial decrease in discipline offenses for all groups. These results suggest that truancy courts . . . may have an impact on truancy for severely truant students, but may have a limited effect on students with mild or moderate [truancy]. (Hendricks, Sale, Evans, McKinley, & DeLozier, p. 173)

Conversely, a 2006 study reported that a Truancy Court Diversion Program (TCDP) did the following:

[It] significantly impacted unexcused absences, unexcused tardies, and academic performance of the elementary and junior high students participating in the program. Elementary participants were more likely to maintain their improved attendance following participation than were junior high participants. Nonetheless, junior high participant grade point averages increased during TCDP and were maintained subsequent to TCDP. TCDP was an effective intervention for improving attendance and academic performance and helping preclude future delinquency. (Shoenfelt & Huddleston, 2006, p. 383)

Whether these types of courts and school interventions are effective long-term is yet to be determined. Some are also being challenged by the American Civil Liberties Union as unlawful and discriminatory, namely school resource officers, truancy courts, zero-tolerance policies, and out-of-school suspensions. The courts and school intervention programs are likely to continue and to transition and change to better meet the needs of the schools and the students involved.

IN PRACTICE 10.2

CONTRA COSTA COUNTY'S FIRST TRUANCY COURT GOES AFTER PARENTS

MARTINEZ—One by one, they approached the bench to answer to the judge.

"He's afraid—he doesn't want to go. I don't know what his issue with school is," Mt. Diablo Unified parent Maria Martinez said through an interpreter when asked why her fifth-grader had missed 51 days of classes the previous academic year and was late for 23 more.

Contra Costa Superior Court Judge Rebecca Hardie's response was swift and emphatic.

"It is your obligation under state law to be sure he's at school every day and on time," she told Martinez and her husband. "You must get your child to school."

For two hours every other Friday, Hardie hears cases that school districts have referred to the District Attorney's Office after exhausting attempts to convince parents that they need to get their child to class. Known as the parent truancy calendar, it's the latest effort among Contra Costa County officials to curtail chronic truancy, which they say costs area schools millions of dollars and leads to crime.

Inspired by a similar undertaking in Alameda County, the court and the District Attorney's Office this fall took a different tactic: Instead of the district attorney charging parents with a misdemeanor in extreme cases as it has done a handful of times in recent years, that office and the courts for the first time are trying to intervene before situations deteriorate.

The truancy court focuses on children ages 12 and below, those too young to be held responsible for their attendance record. Similar courts have been held in San Francisco and Solano counties.

"We're trying to intervene in situations where the parents are the ones who are essentially at fault," said Deputy District Attorney Laura Delehunt, noting that students typically don't start deciding to skip school until they're in their teens, when they have more control over their schedule.

A third-grader, by contrast, doesn't have that measure of independence or ability to get to school on his or her own, she said.

"That's on the parent," Delehunt said, adding that the reasons for truancy among younger students are all over the map—the parent might be using drugs, working two jobs, lack transportation or be distracted by a relationship.

"But what they all have in common is that (lack of) prioritization—most other things come first," she said.

Families' involvement with the legal system begins when Delehunt receives the files of students the law considers chronically truant or absent because they missed 10 percent or more of the school year.

She reviews the facts of each case in deciding whether to charge the parents with an infraction.

Akin to a traffic ticket, the offense doesn't carry any jail time, but parents still must appear in court. Those who plead guilty are placed on probation for one year and face $175 in fines and court fees.

During that period, the judge might require them to attend parenting classes, undergo family counseling or get help for other needs such as kicking a drug habit.

The idea is to identify the factors that are getting in the way of parents fulfilling their legal responsibility to keep their kids in school.

"The attendance problems are a symptom," Delehunt said. "Truancy is typically the tip of the iceberg. There are a whole host of issues that the child and parents are struggling with."

Delehunt and Hardie emphasize that their goal is to help, not harm.

"We want to work with you," Delehunt told the group of defendants who appeared on a summons in mid-October, the first of 17 who have been charged with infractions to date. "This isn't something where we want to . . . punish you."

As such, if a child's attendance shows a dramatic improvement over the next 12 months—Delehunt's looking for a near-perfect record—the court will dismiss the case and waive the monetary penalties.

If parents don't cooperate, however, they'll be charged with a misdemeanor and could end up spending one year in jail and with fines of up to $2,000.

By enforcing the state's Education Code, the hope is to reduce the number of young people who cause—and suffer from—the raft of social ills linked to chronic truancy.

For starters, kids who miss out on school don't master the three R's, can't keep up with their peers and consequently often quit school in frustration and embarrassment.

"Every single day missed is a day behind," Hardie told Pittsburg Unified parent Jamila Al-Malik, whose fifth-grader's spotty attendance history dates back to 2011, when she racked up 47 absences and 30 tardies.

(Continued)

(Continued)

Regardless of whether parents notify school officials that they're keeping their child home, that student is still passing up an opportunity to learn, Hardie added.

Hardie reiterated her point to Pittsburg parents Gary Brown and Stephanie Butler: Their fifth-grade daughter skipped 31 days of school last year and was late to class 41 times.

"The goal is simply to get her to school and get her caught up," Hardie said, adding that showing up for class is a habit that can be developed with practice. Since the hearing, their daughter has had no unexcused absences. "Children learn to read up to the third grade, but then they have to read to learn thereafter," she said, explaining that those who don't master the basics of English and math by then will have trouble in other subjects. "If there's a history of not going to school . . . by the time they're her age, it does become more of a mountain to climb."

Delehunt also tries to disabuse parents of the notions that elementary school absences aren't as important as those in high school and that a child suffers only if he or she is gone for days at a time.

Truancy not only has a direct bearing on the dropout rate but also costs schools huge sums of attendance-based revenue.

In Contra Costa County, 30.4 percent of children in grades K–5 met the Education Code's mildest definition of truancy during the 2013–14 academic year, according to state Attorney General Kamala Harris' 2015 report on elementary school attendance.

By missing at least three days of school or arriving late that many times without a valid reason, they cost schools just over $36 million in state funding, the analysis revealed.

And the financial drain on society as a whole runs into the billions. Studies confirm the connection between a lack of education, low wages and unemployment, which equates to lost tax revenue—earning even a high school diploma can make a significant difference, said Contra Costa District Attorney Mark Peterson.

And plenty of research has concluded that high school dropouts are also more likely to get involved in drugs and gangs, driving up the bill that taxpayers are footing for incarcerating offenders.

"If one kid stays out of prison, it saves all of us $50,000 a year," Peterson said.

Hardie routinely sees the nexus between truancy and crime in the juvenile delinquency cases she hears twice a week.

But statistics aren't deterring her or others working on behalf of the county's youths from tackling these sweeping problems one family at a time.

"If you think about preventing crime, any time that you can do it, you can imagine there's one less jail cell that's filled, one less victim," Delehunt said. "I feel like it's such important work."

Source: "Contra Costa County's Truancy Court Goes After Parents" (2016).

Questions to Consider

1. True or False: Truancy is a delinquent offense that should result in a 48-hour lock-up in a detention facility.

2. Multiple Choice: In cases of truancy,

   a. parents are solely responsible and should be punished to the fullest extent of the law.

   b. the child is solely responsible and should be punished to the fullest extent of the law.

   c. the child should be treated as a status offender.

   d. schools have a responsibility to go to a home and physically bring a child to school.

3. If you were a judge in a truancy court and a 12-year-old claimed to be afraid to go to school, what action would you take? What alternatives would you provide to the child and family? Would you use fines and jail?

Alternative education programs for expelled students have also become more widespread as school districts report increases in the number of students expelled and the length of the expulsion (OJJDP, 1996, p. 65). Such programs include enhanced skills training, community internship programs, and more general attempts to integrate the school and the community in the interests of serving the needs of marginal students and those who do not anticipate attending college. LifeSkills Training programs, implemented by teachers in the classroom, are directed at sixth and seventh graders and are designed to prevent or alleviate tobacco, alcohol, and marijuana use (Mihalic, Irwin, Elliot, Fagan, & Hansen, 2001). Research on alternative education programs shows an increase in graduation rates, attendance, and motivation and a decrease in the negative behaviors that brought the student to the alternative school in the first place (OJJDP, 1996). Illinois's Regional Safe Schools program and Georgia's Mountain Education Center program, both discussed earlier in this chapter, are prime examples of alternative education environments at work.

Wilderness Programs

Wilderness programs had their origins in the forestry camps of the 1930s. These programs involve small, closely supervised groups of juveniles who are confronted with difficult physical challenges that require teamwork and cooperation to overcome them. The intent of the programs is to improve the self-esteem of the juveniles involved while teaching them the value of cooperative interaction. Wilderness programs, which last from roughly 1 month to 1 year or longer, do not typically accept violent juveniles. Some provide counseling and follow-up services, whereas others do not. Juveniles may be sent directly to these programs as an alternative to detention or may participate in the programs after more traditional dispositions have been imposed.

Evaluations of wilderness programs have been fraught with methodological difficulties. Much of the information concerning the success of the programs has been provided by program developers and staff and is anecdotal in nature. Most of the evidence provided under these less-than-ideal conditions shows that the programs lead to somewhat lower recidivism rates than no programs at all, but the effectiveness of the programs is in question.

Restorative Justice Programs

The philosophy of restorative justice centers on the assertion that crime and delinquency affect persons instead of the traditional assertion that crime affects the state. Howard Zehr (2002), viewed as the leading visionary in restorative justice, defined restorative justice as "a process to involve, to the extent possible, those who have a stake in a specific offense and to collectively identify and address harms, needs, and obligations in order to heal and put things as right as possible" (pp. 19–20). Umbreit, Vos, Coates, and Lightfoot (2005) claim that restorative justice "is grounded in the belief that those most affected by crime should have the opportunity to become actively involved in resolving the conflict" (p. 255). Table 10.1 contains a summary of the principles involved in restorative justice.

Restorative justice advocates programs such as victim–offender mediation, victim-impact panels, community service, and community sentencing. Schools have even adopted a variety of programs and approaches commonly used in restorative justice. These programs include restorative dialogue techniques between teachers and students and restorative conferencing that involves students, staff, family, and community members (Fronius, Persson, Guckenburg, Hurley, & Petrosino, 2016). Restorative justice programs are being used in place of punitive approaches to school misbehavior in some states, in response to the school-to-prison pipeline arguments. Research on restorative justice's effectiveness in schools is still unclear, but exploratory studies have shown some promising results in deterring negative student behaviors (Fronius et al., 2016). Traditionally, restorative justice

Table 10.1 Principles of Restorative Justice

- Crime is injury.
- Crime hurts individual victims, communities, and juvenile offenders and creates an obligation to make things right.
- All parties should be a part of the response to the crime, including the victim if he or she wishes, the community, and the juvenile offender.
- The victim's perspective is central to deciding how to repair the harm caused by the crime.
- Accountability for the juvenile offender means accepting responsibility and acting to repair the harm done.
- The community is responsible for the well-being of all its members, including both victim and offender.
- All human beings have dignity and worth.
- Restoration—repairing the harm and rebuilding relationships in the community—is the primary goal of restorative juvenile justice.
- Results are measured by how much repair was done rather than by how much punishment was inflicted.
- Crime control cannot be achieved without active involvement of the community.
- The juvenile justice process is respectful of age, abilities, sexual orientation, family status, and diverse cultures and backgrounds—whether racial, ethnic, geographic, religious, economic, or other—and all are given equal protection and due process.

Source: OJJDP (n.d.).

approaches are designed to hold youth accountable, take responsibility for the needs of the victim, and involve the community in support of the offending youth and victim (McGarrell, 2001).

The question is, how well does restorative justice work in practice? Most studies on restorative justice have focused on satisfaction rates of the participants, not recidivism. Feelings of satisfaction and fairness have consistently been high among the participants (Bradshaw & Roseborough, 2005). But what about recidivism? Walker (1998) indicated the following:

> Evaluations of experimental programs have tended to find slightly lower recidivism rates for offenders receiving restorative justice than for those given traditional sentences of prison or probation. The differences are not always consistent, however, and many questions remain regarding the implementation and outcomes of such programs. (p. 224)

Bradshaw and Roseborough (2005) found in their study that victim–offender mediation and family group conferencing were two restorative programs that showed the most promise in reducing recidivism. De Beus and Rodriguez (2007) found that status offenders and property offenders who participated in restorative justice programs were less likely to recidivate. Other researchers (Hayes, 2005; Rodriguez, 2005) have suggested that the type of offense may make a difference in participant recidivism, with violent offenders responding differently to the programs from property or nonviolent offenders. It has even been suggested that prior offending history is more indicative of recidivism after completing a restorative justice program than type of offense (Hayes & Daly, 2003). Needless to say, there is a necessity for additional research in this area.

Although it is likely that the informal sanctions imposed by family and community are more effective than threats of formal punishment, what happens when there is no sense of family or community? The sense of family and community may well be lacking in drug-ridden and economically ravaged neighborhoods. The concept of restorative justice may make sense for young middle-class offenders involved in minor first offenses but may be totally irrelevant for those living in the most crime-ridden areas of America (Walker, 1998, p. 225). In fact, the failure of these institutions is largely responsible for the development of our current criminal justice system. Although we see some movement toward a social justice approach, there is still little evidence of the rebirth or strengthening of these institutions today (Cox & Wade, 1996, pp. 48–50; Walker, 1998).

Other faith-based initiatives have developed under former president George W. Bush's established Center for Faith Based and Neighborhood Partnerships. Through this office, faith-based organizations apply for grants and funding to support programs aimed at drug prevention, violence prevention, at-risk youth, gang behaviors, and so on. Research on these programs is scarce; however, Ericson (2001) reported that faith-based groups are usually open to developing relationships with other agencies, have poor administrative or organizational structures (e.g., hiring practices, bookkeeping skills), and avoid preaching to the children about religion. Instead, they rely on relationship building and support. Under President Obama, the Center for Faith Based and Neighborhood Partnerships had a focus on grassroots initiatives to reduce poverty and teen pregnancy, while increasing the role of fathers in families (U.S. Department of Health and Human Services, n.d.). Under the new initiatives, faith-based organizations may not play as big a role in restorative justice approaches or crime control as originally thought.

Figure 10.2 is a graphic representation of the balanced-approach mission.

Figure 10.2 The Balanced Approach

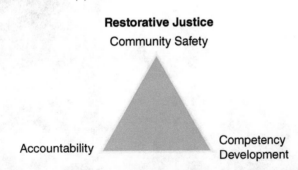

Restorative Justice
Community Safety

Accountability

Competency
Development

Clients/Customers	Goals	Values
Victims	Accountability	When an individual commits an offense, the offender incurs an obligation to individual victims and the community.
Youth	Competency development	Offenders who enter the juvenile justice system should be more capable when they leave than when they entered.
Community	Community safety	Juvenile justice has a responsibility to protect the public from juveniles in the system.

Sources: OJJDP (n.d.). Adapted from Malone, Romig, & Amstrong (1998).

Children and Family Services

As noted in Chapter 8, child protective services (CPS) (children and family services) agencies have goals similar to those of the juvenile justice system. These agencies provide, among other services, day care programs, foster care programs, youth advocacy programs, and advice to unwed mothers. In addition, they investigate reported cases of child abuse and neglect. Children and family services agencies deal with all categories of juveniles covered by most juvenile court acts, provide individual and family counseling services, and are empowered to refer suitable cases to appropriate private agencies. In addition, they can provide financial aid to children and families in need.

Like most state offices, children and family services agencies are often caught up in political change. Although many of these agencies require a bachelor's or master's degree for employment and emphasize the need for professionalism among staff members, skillful and competent administrative personnel are often replaced when the political party in power changes. As a result, the continuity of policies implemented by these agencies frequently leaves much to be desired. Nonetheless, state agencies concerned with providing services to children and families often have considerable power and, when administered appropriately, can provide multiple services to children in trouble. When not administered in the proper way, results can be disastrous.

Federal Programs

The federal government has sponsored many programs that, although not designed specifically as delinquency prevention programs, did encourage children to accept and attain lawful objectives through institutionalized means of education and employment. Examples of some of the varied federal programs

© iStockphoto.com/DGLimages

Early childhood education programs may help to prevent later delinquency.

provide some insight into the value of these programs in preventing delinquency and crime, illustrate the focal points of these programs, and show how they attempt to improve the social ills that result in delinquency (Yablonsky & Haskell, 1988).

There have been a number of federally funded programs aimed at improving educational and occupational opportunities for disadvantaged children. A secondary benefit of many of these programs was believed to be a decrease in the likelihood of delinquency among the children involved. The projects Head Start and Follow Through were designed to help culturally deprived children catch up or keep pace during their preschool and early school years. Previously, many children from culturally and/or economically deprived parents lagged behind other children in verbal and reading skills. Starting far behind in basic skills, many of these children never caught up, and school too often became an experience characterized by failure and rejection. As a result, many dropped out of school as soon as possible, often during their first or second year of high school. Of those who did drop out, many went on to become delinquent. Head Start and Follow Through have shown that children who are socioeconomically disadvantaged can, and do, make progress when parents, teachers, and volunteers focus their efforts on these children (Eitzen & Zinn, 1992, p. 399). Perhaps the most successful federally funded school program to prevent delinquency is the High/Scope Perry Preschool Project in Ypsilanti, Michigan. This program focused on a group of 123 African American 3- and 4-year-olds identified as being at risk for school failure in 1962. Of these children, 58 were assigned to the preschool program, and 65 were assigned to a control group. Data concerning these children was collected periodically for some 40 years. The results of the research showed that children who had participated in the preschool program for 2 and a half hours per day, Monday through Friday, for 2 years (1) had lower rates of delinquency than did the control group, (2) had lower teen pregnancy rates than did the control group, (3) were less likely to be dependent on welfare than were the control group members, and (4) were more likely to graduate from high school than were the control group members (High/Scope Educational Research Foundation, 2002). Demonstrating a trickle-down effect, some states have picked up on this trend by funding prekindergarten programs in public schools and in private day care centers (as done in Georgia). In 2014–2015, more than 1.4 million children attended state-funded pre-K programs. Although funding for pre-K programs had declined during the economic downturn, "state spending topped $6.2 billion, an increase of over $553 million, although two-thirds of this increase can be attributed to New York" (National Institute for Early Education Research, 2015, p. 5).

Along slightly different lines, a number of federal laws providing assistance to the hard-core unemployed were passed. For example, the Manpower Development and Training Act, the Vocational Education Act, the Economic Opportunity Act, the Rehabilitation Program for Selective Service Rejectees, the Comprehensive Employment and Training Act, the Job Training Partnership Act, and the President's Youth Opportunities Campaign had objectives of aiding young people in finding employment by helping them to become more readily employable. The basic assumption underlying these programs has been that employment is an important key to solving the problems of many young people.

The emphasis of youth opportunity centers is to increase employability through counseling or to provide vocational and prevocational training and work training programs. This approach recognizes that if young people, handicapped by inadequate education and lack of occupational skills, are to become employable, they must somehow be provided with additional training. It is hoped that these young people will then be absorbed into the labor market once their performance capabilities are improved.

Similarly, the Job Corps program was directed at individuals 16 to 21 years of age with the principal objective of providing training in basic skills and a constructive work experience. The Job Training Partnership Act of 1981 also promised new hope for young people seeking their first jobs when it replaced the scandal-ridden Comprehensive Employment and Training Act.

All of these programs have been geared toward providing youth with employment opportunities that, it is hoped, will lead them to a better life. The basic underlying assumption seems to be that young people employed in jobs for which they are suited are less likely to engage in delinquent or criminal activity than are young people who are not employed and have little hope of finding any worthwhile employment.

During recent years, the federal government has given attention to the concept of mentoring. In 1992, Congress amended the Juvenile Justice and Delinquency Prevention Act of 1974 to include the Juvenile Mentoring Program (JUMP) because of a growing belief that positive bonds between children and adults can forge actions or behaviors essential to a healthy life (Bilchik, 1998b). The 1998 JUMP report to Congress said the following:

> Historically, the notion of one individual providing caring support and guidance to another individual has been reflected in a variety of arenas. In the clinical mental health field, we talk about bonding and the importance of a child feeling connected to a nurturing adult in the early years of life. In the adoption field, we talk about the need for attachment. In schools, tutors help support successful educational experiences. In juvenile and family court, Court Appointed Special Advocates (CASAs) provide support and advocacy for children in need of assistance. In the substance abuse field, we make use of sponsors to support sobriety. In the business field, we create teams to ensure that new employees have the support they need to be successful in the corporate organizational system. Currently, there are many types of formal mentoring programs generally distinguishable by the goals of their sponsoring organization. Most youth oriented programs recognize the importance of ensuring that each child they serve has at least one significant adult in his/her own life that can be friend, role model, guide, and teacher of values. If that person is not available in the child's family, mentors can help fill the critical gap. (p. 5)

By using JUMP, the federal government helped modify behaviors committed by children that can lead to juvenile delinquency, gang participation, and increased school dropout rates and to enhance the academic performance of the children participating in the program. All JUMP programs have been sponsored by local community organizations with the help of federal grants. Findings indicate that both children and their mentors found the relationship to be rewarding (Novotney, Mertinko, Lange, & Baker, 2000, p. 5). The federal government continues to offer grants that sponsor mentoring programs throughout the United States.

The role of the federal government in programs designed specifically to prevent delinquency has been somewhat limited as a result of the belief that the primary responsibility for these programs rests with the states. Although there have been scattered efforts in the field of juvenile justice by the federal government (e.g., the development of the Children's Bureau in 1912, the development of various federal commissions and programs in 1948, 1950, and 1961), the ones most relevant to prevention occurred in 1968 with the Juvenile Delinquency Prevention and Control Act and in 1974 with the Juvenile Justice and Delinquency Prevention Act. The Juvenile Delinquency Prevention and Control Act permits allocation of federal funds to the states for delinquency prevention programs, and the Juvenile Justice and Delinquency Prevention Act attempts to create a coordinated national program to prevent and control delinquency (OJJDP, 1979). The Juvenile Justice and Delinquency Control Act also called for an evaluation of all federally assisted delinquency programs, a centralized research effort on problems of juvenile delinquency, and training programs for persons who work with delinquents. This law directs spending of funds on diverting juveniles from the juvenile justice system through the use of community-based programs such as group homes, foster care, and homemaker services. In addition, community-based programs and services that work with parents and other family members to maintain and strengthen the family unit are recommended.

The Juvenile Justice Amendments of 1977 made it clear that, in the opinion of Congress, the evolution of juvenile justice in the United States had resulted in excessive and abusive use of incarceration under the rubric of "in the best interests of the child" and that the prohibitions of contact with adult offenders and incarceration of status offenders and nonoffenders (e.g., dependent or neglected children) were to be taken seriously (OJJDP, 1980).

A wide variety of community and state agencies have become involved in delinquency prevention. Most efforts have been independent and uncoordinated. By the 1950s, the delinquency prevention effort in virtually every state and large city was like a jigsaw puzzle of services operating independently. The agencies concerned with delinquency prevention included the schools, recreation departments, public housing authorities, public welfare departments, private social agencies, health departments, and medical facilities. Davidson, Redner, and Amdur (1990) came to the conclusion that although diversion programs can provide positive results, territorial jealousies remain difficult to overcome.

Other Diversion and Prevention Programs/Therapeutic Courts

Although it would be impossible to list and discuss all prevention and diversion programs, we mention a few more here. The concept of teen courts has originated as a way to keep first-time juvenile offenders who commit minor offenses and are willing to admit guilt from being processed in the formal juvenile justice system. Local civic agencies or schools, in conjunction with the police department and the juvenile court, sponsor most of these programs. The courts use four models of design ranging from limited adult involvement to youth tribunals. In the most common teen court model—adult judge model—teens under 17 years of age process the cases by acting as prosecutor, defense counsel, bailiff, and clerk and determine the punishment for the cases by acting as the jury. An adult attorney acts as the judge to ensure the fairness and legality of the sentencing (Butts & Buck, 2000). The offender is required to complete the sentence handed down by the teen jury. If the offender does not abide by the sentencing guidelines, he or she is referred to the juvenile court for formal processing. The goal of these programs is to hold juveniles accountable for their actions and attempt to divert them from further delinquency but not to stigmatize them by formally processing them in the juvenile justice system. Research on teen courts' ability to reduce recidivism has shown few positive results (Forgays, 2008; Hissong, 1991; North Carolina Administrative Office of the Courts, 1995; Seyfrit, Reichel, & Stutts, 1987). Studies on participant satisfaction (Colydas & McLeod, 1997; McLeod, 1999; Reichel & Seyfrit, 1984; Wells, Minor, & Fox, 1998) have been positive as have studies on perceived procedural fairness (Butler-Mejia, 1998) and attitudes toward authority (LoGalbo, 1998; Wells et al., 1998).

Drug courts, a form of therapeutic court, are another attempt to prevent children and adults from continuing deviant behaviors. Drug courts aim to stop the abuse of alcohol and other drugs (AODs) through the use of intensive therapeutic supervision. According to Huddleston, Marlowe, and Casebolt (2008), there were 2,147 drug courts in operation as of the end of 2007 and approximately 70,000 individuals being served by such courts. Recent research has raised some issues regarding drug courts, particularly with regard to graduation rates and offender characteristics. In a review of drug court literature, Stein, Deberard, and Homan (2013) found the following:

One clear trend in the available studies was the dramatic difference in recidivism rates for adolescents who succeed in graduating from drug court, relative to those who do not. In addition, the review revealed that behavior patterns evidenced during drug court participation were most strongly associated with both the probability of graduating successfully from drug court and recidivism (e.g., few in-program arrests, citations, detentions, and referrals; greater length of time in program or amount of treatment; lower use of drug and alcohol use, few positive urine screens, greater school attendance). Unfortunately, non-white participants tend to have a lower probability of graduation from drug court and experience higher recidivism during and following the program. Available juvenile drug treatment court studies confirm a number of reputed adolescent risk factors associated with substance abuse, criminality, treatment failure, and recidivism among adolescents (e.g., higher levels of emotional and behavioral problems, higher levels and severity of pre-program substance abuse, male gender). (p. 159)

Other research has shown that drug courts are effective because they improve substance abuse treatment outcomes, reduce crime, and show greater cost benefits than other strategies. Additionally, the U.S. Government Accountability Office stated in 2005 that adult drug court programs reduce crime by lowering rearrest and conviction rates among graduates of the court (Huddleston et al., 2008, p. 2). The programs have been expanded, with positive results, to youth identified as having drug and alcohol problems. Following the lead of teen and drug courts, other specialty courts have come into existence. Known as problem-solving or therapeutic courts, these courts focus on social issues that emerge in the traditional court system but that cannot be adequately dealt with through traditional court means and sanctions. Problem-solving courts geared primarily at common youth issues include community courts (which focus on quality-of-life offenses), domestic violence courts, family dependency courts (which address the needs of youth who are abused or neglected as a result of parental substance abuse), and mental health courts.

In addition to the prevention and diversion programs already mentioned, there have been a number of attempts to scare juveniles away from delinquent behavior. The best known, although not the earliest, of these programs was publicized nationally through a television film called *Scared Straight*. The film recorded a confrontation between juveniles brought into Rahway State Prison in New Jersey and inmates housed in the prison. Such confrontation was based on the theory that inmates could frighten juveniles to the extent that they would be deterred from committing further delinquent acts. *Scared Straight* reported that of the 8,000 juveniles participating in such sessions through 1978, about 90% had not been in trouble with the law again. Nationwide attention was focused on attempts to frighten juveniles out of delinquency, and such programs were viewed by some as a panacea for delinquency problems (Finkenauer, 1982). However, more objective evaluations of this and other such programs have yielded, at best, mixed results. It is certain that such programs are not a panacea for delinquency, and some appear to increase rather than decrease the frequency of recidivism. In fact, even though this type of program has again gained popularity among television audiences because of A&E's *Beyond Scared Straight* reality series, Lundman (1993) recommended the permanent abandonment of efforts to scare and inform juveniles "straight."

Yet another attempt at preventing delinquency and diverting delinquent children involves the use of community policing models oriented toward juveniles. These programs operate on the assumption that community policing officers are more likely to favor problem-solving and peacekeeping roles with children than are their traditional counterparts (see Chapter 8). Officers who view their roles in these terms may be more likely to try to help children before they get into trouble or to divert them away from the juvenile justice network (Bazemore & Senjo, 1997; Belknap, Morash, & Trojanowicz, 1987).

There are a host of other agencies providing services that complement those of the juvenile justice system. These include YMCAs and YWCAs, both of which often provide counseling and recreation programs. One alarming trend among these agencies is that membership fees have tended to eliminate the opportunity for some children to use the services available. Some YMCA and YWCA programs seem to discourage rather than encourage the participation of children whom we would consider to be most at risk because they have little interaction with adults and few resources.

In many areas, community mental health clinics provide services based on a sliding-fee scale. Other agencies, such as Catholic Social Services, Vocational Rehabilitation Services, and the Boy and Girl Scouts of America, also use a sliding scale to determine fees for counseling, membership, testing, and employment referrals. Still other agencies provide essentially the same services free of charge. These agencies typically include community centers, Big Brother Big Sister volunteer programs, alcohol and drug clinics, and hotline programs. In addition, many colleges and universities offer counseling services free of charge or based on a sliding scale.

Some Criticisms

As indicated previously, delinquency prevention programs usually employ one of two strategies: either (1) reform of society or (2) individual treatment. Both strategies, as generally employed, have had difficulties. Programs oriented toward reforming society have been quite costly in terms of the results produced, depending on whether results are measured in terms of alleviating educational, occupational, and economic difficulties or in terms of reducing delinquency. Lack of coordination among various programs, inter-program jealousy, considerable duplication, and mismanagement have seriously hampered the effectiveness of these programs. As a result, much of the money intended for juveniles with problems ends up in staff salaries, and many of the personnel hired to help supervise, train, and educate these juveniles are tied up in dealing with administrative red tape. In addition, programs attempting to improve societal conditions may take a long time to show results. The extent to which any results can be attributed to a specific program is extremely difficult to measure. As a result, the public is frequently hesitant to finance prevention programs because they have no immediately visible payoffs. In fact, it may be that diversion programs simply do not work either because the concept is flawed or because the current system does not provide an opportunity for them to work. Some see diversion as an interesting concept with "unanticipated negative consequences" (Mays & Winfree, 2000, p. 116).

There are those prevention programs directed at providing individual treatment. These deal with children who have already come into contact with the juvenile justice system and attempt to prevent further contact. As noted previously, there are inherent difficulties in attempting to reform or rehabilitate juveniles after they have become delinquent. Many of the basic assumptions about programs directed at preventing future delinquent acts by those already labeled as delinquent are highly questionable. For example, it is doubtful whether individual therapy will be successful if the juvenile's problems involve family, school, and/or peers. Similarly, the belief that recreational or activity programs, in and of themselves, are beneficial in reducing delinquency seems to be more a matter of faith than a matter of fact at this time.

Another type of individual treatment program attempts to identify juveniles who are likely to become delinquent before a delinquent act is committed. These programs may be called early identification programs or predelinquency detection programs. Although these programs are clearly intended to nip the problem in the bud, they may be criticized for creating the very delinquency they propose to reduce; that is, identifying a juvenile as predelinquent focuses attention on the juvenile as a potential problem child and, therefore, labels him or her in much the same way as official juvenile justice agencies label juveniles as delinquent. In one sense, then, the juvenile is being treated (and sometimes punished) for something that he or she has not yet done. Programs directed toward pure prevention may, unintentionally, lead juveniles to be labeled earlier by identifying them at an earlier stage. This phenomenon is often referred to as net widening (discussed earlier in this chapter).

Some time ago, Edwin M. Schur encouraged the development of an approach to delinquency prevention. We believe (and have suggested at other points in this book) that it has considerable merit. His approach is called radical nonintervention. According to Schur (1973), "The primary target for delinquency policy should be neither the individual nor the local community setting, but rather the delinquency-defining processes themselves" (p. 154). Rather than consistently increasing the number of behaviors society refuses to tolerate, we should develop policies that encourage society to tolerate the "widest possible diversity of behaviors and attitudes" (Schur, 1973, p. 154). Much of the behavior currently considered delinquent is characteristic of adolescence, is nonpredatory in nature, and is offensive only because it is engaged in by juveniles. Because in one sense it is rules that produce delinquents, it might make more sense to change the rules (as we have done at the adult level in terms of alcohol consumption, abortion, and homosexuality) than to attempt to change juveniles or the entire society overnight. One approach, then, would be to make fewer activities delinquent and to concentrate on enforcing rules for violations that may actually be harmful to the juvenile, society, or both. In other cases, our best strategy may be simply to "leave kids alone wherever possible" (Schur, 1973, p. 154).

Supporting Schur's (1973) contention is the fact that the OJJDP (1979) found that a number of programs have no defensible basis whatsoever (e.g., those based on presumed personality differences or biological differences), others are poorly implemented (e.g., behavior modification programs in treatment settings without community follow-up), and still others of questionable merit are based only on preliminary evidence (e.g., most predelinquency identification programs).

Finally, Sherman and colleagues (1997), in a systematic review of literature on crime prevention, concluded that some programs seem to work but that many do not. More important, perhaps, the authors concluded that the programs that work best are those in communities that need them least and that true prevention probably lies outside the realm of criminal justice. Indeed, many programs seem to work where schools and families are stable, but few appear to be successful where schools and families are torn apart by drugs, crime, and violence. Walker (1998), in reviewing this and other studies, concluded the following:

> We found that most current crime [delinquency] policies and proposed alternatives are not effective. We found that both conservatives and liberals are guilty of peddling nonsense with respect to crime policy. . . . The truth about crime policy seems to be that most criminal justice-related policies will not make any significant reduction in crime. (p. 279)

Thus, as we indicated earlier in the book, if we wish to prevent at least some crime and delinquency, we must seek solutions in the broader social structure by focusing on unemployment, poverty, and discrimination; maintaining stable families (whatever their structure); and providing meaningful education for all children.

Child Abuse and Neglect Prevention Programs

Many of the specific programs we have discussed are oriented toward diverting delinquents and preventing delinquency. There are also numerous programs aimed at preventing child abuse and neglect. The majority of these programs are offered by state CPS agencies and, in most cases, are in collaboration with schools, the police, day cares, and community-based agencies. These programs include clothing drives, food pantries, parenting classes, money management classes, anger management classes, and day care cost assistance, just to name a few.

As is the case with delinquency prevention programs, none of them are foolproof—none are a panacea.

CAREER OPPORTUNITY: BIG BROTHER BIG SISTER PROGRAM DIRECTOR

Job description: Work with children and their families interested in forming relationships with adult mentors. Work with adult volunteers who choose to develop mentoring relationships with children. Interview, assess, and train volunteers, children, and families. Supervise and monitor adult-to-child mentoring matches. Facilitate support groups. Be responsible for recruiting children and adult mentors from the community.

Employment requirements: Must have a minimum of a bachelor's degree in social work, counseling, guidance, psychology, or a related field. Must have experience in working directly with children within a social-service agency or similar surroundings, excellent oral and written communication skills, assessment and counseling skills, problem-solving skills, experience with diverse populations, and (usually) some experience in public speaking. Required to work some evenings and, on occasion, weekends.

Beginning salary: Salary ranges from $20,000 to $40,000, depending on the location of the position. Benefits vary by geographical location but typically include paid medical, dental, and vacation as well as a 401(k) plan.

Summary

All practitioners interested in the welfare of juveniles with problems should be familiar with the wide range of programs available in most communities. Teachers should not hesitate to consult personnel from children and family services agencies or law enforcement officials when appropriate or to enter into long-term agreements about sharing information in the interests of intervening appropriately with children in trouble. It is important to remember that the goal of each of these agencies is the same—to provide for the best interests of children. Territorial jealousy must be eliminated, and practitioners must learn to share their expertise with those outside their agency. It is not a sign of failure or weakness to recognize and admit that a particular problem could be dealt with more beneficially by personnel from an agency other than one's own. Concerned practitioners should provide direct services when it is possible and should not hesitate to make referrals when doing so is necessary or desirable.

Probably the best way to combat delinquency and child abuse is to prevent them from occurring in the first place. There are at least three ways to accomplish some form of prevention: (1) changing juvenile behavior, (2) changing the rules governing that behavior, and (3) changing societal conditions leading to that behavior. Although the last named probably holds the most promise for success, it is also the least likely to occur.

By establishing good working relationships among schools, families, and juvenile justice practitioners, early detection of serious juvenile problems may be facilitated, and proper referrals may be made. Clearly, if the old adage that "an ounce of prevention is worth a pound of cure" is true, early detection and the support of the family as the primary institution influencing juvenile behavior are crucial to prevention programs. It is true that educational and vocational projects, community treatment programs, family involvement in intervention, and the use of volunteers and nonprofessionals show some effectiveness. Recreation, individual and group counseling, social casework, and the use of detached workers (gang workers) may also be effective under some conditions.

At the same time, it is clear that many juvenile offenses are of a nonserious nature and that the statutes creating these offenses could be changed. We need to assess the necessity or desirability of many statutes and move to change those that serve no useful purpose and those that do more harm than good.

Practitioners are also in an excellent position to detect and report types of behavior that, in their experience, frequently lead to the commission of serious delinquent acts. Use of their experiences in combination with well-designed research projects will, it is hoped, lead to modified, more satisfactory theories of causation. Recognizing the variety of factors involved, the range of alternative programs available, and the strengths and weaknesses of prevention programs should lead to greater success in dealing with juveniles.

Preventing delinquency and child abuse is more desirable than attempting to rehabilitate delinquents or salvage battered and neglected juveniles from an economic viewpoint, from the viewpoint of the juveniles involved, and from society's viewpoint. It is hoped that commitment by both government and the private sector will facilitate more effective prevention and lead to the abandonment of ineffective programs. Examination of some of the basic assumptions of current prevention programs is essential as is the incorporation of evidence-based practices in those programs that exist or those being developed.

There are a number of agencies operating programs that complement or supplement juvenile justice programs. Coordinating and organizing these programs to eliminate duplication and increase efficiency has been shown to be difficult as the result of territorial jealousy. Nonetheless, the best way to ensure the welfare of juveniles with problems is to share knowledge through interagency cooperation and referral, and budgetary restraints are currently dictating that this be accomplished.

KEY TERMS

diversion   259

drug courts   277

faith-based initiatives   273

Follow Through   275

functionally related agencies   259

Head Start   275

Juvenile Mentoring Program (JUMP)   276

mental health courts   278

net widening   260

postadjudication intervention   255

preadjudication intervention   255

primary prevention   256

pure diversion   259

radical nonintervention   280

restorative justice   271

Scared Straight   278

school-to-prison pipeline   261

secondary diversion   259

secondary prevention   256

social promotion   260

teen courts   277

territorial jealousy   260

tertiary prevention   256

truancy courts   267

wilderness programs   271

Critical Thinking Questions

1. What are the major approaches to delinquency prevention? What are the strengths and weaknesses of each? Discuss some contemporary attempts to prevent delinquency or divert delinquents, and tell why you believe they are effective or ineffective.

2. List some of the assumptions you believe are basic to delinquency prevention and diversion programs. To what extent do you feel each of these assumptions is justified? Why is the public often unwilling to finance prevention programs, and what are the consequences of this unwillingness?

3. What is territorial jealousy? Why does it occur, and what are some of its consequences?

4. Statistics point to the fact that the use of drugs contributes to criminal behavior. Do you think drug courts (and other types of therapeutic courts) can adequately address the causes of drug use and result in reduced juvenile offending? Why or why not?

5. Discuss at least two agencies or programs with goals similar to those of the juvenile justice system. In your opinion, how successful are these agencies in achieving their goals?

6. Discuss some of the attempts currently being made to prevent child abuse and neglect. Are such programs operating in your community?

Suggested Readings

Beale, A. V., & Hall, K. R. (2007). Cyberbullying: What school administrators (and parents) can do. *The Clearing House, 18*, 8–12.

Butts, J. A., & Buck, J. (2000). *Teen courts: A focus on research*. Washington, DC: Office of Juvenile Justice and Delinquency Prevention. Retrieved from www.ncjrs.gov/pdffiles1/ojjdp/183472.pdf

Carnevale Associates. (2006). *A longitudinal evaluation of the new curricula for the D.A.R.E. middle (7th grade) and high school (9th grade) programs: Take charge of your life—Year four progress report*. Retrieved from www.dare.com/home/Resources/documents/DAREMarch06ProgressReport.pdf

Centers for Disease Control and Prevention. (2011). *Youth Risk Behavior Surveillance System (YRBSS)*. Retrieved from www.cdc.gov/HealthyYouth/yrbs/index.htm

Darnell, A. J., & Emshoff, J. G. (2008). *Findings from the evaluation of the D.A.R.E. Prescription and Over-the-Counter Drug Curriculum*. Atlanta, GA: Emstar Research. Retrieved from www.dare.com/home/Resources/documents/DAREReport0821_final.pdf

Dembo, R., Wareham, J., & Schmeidler, J. (2005). Evaluation of the impact of a policy change on diversion program recidivism. *Journal of Offender Rehabilitation, 41*(3), 29–61.

Esbensen, F.-A. (2004). *Evaluating G.R.E.A.T.: A school-based gang prevention program* (Research for policy). Washington, DC: National Institute of Justice.

Esbensen, F.-A., Peterson, D., Taylor, T. J., & Osgood, D. W. (2012). *Is G.R.E.A.T. effective? Does the program prevent gang joining? Results from the National Evaluation of G.R.E.A.T.* St. Louis, MO: University of Missouri–St. Louis. Retrieved from www.umsl.edu/ccj/pdfs/great/GREAT%20Wave%204%20Outcome%20Report

Farrington, D. P., & Welsh, B. C. (2007). *Saving children from a life of crime: Early risk factors and effective interventions*. New York, NY: Oxford University Press.

Federal Bureau of Investigation. (n.d.). *Cyber crime*. Retrieved from https://www.fbi.gov/investigate/cyber

Greenwood, P. (2008). Prevention and intervention programs for juvenile offenders. *Future of Children, 18*(2), 185–210.

Hendricks, M. A., Sale, E. W., Evans, C. J., McKinley, L., & Carter, S. D. (2010). Evaluation of a truancy court intervention in four middle schools. *Psychology in the Schools, 47*(2), 173–183.

Hinduja, S., & Patchin, J. W. (2008). Cyberbullying: An exploratory analysis of factors related to offending and victimization. *Deviant Behavior, 29*, 129–156.

Huddleston, C. W., Marlowe, D. B., & Casebolt, R. (2008). *Painting the current picture: A national report card on drug courts and other problem-solving court programs in the United States*. Alexandria, VA: National Drug Court Institute, Bureau of Justice Statistics. Retrieved from www.ndci.org/sites/default/files/ndci/PCPII1_web%5B1%5D.pdf

Illinois State Board of Education. (2012). *Regional safe schools program: FY 2012 data summary*. Retrieved from www.isbe.state.il.us/research/pdfs/rssp_data_summary12.pdf

Lipsey, M. W., Wilson, D. B., & Cothern, L. (2000). *Effective intervention for serious juvenile offenders*. Retrieved from www.ncjrs.gov/html/ojjdp/jjbul2000_04_6/contents.html

Luxenburg, H., Limber, S. P., & Olweus, D. (2015). *U.S. bullying in schools: 2014 status report*. Center City, MN: Hazelden. Retrieved from http://olweus.sites.clemson.edu/documents/Bullying%20in%20US%20Schools—2014%20Status%20Report.pdf

McCollister, K. E., French, M. T., & Fang, H. (2010). The cost of crime to society: New crime-specific estimates for policy and program evaluation. *Drug and Alcohol Dependence, 108*(1–2), 98–109.

Mihalic, S., Fagan, A., Irwin, K., Ballard, D., & Elliot, D. (2004). *Blueprints for violence prevention*. Washington, DC: U.S. Department of Justice, Office of Juvenile Justice and Delinquency Prevention.

Nelson, L., & Lind, D. (2015). *The school to prison pipeline, explained*. Justice Policy Institute. Retrieved from http://www.justicepolicy.org/news/8775

Office of Juvenile Justice and Delinquency Prevention. (2011). *Department of justice examines impact of bullying in schools: New study recommends strategies to address bullying and support victims*. Retrieved from www.ojp.gov/newsroom/pressreleases/2011/JJ_PR-121611.pdf

PATHS. (2010). PATHS results and recognitions. *Channing-Bete Company*. Retrieved from www.channing-bete.com/prevention-programs/paths/results-recognition.php

Perry, C. L., Komro, K. A., Veblen-Mortenson, S., Bosma, L. M., Farbakhsh, K., Munson, K. A., . . . Lytle, L. A. (2003). A randomized controlled trial of the middle and junior high school D.A.R.E. and D.A.R.E. Plus programs. *Archives of Pediatric and Adolescent Medicine, 157*, 178–184. Retrieved from http://archpedi.ama-assn.org/cgi/reprint/157/2/178?maxtoshow=&hits=10&

RESULTFORMAT=&fulltext=a+randomized+ controlled+trial+of+the+middle+and+junior+high+ school&searchid=1&FIRSTINDEX=0& resourcetype=HWCIT

Puzzanchera, C., Stahl, A., Finnegan, T., Snyder, H., Poole, R., & Tierney, N. (2000). *Juvenile court statistics 1997* (NCJ180864). Washington, DC: Department of Justice, Office of Juvenile Justice and Delinquency Prevention.

Roman, C. G., Kane, M., Baer, D., & Turner, E. (2009). *Community organizations and crime: An examination of the social-institutional processes of neighborhoods.* Washington, DC: Urban Institute Justice Policy Center, Final Research Report. Retrieved from www.ncjrs.gov/pdffiles1/nij/ grants/227645.pdf

Shariff, S., & Johnny, L. (2007). Cyber-libel and cyber-bullying: Can schools protect student reputations and free-expression in virtual environments? *Education Law Journal, 16,* 307–342.

Stein, D. M., Deberard, S., & Homan, K. (2013). Predicting success and failure in juvenile drug treatment court: A meta-analytic review. *Journal of Substance Abuse Treatment, 44*(2), 159–168.

Thornberry, T. P., Huizinga, D., & Loeber, R. (2004). The causes and correlates studies: Findings and policy implications. *Juvenile Justice, 9*(1). Retrieved from www.ncjrs.gov/html/ojjdp/203555/jj2.html

Vincent, G. M., Guy, L. S., & Grisso, T. (2013). *Risk assessment in juvenile justice: A guidebook for implementation.* Chicago, IL: MacArthur Foundation. Retrieved from www .macfound.org

Ybarra, M. L., & Mitchell, K. J. (2004). Youth engaging in online harassment: Associations with caregiver-child relationships, Internet use, and personal characteristics. *Journal of Adolescence, 27,* 319–336.

Zehr, H. (2002). *The little book of restorative justice.* Intercourse, PA: Goodbooks.

$SAGE edge™

Sharpen your skills with SAGE edge at **edge.sagepub.com/coxjj9e**. SAGE edge for students provides a personalized approach to help you accomplish your coursework goals in an easy-to-use learning environment. You'll find action plans, mobile-friendly eFlashcards, and quizzes as well as video and web resources and links to SAGE journal articles to support and expand on the concepts presented in this chapter.

Dispositional Alternatives

11

On completion of this chapter, students should be able to do the following:

- List and describe dispositional alternatives
- Discuss the dispositional phase of the juvenile justice process
- Discuss probation, conditions of probation, and revocation
- Discuss the relationship between probation and restorative justice
- List advantages and disadvantages of foster homes
- List advantages and disadvantages of treatment centers
- Discuss juvenile corrections, dilemmas, and consequences
- Present arguments for and against capital punishment for juveniles
- Address possible solutions to the effects of incarceration

WHAT WOULD YOU DO?

James has been on your caseload for shoplifting for about 4 months. He has had bruises and welts on his arms before, but when asked, he says that they are from falling, roughhousing with his brother, or altercations with kids at school. You have not thought much about them, although you continue to watch him for other signs of abuse. You have also noticed that he is quick to anger, often wears clothes that are inappropriate for the weather, and shies away from being touched.

Today, the community service officer calls you and says that you need to come down to the detention center where the kids are washing cars. He reports that James has some pretty significant marks that he'd like you to look at.

Upon arriving, you see James spraying the water hose and laughing and playing with a couple of the other boys. You walk over to him and start a conversation. You notice he's wearing a long-sleeve shirt and jeans even though it's almost 80 degrees outside. You also notice that he has the sleeves pulled down even though they are getting wet on the ends. After talking for a minute, you ask him to give the water hose to someone else and to step over to the side of the parking lot with you. He does. You ask him about his home life, school, and brother. Then you ask him if there's anything he should tell you or anything he'd like to share. He says no. You ask him if he's been hurt and if he feels safe at home. He shrugs his shoulders and looks away but then

(Continued)

(Continued)

nods yes. You then ask him to pull his sleeves up so you can see his arms. He does so and you see 15 to 20 cuts on each arm starting just at the elbow. Some are deep and have started to scab. Others look similar to cat scratches.

When you ask James about the cuts, he shrugs his shoulders and starts to move away from you and back to the car wash area. You again ask him if they are self-inflicted or if someone cut him. He doesn't say anything. Finally, you get him to stop walking and compassionately ask him who did this to him. He says, "You know my mom . . . she gets mad and stuff." At this point, you decide to ask him if there are other injuries. He pulls up his shirt to reveal slashes on his back and several small cigarette burns on his side. Then he quickly puts his shirt down and jogs back over to where the kids are washing cars. He tries to rejoin the group and doesn't look at you again.

What Would You Do?

1. Do you consider the marks signs of abuse? Why or why not?

2. Who would you contact about the abuse, and what would you state in the report you may be required to file?

3. Would you confront the mother about the cuts and marks? Why or why not?

When attempts to divert a child from the juvenile justice network fail, an adjudicatory hearing is held to determine whether the juvenile should be dismissed or categorized as a delinquent; as a minor in need of supervision (or authoritative intervention); or as an abused, neglected, or dependent child. After adjudication, the judge must make a decision concerning appropriate disposition. The judge uses his or her own expertise and experience, the social background (social summary or predisposition) investigation report, and sometimes the probation officer's or caseworker's recommendation in arriving at a decision.

Many states use a bifurcated hearing process so that the adjudicatory and dispositional hearings are held at different times. This is often preferred because different evidentiary rules apply at the two hearings. Whereas only evidence bearing on the allegations contained in the petition is admitted at the adjudicatory hearing, the totality of the juvenile's circumstances may be heard at the dispositional hearing.

The alternatives available to the judge differ depending on the category in which the juvenile has been placed, but in general they range from incarceration to treatment, foster home placement, or probation. In the *Gault* case, the U.S. Supreme Court specifically declined to comment on the applicability of due process requirements during the dispositional phase of juvenile court proceedings (*In re Gault*, 1967). Thus, we must turn to state statutes or lower-court decisions in analyzing this process. Keep in mind that the purpose of the dispositional hearing is to determine the best way to correct or treat the juvenile in question while protecting society. To accomplish these goals, the court must have available as much information as possible about the juvenile, his or her background (e.g., family, education, legal history), and available alternatives. Evidence pertaining to the welfare of the juvenile is generally admissible at this stage of the proceedings, and the juvenile should be represented by counsel.

Although some nondelinquent juveniles, typically those found to be in need of supervision, may be confined temporarily in specifically designated facilities, the trend had been toward diverting them to other types of programs. In some cases, the child is permitted to remain with the family under the supervision of the court; in others, custody reverts to the state, with placement in a foster or adoptive home. The extent of state intervention has been a subject of considerable controversy, but when the welfare of the child is involved, termination of parental rights may be the only way to provide adequate protection.

Delinquent conduct always involves a violation of the law—unlike some of the other conduct dealt with by the juvenile court. There are numerous available dispositions for juveniles in this category, including probation (release after trial with court supervision) under conditions prescribed by the court, placement in a restrictive or secure facility not operated by the department of corrections, and commitment to a public correctional facility. The latter disposition is generally used as a last resort but may be necessary to protect society. In some cases, restitution is used in addition to probation or as a disposition in and of itself. In other cases, weekend incarceration or community-based correctional programs are used. These programs allow juveniles to remain in the community, where they may attend school, work part-time, and participate in supervised activities. The effectiveness of such programs is an empirical question, and many of these programs are not adequately evaluated.

Youth may be sentenced by the juvenile or specialized court to complete community service. In this instance, youth clean the streets rather than be incarcerated.

Probation

A juvenile delinquent on probation is released into the community with the understanding that his or her continued freedom depends on good behavior and compliance with the conditions established by his or her probation officer and/or the judge. Probation, then, gives the delinquent a second chance to demonstrate that he or she can function in the community. The history of probation goes back to the 14th century, when offenders could be entrusted to the custody of willing citizens to perform a variety of tasks. The founding father of probation is said to be John Augustus, who attended criminal court proceedings during the 1850s and took selected offenders into his home so that they might avoid prison. The city of Boston had hired a probation officer by 1878, other cities and states followed suit, and all states had adopted probation legislation by 1925. The National Probation Act, passed in 1925, authorized federal district court judges to hire probation officers as well (Cromwell, Killinger, Kerper, & Walker, 1985).

A major finding of past presidential commissions has been that the earlier and deeper an offender goes into the juvenile justice system, the more difficult it is for him or her to get out successfully. Unnecessary commitments to correctional institutions often result in "criminalized" juveniles. The revolving door of delinquency and criminality is perpetuated as a result. The fact that there may be a short-term benefit from temporarily removing some juveniles from society should be tempered with the realization that, once released, some juveniles are more likely to jeopardize the community than if they had been processed under adequate probation services in the community where they must eventually prove themselves anyway. Because the goal of the juvenile court is therapeutic rather than punitive, probation is clearly in accord with the philosophy of the court. When circumstances warrant probation, when the juveniles for whom probation is a viable alternative are carefully selected, and when adequate supervision by probation officers is available, probation seems to have potential for success. Failure to take proper precautions in any of these areas, however, jeopardizes chances of success and adds to the criticism of probation as an alternative that coddles delinquents.

Probation is clearly the most frequent disposition handed down by juvenile court judges, accounting for more than 90% of all dispositions in some jurisdictions. Despite pressures exerted by the mass media (in the form of coverage of some exceptionally disturbing offenses committed by probationers), juvenile court judges have generally adopted the philosophy that a juvenile delinquent will usually benefit more from remaining with his or her family or under the custody of other designated persons in the community than from being incarcerated.

In making a disposition, the juvenile court judge traditionally places heavy emphasis on the current offense; the preferences of the complainant; and the juvenile's prior legal history, family background, personal history, peer associates, school record, home, and neighborhood. In addition, consideration is given to whether justice would be best served by granting probation or whether incarceration is necessary for the protection of the public. There are a multitude of other factors considered by judges, including the juvenile's attitude toward the offense and whether the juvenile participated in the offense in a principal or secondary capacity. The degree of aggravation and premeditation, as well as mitigating circumstances, is also considered. This information is provided to the judge in the social background investigation (also known as the social summary report or predisposition report).

Once probation has been granted, certain terms and conditions are imposed on the probationer. Within broad limits, these terms and conditions are left to the discretion of the judge and/or probation officer. The requirements that the probationer obey all laws of the land, attend school on a regular basis, avoid associating with criminals and other persons of ill repute, remain within the jurisdiction, and report regularly to the probation officer for counseling and supervision are general terms and conditions usually imposed by statutory decree. Other requirements that the court may impose include curfews, drug testing, counseling, community service, and restorative justice programming. Although the court has broad discretion in imposing the terms and conditions of probation, these terms and conditions must be reasonable and relevant to the offense for which probation is being granted. For example, in *People v. Dominguez* (1967), a condition that the female defendant could not become pregnant while unmarried was not considered to be related to the robbery for which she was adjudicated delinquent. The appellate court reasoned that a possible pregnancy had no reasonable relationship to future criminality. In *Jones v. Commonwealth* (1946), an order of a juvenile court requiring regular attendance at Sunday school and church was held to be unconstitutional because "no civil authority has the right to require anyone to accept or reject any religious belief or to contribute any support thereto." However, a condition of probation that requires a defendant to pay costs or make restitution is generally upheld provided that the amounts ordered to be paid are not excessive in view of the financial condition of the defendant. Any condition that cannot reasonably be fulfilled within the period fixed by the court is not likely to be upheld.

The importance of adhering to the terms and conditions of probation is stressed because violations constitute a basis for revocation of probation and the imposition or execution of the sentence that could have been given originally by the judge. There are generally three types of violations: (1) technical, (2) rearrest for a new crime or act of delinquency, and (3) absconding or fleeing jurisdiction. A technical violation is usually characterized by the probationer flagrantly ignoring the terms or conditions of probation but not actually committing a new act of delinquency. For example, deliberately associating with delinquent peers might lead to revocation if such behavior was prohibited as a condition of probation. Typically, technical violations include minor infractions on behalf of the probationer. Technical violations are generally worked out between the probationer and probation officer, and they usually do not result in revocation action unless the probationer develops a complete disregard for the terms or conditions of probation. A rearrest or new custody action due to a new act of delinquency is obviously a serious breach of probation. The seriousness of the new act of delinquency is important in determining whether revocation proceedings will be initiated. Most rearrests are viewed by probation officers as serious and usually result in the revocation of probation, although there is some room for discretion. Although absconding or fleeing the juvenile court's jurisdiction may be considered a technical violation, it is generally considered separately and may result in revocation action.

Release on probation is conditional (i.e., probation as conditional release)—that is, the liberty of the probationer is not absolute but rather subject to the terms and conditions being met. Although the probation officer may seek a revocation of probation, the court will ultimately determine whether to revoke probation. When juveniles violate the conditions of supervised release and face revocation of probation, issues of due process with respect to right to counsel and standard of proof arise. In *Morrissey v. Brewer* (1972), the U.S. Supreme Court held that although a parole revocation proceeding is not a part of the criminal prosecution, the potential loss of liberty involved is nevertheless significant enough to entitle the parolee to due process of law. First, the Court held that the parolee is entitled to a preliminary hearing to determine whether there is probable cause to believe that a violation of a condition has occurred. Second, an impartial examiner will conduct the hearing. Finally, notice of the alleged violation, purpose of the hearing, disclosure of evidence to be used against the parolee, opportunity to present evidence on the parolee's own behalf, and limited right to cross-examination are allowed under due process. Subsequently, in *Gagnon v. Scarpelli* (1973), concerning the issue of probation revocation proceedings, the Court held that a probationer was entitled to the same procedural safeguards announced in *Morrissey v. Brewer* (1972), including requested counsel. Previously, in *Mempa v. Rhay* (1967), the Court held that when the petitioner had been placed on probation and his sentence deferred, he was entitled by due process of law to the right to counsel in a subsequent revocation proceeding because the revocation proceeding was a continuation of the sentencing process and, therefore, the criminal prosecution itself. Most courts, in the absence of statute, have held that the probation violation need be established only by a preponderance of the evidence even if the violation is itself an offense.

There are several dispositions available in revocation hearings. If the charges are vacated, the probationer may be restored to probation or the conditions may be altered, may be amended, or may even remain the same. The revocation may be granted with a new disposition generally resulting in an intermediate sanction or a commitment to a juvenile correctional institution. The juvenile may also be sentenced to a treatment center if the revocation was due to behavior requiring treatment such as drug or alcohol abuse.

Although the length of probation varies among states, the maximum term of probation for the juvenile is usually not beyond the maximum jurisdiction of the juvenile court. Most terms of juvenile probation are between 6 months and 1 year, with possible extensions in most states. Probation dispositions are usually indeterminate, leaving the release date up to the discretion of the probation officer. On successful completion of the probation period, or on the recommendation of the probation officer for early discharge, termination of probation releases the juvenile from the court's jurisdiction.

Although probation serves the purpose of keeping the juvenile in the community while rehabilitation attempts are being made, there are some potential dangers built into this disposition. Learning and labeling theories indicate that proper supervision of probationers is essential if rehabilitation is to occur. Otherwise, the juvenile placed on probation may immediately return to the "old gang" or behavior patterns that initially led to his or her adjudication as delinquent.

Similarly, the juvenile placed on probation, while remaining with his or her family, may end up in the same negative circumstances that initially led to delinquent behavior except that he or she has now been labeled and is, more or less, "expected" to misbehave. The labeling process may exaggerate problems in family, school, and peer relations, and the juvenile may find it difficult to meet the expectations established for him or her. In many cases, the only positive role model available is the probation officer, whose caseload may preclude seeing the juvenile for more than a few minutes a week.

To remedy the problems of limited probation officer time and lack of sufficient supervision of the probationer, several strategies are employed. The first of these is electronic monitoring, which uses technology to track the whereabouts of the probationer. A bracelet is placed on the wrist or ankle of the juvenile in question, and his or her whereabouts can be determined by signals transmitted and picked up by a receiver maintained by the probation officer. In some cases, the juvenile is placed under house arrest for a specified period; in other cases, the juvenile may be allowed to go to school or work but must be home during certain hours. A second strategy involves intensive supervision, which is usually reserved for juveniles facing their last chance before incarceration. Probation officers working in intensive supervision programs have limited caseloads, make frequent contacts with their charges, make contacts with the families of the probationers, contact school authorities and/or employers periodically, work with clients at times other than normal working hours, and keep extensive records of their contacts. They typically review the conditions of probation regularly and adjust them as needed. A third strategy involves the use of day reporting centers (DRCs) (in combination with the two strategies discussed previously or by itself). DRCs provide highly structured, nonresidential programs for series juvenile offenders. They offer a wide range of services such as educational or GED classes, drug and alcohol treatment, conflict resolution, life-skills training, and anger management, to name a few. The offender is required to report to the DRC daily for a specified period. The assumptions on which these programs are based are that the probation officer as role model, supervisor, and disciplinarian will be more effective if he or she spends more time with each client and the disposition of probation will be more effective if the client is heavily supervised and involved in diversion programming.

Another attempt at providing better probationary services for delinquents involves contracting with private agencies. The Office of Juvenile Justice and Delinquency Prevention (OJJDP) and other state and local agencies have contracted with private organizations to provide services (e.g., counseling, job readiness skills, and wilderness programs) for probationers to supplement the public services provided. The American Correctional Association (2012) supports the use of private services in its policies, maintaining that the government is ultimately responsible for corrections and should use all resources available to accomplish the goals of corrections. In 2004, the OJJDP (2004a) reported that there are more privately run secure and treatment facilities for juveniles than public facilities, although public facilities hold the majority of juveniles. "In 2010, private facilities accounted for 51% of facilities holding juvenile offenders; however, they held just 31% of juvenile offenders in residential placement" (Hockenberry, 2013, p. 3). In 1999, the American Correctional Association conducted a survey concerning private sector involvement in juvenile corrections. The survey revealed that 46 jurisdictions indicated they had at least one active private-sector contract. The main reason given for such a contract was that private-sector vendors could provide services and expertise that were lacking in the jurisdictions in question (Levinson & Chase, 2000).

One more addition to probation services has been restorative justice practices. Restorative justice (see Chapter 10) is a philosophy that has been adopted by juvenile courts as a supplement to probation services. The roots of restorative justice can be traced to 1974 in Ontario, Canada. The Mennonite Central Committee, through the help of a probation officer, created the first mediation program involving the basic principles of restorative justice. This program, called a victim–offender reconciliation program, used the payment of restitution directly to the victim by the offender as its core. Traditionally, payment of restitution to the victim was handled directly by the probation office in an impersonal manner. By forcing the offender to pay the restitution directly to the victim, the process was construed as a repayment for loss and damages to an individual rather than a state-mandated court fine for a harm done to the state. The success of this program initiated interest in restorative justice in the United States and in other parts of Canada.

Elkhart, Indiana, was the first U.S. city to initiate a victim–offender mediation program during the late 1970s. As the philosophy grew, a nonprofit organization called the Center for Community Justice, based on the restorative justice philosophy, was created in 1979. Since the 1980s, restorative justice has been called by a variety of different names depending on the agency applying its concepts. Although the name may change, the definition and core concepts of restorative justice—accountability, competency, and public safety—remain the same in all programs.

First, accountability in restorative justice is used to explain how offenders are to respond to the harm they have caused to victims and the community. Accountability requires that offenders take personal responsibility for their actions, face those they have harmed, and take steps to repair harm by making amends. Much of the literature regarding restorative justice calls this process "making things right" or "repairing the harm" (Center for Restorative Justice and Mediation, 1996; Restorative Justice for Illinois, 1999). In one state example, Illinois has used the restorative justice philosophy in its juvenile court since 1999 and has been implementing restorative justice programming across the state. As noted in Figure 11.1, many of the programs, discussed shortly, focus on accountability as well as other restorative justice approaches.

Second, restorative justice requires competency on behalf of offenders. Competency is not the mere absence of bad behavior; it is the provision of resources for persons to make measurable gains in educational, vocational, social, civic, and other abilities that enhance their capacity to function as productive citizens (Bazemore & Day, 1996; Restorative Justice for Illinois, 1999). Restorative justice suggests that programs be designed to promote empathy in offenders, to teach effective communication skills to offenders, and to develop conflict resolution skills in offenders. Programs such as victims of crime impact panels (VCIPs), victim–offender mediation programs, and programs sponsored by community-run self-help groups such as Mothers Against Drunk Driving (MADD) strive to teach competency to offenders. One competency program

Figure 11.1 Restorative Justice Practices From Illinois

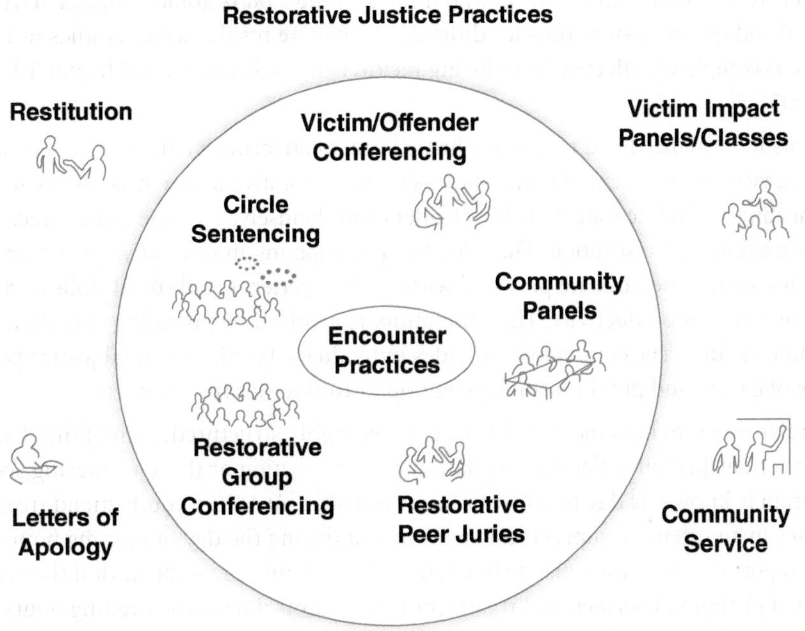

Restorative Justice Practices

Restitution · Victim/Offender Conferencing · Victim Impact Panels/Classes · Circle Sentencing · Community Panels · Encounter Practices · Restorative Group Conferencing · Restorative Peer Juries · Letters of Apology · Community Service

Source: Illinois Balanced and Restorative Justice Initiative (n.d.).

is being used in southeast Missouri for juvenile offenders. This program uses a VCIP to increase empathy levels in juvenile offenders by asking victims of crime to tell offenders how the crimes have affected their lives. MADD offers a similar program by using victim impact panels to build empathy in offenders of drunk driving.

Public safety is the third area of restorative justice. "Public safety is a balanced strategy that cultivates new relationships with schools, employers, community groups, and social agencies" (Restorative Justice for Illinois, 1999, p. 1). Public safety also facilitates new relationships with victims. "The balanced strategy of restorative justice invests heavily in strengthening a community's capacity to prevent and control crime" (Bazemore & Day, 1996, p. 7). The concept of public safety relies heavily on the community. The community, according to restorative justice, should make sure of the following:

The laws which guide citizens' behaviors are carried out in ways which are responsive to our different cultures and backgrounds—whether racial, ethnic, geographic, religious, economic, age, abilities, family status, sexual orientation, and other backgrounds—and all are given equal protection and due process. (Center for Restorative Justice and Mediation, 1985, p. 1)

Restorative justice also proclaims that crime control is not the sole responsibility of the criminal justice system but rather is the responsibility of the members of the community. Sentencing circles, reparative boards, and citizen councils are examples of the public safety concept in application.

Reducing recidivism is typically the baseline for showing that a program is effective. In a review of restorative justice programs, Umbreit, Vos, and Coates (2006) found that reports examining recidivism rates after victim–offender mediation and group circles have been mixed. Rodriguez (2007) found that juveniles in a restorative justice program in Maricopa County, Arizona, were less likely to recidivate than juveniles in the comparison group when controlling for legal and extralegal factors. Hayes and Daly (2003) reported that those juveniles who believe that the reparation plan is arrived at in consensus instead of being forced on them are less likely to reoffend than are those who do not. Studies on restorative justice have been plagued by methodological and quality issues, thus it's difficult to compare results across studies or to say that restorative justice is completely effective in reducing recidivism, as discussed in Chapter 10 (Bradshaw & Roseborough, 2005).

The participants in a balanced and restorative justice system are crime victims, offenders, and the community. Crime victims are essential to the success of the restorative justice process because they are involved in the healing and reintegration of the offenders and themselves. Crime victims receive support, assistance, compensation, and restitution. The offenders participating in restorative justice programs provide repayment to their communities and are provided with work experience and social skills necessary to improve decision making and citizen productivity. The community is involved by providing support to both the offenders and crime victims. The community provides individuals, besides criminal justice personnel, to act as mentors to the offenders and provides employment opportunities for the offenders.

Of late, a popular program has emerged that focuses on highly structured, community-based programming for serious juvenile offenders on "last chance" probation or those reentering society. Mentioned earlier, this program is known as day treatment centers or DRCs. At DRCs, youth attend treatment and educational classes in an intensive supervision environment during the day or evening hours. In most instances, youth report to DRCs immediately following release from school (or work if they are employed) and participate in a plethora of correctional treatment curriculums during the evening hours and on the weekends. Probation officers, parole officers, and day treatment staff meet with the youth to address ongoing needs and risks (OJJDP, 2004b). Research on these programs is ongoing and has focused on a variety of indicators of success to include rehabilitation principles (Ostermann, 2009), client outcomes (Craddock, 2000), recidivism (Craddock & Graham, 2001), and other evaluative criteria (Jones & Lacey, 1999; Van Vleet, Hickert, & Becker, 2006). Martin, Lurigio, and Olson, in a 2003 study of the Cook County, Illinois, DRC program, reported fewer rearrests and reincarcerations for offenders who participated in the treatment and found better reentry results for those who participated in the program for a longer period. In 2009, Solomon investigated the impact of a New York City DRC, which serviced misdemeanor offenders and found a program completion success rate of approximately 80% over the 2 years under investigation. Ostermann (2009) found that membership in DRCs had a positive and statistically significant effect on rearrest when compared to offenders not being supervised. Roy and Barton (2006) have reported that the literature on DRCs represents a range of program completion success as low as 13.5% up to 84% or higher depending on the criteria used to evaluate the program. Winokur Early, Hand, Blankenship, and Chapman (2010) examined the impact of the AMIkids Community-Based Day Treatment Services offered to at-risk and delinquent youth in Florida. Their evaluation found that youth who received services in this program were "significantly less likely to be rearrested, rearrested for a felony offense, adjudicated or convicted for an offense, convicted for a felony offense, and subsequently committed, placed on adult probation, or sentenced to prison within 12 months of release compared with youth who completed residential programming" (p. 2). With regard to postprogram success rates, Roy and Barton (2006) claimed that there have been few studies on this topic and that those that do exist report an arrest rate between 20% and 44%. It should be noted here that few of these studies focus specifically on DRCs dedicated to juvenile offenders only. So, given the relatively recent and increased use of the DRC model with juveniles and the complete gap in research that focuses specifically on youth involved in these programs, readers are cautioned to critically consider the results with regard to reductions in juvenile offending and not to make assumptions that DRCs are more effective in juvenile justice than they may actually be.

Juveniles placed on probation with families or support persons who are concerned and cooperative may benefit far more from this disposition than from placement in a correctional facility. In an attempt to provide this solid foundation for juveniles whose own families are unconcerned, uncooperative, or the source of the delinquent activity or abuse or neglect in question, the juvenile court judge may place the juvenile on probation in a foster home.

Foster Homes

When maintenance of the family unit is clearly not in the juvenile's best interests (or in the family's best interests, for that matter), the judge may place a juvenile in a foster home. Typically, foster homes are reserved for children who are victims of abuse or neglect. Delinquent children may spend a short time in a foster home, but these children seem more suited for treatment facilities and the services they offer. Ideally, foster homes are carefully selected through state and local inspection and are to provide a concerned, comfortable setting in which the juvenile's behavior may be modified or in which the abused or neglected child can be nurtured in safety.

Foster parents provide the supervision and care that are often missing in the juvenile's own family and provide a more constant source of supervision and support than does the probation officer. As a result, the juvenile's routine contacts should provide a more positive environment for change than would be the case if the juvenile were free to associate with former delinquent companions or unconcerned, abusive, or criminal parents. Foster homes are frequently used as viable alternatives for minors who have been abused or neglected, or who are dependent or in need of supervision, because many of these children are caught up in dangerous situations at home. It is often clearly in their best interests to be removed from their natural families.

Foster homes undoubtedly have a number of advantages for children who are wards of the court—provided that the selection process for both foster parents and the children placed with them is adequate. Unfortunately, some couples apply for foster parent status in the belief that the money paid by the state or county for housing such juveniles will supplement their incomes. If this added income is the basic interest of potential foster parents, only limited guidance and assistance for foster children can be expected. In addition, many of these couples soon find that the money paid per foster child is barely adequate to feed and clothe the child and, therefore, does not enhance their incomes. Thus, careful selection of foster parents is imperative; foster parents who may injure or kill children in their care are unsuitable and must be weeded out during the process (see In Practice 11.1). The number of foster children is growing more rapidly than the number of foster parents willing to take on the responsibility. According to the Child Welfare Information Gateway, ending in September 2014, there were approximately 415,129 children in the U.S. foster care system with the majority (46%) of them living in nonrelative foster homes (Child Welfare Information Gateway, 2014). Although this placement may be suitable, and possible, for some, it's not feasible for all.

IN PRACTICE 11.1

FOSTER PARENTS INDICTED FOR MURDER IN DEATH OF 2-YEAR-OLD

A 2-year-old girl in foster care in Henry County, Georgia, was found dead 10 months ago. Her foster parents are accused of malice murder, felony murder, aggravated battery, and child cruelty after the child was found to have a history of injuries going back to more than one month prior to her death. The district attorney believes the foster mother struck the child in the abdomen with such force that the child's pancreas was split. The girl then died from shock resulting from blood loss.

The foster mother's attorney claims the girl's death was a tragic accident and the foster mother had tried to perform the Heimlich maneuver on the child when she was choking on some chicken. According to the attorney, the force used by the foster mother during the maneuver was too excessive and may have injured the girl.

The child had lived with the foster parents for 4 months prior to her death. There was evidence that the 2-year-old child was abused over time and there were injuries noted throughout her body at the time of the autopsy.

Source: Adapted from "Foster parents indicted for murder in death of 2-year-old Laila Daniel"

by Craig Schneider, *The Atlanta Journal-Constitution.* (2016).

Questions to Consider

1. True or False: It is impossible for states to positively identify who will be a "good" foster parent and who will be a "bad" foster parent. It is really just "luck of the draw" for children in foster care.

2. Multiple Choice: If abuse occurred, an autopsy will likely show indications of which of the following?

   a. A swollen tongue

   b. Black on the soles of the feet

   c. Bruises throughout the body in various stages of healing

   d. All of the above

3. According to the article, do the new charges of malice murder, felony murder, aggravated battery, and child cruelty seem warranted? Why or why not?

No matter how careful the juvenile court judge is in selecting children for foster home placement, some placements are likely to involve children whose behavior is difficult to control. As a result, the number of couples willing to provide foster care for delinquent and abused juveniles is never as great as the need. Compounding the issue is that even if a family is willing to care for a child and meets the strenuous requirements, they may not want to foster school-aged teenagers and children with special needs. Foster families must be carefully screened through on-site visitations and interviews and must possess those physical and emotional attributes that will be supportive for any child placed with them. Assuming responsibility for a delinquent, abused, or neglected juvenile placed in one's home requires a great deal of commitment, and many juveniles who might benefit from this type of setting cannot be placed due to the lack of available families and the unwillingness to foster the most needy of abused and neglected children. Alternatives available to the judge in such cases include placement in a treatment center, placement in a group home, and incarceration in a juvenile correctional or shelter care facility. According to the U.S. Department of Health and Human Services (2002) Office of Inspector General, residential facility placements like institutions and group homes are becoming more popular as a result of issues discussed earlier (i.e., lack of foster homes).

Treatment Centers

Throughout this book, it has been indicated that juveniles should be diverted from the juvenile justice system when the offenses involved are not serious and when viable alternatives are available. Status offenders and abused, neglected, or dependent juveniles clearly should not be incarcerated. There may, of course, be times when the only option available to the court is to provide temporary placement in shelter care facilities, foster homes, or group homes when conditions preclude a return to the family. In cases where the juvenile in question may present a danger to himself or herself or to others, or where the juvenile may flee, temporary placement may be necessary.

Placement may also be necessary in cases where the juvenile's family is completely negligent or incapable of providing appropriate care and/or control. Temporary custody of dependent, neglected, and in-need-of-supervision juveniles, as well as nonserious delinquents, should be in an environment conducive to normal relations and contact with the community. Numerous private and public programs directed at such juveniles have emerged during the past decade.

Sentencing a child to a treatment center is often used in conjunction with probation but can be used alone. Children are sent to treatment programs for a variety of reasons, including chemical dependency, behavioral or emotional problems, sexual assault counseling, problems resulting from previous abuse or neglect, and attitudinal or empathy therapy. Facilities such as Boys Town of America specialize in treating children with behavioral problems. This facility uses small family-oriented cottages focused on behavior modification to teach delinquent children how to control impulsive behaviors that may lead to criminal acts. Other treatment centers use positive peer culture treatment programs, play therapy programs, anger management therapy, conflict resolution programs, and life skills programs, to name only a few. Treatment centers are rarely administered by the state, so the juvenile court contracts with private institutions to provide these services. Most delinquent children sentenced to terms in treatment centers are one step away from being sentenced to a correctional institution. Thus, successful completion of the treatment program determines whether the delinquent children will return to society or go to a correctional institution.

Juvenile Corrections

The most severe dispositional alternative available to the juvenile court judge considering a case of delinquency is commitment to a correctional facility. In a 2014 survey of private and public security facilities, 50,821 justice-involved youth who were younger than 21 were included on the census data, so there are clearly some juveniles whose actions cannot be tolerated by the community (Hockenberry, Wachter, & Sladky, 2016). Those who commit predatory offenses or whose illegal behavior becomes progressively more serious might need to be institutionalized for the good of society. For these delinquent juveniles, alternative options may have already been exhausted, and the only remedy available to ensure protection of society may be incarceration. Because juvenile institutions are often very similar to adult prison institutions, incarceration is a serious business with a number of negative consequences for both juveniles and society that must be considered prior to placement.

Although incarcerating juveniles for the protection of society is clearly necessary in some cases, correctional institutions frequently serve as a gateway to careers in crime and delinquency. The notion that sending juveniles to correctional facilities will result in rehabilitation has proved to be inaccurate in most cases. In 1974, Robert M. Martinson completed a comprehensive review of rehabilitation efforts and provided a critical summary of all studies published since 1945. He concluded that there was "pitifully little evidence existing that any prevailing mode of correctional treatment had an appreciable effect on recidivism" (Martinson, 1974, p. 54). Bernard (1992, p. 587) arrived at the same conclusion two decades later. In spite of the fact that most of the research on the effects of juvenile correctional facilities substantiates the conclusions of these authors, we have developed and frequently implement what may be termed an away syndrome. When confronted with a juvenile who has committed a delinquent act, we all too frequently ask, "Where can we send him [or her]?" This away syndrome represents part of a more general approach to deviant behavior that has prevailed for many years in America. The away syndrome applies not only to juveniles but also to the mentally ill, the mentally retarded, the aged, the disabled, and the adult criminal. This approach frequently discourages attempts to find alternatives to incarceration, arises frequently when we become frustrated by unsuccessful attempts at rehabilitation, and is frequently accompanied by an "out-of-sight, out-of-mind" attitude. Our hope seems to be that if we simply send deviants far enough away so that they become invisible, the juveniles and their problems will disappear. However, walls do not successfully hide such problems, nor will they simply go away. Not only do "graduates" from correctional institutions reappear, but also their experiences while incarcerated often seem to solidify delinquent or criminal attitudes and behavior. Most studies of recidivism among institutionalized delinquents lead to the conclusion that although some programs may work for some offenders some of the time, most institutional programs produce no better results than does the simple passage of time.

There are a number of alternative forms of incarceration available. For juveniles whose period of incarceration is to be relatively

The most severe dispositional alternative for juveniles is commitment to a correctional facility.

brief, there are many public and private detention facilities available. Treatment programs and security measures vary widely among these institutions. Both need to be considered when deciding where to place a juvenile. In general, private detention facilities house fewer delinquents and are less oriented toward strict custody than are facilities operated by the state department of corrections. Many of these private facilities provide treatment programs aimed at modifying undesirable behavior as quickly as possible to facilitate an early release and to minimize the effects of isolation. The cost of maintaining a delinquent in an institution of this type may be quite high, and not every community has access to such a facility.

Public detention and juvenile prison facilities frequently are located near larger urban centers and often house large numbers of delinquents in cells or dormitory-type settings. As a rule, these institutions are used only when all other alternatives have been exhausted or when the offenses involved are quite serious. As a result, most of the more serious delinquents are sent to these facilities. In these institutions, concern with custody frequently outweighs concern with rehabilitation. Typically, we see fences, razor wire, and guards at these facilities more often than we see treatment providers.

Secure facilities that house juvenile offenders may use solitary confinement and other restraints, similar to their adult counterparts. Sedlak and McPherson (2010) reported in a survey among youth in residential placement that at least 35% of youth reported being locked up alone or confined to their room with no contact with other residents at some point during their confinement. The majority claimed the isolation was for longer than 2 hours (87%) and more than one-half claimed to have been isolated for more than 24 hours (55%). Fifty-two percent of those isolated for more than 2 hours did not speak to a counselor after the conclusion of the isolation, as suggested by best practices in solitary confinement. Restraints were also reported to have been used on nearly 28% of the respondents in the survey (Sedlak & McPherson, 2010). Restraint types included handcuffs, wristlets, a security belt, chains, or a restraint chair. Juvenile respondents also reported being handcuffed or restrained during transportation to and from the facility and either personally experiencing or witnessing the use of pepper spray. Best practices in juvenile discipline procedures have dictated that restraint chairs and pepper spray only be used as last resorts and distinct protocol be followed when these approaches are exercised (Beyer, 2003; Roush, 1996). As a response to the overuse of solitary confinement in facilities for both juveniles and adults, President Obama asked the Bureau of Prisons to end the practice of using solitary confinement with juveniles. A Sentencing Reform and Corrections Act was also sponsored in the U.S. Congress in 2015 that would lawfully end juvenile solitary confinement in federal facilities; however, it is still pending (U.S. Department of Justice, 2016). States may want to adopt similar policies and consider best practices prior to using solitary confinement and restraints if there is truly a goal of rehabilitation and lowering juvenile recidivism rates upon release. As the discussion of learning and labeling theories indicates, current correctional environments are not the best places to mold juvenile delinquents into useful law-abiding citizens. As noted in the same study by Sedlak and McPherson (2010), most youth (63%) live in units where the majority of other offenders have committed person offenses. "Nearly one-fifth of the less serious career offenders (status offenders, technical parole violators, and youth who report no offense) are placed in living units with youth who have killed someone, and about one-fourth reside with felony sex offenders" (Sedlak & McPherson, 2010, p. 4). On the one hand, mixing less serious offenders with those who have extensive offending backgrounds raises both safety concerns as well as concerns about what the offenders may be learning from one another. On the other hand, placing youth with similar offending histories together may have a reinforcing effect, raising recidivism rates after release (Sedlak & McPherson, 2010). Clearly, sending a delinquent to a correctional facility to learn responsible, law-abiding behavior is like sending a person to the desert to learn how to swim. If our specific intent is to demand revenge of youthful offenders through physical and emotional punishment and isolation, current correctional facilities will suffice. If we would rather have those incarcerated juveniles return to society rehabilitated, a number of changes must be made.

First, we need to be continually aware of the negative effects resulting from isolating juveniles from the larger society—especially for long periods of time. This isolation, although clearly necessary in certain cases, makes reintegration into society difficult. The transition from a controlled correctional environment to the relative freedom of society is not an easy one to make for those who have been labeled as delinquent. This was demonstrated by Krisberg, Austin, and Steele (1989), who found recidivism rates of 55% to 75% among juvenile parolees (and these figures seem to remain fairly accurate today).

Second, it is essential to be aware of the continual intense pressure to conform to institutional standards that characterizes life in most correctional facilities. Although some juvenile institutions provide environments conducive to treatment and rehabilitation, many are warehouses concerned only with custody, control, and order maintenance. Correctional personnel frequently deceive the public, both intentionally and unintentionally, about what takes place in their institutions by providing tours that emphasize orderliness, cleanliness, and treatment orientation. Too often, we fail to see or consider the harsh discipline, solitary confinement, and dehumanizing aspects of correctional facilities. We also often fail to properly consider and treat the 13% to 15% of youth in correctional facilities who identify as lesbian, gay, bisexual, transgendered, or questioning (LGBTQ) (OJJDP, 2014). These youth may feel an overwhelming sense of pressure to conform to standards or face harassment, emotional abuse, physical and sexual assault, or prolonged isolation periods. Even with the implementation of the Prison Rape Elimination Act of 2003 and the requirements that correctional facilities create individualized housing and program placements for transgender and intersex individuals, facilities may not know how to properly treat and protect LGBTQ youth, placing these youth under even more intense pressure. We often fail to realize that the skills needed by all youth to survive in these institutions may be learned very well, but these are not the same skills needed to lead a productive life on the outside. It has been recommended that concerned citizens, prosecutors, public defenders, and juvenile court judges spend a few days in correctional facilities to see whether the state is really acting in the best interests of juveniles who are sent there.

Third, the effects of peer group pressure in juvenile correctional facilities must be considered. There is little doubt that behavior modification will occur, but it will not necessarily result in the creation of a law-abiding citizen. The learning of delinquent behavior may be enhanced if the amount of contact with those holding favorable attitudes toward law violation is increased. Juvenile correctional facilities are typically characterized by the existence of a delinquent subculture that enhances the opportunity for dominance of the strong over the weak and gives impetus to the exploitation of the unsophisticated by the more knowledgeable.

Into this quagmire we sometimes thrust delinquents who become involved in forced homosexual activities, who learn to settle disputes with physical violence or weapons, who learn the meaning of shakedowns and "the hole," and who discover how to "score" for narcotics and other contraband. Juvenile institutions have long been cited in cases of brutal beatings and other inhumane practices among residents (inmates) and between staff and residents. We are then surprised when juveniles leave these institutions with more problems than they had prior to incarceration.

It is clearly counterproductive to send juveniles to educational or vocational training 6 to 8 hours a day only to return them to a cottage or dormitory where "anything goes" except escape. Juveniles who are physically assaulted or gang raped in their dorm at night are seldom concerned about success in the classroom the next day. The delinquent subculture and the existence of gangs in juvenile correctional facilities requires a persona of toughness and the ability to manipulate others. Status is determined largely by position within this delinquent subculture, which often offsets the efforts of correctional staff to effect positive attitudinal and/or behavioral change. Because, as we saw earlier, the behavior demanded within the delinquent subculture is frequently contrary to behavior acceptable to the larger society, techniques for minimizing the negative impact of that subculture must be found.

A fourth problem frequently encountered in juvenile correctional facilities is the assignment to facilities and/or existing programs based on vacancies rather than on the benefit to the particular juvenile. Juveniles who need remedial education may end up in vocational training. Any benefits to be derived from treatment programs, therefore, are minimized.

A fifth problem involves mutual suspicion and distrust among staff members who see themselves as either rehabilitators or custodians. Rehabilitators often believe that custodians have little interest and expertise in treatment, whereas custodians often believe that rehabilitators are "too liberal" and fail to appreciate the responsibilities of custody. The debate between these factions frequently makes it difficult to establish a cooperative treatment program. In addition, juveniles frequently try to use one staff group against the other. For example, they may tell the social worker that they have been unable to benefit from treatment efforts because the correctional officers harass them physically and psychologically, keeping them constantly upset. This kind of report often contributes to the feud between custodians and caseworkers, who occasionally become so concerned with staff differences that the juveniles are left to do mostly as they please.

Finally, the development of good working relationships between correctional staff members and incarcerated juveniles is difficult. The delinquent subculture, the age difference, and the relative power positions of the two groups work against developing rapport in most institutions. Frankly, there is often little contact between treatment personnel and their clients. It is very difficult for the caseworker, who sees each of his or her clients 30 minutes a week, to significantly influence juveniles, who spend the remainder of the week in the company of their delinquent peers and the custodial staff. Because the custodial staff members enforce institutional rules, there is a built-in mistrust between the staff members and their charges. Sedlak and McPherson (2010) found that 43% of youth report living in units with relatively poor youth–staff relationships. Those in secure lock facilities (53%) are almost twice as likely to report negative relationships than those in unlocked units. Forty percent of youth say staff are difficult to get along with, 38% say staff are disrespectful, and 29% say staff are mean. Juveniles in community-based and residential treatment programs report more positive perceptions of staff, in general (Sedlak & McPherson, 2010). Regardless of youth perceptions, correctional officers deal with the day-to-day problems of incarcerated juveniles most frequently but may be treated poorly by caseworkers and not regarded as particularly competent.

Under these circumstances, it is not difficult to see why rehabilitative efforts often end in failure. Fortunately, some changes in the use of correctional institutions appear to be on the horizon. After decades of overincarceration of youth, for even minor offenses, there have been a number of reforms in some states to reduce the use of confinement. In fact, 2014 was the lowest recorded census of youth in confinement since 1975 (Hockenberry, Wachter, & Sladky, 2016). Arizona, Connecticut, Louisiana, Minnesota, and Tennessee are leading the way by reducing the number of youth incarcerated in their states by more than half from 2001 to 2010. Litigation concerning confinement and other administrative criticisms, splitting the juvenile corrections systems from the adult corrections system and partnering it with child welfare systems, improving interagency collaboration and communication, and having state leaders who commit the systems to holistic approaches in juvenile justice seem to be guiding the aggressive changes we see in these states (Juvenile Policy Institute, 2013). Another state that has made dramatic changes to its juvenile system is Missouri. Known as a leader in juvenile justice, Missouri has committed to the Juvenile Detention Alternatives Initiative (JDAI), which was introduced by the Annie E. Casey Foundation. At the end of 2013, this initiative was operating in 250 local jurisdictions in 39 states and the District of Columbia. It has eight main goals: (1) collaboration between the actors in the justice system, (2) collection and use of data to diagnose problems and impact of reforms, (3) admissions screenings to identify which youth are in most need of detention and pose the most threat to society, (4) use of nonsecure alternatives to detention for those who would have been locked up in the past, (5) the expediting of cases through the juvenile system to reduce lengths of stay in detention, (6) flexibility in policies and practices to deal with "special" cases like probation violations, (7) attention to racial disparities in contact and incarceration, and (8) intensive monitoring of the conditions found in confinement (Annie E. Casey Foundation, 2009). As a result of participation in JDAI, counties reported an average daily detention population in 2011 that was 43% lower than the year before, and counties admitted 59,000 fewer youth to detention in 2012 (Annie E. Casey Foundation, 2014). The foundation has publicized the success of the JDAI approach in studies. Whether these states continue their aggressive work toward change and whether these approaches continue to work in lowering the number of incarcerated youth is yet to be seen, as changes to culture, society, and systems take time.

Capital Punishment and Youthful Offenders

Clearly, there are some juveniles who are extremely dangerous to others and who do not appear to be amenable to rehabilitation. Thus, all states have established mechanisms for transferring or waiving jurisdiction to adult court in such cases (as we indicated in Chapter 6). Once this transfer occurs, the accused loses all special rights and immunities and is subject to most of the full range of adult penalties for criminal behavior. In the past, juveniles could be provided "absolute" sentences such as life in prison without parole (Cothern, 2000, p. 1; Dorne & Gewerth, 1998, p. 203); however, the 2010 U.S. Supreme Court decisions in *Graham v. Florida* (see In Practice 11.2), *Jackson v. Hobbs* (2011), *Miller v. Alabama* (2012), and *Montgomery V. Louisiana* (2016) no longer allow life sentences and mandatory life sentences without parole for youth who have not committed homicide. The rulings in the *Jackson* and *Miller* cases essentially struck down 29 state statutes that allow for mandatory sentencing of youth to life in prison without parole, and the Montgomery case applied the ruling retroactively. The U.S. Supreme Court based its decision on the Eighth Amendment, adding that penological theory does not support life sentences without parole for youth who do not commit homicide or have limited culpability, and the sentence is overly severe for a juvenile. The Court went on to say that life without parole is the second most serious punishment available in the United States and that a youth serving such a sentence will spend, on average, more years institutionalized than an adult offender convicted of the same offense, making the penalty cruel and unusual (*Graham v. Florida*, 2010; *Jackson v. Hobbs*, 2011; *Miller v. Alabama*, 2012; *Montgomery v. Louisiana*, 2016). At the time of the *Graham* ruling, there were 129 youth offenders serving life sentences without parole for nonhomicide crimes. The majority of these (77) were in Florida (*Graham v. Florida*, 2010). In yet another decision, in 2005, the U.S. Supreme Court held in *Roper v. Simmons* that states cannot execute offenders (i.e., capital punishment) who are under the age of 18 years. According to the ruling, juveniles are not as culpable as typical criminals, and executing juveniles would violate both the Eighth Amendment and the Fourteenth Amendment (Death Penalty Information Center, n.d.). At the time, the Court's ruling affected 72 juveniles in 12 states.

The first recorded juvenile execution in America occurred in 1642. Since that time, 361 individuals have been executed for crimes they committed as juveniles (Cothern, 2000, p. 3; Streib, 2000). The first case that the U.S. Supreme Court heard on the death penalty for juveniles was *Eddings v. Oklahoma* (1982). In this case, the Court did not rule on the constitutionality of the death penalty for minors, but it did hold that the age of the minor is a mitigating factor to be considered at sentencing. In *Thompson v. Oklahoma* (1988), the Supreme Court found that the Eighth and Fourteenth Amendments prohibited the execution of a person who is under

16 years of age at the time of his or her offense, though only four of the justices fully concurred with this ruling. In *Stanford v. Kentucky* (1989) and in *Wilkins v. Missouri* (1989), the Supreme Court sanctioned the imposition of the death penalty on offenders who were at least 16 years of age at the time of the crime. The decision in *Roper* (2005) overturns these prior judgments.

IN PRACTICE 11.2

GRAHAM V. FLORIDA: THE SUPREME COURT'S USE OF INTERNATIONAL TRENDS WHEN RULING ON LIFE SENTENCES FOR JUVENILES

Recently, the U.S. Supreme Court has ruled that juveniles may not be sentenced to life without parole unless the crime involves the actual death of the victim.

This ruling was controversial but ended with a 6 to 3 vote within the Court. Five justices delivered an opinion led by Justice Anthony Kennedy, arguing that life sentences without parole for juveniles violated the Eighth Amendment's restriction against cruel and unusual punishments. The sixth justice to concur was Chief Justice John Roberts, who agreed that Graham's particular case was too harsh to warrant a sentence of life without parole but would not completely commit to the idea that all juveniles should be exempted from life-without-parole sentences. Rather, Roberts contended that this should be decided on a case-by-case basis.

The specific facts of the case involved Terrance Graham, who committed his crime at the age of 16. In July 2003, Graham and three other juveniles attempted to rob a barbeque restaurant in Jacksonville, Florida. Their crime resulted in injuries to the restaurant manager, who had to get stitches for his head injury. Graham was subsequently arrested for the robbery attempt. Under a plea agreement, the Florida trial court sentenced Graham to probation and withheld adjudication of guilt. Later, Graham violated the terms of his probation by committing additional crimes. The court then adjudicated Graham guilty of his earlier charges, revoked his probation, and sentenced him to life in prison for the burglary. Because Florida has abolished its parole system, the life sentence had essentially left Graham no possibility of release except executive clemency.

In response, the Court held that the Eighth Amendment does not permit a juvenile offender to be sentenced to life in prison without parole for a nonhomicide crime.

In explaining its rationale, Justice Kennedy of the majority noted that "a state need not guarantee the offender eventual release, but if it imposes the sentence of life, it must provide him or her with some realistic opportunity to obtain release before the end of that term" (p. 32).

This ruling was unique because it is the first time that the Court has identified an entire category of offenders (in this case, juveniles) as being exempt from a given type of punishment, aside from the death penalty. In other words, most rulings that exempt a class of offenders (such as mentally challenged offenders or juvenile offenders) have been restricted to the death penalty. Graham departs from this precedent and extends it to include issues related to life-in-prison-without-parole decisions as well. This is important because it represents a wider net of exclusion and because the future implications may include additional rulings that can include other groups or even more limits on sentencing with juvenile offenders.

The *Graham* case is also important for another reason that is discussed in future chapters of this text. In *Graham*, several of the justices (namely Kennedy, Stevens, Ginsburg, Breyer, and Sotomayor) pointed toward both national and international practices that were consistent with this restriction on such long-term sentences for juveniles. The fact that the Court has again used examples from the international legal community is significant because it demonstrates an

(Continued)

(Continued)

ever-increasing trend to consider legislation and legal orientations from other countries when handing down rulings in the United States. This represents the fact that globalization has impacted the juvenile system via the Supreme Court who, from prior precedent such as *Roper v. Simmons* (the Court case that excluded juveniles from the death penalty), has consistently cited trends within the international arena. This demonstrates a willingness and desire of the Court to interlace the U.S. sense of justice for youth to be consistent with the evolving standards of decency that are developing throughout the world, particularly through the influence of organizations such as the United Nations and the World Court.

The tendency for some justices to cite international opinions, protocols, and procedures has been criticized by some, including other justices such as Thomas and Scalia. These justices have consistently opposed the use of international influences on the high court's decisions. It is important to note that the Court has used international trends as a basis for its decision even though a clear majority of states in the United States (37 out of 50 states) have sentences that do allow life without parole for juvenile offenders. Thus, the majority trend in the United States has been reversed based on other criteria, including international influences.

Finally, there is now the possibility that juvenile advocates may press further, looking to reduce the likelihood of juveniles receiving life without parole for crimes where a victim was killed. This would be a likely occurrence, and the *Graham* ruling does provide these advocates with some potential for success. The Court, in past rulings that involve the Eighth Amendment, has referred to an often-cited catchphrase of "the evolving standards of decency that mark the progress of a maturing society" as the basis for generating humanitarian changes in how offenders are sentenced and punished within the justice system.

The question that now remains is just how far those evolving standards of decency are likely to progress, in light of the *Graham* ruling and in light of the fact that the Court continues to include norms in the international community when generating rulings. This question is particularly relevant to high court rulings on juveniles, which continue to reduce the use of potentially punitive sentences for youth. The basis for this is due to the inherent views related to youth and crime; youth are considered more amenable to later change. To give youth life sentences without parole eliminates the consideration that young offenders may, over a long number of years, eventually reduce their likelihood of committing further crimes. Such a presumption runs contrary to the underlying philosophy of our juvenile justice system and, according to the Court, also runs counter to the evolving standards of decency common to a progressive and maturing society. Apparently, due to the Court's current ruling in *Graham*, the definition of the term *society* can and does include norms and trends in countries abroad.

Sources: Liptak (2010); U.S. Supreme Court (2010).

Questions to Consider

1. True or False: The death penalty is never an appropriate sentence for a juvenile.

2. Multiple Choice: Juveniles can receive which of the following types of sentences?

   a. Prison

   b. Capital punishment

   c. Community based

   d. All of the above

3. Although the death penalty was struck down in the *Graham* case, do you think Terrance Graham deserved to die for what he did to his victim? Why or why not?

Possible Solutions

All rehabilitative programs are based on some theoretical orientation to human behavior, running the gamut from individual to group approaches and from nature to nurture. Knowledge of these various approaches is critical for all staff members working in juvenile correctional facilities. Nearly all juvenile institutions use some form of treatment program for the juveniles in custody—counseling on an individual or group basis, vocational and educational training, various types of therapy, recreational programs, and religious counseling. In addition, they provide medical and dental programs of some kind as well as occasional legal service programs. The purpose of these various programs is to rehabilitate the juveniles within the institutions—to turn them into better adjusted individuals and send them back into the community as productive citizens. Despite generally good intentions, however, the goal of rehabilitation has been elusive, and it may be argued that it is better attained outside the walls of institutions.

Solving the problems created by the effects of isolation on incarcerated juveniles is a difficult task. We need to be certain that all available alternatives to incarceration have been explored. We must remember that virtually all juveniles placed in institutions will eventually be released into society. If those juveniles are to be released with positive attitudes toward reintegration, we must orient institutional treatment programs toward that goal. This can be accomplished through educational and vocational programs brought into the institutions from the outside and through work or educational release programs for appropriate juveniles. In addition, attempts to facilitate reintegration through the use of halfway houses or prerelease guidance centers seem to be somewhat successful.

Unfortunately, in many instances correctional staff members begin to see isolation as an end in itself. As a result, attempts at treatment are often oriented toward helping the juveniles adapt to institutional life rather than preparing them for reintegration. Ignoring life on the outside and failing to deal with problems that will be confronted on release simply add to the problem. Provision of relevant educational and vocational programs, employment opportunities on release, and programs provided by interested civic groups should take precedence over concentrating on strict schedules, mass movements, and punishment. The out-of-sight, out-of-mind attitude should be eliminated through the use of programs designed to increase community contact as soon as possible. This is not meant to belittle the importance of institutional educational, vocational, and recreational programs for juvenile delinquents. However, such programs will fail unless they are supported by an intensive continual orientation to success outside the walls of the institution. This will require both correctional personnel and concerned citizens to pull their heads out of the sand in a cooperative effort to serve the best interests of both the incarcerated juveniles and society.

Changes are needed in rehabilitation and treatment programs within the walls of the institution as well. Some programs are based on faulty assumptions. Others fail to consider the problems arising from the transition between the institution and the community upon release. Some further examples should help to illustrate the advantages and disadvantages of different types of treatment programs.

Many institutions rely on individual counseling and psychotherapy as treatment modalities. Treatment of this type is quite costly, and contact with the therapist is generally quite limited. In addition, treatment programs of this type rest on two highly questionable assumptions: (1) that the delinquents involved suffer from emotional or psychological disorders and (2) that psychotherapy is an effective means of relieving such disorders. Most delinquents have not been shown to suffer from such disorders. Whether those who do are suffering from some underlying emotional difficulty or from the trauma of being apprehended, prosecuted, adjudicated, disposed of, and placed in an institution is not clear. Finally, whether psychotherapeutic techniques are effective in relieving emotional or psychological problems when they do exist is a matter of considerable disagreement.

Another type of program involves the use of behavior modification techniques. In programs of this type, the delinquent is rewarded for appropriate behavior and punished for inappropriate behavior. Rewards may be given by the staff, by peers, or by both, with rewards given by both showing the best results. Research on behavior modification programs has shown encouraging results. It is reasonable to assume that most delinquent behavior can be modified under strictly controlled conditions. Although it is possible to control many conditions within the walls of the institution, such controls cannot be applied to the same degree following release. In addition, as indicated earlier, behavior that is punished within the institution may be rewarded on the outside and vice versa. Again, transition from the institutional setting to the community is crucial. There are also ethical issues to consider that concern granting institutional staff members the power to modify behavior while still protecting the rights of juveniles.

Other treatment techniques frequently employed in juvenile facilities center on change within the group. These include the use of reality therapy, group counseling sessions, psychodrama or role-playing sessions, transactional analysis, activity therapy, guided group interaction, and self-government programs. All of these techniques are aimed at getting juveniles to talk through their problems, to take the roles of other people so as to better understand why others react as they do, and to assume part of the responsibility for solving their own problems. All of these seem to be important given that lack of communication, lack of understanding other people's views, and failure to assume responsibility for their own actions characterize many delinquents. Continuing access to behavior modification programs after release could provide valuable help during and after the period of reintegration.

Assuming that we have worthwhile rehabilitation programs in juvenile institutions, serious attempts should be made to match juveniles with appropriate programs and to stop convenience assignments such as those based on program vacancies and ease of transfer. It is important to classify offenders into treatment-relevant types based on juveniles' current behavior, self-evaluations, and past histories. Assignment of youthful offenders to specific programs and living areas based on these categories must be associated with specific types of treatment and training programs. Treatment programs will vary according to juveniles' behavioral characteristics, maturity levels, and psychological orientations. Whereas one behavioral type may benefit from behavior modification based on immediate reinforcement (positive/negative), another behavioral type may benefit more through increasing levels of awareness and understanding. Inappropriate behavior will result in a loss of privileges or points toward a specific goal. Although it may be risky to assume that there are clearly delineated behavioral categories with accompanying treatment for each category, systematic attempts along these lines would appear to be a step in the right direction (Harris & Jones, 1999).

Because the peer group plays such an important role in correctional facilities, some way must be found to use its influence in a positive manner. Some institutions have adopted a positive peer culture orientation in which peers are encouraged to reward one another for appropriate behavior and to help one another eliminate inappropriate behavior. Although correctional staff members frequently believe that these programs are highly successful, in many cases juveniles simply learn to play the game; that is, they make appropriate responses when being observed by staff members but revert to undesirable behavior patterns on their return to the dorm or cottage. This frequently happens because correctional personnel get taken in by their own institutional babble. They sometimes begin to believe that the peer culture they see is positive when it is actually mostly negative. One way to avert this problem is to view rehabilitation as more than an "8 to 5" job. Unfortunately, the problems that confront incarcerated juveniles do not always arise at convenient times for staff members. Assistance in solving these problems should be available when it is needed.

Another beneficial step taken in some institutions has been to move away from the dormitory or large-cottage concept to rooms occupied by two or three juveniles. These juveniles are carefully screened for the particular group in which they are included in terms of seriousness of offense, type of offense, past history of offenses, and so forth. This move holds some promise of success because "rule by the toughest" may be averted for most inmates. In this way, nonviolent offenders, such as auto thieves and burglars, run less risk of being "contaminated" by their more dangerous peers, for example, those who committed offenses involving homicide, battery, sexual assault, or armed robbery. Finally, relationships between therapeutic and custodial staff members, and between all staff members and inmates, need to be improved. The solution is obvious. All staff members in juvenile correctional facilities should be employed on the basis of their sincere concern with preparing inmates for their eventual release and reintegration into society. Distinctions between custodial and treatment staff members should be eliminated, rehabilitation should be the goal of every staff member, and every staff member should be concerned about custody when necessary. Training and educational opportunities should be available to help staff members keep up with new techniques and research.

In some instances, however, it appears that no matter what correctional officials do in traditional programs, some juveniles just won't get the message. To get the attention of such juveniles, programs using shock intervention and/or boot camp principles have been introduced. These programs are usually relatively short in duration (3 to 6 months) with an emphasis on military drill, physical training, and hard labor coupled with drug treatment and/or academic work (Inciardi, Horowitz, & Pottieger, 1993; Klein-Saffran, Chapman, & Jeffers, 1993). The juveniles sent to boot camps may have started to use illegal substances or have minor legal problems that include nonviolent offenses (Boot Camps for Teens, n.d.). Drill-sergeant-like supervisors scream orders at the juveniles, demand strict obedience to all rules, and otherwise try to shock young offenders out of crime while imposing order and discipline. Although these programs have received a good deal of media attention, there is some doubt about their overall effectiveness. Whereas some maintain that the programs build self-esteem and teach discipline, others argue that serious delinquents are unlikely to change their behavior as the result of marching, physical exertion, and shock tactics (MacKenzie & Souryal, 1991). Boot camps are not suitable for all children. Abundant Life Academy (2006) suggested the following:

> There are children that need a more clinical setting than a boot camp. If a child has suicidal issues, is severely depressed, [is] self-mutilating, or has a serious psychiatric diagnosis, they would be better served in a therapeutic boarding school, residential treatment center, or in some cases even a psychiatric hospital. (par. 7)

Boot camps have declined in popularity recently, and a number of states aren't using these programs at all.

Providing concerned and well-trained correctional personnel will not guarantee better relationships with all incarcerated juveniles, but it should improve the overall quality of relationships considerably. Although initial costs of employment may be somewhat higher, the overall costs will not exceed those now incurred by taxpayers who often pay to have the same juveniles rehabilitated time and time again. According to Hibbler (1999), the National Juvenile Corrections and Detention Forum addressed this issue, recognizing that new laws dealing with juveniles have often led to a distancing from the use of appropriate intervention techniques that might help juveniles to grow into responsible adults. Forum participants concluded that incarcerated juveniles should be taught to understand and respect societal rules, that vocational training should be included in their correctional programs, and that bridge programs should be developed to help incarcerated juveniles to complete the transition to society (Hibbler, 1999).

We have focused, for the most part, on dispositional alternatives available to delinquents. There are other types of alternatives available to dependent, addicted, abused, and neglected minors as well. In addition to foster home placement, these include placement of juveniles in their own homes under court supervision (protective supervision); use of orders of protection that detail when, where, and under what circumstances parents or guardians may interact with the juveniles in question; and commitment to drug rehabilitation or mental health programs.

CAREER OPPORTUNITY: RECREATION OFFICER I OR II

Job description: Responsible for facilitating and implementing planned recreational activities for incarcerated juveniles. Facilitate indoor and outdoor supervised sports; conduct group games; organize field trips; and facilitate other recreational programs that meet the varied interests, abilities, and needs of the juveniles. Maintain facility policies and enforce behavior management strategies in the course of recreational programs.

Employment requirements: Requires a 4-year degree with a specialization in recreation, physical education, leisure management, or a closely related field. If without a college education, must possess 4 years of diversified experience in the field of group recreation or physical education; must have graduated from high school; and must have experience in organizing, implementing, scheduling, and overseeing recreation activities. General college education may be substituted for up to 2 years of experience.

Beginning salary: Salary ranges from $22,000 to $36,000. Benefits are provided according to the state benefits program, which usually includes health and life insurance, paid vacations and holidays, and a retirement program.

Summary

It is clear that careful consideration should be given to available alternatives to incarceration of juveniles and that at least some states are taking an aggressive stand against the overuse of incarceration. Probation, whether within the juvenile's own family or in a foster home, has the advantage of maintaining ties between the juvenile and the community. Community corrections, by and large, should be the preferred approach to youthful offenders who do not pose serious threats to society. Proper supervision and careful selection procedures to determine whether a juvenile can benefit from probation are essential. When incarceration is necessary to protect society, programs directed toward the eventual return of the juvenile to society should be stressed.

Changes are required in society's belief that juveniles who are "out of mind" will automatically remain "out of sight." Nearly all of these juveniles will eventually return to society, and efforts must be made to ensure that time spent in institutions produces beneficial results, not negative results. Thus, juveniles should not be randomly assigned to correctional treatment programs, nor can the negative effects of the delinquent subculture that develops in most institutions be ignored. All programs should be routinely evaluated to determine whether they are meeting their goals and the more general goals of rehabilitating juveniles while protecting society.

Critical Thinking Questions

1. What are some of the possible negative consequences of placing juveniles in correctional facilities? In your opinion, what circumstances would warrant such placement? Why?

2. What types of issues may be faced by LGBTQ youth in correctional facilities? Identify one or two best practices for the confinement of LGBTQ youth.

3. What is restorative justice? What are the three primary concepts used in restorative justice? Who is involved in the implementation of restorative justice programs?

4. If you were superintendent of a juvenile correctional facility today, what steps would you take to ensure that juveniles would be better prepared for their return to society? Why would you take these steps?

5. What are the goals of JDAI? Why are states adopting philosophies that keep youth out of facilities, even when it appears that youth are more violent than ever before? Are youth more violent than ever before?

Suggested Readings

Annie E. Casey Foundation. (2009). *Two decades of JDAI: A progress report*. Retrieved from www.aecf .org/MajorInitiatives/~/media/Pubs/Initiatives/ Juvenile%20Detention%20Alternatives%20Initiative/ TwoDecadesofJDAIFromDemonstrationProjecttoNat/ JDAI_National_final_10_07_09.pdf

Bradshaw, W., & Roseborough, D. (2005). Restorative justice dialogue: The impact of mediation and conferencing on juvenile recidivism. *Federal Probation, 69*(2). Retrieved from www.uscourts.gov/FederalCourts/ ProbationPretrialServices/FederalProbationJournal/ FederalProbationJournal.aspx?doc=/uscourts/ FederalCourts/PPS/Fedprob/2005-12/index .html

Champion, D. R., Harvey, P. J., & Schanz, Y. (2011). Day reporting center and recidivism: Comparing offender groups in a western Pennsylvania county study. *Journal of Offender Rehabilitation, 50*(7), 433–446.

Child Welfare Information Gateway. (2009). *Foster care statistics*. Retrieved from www.childwelfare.gov/pubs/ factsheets/foster.cfm

Department of Health and Human Services. (2002). *Recruiting foster parents: Office of the Inspector General*. Retrieved from http://oig.hhs.gov/oei/reports/oei-07- 00-00600.pdf

Hayes, H. (2004). Assessing reoffending in restorative justice conferences. *Australian and New Zealand Journal of Criminology, 38*(1), 77–101.

Hayes, H., & Daly, K. (2003). Youth justice conferencing and reoffending. *Justice Quarterly, 20*, 725–764.

Jackson v. Hobbs, 132 S. Ct. 548 (2011).

Kilgore, D. (2004). Look what boot camp's done for me: Teaching and learning at Lakeview Academy. *Journal of Correctional Education, 55,* 170–185.

Miller v. Alabama, 132 S. Ct. 2455 (2012).

Office of Juvenile Justice and Delinquency Prevention. (2004a). *Juveniles in corrections* (NCJ202885). Washington, DC: Office of Justice Programs. Retrieved from www.ncjrs.gov/html/ojjdp/202885/contents.html

Office of Juvenile Justice and Delinquency Prevention. (2004b). *Model programs guide: Day treatment.* Washington, DC: Office of Justice Programs. Retrieved from www2.dsgonline.com/mpg/program_types_description.aspx?program_type=Day%20 Treatment&continuum=intermediate

Williams, D., & Turnage, T. (2001). Success of a day reporting center program. *The Corrections Compendium, 26*(3), 1–26.

⑤SAGE edge™

Sharpen your skills with SAGE edge at **edge.sagepub.com/coxjj9e**. SAGE edge for students provides a personalized approach to help you accomplish your coursework goals in an easy-to-use learning environment. You'll find action plans, mobile-friendly eFlashcards, and quizzes as well as video and web resources and links to SAGE journal articles to support and expand on the concepts presented in this chapter.

Violent Juveniles and Gangs

12

On completion of this chapter, students should be able to do the following:

- Discuss the history and current status of gangs in the United States
- Assess the various theories of gang development and membership
- Recognize the relationships among gangs, violence, and drugs
- Understand the role of firearms in youth violence
- Understand the relationship between delinquency and gang membership
- Discuss the characteristics of gang members in terms of age, race/ethnicity, gender, monikers, jargon, and graffiti
- Discuss a variety of public and private responses to gang activities
- Assess various alternatives to incarceration for violent juveniles

WHAT WOULD YOU DO?

Tuam Tsu walked down the street alone. It was dark outside, but his path was intermittently lit by streetlights above. It was about 11:30 p.m., and he had only a little way to go. He knew his father and mother were concerned about his whereabouts, but neither of them really knew English and could not do much about his decisions. He came to an area behind a big warehouse that was very dark, and there, in the darkness, were members of what would become his "other family"—persons in the Hmong Nation Society, a street gang consisting of other kids and some adults who were ethnic Hmong. They gathered, and one of them, an adult leader, stepped forward and said in the Hmong language, "Tonight we initiate Tuam Tsu into our family. Tonight he will prove his worth."

During the next 30 minutes, Tuam Tsu was slapped, kicked, beaten, hit with sticks and bats, and basically jumped by five other members of the gang. Tuam Tsu fought back, as best as he could, but his eyes and nose were bruised and bloodied and his whole body ached. It felt as though his leg had been kicked and was broken and his head pounded with welps. All of a sudden, he heard, "Stop! Stop! Stop!" and the beating was over.

One of the members held him upright, and the rest came and hugged him saying, "Much love, homie" and other similar greetings. The adult leader then said, "Welcome to the family, brother Tuam Tsu. Tonight you celebrate!"

They drug him out of the alley into a car and took him to the "family" home. He healed up and

(Continued)

was pumped up with crystal meth and introduced to some young Hmong girls who were "friends of the family." Later that week, one of the gang leaders, Koob Meej, approached Tuam Tsu and asked him about his sister, Lig Paaj. Koob Meej explained that he had his eye on Lig Paaj for quite some time. All he wanted was just one date with her. Tuam Tsu knew that in many cases, gang members "sexed in" girls and that, once this was done, they were essentially property of the gang. Tuam Tsu was, of course, upset about this request but knew that it was not smart to cross a gang member with rank and the punishment could be serious for both him and his sister. Tuam Tsu thought about going to another gang leader, but if he did so and if his objection to Koob Meej's request was denied, he would be in an even worse position.

What Would You Do?

1. What types of concerns have likely influenced Tuam Tsu to join the Hmong Nation Society?

2. What might be an effective way to address Koob Meej's request?

Although there are a number of theoretical attempts to explain why juveniles engage in antisocial conduct, it is well known that many delinquent acts are committed in the company of others (Thornberry & Burch, 1997). As a result, much attention has been given to the role of the gang. Research has focused on two areas: (1) the factors that direct or encourage a juvenile to seek gang membership and (2) the effects of the gang on the behavior of its membership.

Cohen (1955) concluded that much delinquent behavior stems from attempts by lower-class youth to resolve status problems resulting from trying to live up to middle-class norms encountered in the educational system. Juveniles who determine they cannot achieve in this system often seek out others like themselves and form what Cohen called a delinquent subculture. According to Cohen, it is in the company of these "mutually converted" associates that a great deal of delinquency occurs.

According to many scholars (Bursik & Grasmick, 1995; Ritter & Simon, 2013; Valdez, 2007), numerous factors bring juveniles into gangs. Sociological factors and physical factors include place of residence, school attended, location of parks and hangouts, age, race, and nationality. Psychological factors include dependency needs, family rejection, and impulse control. Still, other factors are related to the structure and cohesiveness of the gang and peer group pressure. In the early appraisals of gangs, causation was tied to the theories of the slum community and its inherent attributes of social disorganization (Klein, 2005; Ritter & Simon, 2013; Valdez, 2011).

During the 1920s and 1930s, a group of sociologists at the University of Chicago, including Frederick Thrasher, Frank Tannenbaum, Henry McKay, Clifford Shaw, and William Whyte, conducted a number of studies of gangs in Chicago. According to Thrasher (1927), the gang is an important contributing factor facilitating the commission of crime and delinquency. The organization of the gang and the protection it affords make it a superior instrument for execution of criminal enterprises.

Interest in the relationship between gangs and delinquency waned during the 1960s and 1970s but increased during the late 1980s and early 1990s with reports of gang activities among minority groups both in and out of correctional facilities (Klein, 2005; Valdez, 2011). Chicano gang activity on the West Coast and Chinese and Vietnamese gang activity have received media attention recently as well as attention from the National Institute of Justice (NIJ) and, of course, the Office of Juvenile Justice and Delinquency Prevention

(OJJDP) (Hanser, 2007a; Howell, Egley, Tita, & Griffiths, 2011; Valdez, 2007). It has been suggested that the amount of attention gangs receive is directly related to the ideology of the political party in power, to economic concerns of citizens, and to fear of victimization (Bookin & Horowitz, 1983; McGloin, 2005). Fear of victimization in the form of random and drive-by shootings has captured the attention of the media, the public, and Congress. The gangs of the late 1980s and 1990s were better armed, more violent, and more mobile than their predecessors, and research on gangs once again came into vogue (Howell et al., 2011; Valdez, 2007, 2011).

Over the past two decades, violent crimes committed by juveniles have again received a great deal of attention, much of which has focused on juvenile gangs and the crimes of violence they perpetrate; however, recent findings from researchers seem to run contrary to conventional wisdom. Though there did appear to be a decline in youth violence during the early 2000s, including juvenile gang violence, there was a slow but steady increase in juvenile gang problems from 2000 to 2009, and according to Pyrooz (2016), there are likely many more youth involved in gangs than research has contended in the past (see In Practice 12.1). Interestingly, it is thought that gang activity among youth may be much more transient than has been realized during the past few decades (Pyrooz, 2016).

IN PRACTICE 12.1

DISPELLING MYTHS ABOUT JUVENILE GANG MEMBERS IN THE UNITED STATES

Gangs evoke clear images of certain people, places, and activities—racial and ethnic minority boys, prisons and inner cities, and health risk behaviors such as violence, drug dealing, and weapon carrying. It is also thought that gang membership is a lasting commitment, or at least a commitment that exacts a physically costly toll to exit. Many media commentators and criminal justice officials feel that gangs are running rampant in our neighborhoods and schools. Are these stereotypes accurate?

In a recent study, my colleague Gary Sweeten and I sought to assess the accuracy of these claims. While many studies have explored the extent to which males and minorities are overrepresented in gangs, and how long youth remain in gangs, this research was city-specific rather than general to the United States. Our interests were in painting a national portrait of juvenile gang activity, which is what we did using data from the National Longitudinal Survey of Youth 1997 (NLYS97), representative of youth born between 1980 and 1984.

Patterns and demographics of gang members were tracked among juveniles in the U.S. between ages 5 and 17. Juveniles self-reported their involvement in gangs, including the age at which they joined and left the gang, and patterns of gang membership were tracked over the NLSY97 annual surveys. While there are reasons why youth might under- or over-report membership in a gang, this method of operationalizing gang membership has high reliability and validity. Based on extreme assumptions about missing data and sampling design effects, we placed upper and lower bounds over our estimates to represent the most and least conservative findings. We then linked these findings to demographic and socioeconomic data in the NLSY97 and extrapolated from the 2010 U.S. Census data to produce single age estimates.

Our study revealed several critical findings about juvenile gang membership in the U.S. First, the overall prevalence of gang membership was 2.0%, with extreme lower and upper bounds of 1.2–2.8%. These results suggest that gang membership is rare among youth. Second, gang

(Continued)

(Continued)

membership is strongly age-graded. Age-specific rates of gang membership surpassed 1% by age 10, then rapidly increase during the pre-teen years, peaking at 5% at age 14. By the late teens, rates of gang membership drop back down to 1%. Should those trends persist through adulthood, it would suggest that gang membership is overwhelmingly an adolescent activity.

The third major finding from our study was that there are slightly over 1 million juvenile gang members in the U.S. This figure might sound exceptionally large, but findings from nationally representative surveys of law enforcement identify much fewer juvenile gang members. Our conservative lower bound estimate was 2.2 times as great as what law enforcement reports, suggesting that there are far more gang youth who go undetected in official records, which has tradeoffs that are both good (e.g., reduced risk of labeling) and bad (e.g., missed opportunity for intervention services).

Fourth, gang membership is a highly transient life state. Rarely did youth persist in gangs beyond one or two years. The annual turnover rate in gang membership was 36%—not quite equivalent to restaurant/hospitality industry rates, but youth join and leave gangs quite frequently. Indeed, our results showed that roughly 400,000 youth exited gangs annually. Which also means that gangs constantly had to attract new members, and our results showed that about the same number of youth joined gangs each year.

Finally, while gang members were disproportionately male, black, Latino, from single-parent households, and families that lived below the poverty line, these demographic and socioeconomic characteristics were not monolithic to gang members. Many females, whites, and children from two-parent and middle- and high-income households were also gang members.

The results of this study are important for law enforcement and healthcare professionals. Law enforcement under-recognizes juvenile gang activity, which may be surprising to some who feel police practices do more to net-widen than to reduce criminal stigma. Yet, the powerful image of juvenile gang members promulgated by law enforcement is not entirely accurate, particularly with respect to gender, race, and ethnicity. Relying on law enforcement representations of juvenile gang members runs the risk of type II error.

Another important implication of these results is that they drive home calls for early prevention and intervention, both of which should be in place during the pre- and mid-teen years. Gang membership has lasting consequences that cascade across life domains, including economic, education, family, and health, which is why is it much more effective to prevent gang membership than having to intervene once a youth is active.

Source: Pyrooz (2016).

Questions to Consider

1. True or False: According to Pyrooz, gang membership tends to be long-term once youth are formally admitted.

2. Multiple Choice: The reasons this study is important include which of the following?

   a. Law enforcement is probably underrecognizing juvenile gang activity.

   b. This study demonstrates why early prevention is important.

   c. Gang membership consists of fewer than 500,000 juveniles, the rest being adults.

   d. A & B, but not C.

   e. B & C, but not A.

3. From this new research, how common do you think violent crime might be among juvenile gang members in reality? Explain your reasons why you answer as you do.

As we noted in earlier chapters, one result of this emphasis on juvenile violence is that all states now have laws making it easier to try violent juveniles in adult courts and making it possible to prescribe more severe penalties for such juveniles. To what extent are the concerns about growing violence by juveniles based in fact? What, if anything, can be done to effectively reduce violence by juveniles? In the following sections, we examine these and other questions concerning the involvement of juveniles in violent activities.

Violent Juveniles

Reports of violent juveniles are widespread and are regular parts of newspaper and magazine headlines, television specials on youthful violence, comments on behalf of political officials promising a "get tough" approach (increasing the severity of punishment) to young offenders, and citizen action groups concerned about juvenile violence. Many of the newspaper articles and comments are based on analyses of official statistics that, as we pointed out earlier in the book, can be highly misleading or misinterpreted when it comes to assessing juvenile delinquency.

But are these statistics currently being misinterpreted? If we consider violent juvenile offenders to be those who commit (and, in terms of official statistics, are arrested for) criminal homicide, rape, robbery, or aggravated assault or battery, what has been the trend during recent years? Researchers Sickmund and Puzzanchera (2014) of the National Center for Juvenile Justice found that, during the period from 2001 to 2010, overall juvenile arrests for violent, property, and nonindex crimes decreased across the board (see Table 12.1).

Table 12.1 Juvenile and Adult Arrest Rates, 2001–2010

	Percentage Change in Arrests, 2001–2010	
Most Serious Offense	Juvenile	Adult
Violent Crime Index	−22%	−10%
Murder	−20%	−18%
Forcible rape	−37%	−24%
Robbery	3%	4%
Aggravated assault	−31%	−12%
Property Crime Index	−25%	13%
Burglary	−27%	11%
Larceny-theft	−18%	21%
Motor vehicle theft	−67%	−44%
Weapons law violations	−15%	−1%
Drug abuse violations	−15%	6%
Total	−21%	0%

Source: Sickmund & Puzzanchera (2014).

As can be seen in Table 12.1, juvenile violent crime decreased from 2001 to 2010 in every single category, except robbery, which increased only 3% when averaging male and female juveniles. In fact, the very slight increase in this one category is the only category that increased for juvenile offenders. When compared to adult crime, this is important to note, for adult crime increased in robbery and a number of other offenses.

These decreases are more substantial than those for adult crimes of the same category, and, in many cases, adult crime actually went up rather than down. Consider that increases in adult crime were seen for robbery, burglary, larceny, simple assault, and drug abuse violations, whereas juvenile crime went down in all these categories but robbery.

Thus, these data do not warrant the media hype and public perception that juvenile crime is increasing. Further, crimes such as murder and/or assault are low, numerically, to the other categories but, due to the lethality involved, gain a disproportionate amount of media attention than do the other crimes.

Prior to these recent reports, the picture of juvenile violence looked considerably different. From 1965 to 1990, the overall murder arrest rate for juveniles increased 332%, accompanied by a 79% increase in the number of juveniles who committed murder with guns. Juvenile arrests for murder also showed an increase from 1987 to 1993, when 3,800 juveniles were arrested for murder. By 1999, the number of juvenile arrests for murder had declined to 1,400 (Snyder, 2000, p. 1). All in all, roughly one-third of 1% of 10- to 17-year-olds were arrested for violent crimes in 1999 (p. 6).

The forcible-rape juvenile arrest rates increased by 44% from 1980 to 1991 but declined from 1991 to 1999 when compared with the 1980 rate. Aggravated assault arrest rates more than doubled from 1983 to 1994 and then declined to 24% below the 1994 peak but remained 69% above their 1983 low point. And the juvenile arrest rate for robbery increased 70% from 1988 to 1994 but then declined in 1999 to its lowest levels since at least 1980 (Snyder, 2000, p. 8). Even with the clear decline in official violence by juveniles, fear of such violence persists and is fed by events such as school shootings.

Though media portrayals of teen violence aggravate concerns among the lay public, the reality is that there has been a trend toward lower violent juvenile crime. Although there was a general short-term increase in 2006 of observed violent juvenile crime, this increase proved to be short-lived. Since that time, there has been a notable decline in violent offending, as we have seen earlier in Chapter 3 of this text (see Tables 3.1 and 3.2, which showcase FBI data from 2015). Data from the FBI (2015) indicate that from 2011 to 2015, juvenile arrests for Violent Crime Index offenses consistently decreased.

Although juvenile violent criminal behavior may fluctuate from year to year, it would appear that juvenile crime has consistently declined, casting aside any rational fear of a prolonged epidemic of youth crime anytime in the near future. The media sensationalism associated with juvenile crime has created an image in the minds of many people that youth crime is on an ever-increasing rise; this is not the case according to more recent data on juvenile offending.

Juvenile Homicide and Juvenile Violence

American researchers consistently find that the most common weapons used in juvenile homicides are firearms (Office of Community Oriented Policing Services [COPS], 2007). One study of juvenile homicide offenders by DiCataldo and Everett (2007) found that these youth differed from other violent youth based on two key factors. First, they had a greater availability of and access to firearms. Second, these youth were more prone to use drugs of greater strength and in greater doses at the time of their offending than were other youth. Whereas some researchers have examined other potential causal factors, the accessibility to firearms and the use of substances seem to consistently be a theme in juvenile homicides.

However, the prediction of gun violence is typically considered problematic by social scientists due to the inherent difficulty in predicting low base rate behavior (COPS, 2007). In other words, because juvenile gun violence is not a routinely occurring behavior, there are limited cases to analyze as a means of deriving conclusions. Furthermore, the risk of gun violence changes with the specific motivation for the juvenile's use of a firearm. For example, motivations might be due to any of the following: membership in a gang; victimization and bullying from other juveniles; a desire to mimic others observed; and the intent to harm parents, teachers, or others disliked by the juvenile. These examples are considerably different from one another, and this demonstrates the contextual and subjective element of risk prediction associated with gun violence. Despite the difficulty in prediction, Kaser-Boyd (2002) provided five indicators that serve as warning signs of potential child/juvenile gun violence:

Police stand outside the east entrance of Columbine High School as bomb squads and SWAT teams secure students on April 20, 1999, in Littleton, Colorado, after two masked teens on a "suicide mission" stormed the school and blasted fellow students with guns and explosives before turning the weapons on themselves. Such school-related incidents have continued to occur during recent years.

1. *Exposure to violence, either in the home or in the community.* Although exposure to television violence is not commonly cited, it is a factor in a number of homicides. Furthermore, the preoccupation with violent images is a definite warning sign. This preoccupation is often stimulated by media exposure to violent acts.

2. *A lack of success with the normal tasks of adolescence.* (Two examples are failing in school or having no extracurricular involvement.)

3. *Social rejection and poor social supports.* Alienation and lack of empathy develop in large part from social deprivation.

4. *Intense anger* that has built up from previous events.

5. *An inability to express or resolve intense feelings in adaptive ways* and a proclivity for externalizing defenses or acting out. (p. 198)

It should be noted that young children may provide a variety of clues or indicators of future gun violence in artwork or other similar school assignments (COPS, 2007; Hanser, 2007c). However, teachers, parents, and other child care workers may find it quite difficult to distinguish usual fantasy drawings from those that are true warning signs (Hanser, 2007c). But as children grow older, drawings are not as likely to correlate with future gun violence (Hanser, 2007c); rather, many older juveniles will provide verbal references or warnings that are often dismissed by others who otherwise would be able to prevent the escalation of violence (Hanser, 2007c; Kaser-Boyd, 2002). In either event, most variables are not clearly discernible in many cases, with the possible exception of membership in a gang that has used violence and/or firearms in past gang-related incidents (Hanser, 2007c). Even with this information, most experts agree that there are no truly predictive variables that are particularly effective in distinguishing school firearms offenders from other students

(Kaser-Boyd, 2002). The good news on juvenile firearm homicide is that it is not on the rise; in fact, it has consistently decreased during the past two decades or so (see Figure 12.1). Indeed, research in 2016 released by the Office for Juvenile Justice and Delinquency Prevention (OJJDP) on juvenile homicides by firearms found the following:

1. From 1984 to 1994, the number of firearm-related homicides committed by known juvenile offenders quadrupled.

2. The sharp decline in homicides by known juvenile offenders from 1994 to 2001 was attributable entirely to a decline in homicides by firearm.

3. From 2002 to 2014, the number of nonfirearm-related homicides committed by known juvenile offenders was relatively stable.

4. In the mid-1990s, about 80% of known juvenile homicide offenders were involved in firearm-related homicides; this percentage fell to 62% in 2001 then rose to 72% by 2014.

Most violent crime by juveniles has traditionally been committed by male offenders. However, this has been changing and continues to change. Indeed, though crime by male offenders tended to drop from 2000 to 2004, female crime remained stable or actually increased (Chesney-Lind, 2013; Valdez, 2007). In addition, the types of offenses for which females are arrested and incarcerated have changed (Chesney-Lind, 2013; Valdez, 2007). In some areas of the United States, female gangs have actually assumed a role that is quite distinct and independent from that of local male gangs, and some have even excelled in criminal enterprise ventures such as drug trafficking (Chesney-Lind, 2013; Valdez, 2007).

The heightened involvement of females in violent offenses has been attributed to prior victimization of females (Chesney-Lind, 2013). This has been referred to as the "victim-turned-offender hypothesis" by some researchers (Hanser, 2007c). From an abundance of literature, it is clear that female offenders are often victims of sexual abuse and physical abuse during early childhood and tend to be victims of sexual assault and/or domestic abuse during adulthood (Chesney-Lind, 2013; Hanser, 2007c). The suggestion is that females become violent perpetrators in response to their own victimization, although substance abuse, economic conditions, and dysfunctional family lives have also been linked to violent offending by females (Bloom et al., 2003; Chesney-Lind, 2013).

Figure 12.1 Known Juvenile Homicide Offenders by Firearm Involvement, 1980–2014

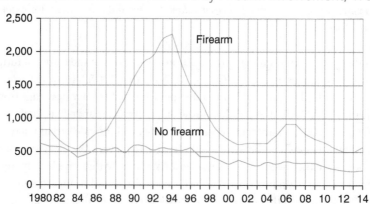

Source: Office of Juvenile Justice and Delinquency Prevention (2016).

Some violent crimes have been attributed to the rebirth of neo-Nazism in the form of "skinhead" groups such as the Nazi Low Riders, White Aryan Resistance, Hammer Skins, World Church of the Creator, and other groups whose members perpetrate hate crimes (Hamm, 1993; Valdez, 2007, 2011; Wooden & Blazak, 2001, p. 131). Whether these groups can be legitimately defined as gangs is a matter of perspective, but they are often excluded from the traditional definition because they are typically organized around the overt ideology of racism rather than as the result of shared culture and experiences (Hamm, 1993). Still, they may be considered as politicized gangs because they use violence for the purpose of promoting political change by instilling fear in innocent people. The debate rages as to whether violent crimes are related to violence in the media (Centerwood, 1992; Kaser-Boyd, 2002; Wooden & Blazak, 2001, pp. 113–114). As a result, there has been considerable pressure and some success in getting television networks to tone down violence and to label programs with violent content as such. Many of the violent crimes attributed to juveniles are drug-related crimes involving gang disputes over drug territories or attempts to steal to get money to buy drugs (McGloin, 2005). And, of course, a great deal of violence is associated with traditional street gangs, as well as neo-Nazi white supremacists.

Gangs

Gangs pose a serious social problem in the United States. It is no secret that in U.S. communities, large and small, the fear wrought by teen gangs has spread rapidly. With gang victimizations reported daily, many people have become virtual prisoners in their own homes. The trepidation caused by gang drive-by shootings causes schools to practice "ducking drills" and people to huddle in their darkened homes, hide their children in bathtubs, and be afraid to let their children play outside. (Peak, 1999, p. 51)

It should be noted that although we once could have referred to gangs as "juvenile" gangs, such a distinction is no longer totally appropriate because many gangs now include older adults among their memberships. Indeed, some researchers and practitioners have noted that gangs can be intergenerational in nature (Howell et al., 2011; Valdez, 2007, 2011). In communities that have intergenerational membership, it is often found that multiple family members—all of different age ranges—may be current or past gang members. In such families, children are essentially socialized into the gang subculture through their families and through the surrounding community. In fact, the majority of citizen members in these communities may be gang members or at least gang sympathizers, making it very difficult for police or community supervision personnel to combat gang activity in these areas (Valdez, 2007).

The "turf" gangs of yesteryear have been replaced in many instances by sophisticated criminal organizations involved in drug trafficking, extortion, murder, and other illegal activities (Egley & Howell, 2012; Howell et al., 2011; Klein, 2005; McGloin, 2005; Valdez, 2007). These street gangs destroy entire neighborhoods, maiming and killing their residents.

Gang signs and symbols may be included in graffiti, which may also identify a gang's turf.

© iStockphoto.com/AnderAguirre

They destroy family life, render school and social programs ineffective, deface property, and terrify decent citizens. Last but not least, they have grown into national organizations that support and encourage criminal activities not only in local neighborhoods but also across the country and internationally (Egley & Howell, 2012). Some 756,000 gang members were thought to be active in more than 29,400 gangs across the United States in 2010 (Egley & Howell, 2012). As seen in Figure 12.2, when examining the national demographics of juvenile gangs, about 46% of all gang members were thought to be Hispanic, 35% were thought to be African American, 11% were thought to be Caucasian, and 7% were thought to be Asian or "other" (National Gang Center, 2013). More than one-third of all youth gangs were thought to have memberships including members of two or more racial groups (McGloin, 2005).

Every city with a population of 250,000 or more reported the presence of gangs (Bilchik, 1999c; McGloin, 2005). Although gang problems continue to be a big-city problem early in the 21st century, they are by no means confined to such cities. In fact, the number of cities with populations of 1,000 to 5,000 reporting gang activities has increased 27 times, and the number of cities with populations of 5,000 to 10,000 reporting gang activities has increased more than 32 times (Miller, 2001, p. x). The number of gang members in rural counties increased by 43% from 1996 to 1998 (Wilson, 2000). Indeed, the largest proportion of gang members involved in burglary or breaking and entering was reported in rural counties (Wilson, 2000, p. xv).

Examining this further, we find that larger cities continue to exhibit the highest rates of prevalence for gang activity when compared to smaller cities, suburban regions, or rural counties (see Figure 12.3). It is speculated that the rates for suburban regions are closest to the rates of large cities due to both having relatively large populations. We contend that this is also simply due to proximity; the suburbs surrounding these larger cities are the most convenient locations into which large city gangs can most readily extend their criminal activity,

Figure 12.2 Race/Ethnicity of Gang Members, 1996–2011

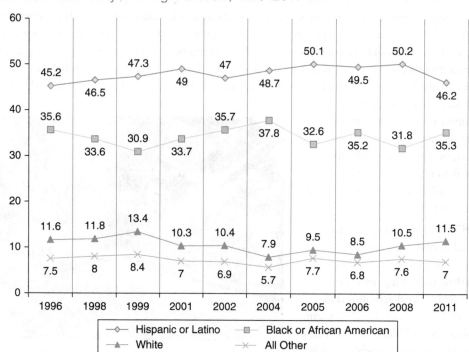

Source: National Gang Center (2013).

Figure 12.3 Reports of Gang Problems by Area Type, 1996–2012

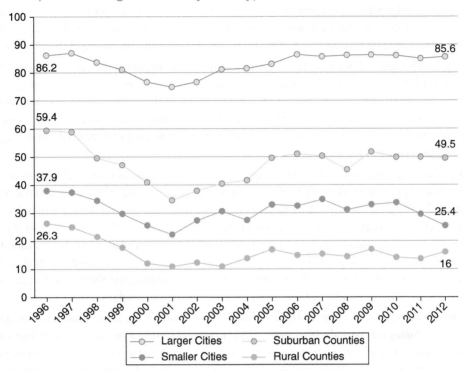

Source: National Gang Center (2013).

without actually having to completely relocate their base of operations. These areas, geographically, are also the next most logical location to which these gangs can expand, if they desire to do so. Further, there is a shifting of inner-city slum and ghetto-based gangs to suburban areas due to growing popularity and iconic portrayals of gang membership among many suburban youth (Howell et al., 2011).

Brief History of Gangs

Thrasher's classic study of juvenile gangs was published in 1927 and included information based on more than 1,300 gangs in the Chicago area, including fraternities, playgroups, and street corner gangs. His study was the first to emphasize the organized purposeful behavior of youth gangs. He found that gangs emerged from the interstitial areas as a result of social and economic conditions, became integrated through conflict, gradually developed an esprit de corps or solidarity, and protected their territory against outsiders much like today's gangs.

According to Thrasher (1927), gangs originate naturally during the adolescent years from spontaneous playgroups, which eventually find themselves in conflict with other groups. As a result of this conflict, it becomes mutually beneficial for individuals to band together in a gang to protect their rights and satisfy needs that their environment and families cannot provide. By middle adolescence, a gang has distinctive characteristics that include a name, a geographical territory, a mode of operation, and usually an ethnic or racial distinction. Thrasher not only analyzed gang behavior and activity but also was concerned about the effect of the local community on gangs. He found that if the environment is permissive and lacks control, gang activity will be facilitated. If there is a high presence of adult crime, a form of hero worshiping occurs with high status given to adult criminals. This type of environment is conducive to, and supportive of, gang behavior.

Although Thrasher did his analysis more than 75 years ago, his conclusions appear to be borne out in terms of contemporary gang and neighborhood activities. Gangs clearly flourish where control of streets and children has been lost and under circumstances where role models are basically older males involved in criminal activity (Valdez, 2005, 2007), as shown in the What Would You Do? feature at the beginning of this chapter.

The Chicago school spurred other studies of gangs that generally supported the earlier images of that school. Shaw and McKay (1942) found that most offenses were committed in association with others in gangs and that most boys were socialized into criminal careers by other offenders in the neighborhood. As indicated earlier, Cohen (1955), in his book *Delinquent Boys*, emphasized that gang juveniles have a negative value system by middle-class standards. This results in a "status frustration" that is acted out in a "nonutilitarian, negativistic" fashion through the vehicle of the gang.

Yablonsky (1962) indicated that violent gangs, at least, are not as well organized and highly structured as some theorists had supposed. In addition, Yablonsky indicated that the police, the public, and the press may help to create and unify gangs by attributing to gangs numerous acts that gangs did not commit. Strong support for Yablonsky's conclusions can be found in Dawley's (1973) book, *A Nation of Lords*, which is an autobiography of sorts about the Vice Lords in Chicago. Over the past decade, however, violent gangs have unquestionably become more organized, with gangs such as El Rukn and the Bloods and Crips illustrating that such organizations extend even into prisons. Other gangs are also demonstrating the ability to organize mobile units and maintain branch units in scattered cities, largely in response to drug markets.

Cohen, Miller, and others (see Chapter 4) further developed theories of gang delinquency during the 1950s and 1960s. During this period, delinquency came to be regarded as a product of social forces rather than individual deviance. Gang members were viewed as basically normal juveniles who, under difficult circumstances, adopted a gang subculture to deal with their disadvantaged socioeconomic positions. Gangs attracted a good deal of attention as a result of their apparent opposition to conventional norms and sometimes were romanticized, as in the popular *West Side Story*.

By the late 1960s and early 1970s, the United States was in a period of social upheaval marked by civil disturbances, racial protests, antiwar demonstrations, and student protests. Labeling theory came into vogue, postulating that members of the lower social class are more likely to be labeled as deviant than are those in the middle and upper classes as a result of the balance of power resting with the latter. Gangs were viewed as a response to injustice and oppression. Control theory was popular with this political faction because it postulated that delinquency was largely an individual matter, developing early in life and occurring due to a lack of internal and external controls. Failure of institutions such as the family, police, and corrections became the focal point of those representing the conservative viewpoint, obviating the need to deal with the social structure and conditions that were the focus of the liberal camp. The latter group continued to view gang members as juveniles in need of help rather than punishment. While these groups argued over the source of responsibility for crime and delinquency in general, developments that would soon lead society to take another look at the gang phenomenon were occurring.

During the 1960s, a Chicago gang known as the Blackstone Rangers (later called the Black P Stone Nation and still later known as El Rukn) emerged as a group characterized by a high degree of organization and considerable influence. The Blackstone Rangers sought and were granted federal funds, as well as funds from private enterprises, to support their activities. This funding gave the gang an appearance of political and social respectability. Street gangs in America were becoming politicized. Miller (1974) stated the following:

[The notion of] transforming gangs by diverting their energies from traditional forms of gang activities—particularly illegal forms—and channeling them into "constructive" activities is probably as old, in the United States, as gangs themselves. Thus, in the 1960s, when a series of social movements aimed at elevating the lot of the poor through ideologically oriented, citizen-executed political activism became widely current, it was perhaps inevitable that the idea be applied to gangs. (p. 410)

Jacobs (1977) offered three explanations as to why Chicago street gangs, as well as those in many other urban areas, became politicized during the 1960s:

1. Street gangs adopted a radical ideology from the militant civil rights movement.
2. Street gangs became committed to social change for their community as a whole.
3. Street gangs became politically sophisticated, realizing that the political system could be used to further their own needs—money, power, and organized growth. (p. 145)

Jacobs maintained that the third explanation is applicable to the Blackstone Rangers and many other large gangs in metropolitan areas. The leadership learned how to use the system to provide capital for the gangs' illegal activities. Gangs showed increased sophistication in organizing their activities along the lines of organized crime. Individual felonies were replaced by major criminal activity involving drugs, weapons, extortion, prostitution, and gambling. Fistfights were replaced by violent acts involving the use of weapons.

During the 1980s, society became increasingly concerned with violence and prescriptions for crime control, and this concern carried over into the 1990s and the new century (Bilchik, 1999c). Attention has once again focused on crime and delinquency resulting from failures of social institutions, inadequate deterrence, and insufficient incapacitation. Deterrence research has become popular, focusing on police, probation, and corrections activities rather than on gang dynamics. Current emphasis is on preventing juveniles from joining gangs through community education and involvement and on bringing to a halt the violent activities of gangs through stricter laws, better prosecution, more severe sanctions, and negotiated peace agreements between feuding gangs.

The last quarter of the 20th century was marked by significant growth in youth gang problems across the United States. In the 1970's, less than half of the states reported youth gang problems, but by the late 1990's, every state and the District of Columbia reported youth gang activity. (Miller, 2001, p. iii)

The states with the largest numbers of gang problem cities have traditionally been California, Florida, Illinois, Ohio, and Texas (Howell et al., 2011; Klein, 2005; McGloin, 2005).

Defining and Identifying Street Gangs

When defining and identifying street gangs, it is important to understand that there is no universally agreed-upon definition of *gang* in the United States. *Gang*, *youth gang*, and *street gang* are terms widely and often interchangeably used in mainstream coverage. Reference to gangs often implies youth gangs. In some cases, youth gangs are distinguished from other types of gangs; how *youth* is defined may vary as well. For this chapter, we use the federal definition of gangs, used by the Department of Justice and the Department of Homeland Security's Immigration and Customs Enforcement (ICE), and available from the National Institute of Justice website, which provides the following:

1. An association of three or more individuals;
2. whose members collectively identify themselves by adopting a group identity, which they use to create an atmosphere of fear or intimidation, frequently by employing one or more of the following: a common name, slogan, identifying sign, symbol, tattoo or other physical marking, style or color of clothing, hairstyle, hand sign or graffiti;

3. whose purpose in part is to engage in criminal activity and which uses violence or intimidation to further its criminal objectives; and

4. whose members engage in criminal activity or acts of juvenile delinquency that if committed by an adult would be crimes with the intent to enhance or preserve the association's power, reputation or economic resources.

The association may also possess some of the following characteristics:

1. The members may employ rules for joining and operating within the association.

2. The members may meet on a recurring basis.

3. The association may provide physical protection of its members from others.

4. The association may seek to exercise control over a particular geographic location or region, or it may simply defend its perceived interests against rivals.

5. The association may have an identifiable structure.

Most of the research literature on gangs focuses primarily on youth gangs rather than adult gangs. One of the premiere authorities on gang activity is the National Gang Center, a research agency cosponsored by the Bureau of Justice Assistance (BJA) and the OJJDP. This federally sponsored research center provided a general description for juvenile gangs as "a group of youths or young adults willing to identify as a 'gang'" (National Gang Center, 2010). Further, it provided the following criteria as being specific to classifying groups of gangs:

• The group has three or more members, generally aged 12 to 24.

• Members share an identity, typically linked to a name, and often other symbols.

• Members view themselves as a gang, and they are recognized by others as a gang.

• The group has some permanence and a degree of organization.

• The group is involved in an elevated level of criminal activity.

Roles and Activities of Juvenile Versus Adult Gang Members

Antisocial and criminal conduct by members of juvenile gangs is not a new phenomenon. Early immigrant groups arriving in this country frequently found themselves located in the worst slums of urban areas, and gangs soon emerged. Among the earliest juvenile gangs were those of Irish background, followed later by Italian and Jewish gangs and eventually by gangs of virtually all ethnic and racial backgrounds. Typically, members of these gangs left gang activities behind as they grew older, married, found employment, and raised families (Howell et al., 2011; Huff, 1996; Siegel, Welsh, & Senna, 2003). Some, however, gravitated to adult gangs and into organized criminal activities (Abadinsky, 2003). The path from juvenile gang membership to adult crime seems to have broadened during recent years, so although it is true that some street gangs are still little more than collections of neighborhood juveniles with penchants for macho posturing, many are emerging as drug terrorism gangs that terrify residents of inner-city neighborhoods. In fact, the National Criminal Justice Reference Service (NCJRS) provides data that demonstrate this observation. For instance, in 1996, 50% of gang members were juveniles (i.e., under 18 years) and 50% were adults (i.e., 18 years or over). However, just 3 years later (in 1999), it was found that roughly 37% were juveniles and 63% were adult offenders (NCJRS, 2005). Figure 12.4 shows how, during the years from 1996 to 2011, juvenile membership composition in gangs has varied but, since 1996, has consistently stayed at or under 40%, meaning that the majority of gang members are actually adult offenders.

Figure 12.4 Proportion of Gang Members Who Are Youth Versus Adult

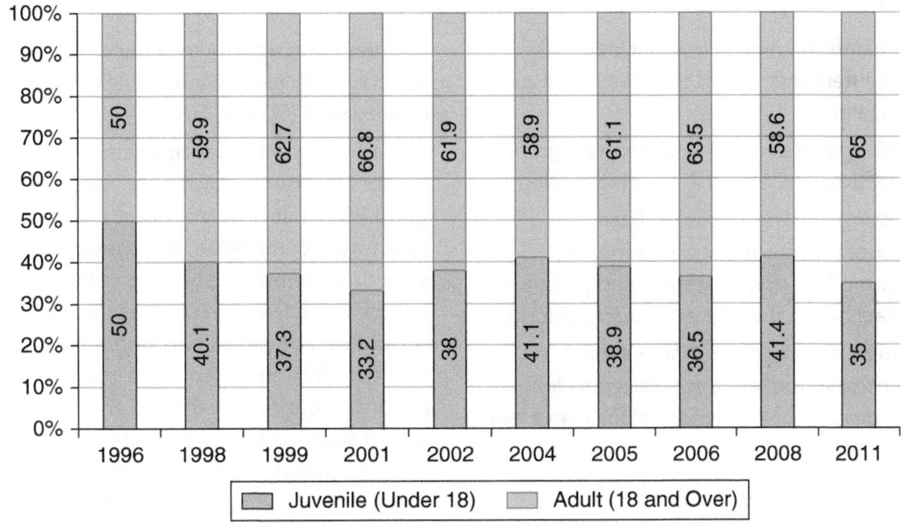

Figure showing stacked bar chart with Juvenile (Under 18) and Adult (18 and Over) values by year:
- 1996: Adult 50, Juvenile 50
- 1998: Adult 59.9, Juvenile 40.1
- 1999: Adult 62.7, Juvenile 37.3
- 2001: Adult 66.8, Juvenile 33.2
- 2002: Adult 61.9, Juvenile 38
- 2004: Adult 58.9, Juvenile 41.1
- 2005: Adult 61.1, Juvenile 38.9
- 2006: Adult 63.5, Juvenile 36.5
- 2008: Adult 58.6, Juvenile 41.4
- 2011: Adult 65, Juvenile 35

Legend: Juvenile (Under 18), Adult (18 and Over)

Source: National Gang Center (2013).

Thus, it is clear that adults have the greatest influence over gang activity. These adult members likewise tend to form the leadership for most street gangs (Valdez, 2005), just as was shown in the What Would You Do? feature at the beginning of this chapter. However, there are indications that many juveniles that do engage in gang activity may be more willing to engage in violence (see In Practice 12.2).

IN PRACTICE 12.2

DEVELOPMENT OF A COMPREHENSIVE COMMUNITY-WIDE GANG PROGRAM MODEL

With funding by the OJJDP, a group of researchers has developed what has often been referred to as the Comprehensive Community-Wide Gang Program Model (Spergel et al., 1994). This model has been widely adopted among agencies and communities that are successful in developing collaborative anti-gang programs, particularly those related to juvenile gang offending. According to Spergel et al. (1994, pp. 2–5), an ideal program should include several components, which are listed as follows:

Addressing the problem. A community must recognize the presence of a gang problem before it can do anything meaningful to address the problem.

Organizing and developing policy. Communities must organize effectively to combat the youth gang problem.

Coordinating and encouraging community participation. A mobilized community is the most promising way to deal with the gang problem.

Making youth accountable. While youth gang members must be held accountable for their criminal acts, they must at the same time be provided an opportunity to change or control their behavior.

Staffing. Youth gang intervention and control efforts require a thorough understanding of the complexity of gang activity in the context of local community life.

(Continued)

(Continued)

Training staff. Training should include prevention, intervention, and suppression in gang problem localities.

Researching and evaluating. Determining what is most effective, and why, is a daunting challenge.

Establishing funding priorities. Based on available research, theory, and experience, community mobilization strategies and programs should be accorded the highest funding priority.

In addition, communities that use this comprehensive model are encouraged to follow a five-step process of implementation. These five steps consist of the following:

1. The community and its leaders acknowledge the youth gang problem.

2. The community conducts an assessment of the nature and scope of the youth gang problem, leading to the identification of a target community or communities and population(s).

3. Through a steering committee, the community and its leaders set goals and objectives to address the identified problem(s).

4. The steering committee makes available relevant programs, strategies, services, tactics, and procedures consistent with the model's five core strategies.

5. The steering committee evaluates the effectiveness of the response to the gang problem, reassesses the problem, and modifies approaches, as needed.

These steps have been tested in several settings by the OJJDP and have been found to be effective throughout various regions of the United States (OJJDP, 2007). Regardless, the exact means by which a community will address a gang problem differs depending on the event or events that draw public attention to the issue. In some cases, a high-profile, often-tragic event occurs that galvanizes the community and stimulates mobilization to address gangs (OJJDP, 2007). In other cases, an increase in public support to address gang activity may build more gradually and may only lack an individual or agency to serve as a catalyst (OJJDP, 2007).

At some point, key agencies and community leaders will begin to openly discuss and address gang issues. It is at this point that a standing task force, committee, or organizational structure (namely a steering committee, as noted in the five-step process just discussed) should be convened and begin to work on implementation of the steps that should follow. It is this steering committee that can provide group leadership to ensure that problems are addressed and can also administrate the collection of initiatives and resources listed by Spergel et al. (1994). This approach has been shown to improve community response to gang problems and has also been shown to empower communities. Such an approach is therefore a positive means of bringing the community together in a manner that is constructive while also eliminating factors that seem to breed juvenile gang membership.

Sources: OJJDP (2007); Spergel et al. (1994).

Questions to Consider

1. True or False: The key component of the Comprehensive Community-Wide Gang Program (Spergel) Model is the integration of police suppression techniques.

2. Multiple Choice: An ideal antigang program should have which of the following components?

   a. Youth accountability

   b. Process to organize and develop policy

   c. Research and evaluation

   d. All of the above

   e. None of the above

3. Explain why this type of intervention approach might be well-suited for diverse communities (hint: this model uses community members themselves).

Street gangs violate civilized rules of behavior, engaging in murder, rape, robbery, intimidation, extortion, burglary, prostitution, and drug trafficking. During the 1990s, drive-by shootings became another tool of gang members who were seeking retribution but were unconcerned about the lives of innocent bystanders often shot in the process (Valdez, 2007). The activities of gangs have become increasingly serious, more sophisticated, and more violent, and they are more likely to involve the use of weapons (Siegel et al., 2003; Valdez, 2007, 2011). Gangs have become problematic in California, where the legislature passed a law making it a felony to belong to a gang known to engage in criminal activities, and other jurisdictions are in the process of establishing similar legislation. Although the constitutionality of these laws has yet to be established, their mere existence indicates how serious the gang problem is perceived to be.

The days when rival gangs fought each other over "turf" and "colors" are a thing of the past. Today, gang conflicts are more in the form of urban guerrilla warfare over drug trafficking (Hanser, 2007a). Gang turf is now drug sales territory. Informers, snitches, and competitors are ruthlessly punished or assassinated. Street warfare and the bloody rampage of gang violence are the norm in many inner cities. As an illustration of these points, it is estimated that 3,340 member-based gang homicides were committed in 1997 (Bilchik, 1999c, p. 15; Valdez, 2007). Gang members commit a disproportionate share of crime for their numbers (Howell et al., 2011; Klein, 2005; McGloin, 2005). Statistical data indicate that although gang membership in a given jurisdiction might not be high and gang members constitute only a small percentage of all criminals, they typically commit more offenses than their non–gang member criminal counterparts (NCJRS, 2005). In large metropolitan areas such as Chicago, New York, Miami, and Los Angeles, gang-related homicides number in the hundreds annually (Valdez, 2007). Many of these homicides result from gang wars and retaliations, and often the victims are innocent bystanders or those unable to defend themselves (Hughes, 2005). The macho image of gang members confronting each other in open warfare is largely a creation of the media. More often, gang killings occur on the streets, in the dark, as a result of gang members in a speeding vehicle firing shots at their intended victim(s). To get a clear understanding of how gangs are closely related to homicide rates, consider that homicide is the second leading cause of death for individuals aged 15 to 24. Further, in cities like Los Angeles and Long Beach, gang homicides account for the majority of murders in this age group (61% and 69%, respectively). As Figure 12.5 shows, a substantial number of homicides are gang-related.

Major gangs have made narcotics trafficking (sale and distribution of drugs) an important source of income, and activities in this area have become even more lucrative with the advent of a street market for a variety of drugs. For instance, Latino street gangs are highly active in the trafficking of heroin and cocaine that originate in Mexico and South America, respectively (Hanser, 2007a; Thompson, 2004). Some of the increase in gang violence is a result of competition over turf ownership related to the sale of these products. Gangs involved in profit-oriented schemes frequently resort to violence to protect their illicit businesses (Hanser, 2007a; Thompson, 2004). With this shift to more business-oriented activities, some gangs have gone underground; members no longer openly display colors or graffiti, sometimes leading to the mistaken assumption that gang activity in a particular area has ceased (Hughes, 2005; Klein, 2005; McGloin, 2005).

On other occasions, even when officials know that gangs are behind a good deal of the illegal activity occurring in their jurisdictions, they deny the importance of gangs for political reasons (Valdez, 2005). Political officials, including some police chiefs, would prefer not to make themselves look bad by admitting that gang activity in their areas is uncontrollable. It is estimated that 42% of youth gangs are involved in the street sale of drugs for the purpose of making a profit for their gangs and that 33% of youth gangs in the United States are involved in the distribution of drugs. Crack cocaine and marijuana are thought by law enforcement agencies to lead the list of drugs sold (Bilchik, 1999c, pp. 22, 25, 28).

Figure 12.5 Estimated Gang-Related Mortality Rates Among 33 Cities Using National Violence Death Reporting System (NVDRS) and/or National Youth Gang Survey Data (NYGS), 2003–2008

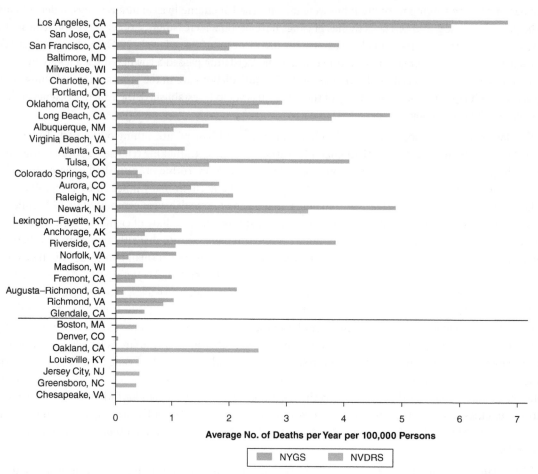

Source: Centers for Disease Control and Prevention (2012). Gang homicides: Five U.S. cities, 2003–2008. *Morbidity and Mortality Weekly Report, 61*(3), 45–51.

An illustration of the drug gang problem can be seen in South Central Los Angeles, where the Bloods and Crips reign (Huff, 1996; Valdez, 2005). These gangs consist of confederations of neighborhood gangs, each with a relatively small number of members. The gangs have traditionally been involved in robbery, home invasion, burglary, and homicide, but they became involved in drug trafficking as a major enterprise with the production of crack cocaine. The Bloods (whose color is red) and the Crips (whose color is blue) date back to the late 1960s and early 1970s and consist of "rollers" or "gangbangers" who are in their 20s and 30s—gang veterans who have made it big in the drug trade (Huff, 1996; Valdez, 2005). These veterans supervise and control the activities of younger members who are involved in drug trafficking and operating and supplying crack houses—activities that bring in millions of dollars a week. The drug trafficking of the Bloods and Crips spread into other cities, including Seattle, Portland, Denver, Kansas City, Des Moines, and even Honolulu and Anchorage (Hieb, 1992). Police sources there say that from January to November 2000, there were some 64 gang-related shootings and 34 gang-motivated gun battles between the Bloods and the Crips (McPhee, 2000). In 2004, more than half of the almost 1,000 homicides committed in Los Angeles and Chicago were considered to be gang related (OJJDP, 2008).

Gang Affiliation and Identification Along Racial Lines

Many gangs throughout the United States have developed along racial or ethnic lines. This was true during the early historical development of gangs when ethnic immigrant groups formed gangs in early American history. It has continued to be the case throughout generations, and, as we have noted, many gangs are multigenerational, with family membership extending back several generations. In these cases, neighborhoods where ethnic and racial groups predominate and where gangs have their homes, there will be a tendency for future members to be drawn from the same racial or ethnic backgrounds of which the gang initially was composed. This process, therefore, gets replicated throughout generations. Further, gangs in prisons tend to be aligned on racial loyalties, which also is true in most juvenile institutions. As youth exit these facilities and rejoin youth on the streets, they "stick with their own" both on the inside and on the outside of institutions. Further, adult members of gangs also continue this very same tendency and, of course, pass this form of loyalty on to more junior gang members.

In Chicago, for example, major street gangs include the Black Disciples or Black Gangster Disciple Nation or Brothers of the Struggle (BOS) who are collectively known as folks. They are in competition with the Vice Lords, also known as the Conservative Vice Lord Nation, who have aligned themselves with other groups such as the Vice Queens and Latin Kings (Main, 2001; Main & Spielman, 2000). These gangs are collectively referred to as people (Babicky, 1993a, 1993b; Dart, 1992). Splinter gangs of people and folks have been found in Minneapolis, Des Moines, Green Bay, and the Quad Cities area of Illinois. Activities include extortion, drug trafficking, and violent crime in the form of homicide, robbery, drive-by shooting, and battery.

Although street gangs are predominantly black and Hispanic, the Simon City Royals (folks) are a white gang that originated in Chicago during the early 1960s. Originally formed to stop the "invasion" of Hispanic gangs into their area of the city, the Royals became actively involved in burglaries and home invasions during the 1980s. As leaders of the gang were imprisoned, they formed alliances with the Black Gangster Disciples for protection, and the alliances continue today (Babicky, 1993a, 1993b; Multijurisdictional Counterdrug Task Force Training [MCTFT], 2010). These alliances were based on agreements with the drug trade and became so strong that Larry Hoover, the leader of the Gangster Disciples, created an official cross-racial alliance between the two gangs and essentially adopted the Simon City Royals as folks, with the same status as traditional Gangster Disciples. This meant that Disciples were then obligated to protect their fellow folks members who were Caucasian. Eventually, the Simon City Royals developed a formal constitution that incorporated the six points (and the six-point star) characteristic of the Folk Nation (MCTFT, 2010).

Latino gangs exist in every major urban area and many suburban areas. Indeed, Latino gangs have spread to various areas of the United States, including cities in the Southwest, Florida, New York, and the city of Chicago. In fact, the NCJRS (2005) estimated that nearly 47% of all gang members are Latino. Furthermore, in states such as Arizona, it is reported that fully 62% of gang members are Latino. Other areas of the Southwest report similar levels of Latino gang activity (NCJRS, 2005).

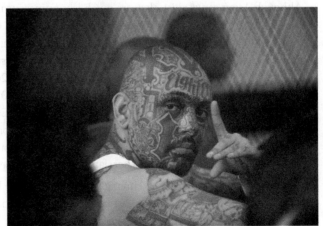

JOHAN ORDONEZ/AFP/Getty Images

Tattoos may be used to signify gang affiliation as well as to express individuality.

Among gangs in general, including Latino gangs, there has been an emergence of gang nations (Attorney General of Texas, 2002; MCTFT, 2010). The term *gang nation* is an informal name for a very large gang that may have several affiliated subsets of members, sometimes stretching across vast areas of the United States (Attorney General of Texas, 2002; MCTFT, 2010). Increasingly, law enforcement officials are considering the Surenos and Nortenos in California, as well as the Mexican Mafia in California and Texas, to be gang nations (Hanser, 2007a). These two Latino gang nations are made up of smaller "sets" that share certain symbols and loyalties. These gang nations have become so large that different sets of the same gang might not even know each other except by recognition of some common sign or insignia (Attorney General of Texas, 2002; MCTFT, 2010). In fact, these sets, although belonging to the same nation, may develop rivalries among themselves while also rallying against a common enemy (Attorney General of Texas, 2002; Hanser, 2007a).

In the United States, there has recently been an emergence of Latino gangs whose membership comes largely from nations in Central America (Hanser, 2007a; Thompson, 2004; Valdez, 2005). During the past decade, gangs have migrated across Central America and into Mexico, ultimately to settle in the United States. This migration has occurred due to military targeting of these gangs in their native nations of El Salvador, Guatemala, and Honduras (Thompson, 2004). The arrival of these new immigrants has generated an unending stream of gang-related violence in many Latino neighborhoods in various areas of California (Hanser, 2007a; Thompson, 2004).

The two largest Central American gangs in the United States are the Mara Salvatruchas (known as MS-13) and the Mara 18 (also known as MS-18), and both of these gangs originated on the streets of Los Angeles (Hanser, 2007a; Thompson, 2004). The Salvatruchas gang was started by the children of refugees from various war-torn countries in Central America (Thompson, 2004). Conversely, the Mara 18 (known as the 18th Street gang) was started by Mexican immigrants who arrived during the 1970s. The 18th Street gang and the Mara Salvatruchas are polar enemies of one another (Hanser, 2007a; Thompson, 2004; Valdez, 2005). Both gangs have experienced tremendous growth, although the MS-13 has gained the greatest national notoriety. Given the sheer numbers of illegal immigrants entering the United States from Mexico, prevention of gang immigrants seems to be virtually impossible for law enforcement agencies in the southwestern region of the United States. In the following chapter, it will become clear that these two gangs have become an international regional threat, their influence spreading from Honduras throughout Central America, Mexico, and various areas of the United States (United Nations, 2003). Their impact on Latino youth in these areas of the Americas is profound—particularly for those Latino youth at risk of gang involvement.

Although Asian gangs exist, they are much less numerous than those consisting of African American or Latino American members. Asian gangs are located mostly in California (particularly Los Angeles), New York, Virginia, and Philadelphia and consist of mainly Chinese, Vietnamese, Cambodian, Korean, and Hmong communities and are involved in a variety of illegal activities such as extortion, protection of illegal enterprises, and summary executions of members of rival gangs (Valdez, 2005). Often, these gang members victimize their own ethnic groups and/or communities (Abadinsky, 2003; Valdez, 2005). Groups like the Tiny Rascal Gangsters have spread from California and are found on the East Coast of the United States as well as in Canada. This gang originated in Cambodia, and many of its original members have immigrated to the United States and Thailand to escape imprisonment in their home country (Kuanliang, 2010). This gang recruits non-Asian members on occasion, with Caucasian and African American members being found in the United States.

Other Asian gangs, such as the Hmong Nation Society, are located in major cities, some suburbs of California, and in some areas of the East Coast. This gang's adopted color is deep red (symbolic of blood), and the gang was largely noted for its violence during the late 1990s. In particular, this gang has been known to commit gang-related sexual assaults of women in Hmong communities, as well as establishing extortion rackets of Asian businesses and being active in the drug trade. It is important to note that Hmong culture is very patriarchal in nature; boys are much more prized than girls in Hmong families. The honor system among the Hmong holds that men drive the wealth of the family, preside over functions, and hold predominant social clout. Thus, members of Hmong and other Laotian descent will tend to be very macho in their beliefs. Often, the acts of sexual assault committed by the Hmong Nation Society on young Hmong women assert their superiority and are designed to disrespect and dishonor families aligned against their gang.

A variety of other Asian gangs exist in California. There are known to be thousands of members of Asian gangs located in Los Angeles and surrounding counties. The activities of these gangs are routinely reported in local newspapers and on local television. These gangs vary as to the specific Asian nationality that predominates as membership. Some gangs may have mixed Asian national descendants and some may even allow non-Asians to become members. In general, these gangs tend to be more difficult for law enforcement to infiltrate and gain intelligence because of language and cultural challenges as well as the fact that there tends to be few Asian police officers (and investigators) when compared to other racial or ethnic groups.

Delinquent and Criminal Gang Activities

Gangs engage in a wide variety of activities, including the following:

1. *Vandalism*—graffiti and wanton destruction
2. *Harassment and intimidation*—to recruit members, to exact revenge on those who report their activities, and so forth
3. *Armed robbery and burglary*—the elderly and, more recently, suburban communities targeted
4. *Extortion* of the following:
   a. *Students in schools*—protection money
   b. *Businesses*—protection money to avoid burglaries, fires, vandalism, and general destruction
   c. *Narcotics dealers*—protection money to operate in a specific geographic area and a percentage of the "take"
   d. *Neighborhood residents*—who pay for the ability to come and go without being harassed and for the "privilege" of not having their property destroyed

Gang crime continues to grow in smaller suburban and even rural communities, which are frequently perceived as easy marks for theft, burglary, robbery, and shoplifting, among other crimes. In other cases, gangs migrate to these areas to avoid the intense competition of drug trafficking in the cities (see In Practice 12.2). The drug trade has been the primary means by which both adult and juvenile gangs generate income to fund their lifestyle. This activity is becoming increasingly more common within the suburban regions of the United States; it is not just an inner-city problem anymore. Table 12.2 provides a recent and detailed overview of the drug involvement (as well as region of operation) associated with many of the more commonly known street gangs.

Nearly every community has experienced wannabes, or juveniles who may wear gang colors and post graffiti in an attempt to emulate big-city gang members. Yet in many communities, gangs have been largely ignored. Part of the reason for the continued expansion of gang activities is the view that such activity is not our problem. Because many street gangs are ethnically oriented, it is easy to perceive the problem as affecting only certain groups or neighborhoods. Because members of traditional gangs are predominantly from the lower social class, gangs are perceived as problematic basically in lower-class areas. However, if gang activity is not dealt with quickly, the consequences soon spread to the larger community, including middle-class neighborhoods, and the problem may become unmanageable (Pattillo, 1998). Osgood and Chambers (2000) analyzed juvenile arrest rates for 264

Table 12.2 Gangs and Drug Trafficking Activity

Name	Primary Areas of Operation	Drugs Trafficked	Affiliations (DTOs)
18th Street	Pacific Southwest	Methamphetamine	Sinaloa Tijuana
Barrio Azteca	Southwest	Cocaine Heroin Marijuana Methamphetamine	Juárez
Bloods	New England New York/New Jersey Southeast Southwest Pacific	Cocaine Heroin Marijuana MDMA	Tijuana Sinaloa
Crips	New England Southeast Southwest Pacific	Cocaine Heroin Marijuana MDMA	Juárez
Gangster Disciples	Great Lakes Pacific Southeast West Central	Cocaine Heroin Marijuana	Sinaloa
Latin Kings	Florida Great Lakes New England New York/New Jersey Mid-Atlantic Pacific Southeast Southwest West Central	Cocaine Heroin Marijuana MDMA	Juárez Sinaloa Gulf Coast
Mara Salvatrucha	Mid-Atlantic New England New York/New Jersey Southeast Southwest West Central Pacific	Cocaine Heroin Marijuana Methamphetamine	Sinaloa Gulf Coast Zetas
Mexican Mafia	Southwest Pacific	Cocaine Marijuana	Sinaloa Tijuana Zetas
Mexikanemi	Southwest	Cocaine Marijuana Methamphetamine	Gulf Coast Zetas
Norteños	Pacific Southwest	Cocaine Marijuana Methamphetamine	Sinaloa Tijuana
Sureños	Pacific Southwest West Central Southeast Southeast	Cocaine Heroin Marijuana Methamphetamine	Sinaloa Tijuana
Texas Syndicate	Southwest	Cocaine Marijuana	Gulf Coast Zetas
Tiny Rascal Gangsters	New England Pacific	Marijuana MDMA	Asian DTOs

Source: National Gang Intelligence Center (2015).

nonmetropolitan counties in four states. They concluded that juvenile violence in nonmetropolitan areas is associated with residential instability, family disruption, ethnic heterogeneity, and population size. Evans, Fitzgerald, and Weigel (1999) found no significant differences in gang membership or pressure to join gangs between rural and urban juveniles. Urban juveniles, however, were more likely to report having friends in gangs and being threatened by gangs than were their rural counterparts.

Gang Membership

Several studies throughout the past four decades have explored why youth join gangs. Decker and Van Winkle (1996) and Valdez (2005) conducted research that examined numerous risk factors that make youth more likely to join gangs. These risk factors were grouped into individual, family, peer group, school, and neighborhood categories. A list of these categories and the risk factors they included is provided in Table 12.3.

Although the various risk factors associated with youth gang membership exist in numerous vantage points, it is interesting to also note that these factors do have an additive effect. Indeed, it is clear that the more risk factors experienced by the youth, the more likely he or she is to join a gang. Hill et al. (2001) examined four

Table 12.3 Categories and Corresponding Risk Factors Associated With Likely Gang Membership

Category	Risk Factor(s)
Individual	Low religious service attendance Early marijuana use Early violence Antisocial beliefs Early drinking Externalizing behaviors Poor refusal skills
Family	Family structure One parent only One parent plus other adults Parental attitudes favoring violence Low bonding with parents Low household income Sibling antisocial behavior Poor family management
Peer group	Association with friends who engage in problem behaviors
School	Learning disabled Low academic achievement Low school attachment Low school commitment Low academic aspirations
Neighborhood	Availability of marijuana Neighborhood youth in trouble Low neighborhood attachment

Source: Hill, Lui, & Hawkins (2001).

Figure 12.6 Odds of Joining a Gang Based on Risk Factors

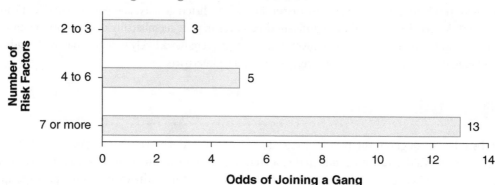

Source: Hill, Lui, & Hawkins (2001).

groups of potentially at-risk youth based on the number of risk factors they possessed. They found that the more risk factors were present in the youth's life, the greater the odds of him or her joining a gang. Indeed, youth who had two or three risk factors were 3 times more likely to join a gang (see Figure 12.6), whereas youth with four to six risk factors were found to be 5 times as likely to join a gang than those who had no risk factors. Finally, youth with seven or more risk factors were 13 times more likely to join a gang when compared to youth with only one or zero risk factors.

Aside from listing the risk factors that can predict likely gang involvement, it is perhaps best to view the likelihood of joining a gang as entailing multiple pushes and pulls upon the juvenile (Decker & Van Winkle, 1996). Pushes are external factors that move a person toward circumstances that breed gang involvement, whereas pulls are internal factors that make gang life attractive to the individual. As has been discussed throughout this text, social and economic factors may essentially push youth into gang membership. This is particularly true if gangs have been well established and are long lasting in the community. In communities where gang membership is commonplace, juveniles join gangs for protection from other gangs and/or are virtually born into gang membership because their parents or family members have been prior members.

Economic factors can also push youth into gang membership. In areas of serious deprivation and where few prosocial opportunities exist, the prospect of joining a gang is enhanced—particularly if the gang is thought to offer material rewards that the youth can readily observe. Seeing other older (and admired) youngsters dressed in new clothes, having rolls of cash, jewelry, and multiple friends can be very enticing to a preteen or teenager. This is particularly true if the youth observes his or her parents working in some type of low-paid employment or if the parents are chronically unemployed. In addition, if the youth's family is unable to afford material goods or provide opportunities for the youngster, it becomes easy to see why, amid a community of little or no opportunities, youth will turn to gangs for their material security; there are seemingly no other truly viable options in their local area. Particularly, there are no options for which they are qualified, whereas gangs are always "hiring" regardless of economic conditions.

Urbanization is another factor that often serves as a push into gang membership. This factor, being a macrolevel influence on gang membership, has been found to impact likely gang membership throughout the United States and other areas of the world. Chapter 13 provides additional discussion regarding urbanization and its impact on worldwide gang membership; in other developing countries, this seems to be a primary factor in breeding the social and economic conditions for gang development. In the United States, urbanization has contributed as a push toward gang growth, but it is perhaps now more the case that the suburbs have become a new and equally common playing ground for gangs. Thus, one could say that suburbanization is a leading factor in gang growth in the United States. *Suburbanization* is a term that refers to the growth of urban sprawl throughout the United States, turning urban centers into large multijurisdictional conglomerates that include large areas of terrain.

Numerous pulls can also entice youth into gang membership. Feelings of connection, involvement, and a sense of identity can provide the emotional basis for joining a gang (Decker & Van Winkle, 1996; Howell, 1998). Indeed, it has been noted that "for some youth, gangs provide a way of solving social adjustment problems, particularly the trials and tribulation of adolescence" (Howell, 1998, p. 5). Further, the attractiveness of the gang may come by way of prestige or status that one may acquire through membership, especially if membership is seen as exclusive or difficult to obtain (Decker & Van Winkle, 1996; Valdez, 2005). The need for a sense of fellowship and brotherhood where psychological and/or emotional needs are met is often cited as a reason for membership among youth—particularly those who come from abusive or neglectful homes (Hanser & Mire, 2011; Valdez, 2005). Considerable research has found that gangs often provide youth with basic human needs related to belonging and a sense of self-worth (Hanser & Mire, 2011; Valdez, 2005). This is even more likely if the individual youth has not been an achiever in school, whether academically or athletically. Thus, the gang can be a surrogate family, of a sort.

This notion of connectedness as a surrogate family was noted even back in the 1940s when Whyte (1943) portrayed the gang as a street corner family. "Gangs are residual social subsystems often characterized by competition for status and, more recently, income opportunity through drug sales" (Curry & Spergel, 1988). Students are encouraged to examine In Practice 12.3 for more details on this topic.

Characteristics

Gang membership can be divided into three categories: (1) leaders, (2) hard-core members, and (3) marginal members. The leaders within gangs usually acquire their positions of power through one of two methods: (1) by being the "baddest" or meanest member or (2) by possessing charisma and leadership abilities. In addition, the leaders tend to be older members who have built up seniority. Hard-core members are those whose lives center on the totality of gang activity. They are generally the most violent, streetwise, and knowledgeable in legal matters. Marginal or fringe members (sometimes referred to as "juniors" or "peewees") drift in and out of gang activity. They are attached to the gang but have not developed a real commitment to the gang lifestyle. They associate with gang members for status and recognition and tend to gravitate toward hard-core membership if no intervention from outside sources occurs (Babicky, 1993a, 1993b; Mays & Winfree, 2000, p. 302).

Age

Gang members ranging from 8 to 55 years of age have been found in various areas of the nation. For many younger juveniles, gang members serve as role models whose behavior is to be emulated as soon as possible to become full-fledged gangbangers. Consequently, these children are often exploited by members of gangs and manipulated into committing offenses such as theft and burglary to benefit the gang as part of their initiation or rite of passage. As gang crimes become more profitable, as in the case of drug franchises, the membership tends to be older. As members become older, they move away from street crime and move up in stature within the gang hierarchy. The younger members maintain the turf-oriented activities, and the adults move into more organized and sophisticated activities.

GANG PROBLEM IS STILL A THREAT, ACCORDING TO THE 2012 NATIONAL YOUTH GANG SURVEY

Researchers Egley, Howell, and Harris (2014) have found that, although there are slightly fewer overall police agencies that report gang activity around the nation, the overall gang problem among law enforcement agencies has remained concentrated in urban areas and seems to be occurring even more in recent years. Indeed, more than 50% of the net increase in the estimated number of gang members in 2012 occurred in areas with larger populations. Consider the following:

1. In 2012, there were an estimated 30,700 gangs (an increase from 29,900 in 2011) and 850,000 gang members (an increase from 782,500 in 2011).

2. It would appear that gang-related homicides have increased throughout the nation, in part, due to increased reporting by agencies. Compared with the previous 5-year average, the number of

gang-related homicides increased by more than 20% in 2012.

3. Across jurisdiction types, prevalence rates of gang activity increased in the early 2000s and, from 2005 onward, seems to have stabilized, overall, with a slight growth trend continuing in larger metropolitan areas.

4. Fifty-five percent of the responding agencies characterized their gang problems as "staying about the same" in 2012, an increase over the percentage of agencies in 2010 and 2011 and the largest percentage that the survey has ever recorded.

When considering #4 above, it begs the question as to how it is, exactly, that police agencies are identifying and classifying gang members to determine the prevalence of their gang problem. Therefore, understanding police procedures for designating individuals as gang

Figure 12.7 Means by Which Police Agencies Designate Persons as Gang Offenders

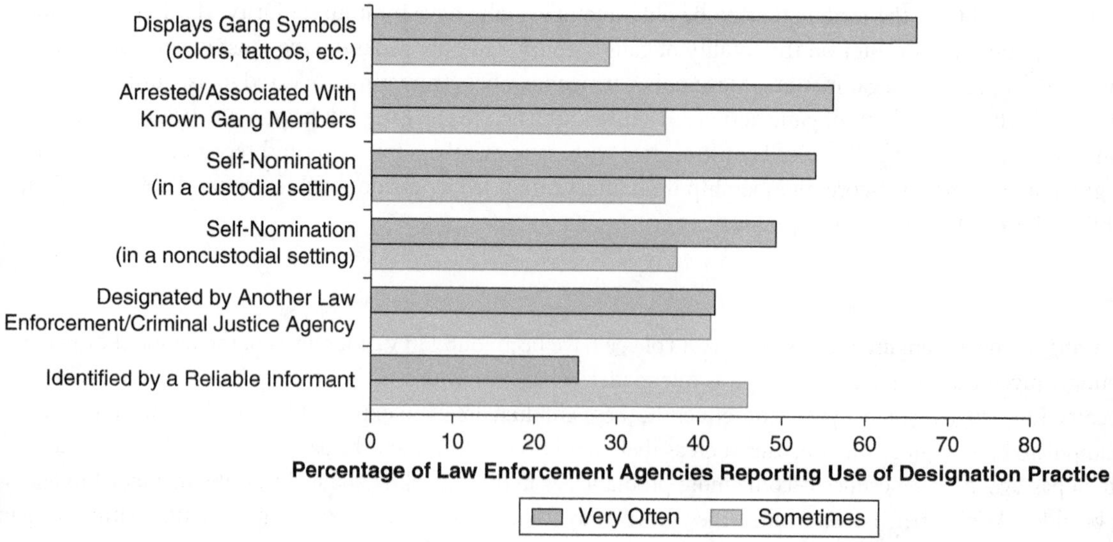

Percentage of Law Enforcement Agencies Reporting Use of Designation Practice

□ Very Often   □ Sometimes

Source: OJJDP (2012).

members can provide insight into the type and range of data that is maintained.

When agency administrators were asked to determine how frequently six common practices for designating an individual as a gang member were used, the following results (see Figure 12.7) were found:

- The display of gang symbols (66% of respondents)
- Suspect has been arrested or associates with known gang members (56%)
- Suspect self-discloses his/her membership while in a jail or prison setting (54%)
- Suspect self-discloses his/her membership while in the community (49%)
- The individual is designated a gang member by another law enforcement agency (42%)
- A reliable informant identifies the suspect as a gang member (25%)

From the information obtained in the 2012 National Youth Gang Survey (NYGS) it is clear that the number of gangs, number of gang members, and gang-related homicides have all increased during the past year. In fact, Egley et al. (2014) note that this increase has been an observed trend that has persisted throughout the past 5 years.

Interestingly, there are fewer gang members in smaller cities, but this good news is offset by the fact that there is a corresponding growth in the concentration of gang activity in largely populated areas, showing that the spread of gang activity outward from larger cities is limited in size and scope. Rather, gang members remain in their familiar urban areas of operation. It may well be that these areas provide more lucrative criminal opportunities than do smaller cities.

What is interesting is that, though gang membership reported by police agencies seems to be growing, researchers like Pyrooz (2016; see In Practice 12.1) contend that even these estimates underrecognize juvenile gang activity. This also means that the traditional methods of antigang measures that law enforcement agencies use (i.e., the use of a dedicated gang officer and/or unit, targeted patrols, and a local gang task force) may need to be reexamined. This lends credence to some of the claims by Sorrells (1980) as well as Freng and Terrance (2013), who contend that policies that address ill community variables will likely be the most effective means of removing the appeal of gang membership from youth who are at risk.

Questions to Consider

1. True or False: Though juvenile crime has been declining, juvenile gang membership seems to have increased during the past year.

2. Multiple Choice: In 2012, there were an estimated _____ gang members around the nation.

   a. 550,000
   b. 650,000
   c. 750,000
   d. 850,000
   e. None of the above

3. Explain how the information from In Practice 12.3 comports with and differs from the contentions of other researchers.

Gender

Street gangs are predominantly male. Although girls have been a part of gangs since the earliest accounts from New York during the early 1800s, their role has traditionally been viewed as peripheral. Thrasher (1927), in his classic study of gangs, discussed two female gangs in Chicago. Females have been described in the literature primarily as sex partners for male gang members or as members of auxiliaries to male gangs (Campbell, 1995). Yet, as we have indicated throughout this book, involvement in crime, including violent crime, among juvenile females has clearly increased over the past decade.

Monikers

Many gang members have monikers, or nicknames, that are different from their given names. In general, these monikers reflect physical or personality characteristics or connote something bold or daring. Often gang members do not know the true identities of other members, making detection and apprehension difficult for law enforcement officials.

Graffiti

Street gang graffiti is unique in its significance and symbolism. Graffiti serves several functions: It is used to delineate gang turf as well as turf in dispute, it proclaims who the top-ranking gang members are, it issues challenges, and it proclaims the gang's philosophy. Placing graffiti in the area of a rival gang is considered an insult and a challenge to the rival gang, which inevitably responds. The response may involve anything from crossing out the rival graffiti to committing drive-by shootings or engaging in other forms of violence. The correct interpretation of graffiti by the police can offer valuable information as to gang activities. Symbols that represent the various gangs are typically included in graffiti and are known as identifiers.

Jargon

Gang members frequently use jargon to exchange information. In fact, understanding gang jargon may be critical to obtaining convictions for gang-related crimes. In 1986, Jeff Fort and several high-ranking members of the Chicago-based El Rukn were charged with plotting acts of terrorism in the United States for a sum of $2.5 million from Libya. The FBI recorded 3,500 hours of telephone conversations, most of which were in code, in this case. A former high-ranking member of El Rukn, who became a prosecution witness, translated portions of the confusing conversations for jurors. Fort was convicted and sentenced to an extended prison term.

Recruitment

Gangs continue to recruit new members to defend their turf and expand criminal activities so as to increase profits (Hughes, 2005). There is often intense competition among new young gang members to prove themselves to the hard-core membership. Brutal initiation rituals in which recruits are severely beaten with fists, feet, and other objects are not uncommon (Hughes, 2005; Mays & Winfree, 2000; Valdez, 2005). This competition results in younger gang members (10–13 years old) being very dangerous. Gang members know that juveniles in this age group are not likely to be prosecuted in adult court, making them particularly valuable in the commission of serious offenses (Hughes, 2005; McGloin, 2005; Szymanski, 2005). Because the young members want the approval of the older gang members, they are highly motivated to prove themselves and are likely to do whatever they are told to do. Recruitment of these new members occurs anywhere juveniles gather—shopping malls, bowling alleys, skating rinks, public parks, neighborhoods, and schools (Hieb, 1992; Huff, 1996; Siegel et al., 2003). There has been an increase in the recruitment of members outside major urban centers and in the number of middle-class juveniles approached as potential members.

One means of recruiting that has increased during the past decade is through the use of technology, including online social media. Social media sites provide gangs with a platform to recruit new members, either through direct communication or indirectly through videos that spread the gang's brand and boast the benefits of the gang lifestyle. Figure 12.8 shows which social media platforms are most often used by street gangs for recruiting and general membership.

A gang in California used social media sites like Instagram, Facebook, YouTube, and Twitter to lure unwitting young girls into the gang lifestyle with rap videos and promises of a glamorous life. These girls

Figure 12.8 Social Media Platforms Most Often Used by Gangs

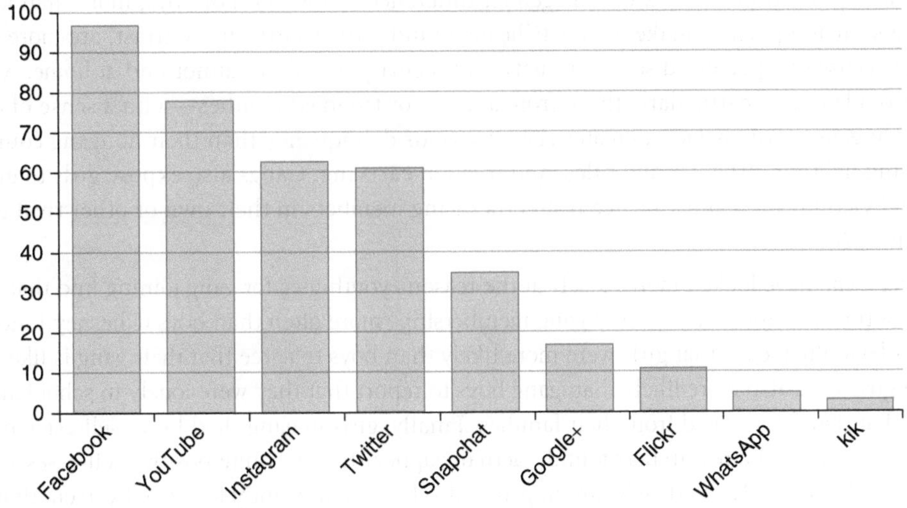

Source: National Gang Intelligence Center (2015).

were then forced into sex trafficking (National Gang Intelligence Center, 2015). In another case, a member of a neighborhood-based gang in the Bronx, New York, posted rap videos on YouTube espousing violence and the gang lifestyle. In response, he received text messages containing requests to join the gang. For example, he received a text message stating, "I'm from Queens but I watch all ya videos. Imma trying be down with the WTG Move." The rapper responded, "You can be WTG under me and b official" in exchange for $125 (National Gang Intelligence Center, 2015). In another case, suspected MS-13 members in Virginia allegedly contacted a middle school student via kik, telling him to join MS-13 and provide names of other middle school students for recruitment (National Gang Intelligence Center, 2015).

Gang members are increasingly moving to messaging platforms, such as Snapchat, kik, and WhatsApp, to communicate. These technologies provide instantaneous communication similar to short message service (SMS) text messaging while providing more anonymity. Gangs with juvenile and adult members rely on technology to stay connected with other members and to help coordinate their illicit activities. This has also become true in cases where some members (usually adult members) are incarcerated. The use of smuggled cell phones and social media platforms enable fast communication and coordination efforts among street gang members; between adult or juvenile gang members in prison; and between prison and street members, whether juvenile or adult (National Gang Intelligence Center, 2015).

Juvenile Girls and Gang Membership

Gang membership is not an exclusively male phenomenon: According to the most recent national data, girls comprise at least one-quarter of the youth in gangs (Chesney-Lind, 2013). Unfortunately, this fact is often obscured because those watching the gang problem—particularly law enforcement—typically pay more attention to the behavior of boys than of girls. Another reason girls in gangs are seemingly out of sight and out of mind is that girls enter gangs—and exit from gang activity—at earlier ages than boys (Chesney-Lind, 2013).

Gangs can offer juvenile males and females a sense of belonging and a perceived sense of fun, excitement, and protection. There are some gender differences, however. For boys, more than for girls, a gang may be seen as a place to make money (Chesney-Lind, 2013). Girls, by contrast, are more likely to join a gang because of a perceived sense of safety and security that they cannot find at home. Although a gang may provide girls—particularly those from abusive or troubled families—with a sense of a surrogate family, girls in gangs actually face a greater risk of serious delinquency than their nongang counterparts, including gang fighting, drug use and sales, and weapon carrying. Gangs also expose girls to greater risk of sexual victimization and violence from other gang members in their own or other rival gangs (Chesney-Lind, 2013).

Researchers who have looked more closely at the reasons youth give for gang joining find that girls tend to "tap an emotional or affective aspect of gang membership" more often than boys (Chesney-Lind, 2013, p. 122). This basically means that girls were more likely than boys to agree that their gang is like family to them. Gang girls were also more likely than gang boys to report that they were lonely in school and with friends and that they felt isolated from their families. Finally, girls in gangs had lower self-esteem than did boys in gangs, who, the researchers found, "actually appear to have quite positive self-assessments" (Chesney-Lind, 2013, p. 122). Girls who are in gangs also have significantly lower self-esteem than girls who are not in gangs (Chesney-Lind, 2013).

As we saw in the opening What Would You Do? feature in this chapter, girls are often around gangs in other roles—such as girlfriend, sister, or daughter—that might put them at risk, even if they are not full-fledged gang members. Although some youth have the *perception* that being in a gang offers fun, excitement, and protection, the *reality* is otherwise (Chesney-Lind, 2013). For girls as well as boys, gang membership increases delinquent behavior (Chesney-Lind, 2013). Table 12.4 shows some of the common self-reported risk behaviors for young women who are in a gang versus young women who are not in a gang.

To address the issue of girls joining gangs, it is important to understand the particular risks that girls confront in their families, schools, and neighborhoods. According to Chesney-Lind (2013), when compared with their non-gang-joining peers, girls who join gangs are more likely to

1. have a history of sexual abuse and trauma,
2. live in a destructive or distraught family,
3. have problematic peer relationships,
4. abuse drugs, and
5. live in dangerous neighborhoods and attend unsafe schools.

Likewise, many girls in gangs also have problematic relationships with other girls. Girls in mixed-sex gangs often fight with other girls because of jealousy over boys. Chesney-Lind points out that because girl gang

Table 12.4 Risk Behaviors of Juvenile Girls in a Gang Versus Not in a Gang

	Girls in a Gang	Girls Not in a Gang
Carried concealed weapon	79%	30%
Been in a gang fight	90%	9%
Attacked with a weapon to cause serious injury	69%	28%

Source: Chesney-Lind (2013).

members generally identify more with males than with females, they may exhibit the following gendered means of aggressing against other female gang members:

1. They may ignore male violence toward females, especially one whom they do not like.
2. They may blame other girls for male infidelity.
3. Some will use their sex appeal to set up rival gang members.
4. They may be complicit actors in grooming girls for sexual assault by male gang members.

All this can lead to a system of sexual inequality that encourages male violence and contributes to girls seeing themselves through the eyes of males. Because relationships are so important to girls, and because girls say they are drawn to gangs for a sense of belonging, it is important that prevention programs focus on promoting a girl's access to positive peer groups—like culturally appropriate, school-based empowerment programs—while giving them the skills to critically challenge destructive cultural themes. Finally, given that youth in gangs tend to come from diverse groups, it is important that interventions be culturally relevant and appropriate whenever possible. In Practice 12.4 highlights this fact.

IN PRACTICE 12.4

FEMALE JUVENILE GANG MEMBER DIVERSITY AND CULTURALLY COMPETENT APPROACHES TO INTERVENTION

Girls, Gangs, and Cultural Context

Cultural context is an important factor in understanding why some girls join a gang. For example, Latina and Hispanic girls must negotiate the traditional gender-role ideologies of machismo and marianismo. Machismo dictates that Latino boys and men should be tough, sexually assertive, and dominating; marianismo stresses that girls and women should be submissive and passive in their relationships with boys and men.

Young Latinas often resent such constraints. In one study of Latina and Portuguese mothers and daughters in the late 1990s, researchers found that some Latina girls chafed at controls imposed on them, saying that their parents were "too concerned" about their safety. They also reported feeling constrained and frustrated as they saw their mothers being bound by a culture that expected them to "do everything for everybody." The girls said that, if they complained about

people taking advantage of their mothers, their mothers got angry.

Many African-American girls must learn to cope with both sexism and racism, to say nothing of dangerous communities. Research has shown that some African-American mothers teach their daughters "race-related resistance strategies," like how not to fall prey to corrosive effects of the white standard of American beauty. Black mothers may also ensure that their daughters learn two cultural scripts: one for living in the white world and another for living as an African-American. Other research has found that because many African-American girls grow up in very violent neighborhoods, their women may also teach their daughters to "physically defend themselves" because they do not want them to become "a statistic."

In fact, conflicts between African-American mothers and their daughters might well escalate precisely *because* the girls learn resistance strategies from their mothers. As Dr. Nikki

(Continued)

(Continued)

Jones, from the University of California at Santa Barbara, has noted in her book, *Between Good and Ghetto: African American Girls and Inner City Violence*, published in 2010, African-American mothers defended their attempts to curtail their daughters' "freedom" by pointing to the "often hostile and dangerous environments" that their teens lived in as well as the fact that "they were also less likely to be given a break when they err than white teens."

Female African-American gang members differ from Latina and Hispanic gang members in one very interesting way: how they feel about their futures, especially heterosexual marriage. Seventy-five percent of African-American girls—and only 43 percent of the Latinas—agreed with the statement, "The way men are today, I'd rather raise my kids myself." Similarly, when asked about the statement, "All a woman needs to straighten out her life is to find a good man," 29 percent of Latinas—and none of the African-American girls—agreed.

Prevention efforts must be shaped by the cultures in which they operate; they must be cognizant of the dynamics between girls and their mothers, in particular, because research shows that, although these relationships are important, they are likely to be strained with respect to girls who are at the greatest risk.

Source: Chesney-Lind (2013).

Questions to Consider

1. True or False: The term that identifies culturally driven submission qualities in Latina girls is *marianismo*.

2. Multiple Choice: Which group of mothers has their daughters learn two cultural scripts?

   a. Latino American

   b. African American

   c. Native American

   d. Asian American

3. According to In Practice 12.4, African American juvenile female gang members differ from Latina gang members in how they perceive their future. Describe and discuss this difference in perception.

Response of Justice Network to Gangs

The problems presented by juvenile gangs are not easily addressed. In large part, the origins of these problems are inherent in the social and economic conditions of inner-city neighborhoods across the United States, and the issue is complicated by the continued existence of racial and ethnic discrimination in the educational and social arenas (Decker, 2008; Ritter & Simon, 2013). These conditions are largely beyond the control of justice officials, whose efforts are hampered greatly as a result. Because we appear to be unwilling to confront the basic socioeconomic factors underlying gang involvement, our options are limited largely to responding to the actions of gang members after they have occurred (Decker, 2008; McGloin, 2005; Walker et al., 2004). In general, the response in these terms has been to propose, and often pass, legislation creating more severe penalties for the offenses typically involved—specifically, drug-related and weapons-related offenses (Ritter & Simon, 2013). Recognizing the fact that gangs are now more mobile and that splinter gangs exist in numerous communities, law enforcement officials have attempted to respond by establishing cooperative task forces of combined federal, state, and local authorities who share information and other resources to combat gang-related activities.

At the federal level, several past presidents have called for a war on drug trafficking and appointed a drug czar to oversee efforts in this area. President Bill Clinton appointed Lee Brown, a former Houston police chief and New York City police commissioner, to the post. Prosecutors at the federal and state levels have become involved in extremely complex, expensive cases to incarcerate known gang leaders and to send a message to gangs that their behavior is not to be tolerated. Gang crimes units and specialists have emerged in most large urban, and some medium-sized, police departments. School liaison programs (discussed in Chapter 8) have been implemented in the hope of reducing gang influence in the schools (Brown, 2006; Ervin & Swilaski, 2004; Valdez, 2007, 2011). Parent groups have mobilized to combat the influence of gangs on children, and media attention has focused on the consequences of ignoring gang-related crimes (Decker, 2008; Ritter & Simon, 2013). There is now considerable effort directed toward controlling gang activities. Whether such effort is properly organized, coordinated, and directed and whether the effort will have the desired consequences remain empirical questions.

In 2013, the National Institute of Justice, in partnership with the OJJDP, awarded grants to five communities to implement and test the Spergel model intended to reduce gang crime and violence. This model involves developing a coordinated team approach to delivering services and solving problems (Burch & Kane, 1999). Strategies involved include mobilization of community leaders and residents; use of outreach workers to engage juveniles in gangs; access to academic, economic, and social opportunities; and gang suppression activities. Such collaborative efforts that use resources from multiple agencies in the community have been widely adopted throughout the nation (Ervin & Swilaski, 2004; Hanser, 2007c; Hughes, 2005; Ritter & Simon, 2013).

Public, Legislative, and Judicial Reaction

There is little doubt that some violent juveniles must be dealt with harshly and incarcerated for the protection of society in spite of the fact that processing these juveniles as adults clearly violates the philosophy of the juvenile court network by labeling them as criminals at an early age and by placing them in incarceration with automatic transfer to adult facilities at the age of majority (McGloin, 2005; Moffitt & Caspi, 2001; Szymanski, 2005). As we have seen, public perception that there was a dramatic increase in violent and serious crime by juveniles during the 1980s and 1990s resulted in considerable pressure on legislators to pass new, more stringent laws relating to the prosecution and incarceration of violent juvenile offenders (Siegel et al., 2003; Szymanski, 2005). As noted in Chapter 5, the juvenile court acts of many states have been amended to remove juveniles charged with criminal homicide, rape, or armed robbery from the jurisdiction of the juvenile court if they were over a certain age at the time they committed the offense.

However, legislative attempts to solve crime problems by passing tougher laws, such as mandatory sentencing laws (e.g., for drug crimes) and "three strikes" laws (after the third offense, they "throw away the key"), have resulted in less than desirable outcomes (Clear & Cole, 2003; Walker et al., 2004). Walker (1998), for example, concluded that "three strikes and you're out laws are a terrible crime policy" because there is no evidence that they reduce serious crime and considerable evidence that they lead to the incarceration of many people who would not commit other crimes anyway (p. 140; see also Clear & Cole, 2003).

Gang suppression, gang sweeps, zero-tolerance policies, and loitering ordinances are tactics employed by the police to minimize gang activity (Valdez, 2011). Attention has been focused on developing partnerships between the police and other community agencies in an attempt to intervene in gang activities. In the city of Reno, Nevada, for example, police decided to focus on the top 5% of gang members using a repeat-offender program to target them. At the same time, the police coordinated efforts to deal with the 80% of gang members who are not considered hard core. A community action team (CAT) was formed to accomplish these tasks, interview and develop intelligence on gang members, deal with the families of gang wannabes, develop neighborhood advisory groups (NAGs), and implement an improved media policy. This collaborative effort has resulted in increasingly positive evaluations of police performance and reduced amounts of gang violence (Valdez, 2011).

Alternatives to Incarceration for Violent Juveniles

Although numerous causes of youth violence have been posited, solutions have been less apparent. Should we censor the media? Are more prisons or longer sentences the answer? Does gun control help? Is the juvenile justice network, as currently conceived, out of date and ill-equipped to handle violent juveniles? Should we provide more family support?

In his study of juvenile homicide, Sorrells (1980) found that a disproportionate number of juveniles who commit this offense come from communities with a high incidence of poverty and infant mortality (see also Freng & Terrance, 2013). He also noted that such offenders are products of "violent chaotic families." As alternatives to incarceration, the research by Sorrells (1980) and others (Freng & Terrance, 2013) has led to suggestions to identify high-risk communities and pool agency resources in those communities as a means of preventing community issues that encourage violent juvenile crime (Freng & Terrance, 2013; Ritter & Simons, 2013). In addition, schools and community youth groups can implement screening of violent juveniles for emotional problems, develop treatment programs focusing on resolving such emotional problems, and remove children from violent chaotic families where possible (Ritter & Simon, 2013).

Other researchers have provided general support for Sorrells's (1980) findings and made similar recommendations (Freng & Terrance, 2013). These researchers note that community and environmental factors play a critical role in the creation of youth gangs. In current U.S. society, Freng and Terrance (2013) further note that members of racial/ethnic minority groups are much more likely than Caucasians to live in disadvantaged communities with characteristics that exacerbate risk for gang joining. This, then, helps to explain the common question related to the overrepresentation of minority youth as gang members. Some of the macro-level variables that Freng and Terrance (2013) identify include the following:

- Concentrated poverty

- Social and geographic isolation

- Resource-deprived social institutions, such as schools and hospitals

- Rundown and decaying housing

- Relatively high rates of crime and violence

- A criminal justice system that removes a disproportionate share of residents—particularly young men—from the area

Although there is no doubt that the community in which an individual develops has important implications for youth's likelihood of joining gangs, the reality is that few programs have the means to change these larger societal factors. Consequently, most evidence-based practices have focused on individual-level characteristics that are assumed to be more easily addressed. To truly reduce youth gang joining and violence, however, we must address the conditions that create the types of communities where gangs thrive.

Programs that focus on changing the structure of communities—by reducing pro-delinquent opportunities and promoting prosocial opportunities—will most likely provide the greatest return on investment in terms of effectively addressing the root causes of gang membership and violence (Freng & Terrance, 2013; also see In Practice 12.2). Whereas this would not be an easy task, it is probably the most realistic approach to actually reducing gang affiliation. For this to be realized, policymakers will need to make a concerted effort to address factors such as the concentration of high unemployment, the increase in households where the father is absent, the disruption these areas experience as a result of higher levels of mental and physical illness and other disabling conditions, and the overburdened health care system and community services (Freng & Terrance, 2013). It is worth noting that the policymaking approaches cited by Freng and Terrance (2013) are much different from those noted in our previous section where tougher laws, such as mandatory sentencing laws (e.g., for drug crimes), "three strikes" laws, and zero-tolerance policies, have been showcased as the approach of choice.

Going further, schools and teachers can also play important roles in preventing violence and gang membership (Ritter & Simon, 2013). The GREAT (Gang Resistance Education and Awareness Training) program (discussed in Chapter 7), taught by police in the schools, may help juveniles to resist gangs. Parents and teachers can work together to improve the interpersonal, cognitive, and problem-solving skills of juveniles. This approach focuses on modifying thinking processes rather than behaviors themselves. The GREAT program helps children learn to solve interpersonal problems by focusing on means–ends thinking (a step-by-step approach to pursuing goals), weighing pros and cons (of carrying out behaviors), thinking of alternative solutions, and thinking about consequences (the ability to think about different outcomes from a specific behavior). Although more research needs to be done, there is some evidence that teaching children such skills at very young ages can help them to develop prosocial attitudes and behaviors that last well into adulthood (Hanser, 2007c; Ritter & Simon, 2013).

An abundance of research has sought to differentiate between long-term and repeat juvenile offenders and those who are likely to eventually desist from further crime, including gang offenders (Moffitt, 1993; Moffitt & Caspi, 2001; Pyrooz, 2016; Szymanski, 2005). Because some juveniles persist in violent behavior even after conventional interventions are used, some researchers have concluded that it may be necessary to deal with juveniles who engage in progressively more serious assaultive behavior by commitment to a detention facility for a 3- to 6-month period (thereby preventing recidivism in the community during this very high-risk period), during which time the juvenile's behavior is stabilized and brought under control (Moffitt, 1993; Moffitt & Caspi, 2001; Szymanski, 2005). Many researchers and authors maintain that effectively targeting and detaining select juveniles most likely to recidivate can produce maximal results in recidivism outcomes (Hanser, 2007c; Moffitt, 1993; Moffitt & Caspi, 2001; Szymanski, 2005).

Because of past research on juvenile detention and juvenile treatment outcomes, many researchers and advocates now call for a comprehensive strategy aimed at eliminating all risk factors for further delinquency, including gang involvement (Evans & Sawdon, 2004; Hanser, 2007c; Ritter & Simon, 2013; Valdez, 2007; Wolf & Gutierrez, 2012). This strategy called for a wide spectrum of services and sanctions to be used to protect potential and current delinquents from the womb to school and beyond (Clear & Cole, 2003; Ervin & Swilaski, 2004; Evans & Sawdon, 2004; Hanser, 2007c; Wolf & Gutierrez, 2012).

Unfortunately, getting to and treating potentially violent juveniles is not an easy task. Although the proportion of juveniles who commit violent crimes is relatively small, this group commits a sizable number of offenses (Moffitt, 1993). Protecting the best interests of children is clearly an important goal of the juvenile justice network, but so is protection of society (Hanser, 2007c; Siegel et al., 2003). It may well be that police, prosecutors, and judges need to deal with violent juveniles earlier and more severely than they have done in the past (Szymanski, 2005). Although giving juveniles the benefit of the doubt in early encounters with the police and courts may be well intentioned, in the case of violent offenders at least, it is also dangerous to others (Hanser, 2007c). It is clear that violence becomes a pattern of behavior when intervention either does not occur or is not effective (Moffitt, 1993). In the interests of protecting society and attempting to rehabilitate violent juveniles by delivering the best programs available as early as possible, violent juveniles must be identified, apprehended, and evaluated or judged as soon as possible (Ritter, Simon, & Mahendra, 2013).

It seems that many of the factors involved in improving opportunities for juveniles while reducing delinquency lie outside the scope of the traditional juvenile justice system. It is because of this that antigang programs must incorporate comprehensive intervention that assists these juveniles in separating themselves from their gang affiliation. This can be particularly challenging when juveniles come from neighborhoods where gang activity is quite prevalent. In response to the challenges in reforming youth gang members, many areas throughout the United States and Canada have developed gang exit programs for youthful gang members. We now turn our focus to these programs.

Establishing a Juvenile Gang Exit Program

Effective gang intervention programs must include community advocacy that can facilitate a sense of cohesion among neighborhoods so that these communities will not be intimidated by gangs and gang activity. One such program in Toronto, Canada, addresses this issue through a regimen that has three specific components: (1) assessment and intake, (2) intensive training and personal development, and (3) case management (Evans & Sawdon, 2004; Hanser, 2007c).

The assessment and intake phase examines the interest and motivation of the individual gang member, the amount of gang involvement by that member, and the gang member's family and social history (Evans & Sawdon, 2004). The next phase is referred to as the gang-member-intensive-training-and-personal-development phase and consists of two separate curricula—(1) one for male gang members and (2) the other for female gang members—that address different aspects relevant to both genders (Evans & Sawdon, 2004; Hanser, 2007c). Female gang members have special issues that are not relevant to male gang offenders as frequently, including child-rearing concerns, the fear of sexual victimization, and issues related to childhood molestation (Hanser, 2007c; Wolf & Gutierrez, 2012). Likewise, male gang members may have issues related to the definitions of masculinity, lack of respect for the female population, and other problems that are not usually pertinent to female offenders (Hanser, 2007c). Both curricula include 60 hours of intensive training and interactional exercises addressing typical topics such as anger management, racism, and communication skills. The last phase of this intervention is the gang member case management phase and includes individualized therapeutic sessions as well as ongoing group meetings for ex-gang members. This phase is designed to be a relapse or recidivism prevention mechanism for prior gang members.

One aspect of this intervention program that is particularly effective is the use of group facilitators who are also prior gang members (Evans & Sawdon, 2004; Hanser, 2007c). These staff members maintain community connections by visiting local community centers and other youth services and/or recreational establishments to provide information pertaining to the program. Staff members are likewise given training in leadership skills, empathy building, and counseling as well as in the development of their own personal stories that help the juveniles to identify with staff members during their outreach role as well as their role as facilitator during group sessions (Evans & Sawdon, 2004; Hanser, 2007c).

Overall, this program has been found to be quite effective in terms of both treatment and outreach to gang members in the community. In addition to the initial treatment regimen and the relapse sessions, this program attempts to separate juveniles from their gang-oriented surroundings. This is often necessary because prior gang members must otherwise combat members from their prior gangs. Furthermore, the tug of the gang subculture tends to be powerful, and this makes the juveniles more likely to recidivate (Hanser, 2007c). Thus, the gang exit strategy will employ a combination of individualized and group interventions while relocating prior gang members to an area that is not as likely to pull the youthful offenders back into gang activity (Evans & Sawdon, 2004; Hanser, 2007c).

One other example of an effective intervention and exit program that is designed specifically for female gang members wishing to leave the gang life can be found in Los Angeles. A nonprofit organization, Girls & Gangs, serves young girls ages 12 to 18 who are involved in gangs and/or the juvenile justice system (Wolf & Gutierrez, 2012). This nonprofit organization provides prerelease and postrelease assistance that is gender-responsive and addresses gender-specific issues for these young girls. A variety of case management, mentoring, life skills training, and advocacy are provided. In addition, healing from underlying trauma or abuse (both in families and within the gang) are addressed. The Girls & Gangs program works with officially initiated female members as well as those who are involved with a gang but have not yet been jumped-in or sexed-in to the gang. The program helps these women with child-rearing challenges and provides classes and therapeutic sessions related to gender roles and power dynamics between males and females, both in the gang life and in society in general (Wolf & Gutierrez, 2012).

CAREER OPPORTUNITY: D.A.R.E. OFFICER

Job description: Work full-time as certified police officer teaching the D.A.R.E. program curricula to local schoolchildren from fifth grade through high school. Act as role model in the classroom, drawing attention to the hazards of drug and alcohol use, peer pressure, and violence as well as the issues involved in racial and gender stereotyping. Trained in the D.A.R.E. curricula at a training center sponsored by the national D.A.R.E. program.

Employment requirements: Required to be full-time uniformed police officer with at least 2 years of policing experience. Must have met at least the minimum training standards set by the local policing agency and must go through an oral interview during the D.A.R.E. screening process. In addition, the officer and his or her agency must have an agreement with the local school district to teach the D.A.R.E. curricula at the school. Other qualities important to the position include a demonstrated ability to interact and relate well with children; good oral and written communication skills; organization skills; promptness; the ability to develop personal relationships; and flexibility and ability to handle unexpected situations, statements, and actions. Must successfully complete 80 hours of training to be certified to teach the core curriculum and the K–4 program. If teaching at the high school level, in the D.A.R.E. parent program, or in special education classes, must complete an additional 40 hours of training and teach the core curriculum for at least two semesters prior to the additional training.

Beginning salary: Salary varies from jurisdiction to jurisdiction. Good benefits and retirement packages are typically included.

Summary

Violence by and against juveniles has received considerable attention during the early 2000s. Stories appeared in the mass media that led many to believe that violence committed by juveniles was an epidemic, whereas current official statistics and other sources of information indicate that violent acts committed by juveniles have actually decreased during recent years. Regardless, there is little doubt that those juveniles who commit violent offenses deserve our immediate attention because research indicates that they are likely to continue to commit such acts unless early effective intervention occurs. Careful screening of juveniles to ensure that only those who actually commit violent acts are processed according to laws intended to deal with such offenders is imperative in terms of costs to both the juveniles involved and society.

Our society is confronted by a multitude of problems relating to gangs. Preventing juveniles from becoming involved in gang activities, particularly in inner-city neighborhoods, is extremely difficult if not impossible. Juveniles who do not join gangs voluntarily risk their lives as well as the lives of their family members. Thus, early identification of new recruits and comprehensive knowledge concerning the membership and actions of existing gangs are essential. Identification of juveniles who are in the process of becoming gang members may be accomplished through a variety of means. Sudden changes in friendships; minor but chronic problems with police, school, and family; wearing the same color patterns daily (although colors now appear to be diminishing in importance as a symbol of gang membership); discovery of strange logos or insignia on juveniles' bodies, notebooks, or clothing; use of new nicknames (monikers); flashing of hand signs; and unexplained money may be signs of impending or actual gang involvement (Valdez, 2007). Spotting the signs of pre- or early gang activity is, of course, largely up to parents and teachers, who then need to take appropriate action to address the issue (Ritter, Simon, & Mahendra, 2013; Valdez, 2007).

Even early intervention does not ensure that gang influence will be reduced given that the juveniles in question are most likely to be returned to the neighborhoods in which the gangs operate or, in some cases, to a correctional facility that is also largely controlled by gangs (Ritter, Simon, & Mahendra, 2013). Incarceration of adult gang leaders may have some impact, but evidence indicates that these leaders often continue to control gang activities on the outside while they are in prison and frequently control the gangs within the prisons themselves.

The best available strategy is to identify the signs of gang activities as early as possible (Pyrooz, 2016) and prosecute gang members to the full extent of the law so as to send gang leaders the message that their actions will not be tolerated by the community. These programs are often referred to as zero-tolerance programs, meaning that no amount of gang activity will be accepted. Such action by the community and justice network may persuade gang leaders looking to expand their spheres of influence to move elsewhere. Where gangs are already clearly established, as in most metropolitan areas, a massive coordinated effort addressing socioeconomic conditions as well as criminal behavior will be required if gang behavior is to be brought under some degree of control. Some such efforts are now being made, and careful evaluation of their impact is crucial.

Gang activities have a long history in the United States, but attention has been redirected toward gangs recently as a result of their involvement with drug trafficking and gunrunning, which are multimillion-dollar enterprises. The complexion of gangs has changed somewhat over the years, and referring to gangs as "juvenile" gangs is not totally appropriate at this time due to the strong influence of adult gang leaders who supervise, organize, and control gang activities.

Juveniles continue to join gangs to attain status and prestige lacking in the domestic and educational arenas. Gang members continue to fight territorial wars, wear colors, extort protection money, and exclude from membership those from different racial or ethnic groups. Gangs exist in all urban areas, have extensive organizations in most prisons, and are spreading out to medium-sized and even smaller cities.

Gang involvement in violent activities—sometimes random and sometimes carefully planned—has received a good deal of attention from both the media and justice officials. The latter are organizing to better combat gang activities, but their success has yet to be carefully evaluated. Similarly, get-tough legislation has been passed at all levels, but the impact of such legislative action remains in question.

Critical Thinking Questions

1. Is violence committed by juveniles on the increase in the United States? Support your answer. In your opinion, are adults in the United States afraid of juveniles? Should they be?

2. Is probation likely to be effective in deterring violent juveniles from recidivating? Why or why not? Are there more effective programs for deterring violent juveniles?

3. What are the relationships among guns, drugs, and violence? Would gun control cut down on the number of violent crimes committed by juveniles? Against juveniles?

4. Describe the conditions under which gang membership is most likely to be attractive to juveniles. What kinds of responses do we, as a society, need to make to help control gangs?

5. Are there major differences in reasons for joining gangs and behaviors engaged in while in gangs between male and female gang members? Are female gang members more similar to or different from their male counterparts today regarding criminal activity?

Suggested Readings

Chesney-Lind, M. (2013). How can we prevent girls from joining gangs? In N. M. Ritter & T. R. Simon (Eds.), *Changing course: Preventing gang membership: Executive summary* (pp. 121–133). Washington, DC: National Institute of Justice.

Decker, S. H. (2008). *Strategies to address gang crime: A guidebook for local law enforcement.* Washington, DC: Office of Community Oriented Policing Services.

Evans, D. G., & Sawdon, J. (2004, October). The development of a gang exit strategy: The Youth Ambassador's Leadership and Employment Project. *Corrections Today.* Retrieved from www.cantraining.org/BTC/docs/Sawdon%20Evans%20CT%20Article.pdf

Freng, A., & Terrance, T. J. (2013). Race and ethnicity: What are their roles in gang membership? In N. M. Ritter & T. R. Simon (Eds.), *Changing course:*

Preventing gang membership: Executive summary (pp. 135–149). Washington, DC: National Institute of Justice.

Howell, J. C., Egley, A., Tita, G. E., & Griffiths, E. (2011). *U.S. gang problem trends and seriousness, 1996–2009.* Washington, DC: Office of Juvenile Justice and Delinquency Prevention.

National Criminal Justice Reference Service. (2005). *Gangs: Facts and figures.* Washington, DC: U.S. Department of Justice. Retrieved from www.ncjrs.org/spotlight/gangs/facts.html

National Gang Intelligence Center. (2015). *National gang report—2015.* Washington, DC: Author.

Office of Community Oriented Policing Services. (2009). *The stop snitching phenomenon: Breaking the code of silence.* Washington, DC: Author.

Office of Juvenile Justice and Delinquency Prevention. (2016). *Statistical briefing book*. Retrieved from http://www.ojjdp.gov/ojstatbb/offenders/qa03103.asp?qaDate=2014

Pyrooz, D. (2016). *Dispelling myths about juvenile gang members in the United States*. Washington, DC: National Institutes of Health.

Ritter, N. M., Simon, T. R., & Mahendra, R. R. (2013). *Changing course: Preventing gang membership*. Washington, DC: National Institute of Justice.

Valdez, A. (2009). *Gangs: A guide to understanding street gangs* (5th ed.). San Clemente, CA: LawTech.

Valdez, A. (2011). *Gangs across America: Histories and sociology* (2nd ed.). San Clemente, CA: LawTech.

Wolf, A. M., & Gutierrez, L. (2012). *It's about time: Prevention and intervention services for gang-affiliated girls*. Los Angeles, CA: Institute for Youth, Education, & Families. Retrieved from http://kern.org/schcom/wp-content/uploads/sites/28/2015/06/GirlsinGangs.pdf

$SAGE edge™

Sharpen your skills with SAGE edge at **edge.sagepub.com/coxjj9e**. SAGE edge for students provides a personalized approach to help you accomplish your coursework goals in an easy-to-use learning environment. You'll find action plans, mobile-friendly eFlashcards, and quizzes as well as video and web resources and links to SAGE journal articles to support and expand on the concepts presented in this chapter.

Global Issues in Juvenile Justice

13

WHAT WOULD YOU DO?

The sun was barely rising in the distance, and Khalid watched as many people throughout the town began to scurry about. He was high up on the hill and could look down on the town and see the various merchants and vendors setting out their merchandise. Khalid watched one merchant in particular who sold a number of food items (dates, fruit, dried meat, and some trinkets). He watched intently as the merchant set up his section at the bazaar and noticed that his friend Achmed approached the man just as planned. Achmed came just as the man was open for business and asked to buy some dates. Achmed paid the man and then walked off. At this time, Khalid watched as the man eventually turned and placed the coins in a small belt pouch that he wore loosely at his side.

Using his binoculars, Khalid examined the pouch and saw where it was tethered to the belt, underneath a loose-fitting shirt. Khalid watched

throughout the day as the man filled the pouch with coins from customers. During the day, his friend Achmed would come and visit and ask about what was observed. Achmed brought Khalid some of the dates and some water and, later that afternoon, went back down into the town as planned. About 30 minutes later, Khalid did the same.

You are across the street, waiting on a friend, and look over at the wares sold by the produce merchant. You observe a boy who introduces himself as Achmed to the vendor who sold the dates. You can hear the boy pleading with the vendor, saying, "Mister, your dates were bad. They made me sick, and I want my money back!"

The vendor states, "No, child, there is no money back . . . and my fruit is good. You are wrong!"

At that time, you observe Achmed holding his stomach, showing signs of impending

(Continued)

regurgitation, positioning himself so that he would likely discharge his vomit on the man's merchandise that sat out on the counter. At this point, you see the vendor begin to holler obscenities at Achmed, walking from behind his counter. . . . All while you observe another young boy approach quietly behind the man. While the man chastises Achmed and bellows at the youngster, the other boy looks about, and with a quick motion, he uses a thin razor knife to loosen the money pouch from the vendor's belt. The pouch comes loose and, while bumping into the man, the boy quickly grabs the pouch and says, "Excuse me, sir. This boy is making it difficult for everyone. I just need by, if I may. . . ." The young boy continues to walk by while Achmed continues taunting and jeering at the vendor from a distance. Eventually, Achmed leaves, acting obviously disappointed that he did not get his money back.

The vendor smiles and says to Achmed, "I notice that you have not thrown up. . . . Perhaps my dates are not so bad, after all?!" Then he adds, "Be gone with you!"

You observe Achmed leave, kicking dust at the man in the filthy street and then scurrying past you, almost running into you. He goes to the edge of the building where you are standing and says, "Psst . . . Khalid, where are you?"

"Over here. Catch up, quickly, before he finds out!" says the voice of a young boy.

You watch Achmed go into the alley and, following just a bit, hear him say, "Ha ha ha, Khalid, it worked! That old man did not know at all!"

The boys turn a bit, see you at the end of the alleyway, and take off into a covered section of the mazelike alleys of the bazaar.

A couple of minutes later, you see another customer approach the vendor to make a purchase. The customer extends his hand to provide a payment and, when the vendor reaches down to place the new revenue into his pouch, his face has a look of sheer and utter panic. He fumbles around, takes the money from the customer, and after letting the customer go, he begins to yell out loud. There are tears in his eyes as he begins to close shop, obviously deciding to quit for the day.

As he carries merchandise, his daughter, a young girl of 12 years old, is on crutches and tries to help him as well. They make their way roughly in your direction, and, at that point, the girl looks at you and says, "Hi mister, you have been here a while. So, I was wondering if you may have seen the person who stole my father's money? He is working so that I can go to the hospital for treatment."

You look at her, wondering why she picked you of all people to ask.

What Would You Do?

1. Given the circumstances, would you tell the vendor's daughter what you knew about the crime? Why or why not?

2. How serious is this crime, in your opinion, when considering all persons impacted and/or involved?

J uvenile crime is a major issue throughout the world. The various issues discussed throughout this text are encountered among other countries and other cultures in the global community. Indeed, issues related to youth, delinquent behavior, and the processing of youth who commit these behaviors are common on a worldwide scale. Because of this, we would be remiss if we failed to include some type of attention on international juvenile justice. This chapter addresses numerous juvenile justice issues around the world. We have included details and emphases that are consistent with the earlier chapters in this text. However, it should be clear that the chapter is by no means exhaustive because an entire text could be written on multinational juvenile justice issues alone.

Problems With Delinquency in the Global Community

Simply put, juvenile delinquency is a worldwide problem that has ebbed and flowed in focus and attention just as it has in the United States. The effects of globalization have impacted the juvenile justice arena—just as they have numerous other areas of criminal justice operations. *Globalization* refers to the increased connectivity and interdependence that has evolved among countries; this sense of interconnection has been fostered by technological advances as well as cultural shifts. Despite commonalities throughout the world, there is still a wide degree of variability in the way in which delinquency is measured from country to country around the world, and this makes it difficult to determine the exact extent of delinquency and its impact on the global community. In fact, there are a number of points in any juvenile system where data may not be accurately recorded; this can and does cause numerous problems for juvenile systems within the bounds of independent nations and makes it very difficult to accurately compare data within systems from country to country (United Nations Office on Drugs and Crime [UNODC], 2011). This is even more true for nations where information systems are not fully automated or where technology is limited. We provide Table 13.1 as an example of the various types of data that the United Nations contends should be kept in information systems of member countries.

Table 13.1 Minimal Information That Should Be Recorded by Juvenile Justice Information Systems

Information Source	Example of Minimum Information That Should Be Recorded by Newly Developed Information Systems	Notes
Police or law enforcement authority	For each child arrested: • Name, identification number, date of birth, gender and ethnicity, address and details of parents or guardian and legal representative • Date of arrest and reason for arrest • Details of charge (where relevant) • Details of diversion (where relevant) For each child detained: • Room/cell location and degree of separation from adults • Date of visits from parents, guardian, or adult family members • Details and dates of hearings before a competent authority to consider the issue of release	It is helpful if a unique code is assigned to each child's file. The competent authority and any subsequent place of detention can also use the same code to improve information flows between different bodies and institutions.
Competent authority or public prosecutor	For each child within the jurisdiction of the competent authority: • Registration of the case, including the assignment of a case identification number and the opening of a file folder to contain all relevant documents for that case • Basic details about the child, including name, date of birth, gender, ethnicity, address, and details of parents or guardian and legal representative • Date of arrest and details of charge	A comprehensive case record for each child ensures control of a case. There is a close connection between effective record management and fairness, transparency, and accountability in competent authorities.

(Continued)

Table 13.1 (Continued)

Information Source	Example of Minimum Information That Should Be Recorded by Newly Developed Information Systems	Notes
	• Status of case (e.g., pending first hearing, pending sentencing, or under appeal) including details of whether the child is held in presentence detention, updated upon any change • List of case actions, such as filing of evidence, charge sheets, pleadings, or social inquiry reports, including dates of such actions • List of hearings with dates • List of judicial actions, such as diversion, judgments, or orders, including dates • Details of the implementation of measures after judgment, including (where applicable) details of supervision of the sentence by the competent authority • Details of the end of measures and case closure	To prevent children from waiting a long time to have their case heard, case records should show clearly the status of the case and dates of actions and hearings.
Place of detention	As each child enters the place of detention: • Name, identification number, date of birth, gender and ethnicity, address, and details of parents or guardian and legal representative • Date of entry to the place of detention • Date of arrest • The situation of the child prior to entry into the place of detention (e.g., arrest, held in another place of detention, or bail) • Category of offense/reason for detention including details of sentence where applicable and expected date of release • Details of the assessment of the child's needs made on entry to the place of detention, including medical examination results Situation of each child in detention: • Whether detained presentence or after sentencing, including the date of any change of status • Room/cell location and degree of separation from adults • Date of visits from parents, guardian, or adult family members As each child leaves the place of detention: • Date of leaving detention • Reason for leaving detention (e.g., sentencing, completion of sentence, release on parole) • Registration for structured aftercare where applicable General information: • Date and details of independent inspection visits carried out • Record of complaints made and outcome	Information should be recorded for every individual child entering the place of detention and updated as appropriate. The information system may consist of a manual log book, an individual paper file for each child, or a computer database with a record for each child. Care should be taken to record personal details accurately.

Source: UNODC (2006).

Regardless of the limitations in data collection and measurement and regardless of whether we can adequately compare juvenile systems around the world, one thing is clear—delinquency is a growing problem around the world. To illustrate this, consider the following quote from the United Nations (2003):

> Statistical data indicate that in virtually all parts of the world, with the exception of the United States, rates of youth crime rose in the 1990s. In Western Europe, one of the few regions for which data are available, arrests of juvenile delinquents and under-age offenders increased by an average of around 50 percent between the mid-1980s and the late 1990s. The countries in transition have also witnessed a dramatic rise in delinquency rates; since 1995, juvenile crime levels in many countries in Eastern Europe and the Commonwealth of Independent States have increased by more than 30 percent. Many of the criminal offences are related to drug abuse and excessive alcohol use. (p. 189)

The rise in serious delinquency has been especially noteworthy in Europe, where both eastern and western European countries noted sharp increases during the late 1990s and early parts of the second millennium, presumably due to social and economic upheaval and change that occurred throughout the continent. In Africa, various parts of Asia, and Latin America, industrialization is considered one of the key reasons for the rise in economic-based, nonviolent offenses observed among youth in these regions. Further still, prosperous countries in the Arab world are also reporting increases in delinquency.

The *World Youth Report* (United Nations, 2003), a comprehensive document describing juvenile delinquency around the world, indicates that the number of children in especially difficult circumstances is estimated to have increased from 80 million to 150 million between 1992 and 2000. Although most would agree that these youth are at increased risk of committing acts of delinquency, the UNODC pointed out that it is difficult to develop agreement on something as simple as a definition of what constitutes a delinquent. The UNODC noted that not every child who comes into contact with the juvenile justice or adult criminal justice system should be counted as a delinquent. In discussing this point, the UNODC pointed toward indicators that specifically place the youngster in conflict with the law. This term, *conflict with the law*, offers a set of criteria that provides practitioners with a working and usable definition of delinquent youth. These criteria, or indicators, have been found to be common around the world and are necessary due to the wide variety of situations encountered from country to country.

For instance, consider that youth who are placed into detention may be provided such security for various reasons and that the legitimate grounds for detention may vary considerably by jurisdiction. Thus, children in some nations may be placed into a detention facility by a social worker due to the lack of a primary caregiver and/or the need for basic supervision, care, and protection. Consider some of the other following situations:

> A street child may be arrested by the police and detained in order to keep him off the streets for a while. A child's family may even simply take him or her to the local prison due to an allegedly troublesome nature. Indeed, a large majority of children are in detention because of underlying welfare issues that manifest themselves as delinquent behavior. (UNODC, 2006, p. 26)

The examples listed demonstrate that it may be quite difficult to determine when a child is in conflict with the law. The statutes and policies that control whether a child is formally in conflict with the law vary, depending on the social context within a given country.

Experts with UNODC noted gray areas in determining youth who are at risk of delinquency. Youth in irregular situations may be those who spend most of their time on the streets and those who may not commit a true offense under that nation's law, but may, nonetheless, find themselves placed in a secure detention facility after being arrested by the police. This is often couched as the best means of protecting the child, but in actuality, this sets a tone of criminalization for the child. In such cases, it is best that these youth are regarded as in need of care and protection and subject to the concern of a social or welfare officer (UNODC, 2006). However, complications can arise when countries use the same basic facilities for youth under the jurisdiction of child protection services, social services, and/or the juvenile justice system. In such cases, youth may be processed in such a manner that their likelihood of future misbehavior is increased, not decreased (UNODC, 2006).

Characteristics of Juvenile Delinquents Around the World

The *World Youth Report* (United Nations, 2003) noted that around the world youth who are most at risk of becoming delinquent share similar characteristics such as parental alcoholism, poverty, breakdowns in the family, and abusive family dynamics. In developing countries, youth may face the death of one or both parents during periods of armed conflict and can be orphaned without the basic necessities to sustain themselves. In war-torn areas of the world, orphaned youth may band together as a means of survival. The movie *Turtles Can Fly* provides a very good depiction of how youth may form into virtual families out of necessity to support themselves, engaging in various activities such as the removal of mines from fields. Naturally, many of these youth die or are maimed in the process of completing such work. With such stark conditions, it is easy to understand why these youth might resort to theft and other forms of delinquency in a world that is barbaric when compared to most standards that exist in the United States.

There is one single common variable that tends to emerge among all countries that report serious increases in delinquency—urbanization. Given our prior theoretical readings in this text, it is not surprising to find that, as conditions become more congested and as family systems around the world become fragmented due to modern work demands and economic circumstances, similar symptoms of delinquency among youth begin to emerge, regardless of the cultural and/or national background they may have.

Indeed, it would seem to be true that delinquency is, at least in concept, a universal phenomenon in which youth engage in similar types of behavior all around the world. Further, the demographics and factors that exacerbate delinquent activity around the world are also very similar, though in some countries the social, political, and economic circumstances may be much more dire and dangerous than in others. In those areas of the world where warfare, famine, or disaster are not a primary threat to the social order, delinquency is still common, and it has even been speculated that delinquency is simply a natural by-product of modernization in developed countries. In essence, it may well be that delinquency could be seen as a natural part of the life cycle for youth who are westernized. Evidence that delinquency is becoming normalized throughout the world can be found in the statements of the *United Nations Guidelines for the Prevention of Juvenile Delinquency* (United Nations, 1990a), which noted that "youthful behaviour or conduct that does not conform to overall social norms and values is often part of the maturation and growth process and tends to disappear spontaneously in most individuals with the transition to adulthood" (p. 2). It would then appear that a large majority of youth tend to commit some type of minor offense (either status or otherwise) during their formative years, yet they do not tend to become long-term criminals in the majority of cases.

As with the United States, it is clear that delinquency and crime are correlated with gender. International police data show that the delinquency rate of male juvenile offenders is more than double that of juvenile females. Indeed, the number of male juvenile suspects for every 100,000 members of the designated age group is more than 6 times the corresponding figure for females; for those in the youth category, the male–female suspect ratio is even higher, at 12.5 to 1 (United Nations, 2003). There are many reasons why this is the case. Among others, it tends to be true that girls are subject to stronger family control than are boys. Cultural concepts are such that society at large is less tolerant of deviant behavior among young women than among young men. In addition, aggression and violence play an important role in the construction of masculinity and sexuality in patriarchal societies, the primary objective being to reinforce and maintain the status and authoritative position of men (Hearn, 1998).

Delinquency may be a typical characteristic at one time or another among youth, but it does not tend to be a solitary activity. Rather, youth tend to engage in delinquent acts with other youth, which often leads to the development of delinquent groups of youth. Among those youth who tend to continue into adult criminal activities, many around the world tend to do so with the socialization and assistance of subcultural groups of like-minded youth (recall the discussion earlier of orphaned youth who ban together for survival). Further, the statistics around the world demonstrate that delinquency is typically a group activity, with approximately two-thirds of all acts of delinquency being committed by groups of youth. Although this is true among nations around the world, it is particularly true among larger and more populous countries. For instance, consider data from the Russian Federation: The rate of delinquent and/or criminal behavior among groups of youth is about 3 to 4 times higher than that of adult offenders. When considering age ranges, juvenile group crime is most prevalent among 14-year-olds and least prevalent among 17-year-olds. These rates are higher for theft, robbery, and rape and lower for various violent offenses (United Nations, 2003).

The *World Youth Report* (United Nations, 2003) pointed toward the similarities in basic characteristics of juvenile groups:

> Juvenile peer groups are noted for their high levels of social cohesiveness, hierarchical organization, and a certain code of behaviour based on the rejection of adult values and experience. The subcultural aspect of juvenile group activities is rarely given the attention it deserves. Different juvenile groups adopt what amounts to a heterogeneous mix, or synthesis, of predominant (class-based) values, which are spread by the entertainment industry, and intergenerational (group-based) values, which are native to the family or neighbourhood. Subcultures can be defined as particular lifestyle systems that are developed in groups. (p. 191)

These observations are important because this demonstrates that youthful behavior, both delinquent and prosocial, develops within the context of the peer group. Just as is the case with traditional peer groups, delinquent subcultures reflect the attempts of youth to resolve challenges presented by society. In the process, these groups set up their own rules and mores, often counter to those that are traditional, involving alcohol, drugs, risk taking, and even violence. Indeed, some groups tend to use violence as a means of solving interpersonal conflicts. Thus, the atmosphere created is an important mediating factor contributing to delinquent behavior.

Lending credence to the criminological theories discussed in Chapter 4, we can apply differential association theory as an example in this discussion. As readers may recall, differential association entails circumstances where youth are exposed to messages supportive of criminal behavior that exceed messages counter to engaging in criminal behavior. Given that youth involved in delinquency are receiving group messages (i.e., peer pressure) to engage in delinquent behaviors (such as drug use, vandalism, and even violent actions such as bullying), it is clear that the theoretical explanations in Chapter 4 apply to youth both in the United States and in other areas of the world.

Juveniles as Victims of Crime

From a global perspective, violence and conflict are serious and pervasive developmental challenges that confront many youth today. A peaceful and stable environment is a requisite for positive youth development.

Yet young people in many parts of the world are caught in a vortex of violence and armed conflict that is rarely of their own making. Close to 600 million youth live in fragile or conflict-affected areas (Commonwealth Secretariat, 2016).

The physical and mental toll that unstable and violent environments inflict on youth around the world is hard to imagine, but perhaps even harder to estimate is the harm it is doing to their long-term health and future opportunities (Commonwealth Secretariat, 2016). Violent environments can affect short- and long-term youth development outcomes: The problem is particularly acute in fragile states, where an underdeveloped youth population can easily fall prey to violence or become perpetrators of violence themselves (United Nations, 2012). These same environments also tend to have high rates of poverty and unemployment. In such cases, youth are likely to commit petty crimes like picking pockets or other crimes like prostitution as a means of gaining income for themselves or even their families. In fact, these youth are commonly pressured into these activities by other individuals, such as major criminals, under threat of harm to their person and relatives (United Nations, 2012). Thus, many youth throughout the world are viewed and treated as pawns for exploitation or powerless victims of violence and conflict.

Research by the Commonwealth Secretariat (2016) has found that youth are frequently the victims of violence around the world. Globally, physical violence would seem to be a major aspect in the lives of children and young people and continues to be a serious threat to their health and development. One in every three young people lives in a fragile or conflict-affected area. An estimated 200,000 homicides occur worldwide among youth each year, which make up 43% of the total homicides each year (Commonwealth Secretariat, 2016, p. 95). Eight out of ten young homicide victims are male, and nearly all these deaths occur in less affluent countries (Commonwealth Secretariat, 2016, p. 95).

Juvenile Exploitation and Delinquency

In prior chapters of this text, we have discussed how various forms of abuse and neglect can impair youth and also increase the likelihood that they will commit acts of delinquency. In families where abuse, dysfunction, or neglect is encountered, youth around the world are more prone to engage in substance abuse, vandalism, or other forms of delinquency. Those from seriously abusive homes may be inclined to become runaways and/or may join street gangs as a form of support and survival away from their families. All these types of circumstances are commonly found among youth worldwide.

However, there is one type of victimization encountered in the international environment that tends to be distinct from those in the United States—human trafficking. In many underdeveloped countries, youth may be abducted and trafficked to other more developed nations in Europe, the Americas, and Japan (Hanser, 2007b). The youth frequently suffer from double victimization. Double victimization occurs when youth experience abuse and, in reaction, engage in delinquent behaviors that later result in labeling and punishment from the state for their delinquent and/or criminal activity. Hanser (2010) noted specific circumstances where juveniles who are victims of trafficking have been "discovered" in various countries to be delinquent (Shared Hope International, 2008). In many of these cases, these youth may be forced into child prostitution and, though forced into such forms of victimization, may be inappropriately labeled "delinquent" by juvenile officers who consider such youth as vagrant and/or willing participants (Hanser, 2007b, 2010; Shared Hope International, 2008). This is particularly true for teenage girls in countries where the sex trade flourishes. In many cases, law enforcement in these countries may simply turn a blind eye to such victimization (Hanser, 2007b; UNODC, 2009).

Juvenile Exploitation in
Underdeveloped and War-Torn Areas

In various regions of the world, countries are underdeveloped and not industrialized as are the United States, Europe, and Australia. In some of these countries, armed conflicts may be pervasive and ongoing. The violence associated with these circumstances often has long-lasting consequences for youth, including physical injury, trauma, the loss of family and friends, and premature death. Associated with these circumstances are additional risks such as increased early use of tobacco, alcohol, or other drugs as well as sexual victimization. From a societal standpoint, access to health care, education, employment, or other social services is usually disrupted long-term.

The mortality of young males is disproportionately impacted due to their recruitment as fighters in these war zone regions, although it is young women and girls who are particularly hard hit by violent conflicts, for they tend to become the poorest of the poor (Commonwealth Secretariat, 2016). Young women and girls usually face serious psychological effects and, along with very young children, constitute the largest number of forcibly displaced persons, particularly in refugee camps and such. Further, women and young girls are often the focus of war crimes that include sexual assault and physical violence. This is sometimes a deliberate strategy of war and serves to terrorize and humiliate the community long after the conflict has subsided.

Because of these circumstances, female youth face reproductive health risks and may even be coerced into childhood marriages because parents may see the early marriage as a way to give their young daughter some long-term assistance and to legitimize the birth of her child that resulted from the war crime of rape. Although wartime conflicts impair the childhoods of both male and female youth, it would seem that girls often have more disadvantaged outcomes when compared with boys.

Regardless of gender, hundreds of thousands of youth are associated with state and nonstate armed militant groups (see In Practice 13.1). The prominence of civilian casualties, including children and youth, in modern-day conflicts shows how notions of warfare have evolved into a landscape where there is an increased use of improvised explosive devices and new technologies, where hostilities increase in urban or densely populated areas, and where there is a blurring of the distinction between civilians and militants (Office of the Special Representative of the Secretary-General for Children and Armed Conflict, 2013). In some countries, young children, preteens, and teens are used as suicide bombers. Likewise, in some countries, schools are attacked in a systematic manner that puts children at risk and prevents their ability to attain an education.

Research has shown that the top three countries where youth are impacted by armed conflict, civil unrest, and natural disasters are Pakistan, Angola, and Haiti (Commonwealth Secretariat, 2016). In these countries, violent conflict has been encountered in the past decade but is further exacerbated by pervasive criminal and interpersonal violence. In other words, it is speculated that countries affected by armed conflict tend to also have a multiplicity of other correlating and coalescing variables that make conditions further detrimental for youth. The combination of various detrimental variables is especially acute in low- and middle-income nations that are politically and economically fragile (Commonwealth Secretariat, 2016). The poor and corrupt governance often associated with these countries makes them all the more susceptible to internal conflicts and less able to overcome setbacks from national disasters. This, in turn, sets a cycle of continued impoverishment and misery amid which youth find themselves, with few prospects for the future.

CHILDREN AND ARMED CONFLICT

Definition of a Child Soldier

A child associated with an armed force or armed group refers to any person below 18 years of age who is, or who has been, recruited or used by an armed force or armed group in any capacity, including but not limited to children, boys and girls, used as fighters, cooks, porters, spies or for sexual purposes.

Child Recruitment and Use

Hundreds of thousands of children are used as soldiers in armed conflicts around the world. Many children are abducted and beaten into submission, others join military groups to escape poverty, to defend their communities, out of a feeling of revenge or for other reasons.

Combat and Support Roles

In many conflicts children take direct part in combat. However, their role is not limited to fighting. Many girls and boys start out in support functions that also entail great risk and hardship. One of the common tasks assigned to children is to serve as porters, often carrying heavy loads, including ammunition or injured soldiers. Some children act as lookouts, messengers, cooks or other routine duties. Girls are particularly vulnerable. They are often forced to serve as sexual slaves. Moreover, the use of children for acts of terror, including as suicide bombers, has emerged as a phenomenon of modern warfare.

A Long Healing Process

Regardless of how children are recruited and of their roles, child soldiers are victims, whose participation in conflict bears serious implications for their physical and emotional well-being. They are commonly subject to abuse and most of them witness death, killing, and sexual violence. Many are forced to perpetrate these atrocities and some suffer serious long-term psychological consequences. The reintegration of these children into civilian life is a complex process.

Prohibition Under International Law

Human rights law declares 18 as the minimum legal age for recruitment and use of children in hostilities. Recruiting and using children under the age of 15 as soldiers is prohibited under international humanitarian law—treaty and custom—and is defined as a war crime by the International Criminal Court. Parties to conflict that recruit and use children are listed by the Secretary-General in the annexes of his annual report on children and armed conflict.

Source: United Nations Office on Drugs and Crime (2016).

Questions to Consider

1. True or False: The minimum age allowed by the UN to recruit and use children in hostilities is 15 years old.

2. Multiple Choice: Children recruited into armed conflict often do which of the following?

   a. Act as porters of ammunition

   b. Act as porters for injured soldiers

   c. Act as lookouts and messengers

   d. All of the above

3. Explain why recruiting and using children who are below the minimum legal age for armed conflict is defined as a war crime.

In 2009 and 2011, the secretary-general for children and armed conflict revised the listing criteria of parties that recruit or use child soldiers to include the killing and maiming of children, sexual violence against children, and attacks on schools and hospitals. From a global perspective, it has been found that this listing of parties complicit in these crimes against children serves as a powerful tool to get violators to end these practices, particularly political leaders and their cronies. This is a public list that indicates to the world where these criminal groups are located, which can result in the United Nations taking action and imposing sanctions. Sanctions often are placed unless the country agrees to the immediate release and reintegration of children, the criminalization of child recruitment through national legislation, and allowing full access for UN staff into military installation to confirm that children are not used as combatants. As of 2017, numerous action plans to end violations against children have been signed by dozens of armed forces and conflict groups, resulting in the release of thousands of children. See In Practice 13.2 for the recommendations of the special representative of the secretary-general for children and armed conflict to protect youth.

IN PRACTICE 13.2

SECRETARY-GENERAL FOR CHILDREN AND ARMED CONFLICT GENERAL RECOMMENDATIONS TO PROTECT YOUTH DURING WARTIME CIRCUMSTANCES

1. **Securing universal compliance with international norms and standards** — The international community should strive for universal adherence to international standards, including the Optional Protocol to the Convention on the Rights of the Child on the involvement of children in armed conflict, that protect children from the adverse effects of war.

2. **End impunity for violations against children** — Member States must ensure systematic and timely investigation and prosecution of crimes against children and youth in the context of armed conflict and provide assistance to victims.

3. **Strengthening the monitoring and reporting mechanism** — Member States, United Nations entities and non-governmental organizations must continue to enhance the existing common framework to timely collect information on violations against children and youth.

4. **Promote justice for children** — Member States need to uphold international standards on juvenile justice with detention used only as a last resort and a guarantee that detained juveniles be separated from detained adults.

5. **Support inclusive reintegration strategies** — Stakeholders should ensure that release and reintegration strategies are in line with the Paris Commitments and Principles. Strategies should ensure long-term sustainability and community-based approaches, with emphasis on education and employment.

6. **Integrate children's rights in peacemaking, peacebuilding and preventive actions** — All peacemaking and peacebuilding processes should be child-sensitive, including specific provisions in peace agreements.

7. **Increase the participation of and support for children and youth** — The participation of children and youth in the child rights agenda is a key element to future work in this area.

Source: Office of the Special Representative of the Secretary-General for Children and Armed Conflict (2013).

Questions to Consider

1. True or False: The participation of youth in the child rights agenda is a key element to future work to protect youth during wartime circumstances.

2. Multiple Choice: Stakeholders should do which of the following?

   a. Ensure reintegration strategies are in line with the Paris Commitments and Principles

   b. Use strategies that emphasize education and employment

   c. Use strategies that ensure long-term sustainability

   d. All of the above

   e. A & B, but not C

Urbanization and Delinquency in Developed Countries

As one might guess, it has been found that countries with more urbanized populations tend to have higher rates of official juvenile offenses. Multiple theories can serve as explanatory mechanisms for this connection, but for the most part, researchers have found that it is the breakup of the family—caused by urbanization and employment shifts—that has led to the correlation between youth crime and concentrated populations. According to the United Nations, the higher rates are attributable to differences in social control and cohesion. It seems that rural communities have more closely networked family systems that provide better forms of supervision and control over the behavior of youth. In many cases, smaller communities—where most members of the community know one another personally—allow for informal means of addressing misbehavior of youth.

Areas such as urban settings, where more people are in contact with one another, allow for more criminal opportunities. Also, in these more populous regions where industrialization leads to virtual strangers living next to one another, more formal forms of legal and judicial processing are implemented. The impersonal nature by which these urban areas address youth crime serves to magnify the problem. It is for these reasons that it is thought that the ongoing process of urbanization in developing countries contributes to juvenile involvement in criminal behavior. The basic features of the urban environment foster the development of new forms of social behavior that emerge as informal forms of social control (e.g., family) are weakened. These conditions are generated by the higher population density and degree of heterogeneity typically found in urban areas.

In various industrialized countries, increased prosperity and the availability of a growing range of consumer goods have led to increased opportunities for juvenile crime, including theft, vandalism, and the destruction of property. With these social changes seen during the past few years, it has been observed that "the extended family has been replaced by the nuclear family as the primary kinship group" and "the informal traditional control exercised by adults (including parents, relatives and teachers) over young people has gradually declined" (United Nations, 2003, p. 1999). Throughout this process, effective substitutes have not been developed. Related to this is the fact that insufficiency of parental supervision has become common and has been found to be one of the strongest predictors of delinquency throughout the world.

Urbanization and modernization have not translated to wealth and prosperity for everyone. Among many developing countries, there is a growing population of "have-nots," people who are disadvantaged and experience deprivation in relation to the wealth that may exist around them in urban and modernized areas. These lower-income families may be immigrants or persons who have recently come from rural areas of a country to a more urban setting. Social and economic shifts have created a distinct gap between the rich and the poor, and some populations (e.g., minority groups and immigrants) have been excluded from success due to the emergence of social obstacles. Similar to what occurs in the United States, welfare systems in industrialized nations have provided relief but have not eliminated the meager standards by which some groups subsist. This, together with the increased dependence of low-income families on different forms of social services, has led to the development of a new class of poverty-ridden persons in many industrialized areas of the world (UNICEF, 2012).

Further exacerbating these problems is the fact that in many urban areas around the world, migration has led to overpopulation and to further burgeoning of slums. This has created dangerous communities that are avoided by most other citizens, which, in turn, further isolates the slum area and distances access to social and economic benefits in the larger society. These areas are often so chaotic and violent that local police and other security forces are hesitant to enter. According to estimates from UNICEF, one out of every three city dwellers—which amounts to nearly 1 billion persons—live in slum conditions. Further, these slums, which are characterized by social exclusion and lack of social support systems, are prevalent in developing countries where urbanization has occurred rapidly but the spread of wealth, technology, and access to education has been restricted to a small segment of the population. This problem impacts some areas of the world more than others, with the sub-Saharan African region having the highest percentage (71%) of its urban population forced to live in slums (UNICEF, 2012, p. 3). Slum development is also problematic in southern Asia, where approximately 57% of city residents live in slums; East Asia, where about 34% of urban residents live in slums; and Latin America, where about 30% of persons in city areas live in slums (UNICEF, 2012, p. 3).

Age of Responsibility

Determining the age of responsibility is an important consideration for international research with juveniles. The age at which a person becomes an adult differs in countries throughout the world. Earlier chapters of this text have discussed this important issue within the United States, marking a degree in variance between a number of states. Research has shown that the age of criminal responsibility can range from 7 to 18, depending on the country (UNODC, 2006, 2011). Currently, the UN does not specify a minimum age of criminal responsibility. However, it has criticized nations that set the minimum age at 12 or less. The primary philosophy is explained in official commentary to the *United Nations Standard Minimum Rules for the Administration of Juvenile Justice*, also known as the Beijing Rules of 1985 (see In Practice 13.6 later in the chapter for additional details).

Making matters more complicated is the fact that many nations have more than one age of criminal responsibility depending on the category of offense committed. In addition, countries that make use of an administrative system for minor offenses may define the age at which a child can be subject to administrative sanctions. As a general rule, where the age of criminal responsibility is especially high, such as 17 or 18, it is likely that the country's juvenile justice system is mainly welfare oriented. Under such a system, children are not described as having committed an offense because delinquent behavior of children is viewed as a welfare, social, or educational issue (UNODC, 2006). Nonetheless, these types of systems may still sentence children to secure institutions. The intent of this action is therapeutic rather than punitive. This is distinct from an enforcement approach that relies on police intervention.

Delinquency in Various World Regions

Although certain aspects of juvenile delinquency are universal, others vary from one region to another. This section provides the student with an overview of delinquency in various regions of the world. This topic alone could serve as the basis for an entire text in and of itself. The purpose here is simply to provide readers with some idea of the global picture related to delinquency. This section, though broad in scope, is followed by another more specialized section that focuses on juvenile gang offenders in various areas of the world. Students will see that many of the issues found around the world are similar to those in the United States but, at the same time, have different nuances shaped by internal and external factors unique to that region or country. We now proceed with a regional analysis of delinquency.

Africa

Throughout the African continent, delinquency tends to be attributed primarily to poverty, malnutrition, and unemployment. These factors are the result of marginalization of juveniles in the already severely disadvantaged segments of society. Rapid population growth has been experienced in Africa, and the population seems to be getting correspondingly younger over time. This is coupled with the fact that few new jobs are developed in Africa, which has resulted in half of all families living in poverty. Many of the urban poor live in slum and squatter settlements with unhealthy housing. One of the most serious problems is the great number of street and orphaned children, whose numbers have been growing as a result of continuous and multiple armed conflicts, the advent of HIV/AIDS, and the breakdown of the traditional tribal culture and family influence on children. Juvenile delinquency is on the rise, with the primary offenses being theft, robbery, smuggling, prostitution, the abuse of narcotic substances, and drug trafficking among young offenders.

Asia

In Asian countries, juvenile crime and delinquency are largely urban phenomena. As is true elsewhere, young people constitute the most criminally active segment of the population. The most noticeable trends in the region are the rise in the number of violent acts committed by young people, the increase in drug-related offenses, and the marked growth in female juvenile delinquency. The financial crisis that hit some countries in East and Southeast Asia in the late 1990s created economic stagnation and contraction, leading to large-scale youth unemployment.

Some countries are facing great difficulty because they are located near or within the "Golden Crescent" or the "Golden Triangle"—two areas of Asia where massive amounts of opium are grown and produced. Drug traffickers frequently recruit adolescents to serve in this industry, and many become addicted to drugs while involved in this criminal activity.

Latin America

In Latin America, the young have been the hardest hit by the economic problems linked to the debt crisis in the region, evidenced by the extremely high unemployment rates prevailing within this group. Juvenile delinquency is particularly acute and is often associated with the problem of homelessness among children and adolescents. Government corruption and constant military skirmishes in countries such as Nicaragua, El Salvador, Guatemala, and Honduras create environments conducive to crime and delinquency.

Middle East

In the Middle East, there is less indication that serious problems with juvenile delinquency exist. However, affluent nations such as Saudi Arabia and the United Arab Emirates have more problems with juvenile offenders than do other nations in the Middle East (Reichel, 2005). Otherwise, issues associated with juvenile delinquency vary from one country to another. Some countries have experienced socioeconomic difficulties, while others have become prosperous. In the latter group, delinquency may occur in connection with migrants seeking employment, or it may be linked to factors such as continued urbanization, sudden affluence, rapid changes in the economy, and the increasing heterogeneity of the population. The conflict between traditional Arab-Islamic values and modern views imported from other areas of the world seems to be a common problem for countries in this area of the world.

Eastern Europe

In eastern European countries and among those countries that were once part of the former Soviet Union, families are becoming more dysfunctional. Indeed, the number of parents deprived of their child-rearing rights is increasing annually. These parents are often alcoholics, drug addicts, and people who have mental health issues or criminal backgrounds. Factors such as unemployment and low family income are the main contributors to juvenile delinquency in many parts of this region. There are few, if any, social services in these countries, which creates a dismal picture for youth.

Juvenile Gangs Around the World

Serious gang problems among youth are also seen in other countries and, in many cases, are idealized just as is done via the media and music of youth in the United States. Among such youth, aggression may be considered an acceptable, preferable, and courageous approach to problem solving. In fact, youth who are willing to engage in violence may derive status and prestige among their cohorts, which serves to socially reinforce this type of behavior in the future. Indeed, street and gang activity among young people roaming the streets has become a normal presence in many urban areas of the developing world, especially in those cities characterized by slums.

According to UNICEF (2012), the data suggest that tens of millions of children and youth live or work on the street and that the majority of them reside in the most populous cities of sub-Saharan Africa, Latin America, and India. This is usually because their families are incapable of supporting them or because they have little choice but to opt for street life over the hardship of their domestic situation. On the street, many become involved in a variety of clandestine activities, such as begging, prostitution, or petty crime (UNICEF, 2012). In such situations, they are more likely to become involved in criminal activities with adult traffickers, being enticed by the notion of quick and easy money and a desire for recognition from their peer group. In some cases, they may become involved to gain protection from juvenile gangs and/or violence committed by adult criminals on the same streets. In other cases, they may seek protection from the police—the very people who are expected to protect them (UNICEF, 2012).

Young urban dwellers who engage in illegal activities often gather in gangs, which provide both an organized process of maximizing shared profits and protection from others who may cause harm (United Nations, 2012). In many cases, these gangs are a primary source of instability within urban regions. In some regions youth gangs are pervasive within cities and, to make matters worse, are in league with major criminal syndicates who commit trafficking crimes related to prostitution, weapons, drugs, and/or illegally traded goods (United Nations, 2012). For instance, in the Caribbean, gang members have been found to be 20 times more likely to sell drugs than were nonmembers and 35 times more likely to collaborate with drug dealers (United Nations, 2012, p. 4). Worldwide, the youth most likely to participate in delinquent or violent activities are part of a gang, though this association tends to be higher for theft, robbery, and rape and lower for premeditated murder and assault with the intent to inflict grievous bodily harm (United Nations, 2012).

It would appear that the most likely youth groups to engage in delinquent behaviors are members of territorial gangs. Indeed, juvenile gang members commit a much greater number of offenses, per person, than do non–gang members (Hanser, 2007c). United Nations research reveals that the most frequent offenses committed by gang members are fighting, street extortion, and school violence. These types of offenses are similar to those found among youth gangs in the United States. Because juvenile gangs are a clear and identifiable problem in numerous areas of the world, we cover this phenomenon in more detail in the subsection that follows.

Mexico and Central America

In Mexico, juvenile gangs can be found in various urban areas. Studies have found that perhaps 1,500 street gangs exist in Mexico City alone. These street gangs may range from a handful of members to full-blown international gangs such as MS-13 (Mara Salvatruchas) and MS-18 (Mara 18) (see Chapter 12 for more information on these gangs). Youth gangs in Mexico are normally referred to as *pandillas* not *maras*, fight for territorial control over *barrios*, and carry homemade arms or arms often acquired through the robbery of private security guards. These gangs are typically composed of youths from marginal urban neighborhoods (USAID, 2006). Such gangs tend to have teen members but recruit very young members—younger than age 12—who serve as lookouts and drug couriers for older gang members. The younger members may be given humorous or derogatory names such as "pee wee league" or "diaper brigade," which denotes their lower status in the gang pecking order.

In Central America, the youth gang problem is very serious and often leads to what is later an adult gang problem. For instance, in Honduras, the population is fairly young: 41% are under the age of 15, and 20% are 15 to 24 years old. Further, in that country, about 6% of the youth population is illiterate. Twenty-nine percent of children drop out of school before the eighth grade, further limiting the chances that these youth will be able to compete in the legitimate workforce. These factors create a fertile breeding ground for young members who are recruited by older youth and adult leaders of these gangs. See In Practice 13.3 for more on recruitment into the gang life.

Indeed, the current level of youth violence in Honduras is among the worst in Central America. The gang phenomenon is considered by many as one of the biggest problems affecting Honduras. According to police statistics, at the end of 2003, there were 36,000 gang members in Honduras alone (USAID, 2006).

Gangs have established themselves throughout Honduras, El Salvador, Guatemala, and Nicaragua. As in Mexico, MS-13 and MS-18 have proliferated and are well entrenched throughout Honduras and the remainder of Central America. Since the late 1980s, an internationalization of the gang problem has occurred. Indeed, many MS-13 and MS-18 gang members immigrated illegally into the United States; this includes both juvenile and adult members. Over time, the United States deports these members back to their home country, which has resulted in a large number of MS-13 and MS-18 in Central America who have extensive experience in the United States. These gang members, once released into Honduran society, actively recruit young gang members, perpetuating membership across generations. In the process, these gangs also recruit members across borders because they actively recruit youth in the United States, particularly Latino American youth from disadvantaged areas of California. Over time, this has led to the growth of MS-13 due to increased membership of U.S. citizens, usually of Mexican or Central American origin.

As in the United States, growth of MS-13 and MS-18 has occurred in Honduras and, to a lesser extent, El Salvador, Guatemala, and Nicaragua due to the broad assimilation of small-scale street gangs into the MS-13 and MS-18 gangs. As this assimilation took place, members of smaller gangs began to imitate the two main rival gangs, adopting the hand signs, clothing, and language that originated on the streets of Los Angeles. It is in this manner that an almost symbiotic relationship is shared between members of these gangs in the United States and

Jan Sochor/Latincontinent/Getty Images

In El Salvador, a member of the MS-13 in the Tonacatepeque penitentiary for underage prisoners is shown.

YOUTH GANGS, HUMAN TRAFFICKING, AND RECRUITMENT THROUGH ROMANTIC FRIENDSHIPS

The recruitment of victims is an essential part of the trafficking process. Though the recruitment can happen in many ways, it often involves deception. The victim may be deceived about work conditions such as the type of job, the workplace, and the salary. In other cases, criminals deceive by feigning a romantic interest and entering into a relationship with the victim in order to gain her trust. Victims of this type of recruitment are often underage but may also be adults. Generally, the perpetrator is male and the victim female. As the "relationship" develops, the exploiter manipulates and/or coerces the victim into sexual exploitation, from which he obtains the profits.

One example that occurred in Canada involved 10 males—including one minor boy— who were convicted of trafficking four underage girls. The sentences ranged from 1 to 3 years of imprisonment. The offenders were part of a "street gang" who carried out a relatively extensive trafficking operation in which the minor boy was the recruiter. He operated at schools where he could easily make contacts with multiple underage girls. Some of the girls fell in love with him, and once trust had been established, the girls were introduced to the other, older gang members. The victims were then forced, under threats of violence, to abide by strict rules and provide sexual services for payments the traffickers then collected. Here, the recruitment through the feigned romantic relationship was one part of a larger scheme to exploit several girls.

Several points of importance related to this incident dovetail with what has been discussed in this text regarding youth gang members, issues of juvenile crime, juvenile victimization, and human trafficking. This incident involved gang membership but used a juvenile member of the group who was the primary perpetrator involved to access the young victim. Further, this shows that trafficking does not necessarily need to use physical violence. Rather, the use of deception to connive and delude the victim is often used.

Source: United Nations Office on Drugs and Crime (2014).

Questions to Consider

1. True or False: In most cases where feigning romantic interest is used to lure victims of human trafficking, the victim is underage.

2. Multiple Choice: Which techniques do traffickers use to acquire new victims?

   a. Using deception about work conditions

   b. Feigning a romantic interest and entering into a relationship with the victim

   c. Threatening deportation of the victim

   d. A & B, but not C

   e. A & C, but not B

3. From the scenario outlined, explain how youth can be both perpetrators and victims of crime.

Central America. Members of these gangs circulate back and forth into and out of the United States and into and out of jail and/or prison. Throughout the process, they recruit young members and even have children who later become members of these gangs. Thus, these "street gangs" are intergenerational and international in scope, using juvenile members for petty aspects of the day-to-day gang operations and refining them into more sophisticated members by the time they reach adulthood. Both MS-13 and MS-18 play upon the various misfortunes of the regions in which they operate when recruiting new members. In Practice 13.4 discusses gang resistance education in Central America.

GANG RESISTANCE EDUCATION AND TRAINING IN CENTRAL AMERICA: AN UPDATE FROM 2012

In November 2009, the Gang Resistance Education and Training (G.R.E.A.T.) Program broke ground in its international efforts by piloting a training in Central America. Since that successful pilot, the Regional Gang Initiative, funded by the U.S. Department of State, has provided G.R.E.A.T. Officer Trainings, G.R.E.A.T. Families Trainings, G.R.E.A.T. Officer in Service Trainings, and a bilingual Web site.

At this point, well over 100 officers from seven Central American countries have been certified to teach the G.R.E.A.T. curriculum in middle and elementary schools, and around 12,000 students have graduated from the Program.

Jim Rose, Regional Gang Advisor for the Bureau of International Narcotics and Law Enforcement Affairs, U.S. Department of State, had once reported that G.R.E.A.T. was quickly becoming a success, and with its current progress in the region, he foresaw a day when every student in Central America will be exposed to the program during elementary and/or middle school.

During the past few years, there has been tremendous support for the G.R.E.A.T. program in Central America. Consider that, in 2015, the nation of Honduras bussed in nearly 950 G.R.E.A.T. students from several different schools who had completed the elementary and/or middle school curriculum. Select students from each school were recognized individually and given certificates for their schools/grades. The ceremony also honored the 48 newly certified G.R.E.A.T. instructors who had just completed the training.

According to a recent BBC News article, "Central America drug gang violence is at 'alarming levels.'" At this time, it is estimated that approximately 10 percent of the population in El Salvador, Honduras, and Guatemala have fled the region due to excessive violence. In fact, approximately 48,000 homicides occurred between 2011 and 2014, with many due to gang violence. In response, numerous people migrate to the United States, travelling north through Mexico. Among these migrants are thousands and thousands of unaccompanied children of various ages who traveled in groups, north, to the United States border. These youth report forced gang recruitment, extortion, the lack of resources, and complete apathy among many governmental workers as their reasons for leaving their home country. As a result and among other things, it is hoped by the United States that gang awareness in these countries-of-origin will help to stem the tide of child migrants at the border of the United States. To further demonstrate how overwhelming this problem has been, consider that there are currently 900 street gangs and 70,000 members in Central America.

Sources: G.R.E.A.T. Program (2016); National Gang Center (2012).

Questions to Consider

1. True or False: One reason that the United States has shared the G.R.E.A.T. approach with countries in Central America is to help stem the tide of youth migrants at the U.S. border.

2. Multiple Choice: Which countries have had approximately 10% of their citizens move away due to concerns for safety and security?

   a. El Salvador
   b. Honduras
   c. Guatemala
   d. All of the above
   e. None of the above

3. In your opinion, how successful has the Gang Resistance Education and Training (G.R.E.A.T.) Program been in Central America and Mexico?

In Mexico and Central America, gang members can be organized into the following four categories: (1) sympathizers, (2) recruits, (3) members, and (4) leaders. Sympathizers start as lookouts on sidewalk corners and later become involved in selling drugs and other crimes. A sympathizer is voluntarily "jumped" (or beaten) into the gang 2 to 3 years later. It has been reported by some gang experts that the MS-13 require that the beating last for 13 seconds, a symbolic marker for the gang's number. Adding to the overall crime problem associated with gangs is the fact that before the new gang members are jumped, they are required to kill or commit a crime.

Youth in Mexico and Central America who will possibly join a gang are characterized by several risk factors that make them susceptible to gang membership. The majority of youths in this group are poor, live in marginalized urban areas, have limited or no educational or job opportunities, and represent the lowest level of the gang membership, carrying the least amount of status. With continued exposure to gang subcultures and mores, these youth become well versed and more sympathetic to gang life. Such youth are more likely to stay entrenched in gang membership if their basic needs such as income and fulfilling social ties are not satisfied in other ways.

Africa

Research on juvenile gangs in Africa tends to focus on the nation of South Africa or the region of West Africa, because of their modernized society that breeds the conditions for gang membership (Pinnock, 1996). In both areas of Africa, urbanization and economic factors have been considered as primary contributors to the emerging gang problem. However, it should be noted that Africa, in general, is characterized by a

MARVIN RECINOS/AFP/Getty Images

Two juvenile gang members display gang signs while cuffed and in custody.

great deal of political instability and corruption, with this being particularly true in Western African nations such as Nigeria, Dakar, and Senegal.

In South Africa, the need to earn a wage and the adjustment to urbanization have impacted the family system, which has not effectively adapted to the newer form of society. In the process, extended-family support systems and their role of extending guidance, mentorship, and discipline to youth have all but disappeared. This has affected youth in a very profound manner that results in many spending more time on the streets in urban areas of South Africa and developing criminal associations.

Pinnock (1996) contended that gangs, similar to traditional society, provide support and a sense of direction to youth who feel accepted by the gang culture. As we saw in Chapter 12, this same desire for belonging and acceptance is found among many youth who join gangs in the United States. Many marginalized youth in South Africa found the acceptance they desired within the structure of street gangs. Others gravitated toward the emerging political groups that rose against apartheid and the government. Street culture and the involvement of youth in street gangs or political formations is not homogeneous but is composed of a variety of groups established to meet the different needs of youth.

Youth in some major towns in South Africa grow up spending their time on the streets. Many of these juveniles, particularly the males, are drawn into gangs due to prior family affiliations; they may have even been born into a world of gang membership. It is not uncommon for youth to have parents who are, or were, gang members, so they naturally take on the inherited roles from their parents who were involved in the gang life. Yet again, this demonstrates how theoretical explanations like differential association and subcultural theories explain how gang membership is perpetuated across generations. Youth often model the behaviors seen in their dysfunctional parents and seek out the feelings of inclusion offered by gangs. This is reinforced by the understanding that gang life can provide opportunities for economic improvement and for gaining a sense of power, acceptance, and purpose (Pinnock, 1996).

Gang operations in South Africa tend to center on the supply and trade of drugs in the community, in surrounding areas, and, at an even higher level, internationally (Dissel, 1997). As with gangs in Mexico and Central America, it is common for adults to lead gangs that have operations extending past mere local street operations. Nevertheless, these youth play an important role in the drug trafficking process perpetuated by organized adult criminals in the areas of South Africa.

Asia

Juvenile gangs emerged and caught media headlines in Japan, with initial reports surfacing in the late 1990s and early 2000s. Most government and media portrayals indicated that these gangs were more of a nuisance than a serious threat. The largest nuisance has been juvenile biker gangs who are seen as one of the key contributors to juvenile crime, including serious crimes (Kattoulas, 2001). As early as 1999, the National Police Agency in Japan produced data that demonstrated that these biker gangs, known as Bosozoku Gangs, were responsible for more than 80% of serious crimes committed by juveniles (Kattoulas, 2001).

In addition, it has been made public by the National Police Agency that the Bosozoku Gangs are linked to the *Yakuza*, the broad term used for members of the various Japanese organized crime syndicates. The Yakuza, known for their tattoos and penchant for violence, often recruit members from these biker gangs as the juveniles mature and become adults. Further, it has been indicated that these juvenile biker gangs provide tribute to the Yakuza, thereby lining the pockets of the adult mobsters.

Fortunately, it has been found recently that these gangs are in a state of decline. They tend to ride expensive motorbikes and wear flamboyant outfits and are easily identified by police. Further, economic factors have apparently restricted the ability of youth to purchase these bikes and other articles that were customary for these gangs in the early part of this decade. Theft of bikes and other types of procurement do not seem to be effective enough to supplement gang activity due to police crackdowns on these juvenile gangs during the past few years. These crackdowns have reduced the spread of juvenile biker gangs in Japan. Nevertheless, they represent a unique type of youthful delinquency that is worth mention among the East Asian region of the world.

In the People's Republic of China, juvenile crime has increased, and juvenile gangs have been specifically cited for serious crimes such as assault and rape (BBC News, 2007). The rise in youth gangs has been attributed to immigration, globalization, modernization, and economic shifts that have impacted families. Among many rural families, youth are left with elderly relatives while parents go into the cities for employment (BBC News, 2007). The breakdown in the traditional Chinese family structure is further aggravated by technological influences from the Internet and other sources where the youth subculture is unduly influenced.

In other countries, such as South Korea, Thailand, and Taiwan, youth gangs exist, but they are typically local and engage in only petty delinquency. In most cases, they are seen as being fairly harmless and more of a simple inconvenience than anything else. Even though youth crime has risen in most East Asian countries, the existence of youth gang-related crime in these other countries is not cited as a problem. Thus, it would appear that juvenile gangs in Asia are, for the most part, not a widespread or serious issue except in certain specific countries, such as Japan and China, as well as Hong Kong and Taiwan.

Europe

Juvenile crime in Europe has been given a great deal of attention during the past decade (Fitzgerald, Stevens, & Hale, 2004). Indications are that youth crime has increased and, as with other areas of the world, much of the cause is attributed to urbanization and modernization, along with immigration and economic factors. However, some countries began to see a rise in juvenile gangs that, while loosely organized, were aligned along either racial or ethnic ties, such as has been noted among Muslim youth in France (Hanser & Caudill, 2002). The emergence of these gangs has much to do with the sense of powerlessness that these youth experience, poor economic conditions, a sense of identity crisis as immigrants with few opportunities, and a sense of cultural isolation from mainstream French society (Hanser & Caudill, 2002; Radu, 2005).

In Germany, juvenile gangs are also reported as a problem and seem to focus more around ethnic issues. Youth gangs in Germany tend to be traditional German youth who have embraced neo-Nazi ideologies, largely in reaction to the immigration of eastern Europeans and other foreigners into Germany (Decker, 2005; Klein, Weerman, & Thornberry, 2006). These youth typically promote supremacist viewpoints and commit crimes of vagrancy and hate crimes against minorities and immigrants. In recent years, as the rate of immigration into Germany has stabilized, the level of violence associated with youth gangs has declined (Decker, 2005; Klein et al., 2006).

Throughout the remainder of Europe, juvenile gangs exist but are not the focus of as much media attention. The factors associated with their development tend to include shifts in immigration and ethnicity, urbanization, national influences, and local neighborhood circumstances related to gang development in several European countries. Klein and colleagues (2006) conducted research on juvenile gangs in over a dozen countries throughout Europe and found a wide pattern of violent behavior within these groups. They also found that the level of violence among these youth was greater than among nongang youth and that the violence was less serious than that committed by juvenile gangs in the United States. The reasons for this less serious violent crime (when compared with the United States) were thought to be linked with the tighter control on handguns in Europe and the fact that youth gangs were not usually linked to territory or organized criminal syndicates and/or drug trafficking activity.

Australia

Rob White, one of the most preeminent researchers on youth gangs in Australia, has provided the most relevant and recent research on this issue. According to White, there is a widespread public perception that juvenile gangs have become a serious concern in Australia. White (2004) further contended that this perception is increased by politicians who add hype to the portrayal of the problem to gain attention and public support. Nevertheless, White (2004) said there is very little empirical data that allow researchers or agencies to know how many gangs and/or gang members exist throughout the nation. There is also a corresponding lack of data on the types of crimes committed by these gangs and/or the motivations behind these groups.

Among the scant research that does exist, it has been speculated that the social dynamics of youth group formation have been impacted by modern-day information access (the Internet and popular-media culture) as well as aggravation related to economic inequalities experienced by immigrants. As a means of rectifying these issues, White (2004) called for community collaboration and community policing techniques to reduce crime-producing conditions that lead to youth gang formation. In promoting this approach, White (2004) pointed toward the extensive research conducted by gang and community policing researchers in the United States, demonstrating the back-and-forth learning process that nations can develop when addressing social issues such as youth gangs and criminal activity.

International Approaches to Preventing Juvenile Gangs

The *World Youth Report* (United Nations, 2003) made it clear that if gang prevention efforts are to be effective, they must take into account both individual motivations and group dynamics. Although this is true, such programs must also take into account the severe forms of deprivation that many youth experience, especially in developing countries. In addition, it is likely that delinquency will only be reduced if developing countries become more stable and less corrupt because instability and corruption are invitations to organized crime syndicates to exercise influence over communities. When organized crime has strong influence over a region, youth involved in crime serve as the breeding ground for recruits into organized criminal activity. Juvenile gangs, in particular, serve as a very good source of recruits for organized criminal groups.

In some countries, such as the Russian Federation, Japan, and Honduras, juvenile gangs have a direct link to adult criminal groups and are therefore undaunted by official forms of sanction. They view their activity as the first step into what might be seen as a career track; facing legal sanctions and penalties is simply a rite of passage that indicates their maturity into the world of crime. With these types of structures in place, it is virtually impossible to effectively implement gang prevention programs and even less likely that gang exit strategies discussed in Chapter 12 can be successfully provided.

In addition, prevention and intervention programs cannot be viewed in a "one-size-fits-all" fashion; what works in one country will not necessarily work in another. Countries around the globe will need to implement combined approaches that consist of prevention, intervention, and suppression strategies. Only when these three aspects are successfully implemented can gang exit strategies be realistically developed within emergent countries. For these programs to be optimally effective, they should consist of the following:

1. Prevention efforts that use community policing techniques so that a rapport can be developed with youth and police
2. Interventions that include restorative justice applications, creating "buy in" from victims and avoiding the effects of stigmatization for youthful offenders

3. Suppression techniques specifically targeted at disrupting juvenile links with larger organized criminal syndicates

The *World Youth Report* (United Nations, 2003) noted that juvenile gang members do not necessarily lack the desire to live within socially approved boundaries. In fact, as we have seen in this and previous chapters, youth often engage in delinquency, including gang membership, because of factors related to home life or external influences. As such, many see the gang as their only family and support. When shown another path, and when that path is realistic when considering their circumstances, many will be likely to consider options other than gang life. This is particularly true if the previously listed aspects (prevention, intervention, and suppression) of gang reduction are implemented. In addition, the prevention of juvenile gang activity and juvenile delinquency in general should be considered a multifaceted project. Students should refer to In Practice 13.2 for details on what the United Nations has identified as necessary for model prevention programs.

As it stands, the *World Youth Report* (United Nations, 2003) noted that in most countries, "most rehabilitation initiatives are not working to redirect the energies or potential of gang members into socially desirable activities" (p. 206). We agree with this appraisal of gang reduction programs around the world and would, therefore, encourage practitioners around the world to develop new and innovative strategies for solving the juvenile gang epidemic that has proliferated throughout many urban areas of the globe.

Human Trafficking and Youth Exploitation

During recent years, the existence of human trafficking has been recognized as one of the many unrecognized scourges that face the global community. The exploitation of humans as slaves is the key profit base for criminal traffickers. Exploitation and trafficking can occur by using nonviolent methods of deception (see In Practice 13.3), or it can be overt and violent, with entire armed militant groups serving as perpetrators (see In Practice 13.1).

We have seen that, for the most part, the victimization of young girls tends to be more common, with sexual slavery being a frequent form of exploitation. This is not to say that some male youth are not also forced into sexual slavery, but the majority of these victims are young girls and women (see Figure 13.2). Another frequent form of exploitation of youth is making them perform labor. In this area of exploitation, males are selected more often as victims than females (see Figure 13.2). The types of forced labor that may be required are broad and limited only by the demands of the buyer. Examples of the types of work trafficked youth may be forced to perform include manufacturing, cleaning, construction, textile production, catering, and domestic servitude.

Figure 13.2 Gender Breakdown of Detected Victims of Trafficking for Sexual Exploitation and Forced Labor

Left: Gender breakdown of detected victims of trafficking for sexual exploitation, 2010–2014
Right: Gender breakdown of detected victims of trafficking for forced labor, 2010–2014
Source: United Nations Office on Drugs and Crime (2014).

Figure 13.3 shows the most common types of exploitation of youth by region of the world. Whereas in most regions it would appear that sexual exploitation is the most common category, forced labor has become more common throughout the years. Nevertheless, in Europe and Central Asia (66%), Africa and the Middle East (53%), and the Americas (48%), sexual exploitation is the primary demand for youth who are trafficked, particularly female youth. The reasons for these fluctuations by region usually depend on whether each country is a demand country or a supply country. In general, the more affluent nations in North America,

---

IN PRACTICE 13.5

BOKO HARAM ABDUCTS GIRLS EN MASSE TO BE FUTURE WIVES OF MILITANT MEMBERS

The radicalized Islamic group Boko Haram has been in armed conflict with the government of Nigeria for a number of years. Members of Boko Haram wish to establish an Islamic haven in Nigeria. Among other things, Boko Haram contends that Western-style education is corrupt because it causes doubt in the minds of followers as to the veracity of the Islamic faith. During 2013 and 2014, the Nigerian army managed to repel Boko Haram forces, driving them back into mountainous regions, where Boko Haram was forced to focus attacks on civilian sites rather than military targets.

During the years of this insurgency group's mayhem, various schools for children were attacked, with several hundred students killed over the years. As a result of the chaos and instability in various regions of Nigeria, thousands of youth have been prevented from attending school. Throughout these years, Boko Haram was known to kidnap young girls, making them serve as cooks, servants, and/or sex slaves. Key to the beliefs of Boko Haram is that women, especially young girls, do not have a need for education because, according to Boko Haram, this distracts them from other duties with which they are tasked.

Aside from what has been noted so far, it was the incident on April 14, 2014, that caught the eye of the world's media. Boko Haram attacked the Government Girls Secondary School in Chibok, Nigeria. During this raid, several Boko Haram members were dressed as school security guards and broke into the school. They encouraged the girls to leave the school and follow them, under the guise that they were taking the girls to safety. These girls were taken off by truck to remote areas of northeast Nigeria where Boko Haram was known to have several fortified camps.

It was reported that 267 young girls were abducted during the raid. During the next few months, some girls were released and others escaped, over time, on their own. To this day, well over a hundred of these girls remain captives of Boko Haram, with release being nowhere in sight anytime soon.

Source: Written from personal research by Robert Hanser.

Questions to Consider

1. True or False: Key to the beliefs of Boko Haram is the idea that women should be subservient to men.

2. Multiple Choice: Boko Haram is an extremist group active in which country?

   a. South Africa

   b. Tanzania

   c. Nigeria

   d. None of the above

3. In your opinion, considering readings in prior chapters on abuse, what might be some reasons for a young girl to refuse to leave her Boko Haram captors, even when given the chance months later?

Figure 13.3 Forms of Exploitation Among Detected Trafficking Victims, by Region

Region	Sexual exploitation	Forced labor, servitude, and slavery	Other forms of exploitation
Africa and the Middle East	53%	37%	10%
Americas	48%	47%	4%
East Asia, South Asia, and Pacific	26%	64%	10%
Europe and Central Asia	66%	26%	8%

Source: United Nations Office on Drugs and Crime (2014).

Europe, and Australia are the demand countries, whereas countries that are not affluent tend to be primarily supply nations from which a disproportionate number of youth are trafficked.

International Administration of Juvenile Justice

In 1985, the United Nations produced a document titled *United Nations Standard Minimum Rules for the Administration of Juvenile Justice*. This document is often referred to as the Beijing Rules of 1985 because it was developed during a United Nations meeting in Beijing. The document set the initial stage and tone for how juvenile justice programs should be administered. Although this document is not legally binding, it has served as an official reference point since its inception. The primary impetus behind the document was to encourage the humanitarian treatment of juvenile offenders. In Practice 13.6 provides students with a modified version of the Beijing Rules.

Four years after the Beijing Rules were created, the UN developed another legal instrument known as the *Convention on the Rights of the Child* (CRC) (1989). The CRC was different from the Beijing Rules because it was legally binding upon member nations who signed this document. Further, it was considered "in bad taste" for nations to not adopt these practices. Those nations signing the treaty agree to abide by its standards, associated national laws, policies, and procedures (Reichel, 2005). The CRC has become one of the most universally accepted treaties around the world. Currently, only two countries have not ratified and signed this document—(1) Somalia and (2) the United States (Reichel, 2005).

UNITED NATIONS STANDARD MINIMUM RULES FOR
THE ADMINISTRATION OF JUVENILE JUSTICE (THE BEIJING RULES)

Part One. General principles

Member States shall endeavor to develop conditions that will ensure for the juvenile a meaningful life in the community, which, during that period in life when she or he is most susceptible to deviant behavior, will foster a process of personal development and education that is as free from crime and delinquency as possible.

Sufficient attention shall be given to positive measures that involve the full mobilization of all possible resources, including the family, volunteers and other community groups, as well as schools and other community institutions, for the purpose of promoting the well-being of the juvenile, with a view to reducing the need for intervention under the law, and of effectively, fairly and humanely dealing with the juvenile in conflict with the law.

Part Two. Age of criminal responsibility

In those legal systems recognizing the concept of the age of criminal responsibility for juveniles, the beginning of that age shall not be fixed at too low an age level, bearing in mind the facts of emotional, mental and intellectual maturity.

Part Three. Adjudication and disposition

The proceedings shall be conducive to the best interests of the juvenile and shall be conducted in an atmosphere of understanding, which shall allow the juvenile to participate therein and to express herself or himself freely.

Part Four. Non-institutional treatment

Efforts shall be made to provide juveniles, at all stages of the proceedings, with necessary assistance such as lodging, education or vocational training, employment or any other assistance, helpful and practical, in order to facilitate the rehabilitative process.

Part Five. Institutional treatment

Juveniles in institutions shall be kept separate from adults and shall be detained in a separate institution or in a separate part of an institution also holding adults. Young female offenders placed in an institution deserve special attention as to their personal needs and problems. They shall by no means receive less care, protection, assistance, treatment and training than young male offenders. Their fair treatment shall be ensured.

Part Six. Juvenile reentry

Efforts shall be made to provide semi-institutional arrangements, such as half-way houses, educational homes, day-time training centers and other such appropriate arrangements that may assist juveniles in their proper reintegration into society.

Part Seven. Research, planning, policy formulation and evaluation

The utilization of research as a basis for an informed juvenile justice policy is widely acknowledged as an important mechanism for keeping practices abreast of advances in knowledge and the continuing development and improvement of the juvenile justice system. The mutual feedback between research and policy is especially important in juvenile justice. With rapid and often drastic changes in the life-styles of the young and in the forms and dimensions of juvenile crime, the societal and justice responses to juvenile crime and delinquency quickly become outmoded and inadequate.

Source: United Nations (1990b).

Questions to Consider

1. True or False: According to the Beijing Rules, reentry of juvenile offenders is a practice expected to be used.

Further, consider the case of *Roper v. Simmons*, where the Court looked to the laws and standards of several other industrialized countries as additional support for determining whether national consensus against the death penalty was consistent with worldwide cultural shifts. To be clear, the Court did not rely on its analysis of other countries when making its ruling nor was it under any obligation to do so. Rather, the U.S. Supreme Court did what it rarely does, which was to use legalistic evolution around the world as a means of supporting the rationale for its decision. Although this was not completely unheard of (the Court has examined foreign laws in other cases as supporting commentary), it was unusual and also represented the impact that globalization has had on all countries, including the United States. In fact, the decision to use precedent and legal developments in the global community drew criticism from some members of Congress who felt that the interpretation of law in the United States should be strictly based on the interpretation of the U.S. Constitution. Whether the Court was "out of bounds" in its analysis is a matter of judgment concerning the age-old arguments centering on judicial restraint. For our purposes, it is important to understand that juvenile law in the United States has been, and will continue to be, impacted by developments around the world.

One of the most important reasons why the United States has not ratified this treaty is because during the time of its creation, the United States allowed the death penalty for juveniles whose crime was committed prior to their 18th birthday. Because Article 37 of the CRC expressly prohibits capital punishment for juveniles, the United States was initially in direct conflict with the legally binding document. At that time, only seven countries (Congo, Iran, Nigeria, Pakistan, Saudi Arabia, Yemen, and the United States) were known to have executed juvenile offenders, being either nonsignatory nations or having only eliminated this practice at a later period after the creation of the CRC. At the time of the document's drafting, 22 U.S. states allowed the death penalty for persons who were under the age of 18 at the time they committed their crime. However, readers may recall the more recent U.S. Supreme Court ruling *Roper v. Simmons* (2005), where the Court invalidated the execution of juveniles who were under 18 at the time of the crime commission. Obviously, this ruling changes the political and social landscape for the United States in regard to signing the CRC.

From 1990 until the 2005 ruling in *Roper*, the United States had committed the majority of juvenile executions. In his arguments against the death penalty, Justice Kennedy pointed out that all of these countries, save the United States, had either completely abolished the death penalty for youth or had provided strong public statements and legal mechanisms that disavowed the use of the death penalty with juvenile offenders. The United States stood as the most ardent and passionate supporter of the practice. Thus, it is clear that the *Roper* decision generated a good deal of international controversy and debate, with legal scholars from countries around the world watching with keen interest. Whether the United States will eventually sign the CRC is still to be decided. In 2002, during the United Nations Special Session on Children, various members of the U.S. delegation again declined to sign the CRC. This occurred in spite of the fact that the United States was an active participant in the drafting and creation of the document.

Since the Special Session on Children in 2002, a number of children's advocates have pushed for the U.S. adoption of this document. As of 2017, the United States had yet to adopt this document. One organization, known as the Campaign for U.S. Ratification of the *Convention on the Rights of the Child* (CRC), is a volunteer-driven network of academics, attorneys, child and human rights advocates, educators, members of religious and faith-based communities, physicians, representatives from nongovernmental organizations (NGOs), students, and other concerned citizens who seek to bring about U.S. ratification and implementation of the CRC. According to its website, its campaign began shortly after the Special Session on Children in 2002. As of 2017, the following passage remained on this group's website and describes the organization's development:

Through the leadership of the Child Welfare League of America (CWLA), a core group of child advocates convened the first meeting of the Campaign for U.S. Ratification of the CRC in August 2002. Participants focused on efforts needed to build a national coalition. In 2003, representatives from more than 50 U.S. non-governmental organizations met in Washington, DC for a two day strategy session entitled "Moving the CRC Forward in the United States." Out of this effort, the Campaign for U.S. Ratification of the CRC was formalized. From its origins, the Campaign has grown to encompass membership from 200 organizations and academic institutions. (Campaign for U.S. Ratification of the *Convention on the Rights of the Child* [CRC], n.d.)

Most likely, in time, the United States will ratify this document because it has become an increasing source of embarrassment and makes it difficult for the United States to admonish other countries that have exploitative practices that involve children. The fact that it has not adopted this document serves as a political barb that sticks the United States whenever it attempts to promote enforcement of child welfare issues or matters of human rights that impact youth around the world. President Barack Obama made public mention that it is an embarrassment that this document has not been ratified. The U.S. Senate must approve the treaty with two-thirds majority, but so far, the CRC has not been put before the Senate. Although this is expected to eventually happen, there has been no set timeline. Eventually, with internal political pressure from child advocates within the country and external political pressure from abroad, it will simply make good sense for the United States to become a signatory.

Reichel (2005) noted that when nations agree to sign the CRC, they are allowed to state reservations they have regarding any of its specific provisions. This process allows signatory countries to avoid being bound by specific provisions as long as the majority of other signatory nations do not object to these disagreements. Reichel (2005) presented an example where Australia, Canada, and numerous other countries lodged reservations with the provision that during times of detention, juvenile offenders cannot be detained with adult offenders in the same detention facility. These countries contend that, although they agree with the spirit of the provision, it is not always logistically feasible to provide separate accommodations. Despite this, these countries indicate understanding that such youth should be afforded concerns for safety and security to ensure that juveniles in detention are not victimized by adults in detention.

Other countries in the Middle East have also indicated disagreements related to the use of the CRC when provisions conflict with Islamic law. Based on religious factors, these nations have been allowed to be signatories to the CRC while at the same time maintaining tenets of the Muslim faith. Within the convention's signatory content, reservations by Muslim nations are documented. For instance, as noted within the CRC, the nation of Iran has the following reservation on file:

[It] reserves the right not to apply any provisions or articles of the Convention that are incompatible with Islamic Laws and the international legislation in effect. (United Nations, 1990c, p. 4)

Within the signatory documents, it can be seen that nine countries filed objections to this reservation and the other similarly worded reservations filed by different Middle Eastern nations. These objecting countries included Austria, Denmark, Finland, Germany, Ireland, the Netherlands, Norway, Portugal, and Sweden (United Nations, 2007). From other supporting documents, it is clear that these objecting nations filed their objections simultaneously and for similar reasons—the belief that a general reference to religious law without specification of its content lacks clarity in determining the extent to which reserving states (Iran, Saudi Arabia, Oman, Pakistan, and other Arab nations) commit themselves to the CRC.

From these examples of reservations and objections to those reservations, all held by multiple nations for multiple reasons, it is clear that consensus on the CRC does not exist around the world. Nevertheless, the entire world has been able to agree, at least in terms of philosophy, that juveniles warrant different treatment from adults and that this treatment must be geared toward correction rather than punishment (these, of course, were the very concerns upon which a separate juvenile justice network is based in the United States). Thus, the CRC remains an important international document that sets forward minimal standards for processing juvenile offenders and has created a global culture that acknowledges the unique issues related to children who are found errant (Reichel, 2005).

International Standards and Documents

Among other documents, conferences, and World Court rulings, it is the CRC, the *United Nations Standard Minimum Rules for Administration of Juvenile Justice* (produced in 1985, and often referred to as the Beijing Rules), and the *United Nations Guidelines for Prevention of Juvenile Delinquency* (written in 1990, also known as the Riyadh Guidelines) are most important in shaping the international juvenile justice response. The prevention guidelines were drafted in 1990 and represent the most recent of the three documents discussed in this chapter.

The Beijing Rules encourage diversion mechanisms rather than formal court processes for all but the most serious of juvenile offenders. The Riyadh Guidelines of 1990 consider most youth offending to be a part of the growing process—something routinely engaged in by youngsters that they eventually mature out of. This is consistent with criminological research that has found that many offenders "age out" of the criminal lifestyle.

The key to understanding the long-term implications of juvenile delinquency around the world is to perhaps view delinquency as a dual taxonomy (Moffitt, 1993). According to this theoretical basis, most youth engage in delinquency that is short-term, peer-group based, and part of the process of adolescent development and maturation. For the majority of youth who commit delinquent acts, they will likely age out by early adulthood; this observation is noted around the world (Moffitt, 1993; Reichel, 2005; United Nations, 2003). However, among those youth who commit violent crimes, become true members of a criminal gang, and/or have serious crimes perpetrated against them, there is a likelihood that they will persist in crime throughout the course of their life (Moffitt, 1993). This means that early intervention efforts are critical to curbing the likelihood that a youngster will reach a point where his or her aberrant behavior becomes a lifelong trajectory rather than one limited to the adolescent years of development. Thus, it is clear that the international community and the global culture should identify juvenile delinquency and juvenile welfare as problems that warrant corrective solutions rather than punitive reactions. It would appear that the world, for the most part, agrees that youth who offend are in need of assistance and guidance rather than harsh discipline (returning us full circle to the foundation upon which the first juvenile court in the United States was built in 1899).

Use of Restorative Justice With Young Offenders Around the World

Restorative justice has been discussed throughout this text as a means of addressing delinquent activity. What may not be widely known is that restorative justice processes in the United States were largely borrowed from other countries—particularly European countries (Reichel, 2005). Thus, the use of restorative justice applications is one that has international roots. Nations such as Australia, Canada, Germany, Japan, and New Zealand have long histories of integrating restorative justice techniques into their official response to problems with delinquency. The *United Nations Basic Principles on the Use of Restorative Justice Programmes in Criminal Matters* provides a clear example of how restorative justice processes have been widely adopted within the international community. This document notes that obvious disparities with respect to "power imbalances and the parties' age, maturity or intellectual capacity should be taken into consideration in referring a case to and in conducting a restorative process" (United Nations, 2000, p. 3). These principles point toward the fact that various forms of crime mediation should be free from coercion, manipulation, or exploitation—for both the victim and the juvenile offender. This is important because it points the way for informal means of handling youth that can avoid the stigmatization of official courtroom processing.

As noted earlier, many juveniles begin their delinquent and/or criminal activity with minor acts. Those who persist tend to progressively commit more crimes, which eventually leads to violent criminal activity. In these cases, youth will often gravitate toward other youth (whether as informal groups or formal gang structures) prone to criminal behavior. As the youth go along this trajectory, they acquire definitions favorable to crime, become labeled by others in their community as delinquent or criminal, and then move into more long-term criminal histories. Restorative justice provides one mechanism (among others) where youth can make amends with the victim without the formal experience of a country's court system and, perhaps, without the formal labels. This type of approach often yields more flexible solutions that seem to benefit the victim and the young offender more than stiff sanctions usually do (Reichel, 2005).

CAREER OPPORTUNITY: UNICEF PROGRAM SPECIALIST IN ADOLESCENT DEVELOPMENT

Job description: The person working in this position is responsible for providing program support for UNICEF's approach to holistic and positive survival, development, protection, and participation for extremely vulnerable adolescents in underdeveloped and developing countries. The program specialist will work in accordance with the organizational and international framework of policies and procedures. Experience with child protection issues and emergency or transition situations is commonplace for adolescent development program specialists. Other areas of responsibility may include child poverty and poverty reduction strategies as well as working with institutional reforms related to migration, particularly for migrant children, women, and families.

Employment requirements: The following general requirements are common to most all positions working with youth at UNICEF:

- Education: Master's degree in a field relevant to the work of UNICEF or equivalent professional experience

- Experience: Relevant professional work experience, some of which has been obtained in a developing country, at least 5 years for midcareer and 2 to 3 years for an entry-level position
- Language: Proficiency in English and in another United Nations working language (Arabic, Chinese, French, Russian, and Spanish). Knowledge of the local language of a duty station where the position is based is an asset.

Beginning salary: Salaries for professional staff are set by the International Civil Service Commission and include base salaries that are standardized but have additional enhancements for employees who are stationed in affluent areas of the world. As of January 2010, the absolute lowest entry-level salary for professionals (most all child and adolescent workers are considered professional employees) was around $50,000 to start and could go up—depending on the professional category (ranging from P1 to P5)—to approximately $140,000 a year. These are nonsupervisory positions. For supervisory positions (director positions), salaries can nearly reach $168,000.

It is important to note that these are base salaries only and are the lowest-end salary that employees will make—usually if they are stationed in a less developed area of the world where living expenses are considerably less than in the United States. If an employee is stationed in an industrialized area or a developed country, salaries are given standardized adjustments that can be quite considerable.

The salary level for professional staff is based on the notion that the International Civil Service Commission should be able to recruit staff from its member states, including those states that have economies where personnel are paid much higher. Because of this, the salaries for professional staff are set by reference to the highest-paying national civil service system. This should make it clear that UNICEF and other affiliates of the United Nations are good organizations to work within, at least when considering pay scales.

In addition, UNICEF's policies and protections for these employees have numerous benefits related to family issues, work–life fitness and health, as well as protections for a diverse work group. UNICEF is committed to maintaining a balanced gender and geographical employee composition. Other benefits and entitlements include the following:

- Annual leave
- Dependency allowance
- Rental subsidy
- Education grant
- Pension scheme
- Medical and dental insurance
- Home leave
- Life insurance
- Paid sick leave
- Family leave
- Family visit
- Maternity and paternity adoption leave
- Special leave

Summary

When comparing juvenile delinquency around the world, it is clear that juvenile misbehavior is a common phenomenon throughout all of humanity. It would appear that delinquency is to be expected and that the dynamics related to offending are very similar around the world. Further, the causal factors associated with juvenile offending are similar. Whether the youngster is subjected to abuse, neglect, dysfunctional family lifestyles, states of poverty and deprivation, urbanization, social messages that are procriminal, or media influences that provide fuel for an aberrant youth subculture, the reasons seem to be similar in various parts of the world. Youth from modernized regions where family instability has emerged are particularly vulnerable to becoming delinquent. Other youth who are from war-ravaged countries or regions of great instability are also at risk of committing delinquent acts, in many cases as a means of survival. It appears that youth suffer serious forms of victimization that set the stage for their own future tendency to victimize others.

Juvenile gangs have been given special focus in this chapter because they have emerged throughout the past decade as a specific and serious international concern. In various areas of the world, youth have banded together and engaged in various types of crimes. It would seem that youth who join gangs do so for very similar reasons, regardless of the region of the world where they are located. Many join gangs for acceptance and a sense of belonging. Many come from dysfunctional family systems or from backgrounds of serious deprivation and/or violence. Many juvenile gangs are connected to other more serious criminal organizations that are usually run by adults. This means that juvenile gangs tend to be a primary source of later members of various criminal organizations. It is important to keep in mind that those members who join gangs in various areas of the world tend to do so to have basic needs met, but it is those who are prone to acts of violent crime and/or suffer from serious deprivations that are most likely to continue their criminal activity into adulthood.

The standards and guidelines for addressing juvenile offending have been set by the United Nations through three key documents. These documents include the *United Nations Standard Minimum Rules for the Administration of Juvenile Justice* (the Beijing Rules), the *United Nations CRC* (1989), and the *United Nations Guidelines for the Prevention of Juvenile Delinquency* (the Riyadh Guidelines). When combined, each of these three documents provides a unified set of protocols that guide signatory nations toward a civilized and humane means of addressing juvenile offending throughout the world. Although cultural, religious, and political factors may impact the specific means by which these documents are integrated into a particular nation's juvenile justice system, it is clear that a basic philosophical framework has emerged within the global community that enshrines reformative approaches to juvenile justice processes. It is equally clear that most of the tenets contained in these documents can be found in juvenile court acts in every state in the United States and reflect the historical approaches used in the U.S. juvenile justice system.

KEY TERMS

Beijing Rules of 1985   361

Bosozoku Gangs   368

Campaign for U.S. Ratification of the *Convention on the Rights of the Child* (CRC)   376

conflict with the law   353

Convention on the Rights of the Child (CRC) (1989)   373

developing countries   354

double victimization   356

globalization   351

Riyadh Guidelines of 1990   377

United Nations Basic Principles on the Use of Restorative Justice Programmes in Criminal Matters   378

urbanization   354

World Youth Report   353

Critical Thinking Questions

1. In your opinion, how should the United Nations work to eradicate juvenile gangs in different areas of the world? Be sure to explain the reasons for your answer.

2. Recently, the nation of Somalia has considered becoming a signatory with the CRC. This would mean that the United States would be the only nation to not officially support the document. From an international relations standpoint, how do you think this impacts the ability of the United States to provide input on juvenile issues?

3. Discuss some of the challenges in defining juvenile delinquency in the international community. In addition, explain how the age of responsibility in different nations serves to further complicate our ability to achieve any one specific definition.

4. Discuss the major documents drafted by the United Nations to address the processing of juvenile offenders. From what you can tell, do these documents seem to address issues consistent with the prior chapters of your text related to juvenile justice in the United States? Explain your answer.

Suggested Readings

Shoemaker, D. (1996). *International handbook on juvenile justice.* Westport, CT: Greenwood Press.

Svevo-Cianci, K., & Lee, Y. (2010). Twenty years of the *Convention on the Rights of the Child*: Achievements in and challenges for child protection implementation, measurement and evaluation around the world. *Child Abuse & Neglect, 34*(1), 1–4.

Tonry, M., & Doob, A. N. (2004). *Youth crime and youth justice: Comparative and cross-national perspectives.* Chicago, IL: University of Chicago Press.

Webb, V. J., Ren, L., Zhao, J., He, N., & Marshall, I. (2011). A comparative study of youth gangs in China and the United States: Definition, offending, and victimization. *International Criminal Justice Review, 21*(3), 225–242.

Winterdyke, J. (2002). *Juvenile justice systems: International perspectives* (2nd ed.). Toronto, Canada: Canadian Scholars' Press.

$SAGE edge™

Sharpen your skills with SAGE edge at **edge.sagepub.com/coxjj9e**. SAGE edge for students provides a personalized approach to help you accomplish your coursework goals in an easy-to-use learning environment. You'll find action plans, mobile-friendly eFlashcards, and quizzes as well as video and web resources and links to SAGE journal articles to support and expand on the concepts presented in this chapter.

The Future of Juvenile Justice

14

On completion of this chapter, students should be able to do the following:

- Evaluate the extent to which the goals of the juvenile justice system have been met early in the 21st century
- Suggest alternatives for the future of the juvenile justice system
- Explain the restorative justice and "get tough" approaches to juvenile justice
- Discuss the possible demise of the juvenile justice system
- Discuss ways of improving on the current juvenile justice system

WHAT WOULD YOU DO?

This What Would You Do? is different because it is located at the end of the book. As a conclusion to the book, we wanted you to consider your own personal growth throughout the course with regard to understandings in juvenile justice. We also wanted you to consider challenges that are ongoing in the system itself and how you may contribute to positive changes in the system.

At the beginning of each chapter of the textbook, you have been exposed to situations that are common in juvenile justice. Each one represents a daily challenge to the system and to the various people working in juvenile justice. As

you read this chapter, reflect on your responses to each of the chapter What Would You Do? situations and decide if your reactions and views have changed over the course of the book. In other words, would you respond differently now than you would have at the beginning of the text? If so, how have your perceptions of youth, the juvenile justice system, and those working in the system changed? Have you changed the way you view society and how it handles children? Considering all that you know now, what changes would you recommend for the future of juvenile justice?

Throughout this book, we have discussed in varying detail the philosophies of the juvenile justice system, the procedural requirements of that system, and some of the major problems with the system as it now operates. We have seen that the juvenile justice system is subject to numerous stresses and strains from within. The good intentions are sometimes met with less than desirable results; thus, change and trial and error are imperative. We have arrived at a number of conclusions—some of which are supported by empirical evidence and others of which are more or less speculative—based on our observations and those of concerned practitioners and citizens.

The initial underlying assumption of the juvenile justice system is that juveniles with problems should be treated and/or educated rather than punished. Adult and juvenile justice systems in the United States were separated because of the belief that courts should act in the best interests of juveniles and because of the belief that association with adult offenders would increase the possibility that juveniles would become involved in criminal careers. The extent to which we have achieved the goals of the juvenile justice system continues to be debated. Where do we go from here? Although it is always risky to speculate, it appears to us that there are four more or less distinct possibilities for the future of the juvenile justice system.

Possibilities for the Future of Juvenile Justice

Possibility number one is that the juvenile justice system will cease to exist as a separate entity. Possibility number two is that the juvenile system will begin to rely heavily on hybrid sentencing with regard to violent juveniles. Possibility number three is that the restorative or balanced justice movement will triumph, and we will return to a more caring personal approach to juvenile justice. Possibility number four, as Lindner (2004) pointed out, is based on the fact that the juvenile court today is more focused on accountability and punishment than ever before. So, those who support the "get tough" or "just deserts" approach will reform the juvenile justice system, resulting in an increasing number of juveniles being processed in the adult justice system. "A popular view [among policymakers and supporters of get tough] is that, to protect the public safety, youth who commit serious or violent acts should be subject to the same punishments as apply to adults" (Bishop, 2004, p. 635). Unruh, Povenmire-Kirk, and Yamamoto (2009) argued that at present "adolescents involved in the juvenile justice system face multiple challenges on their pathway to adulthood. These adolescents not only have an increased risk of committing future crimes [but] are further at risk of not becoming healthy, productive adults" (p. 201). Although many states have adopted the get-tough approach and are now operating in full swing with transfers to adult court, this philosophy is contradictory to the purpose of juvenile court.

> There is little argument that the current juvenile justice system is indeed in turmoil and lacks the foresight and preventive measures required for lasting reform. The challenge before us is to move from the rhetoric to the reality of what we are going to do to save their [juveniles'] lives and our collective futures. (Hatchette, 1998, pp. 83–84)

If this sounds familiar, it may be because it has been the theme throughout this text. Ohlin (1998) noted the following:

> Confidence in the ability of our institutional system to control juvenile delinquency has been steadily eroding. Public insecurity, fear, and anxiety about youth crime are now intense and widespread, despite the juvenile court and probation system and the training schools that have evolved over the past century. (p. 143)

Lindner (2004) echoed this statement by pointing out that public perception has been that juvenile crimes are becoming more and more serious. The public has also perceived that the juvenile justice system is too lenient on offenders. Public outcry has led to more punitive laws, increased waivers to adult court, and a shift from the best interests of the child to punishment. In actuality, however, "the rate of juvenile violent crime arrests has consistently decreased since 1994, falling to a level not seen since at least the 1970s" (Snyder & Sickmund, 2006, p. 2), and juveniles in secure youth facilities have also declined over the last decade.

Unfortunately, get-tough proponents are not choosing to advertise the decreased crime rates; instead, they have focused on the upswing in juvenile violence over the past few years.

Barriers to Change in Juvenile Justice

Uniformity of juvenile law has yet to be achieved. Many citizens still adopt an "out-of-sight, out-of-mind" attitude toward juveniles with problems, and both citizens and practitioners are often frustrated by our supposed failure to curb delinquency and abuse or neglect in spite of the millions of dollars invested in the enterprise. We continue to refuse to address the larger societal issues of poverty, dysfunctional families, failed educational systems, race, class, and gender as they relate to crime and delinquency (Ohlin, 1998, p. 152). One could write an entire text on these issues, alone, for they all contribute to the current state of affairs in juvenile justice today. Among these, however, that we have decided to look at more closely is the role of race and racial representation in the juvenile justice system.

Currently, minority youth who identify as being African American, Latino, Asian/Pacific Islander, or Native American constitute a little more than 30% of the entire U.S. population. These minority groups have suffered from generations of social inequality and disparate opportunity. *Social inequality* is a term for circumstances of disparate treatment and opportunity for groups of people based on ethnicity, gender, or other characteristics. Racial discrimination is a form of social inequality that includes experiences that result from legal and/or nonlegal types of discrimination based on the racial identification of the individual. Racial discrimination can occur at both the personal and institutional level. We have discussed, in prior chapters, how norms and processes throughout society collectively work against the individual who is the subject of disparate treatment, but we wanted to more squarely address both disparity and discrimination in the context of society's means or processing minority youth.

Indeed, many authors claim that institutional discrimination is the primary reason for group differences in material wealth and living conditions, such as poverty, education, employment, access to medical care, and political power, including control of the media, political influence, and community finances (Hsia, 2004; Phillips, Settles-Reaves, Walker, & Brownlow, 2009). Exposure to both individual and institutional discrimination is stressful and also leads to frustration and feelings of hopelessness for many racial minorities. This stress and these feelings of frustration are related to negative health outcomes among minority groups (Phillips et al., 2009). See In Practice 14.1 for a closer view of how responses from the justice system may be currently ill-equipped to address minority youth who make contact with the juvenile justice system, thereby contributing to the problem and making matters worse, not better.

Phillips et al. (2009) provide research in which they examine a theory of racial inequality and social integration that examines social factors where racial discrimination is associated with negative mental and physiological health outcomes. They note that, as youth detect contradictions between opportunities in broader society and the lack of opportunity in their own lives, stress and frustration are often experienced. Racial discrimination increases frustrations, reinforces perceptions of unfairness (inequality), and further limits options to achieve life goals.

In the education system, African American and Latino youth, especially males, are highly likely to report negative encounters where their access to education is diminished. On the other hand, Asian youth have indicated higher levels of racist treatment from their peer group at school (such as racial epithets, social rejection, and physical threats). African American female youth tend to report negative racially based treatment more than any other female racial group in the school setting. Finally, African American youth of both genders tend to report racial discrimination as they grow older, on into adulthood. As

DISPARITY IN JUVENILE DETENTION AND INCARCERATION

During the late 1980s and early 1990s, the issue of disparate minority representation in juvenile lockdowns had become a topic of controversy. Most of the data available on this issue emerged during the late 1990s and during the early parts of the new millennium. As a result of the data produced during the 1990s and into the millennium that followed, it became clear that the reasons for the disparity in juvenile confinement are many. Indeed, most all published literature on this issue notes that these statistics are not likely to be due to a racist system. Whereas we cannot possibly answer this question within the scope of one discussion within one section of a single textbook, it should be clear to students that throughout the history of corrections in the United States, African American men and women have been disproportionately incarcerated. Given the various historical precedents associated with the civil rights era and other indicators that our society held minorities in a weakened position, and given the common knowledge regarding the existence of institutional racism that officially existed up until the 1960s, it is not unreasonable to presume that, in some cases, racism may be part of the explanation.

Recent research by Huizinga, Thornberry, Knight, and Lovegrove (2007) investigated the often stated reason given for disparate minority confinement—that it simply reflects the difference in offending rates among different racial/ethnic groups—and they found no support in their rigorous study examining disparate minority contact with the justice system. Huizinga et al. (2007) note that "although self-reported offending is a significant predictor of which individuals are contacted/referred, levels of delinquent offending have only marginal effects on the level of DMC" (p. i). They found these results in terms of both total offending as well as more focused data that examined violent offenses and property offenses separately. Thus, it would appear that minority youth are no more delinquent than Caucasian youth.

The work of Hsia (2004) was a compilation of surveys and official investigation into the juvenile correctional systems of all 50 states. Hsia (2004) notes the following reasons for why such disparities existed in many state systems:

1. *Racial stereotyping and cultural insensitivity.* Eighteen states identified racial stereotyping and cultural insensitivity—both intentional and unintentional—on the part of the police and others in the juvenile justice system (e.g., juvenile court workers and judges) as important factors contributing to higher arrest rates, higher charging rates, and higher rates of detention and confinement of minority youth. The demeanor and attitude of minority youth can contribute to negative treatment and more severe disposition relative to their offenses. The belief that minority youth cannot benefit from treatment programs also leads to less frequent use of such options.

2. *Lack of alternatives to detention and incarceration.* Eight states identified the lack of alternatives to detention and incarceration as a cause of the frequent use of confinement. In some states, detention centers are located in the state's largest cities, where most minority populations reside. With a lack of alternatives to detention, nearby detention centers become "convenient" placements for urban minority youth.

3. *Misuse of discretionary authority in implementing laws and policies.* Five states observed that laws and policies that increase juvenile justice professionals' discretionary authority over youth

(Continued)

(Continued)

contribute to harsher treatment of minority youth. One state notes that "bootstrapping" (the practice of stacking offenses on a single incident) is often practiced by police, probation officers, and school system personnel.

4. *Lack of culturally and linguistically appropriate services.* Five states identified the lack of bicultural and bilingual staff and the use of English-only informational materials for the non-English-speaking population as contributing to minorities' misunderstanding of services and court processes and their inability to navigate the system successfully.

Based on the research by Hsia (2004), it is the general contention of this author that much of the reason the disproportionate confinement exists among minority youth has to do with a confluence of issues that plague members of society who have suffered from historical trauma and, generation after generation, have been restricted from access to material, educational, and social resources. Indeed, issues such as poverty, substance abuse, few job opportunities, and high crime rates in predominantly minority neighborhoods place minority youth at higher risk for delinquent behaviors. Moreover, concerted law enforcement targeting of high-crime areas yields higher numbers of arrests and formal processing of minority youth. At the same time, these communities have fewer positive role models and fewer service programs that function as alternatives to confinement and/or support positive youth development.

Further, it has been found that a disproportionate number of youth in confinement came from low-income, single-parent households (female-headed households, in particular) and households headed by adults with multiple low-paying jobs or unsteady employment. Family disintegration, diminished traditional family values, parental substance abuse, and insufficient supervision contribute to delinquency development. Poverty reduces minority youths' ability to access existing alternatives to detention and incarceration as well as competent legal counsel. Thus, all of these factors, being associated with historical deprivations over time, have contributed and culminated in the state of affairs that we now witness among minority juveniles in the United States.

Sources: Hsia (2004); Huizinga, Thornberry, Knight, & Lovegrove (2007).

Questions to Consider

1. True or False: Racial minorities face the same issues as whites in the United States.

2. Multiple Choice: A disproportionate number of incarcerated youth come from which of the following?

   a. Single-parent homes
   b. Low-income homes
   c. Households where parents hold more than one low-paying job
   d. All of the above

3. Based on what you've learned throughout the book, identify one reason why minorities may be disproportionately incarcerated and one way in which we can lower incarceration rates of minorities.

can be seen, many minorities tend to report racially based discrimination that begins early in life and continues throughout their life span.

The ability to adaptively cope with racial discrimination is a very important developmental challenge for many minority youth. These youth, like nonminority youth, must build a healthy self-concept, work through psychological stress, and make life-course adjustments that entail periods of storm and stress. Unlike their nonminority counterparts, they also must develop effective coping skills when faced with racial discrimination—over which they have no power and little influence. Further, they must deal with persons who undermine their ability to achieve goals for reasons that have no logical basis. During their teens, these youth often have a good understanding about social power and are often greatly impacted by experiences, whether direct or vicarious, where racial discrimination has been inflicted against them, their friends, or their family. In many instances, prolonged feelings of anger and bitterness may exist due to these injustices.

For minority parents, their ability to socialize their own children is usually impacted by their own experiences with

This type of mural is common in many Latino American neighborhoods where youth express their sense of pride in cultural heritage through art that is open for the entire community to see.

racial discrimination. Indeed, in some communities where parents have experienced racial discrimination from law enforcement, they may instruct their children to not trust Caucasian police officers. The Black Lives Matter movement, which began in Ferguson, Missouri, may have been borne from some of the messages taught over time. The shooting of 18-year-old Michael Brown in Ferguson, Missouri, was considered by many to be the result of long-term racial bias in policing and a court system that generated revenue from the poor and minorities ("Judge Approves Ferguson Deal," 2016). Protests after the shooting aimed to bring to light the biases and the differential treatment of minorities by police. In the year since the shooting and protests, the Department of Justice has reached an agreement with the City of Ferguson to make changes to the police force, training, and use of force policies, among other things; however, citizens in Ferguson still do not trust that systemic changes will result and continue to spread a message of suspicion of city officials and the police ("Judge Approves Ferguson Deal," 2016). The Black Lives Matter movement may have started as a protest against police violence, but it has expanded to include other issues facing minority communities, including failing schools, inadequate housing, a lack of political input, and economic unfairness. The messages of mistrust of the government, police, court system, and educational system are apparent from those involved with the movement and do not seem to be letting up anytime soon. Although their own previous experiences may be valid, this type of message being given to youth instantly creates friction between the child and police officers in general and between the child and Caucasian officers in particular. Further, this obviously sets a racist tone that permeates the neighborhood because multiple children are given the same message.

The same circumstances may exist within school systems, where minority parents who have experienced racism may instruct their children not to trust teachers of a given color or cultural background. There is research that some African American mothers report vicarious experiences of racism when they sense or observe racial discrimination that has been leveled at their children. Often, these parents will socialize their children to not trust certain racial groups of teachers. With this said, we also would like to point out that the opposite of this is also equally true; some Caucasian families may instruct their children not to trust minority teachers, thereby reinforcing prejudice and racism. Until issues related to race, racism, cultural difference, poverty, and the need for a balanced society are fully mitigated and resolved, it is likely that our ability to truly revitalize the juvenile justice system will continue to be at least partially impaired.

Possible Improvements to the Juvenile Justice System

As we can see, there is undoubtedly room for a great deal of improvement in society in general and in the juvenile justice system in particular. As we have indicated, to some extent, such improvement depends on changes in societal conditions such as poverty, unemployment, and discrimination. However, we cannot, amid this slow process of social change, sit idly by, waiting for when times are perfect for additional reform in our juvenile justice system. For instance, consider that changes in the family and in the educational system that improve our ability to meet the needs of juveniles are also crucial. Changes in the rules that govern juveniles may be appropriate in some instances. Making better use of the information made available to us by researchers and practitioners is yet another way to improve the system. In the end, taking a rational, calculated approach to delinquency and abuse or neglect will pay better dividends than will adhering to policies developed and implemented as a result of fear and misunderstanding.

Bilchik (1998a) concluded the following:

A revitalized juvenile justice system needs to be put into place and brought to scale that will ensure immediate and appropriate sanctions, provide effective treatment, reverse trends in juvenile violence, and rebuild public confidence in and support for the juvenile justice system. (p. 89)

Such a revitalized juvenile justice system would include swift intervention with early offenders, an individualized comprehensive needs assessment, transfer of serious or chronic offenders, and intensive aftercare. This system would require the coordinated efforts of law enforcement, treatment, correctional, judicial, and social service personnel. This approach to delinquency control represents a form of community programming that might help to reintegrate troubled youth into mainstream society rather than further isolate and alienate them (Bazemore & Washington, 1995; Zaslaw & Balance, 1996). To accomplish this goal, the resistance to change that characterizes most institutions must be overcome.

Revitalizing the juvenile justice system is clearly a complex undertaking. Cohn (2004) indicated that revitalizing the system includes focusing on "areas of attention and repair" (p. 43) such as the following:

1. Excessive caseloads that preclude meaningful interventions by an assumed well-trained staff
2. The failure to recognize that not the offender but the community is the real "customer" of services
3. Little understanding of the relationship among planning, change, and social policy
4. Political, hardline rhetoric leading to inappropriate changes in the juvenile code, including automatic waivers to criminal courts
5. The changing character of youthful offenders, especially in terms of substance abuse and the use of weapons when committing offenses
6. Inadequate kinds and availability of treatment programs for detained youths and for probationers and those in aftercare and, for those that work, inadequate replication efforts
7. A stubborn refusal by some significant actors to work collaboratively in defining and resolving problems of a mutual nature such as diversion or graduated sanctions
8. The failure of the "leadership" to deal head-on with inappropriate and "wrong" changes in juvenile codes, especially in terms of waivers

9. The failure of judges to provide the leadership when it comes to advocacy

10. The lack of meaningful diversion programs, including the need for more informal processes for nonviolent offenders

11. The lack of meaningful programs that involve the families (parents) of offenders

12. The failure to engage in advocacy for needed programs in the community for youth and their families

13. Too much complacency (status quo), which results in lack of appropriate planning

14. The failure to involve critical stakeholders in the development of agency-based policies and procedures

15. Inadequate involvement of subordinate staff in identifying and implementing agency mission and goals

16. Inadequate staff development and training programs that are based on the identification of core competencies

17. The failure to recognize the need for and value of wraparound services and programs, resulting in poor case management by too many case managers in too many agencies in any given case situation (i.e., the failure to recognize that too few offenders and their families receive disproportionately high levels of human services)

18. Inadequate development of ongoing and meaningful communication with superordinates and appropriate stakeholders, which results in too many being unaware of "what works"

19. The failure to design and implement a total, systems-based information technology program that enhances data sharing

20. The ongoing failure to evaluate programs to determine worthiness that should lead to decisions about program continuation, expansion, or abandonment

21. The failure to develop and implement program and operational standards

22. The failure to think systemically

23. The problem of too much stupidity!

Material from "Juvenile Justice in Transition: Is There a Future?," originally published in *Federal Probation* (Cohn, 1999b). Reprinted with permission of the author.

Basically, revitalizing the system means acknowledging that changes are needed within the structure of the system and within the individual agencies operating as part of the system. It does not mean focusing on harsher punishments or accountability. Revitalization puts juveniles and treatment first while fixing the broken aspects of juvenile justice. As Califano and Colson (2005) indicated, the goal of the juvenile justice system is protection and reform of young people who commit crimes, "but the reality is a grim, modern version of Charles Dickens' *Oliver Twist*. Instead of providing care and rehabilitation, many facilities are nothing more than colleges for criminality" (p. 34). With this in mind, Gaudio (2010) suggested that states offer rehabilitation to nonviolent youth drug offenders, rather than incarcerating them. These changes may include the increased use of specialty courts such as drug courts, youth courts, truancy courts, and so forth, discussed earlier in the textbook.

We believe that the first possibility, the complete demise of the juvenile justice system, is unlikely simply because the goals of the system are worthy and not likely to be abandoned completely. In addition, the separate juvenile justice system employs a large supporting staff that is unlikely to be summarily dismissed, especially in light of the restorative justice movement. Based on current trends, it appears likely that the juvenile justice system will continue to provide separate services for juveniles but with an increase in the number of crimes for which waivers to adult court are used and with an increase in hybrid sentencing. Moore (2001–2002) suggested that the use of blended sentences is creating a third criminal justice system. As discussed previously, blended sentences allow juveniles to be sentenced to adult and juvenile dispositions by both adult court judges and juvenile court judges. This raises the following question: When is a juvenile offender a juvenile, and when is he or she an adult? Instead of classifying juvenile offenders as one or the other, hybrid or blended sentences allow the convenience and benefits of both courts. Juveniles are given a second chance by being allowed to rely on the juvenile court for rehabilitation while knowing that the adult court sanctions apply if rehabilitation fails. "By focusing on blending both juvenile and adult criminal sentences, the courts are moving away from an all-or-nothing approach and recognizing the lack of a bright-line rule to define a juvenile versus an adult" (Moore, 2001–2002, p. 138). At the same time, it may be that juvenile justice personnel can do a more effective job of dealing with less serious juvenile offenders. Jennings, Gibson, and Lanza-Kaduce (2009), in a study of some 300 youth, concluded that with respect to status offenders both deterrence and normalization-based rationales showed more positive results than the typical treatment-based approach and that "viewing status offending as normal adolescent behavior (i.e., normalization) has the most beneficial effect on self-concept" (p. 198).

It is unlikely that restorative justice advocates will withdraw from the field of battle in the juvenile justice system. They have gained momentum early in the 21st century because they have focused on caring for victims too long forgotten by those in the juvenile justice system, and that is not likely to change in the near future. They have successfully infiltrated every type of agency working with juveniles, and in a way, the policies they advocate fit rather well with the "just deserts" model because, in addition to being processed through the courts, offenders are forced to confront their victims in the interest of making both "whole" again. Restorative justice may not work for all juvenile offenders and all types of offenses; however, it appears to be successful with those who can be reintegrated into the community after a mistake or a minor wrongful act. As long as proponents realize this and practitioners understand its limitations, it may well work to promote dignity and self-respect, as well as lowered recidivism, in those served by its programs (Schetky, 2009). To the extent, if any, that such programs prove to be uncomfortable for offenders, this may be viewed as another form of punishment in addition to, or in the place of, judicial punishment.

This old and dilapidated building was once a hospital for a variety of patients, including the mentally ill and youth who had behavioral problems. This is a symbolic example of a time that is gone as the juvenile justice system moves into the modern era.

We might close by looking at the future of gangs and efforts to deal with them as a way of summarizing the future of the juvenile justice system. The contemporary cycle of youth gang activities is likely to continue because members who are imprisoned manage to maintain some gang-related activities even while in prison and because recruitment, given the conditions outlined previously, is no problem. As Postman (1991) put it, we can ill afford to "hurtle into the future with our eyes fixed firmly on the rearview mirror" (cited in Osborne & Gaebler, 1992, p. 19). Papachristos (2005) put it this way:

No amount of law enforcement will rid the world of gangs. Strategies at all levels must move beyond simple arrests and incarceration to consider the economic structures of the cities and neighborhoods that breed street gangs. Otherwise, there will be nothing there to greet them but the waiting and supportive arms of the gang. (p. 55)

Community programs aimed at alleviating the causes of gang membership as well as providing opportunities for those inclined to gang membership will need to be given priority if we hope to confront the gang problem. Support for the police is essential but so is support for myriad community programs directed at high-risk youth. The best efforts of school personnel, social services professionals, nonprofit organizations, and the community at large will also be necessary. Only by producing our best efforts in this regard can we hope to maintain the integrity of the juvenile justice system while providing appropriate alternatives for juveniles who cannot, or will not, be helped through education, treatment, care, concern, and opportunity.

This is more important than ever because, as one can tell, these youth will need a full range of services that are likely provided on a continuum that addresses the multiplicity of problems that these youth present. One issue tends to compound the severity of another, making the entire treatment process difficult to unravel. For instance, consider the vignette at the beginning of this chapter, which makes it clear that juveniles will continue to be substance abuse offenders in need of services that include appropriate assessment, treatment, and case management, as well as supervision. As we can see from Figure 14.1, the various aspects of juvenile processing all work together as part of the juvenile justice system. It is our contention that if the juvenile justice system were to disappear then so too would any possibility of truly addressing the myriad corollary issues that influence long-term delinquency and/or later adult criminality.

Figure 14.1 Elements of a Model Juvenile Intervention System

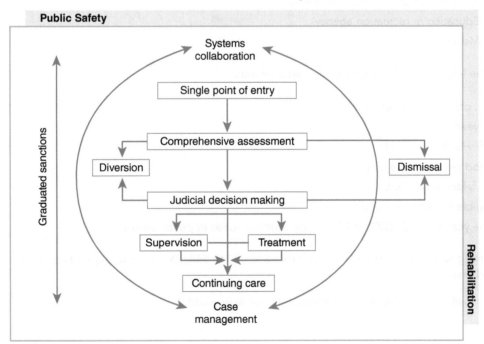

Source: VanderWaal, McBride, Terry-McElrath, & VanBuren (2001).

CAREER OPPORTUNITY: YOUTH CORRECTIONAL COUNSELOR (STATE OF CALIFORNIA)

Job description: The Youth Correctional Counselor will counsel young offenders in their day-to-day activities, programming, and adjustment. Will engage in casework with individual and small-group counseling sessions for approximately 10 to 12 young offenders. Is tasked with classification of young offenders to ensure appropriate placement for living arrangements, academic study, and vocational programming. Also conducts large-group psychoeducational sessions in the facility. Prepares treatment plans and summaries for each young offender.

Employment requirements: Any one of the following:

Experience: One year of experience of service in the state of California maintaining security, custody, and supervision of young offenders in a secure facility.

or

> *Education:* A 4-year degree from a college or university.

or

> Sixty hours of college credit plus 2 years' experience with youth in any of the following combinations:

> 1. Youth correctional agency
> 2. Parole or probation department
> 3. Family, children, or youth guidance center
> 4. Juvenile bureau of law enforcement
> 5. Education or recreation agency
> 6. Mental health facility

Plus the following additional minimum requirements:

> U.S. citizenship (or applied)
> 21 years old
> U.S. HS diploma/GED
> Good physical condition
> No felony convictions
> Eligible to own/possess a firearm
> One year as a CO, YCO, or MTA or performing duties of peace officer

Beginning salary: $48,000 in California. From $36,000 to $48,000 per year, depending on area of the United States.

Source: California Department of Corrections and Rehabilitation (2013).

Indeed, issues related to substance abuse will likely continue to be correlated with most all other acts of delinquency and crime that we associate with these young offenders. This is what some have defined as the juvenile drug-crime cycle (VanderWaal et al., 2001). In addition, they will likely present with a number of co-occurring disorders such as depression, anxiety, and cognitive deficits. This has been found to be particularly true for youth placed in detention or some other type of institutional environment (Sedlak & McPherson, 2010). When combined with their young age and the irreparable damage done to their neurophysiological well-being, it becomes clear that this issue is multifaceted. These youth will also tend to be less healthy both physically and emotionally. Maghan (1999) has noted that future offenders will tend to be the following:

Members of racial minority groups

Unhealthy (average of 10 years older than physical age)

Infected with sexually transmitted diseases, HIV, or tuberculosis

Overly emotional and lack impulse control

Having children of their own

Gang affiliated

Unmarried

From single-parent households

So far, Maghan (1999) has been correct in his prediction, even though that prediction was made over 14 years ago. Whereas his observations are important, it is equally important to note that the characteristics just listed have been observed among juvenile offenders around the world. Indeed, youth in various industrialized nations all exhibit similar demographic and lifestyle trends. The effects of urbanization and modernization on family systems have been detrimental, and problems with high rates of poverty have exacerbated these negative effects on youth. In reaction to these changes, youth are exhibiting behaviors that place them at greater risk for negative health effects, both physically and mentally. The Internet, television, the media, and modern youth culture have proliferated around the world due to advances in communications technology and the effects of globalization. From our previous chapter, it would appear that similarities in criminal and delinquent behaviors exist as well.

KEY TERMS

Black Lives Matter movement 387

"get tough" or "just deserts" approach 383

hybrid sentencing 383

juvenile drug-crime cycle 393

restorative or balanced justice 383

revitalized juvenile justice 388

Critical Thinking Questions

1. In your opinion, what are the most important issues facing the juvenile justice system today? How will this affect juvenile justice in the future? Be sure to explain the reasons for your answer.

2. If the juvenile justice system were to be eliminated, what are the major concerns the adult system would have to address? What potential economic costs or gains would occur?

3. Consider the predictions of Maghan (1999) regarding the characteristics of future juvenile offenders. His predictions were made nearly 15 years ago. In your opinion, was Maghan correct in his predictions? Why or why not? Can you identify these characteristics in youth you know? Provide one example.

Suggested Readings

Cullen, F. T. (2011). Beyond adolescence-limited-criminology: Choosing our future—the American Society of Criminology 2010 Sutherland Address. *Criminology, 49*(2), 287–330.

Garland, B., Melton, M., & Hass, A. (2012). Public opinion on juvenile blended sentencing. *Youth Violence & Juvenile Justice, 10*(2), 135–154.

Gaudio, C. (2010). A call to Congress to give back the future: End the "war on drugs" and encourage states to reconstruct the juvenile justice system. *Family Court Review, 48*(1), 212–227.

Gibson, C. L., Swatt, M. L., Miller, J., Jennings, W. G., & Gover, A. R. (2012). The causal relationship between gang joining and violent victimization: A critical review and directions for future research. *Journal of Criminal Justice, 40*(6), 490–501.

Hsia, H. M. (2004). *Disproportionate minority confinement 2002 update*. Washington, DC: Office of Juvenile Justice and Delinquency Prevention.

Huizinga, D., Thornberry, T., Knight, K., & Lovegrove, P. (2007). *Disproportionate minority contact in the juvenile justice system: A study of differential minority arrest/referral to court in three cities*. Washington, DC: United States Department of Justice.

Jennings, W., Gibson, C., & Lanza-Kaduce, L. (2009). Why not let kids be kids? An exploratory analysis of the relationship between alternative rationales for managing status offending and youths' self-concepts. *American Journal of Criminal Justice, 34*(3), 198–212.

Maghan, J. (1999). Corrections countdown: Prisoners at the cusp of the 21st century. In P. M. Carlson & J. S. Garrett (Eds.), *Prison and jail administration: Practice and theory* (pp. 199–206). Gaithersburg, MD: Aspen Publications.

Ousey, G., Wilcox, P., & Fisher, B. (2011). Something old, something new: Revisiting competing hypotheses of the victimization-offending relationship among adolescents. *Journal of Quantitative Criminology, 27*(1), 53–84.

Phillips, K. S., Settles-Reaves, B., Walker, D., & Brownlow, J. (2009). Social inequality and racial discrimination: Risk factors for health disparities in children of color. *Pediatrics, 124*, 176–186.

Schetky, D. H. (2009). Restorative justice: An alternative model whose time has come. *The Brown University Child and Adolescent Behavior Newsletter, 25*(9), 5–7.

Unruh, D., Povenmire-Kirk, T., & Yamamoto, S. (2009). Perceived barriers and protective factors of juvenile offenders on their developmental pathway to adulthood. *Journal of Correctional Education, 60*(3), 201–224.

Walls, J. (2013, March 25). *Georgia's troubled effort to reduce juvenile crime*. The Center for Public Integrity. Retrieved from www.publicintegrity.org/2013/03/25/12369/georgias-troubled-effort-reduce-juvenile-crime

⑤SAGE edge™

Sharpen your skills with SAGE edge at edge.sagepub.com/coxjj9e. SAGE edge for students provides a personalized approach to help you accomplish your coursework goals in an easy-to-use learning environment. You'll find action plans, mobile-friendly eFlashcards, and quizzes as well as video and web resources and links to SAGE journal articles to support and expand on the concepts presented in this chapter.

Appendix

Uniform Juvenile Court Act

The Uniform Juvenile Court Act was drafted by the National Conference of Commissioners on Uniform State Laws and approved and recommended for enactment in all the states at its annual conference meeting in its seventy-seventh year, Philadelphia, Pennsylvania, July 22–August 1, 1968. Approved by the American Bar Association at its meeting at Philadelphia, Pennsylvania, August 7, 1968.

Section 1. [Interpretation.]

This Act shall be construed to effectuate the following public purposes:

1. to provide for the care, protection, and wholesome moral, mental, and physical development of children coming within its provisions;

2. consistent with the protection of the public interest, to remove from children committing delinquent acts the taint of criminality and the consequences of criminal behavior and to substitute therefore a program of treatment, training, and rehabilitation;

3. to achieve the foregoing purposes in a family environment whenever possible, separating the child from his parents only when necessary for his welfare or in the interest of public safety;

4. to provide a simple judicial procedure through which this Act is executed and enforced and in which the parties are assured a fair hearing and their constitutional and other legal rights recognized and enforced; and

5. to provide simple interstate procedures which permit resort to cooperative measures among the juvenile courts of the several states when required to effectuate the purposes of this Act.

Section 2. [Definitions.]

As used in this Act:

1. "child" means an individual who is:

   i. under the age of 18 years; or

   ii. under the age of 21 years who committed an act of delinquency before reaching the age of 18 years; [or]

   iii. under 21 years of age who committed an act of delinquency after becoming 18 years of age and is transferred to the juvenile court by another court having jurisdiction over him;

2. "delinquent act" means an act designated a crime under the law, including local [ordinances] [or resolutions] of this state, or of another state, if the act occurred in that state, or under federal law, and the crime does not fall under paragraph (iii) of subsection (4) [and is not a juvenile traffic offense as defined in section 44] [and the crime is not a traffic offense as defined in Traffic Code of the State] other than [designate the more serious offenses which should be included in the jurisdiction of the juvenile court such as drunken driving, negligent homicide, etc.];

3. "delinquent child" means a child who has committed a delinquent act and is in need of treatment or rehabilitation;

4. "unruly child" means a child who:

    i. while subject to compulsory school attendance is habitually and without justification truant from school;

    ii. is habitually disobedient of the reasonable and lawful commands of his parent, guardian, or other custodian and is ungovernable; or

    iii. has committed an offense applicable only to a child; and

    iv. if any of the foregoing is in need of treatment or rehabilitation;

5. "deprived child" means a child who:

    i. is without proper parental care or control, subsistence, education as required by law, or other care or control necessary for his physical, mental, or emotional health, or morals, and the deprivation is not due primarily to the lack of financial means of his parents, guardian, or other custodian;

    ii. has been placed for care or adoption in violation of law; [or]

    iii. has been abandoned by his parents, guardian, or other custodian; [or]

    iv. is without a parent, guardian, or legal custodian;

6. "shelter care" means temporary care of a child in physically unrestricted facilities;

7. "protective supervision" means supervision ordered by the court of children found to be deprived or unruly;

8. "custodian" means a person, other than a parent or legal guardian, who stands in loco parentis to the child or a person to whom legal custody of the child has been given by order of a court;

9. "juvenile court" means the [here designate] court of this state.

Section 3. [Jurisdiction.]

a. The juvenile court has exclusive original jurisdiction of the following proceedings, which are governed by this Act:

    1. proceedings in which a child is alleged to be delinquent, unruly, or deprived [or to have committed a juvenile traffic offense as defined in section 44;]

    2. proceedings for the termination of parental rights except when a part of an adoption proceeding; and

    3. proceedings arising under section 39 through 42.

b. The juvenile court also has exclusive original jurisdiction of the following proceedings, which are governed by the laws relating thereto without regard to the other provisions of this Act:

    1. proceedings for the adoption of an individual of any age;

    2. proceedings to obtain judicial consent to the marriage, employment, or enlistment in the armed services of a child, if consent is required by law;

    3. proceedings under the Interstate Compact of Juveniles; [and]

    4. proceedings under the Interstate Compact on the Placement of Children; [and]

    5. proceedings to determine the custody or appoint a guardian of the person of a child.

Section 4. [Concurrent Jurisdiction.]

The juvenile court has concurrent jurisdiction with [_____] court of proceedings to treat or commit a mentally retarded or mentally ill child.

Section 5. [Probation Services.]

a. [In [counties] of over _____ population] the [_____] court may appoint one or more probation officers who shall serve [at the pleasure of the court] [and are subject to removal under the civil service laws governing the county]. They have the powers and duties stated in section 6. Their salaries shall be fixed by the court with the approval of the [governing board of the county]. If more than one probation officer is appointed, one may be designated by the court as the chief probation officer or director of court services, who shall be responsible for the administration of the probation services under the direction of the court.

b. In all other cases the [Department of Corrections] [state] [county] child welfare department] [or other appropriate state agency] shall provide suitable probation services to the juvenile court of each [county]. The cost thereof shall be paid out of the general revenue funds of the [state] [county]. The probation officer or other qualified person assigned to the court by the [Department of Corrections] [state [county] child welfare department] [or other appropriate state agency] has the powers and duties stated in section 6.

Section 6. [Powers and Duties of Probation Officers.]

a. For the purpose of carrying out the objectives and purposes of this Act and subject to the limitations of this Act or imposed by the Court, a probation officer shall:

1. make investigations, reports, and recommendations to the juvenile court;

2. receive and examine complaints and charges of delinquency, unruly conduct or deprivation of a child for the purpose of considering the commencement of proceedings under this Act;

3. supervise and assist a child placed on probation or in his protective supervision or care by order of the court or other authority of law;

4. make appropriate referrals to other private or public agencies of the community if their assistance appears to be needed or desirable;

5. take into custody and detain a child who is under his supervision or care as a delinquent, unruly or deprived child if the probation officer has reasonable cause to believe that the child's health or safety is in imminent danger, or that he may abscond or be removed from the jurisdiction of the court, or when ordered by the court pursuant to this Act. Except as provided by this Act a probation officer does not have the powers of a law enforcement officer. He may not conduct accusatory proceedings under this Act against a child who is or may be under his care or supervision; and

6. perform all other functions designated by this Act or by order of the court pursuant thereto.

b. Any of the foregoing functions may be performed in another state if authorized by the court of this state and permitted by the laws of the other state.

Section 7. [Referees.]

a. The judge may appoint one or more persons to serve at the pleasure of the judge as referees on a full or part-time basis. A referee shall be a member of the bar [and shall qualify under the civil service regulations of the Country]. His compensation shall be fixed by the judge [with the approval of the [governing board of the Country] and paid out of [_____].

b. The judge may direct that hearings in any case or class of cases be conducted in the first instance by the referee in the manner provided by this Act. Before commencing the hearing the referee shall inform the parties who have appeared that they are entitled to have the matter heard by the judge. If a party objects the hearing shall be conducted by the judge.

c. Upon the conclusion of a hearing before a referee he shall transmit written findings and recommendations for disposition to the judge. Prompt written notice and copies of the findings and recommendations shall be given to the parties to the proceeding. The written notice shall inform them of the right to a rehearing before the judge.

d. A rehearing may be ordered by the judge at any time and shall be ordered if a party files a written request therefore within 3 days after receiving the notice required in subsection (c).

e. Unless a rehearing is ordered the findings and recommendations become the findings and order of the court when confirmed in writing by the judge.

Section 8. [Commencement of Proceedings.]

A proceeding under this Act may be commenced:

1. by transfer of a case from another court as provided in section 9;

2. as provided in section 44 in a proceeding charging the violation of a traffic offense; or

3. by the court accepting jurisdiction as provided in section 40 or accepting supervision of a child as provided in section 42; or

4. in other cases by the filing of a petition as provided in this Act. The petition and all other documents in the proceeding shall be entitled "In the interest of _____, a [child] [minor] under [18] [21] years of age."

Section 9. [Transfer from other Courts.] If it appears to the court in a criminal proceeding that the defendant [is a child] [was under the age of 18 years at the time the offense charged was alleged to have been committed], the court shall forthwith transfer the case to the juvenile court together with a copy of the accusatory pleading and other papers, documents, and transcripts of testimony relating to the case. It shall order that the defendant be taken forthwith to the juvenile court or to a place of detention designated by the juvenile court, or release him to the custody of his parent, guardian, custodian, or other person legally responsible for him, to be brought before the juvenile court at a time designated by that court. The accusatory pleading may serve in lieu of a petition in the juvenile court unless that court directs the filing of a petition.

Section 10. [Informal Adjustment.]

a. Before a petition is filed, the probation officer or other officer of the court designated by it, subject to its direction, may give counsel and advice to the parties with a view to an informal adjustment if it appears;

1. the admitted facts bring the case within the jurisdiction of the court;

2. counsel and advice without an adjudication would be in the best interest of the public and the child; and

3. the child and his parents, guardian or other custodian consent thereto with knowledge that consent is not obligatory.

b. The giving of counsel and advice cannot extend beyond 3 months from the day commenced unless extended by the court for an additional period not to exceed 3 months and does not authorize the detention of the child if not otherwise permitted by this Act.

c. An incriminating statement made by a participant to the person giving counsel or advice and in the discussions or conferences incident thereto shall not be used against the declarant over objection in any hearing except in a hearing on disposition in a juvenile court proceeding or in a criminal proceeding against him after conviction for the purpose of a pre-sentence investigation.

Section 11. [Venue.]

A proceeding under this act may be commenced in the [county] in which the child resides. If delinquent or unruly conduct is alleged, the proceeding may be commenced in the [county] in which the acts constituting the alleged delinquent or unruly conduct occurred. If deprivation is alleged, the proceeding may be brought in the [county] in which the child is present when it is commenced.

Section 12. [Transfer to Another Juvenile Court Within the State.]

a. If the child resides in a [county] of the state and the proceeding is commenced in a court of another [county], the court, on motion of a party or on its own motion made prior to final disposition, may transfer the proceeding to the county of the child's residence for further action. Like transfer may be made if the residence of the child changes pending the proceeding. The proceeding shall be transferred if the child has been adjudicated delinquent or unruly and other proceedings involving the child are pending in the juvenile court of the [county] of his residence.

b. Certified copies of all legal and social documents and records pertaining to the case on file with the clerk of the court shall accompany the transfer.

Section 13. [Taking into Custody.]

a. A child may be taken into custody:

1. pursuant to an order of the court under this Act;

2. pursuant to the laws of arrest;

3. by a law enforcement officer [or duly authorized officer of the court] if there are reasonable grounds to believe that the child is suffering from illness or injury or is in immediate danger from his surroundings, and that his removal is necessary; or

4. by a law enforcement officer [or duly authorized officer of the court] if there are reasonable grounds to believe that the child has run away from his parents, guardian, or other custodian.

b. The taking of a child into custody is not an arrest, except for the purpose of determining its validity under the constitution of this State or of the United States.

Section 14. [Detention of Child.]

A child taken into custody shall not be detained or placed in shelter care prior to the hearing on the petition unless his detention or care is required to protect the person or property of others or of the child because the child may abscond or be removed from the jurisdiction of the court or because he has no parent, guardian, or custodian or other person able to provide supervision and care for him and return him to the court when required, or an order for his detention or shelter care has been made by the court pursuant to this Act.

Section 15. [Release or Delivery to Court.]

a. A person taking a child into custody, with all reasonable speed and without first taking the child elsewhere, shall:

   1. release the child to his parents, guardian, or other custodian upon their promise to bring the child before the court when requested by the court, unless his detention or shelter care is warranted or required under section 14; or

   2. bring the child before the court or deliver him to a detention or shelter care facility designated by the court or to a medical facility if the child is believed to suffer from a serious physical condition or illness which requires prompt treatment. He shall promptly give written notice thereof, together with a statement of the reason for taking the child into custody, to a parent, guardian, or other custodian and to the court. Any temporary detention or questioning of the child necessary to comply with this subsection shall conform to the procedures and conditions prescribed by this Act and rules of court.

b. If a parent, guardian, or other custodian, when requested, fails to bring the child before the court as provided in subsection (a) the court may issue its warrant directing that the child be taken into custody and brought before the court.

Section 16. [Place of Detention.]

a. A child alleged to be delinquent may be detained only in:

   1. a licensed foster home or a home approved by the court;

   2. a facility operated by a licensed child welfare agency;

   3. a detention home or center for delinquent children which is under the direction or supervision of the court or other public authority or of a private agency approved by the court; or

   4. any other suitable place or facility, designated or operated by the court. The child may be detained in a jail or other facility for the detention of adults only if the facility in paragraph (3) is not available, the detention is in a room separate and removed from those for adults, it appears to the satisfaction of the court that public safety and protection reasonably require detention, and it so orders.

b. The official in charge of a jail or other facility for the detention of adult offenders or persons charged with crime shall inform the court immediately if a person who is or appears to be under the age of 18 years is received at the facility and shall bring him before the court upon request or deliver him to a detention or shelter care facility designated by the court.

c. If a case is transferred to another court for criminal prosecution the child may be transferred to the appropriate officer or detention facility in accordance with the law governing the detention of persons charged with crime.

d. A child alleged to be deprived or unruly may be detained or placed in shelter care only in the facilities stated in paragraphs (1), (2), and (4) of subsection (a) and shall not be detained in a jail or other facility intended or used for the detention of adults charged with criminal offenses or of children alleged to be delinquent.

Section 17. [Release from Detention or Shelter Care—Hearing—Conditions of Release.]

a. If a child is brought before the court or delivered to a detention or shelter care facility designated by the court the intake or other authorized officer of the court shall immediately make an investigation and release the child unless it appears that his detention or shelter care is warranted or required under section 14.

b. If he is not so released, a petition under section 21 shall be promptly made and presented to the court. An informal detention hearing shall be held promptly and not later than 72 hours after he is placed in detention to determine whether his detention or shelter care is required under section 14. Reasonable notice thereof, either oral or written, stating the time, place, and purpose of the detention hearing shall be given to the child and if they can be found, to his parents, guardian, or other custodian. Prior to the commencement of the hearing, the court shall inform the parties of their right to counsel and to appointed counsel if they are needy persons, and of the child's right to remain silent with respect to any allegations of delinquency or unruly conduct.

c. If the child is not so released and a parent, guardian, or custodian has not been notified of the hearing, did not appear or waive appearance at the hearing, and files his affidavit showing these facts, the court shall rehear the matter without unnecessary delay and order his release unless it appears from the hearing that the child's detention or shelter care is required under section 14.

Section 18. [Subpoena.]

Upon application of a party the court or the clerk of the court shall issue, or the court on its own motion may issue, subpoenas requiring attendance and testimony of witnesses and production of papers at any hearing under this Act.

Section 19. [Petition—Preliminary Determination.]

A petition under this Act shall not be filed unless the [probation officer,] the court, or other person authorized by the court has determined and endorsed upon the petition that the filing of the petition is in the best interest of the public and the child.

Section 20. [Petition—Who May Make.]

Subject to section 19 the petition may be made by any person, including a law enforcement officer, who has knowledge of the facts alleged or is informed and believes that they are true.

Section 21. [Contents of Petition.]

The petition shall be verified and may be on information and belief. It shall set forth plainly:

1. the facts which bring the child within the jurisdiction of the court, with a statement that it is in the best interest of the child and the public that the proceeding be brought and, if delinquency or unruly conduct is alleged, that the child is in need of treatment or rehabilitation;

2. the name, age, and residence address, if any, of the child on whose behalf the petition is brought;

3. the names and residence addresses, if known to petitioner, of the parents, guardian, or custodian of the child and of the child's spouse, if any. If none of his parents, guardian, or custodian resides or can be found within the state, or if their respective places of residence address are unknown, the name of any known adult relative residing within the [county], or, if there be none, the known adult relative residing nearest to the location of the court; and

4. if the child is in custody and, if so, the place of his detention and the time he was taken into custody.

Section 22. [Summons.]

a. After the petition has been filed the court shall fix a time for hearing thereon, which, if the child is in detention, shall not be later than 10 days after the filing of the petition. The court shall direct the issuance of a summons to the parents, guardian, or other custodian, a guardian ad litem, and any other persons as appear to the court to be proper or necessary parties to the proceeding, requiring them to appear before the court at the time fixed to answer the allegations of the petition. The summons shall also be directed to the child if he is 14 or more years of age or is alleged to be a delinquent or unruly child. A copy of the petition shall accompany the summons unless the summons is served by publication in which case the published summons shall indicate the general nature of the allegations and where a copy of the petition can be obtained.

b. The court may endorse upon the summons an order directing the parents, guardian or other custodian of the child to appear personally at the hearing and directing the person having the physical custody or control of the child to bring the child to the hearing.

c. If it appears from affidavit filed or from sworn testimony before the court that the conduct, condition, or surroundings of the child are endangering his health or welfare or those of others, or that he may abscond or be removed from the jurisdiction of the court or will not be brought before the court, notwithstanding the service of the summons, the court may endorse upon the summons an order that a law enforcement officer shall serve the summons and take the child into immediate custody and bring him forthwith before the court.

d. The summons shall state that a party is entitled to counsel in the proceedings and that the court will appoint counsel if the party is unable without undue financial hardship to employ counsel.

e. A party, other than the child, may waive service of summons by written stipulation or by voluntary appearance at the hearing. If the child is present at the hearing, his counsel, with the consent of the parent, guardian or other custodian, or guardian ad litem, may waive service of summons in his behalf.

Section 23. [Service of Summons.]

a. If a party to be served with a summons is within this State and can be found, the summons shall be served upon him personally at least 24 hours before the hearing. If he is within the State and cannot be found, but his address is known or can with reasonable diligence be ascertained, the summons may be served upon him by mailing a copy by registered or certified mail at least 5 days before the hearing. If he is without this State but he can be found or his address is known, or his whereabouts or address can with reasonable diligence be ascertained, service of the summons may be made either by delivering a copy to him personally or mailing a copy to him by registered or certified mail at least 5 days before the hearing.

b. If after reasonable effort he cannot be found or his post office address ascertained, whether he is within or without this State, the court may order service of the summons upon him by publication in accordance with [Rule] [Section]————[the general service by publication statutes]. The hearing shall not be earlier than 5 days after the date of the last publication.

c. Service of the summons may be made by any suitable person under the direction of the court.

d. The court may authorize the payment from [county funds] of the costs of service and of necessary travel expenses incurred by persons summoned or otherwise required to appear at the hearing.

Section 24. [Conduct of Hearings.]

a. Hearings under this Act shall be conducted by the court without a jury, in an informal but orderly manner, and separate from other proceedings not included in section 3.

b. The [prosecuting attorney] upon request of the court shall present the evidence in support of the petition and otherwise conduct the proceedings on behalf of the state.

c. If requested by a party or ordered by the court the proceedings shall be recorded by stenographic notes or by electronic, mechanical, or other appropriate means. If not so recorded full minutes of the proceedings shall be kept by the court.

d. Except in hearings to declare a person in contempt of court [and in hearings under section 44], the general public shall be excluded from hearings under this Act. Only the parties, their counsel, witnesses, and other persons accompanying a party for his assistance, and any other persons as the court finds have a proper interest in the proceeding or in the work of the court may be admitted by the court. The court may temporarily exclude the child from the hearing except while allegations of his delinquency or unruly conduct are being heard.

Section 25. [Service by Publication— Interlocutory Order of Disposition.]

a. If service of summons upon a party is made by publication the court may conduct a provisional hearing upon the allegations of the petition and enter an interlocutory order of disposition if:

1. the petition alleges delinquency, unruly conduct, or deprivation of the child;

2. the summons served upon any party (i) states that prior to the final hearing on the petition designated in the summons a provisional hearing thereon will be held at a specified time and place, (ii) requires the party who is served other than by publication to appear and answer the allegations of the petition at the provisional hearing, (iii) states further that findings of fact and orders of disposition made pursuant to the provisional hearing will become final at the final hearing unless the party served by publication appears at the final hearing, and (iv) otherwise conforms to section 22; and

3. the child is personally before the court at the provisional hearing.

b. All provisions of this Act applicable to a hearing on a petition, to orders of disposition, and to other proceedings dependent thereon shall apply under this section, but findings of fact and orders of disposition have only interlocutory effect pending the final hearing on the petition. The rights and duties of the party served by publication are not affected except as provided in subsection (c).

c. If the party served by publication fails to appear at the final hearing on the petition the findings of fact and interlocutory orders made become final without further evidence and are governed by this Act as if made at the final hearing. If the party appears at the final hearing the findings and orders shall be vacated and disregarded and the hearing shall proceed upon the allegations of the petition without regard to this section.

Section 26. [Right to Counsel.]

a. Except as otherwise provided under this Act a party is entitled to representation by legal counsel at all stages of any proceedings under this Act and if as a needy person he is unable to employ counsel, to have the court provide counsel for him. If a party appears without the counsel the court shall ascertain whether he knows of his right thereto and to be provided with counsel by the court if he is a needy person. The court may continue the proceeding to enable a party to obtain counsel and shall provide counsel for an unrepresented needy person upon his request. Counsel must be provided for a child not represented by his parent, guardian, or custodian. If the interests of 2 or more parties conflict, separate counsel shall be provided for each of them.

b. A needy person is one who at the time of requesting counsel is unable without undue financial hardship to provide for full payment of legal counsel and all other necessary expenses for representation.

Section 27. [Other Basic Rights.]

a. A party is entitled to the opportunity to introduce evidence and otherwise be heard in his own behalf and to cross-examine adverse witnesses.

b. A child charged with a delinquent act need not be a witness against or otherwise incriminate himself. An extrajudicial statement, if obtained in the course of violation of this Act or which would be constitutionally inadmissible in a criminal proceeding, shall not be used against him. Evidence illegally seized or obtained shall not be received over objection to establish the allegations made against him. A confession validly made by the child out of court is insufficient to support an adjudication of delinquency unless it is corroborated in whole or in part by other evidence.

Section 28. [Investigation and Report.]

a. If the allegations of a petition are admitted by a party or notice of a hearing under section 34 has been given the court, prior to the hearing on need for treatment or rehabilitation and disposition, may direct that a social study and report in writing to the court be made by the [probation officer] of the court, [Commissioner of the Court or other like officer] or other person designated by the court, concerning the child, his family, his environment, and other matters relevant to disposition of the case. If the allegations of the petition are not admitted and notice of a hearing under section 34 has not been given the court shall not direct the making of the study and report until after the court has heard the petition upon notice of hearing given pursuant to this Act and the court has found that the child committed a delinquent act or is an unruly or deprived child.

b. During the pendency of any proceeding the court may order the child to be examined at a suitable place by a physician or psychologist and may also order medical or surgical treatment of a child who is suffering from a serious physical condition or illness which in the opinion of a [licensed physician] requires prompt treatment, even if the parent, guardian, or other custodian has not been given notice of a hearing, is not available, or without good cause informs the court of his refusal to consent to the treatment.

Section 29. [Hearing—Findings—Dismissal.]

a. After hearing the evidence on the petition the court shall make and file its findings as to whether the child is a deprived child, or if the petition alleges that the child is delinquent or unruly, whether the acts ascribed to the child were committed by him. If the court finds that the child is not a deprived child or that the allegations of delinquency or unruly conduct have not been established it shall dismiss the petition and order the child discharged from any detention or other restriction theretofore ordered in the proceeding.

b. If the court finds on proof beyond a reasonable doubt that the child committed the acts by reason of which he is alleged to be delinquent or unruly it shall proceed immediately or at a postponed hearing to hear evidence as to whether the child is in need of treatment or rehabilitation and to make and file its findings thereon. In the absence of evidence to the contrary evidence of the commission of acts which constitute a felony is sufficient to sustain a finding that the child is in need of treatment or rehabilitation. If the court finds that the child is not in need of treatment or rehabilitation it shall dismiss the proceeding and discharge the child from any detention or other restriction theretofore ordered.

c. If the court finds from clear and convincing evidence that the child is deprived or that he is in need of treatment or rehabilitation as a delinquent or unruly child, the court shall proceed immediately or at a postponed hearing to make a proper disposition of the case.

d. In hearings under subsections (b) and (c) all evidence helpful in determining the questions presented, including oral and written reports, may be received by the court and relied upon to the extent of its probative value even though not otherwise competent in the hearing on the petition. The parties or their counsel shall be afforded an opportunity to examine and controvert written reports so received and to cross-examine individuals making the reports. Sources of confidential information need not be disclosed.

e. On its motion or that of a party the court may continue the hearings under this section for a reasonable period to receive reports and other evidence bearing on the disposition or the need for treatment or rehabilitation. In this event the court shall make an appropriate order for detention of the child or his release from detention subject to supervision of the court during the period of the continuance. In scheduling investigations and hearings the court shall give priority to proceedings in which a child is in detention or has otherwise been removed from his home before an order of disposition has been made.

Section 30. [Disposition of Deprived Child.]

a. If the child is found to be a deprived child the court may make any of the following orders of disposition best suited to the protection and physical, mental, and moral welfare of the child:

1. permit the child to remain with his parents, guardian, or other custodian, subject to conditions and limitations as the court prescribes, including supervision as directed by the court for the protection of the child;

2. subject to conditions and limitations as the court prescribes transfer temporary legal custody to any of the following:

   i. any individual who, after study by the probation officer or other person or agency designated by the court, is found by the court to be qualified to receive and care for the child;

   ii. an agency or other private organization licensed or otherwise authorized by law to receive and provide care for the child; or

   iii. the Child Welfare Department of the [county] [state,] [or other public agency authorized by law to receive and provide care for the child;]

   iv. an individual in another state with or without supervision by an appropriate officer under section 40; or

3. without making any of the foregoing orders transfer custody of the child to the juvenile court of another state if authorized by and in accordance with section 39 if the child is or is about to become a resident of that state.

b. Unless a child found to be deprived is found also to be delinquent he shall not be committed to or confined in an institution or other facility designed or operated for the benefit of delinquent children.

Section 31. [Disposition of Delinquent Child.]

If the child is found to be a delinquent child the court may make any of the following orders of disposition best suited to his treatment, rehabilitation, and welfare:

1. any order authorized by section 30 for the disposition of a deprived child;

2. placing the child on probation under the supervision of the probation officer of the court or the court of another state as provided in section 41, or [the Child Welfare Department operating within the county,] under conditions and limitations the court prescribes;

3. placing the child in an institution, camp, or other facility for delinquent children operated under the direction of the court [or other local public authority;] or

4. committing the child to [designate the state department to which commitments of delinquent children are made or, if there is no department, the appropriate state institution for delinquent children].

Section 32. [Disposition of Unruly Child.]

If the child is found to be unruly the court may make any disposition authorized for a delinquent child except commitment to [the state department or state institution to which commitment of delinquent children may be made]. [If after making the disposition the court finds upon a further hearing that the child is not amenable to treatment or rehabilitation under the disposition made it may make a disposition otherwise authorized by section 31.]

Section 33. [Order of Adjudication—Non-Criminal.]

a. An order of disposition or other adjudication in a proceeding under this Act is not a conviction of crime and does not impose any civil disability ordinarily resulting from a conviction or operate to disqualify the child in any civil service application or appointment. A child shall not be committed or transferred to a penal institution or other facility used primarily for the execution of sentences of persons convicted of a crime.

b. The disposition of a child and evidence adduced in a hearing in juvenile court may not be used against him in any proceeding in any court other than a juvenile court, whether before or after reaching majority, except in dispositional proceedings after conviction of a felony for the purposes of a pre-sentence investigation and report.

Section 34. [Transfer to Other Courts.]

a. After a petition has been filed alleging delinquency based on conduct which is designated a crime or public offense under the laws, including local ordinances, [or resolutions] of this state, the court before hearing the petition on its merits may transfer the offense for prosecution to the appropriate court having jurisdiction of the offense if:

   1. the child was 16 or more years of age at the time of the alleged conduct;
   2. a hearing on whether the transfer should be made is held in conformity with sections 24, 26, and 27;
   3. notice in writing of the time, place, and purpose of the hearing is given to the child and his parents, guardian, or other custodian at least 3 days before the hearing.
   4. the court finds that there are reasonable grounds to believe that

      i. the child committed the delinquent act alleged;
      ii. the child is not amenable to treatment or rehabilitation as a juvenile through available facilities;
      iii. the child is not committable to an institution for the mentally retarded or mentally ill; and
      iv. the interests of the community require that the child be placed under legal restraint or discipline.

b. The transfer terminates the jurisdiction of the juvenile court over the child with respect to the delinquent acts alleged in the petition.

c. No child, either before or after reaching 18 years of age, shall be prosecuted for an offense previously committed unless the case has been transferred as provided in this section.

d. Statements made by the child after being taken into custody and prior to the service of notice under subsection (a) or at the hearing under this section are not admissible against him over objection in the criminal proceedings following the transfer.

e. If the case is not transferred the judge who conducted the hearing shall not over objection of an interested party preside at the hearing on the petition. If the case is transferred to a court of which the judge who conducted the hearing is also a judge he likewise is disqualified from presiding in the prosecution.

Section 35. [Disposition of Mentally Ill or Mentally Retarded Child.]

a. If, at a dispositional hearing of a child found to be a delinquent or unruly child or at a hearing to transfer a child to another court under section 34, the evidence indicates that the child may be suffering from mental retardation or mental illness the court before making a disposition shall commit the child for a period not exceeding 60 days to an appropriate institution, agency, or individual for study and report on the child's mental condition.

b. If it appears from the study and report that the child is committable under the laws of this state as a mentally retarded or mentally ill child the court shall order the child detained and direct that within 10 days after the order is made the appropriate authority initiate proceedings for the child's commitment.

c. If it does not appear, or proceedings are not promptly initiated, or the child is found not to be committable, the court shall proceed to the disposition or transfer of the child as otherwise provided by this Act.

Section 36. [Limitations of Time on Orders of Disposition.]

a. An order terminating parental rights is without limit as to duration.

b. An order of disposition committing a delinquent or unruly child to the [State Department of Corrections of designated institution for delinquent children,] continues in force for 2 years or until the child is sooner discharged by the [department or institution to which the child was committed]. The court which made the order may extend its duration for an additional 2 years, subject to like discharge, if:

   1. a hearing is held upon motion of the [department or institution to which the child was committed] prior to the expiration of the order;

   2. reasonable notice of the hearing and an opportunity to be heard is given to the child and the parent, guardian, or other custodian; and

   3. the court finds that the extension is necessary for the treatment or rehabilitation of the child.

c. Any other order of disposition continues in force for not more than 2 years. The court may sooner terminate its order or extend its duration for further periods. An order of extension may be made if:

   1. a hearing is held prior to the expiration of the order upon motion of a party or on the court's own motion;

   2. reasonable notice of the hearing and opportunity to be heard are given to the parties affected;

   3. the court finds that the extension is necessary to accomplish the purposes of the order extended; and

   4. the extension does not exceed 2 years from the expiration of prior order.

d. Except as provided in subsection (b) the court may terminate an order of disposition or extension prior to its expiration, on or without an application of a party, if it appears to the court that the purposes of the order have been accomplished. If a party may be adversely affected by the order of termination the order may be made only after reasonable notice and opportunity to be heard have been given to him.

e. Except as provided in subsection (a) when the child reaches 21 years of age all orders affecting him then in force terminate and he is discharged from further obligation or control.

Section 37. [Modification or Vacation of Orders.]

a. An order of the court shall be set aside if (1) it appears that it was obtained by fraud or mistake sufficient therefore in a civil action, or (2) the court lacked jurisdiction over a necessary party or of the subject matter, or (3) newly discovered evidence so requires.

b. Except an order committing a delinquent child to the [State Department of Corrections or an institution for delinquent children,] an order terminating parental rights, or an order of dismissal, an order of the court may also be changed, modified, or vacated on the ground that changed circumstances so require in the best interest of the child. An order granting probation to a child found to be delinquent or unruly may be revoked on the ground that the conditions of probation have not been observed.

c. Any party to the proceeding, the probation officer or other person having supervision or legal custody of or an interest in the child may petition the court for the relief provided in this section. The petition shall set forth in concise language the grounds upon which the relief is requested.

d. After the petition is filed the court shall fix a time for hearing and cause notice to be served (as a summons is served under section 23) on the parties to the proceeding or affected by the relief sought. After the hearing, which may be informal, the court shall deny or grant relief as the evidence warrants.

Section 38. [Rights and Duties of Legal Custodian.]

A custodian to whom legal custody has been given by the court under this Act has the right to the physical custody of the child, the right to determine the nature of the care and treatment of the child, including ordinary medical care and the right and duty to provide for the care, protection, training, and education, and the physical, mental, and moral welfare of the child, subject to the conditions and limitations of the order and to the remaining rights and duties of the child's parents or guardian.

Section 39. [Disposition of Non-Resident Child.]

a. If the court finds that child who has been adjudged to have committed a delinquent act or to be unruly or deprived is or is about to become a resident of another state which has adopted the Uniform Juvenile Court Act, or a substantially similar Act which includes provisions corresponding to sections 39 and 40, the court may defer hearing on need for treatment or rehabilitation and disposition and request by any appropriate means the juvenile court of the [county] of the child's residence or prospective residence to accept jurisdiction of the child.

b. If the child becomes a resident of another state while on probation or under protective supervision under order of a juvenile court of this State, the court may request the juvenile court of the [county] of the state in which the child has become a resident to accept jurisdiction of the child and to continue his probation or protective supervision.

c. Upon receipt and filing of an acceptance the court of this State shall transfer custody of the child to the accepting court and cause him to be delivered to the person designated by that court to receive his custody. It also shall provide that court with certified copies of the order adjudging the child to be a delinquent, unruly, or deprived child, of the order of transfer, and if the child is on probation or under protective supervision under order of the court, of the order of disposition. It also shall provide that court with a statement of the facts found by the court of this State and any recommendations and other information it considers of assistance to the accepting court in making a disposition of the case or in supervising the child on probation or otherwise.

d. Upon compliance with subsection (c) the jurisdiction of the court of this State over the child is terminated.

Section 40. [Disposition of Resident Child Received from Another State.]

a. If a juvenile court of another state which has adopted the Uniform Juvenile Court Act, or a substantially similar Act which includes provisions corresponding to sections 39 and 40, requests a juvenile court of this State to accept jurisdiction of a child found by the requesting court to have committed a delinquent act or to be an unruly or deprived child, and the court of this State finds, after investigation that the child is, or is about to become, a resident of the [county] in which the court presides, it shall promptly and not later than 14 days after receiving the request issue its acceptance in writing to the requesting court and direct its probation officer or other person designated by it to take physical custody of the child from the requesting court and bring him before the court of this State or make other appropriate provisions for his appearance before the court.

b. Upon the filing of certified copies of the orders of the requesting court (1) determining that the child committed a delinquent act or is an unruly or deprived child, and (2) committing the child to the jurisdiction of the juvenile court of this State, the court of this State shall immediately fix a time for a hearing on the need for treatment or rehabilitation and disposition of the child or on the continuance of any probation or protective supervision.

c. The hearing and notice thereof and all subsequent proceedings are governed by this Act. The court may make any order of disposition permitted by the facts and this Act. The orders of the requesting court are conclusive that the child committed the delinquent act or is an unruly or deprived child and of the facts found by the court in making the orders, subject only to section 37. If the requesting court has made an order placing the child on probation or under protective supervision, a like order shall be entered by the court of this State. The court may modify or vacate the order in accordance with section 37.

Section 41. [Ordering Out-of-State Supervision.]

a. Subject to the provisions of this Act governing dispositions and to the extent that funds of the [county] are available the court may place a child in the custody of a suitable person in another state. On obtaining the written consent of a juvenile court of another state which has adopted the Uniform Juvenile Court Act or a substantially similar Act which includes provisions corresponding to sections 41 and 42 the court of this State may order that the child be placed under the supervision of a probation officer or other appropriate official designated by the accepting court. One certified copy of the order shall be sent to the accepting court and another filed with the clerk of the [Board of County Commissioners] of the [county] of the requesting court of this State.

b. The reasonable cost of the supervision including the expenses of necessary travel shall be borne by the [county] of the requesting court of this State. Upon receiving a certified statement signed by the judge of the accepting court of the cost incurred by the supervision the court of this State shall certify if it so appears that the sum so stated was reasonably incurred and file it with [the appropriate officials] of the [county] [state] for payment. The [appropriate officials] shall thereupon issue a warrant for the sum stated payable to the [appropriate officials] of the6[county] of the accepting court.

Section 42. [Supervision Under Out-of-State Order.]

a. Upon receiving a request of a juvenile court of another state which has adopted the Uniform Juvenile Court Act, or a substantially similar act which includes provisions corresponding to sections 41 and 42 to provide supervision of a child under the jurisdiction of that court, a court of this State may issue its written acceptance to the requesting court and designate its probation or other appropriate officer who is to provide supervision, stating the probable cost per day therefore.

b. Upon the receipt and filing of a certified copy of the order of the requesting court placing the child under the supervision of the officer so designated the officer shall arrange for the reception of the child from the requesting court, provide supervision pursuant to the order and this Act, and report thereon from time to time together with any recommendations he may have to the requesting court.

c. The court in this state from time to time shall certify to the requesting court the cost of supervision that has been incurred and request payment therefore from the appropriate officials of the [county] of the requesting court to the appropriate officials of the [county] of the accepting court.

d. The court of this State at any time may terminate supervision by notifying the requesting court. In that case, or if the supervision is terminated by the requesting court, the probation officer supervising the child shall return the child to a representative of the requesting court authorized to receive him.

Section 43. [Powers of Out-of-State Probation Officers.]

If a child has been placed on probation or protective supervision by a juvenile court of another state which has adopted the Uniform Juvenile Court Act or a substantially similar act which includes provisions corresponding to this section, and the child is in this State with or without the permission of that court, the probation officer of that court or other person designated by that court to supervise or take custody of the child has all the powers and privileges in this State with respect to the child as given by this Act to like officers or persons of this State including the right of visitation, counseling, control, and direction, taking into custody, and returning to that state.

Section 44. [Juvenile Traffic Offenses.]

a. Definition. Except as provided in subsection (b), a juvenile traffic offense consists of a violation by a child of:

1. a law or local ordinance [or resolution] governing the operation of a moving motor vehicle upon the streets or highways of this State, or the waterways within or adjoining this State; or

2. any other motor vehicle traffic law or local ordinance [or resolution] of this State if the child is taken into custody and detained for the violation or is transferred to the juvenile court by the court hearing the charge.

b. A juvenile traffic offense is not an act of delinquency unless the case is transferred to the delinquency calendar as provided in subsection (g).

c. Exceptions. A juvenile traffic offense does not include a violation of: [Set forth the sections of state statutes violations of which are not to be included as traffic offenses, such as the so-called negligent homicide statute sometimes appearing in traffic codes, driving while intoxicated, driving without, or during suspension of, a driver's license, and the like].

d. Procedure. The [summons] [notice to appear] [or other designation of a ticket] accusing a child of committing a juvenile traffic offense constitutes the commencement of the proceedings in the juvenile court of the [county] in which the alleged violation occurred and serves in place of a summons and petition under this Act. These cases shall be filed and heard separately from other proceedings of the court. If the child is taken into custody on the charge, sections 14 to 17 apply. If the child is, or after commencement of the proceedings becomes, a resident of another [county] of this State, section 12 applies.

e. Hearing. The court shall fix a time for hearing and give reasonable notice thereof to the child, and if their address is known to the parents, guardian, or custodian. If the accusation made in the [summons] [notice to appear] [or other designation of a ticket] is denied an informal hearing shall be held at which the parties have the right to subpoena witnesses, present evidence, cross-examine witnesses, and appear by counsel. The hearing is open to the public.

f. Disposition. If the court finds on the admission of the child or upon the evidence that he committed the offense charged it may make one or more of the following orders:

1. reprimand or counsel with the child and his parents;

2. [suspend] [recommend to the [appropriate official having the authority] that he suspend] the child's privilege to drive under stated conditions and limitations for a period not to exceed that authorized for a like suspension of an adult's license for a like offense;

3. require the child to attend a traffic school conducted by public authority for a reasonable period of time; or

4. order the child to remit to the general fund of the [state] [county] [city] [municipality] a sum not exceeding the lesser of $50 or the maximum applicable to an adult for a like offense.

g. In lieu of the preceding orders, if the evidence indicates the advisability thereof, the court may transfer the case to the delinquency calendar of the court and direct the filing and service of a summons and petition in accordance with this Act. The judge so ordering is disqualified upon objection from acting further in the case prior to an adjudication that the child committed a delinquent act.

Section 45. [Traffic Referee.]

a. The court may appoint one or more traffic referees who shall serve at the pleasure of the court. The referee's salary shall be fixed by the court [subject to the approval of the [Board of County Commissioners].

b. The court may direct that any case or class of cases arising under section 44 shall be heard in the first instance by a traffic referee who shall conduct the hearing in accordance with section 44. Upon the conclusion of the hearing the traffic referee shall transmit written findings of fact and recommendations for disposition to the judge with a copy thereof to the child and other parties to the proceedings.

c. Within 3 days after receiving the copy the child may file a request for a rehearing before the judge of the court who shall thereupon rehear the case at a time fixed by him. Otherwise, the judge may confirm the findings and recommendations for disposition which then become the findings and order of disposition of the court.

Section 46. [Juvenile Traffic Offenses—Suspension of Jurisdiction.]

a. The [Supreme] court, by order filed in the office of the [ ] of the [county,] may suspend the jurisdiction of the juvenile courts over juvenile traffic offenses or one or more classes effective and offenses committed thereafter shall be tried by the appropriate court in accordance with law without regard to this Act. The child shall not be detained or imprisoned in a jail or other facility for the detention of adults unless the facility conforms to subsection (a) of section 16.

b. The [Supreme] court at any time may restore the jurisdiction of the juvenile courts over these offenses or any portion thereof by like filing of its order of restoration. Offenses committed thereafter are governed by this Act.

Section 47. [Termination of Parental Rights.]

a. The court by order may terminate the parental rights of a parent with respect to his child if:

1. the parent had abandoned the child;
2. the child is a deprived child and the court finds that the conditions and causes of the deprivation are likely to continue or will not be remedied and that by reason thereof the child is suffering or will probably suffer serious physical, mental, moral, or emotional harm; or
3. the written consent of the parent acknowledged before the court has been given.

b. If the court does not make an order of termination of parental rights it may grant an order under section 30 if the court finds from clear and convincing evidence that the child is a deprived child.

Section 48. [Proceeding for Termination of Parental Rights.]

a. The petition shall comply with section 21 and state clearly that an order for termination of parental rights is requested and that the effect thereof will be as stated in the first sentence of Section 49.

b. If the paternity of a child born out of wedlock has been established prior to the filing of the petition, the father shall be served with summons as provided by this Act. He has the right to be heard unless he has relinquished all parental rights with reference to the child. The putative father of the child whose paternity has not been established, upon proof of his paternity of the child, may appear in the proceedings and be heard. He is not entitled to notice of hearing on the petition unless he has custody of the child.

Section 49. [Effect of Order Terminating Parental Rights.]

An order terminating the parental rights of a parent terminates all his rights and obligations with respect to the child and of the child to him arising from the parental relationship. The parent is not thereafter entitled to notice of proceedings for the adoption of the child by another nor has he any right to object to the adoption or otherwise participate in the proceedings.

Section 50. [Commitment to Agency.]

a. If, upon entering an order terminating the parental rights of a parent, there is no parent having parental rights, the court shall commit the child to the custody of the [State County Child Welfare Department] or a licensed child-placing agency, willing to accept custody for the purpose of placing the child for adoption, or in the absence thereof in a foster home or take other suitable measures for the care and welfare of the child. The custodian has authority to consent to the adoption of the child, his marriage, his enlistment in the armed forces of the United States, and surgical and other medical treatment for the child.

b. If the child is not adopted within 2 years after the date of the order and a general guardian of the child has not been appointed by the [_____] court, the child shall be returned to the court for entry of further orders for the care, custody, and control of the child.

Section 51. [Guardian ad litem.]

The court at any stage of a proceeding under this Act, on application of a party or on its own motion, shall appoint a guardian ad litem for a child who is a party to the proceeding if he has no parent, guardian, or custodian appearing on his behalf or their interests conflict with his or in any other case in which the interests of the child require a guardian. A party to the proceeding or his employee or representative shall not be appointed.

Section 52. [Costs and Expenses for Care of Child.]

a. The following expenses shall be a charge upon the funds of the county upon certification thereof by the court:

   1. the cost of medical and other examinations and treatment of a child ordered by the court;
   2. the cost of care and support of a child committed by the court to the legal custody of a public agency other than an institution for delinquent children, or to a private agency or individual other than a parent;
   3. reasonable compensation for services and related expenses of counsel appointed by the court for a party;
   4. reasonable compensation for a guardian ad litem;
   5. the expense of service of summons, notices, subpoenas, travel expense of witnesses, transportation of the child, and other like expenses incurred in the proceedings under this Act.

b. If, after due notice to the parents or other persons legally obligated to care for and support the child, and after affording them an opportunity to be heard, the court finds that they are financially able to pay all or part of the costs and expenses stated in paragraphs (1), (2), (3), and (4) of subsection (a), the court may order them to pay the same and prescribe the manner of payment. Unless otherwise ordered payment shall be made to the clerk of the juvenile court for remittance to the person to whom compensation is due, or if the costs and expenses have been paid by the [county] to the [appropriate officer] of the [county].

Section 53. [Protective Order.]

On application of a party or on the court's own motion the court may make an order restraining or otherwise controlling the conduct of a person if:

1. an order of disposition of a delinquent, unruly, or deprived child has been or is about to be made in a proceeding under this Act;
2. the court finds that the conduct (1) is or may be detrimental or harmful to the child and (2) will tend to defeat the execution of the order of disposition; and
3. due notice of the application or motion and the grounds therefore and an opportunity to be heard thereon have been given to the person against whom the order is directed.

Section 54. [Inspection of Court Files and Records.]

[Except in cases arising under section 44] all files and records of the court in a proceeding under this Act are open to inspection only by:

1. the judge, officers, and professional staff of the court;
2. the parties to the proceeding and their counsel and representatives;
3. a public or private agency or institution providing supervision or having custody of the child under order of the court;

4. a court and its probation and other officials or professional staff and the attorney for the defendant for use in preparing a pre-sentence report in a criminal case in which the defendant is convicted and who prior thereto had been a party to the proceeding in juvenile court;

5. with leave of court any other person or agency or institution having a legitimate interest in the proceeding or in the work of the court.

Section 55. [Law Enforcement Records.]

Law enforcement records and files concerning a child shall be kept separate from the records and files of arrests of adults. Unless a charge of delinquency is transferred for criminal prosecution under section 34, the interest of national security requires, or the court otherwise orders in the interest of the child, the records and files shall not be open to public inspection or their contents disclosed to the public; but inspection of the records and files is permitted by:

1. a juvenile court having the child before it in any proceeding;

2. counsel for a party to the proceeding;

3. the officers of public institutions or agencies to whom the child is committed;

4. law enforcement officers of other jurisdictions when necessary for the discharge of their official duties; and

5. a court in which he is convicted of a criminal offense for the purpose of a pre-sentence report or other dispositional proceeding, or by officials of penal institutions and other penal facilities to which he is committed, or by a [parole board] in considering his parole or discharge or in exercising supervision over him.

Section 56. [Children's Fingerprints, Photographs.]

a. No child under 14 years of age shall be fingerprinted in the investigation of a crime except as provided in this section. Fingerprints of a child 14 or more years of age who is referred to the court may be taken and filed by law enforcement officers in investigating the commission of the following crimes: [specifically such crimes as murder, non-negligent manslaughter, forcible rape, robbery, aggravated assault, burglary, housebreaking, purse snatching, and automobile theft].

b. Fingerprint files of children shall be kept separate from those of adults. Copies of fingerprints known to be those of a child shall be maintained on a local basis only and not sent to a central state or federal depository unless in the interest of national security.

c. Fingerprint files of children may be inspected by law enforcement officers when necessary for the discharge of their official duties. Other inspections may be authorized by the court in individual cases upon a showing that it is necessary in the public interest.

d. Fingerprints of a child shall be removed from the file and destroyed if:

1. a petition alleging delinquency is not filed, or the proceedings are dismissed after either a petition if filed or the case is transferred to the juvenile court as provided in section 9, or the child is adjudicated not to be a delinquent child; or

2. the child reaches 21 years of age and there is no record that he committed a criminal offense after reaching 16 years of age.

e. If latent fingerprints are found during the investigation of an offense and a law enforcement officer has probable cause to believe that they are those of a particular child he may fingerprint the child regardless of age or offense for purposes of immediate comparison with the latent fingerprints. If the comparison is negative the fingerprint card and other copies of the fingerprints taken shall be immediately destroyed. If the comparison is positive and the child is referred to the court, the fingerprint card and other copies of the fingerprints taken shall be delivered to the court for disposition. If the child is not referred to the court, the fingerprints shall be immediately destroyed.

f. Without the consent of the judge, a child shall not be photographed after he is taken into custody unless the case is transferred to another court for prosecution.

Section 57. [Sealing of Records.]

a. On application of a person who has been adjudicated delinquent or unruly or on the court's own motion, and after a hearing, the court shall order the sealing of the files and records in the proceeding, including those specified in sections 55 and 56, if the court finds:

1. 2 years have elapsed since the final discharge of the person;
2. since the final discharge he has not been convicted of a felony, or of a misdemeanor involving moral turpitude, or adjudicated a delinquent or unruly child and no proceeding is pending seeking conviction or adjudication; and
3. he has been rehabilitated.

b. Reasonable notice of the hearing shall be given to:

1. the [prosecuting attorney of the county];
2. the authority granting the discharge if the final discharge was from an institution or from parole; and
3. the law enforcement officers or department having custody of the files and records if the files and records specified in sections 55 and 56 are included in the application or motion.

c. Upon the entry of the order the proceeding shall be treated as if it never occurred. All index references shall be deleted and the person, the court, and law enforcement officers and departments shall properly reply that no record exists with respect to the person upon inquiry in any matter. Copies of the order shall be sent to each agency or official therein named. Inspection of the sealed files and records thereafter may be permitted by an order of the court upon petition by the person who is the subject of the records and only by those persons named in the order.

Section 58. [Contempt Powers.]

The court may punish a person for contempt of court for disobeying an order of the court or for obstructing or interfering with the proceedings of the court or the enforcement of its orders subject to the laws relating to the procedures therefore and the limitations thereon.

Section 59. [Appeals.]

a. An aggrieved party, including the state or a subdivision of the state, may appeal from a final order, judgment, or decree of the juvenile court to the [Supreme Court] [court of general jurisdiction] by filing written notice of appeal within 30 days after entry of the order, judgment, or decree, or within any further time the [Supreme Court] [court of general jurisdiction] grants, after entry of the order, judgment, or decree. [The appeal shall be heard by the [court of general jurisdiction] upon the files, records, and minutes or transcript of the evidence of the juvenile court, giving appreciable weight to the findings of the juvenile court.] The name of the child shall not appear on the record on appeal.

b. The appeal does not stay the order, judgment, or decree appealed from, but the [Supreme Court] [court of general jurisdiction] may otherwise order on application and hearing consistent with this Act if suitable provision is made for the care and custody of the child. If the order, judgment or decree appealed from grants the custody of the child to, or withholds it from, one or more of the parties to the appeal it shall be heard at the earliest practicable time.

Section 60. [Rules of Court.]

The [Supreme] Court of this State may adopt rules of procedure not in conflict with this Act governing proceedings under it.

Section 61. [Uniformity of Interpretation.]

This Act shall be so interpreted and construed as to effectuate its general purpose to make uniform the law of those states which enact it.

Section 62. [Short Title.]

This Act may be cited as the Uniform Juvenile Court Act.

Section 63. [Repeal.]

The following Acts and parts of Acts are repealed:

1.

2.

3.

Section 64. [Time of Taking Effect.]

This Act shall take effect. . . .

Glossary

This glossary summarizes the key terms used throughout this textbook. Readers should refer to this glossary to refresh their knowledge of discussions and case studies explored in chapters, tables, and In Practice boxes.

Abused and Neglected Child Reporting Act: Legislation that designates the state agency for investigating reports of child abuse and neglect and also lists persons mandated to report such abuse and neglect.

Adjudicatory hearing: Hearing similar to a trial in adult court. The merits of the case are heard and determined by the court.

Age ambiguity: A problem due to the difficulty in setting agreed-on lower- and upper-limit legal age definitions, resulting in substantial ambiguity with respect to age definitions.

Age of responsibility: Created nearly 2,000 years ago with origins in both Roman civil law and later canon (church) law. It made distinctions between juveniles and adults based on the notion of a minimum age of responsibility.

Alternatives to incarceration: Community-based programs that provide other sanctioning options besides a sentence to jail or prison. These community-based efforts can likewise be aimed at preventing juveniles from falling into crime within that community so as to avoid later potential incarceration.

Anomalies: Individuals thought to be incapable of resisting the impulse to commit crimes except under very favorable circumstances.

Anomie theory: Sociological theory of criminal causation that generally refers to a state of "normlessness" in society.

Atavists: A biological theory of criminal causation developed during the 19th century by Cesare Lombroso. It argued that criminals are anthropological throwbacks to an undeveloped phase in human evolution and that this atavistic quality is indicated by physical abnormalities.

Automatic waiver: Waiver that is automatically initiated to waive the exclusive jurisdiction of the juvenile court when specific offenses are allegedly committed by a juvenile.

Away syndrome: Approach that discourages attempts to find alternatives to incarceration, frequently arises in reaction to unsuccessful attempts at rehabilitation, and frequently is accompanied by an "out-of-sight, out-of-mind" attitude.

Bail: Release from custody pending trial after payment of a court-ordered sum.

Behavioral definitions: Definitions holding that those whose behavior violates statutes applicable to them are offenders whether or not they are officially labeled.

Behaviorists: Proponents of empirical, objective approaches of observing and measuring behavior.

Beijing Rules of 1985: A document produced by the United Nations titled *United Nations Standard Minimum Rules for the Administration of Juvenile Justice*, which is often referred to as the Beijing Rules due to the fact that it was developed during a UN meeting held in Beijing. Even though this document is not legally binding, it has served as an official reference point for how juvenile justice programs should be administered. The primary impetus behind the document was to encourage the humanitarian treatment of juvenile offenders.

Beyond a reasonable doubt: Standard of proof applied for the resolution of delinquency cases. On a scale of 1% to 100%, proof beyond a reasonable doubt would typically be 95% to 100% certain.

Biological theories: Theories that emphasize the belief that offenders differ from nonoffenders in some physiological way.

Biosocial criminology: A crime-study discipline that views behavior as the product of interaction between a physical environment and a physical organism and holds that contemporary criminology should represent a merger of biology, psychology, and sociology.

Black Disciples: Also known as the Black Gangster Disciple Nation or Brothers of the Struggle (BOS), a Chicago-based gang whose members are collectively known as "folks." They are in competition with the Vice Lords.

Black Lives Matter movement: A movement that began in Ferguson, Missouri, after a police use-of-force shooting meant to draw attention to a long-term racial bias in policing and court system that has generated revenue from the poor and minorities. The movement has expanded to draw attention to other issues facing minority communities, to include failing schools, inadequate housing, a lack of political input, and economic unfairness.

Blackstone Rangers: Original name of El Rukn, a Chicago gang that has emerged as a group characterized by a high degree of organization and considerable influence.

Blended sentencing: Allows juvenile and/or adult courts to impose adult sanctions and juvenile sanctions on certain types of juveniles. The adult sanction may be suspended so long as the child remains in compliance with the juvenile court. If the child violates the juvenile sanction, the adult sentence is then imposed.

Bloods and Crips: Two gangs identified by the color red (Bloods) and the color blue (Crips). These gangs are enemies of one another, and each dates back to the late 1960s and early 1970s in South Central Los Angeles. They consist of "rollers" or "gang-bangers" who are in their 20s and 30s, gang veterans who have made it big in the drug trade. These veterans supervise and control the activities of younger members who are involved in drug trafficking and operating and supplying crack houses, activities that bring in millions of dollars a week. The drug trafficking of the Bloods and Crips spread into other cities, including Seattle, Portland, Denver, Kansas City, Des Moines, and even Honolulu and Anchorage.

Boot camp: Residential correctional facility where drill instructors replicate training techniques used in boot camps of the armed forces, adapting their methods to the special needs of juvenile offenders. The purpose is to "shock" residents into socially productive conformity over a period of 30 to 120 days.

Bosozoku Gangs: Juvenile biker gangs in Japan who have been thought to be responsible for more than 80% of serious crimes committed by juveniles in that country.

Breed v. Jones: The U.S. Supreme Court ruling that trying a juvenile as an adult in criminal court for the same crime that previously had been adjudicated in juvenile court violates the double jeopardy clause of the Fifth Amendment when the adjudication involves violation of a criminal statute.

Broken homes: Homes disrupted through divorce, separation, or desertion.

Bullying: Involves the use of force or coercion to abuse, harass, or intimidate others.

Campaign for U.S. Ratification of the *Convention on the Rights of the Child* (CRC): A group of legal experts and children's advocates who seek to have the United States sign for adoption of the standards associated with the CRC.

Capital punishment: Death penalty.

Chancery courts: Courts that operated under the guidance of the king's chancellor and were created to consider petitions of those in need of special aid or intervention, such as women and children left in need of protection and aid by reason of divorce, death of a spouse, or abandonment, and to grant relief to such persons. Through the chancery courts, the king exercised the right of *parens patriae*.

Child death review teams: Teams composed of experts with medical, social services, and/or law enforcement backgrounds that review suspicious deaths of children and statutory changes facilitating the prosecution of those involved in child maltreatment.

Child neglect: Neglect that involves an individual under the age of 18 whose parent or person responsible for the child's welfare does not provide the proper or necessary support, education as required by law, or medical or other remedial care recognized under state law as necessary, including adequate food, shelter, clothing, or who abandons the child.

Child-savers movement: Mid-19th-century movement in the United States that sought to rescue children from unwholesome and dangerous environments. A fundamental tenet of the movement was that juveniles should receive treatment rather than punishment.

Children and family services: Personnel who do not actually work for the juvenile courts but still play a major role in the investigation, presentation of evidence, and dispositional recommendations in abuse and neglect cases.

Classical theory: Theoretical school holding that individuals are responsible for their deviant behavior. Punishments for these transgressors should always be proportional and never excessive. This theory was popular during the late 18th and early 19th centuries and was revived during the late 20th century in the United States.

Clear and convincing evidence: Standard of proof used in some circumstances that does not rise to the level of proof beyond a reasonable doubt but does exceed that which is based on a preponderance of the evidence.

On a scale of 1% to 100%, clear and convincing evidence would typically be approximately 80% certainty.

Cognitive behavioral therapy (CBT): According to this form of therapy, once individuals become conscious of their own thoughts and behaviors and the attitudes, beliefs, and values underlying those thoughts and behaviors, they can make positive changes to each with the assistance of a trained therapist.

Common law: Law based on custom or use. Under common law, children under the age of 7 were presumed to be incapable of forming criminal intent and, therefore, were not subject to criminal sanctions.

Concentric-zone theory: Theory holding that zones of transition between residential and industrial neighborhoods consistently have the highest rates of crime and delinquency. It is commonly associated with the work of Earnest Burgess.

Conceptual schemes: Schemes that suggest relationships between variables but do not meet the requirements for theory.

Concurrent jurisdiction: Term indicating that two or more courts have jurisdiction over a potential case. For example, certain criminal acts may be concurrently under the jurisdiction of both the juvenile court and the criminal court.

Conditioning: Process of rewarding for appropriate behavior and/or punishing for inappropriate behavior through which any type of social behavior can be taught.

Conflict, radical, critical, and Marxist theories: Theories that focus on whole political and economic systems and on class relations in those systems. Conflict theorists argue that conflict is inherent in all societies, not just capitalist societies, and focus on conflict resulting from gender, race, ethnicity, power, and other relationships.

Conflict with the law: Provides a set of criteria that provides practitioners with a working and usable definition of delinquent youth. These criteria, or indicators, have been found to be common around the world and are necessary due to the wide variety of situations that are encountered from country to country.

Continuance under supervision: Where the judge postpones adjudication and specifies a time period during which he or she (through court officers) will observe the juvenile.

Control theories: Theories assuming that all of us must be held in check or "controlled" if we are to resist the temptation to commit criminal or delinquent acts.

Convention on the Rights of the Child (CRC) (1989): The first legally binding international document to incorporate the full range of human rights afforded to children throughout the world.

Court-appointed counsel: Attorneys who are either private attorneys appointed by the court or public defenders.

Court Appointed Special Advocate (CASA): A volunteer who works closely with the Department of Children and Family Services on abuse and neglect cases.

Crack: A cocaine-based stimulant drug that is inexpensive to manufacture and is much more affordable for drug users than is cocaine.

Criminal sexual abuse: Abuse that involves the intentional fondling of the genitals, anus, breasts, or any other part of the body, through the use of force or threat of force or of a victim (child) unable to understand the nature of the act, for the purpose of sexual gratification.

Criminal sexual assault: Assault that involves contact with or intrusion into the sex organ, anus, mouth, or other body part by the sex organ of another, or some other object wielded by another, with accompanying force or threat of force or of a victim (child) unable to understand the nature of the act.

Criminal subculture: Subculture in which juveniles are encouraged and supported by well-established conventional and criminal institutions.

D.A.R.E. (Drug Abuse Resistance Education): A program that emphasizes drug awareness education for elementary school students. Police officers from local station houses teach children about the different types of drugs, their effects, and how to recognize them. Officers also explain how to say no when drugs are offered.

Day reporting centers (DRCs): Structured, community-based programs where intensive supervision and services are provided to youth postadjudication. The goals are to protect the community and divert future criminal behavior.

Defense counsel: Attorney for the juvenile who is processed through the juvenile court system.

Delinquency and drift: Theory that firm commitment to subcultural values is not necessarily a precursor of delinquent behavior, as argued by Sykes and Matza. Using techniques of neutralization, juveniles drift in and out of the delinquent subculture over time.

Delinquency, neglect, abuse, and dependency cases: Cases or occurrences where findings of delinquency, neglect, abuse, and dependency have been made.

Delinquent subculture: Grouping of young people who "mutually convert" associates in the commission of delinquent activity.

Demonology: Ancient belief holding that human deviance is the product of evil otherworldly forces such as demons and devils. Remedies included exorcism of the evil spirits, which often involved ordeals of pain.

Detention: Period between when a juvenile is taken into custody and prior to a hearing before the juvenile court. It is roughly comparable to the adult concept of being "jailed" because in both circumstances a suspect is temporarily housed in a detention facility pending further processing.

Detention hearing: Court hearing to determine whether detention is required.

Deterrence theory: Punishment alternative based on the fear of swift and severe punishment. In theory, harsh punishment deters individuals who might otherwise be prone to break the law as well as those who have already violated the law.

Developing countries: Countries that are not fully stable, industrialized, and free from political or economic duress. Characterized by weak or corrupt governments with depressed economies and few opportunities for the average citizen.

Discretionary waiver: Waiver that may be left to the juvenile court judge to decide after a petition for a waiver has been filed and a hearing has been conducted on the advisability of granting the waiver. In general, the criteria used by juvenile court judges to determine the granting or denying of waivers of juveniles to criminal courts are rather vague and, for the most part, quite subjective.

Dispositional hearing: Hearing similar to the sentencing hearing in adult court. The court rules on what should become of the juvenile subsequent to the adjudication.

Disproportionate minority contact (DMC): Refers to the disproportionate number of minority youth who come into contact with the juvenile justice system.

Diversion: Conceptual underpinning for community-based programs. This is a process that diverts juveniles away from the formal and authoritarian components of the juvenile justice system. Programs may be coordinated by youth agencies, juvenile courts, or the police.

Double jeopardy: Criminal prosecution of a juvenile subsequent to proceedings in juvenile court involving the same act. In *Breed v. Jones*, the U.S. Supreme Court unanimously ruled that the Fifth Amendment's prohibition against double jeopardy precludes such criminal prosecution.

Double victimization: Occurs when youth experience abuse and, in reaction, engage in delinquent behaviors that later result in labeling and punishment from the state for their delinquent and/or criminal activity.

Dropouts: Juveniles who do not complete their secondary education. The term is also used to describe persons who do not participate throughout the full duration of a study.

Drug courts: Courts that attempt to prevent children and adults from continuing deviant drug-using behaviors. These courts aim to stop the abuse of alcohol and other drugs through the use of intensive therapeutic supervision.

Due process: Observing constitutional guarantees and rules of exclusion when processing court cases.

Ecological/social disorganization approach: Approach that focuses on the geographic distribution of delinquency. It is commonly associated with the work of Shaw and McKay.

El Rukn: Chicago gang that was previously known as the Blackstone Rangers and later was called the Black P Stone Nation until it was called by the current name. This gang has emerged as a group characterized by a high degree of organization and considerable influence.

Electronic monitoring: Form of supervision that requires the juvenile to wear an anklet or other such device that allows the community supervision agency to electronically monitor the location of the juvenile on supervision.

Emotional or psychological abuse: Injury to the intellectual or psychological capacity of a child, as evidenced by a discernible and substantial impairment in the ability to function within the normal range of performance and behavior.

Era of socialized juvenile justice: The period between 1899 and 1967 in the United States. During this era, juveniles were considered not as miniature adults but rather as persons with less than fully developed morality and cognition.

Exclusive jurisdiction: Term indicating that the juvenile court will be the only tribunal legally empowered to proceed and that all other courts are deprived of jurisdiction.

Faith-based initiatives: Initiatives that are intended to strengthen and expand social services offered to the needy (in particular those in poverty). Faith-based organizations can apply for grants and funding to support programs aimed at drug prevention, violence prevention, at-risk youth, and gang behaviors.

Family violence: Intentional violence committed, attempted, or threatened by spouses, ex-spouses, common-law spouses, boyfriends, or girlfriends past or present, and/or child abuse.

Feminism: Approach to studying crime and delinquency that focuses on women's experiences, typically in the areas of victimization, gender differences in crime, and differential treatment of women by the justice network.

Folks: One of two alliances of gangs, or "sets," formed in Chicago. Along with the "people," the "folks" is an amalgamation of gangs that cuts across racial and ethnic identities. These alliances are not quite mega-gangs but rather groupings that identify fellow members as allies.

Follow Through: Similar to Head Start, program designed to help culturally deprived children catch up or keep pace during their preschool and early school years.

Foster homes: Nonsecure residential facilities that expand the concept of family replication by loosening the institutional restrictions found in group homes with a small number of supervisors and residents. Foster care is generally limited to victims of abuse and neglect rather than to lawbreakers. It attempts to substitute a foster family for a child's biological family.

Fourth Amendment: Protection afforded against illegal search and seizure that extends to juveniles.

Freewill approach: Crime control based on the belief that humans exercise free will and that human behavior results from rationally calculating rewards and costs in terms of pleasure and pain.

Functionally related agencies: Agencies that have goals similar to those of the juvenile justice system—namely, improving the quality of life for juveniles by preventing offensive behavior, providing opportunities for success, and correcting undesirable behavior.

Gault case: The U.S. Supreme Court ruling that in hearings that may result in institutional commitment, juveniles have the right to counsel, the right to confront and cross-examine witnesses, the right to remain silent, the right to a transcript of the proceedings, and the right to appeal.

"Get tough" or "just deserts" approach: Approach that would have an increasing number of juveniles processed within the adult justice network.

Globalization: Refers to the increased connectivity and interdependence that has evolved among countries; this sense of interconnection has been fostered by technological advances as well as cultural shifts.

Graffiti: Various forms of painted and coded messages that are placed on buildings throughout the community as a means of communicating to allied and rival gang members. Street gang graffiti is unique in its significance and symbolism. Graffiti serves several functions; it is used to delineate gang turf as well as turf in dispute, it proclaims who the top-ranking gang members are, it issues challenges, and it proclaims the gang's philosophy.

Graham v. Florida: A 2010 decision by the Supreme Court of the United States in which it was held that juvenile offenders cannot be sentenced to life imprisonment without parole for nonhomicide offenses.

GREAT (Gang Resistance Education and Awareness Training): A program based on assumptions similar to, and also subject to criticisms similar to, those of the D.A.R.E. program. These gang resistance programs train police officers to conduct comprehensive anti-gang education programs for juveniles who are not yet in high school.

Guardian ad litem: Court-appointed representative for juveniles who have been abused or neglected or who are dependent. He or she represents the personal interests of juveniles who are deemed unable to do so on their own behalf because of their immaturity.

Head Start: Federal program that delivers preschool and early school educational services to children from poor or culturally marginalized environments. The program provides instruction in basic reading and verbal skills for children who might otherwise grow up with poor skills and thereby an increased possibility of future delinquency or criminality.

Hmong Nation Society: One of the more commonly known street gangs with membership that is exclusively of Hmong ancestry. Thought to have originated in the Stockton City area of California.

Holmes case: The U.S. Supreme Court ruling that because juvenile courts are not criminal courts, the constitutional rights guaranteed to accused adults do not apply to juveniles.

House of refuge: A type of institution founded during the 1820s to house vagrant and criminal juveniles. Houses of refuge are a typical example of Enlightenment-era juvenile justice reforms.

Human trafficking: A form of human slavery that includes forced labor, domestic servitude, and commercial sex trafficking.

Hybrid sentencing: Means of matching a juvenile's sentence to the specific issues and circumstances associated with that offender. These sentences also allow juveniles to be sentenced to adult and juvenile dispositions by both adult court judges and juvenile court judges. Instead of classifying individuals as juveniles or adults, hybrid sentences allow the convenience and benefits of both courts. Juveniles are given a second chance by being allowed to rely on the juvenile court for rehabilitation while being aware that the adult court sanctions apply if rehabilitation fails.

Id, ego, and superego: Three components of the human conscious psyche according to psychoanalytic theory. The id involves instinctual and reactionary impulses, whereas the superego involves the moral sense of self. Both are balanced by the ego, a psychic component that mediates between the two extreme components of the human psyche.

Illegitimate opportunity structure: Scenario that where illegitimate opportunities are available, juveniles who are experiencing strain or anomie are attracted to that structure and are likely to become involved in delinquent activities.

In loco parentis: Latin term meaning "in the place of parents."

In need of supervision: Nondelinquent category to identify juveniles who commit status offenses but do not engage in aberrant behaviors that are serious enough to warrant a classification as delinquent.

Integrated theories: Theories that attempt to combine two or more preexisting theories so as to provide more comprehensive explanations for criminal and delinquent behaviors.

Intensive supervision: Probation program mandated for persons who may pose a risk of flight or noncompliance with the terms of probation. Adult intensive supervision was originally designed during the 1980s to lower costs and reduce prison overcrowding. It is an intensified version of standard probation and emphasizes increased surveillance, more frequent contacts with probation officers, and enhanced control over participants. Electronic monitoring is commonplace.

Internet exploitation: Exploitation that occurs when child sexual predators use the Internet as a means of communicating with potential victims. Because of its anonymity, rapid transmission, and often unsupervised nature, the Internet has become a medium of choice that predators use to contact juveniles and transmit and/or receive child pornography.

Internet offending: Criminal acts that may include exchanging child pornography, locating potential victims for sexual abuse, engaging in inappropriate sexual communication, and corresponding with other individuals who may have a deviant sexual interest in children. It may include the use of websites, newsgroups, chat rooms, e-mail, discussion, and bulletin boards.

Interrogation: Questioning by police. While in custody, juveniles have rights similar to those of adults with respect to interrogation.

Intervention: With respect to child abuse, a process that begins with someone reporting the abuse or suspected abuse, moves into the investigatory stage that typically involves a home visit and interviews with the parties involved, and then moves to risk assessment and a decision concerning what type of action, if any, to take.

Jackson v. Hobbs: A 2011 U.S. Supreme Court case heard at the same time as *Miller v. Alabama* where the Court held that mandatory sentences of life in prison without the possibility of parole are unconstitutional for juvenile offenders.

Jargon: Terminology used by gang members. It can be very useful for practitioners to know and understand. Understanding gang jargon may be critical to obtaining convictions for gang-related crimes.

John Augustus: Founding father of probation.

Juvenile court judges: Central participants in a juvenile court system who sit as the final arbiter for disputes and problems brought before the court. A juvenile court judge is vested with the authority of the state, tangibly and personally representing *parens patriae*.

Juvenile Detention Alternatives Initiative (JDAI): A reform initiative that focuses on changing policies, practices, and programs to reduce secure confinement of youth, improve public safety, reduce costs for youth corrections, reduce racial disparities and bias, and encourage juvenile justice reforms overall.

Juvenile drug-crime cycle: When substance abuse is strongly correlated with other acts of delinquency and crime, and vice versa, being unclear which comes first or which comes second for young offenders.

Juvenile Mentoring Program (JUMP): Supports one-to-one mentoring relationships for youth at risk of becoming involved in delinquency, gangs, and educational failure.

Juvenile probation officer: Key figure at all levels of the juvenile justice system. He or she may arrange a preliminary conference among interested parties that may result in an out-of-court settlement between an alleged delinquent and the injured party or between parties in cases of abuse or neglect. After an adjudicatory hearing, the juvenile probation officer is often charged with conducting a social background investigation. This investigation is used to help the judge make a dispositional decision. This officer is also charged with supervising those juveniles who are placed on probation and released into the community as well as parents who have been deemed to have committed neglect or abuse.

Kent case: U.S. Supreme Court ruling that during waiver hearings, juveniles are entitled to a hearing that includes the essentials of due process required by the Fourteenth Amendment.

Labeling process: Process whereby reactions of society, family, and the justice system can exaggerate problems in family, school, and peer relations, and the juvenile may find it difficult to meet the expectations established for him or her.

Labeling theory: Theory holding that society's reaction to deviant behavior is crucially important in understanding who becomes labeled as deviant.

Latchkey children: School-age children who return home from school to empty houses. Estimates indicate that there may be as many as 10 million children left unsupervised after school.

Latin Kings: Largely Hispanic gang whose members are aligned with the Vice Lords. This gang is known as the "people," and its members typically are not aligned with the Black Gangster Disciples or Simon City Royals.

"Lawgiver" judge: Judge who is primarily concerned that all procedural requirements are fulfilled in court proceedings.

Learning disabled: Possessing deficits in learning processes such as poor reading ability, lack of ability to memorize or follow directions, and incapability to distinguish or otherwise manage letters or numerals.

Learning theory: Theory holding that people learn behaviors through various forms of reinforcements, punishments, and social observations.

Legal definitions: Definitions holding that only those who have been officially labeled by the courts are offenders.

Legalistic approach: Formal and official approach with strict adherence to constitutional safeguards.

Mandated reporters: Reporters who are required to report suspected cases of abuse to the state.

McKeiver v. Pennsylvania: U.S. Supreme Court ruling that the due process clause of the Fourteenth Amendment does not require jury trials in juvenile court.

Mens rea: Latin term for "guilty mind." It centers on the question of when and under what circumstances children are capable of forming criminal intent.

Mental health courts: Problem-solving courts that combine community mental health treatment with judicial supervision and support.

Methamphetamines: Stimulant drug, also known as "meth," that is manufactured easily and sold inexpensively.

Miller v. Alabama: A 2012 U.S. Supreme Court case in which the Court held that mandatory sentences of life without the possibility of parole are unconstitutional for juvenile offenders.

Monikers: Gang member nicknames that are different from members' given names. In general, these monikers reflect physical or personality characteristics or connote something bold or daring.

Montgomery v. Louisiana: A 2016 U.S. Supreme Court case in which the Court found that its previous ruling in Miller v. Alabama (2012) (that a mandatory life sentence without parole should not apply to juveniles convicted of murder) should be applied retroactively.

Munchausen syndrome by proxy (MSBP): Form of child abuse in which the abuser fabricates (or sometimes creates) an illness in the child victim. The child is then taken to a physician, usually by the mother, who knows that hospitalization for tests and observation is likely to be recommended because the symptoms are described as severe, but no apparent cause exists.

Narcotics trafficking: Illicit sale and distribution of narcotic drugs.

National Center for Juvenile Justice: The research division of the National Council of Juvenile and Family Court Judges and the oldest juvenile justice research group in the United States.

National Center on Child Abuse and Neglect: Organization that publishes data on abuse and neglect of children.

National Children's Advocacy Center: Organization that publishes data on abuse and neglect of children in tandem with a number of other agencies.

National Crime Victimization Survey (NCVS): Data derived from annual household surveys conducted by the U.S. Department of Justice's Bureau of Justice Statistics in collaboration with the U.S. Census Bureau. It is usually made twice annually and asks approximately 40,000 to 50,000 respondents whether members of their households have been victims of crimes.

National Incident-Based Reporting System (NIBRS): System developed to collect information on each single crime occurrence. Under this reporting system, policing agencies report data on "offenses known to the police" (offenses reported to or observed by the police) instead of only those "offenses cleared by arrest," as was done in the original crime reporting process of the Uniform Crime Reports (UCRs).

National Probation Act: Passed in 1925, legislation that authorized federal district court judges to hire probation officers as well.

Neoclassical approach: Modification of the classical school that occurred during the early 19th century. It recognizes that juveniles and mentally ill adults do not make the same rational choices as do mature sane adults. Therefore, special consideration should be given to these classes of offenders.

Neo-Nazism: Variety of white supremacist gangs in the form of skinhead groups such as the Nazi Low Riders, White Aryan Resistance, Hammer Skins, World Church of the Creator, and other groups whose members perpetrate hate crimes.

Net widening: A process whereby youth are brought to the attention of juvenile authorities when they otherwise would not be labeled, thereby increasing rather than decreasing stigmatization.

Neurocriminology: A form of criminology that uses brain imaging techniques to study, predict, and prevent criminal behavior.

Notification: Notice that must be given to all parties concerned before a proceeding.

Offenses known to the police: Offenses reported to or observed by the police.

Office of Juvenile Justice and Delinquency Prevention (OJJDP): Organization that coordinates national policy for preventing juvenile delinquency and victimization. Established under the Juvenile Justice and Delinquency Prevention Act of 1974, it conducts independent research, assists experts and agencies in program evaluation, and recommends initiatives for delinquency prevention and treatment.

Official procedures: Clearly delineated guidelines that officers must follow when they formally process juveniles. These procedures are written into juvenile court acts and are reflected in internal procedures adopted by law enforcement agencies.

Olweus Bullying Prevention Program: A comprehensive schoolwide program for use in elementary, middle, or junior high schools. The program's goals are to reduce and prevent bullying problems among schoolchildren and to improve peer relations at school.

Overpolicing: Policing of a given area that is much more than would typically be necessary to maintain public order.

Parens patriae: Concept of the monarch as "father of the country." It is an ancient English doctrine allowing the state to intervene as a surrogate parent in the best interests of children whose parents have failed in their duties to protect, care for, and control them.

"Parent figure" judge: Judge who is often genuinely concerned about the total well-being of juveniles who appear before the court.

Pedophile: Criminal offender who seeks out children for purposes of sexual gratification.

Pedophilia: An ongoing sexual attraction to prepubertal children.

People: One of two alliances of gangs, or "sets," formed in Chicago. Along with the "folks," the "people" is an amalgamation of gangs that cuts across racial and ethnic identities. These alliances are not quite megagangs but rather groupings that identify fellow members as allies.

Personality inventories: Psychological assessment tools examining people's personality characteristics.

Petition: Form process whereby a party initiates proceedings in a court of law.

Phrenology: Study of the shape of the skull.

Police discretion: Exercise of judgment by individual officers on what type of action to take in a particular situation.

Police observational studies: Observations provided by researchers that help in better assessing the extent of unofficial or hidden delinquency, abuse, and neglect.

Police–school liaison officers (PSLOs): Officers located in schools who serve as sources of information and counselors for students.

Politicized gangs: Gangs that use violence for the purpose of promoting political change by instilling fear in innocent people.

Positive peer culture: Orientation used in some treatment programs in which the youthful offender is surrounded by a positive and prosocial set of peers in the program.

Positivist school of criminology: Deterministic approach to criminality and delinquency. This approach holds that biology, culture, and social experiences can be sources of deviant behavior.

Postadjudication intervention: Intervention that is provided after the adjudication phase.

Postclassical theory: Theory involving the notion that people rationally

consider the risks and rewards before they commit crimes. It is also called rational choice theory.

Preadjudication intervention: Intervention that is provided before the adjudication phase.

Preliminary conference: Voluntary meeting arranged by a juvenile probation officer with the victim, the juvenile, and typically the juvenile's parents or guardian in an attempt to negotiate a settlement without taking further official action. Juvenile court acts clearly indicate those persons who are eligible to file a petition.

Preservice and in-service training: Training given to law enforcement personnel. Preservice training is the initial academy-level training given to personnel when they begin their careers in law enforcement or corrections. In-service training is additional training provided while the officers are employed with their respective agencies.

Primary prevention: Intervention with juveniles who have not yet begun breaking the law or otherwise engaging in antisocial deviance.

Private counsel: Attorneys who are sometimes retained or appointed to represent the interests of juveniles in court.

Private detention facilities: Detention facilities that tend to house fewer delinquents than do public facilities and are less oriented toward strict custody than are facilities operated by the state department of corrections.

Probation: Sentence that is served in the community under supervision by a probation officer. The offender's sentence begins and ends in the community, assuming that he or she complies with the terms of probation.

Probation as conditional release: Community supervision that is purely conditional on offenders' compliance with any variety of court-mandated requirements set by the judge.

Progressive Era: The period from 1900 to 1918 characterized by extensive social reform including the growth of the women's suffrage movement, the campaign against child labor, and the fight for the 8-hour workday.

Prosecutor or state's attorney: Official who makes the final decision about whether a juvenile will be dealt with in juvenile court. The prosecutor carries forth charges against the juvenile.

Psychoanalytic approach: Theory proposed by Sigmund Freud arguing that humans have three personality components: (1) the id, (2) ego, and (3) superego. Human personalities also progress through several phases of childhood development. Failure to progress through these phases in a healthy manner can lead to deviant behavior, as can failure to develop a healthy balance among the id, ego, and superego.

Psychological factors: Factors related to a juvenile's likelihood of future involvement in delinquency. These include dependency needs, family rejection, and impulse control.

Psychological theories: Theories that have their basis in the field of psychology as opposed to sociology.

Psychopath: Aggressive criminal who acts impulsively for no apparent reason.

Public detention and juvenile prison facilities: Detention facilities that are frequently located near large urban centers and often house large numbers of delinquents in a cottage- or dormitory-type setting and juvenile prison facilities are similar to minimum, medium, and maximum adult correctional facilities and securely house violent youth sentenced to 1 or more years in prison.

Pure diversion: Also known as preadjudicatory diversion. This is a process of immediate diversion, meaning that young offenders are sent directly into community-based programs before they are adjudicated by a juvenile court and processed into the formal juvenile justice system.

Purpose statement of a juvenile court act: Statement that spells out the intent or basic philosophy of the act.

Pushes and pulls: Affect the likelihood of the youth joining a gang. Pushes are external factors that move a person toward circumstances that breed gang involvement whereas pulls are internal factors that make gang life attractive to the individual.

Radical nonintervention: Approach that encourages law and policymaking organizations to be tolerant of the widest possible diversity of behaviors and attitudes. Such a process would then limit the amount of intervention necessary with juveniles.

Rational choice theory: Theory involving the notion that people rationally consider the risks and rewards before they commit crimes. It is also called postclassical theory.

Reform schools: Juvenile facilities established during the child-savers era in the mid-19th-century United States. They were a programmatic counterpoint to houses of refuge in that the reform schools sought to create a nurturing environment rather than a harsh correctional one. Education and trade or craft were emphasized, as were homelike environments.

Restorative justice: Type of justice in which the core concepts of accountability, competency, and public safety are used in mediation that includes the crime victim(s), the offender(s), and the community.

Restorative or balanced justice: Type of justice that uses mediation that includes the victim(s), the offender(s), and the community, as with restorative justice. The term *balanced justice* is used in some cases because this type of justice addresses all parties rather than focusing on only one party (i.e., the offender) to the exclusion of others.

Revitalized juvenile justice: Justice system that includes swift intervention with early offenders, an individualized comprehensive-needs assessment, transfer of serious or chronic offenders, and intensive aftercare. Such a system requires the coordinated efforts of law enforcement, treatment, correctional, judicial, and social-services personnel.

Revocation of probation: Cessation of probation with a corresponding imposition or execution of the sentence that could have been given originally by the judge.

Riyadh Guidelines of 1990: Guidelines that are broad and all-encompassing providing a multifaceted approach to delinquency prevention. Referred to as the Riyadh Guidelines because they were adopted by the United Nations General Assembly at a meeting in Riyadh, Saudi Arabia, these guidelines provide insight into what a model program would entail. The guidelines consist of five broad components that include (1) general prevention; (2) socialization processes; (3) social policy; (4) legislation and juvenile justice administration; and (5) research, policy development, and coordination.

Role identity confusion: Confusion that occurs when probation officers are unclear about the expectations placed on them when they attempt to balance the competing interests of their "policing" role and their "reform"-oriented role.

Roper v. Simmons: A 2005 case in which the U.S. Supreme Court held that states cannot execute offenders who are under the age of 18.

Routine activities theory: Approach in which crime is simply a function of people's everyday behavior.

Scared Straight: First popularized in the 1978 film *Scared Straight*, program in which groups of young offenders spend a day in a maximum-security prison. They tour the facility and are placed in a graphic and intensive encounter session with hardened adult convicts.

School-to-prison pipeline: A term used to describe children who have trouble at school, such as out-of-school suspensions, but end up in the juvenile justice system because of increased use of zero-tolerance policies, police in schools, physical restraints, and automatic suspensions.

Scientific theory: Set of two or more related, empirically testable assertions (statements of alleged facts or relationships among facts about a particular phenomenon), as defined by Fitzgerald and Cox.

Scope of a juvenile court act: Scope that is indicated by sections dealing with definitions, age, jurisdiction, and waiver.

Secondary diversion: Also known as postadjudicatory diversion. This refers to the release of juveniles who have already been processed into the formal juvenile justice system. They are released into community-based programs prior to final disposition.

Secondary prevention: Intervention with juveniles who have only recently begun engaging in antisocial deviance and are in an early phase of committing relatively minor or status offenses. This is usually predelinquency prevention.

Self-report studies: Studies constructed to resolve the false dichotomy between labeled and nonlabeled juveniles. They use self-reported data that inquire about respondents' own criminal behavior within a specified period.

Sexual abuse: Abuse that consists of the involvement of children in sexual activity to provide sexual gratification or financial benefit to the perpetrator, including contacts for sexual purposes, prostitution, pornography, or other sexually exploitative activities.

Sexual exploitation: Expanded statutory definition of sexual abuse. Such statutes typically include references to exploitation for pornographic purposes and to prostitution.

Shelter care: Nonsecure residential facilities that temporarily house juveniles. Shelters are typically used as temporary housing for status offenders and others while they await final placement to another facility or their family homes. Most shelters are not designed to treat or punish juveniles.

SHOCAP (Serious Habitual Offender Comprehensive Action Program): A multidisciplinary interagency case management and information-sharing system intended to help the agencies involved make informed decisions about juveniles who repeatedly engage in delinquent acts.

Shock intervention: Term used synonymously with *boot camp*. The purpose is to "shock" residents into socially productive conformity.

Simon City Royals: Part of the "folks" alignment in gang membership. This group is a Caucasian gang that originated in Chicago during the early 1960s. Originally formed to stop the "invasion" of Hispanic gangs into their area of the city, the Royals became actively involved in burglaries and home invasions during the 1980s. As leaders of the gang were imprisoned, they formed alliances with the Black Gangster Disciples for protection, and the alliances continue today.

Sixth Amendment: Declaration that in all criminal prosecutions, the accused enjoys the right to a speedy and public trial. However, juvenile court acts prohibit public hearings on the grounds that opening such hearings would be detrimental to the children.

Social background investigations: Investigations that typically include information about the children, the children's parents, school, work, and general peer relations, as well as other environmental factors.

Social disorganization: Urban theory holding that poor urban communities are innately dysfunctional and give rise to criminal behavior.

Social factors: Various factors that are not physiological in nature and that may increase the risk of problems such as abusing drugs and engaging in delinquent behavior.

Social promotion: When teachers pass troubled juveniles on to their colleagues by refusing to fail these "problem youth."

Socialization process: Process of learning moral and social norms of behavior, as defined within children's immediate environment.

Socioeconomic status: Individuals' social and economic position within society.

Sociological factors: Factors that may include a person's place of residence, school attended, age, race, nationality, and the like.

Sociological theories: Theories that look for causes of delinquency in society as well as in the individual.

Somatotypes: Theory of delinquent and criminal causation that classifies three body types as determinants of deviant behavior: (1) *mesomorphs*, who are muscular, sinewy, narrow in waist and hips, and broad-shouldered; (2) *ectomorphs*, who are fragile, thin, narrow, and delicate; and (3) *endomorphs*, who are pudgy, round, soft, short-limbed, and smooth-skinned. A predominance of mesomorphic traits is theoretically found in delinquents and criminals.

Spergel model: Model that involves developing a coordinated team approach to delivering services and solving problems. Strategies involved include mobilization of community leaders and residents; use of outreach workers to engage juveniles in gangs; access to academic, economic, and social opportunities; and gang-suppression activities.

Standard of preponderance of evidence: Standard of proof applied for the resolution of status offense cases. It technically refers to the greater weight of evidence that is more credible and convincing to the mind.

Stationhouse adjustment: Decision that occurs when a juvenile is brought into a police stationhouse and his or her parents are called in for consultation. Officers can release the juvenile into the parents' custody, thereby ending the case prior to official processing into the juvenile justice system.

Status offenses: Legal offenses applicable only to children and not to adults.

Strain theory: Sociological theory of criminal causation that generally refers to a state of "normlessness" in society. Modern strain theory focuses on the availability of goals and means. When the greater society encourages its members to use acceptable means to achieve acceptable goals—and not all members have an equal availability of resources to achieve these goals—members may resort to illegitimate and illicit means.

Street corner adjustment: Informal response that officers may take to nonserious delinquency and/or vagrancy to resolve nuisance behavior committed by juveniles.

Street corner family: Based on the idea that the gang is the member's family and that gangs satisfy deep-seated needs of adolescents. It is associated with the work of William F. Whyte, who portrayed the gang as a "street corner family."

Street gangs: Gangs that routinely engage in criminal behavior such as drug trafficking, burglary, vehicular theft, and assault.

Suburbanization: The growth of urban sprawl throughout the United States, turning urban centers into large multijurisdictional conglomerates that include large areas of terrain.

Taking into custody: When an officer detains a juvenile and keeps him or her under supervision, watch, and/or guard. When delinquency is the alleged reason for taking into custody, law enforcement officers must adhere to appropriate constitutional guidelines.

Technical violation: Minor infraction committed by the probationer while on community supervision. Technical violations are generally worked out between the probationer and the probation officer, and they usually do not result in revocation action unless the probationer develops a complete disregard for the terms or conditions of probation.

Techniques of neutralization: Mental defenses to delinquency internalization that include (1) denial of responsibility (for the consequences of delinquent actions), (2) denial of injury (to the victim or larger society), (3) denial of a victim (the victim "had it coming"), (4) condemnation of the condemners (as hypocrites or spiteful), and (5) appeal to higher loyalties (e.g., to the gang), as defined by Sykes and Matza. Using these techniques, juveniles drift in an out of the delinquent subculture over time.

Teen courts: Courts made up of teens under 17 years of age who process cases by acting as prosecutor, defense counsel, bailiff, and clerk and who determine the punishment for the cases by acting as the jury. An adult attorney acts as the judge to ensure the fairness and legality of the sentencing. Offenders are required to complete the sentences handed down by the teen jury.

Territorial jealousy: Belief commonly held by agency personnel that attempts to coordinate efforts are actually attempts to invade the territory they have staked out for themselves.

Tertiary prevention: Intervention with juveniles who have engaged in serious and chronic deviance and who have already entered the juvenile justice system. These juveniles are technically in need of treatment rather than prevention because efforts to prevent the onset of delinquency have failed. These juveniles should be approached within the context of rehabilitation rather than prevention.

Theory of differential anticipation: Developed by Glaser, theory that combines differential association and control theory and is compatible with biological and personality theories. It assumes that a person will try to commit a crime wherever and whenever the expectations of gratification from doing so—as a result of social bonds, differential learning, and perceptions of opportunity—exceed the unfavorable anticipations from these sources.

Theory of differential association: Developed by Sutherland, theory that combines some of the principles of behaviorism (or learning theory) with the notion that learning takes place in interaction within social groups.

Therapeutic approach: Informal and unofficial approach, being grounded in approaches that emphasize treatment and/or casework.

Totality of circumstances: Approach that considers surrounding contextual facts in determining the validity of the waiver. Circumstances considered include the age, competency, and educational level of the juvenile; his or her ability to understand the nature of the charges; and the methods used in and length of the interrogation.

Trephining: Process that consists of drilling holes in the skulls of those perceived as deviants to allow the evil spirits to escape.

Truancy courts: Attempt to address the underlying causes of the child's failure to attend school; may be held on school property.

Types of neglect: Consist of physical, emotional, and educational neglect.

Underclass: Socioeconomic designation in which large numbers of inner-city poor people are caught in a chronic generational cycle of poverty, low educational achievement, teenage parenthood, chronic unemployment, and welfare dependence. Theorists argue that antisocial behaviors become norms within chronically impoverished inner-city environments.

Uniform Crime Reports (UCRs): Reports published annually by the Federal Bureau of Investigation (FBI) providing a compilation of arrest data and categorizing offenses as Part I or Part II offenses. They are often referred to by the acronym UCRs. Police agencies submit information on clearances (arrest data) to the FBI annually. The FBI then constructs a statistical profile of crime in the United States based on these arrest data.

Uniform Juvenile Court Act: Act providing judicial procedures so that all parties are assured of fairness and recognition of legal rights.

United Nations Basic Principles on the Use of Restorative Justice Programmes in Criminal Matters: A document published by the United Nations that provides a clear example of how restorative justice processes have been widely adopted within the international community.

Unofficial probation: Option that occurs when the prosecutor indicates that he or she has a prosecutable case but also indicates that prosecution will be withheld if the suspect in question agrees to behave according to certain guidelines.

Unofficial sources of data: Methods for determining just how much crime or delinquency remains hidden from official measures of such behavior.

Unruly children: Children who may be disposed of by the court in any authorized disposition allowable for the delinquent except commitment to the state correctional agency. However, if an unruly child is found to be not amenable to treatment under the disposition, the court, after another hearing, may make any disposition otherwise authorized for the delinquent.

Urbanization: The process whereby societies move from agricultural and rural economies and living standards to those based on production, service industries, or information-related businesses that lead to the development of more urban settings.

Vice Lords: Also known as the Conservative Vice Lord Nation, gang whose members have aligned themselves with other groups such as the Latin Kings. These gangs are collectively referred to as "people" and are enemies of the Black Gangster Disciples.

Vice Queens: Female partner group of the Vice Lords. This female gang has broken the gender mold and engages in strong-arming, auto theft, and aggressive and violent behaviors.

Victim–offender mediation program: Programs that have a strong grounding in restorative justice principles by bringing the victim and the offender together in mediation. The desired result is closure and emotional healing on the part of the victim, with accountability and remorse being observed on the part of the offender.

Victim–offender reconciliation program: Program that brings the victim and the offender together to reconcile a criminal wrong that the offender has committed against the victim. It is a much more informal process than are standard court proceedings.

Victim survey research: Survey research that is derived from data provided by victims of crime.

Victims of crime impact panels (VCIPs): Community-based panels that strive to teach competency to offenders. They also attempt to develop offender empathy for understanding the impacts on the victims.

Violent Crime Index offenses: Consist of murder, forcible rape, robbery, and aggravated assault.

Wannabes: Youngsters who emulate older gang members by imitating their dress, speech, and symbols. These young imitators want to be identified as gang members and frequently aspire to joining the group.

White v. Illinois: U.S. Supreme Court ruling that affirmed the use of hearsay statements in child sexual abuse cases. In this case, the 4-year-old child victim did not testify, but others to whom she had talked about the assault (her mother, a doctor, a nurse, and a police officer) were allowed to testify.

Wilderness programs: Juvenile corrections programs centered on minimum-security residential correctional institutions that are located in rural settings. These programs are usually reserved for first-time offenders and/or juveniles who have committed minor offenses. Examples include forestry camps, ranches, and well-established programs such as Outward Bound.

Winship case: U.S. Supreme Court ruling that the standard of proof for conviction of juveniles should be the same as that for adults in criminal court—proof beyond a reasonable doubt—in juvenile court proceedings involving delinquency.

World Youth Report: A comprehensive document published by the United Nations that describes juvenile delinquency around the world.

XYY chromosome: Research suggesting that men with an XYY chromosomal pattern are more prevalent in prison populations than in society. These "supermales" are theoretically more aggressive than typical XY males.

Youth culture: Lifestyles that are peculiar to social associations of young people. There is no single youth culture but rather an assortment of lifestyles and selected identifications.

Youth-Focused Community Policing (YFCP): A program providing information-sharing activities that promote proactive partnerships among the police, juveniles, and community agencies cooperating to identify and address juvenile problems in a manner consistent with a community policing philosophy.

References

1 No. 18, The People & C., Respondent, v. Ricky Mitchell, Appellant (2004 NY Int. 49).

18 U.S.C. § 2251A(a) (2003).

18 U.S.C. § 2422(b) (2003).

18 U.S.C. 1466A (2008).

18 U.S.C. 1470 (2008).

18 U.S.C. 1591 (2008).

32A-1-1 NMSA. (1978).

Abadinsky, H. (2003). *Organized crime* (7th ed.). Belmont, CA: Wadsworth/Thomson Learning.

Abadinsky, H., & Winfree, L. T., Jr. (1992). *Crime and justice* (2nd ed.). Chicago, IL: Nelson-Hall.

Abundant Life Academy. (2006). *Boot camps are proving a helping hand for troubled teens.* Retrieved from www.restoretroubledteens.com/Boot-Camps-for-Teens.html

Ackerman, W. V. (1998). Socioeconomic correlates of increasing crime rates in smaller communities. *Professional Geographer, 50,* 372–387.

Adams, B., & Addie, S. (2011). *Delinquency cases waived to criminal court, 2008* (OJJDP Fact Sheet). Washington, DC: U.S. Department of Justice, Office of Juvenile Justice and Delinquency Prevention. Retrieved from www.ojjdp.gov/pubs/236481.pdf

Adams, N., & Connor, B. T. (2008). School violence: Bullying behaviors and the psychosocial school environment in middle schools. *Children & Schools, 30,* 211–221.

Adler, A. (1931). *What life should mean to you.* London, UK: Allen & Unwin.

Administration for Children and Families. (2008). *Child maltreatment 2008.* Washington, DC: U.S.

Department of Health and Human Services. Retrieved from www.acf.hhs.gov/programs/cb/pubs/cm08/figure3_5.htm

Administration for Children and Families. (2014). *Child maltreatment 2014.* Washington, DC: U.S. Department of Health and Human Services.

Agnew, R. (1985). A revised strain theory of delinquency. *Social Forces, 64,* 151–167.

Agnew, R. (1992). Foundation for a general strain theory of crime and delinquency. *Criminology, 30*(1), 47–87.

Agnew, R. (2001). Building on the foundation of general strain theory: Specifying the types of strain most likely to lead to crime and delinquency. *Journal of Research in Crime and Delinquency, 38,* 319–363.

Agnew, R. (2007). *Pressured into crime: An overview of general strain theory.* New York, NY: Oxford University Press.

Akers, R. L. (1964). Socioeconomic status and delinquent behavior: A retest. *Journal of Research in Crime and Delinquency, 10,* 38–46.

Akers, R. L. (1985). *Deviant behavior: A social learning approach* (3rd ed.). Belmont, CA: Wadsworth.

Akers, R. L. (1992). Linking sociology and its specialties: The case of criminology. *Social Forces, 71,* 1–16.

Akers, R. L. (1994). *Criminological theories: Introduction and evaluation.* Los Angeles, CA: Roxbury.

Akers, R. L. (1998). *Social learning and social structure: A general theory of crime and deviance.* Boston, MA: Northeastern University Press.

Akers, R. L., & Sellers, C. S. (2004). *Criminological theories: Introduction,*

evaluation, and application (4th ed.). Los Angeles, CA: Roxbury.

Alabama Code, 208, Title 12, Chapter 15, Section 12:15:102 (2013).

Alachua County Sheriff's Office. (2012). *SHOCAP.* Retrieved from http://acso.us/pdfs/Annual%20Report%202009%20Final%2005%202010.pdf

Allen, T. T. (2005). Taking a juvenile into custody: Situational factors that influence police officers' decisions. *Journal of Sociology and Social Welfare, 32,* 121–129.

Alston, F. K. (2013). *Latch key children.* New York, NY: NYU Child Study Center. Education.com. Retrieved from www.como.gov/ParksandRec/About_Us/documents/latch-key-children-education-2010.pdf

Alwin, D. F., & Thornton, A. (1984). Family origins and the schooling process: Early versus late influence of parental characteristics. *American Sociological Review, 49,* 784–802.

American Association for Marriage and Family Therapy. (2002). *Child abuse & neglect.* Retrieved from www.aamft.org/imis15/Content/Consumer_Updates/Child_Abuse_and_Neglect.aspx

American Bar Association. (1977). *Standards relating to counsel for private parties.* Cambridge, MA: Ballinger.

American Correctional Association. (2012). *Public correctional policies: 2012.* Retrieved from http://edpdlaw.com/ACA%20Policies.pdf

American Humane. (2008). *What should I know about reporting child abuse and neglect?* Retrieved from www.americanhumane.org/about-us/newsroom/fact-sheets/reporting-child-abuse-neglect.html

American Psychological Association. (2004). *School bullying is nothing new but psychologists identify new ways to prevent it.* Retrieved from www.apa.org/research/action/bullying.aspx

Americans for Divorce Reform. (2005, September 21). *Children of divorce: Crime statistics.* Retrieved from www.marriagedebate.com/pdf/imapp.crimefamstructure.pdf

Anderson, E. (1990). *Streetwise.* Chicago, IL: University of Chicago Press.

Aniskievicz, R., & Wysong, E. (1990). Evaluating DARE: Drug education and the multiple meanings of success. *Policy Studies Review, 9,* 727–747.

Annie E. Casey Foundation. (2009). *Two decades of JDAI: A progress report.* Baltimore, MD: Author. Retrieved from www.aecf.org/MajorInitiatives/~/media/Pubs/Initiatives/Juvenile%20Detention%20Alternatives%20Initiative/TwoDecadesofJDAIFromDemonstrationProjecttoNat/JDAI_National_final_10_07_09.pdf

Annie E. Casey Foundation. (2014). *Juvenile detentions alternative initiative: 2014 progress report.* Baltimore, MD: Author. Retrieved from www.aecf.org/m/resourcedoc/aecf-2014JDAIProgressReport-2014.pdf

Anwar, S., & Loughgran, T. A. (2011). Testing a Bayesian learning theory of deterrence among serious juvenile offenders. *Criminology, 49*(3), 667–698.

Arda, T. B, & Ocak, S. (2012). Social competence and promoting alternative thinking strategies—PATHS preschool curriculum. *Educational Sciences: Theory & Practice, 12*(4), 2691–2698.

Arkansas Code Ann. § 12-12-503 (12)(b) (2001).

Armagh, D. (1998). A safety net for the Internet: Protecting our children. *Juvenile Justice Journal, 5*(1), 9–15. Retrieved from www.ojjdp.ncjrs.gov/jjjournal/jjjournal598/net.html

Armour, J., & Hammond, S. (2009, January). *Minority youth in the juvenile justice system: Disproportionate minority contact.* Washington, DC: National Conference of State Legislatures. Retrieved from www.ncsl.org

Arnold, H., & Rockinson-Szapkiw, A. J. (2012). Bullying in the school system: What does it look like? *Conflict Resolution & Negotiation Journal, 2012*(3), 68–79.

Aslanian, S. (2016, May 12). *Victims, not criminals: Rebranding teen sex trafficking.* Retrieved from www.americanradioworks.org/segments/victims-teen-sex-trafficking

Attorney General of Texas. (2002). *Gangs in Texas 2001: An overview.* Retrieved from www.oag.state.tx.us/AG_Publications/pdfs/2001gangrept.pdf

Augustyn, M., & McGloin, J. (2013). The risk of informal socializing with peers: Considering gender differences across predatory delinquency and substance use. *Justice Quarterly, 30*(1), 117–143.

Australian Bureau of Statistics. (2005). *Personal safety survey Australia* (Cat No. 4906.0). Canberra, Australia: Author. Retrieved from www.ausstats.abs.gov.au/ausstats/subscriber.nsf/0/056A404DAA576AE6CA2571D00080E985/$File/49060_2005%20(reissue).pdf

Ayers, S., Wagaman, M. M., Geiger, J., Bermudez-Parsai, M., & Hedberg, E. E. (2012). Examining school-based bullying interventions using multilevel discrete time hazard modeling. *Prevention Science, 13*(5), 539–550.

Babicky, T. (1993a). *Gangs fact sheets: A reference guide.* Springfield, IL: Illinois Department of Corrections.

Babicky, T. (1993b). *Gangs and gang activity.* Springfield, IL: Illinois Department of Corrections.

Backstrom, J. C., & Walker, G. L. (2006). The role of the prosecutor in juvenile justice: Advocacy in the courtroom and leadership in the community. *William Mitchell Law Review, 32*(3), 964–988.

Bahr, S. J., Masters, A. L., & Taylor, B. M. (2012). What works in substance abuse treatment programs for offenders? *Prison Journal, 92*(2), 155–174.

Barlow, H. D. (2000). *Criminal justice in America.* Upper Saddle River, NJ: Prentice Hall.

Baron, R., Feeney, F., & Thornton, W. (1973). Preventing delinquency through diversion: The Sacramento County 601 diversion project. *Federal Probation, 37,* 13–18.

Baron, S. W. (2004). General strain, street youth, and crime: A test of Agnew's revised theory. *Criminology, 42,* 457–483.

Bartollas, C. (1993). *Juvenile delinquency* (3rd ed.). New York, NY: Macmillan.

Battistich, V., & Hom, A. (1997). The relationship between students' sense of their school as a community and their involvement in problem behaviors. *American Journal of Public Health, 87,* 1997–2001.

Bauer, L., Guerino, P., Nolle, K. L., Tang, S.-W., & Chandler, K. (2008, October). *Student victimization in U.S. schools: Results from the 2005 School Crime Supplement to the National Crime Victimization Survey.* Washington, DC: U.S. Department of Education. Retrieved from http://nces.ed.gov/pubs2009/2009306.pdf

Baumer, E., & Lauritsen, J. L. (2009). Reporting crime to the police, 1973–2005: A multivariate analysis of longterm trends in the NCS and NCVS. *Criminology, 48*(1), 131–185.

Bazemore, G., & Day, S. E. (1996). Restoring the balance: Juvenile and community justice. *Juvenile Justice, 3*(1), 3–14.

Bazemore, G., & Senjo, S. (1997). Police encounters with juveniles revisited: An exploratory study of themes and styles in community policing. *Policing: An International Journal of Police Strategy and Management, 20,* 60–82.

Bazemore, G., & Washington, C. (1995). Charting the future of the juvenile justice system: Reinventing mission and management. *Spectrum: The Journal of State Government, 68*(2), 51–66.

BBC News. (2007). *China youth crime "in rapid rise."* Retrieved from http://news.bbc.co.uk/2/hi/asia-pacific/7128213.stm

Beale, A. V., & Hall, K. R. (2007). Cyber bullying: What school administrators (and parents) can do. *The Clearing House, 18,* 8–12.

Beaver, K. M., Gibson, C. L., DeLisi, M., Vaughn, M. G., & Wright, J. P. (2012). The interaction between neighborhood disadvantage and genetic factors in the prediction of antisocial outcomes. *Youth Violence and Juvenile Justice, 10*(1), 25–40.

Becker, H. S. (1963). *The outsiders.* New York, NY: Free Press.

Beirne, P., & Quinney, R. (1982). *Marxism and the law.* New York, NY: Wiley.

Belknap, J., Morash, M., & Trojanowicz, R. (1987). Implementing a community policing model for work with juveniles. *Criminal Justice and Behavior, 14,* 211–245.

Bell, D. J., & Bell, S. (1991). The victim-offender relationship as a determinant factor in police dispositions of family violence incidents: A replication study. *Policing and Society, 1,* 225–234.

Benekos, P. J., & Merlo, A. V. (2008). Juvenile justice: The legacy of punitive policy. *Youth Violence and Juvenile Justice, 6*(8), 28–46.

Benekos, P. J., Merlo, A. V., & Puzzanchera, C. M. (2011). Youth, race, and serious crime: Examining trends and critiquing policy. *International Journal of Police Science & Management, 13*(2), 132–148.

Berman, G., & Fox, A. (2009). *Lessons from the battle over D.A.R.E.: The complicated relationship between research and practice.* New York, NY: Center for Court Innovation. Retrieved from www.ojp.usdoj.gov/BJA/pdf/CCI_DARE.pdf

Bernard, T. J. (1990). Twenty years of testing theories: What have we learned and why? *Journal of Research in Crime and Delinquency, 27,* 325–347.

Bernard, T. J. (1992). *The cycle of juvenile justice.* New York, NY: Oxford University Press.

Bernburg, J. G., Krohn, M. D., & Rivera, C. J. (2006). Official labeling, criminal embeddedness, and subsequent delinquency: A longitudinal test of labeling theory. *Journal of Research in Crime and Delinquency, 43*(1), 67–88.

Beyer, M. (2003). *Best practices in juvenile accountability: Overview. JAIBG Bulletin.* Washington, DC: U.S. Department of Justice, Office of Justice Programs, Office of Juvenile Justice and Delinquency Prevention.

Bilchik, S. (1998a). A juvenile justice system for the 21st century. *Crime & Delinquency, 44,* 89–101.

Bilchik, S. (1998b). *Juvenile Mentoring Program: 1998 report to Congress.* Washington, DC: U.S. Department of Justice.

Bilchik, S. (1999a). *Juvenile justice: A century of change.* Washington, DC: U.S. Department of Justice.

Bilchik, S. (1999b). *OJJDP research: Making a difference for juveniles.* Washington, DC: U.S. Department of Justice.

Bilchik, S. (1999c). *1997 National Youth Gang Survey.* Washington, DC: U.S. Department of Justice.

Bishop, D. (2004). Injustice and irrationality in contemporary youth policy. *Criminology and Public Policy, 3,* 633–644.

Bishop, S. J., Murphy, J. M., & Hicks, R. (2000). What progress has been made in meeting the needs of seriously maltreated children? The course of 200 cases through the Boston Juvenile Court. *Child Abuse & Neglect, 24,* 599–610.

Bishop, T. (2010, March 3). 3 reputed cult members convicted in toddler's death. *Baltimore Sun.* Retrieved from http://articles.baltimoresun.com/2010-03-03/news/bal-md.cult03mar03_1_toddler-s-death-steven-bynum-trevia-williams

Bjerregaard, B. (2010). Gang membership and drug involvement: Untangling the complex relationship. *Crime and Delinquency, 56*(1), 3–34.

Black, D. J., & Reiss, A. J., Jr. (1970). Police control of juveniles. *American Sociological Review, 35,* 63–77.

Blackstone, W. (1803). *Commentaries on the laws of England* (12th ed., Vol. 4). London, UK: Strahan.

Blair, S. L., Blair, M. C. L., & Madamba, A. B. (1999). Racial/ethnic differences in high school students' Blumberg academic performance: Understanding the interweave of social class and ethnicity in family context. *Journal of Comparative Family Studies, 30,* 539–555.

Blankenship, R. L., & Singh, B. K. (1976). Differential labeling of juveniles: A multivariate analysis. *Criminology, 13,* 471–490.

Bloom, B., Owen, B., & Covington, S. (2003). *Gender responsive strategies: Research, practice, and guiding principles for women offenders.* Washington, DC: National Institute of Corrections.

Blumberg, A. S. (1967). *Criminal justice.* Chicago, IL: Quadrangle.

Bohm, R. M. (2001). *A primer on crime and delinquency theory* (2nd ed.). Belmont, CA: Wadsworth.

Bohnstedt, M. (1978). Answers to three questions about juvenile diversion. *Journal of Research in Crime and Delinquency, 15,* 109–123.

Boisvert, D., Wright, J., Knopik, V., & Vaske, J. (2012). Genetic and environmental overlap between low self-control and delinquency. *Journal of Quantitative Criminology, 28*(3), 477–507.

Bookin, H., & Horowitz, R. (1983). The end of the youth gang: Fad or fiction? *Criminology, 21,* 585–602.

Boot Camps for Teens. (n.d.). *Welcome to boot camps for teens.* Retrieved from www.bootcampsforteens.com

Booth, A., & Osgood, D. W. (1993). The influence of testosterone on deviance in adulthood: Assessing and explaining the relationship. *Criminology, 31*, 93–117.

Bossler, A. M., Holt, T. J., & May, D. C. (2012). Predicting online harassment victimization among a juvenile population. *Youth & Society, 44*(4), 500–523.

Botch, D. (2006). Reforming the American justice system. *Public Administration Review, 66*, 640–643.

Bottrell, D., Armstrong, D., & France, A. (2010). Young people's relations to crime: Pathways across ecologies. *Youth Justice, 10*(1), 56–72.

Bouffard, J. A. (2007). Predicting differences in the perceived relevance of crime's costs and benefits in a test of rational choice theory. *International Journal of Offender Therapy and Comparative Criminology, 51*(4), 461–485.

Bowker, A., & Sullivan, M. (2010, July). *Sexting: Risky actions and overreactions.* FBI Law Enforcement Bulletin. Washington, DC: Federal Bureau of Investigation. Retrieved from https://leb.fbi.gov/2010/july/sexting-risky-actions-and-overreactions

Bowman, J. H., Krohn, M. D., Gibson, C. I., & Stogner, J. M. (2012). Investigating friendship quality: An exploration of self-control and social control theories' friendship hypotheses. *Journal of Youth and Adolescence, 41*(11), 1526–1540.

Bradley, C. M. (2006, March/April). The right decision on the juvenile death penalty. *Judicature, 89*, 302–305. Retrieved from http://proquest.umi .com/pqdweb?did=1039951891& sid=3&Fmt=3&clientId=59796&RQ T=309&VName=PQD

Bradshaw, W., & Roseborough, D. (2005). Restorative justice dialogue: The impact of mediation and conferencing on juvenile recidivism. *Federal Probation, 69*(2), 15–21. Retrieved from http://heinonline.org/HOL/LandingPage?collection=jour nals&handle=hein.journals/fedpro69&div=21&id=&page=

Braithwaite, J. (1989). *Crime, shame, and reintegration.* New York, NY: Cambridge University Press.

Braun, C. (1976). Teacher expectations: Sociopsychological dynamics. *Review of Educational Research, 46*, 185–213.

Breed v. Jones, 421 U.S. 519, 95 S. Ct. 1779 (1975).

Broaddus, E. T., Scott, K. E., Gonsalves, L. M., Parrish, C., Rhodes, E. L., Donovan, S. E., & Winch, P. J. (2013). Building connections between officers and Baltimore City youth: Key components of a police–youth teambuilding program. *Journal of Juvenile Justice, 3*(1), 1–4. Retrieved from www .journalofjuvjustice.org/JOJJ0301/article04.htm

Brown, B. (2006). Understanding and assessing school police officers: A conceptual and methodological comment. *Journal of Criminal Justice, 34*, 591–598.

Brown, J., Cohen, P., Johnson, J., & Salzinger, S. (1998). A longitudinal analysis of risk factors for child maltreatment: Findings of a 17-year prospective study of officially recorded and self-reported child abuse and neglect. *Child Abuse & Neglect, 22*, 1065–1078.

Brown, J. R., Aalsma, M. C., & Ott, M. A. (2013). The experiences of parents who report youth bullying victimization to school officials. *Journal of Interpersonal Violence, 28*(3), 494–518.

Brown, S. A. (2012, June). *Trends in juvenile justice state legislation 2001–2011.* Washington, DC: National Conference of State Legislatures. Retrieved from www.ncsl.org/documents/cj/TrendsInJuvenileJustice.pdf

Brown, S. L. (2004). Family structure, family processes, and adolescent delinquency: The significance of parental absence versus parental gender. *Journal of Research in Crime and Delinquency, 41*(1), 58–81.

Browning, C. R., Byron, R. A., Calder, C. A., Krivo, L. J., Kwan, M.-P.,

Lee, J.-Y., & Peterson, R. D. (2010). Commercial density, residential concentration, and crime: Land use patterns and violence in neighborhood context. *Journal of Research in Crime and Delinquency, 47*(3), 329–357.

Browning, K., & Loeber, R. (1999, February). *Highlights of findings from the Pittsburgh Youth Study* (OJJDP Fact Sheet No. 95). Washington, DC: U.S. Department of Justice.

Buerger, M. E., Cohn, E. G., & Petrosino, A. J. (2000). Defining the hot spots of crime. In R. W. Glensor, M. E. Corriea, & K. J. Peak (Eds.), *Policing communities: Understanding crime and solving problems* (pp. 138–150). Los Angeles, CA: Roxbury.

Bugliosi, V. (1997). *Outrage: 5 reasons why O. J. Simpson got away with murder.* Seattle, WA: Island Books.

Buka, S. L., Stichick, T. L., Birdthistle, I., & Earls, F. J. (2001). Youth exposure to violence: Prevalence, risks, and consequences. *American Journal of Orthopsychiatry, 71*(3), 298–310.

BullyingStatistics.com. (2009). *Cyber bullying.* Retrieved from www .bullyingstatistics.org/content/cyber-bullying.html

Bumphus, V. W., & Anderson, J. F. (1999). Family structure and race in a sample of criminal offenders. *Journal of Criminal Justice, 27*, 309–320.

Burch, J., & Kane, C. (1999, July). *Implementing the OJJDP comprehensive gang model* (OJJDP Fact Sheet No. 112). Washington, DC: U.S. Department of Justice.

Bureau of Justice Assistance. (2003). *Juvenile drug courts: Strategies in practice.* Washington, DC: U.S. Department of Justice.

Bureau of Justice Statistics. (2005). *Family violence statistics: Including statistics on strangers and acquaintances.* Washington, DC: U.S. Department of Justice, Office of Justice Programs. Retrieved from www.bjs .gov/content/pub/pdf/fvs02.pdf

Bureau of Justice Statistics. (2007). *Federal prosecution of child sexual exploitation offenders, 2006.* Washington, DC: U.S. Department of Justice. Retrieved from www.bjs.gov/content/pub/pdf/fpcseo06.pdf

Bureau of Justice Statistics. (2012). Table 17.1 Percentage of students ages 12–18 who reported being afraid of attack or harm, by location and selected student and school characteristics: Various years, 1995–2007. In *Indicators of school crime and safety 2011.* Washington, DC: U.S. Government Printing Office.

Bureau of Labor Statistics. (2011). *Police officer.* Retrieved from www.bls.gov/k12/law01.htm

Bureau of Labor Statistics. (2017, April). *Employment projections.* Retrieved from https://www.bls.gov/emp/ep_chart_001.htm

Burgess, E. W. (1952). The economic factor in juvenile delinquency. *Journal of Criminal Law, 43,* 29–42.

Burgess, R. L., & Akers, R. L. (1968). A differential association-reinforcement theory of criminal behavior. *Social Problems, 14,* 128–147.

Bursik, R. J., & Grasmick, H. G. (1995). The effect of neighborhood dynamics on gang behavior. In M. Klein, C. L. Maxson, & J. Miller (Eds.), *The modern gang reader* (pp. 114–123). Los Angeles, CA: Roxbury.

Butler-Mejia, K. (1998). *Seen but not heard: The role of voice in juvenile justice* (Unpublished master's thesis). George Mason University, Fairfax, VA.

Butts, J. A. (1997). Necessarily relative: Is juvenile justice speedy enough? *Crime & Delinquency, 43,* 3–23.

Butts, J. A., & Buck, J. (2000). *Teen courts: A focus on research.* Washington, DC: Office of Juvenile Justice and Delinquency Prevention. Retrieved from www.ncjrs.gov/pdffiles1/ojjdp/183472.pdf

Bynum, J. E., & Thompson, W. E. (1992). *Juvenile delinquency* (2nd ed.). Boston, MA: Allyn & Bacon.

Bynum, J. E., & Thompson, W. E. (1999). *Juvenile delinquency* (4th ed.). Boston, MA: Allyn & Bacon.

Cadzow, S. P., Armstrong, K. L., & Fraser, J. A. (1999). Stressed parents with infants: Reassessing physical abuse risk factors. *Child Abuse & Neglect, 23,* 845–853.

Califano, J. A., Jr., & Colson, C. W. (2005, January). Criminal neglect. *USA Today,* pp. 34–35.

California Code, Welfare and Institutions Code, art. 6, Dependent Children—jurisdiction (2010).

California Department of Corrections and Rehabilitation. (2013). *Youth correctional counselor careers.* Sacramento, CA: Author.

California Senate Bill 9. (2012). Chapter 828. An act to amend Section 1170 of the Penal Code, relating to sentencing. Retrieved from http://leginfo.legislature.ca.gov/faces/billNavClient.xhtml?bill_id=201120120SB9

Campaign for U.S. Ratification of the Convention on the Rights of the Child (CRC). (n.d.). *About us.* Retrieved from http://childrightscampaign.org/crcindex.php?sNav=about_snav.php&sDat=about_dat.php

Campbell, A. (1995). Female participation in gangs. In M. W. Klein, C. L. Maxson, & J. Miller (Eds.), *The modern gang reader* (pp. 70–77). Los Angeles, CA: Roxbury.

Canter, R. (1982). Family correlates of male and female delinquency. *Criminology, 20,* 149–167.

Carbone-Lopez, K., Esbensen, F., & Brick, B. T. (2010). Correlates and consequences of peer victimization: Gender differences in direct and indirect forms of bullying. *Youth Violence & Juvenile Justice, 8(4),* 332–350.

Carelli, R. (1990, June 28). Court backs sparing children in abuse cases. *Peoria Journal Star,* p. A2.

Carnevale Associates. (2006). *A longitudinal evaluation of the new curricula for the D.A.R.E. middle (7th grade) and high school (9th grade) programs: Take charge of your life—Year four progress report.* Retrieved from www.dare.com/home/Resources/documents/DAREMarch06ProgressReport.pdf

Cauchon, D. (1993, October 11). Studies find drug program not effective. *USA Today,* pp. 1A–2A.

Cavan, R. S. (1969). *Juvenile delinquency: Development, treatment, control* (2nd ed.). Philadelphia, PA: J. B. Lippincott.

Center for Children and Families. (2012). *CASA for children.* Retrieved from http://cfcnela.org/CASAResources.htm

Center for Restorative Justice and Mediation. (1985). *Principles of restorative justice.* St. Paul, MN: University of Minnesota, School of Social Work.

Center for Restorative Justice and Mediation. (1996). *Restorative justice: For victims, communities and offenders—What is restorative justice?* St. Paul, MN: University of Minnesota, School of Social Work.

Centers for Disease Control and Prevention. (2011). *Youth Risk Behavior Surveillance System (YRBSS).* Retrieved from www.cdc.gov/HealthyYouth/yrbs/index.htm

Centers for Disease Control and Prevention. (2012). Gang homicides: Five U.S. cities, 2003–2008. *Morbidity and Mortality Weekly Report, 61(3),* 45–51.

Centers for Disease Control and Prevention. (2013). *Understanding school violence: Fact sheet.* Retrieved from www.cdc.gov/violenceprevention/pdf/school_violence_fact_sheet-a.pdf

Centers for Disease Control and Prevention. (2016). *Sexual violence: Consequences.* Washington, DC: National Center for Injury Prevention and Control. Retrieved from www.cdc.gov/violenceprevention/sexualviolence/consequences.html

Centerwood, B. S. (1992). Television and violence: The scale of the problem and where to go from here. *Journal of the American Medical Association, 267*, 3059–3063.

Chambliss, W. J. (1973). The saints and the roughnecks. *Society, 11*, 24–31.

Chambliss, W. J. (1984). *Criminal law in action* (2nd ed.). New York, NY: Wiley.

Chambliss, W. J., & Mandoff, M. (1976). *Whose law, what order?* New York, NY: Wiley.

Champion, D. (2002). *Probation, parole, and community corrections* (4th ed.). Upper Saddle River, NJ: Prentice Hall.

Charton, S. (2001, July 16). Sheriff says making kids shovel manure stinks. *Chicago Sun-Times*, p. 28.

Chawla, M. J. (2006, December 20). The role of referees in district court. *The Hennepin Lawyer*. Retrieved from http://hennepin.timber lakepublishing.com/article .asp?article=1079&pape r=1&cat=148

Cheesman, F. (2011). *A decade of NCSC research on blended sentencing of juvenile offenders: What have we learned about "who gets a second chance?"* Retrieved from www.ncsc .org/sitecore/content/microsites/ future-trends-2011/home/Special-Programs/4-4-Blended-Sentencing-of-Juvenile-Offenders.aspx

Chesney-Lind, M. (1989). Girl's crime and woman's place: Toward a feminist model of female delinquency. *Crime & Delinquency, 35*, 5–29.

Chesney-Lind, M. (1999). Challenging girls' invisibility in juvenile court. *Annals of the American Academy of Political & Social Science, 564*, 185–202.

Chesney-Lind, M. (2013). How can we prevent girls from joining gangs? In N. M. Ritter & T. R. Simon (Eds.), *Changing course: Preventing gang membership: Executive summary* (pp. 121–133). Washington, DC: National Institute of Justice.

Child Abuse Prevention and Treatment Act (CAPTA), 42 U.S.C. § 5101 (2010).

Child Trends DataBank. (2013). *Unsafe at school*. Retrieved from http://childtrendsdatabank .org/?q=node/323

Child Welfare Information Gateway. (2006). *Child neglect: A guide for prevention, assessment and intervention*. Retrieved from www .childwelfare.gov/pubs/ usermanuals/neglect/chaptersix.cfm

Child Welfare Information Gateway. (2009). *Definitions of child abuse and neglect: Summary of state laws*. Retrieved from www.childwelfare .gov/systemwide/laws_policies/ statutes/define.cfm

Child Welfare Information Gateway. (2013a). *Child maltreatment 2011: Summary of key findings*. Washington, DC: U.S. Department of Health and Human Services, Children's Bureau. Retrieved from www.childwelfare.gov/ pubs/factsheets/canstats .pdf#Page=2&view=What%20 Were%20the%20Most%20 Common%20Types%20of%20 Maltreatment?

Child Welfare Information Gateway. (2013b). *How the child welfare system works*. Washington, DC: U.S. Department of Health and Human Services. Retrieved from www.childwelfare.gov/ pubs/factsheets/cpswork. pdf#page=3&view=What%20 Happens%20When%20Possible%20 Abuse%20or%20 Neglect%20Is%20 Reported

Child Welfare Information Gateway. (2014). *Foster care statistics: 2014*. Retrieved from www. childwelfare.gov/pubPDFs/foster .pdf#page=3&view=Children%20 in,%20entering,%20and%20 exiting%20care

Child Welfare Information Gateway. (2015). *Mandatory reporters of child abuse and neglect*. Retrieved from www.childwelfare.gov/ pubPDFs/manda.pdf#page=1& view=Introduction

Child Welfare Information Gateway. (2016). *Definitions of child abuse and neglect*. Washington, DC: U.S. Department of Health and Human Services, Children's Bureau. Retrieved from www.childwelfare .gov/pubPDFs/define.pdf

Children's Bureau. (1969). *Legislative guide for drafting family and juvenile court acts*. Washington, DC: U.S. Government Printing Office.

Children's Defense Fund. (2006). *Poverty*. Retrieved from cdf. childrensdefense.org/site/ PageServer?pagename=OH_kids_ count_maps_2006

Christensen, H., Pallister, E., Smale, S., Hickie, I. B., & Calear, A. L. (2010). Community-based prevention programs for anxiety and depression in youth: A systematic review. *Journal of Primary Prevention, 31*(3), 139–170.

Chu, J. (2005, August 8). You wanna take this online? Cyberspace is the 21st century bully's playground where girls play rougher than boys. *Time*. Retrieved from www.time.com/time/magazine/ article/0,9171,1088698,00.html

Church, W. T., II, Wharton, T., & Taylor, J. K. (2009). Examination of differential association and social control theory: Family systems and delinquency. *Youth Violence and Juvenile Justice, 7*(1), 3–15.

City of Camdenton Police Department. (2007). *City of Camdenton annual report 2007*. Retrieved from www .camdentoncity.com/Police/PA2007 .pdf

City of Tallahassee. (2013). *Tallahassee Police Athletic League, Inc.* Retrieved from www.volunteermatch.org/ search/org21381.jsp

City of Wichita Police Department. (2010). *Police-school liaison program*. Retrieved from www.wichita .gov/CityOffices/Police/Schools/ SchoolLiaison

Clark, J. P., & Tifft, L. L. (1966). Polygraph and interview validation of self-reported deviant behavior. *American Sociological Review, 4*, 516–523.

Clark, P. (2011). Preventing future crime with cognitive behavioral therapy. *American Jails, 25*(1), 45–48.

Clear, T. R., & Cole, G. F. (2003). *American corrections* (6th ed.). Belmont, CA: Wadsworth/Thomson Learning.

Clemson University. (2013). *The Olweus bullying prevention program*. Retrieved from www.clemson.edu/olweus/

Cloward, R. A., & Ohlin, L. E. (1960). *Delinquency and opportunity*. Glencoe, IL: Free Press.

Cobbina, J. E., Like-Haislip, T. Z., & Miller, J. (2010). Gang fights versus cat fights: Urban young men's gendered narratives of violence. *Deviant Behavior, 31*(7), 596–853.

Cohen, A. K. (1955). *Delinquent boys: The culture of the gang*. Glencoe, IL: Free Press.

Cohn, A. W. (1999a). Juvenile focus. *Federal Probation, 58*, 87–91.

Cohn, A. W. (1999b). Juvenile justice in transition: Is there a future? *Federal Probation, 62*(2), 61–67.

Cohn, A. W. (2004). Planning for the future of juvenile justice. *Federal Probation, 68*(3), 39–44.

Colorado Revised Statutes, 19-2-107 (2002).

Colorado Revised Statutes, 19-2-110 (2012).

Colorado Revised Statutes Annotated, 19-2-511 (1) (2009).

Colydas, V., & McLeod, M. (1997). *Colonie (NY) youth court evaluation* (Unpublished manuscript). Russell Sage College, Troy, NY.

Commonwealth Secretariat. (2016). *Global youth development index and report—2016*. London, UK: Commonwealth Secretariat.

Conklin, J. E. (1998). *Criminology* (6th ed.). Boston, MA: Allyn & Bacon.

Connecticut General Statutes Annotated, sec. 46b-133b (2012).

Consolidated Laws of New York Annotated, McKinney (1975).

Contra Costa County's truancy court goes after parents. (2016, January 2). *East Bay Times*. Retrieved from www.eastbaytimes.com/2016/01/02/contra-costa-countys-first-truancy-court-goes-after-parents

Coohey, C. (1998). Home alone and other inadequately supervised children. *Child Welfare, 77*, 291–310.

Costanza, S. E., & Kilburn, J. C., Jr. (2004). Circling the welcome wagons: Area, income, race, and legal handgun concealment. *Criminal Justice Review, 29*, 289–303.

Costello, B. J., & Vowell, P. R. (1999). Testing control theory and differential association: A reanalysis of the Richmond Youth Project data. *Criminology, 37*, 815–842.

Cote, S. (2002). *Criminological theories: Bridging the past to the future*. Thousand Oaks, CA: Sage.

Cothern, L. (2000, November). *Juveniles and the death penalty*. Washington, DC: U.S. Department of Justice, Coordinating Council on Juvenile Justice and Delinquency Prevention.

Covington, J. (1984). Insulation from labeling: Deviant defenses in treatment. *Criminology, 22*, 619–643.

Cox, S. M. (1975). Review of "Critique of Legal Order." *Teaching Sociology, 3*(1), 97–99.

Cox, S. M., & Wade, J. E. (1996). *The criminal justice network: An introduction*. Boston, MA: McGraw-Hill.

Craddock, A. (2000). *Exploratory analysis of client outcomes, costs, and benefits of day reporting centers—Final report* (NIJ Grant No. 97-IJ-CX-0006). Retrieved from www.ncjrs.gov/pdffiles1/nij/grants/182365.pdf

Craddock, A., & Graham, L. A. (2001). Recidivism as a function of day reporting center participation. *Journal of Offender Rehabilitation, 34*, 81–100.

Creaney, S. (2012). Risk, prevention and early intervention: Youth justice responses to girls. *Safer Communities, 11*(2), 111–120.

Cromwell, P. F., Jr., Killinger, G. G., Kerper, H. B., & Walker, C. (1985). *Probation and parole in the criminal justice system* (2nd ed.). St. Paul, MN: West.

Crosson-Tower, C. (1999). *Understanding child abuse and neglect* (4th ed.). Boston, MA: Allyn & Bacon.

C.R.S. 19-2-509 (2012).

Cruz, B. K., & Cruz J. A. (2007). *Age-graded attachment theory: Conduct disorder and juvenile delinquency*. National Social Science Association. Retrieved from www.nssa.us/journals/2008-29-2/2008-29-2-03.htm

Cunningham, S. M. (2003). The joint contribution of experiencing and witnessing violence during childhood on child abuse in the parent role. *Violence and Victims, 18*, 619–639.

Curran, D. J., & Renzetti, C. M. (1994). *Theories of crime*. Boston, MA: Allyn & Bacon.

Curry, G. D., & Spergel, I. A. (1988). Gang homicide, delinquency, and community. *Criminology, 26*, 381–405.

Cyr, M., McDuff, P., Wright, J., Theriault, C., & Cinq-Mars, C. (2005). Clinical correlates and repetition of self-harming behaviors among female adolescent victims of sexual abuse. *Journal of Child Sexual Abuse, 14*(2), 49–68.

Daly, K., & Chesney-Lind, M. (1988). Feminism and criminology. *Justice Quarterly, 5*, 497–538.

D.A.R.E. (2012). *New D.A.R.E. middle school curriculum—"Keepin' it REAL."* Retrieved from www.dare.com/newdare.asp

Darnell, A. J., & Emshoff, J. G. (2008). *Findings from the evaluation of the D.A.R.E. Prescription and Over-the-Counter Drug Curriculum*. Atlanta, GA: Emstar Research. Retrieved from www.dare.com/home/Resources/documents/DAREReport0821_final.pdf

Dart, R. W. (1992). *Street gangs*. Chicago, IL: Chicago Police Department.

Davidson, H. (1981). The guardian ad litem: An important approach to the protection of children. *Children Today, 10*(2), 20–23.

Davidson, N. (1990). Life without father. *Policy Review, 51*, 40–44.

Davidson, W. S., Redner, R., & Amdur, R. L. (1990). Alternative treatments for troubled youth: The case of diversion from the justice system. New York, NY: Plenum.

Davis, K. C. (1975). *Police discretion*. St. Paul, MN: West.

Davis, N. J. (1999). Youth crisis: Growing up in a high-risk society. Westport, CT: Praeger.

Davis, S. M. (2001). *Rights of juveniles*. New York, NY: Clark Boardman/West.

Dawkins, M. P. (1997). Drug use and violent crime among juveniles. *Adolescence, 32*, 395–405.

Dawley, D. (1973). *A nation of lords*. New York, NY: Doubleday.

Dean, A. (2017, January 4). Woman arrested for starving her children. *Dawson County News*.

Death Penalty Information Center. (n.d.). *DPIC summary of Roper v. Simmons*. Retrieved from www.deathpenaltyinfo.org/article.php?scid=38& did=885

de Beus, K., & Rodriguez, N. (2007). Restorative justice practice: An examination of program completion and recidivism. *Journal of Criminal Justice, 35*(3), 337–347.

Decker, S. H. (2005). *European street gangs and troublesome youth groups: Violence prevention and policy*. Lanham, MD: AltaMira Press.

Decker, S. H. (2008). *Strategies to address gang crime: A guidebook for local law enforcement*. Washington, DC: Office of Community Oriented Police Services.

Decker, S. H., & Van Winkle, B. (1996). *Life in the gang: Family, friends, and violence*. New York, NY: Cambridge University Press.

Defense: Police never read rights to teen suspect in Mercer Co. murder. (2016). Retrieved from www.wkyt.com/content/news/Defense-Police-never-read-rights-to-teen-suspect-in-Mercer-Co-murder-398203531.html

DeLisi, M. M., Wright, J. P., & Vaughn, M. G. (2010). Nature and nurture by definition means both: A response to males. *Journal of Adolescent Research, 25*(1), 24–30.

Dembo, R., Wareham, J., & Schmeidler, J. (2005). Evaluation of the impact of a policy change on diversion program recidivism. *Journal of Offender Rehabilitation, 41*(3), 29–61.

Demuth, S., & Brown, S. L. (2004). Family structure, family processes, and adolescent delinquency: The significance of parental absence versus parental gender. *Journal of Research in Crime and Delinquency, 41*, 58–81.

Dennis, J. P. (2012). Girls will be girls: Childhood gender polarization and delinquency. *Feminist Criminology, 7*(3), 220–233.

Denno, D. W. (1994). Gender, crime, and the criminal law defenses. *Journal of Criminal Law and Criminology, 85*, 80–180.

Dentler, R. A., & Monroe, L. J. (1961). Early adolescent theft. *American Sociological Review, 26*, 733–743.

DePaul, J., & Domenech, L. (2000). Childhood history of abuse and child abuse potential in adolescent mothers: A longitudinal study. *Child Abuse & Neglect, 24*, 701–713.

DiLillo, D., Tremblay, G. C., & Peterson, L. (2000). Linking childhood sexual abuse and abusive parenting: The mediating role of maternal anger. *Child Abuse & Neglect, 24*, 767–779.

Dissel, A. (1997). *Youth, street gangs, and violence in South Africa*. Johannesburg, South Africa: Centre for the Study of Violence and Reconciliation. Retrieved from www.csvr.org.za/wits/papers/papganga.htm

Dorne, C., & Gewerth, K. (1998). *American juvenile justice: Cases, legislation, and comments*. San Francisco, CA: Austin & Winfield.

Drowns, R. W., & Hess, K. M. (1990). *Juvenile justice*. St. Paul, MN: West.

Drug Policy Alliance. (2010). *D.A.R.E. fact sheet*. Retrieved from www.drugpolicy.org/library/factsheets/dare/index.cfm

Dugdale, R. L. (1888). *The Jukes: A study in crime, pauperism, disease, and heredity*. New York, NY: Putnam.

Dukes, R. L., Stein, J. A., & Ullman, J. B. (1997). Long term impact of Drug Abuse Resistance Education (D.A.R.E.). *Evaluation Review, 21*, 483–500.

Durkin, K. F. (1997). Misuse of the Internet by pedophiles: Implications for law enforcement and probation practice. *Federal Probation, 61*, 14–18.

Echeburua, E., Fernandez-Montalvo, J., & Baez, C. (2000). Relapse prevention in the treatment of slot-machine pathological gambling. *Behavior Therapy, 31*, 351–364.

Eddings v. Oklahoma, 455 U.S. 104 (1982).

Edwards, L. P. (2005). The role of the juvenile court judge revisited. *Juvenile and Family Court Journal, 56*(1), 33–45.

Egley, A., & Howell, J. C. (2012). *Highlights of the 2010 National Youth Gang Survey*. Washington, DC: Office of Juvenile Justice and Delinquency Prevention.

Egley, A., Howell, J. C., & Harris, M. (2014). *Highlights of the 2012 National Youth Gang Survey*. Washington, DC: Office of Juvenile Justice and Delinquency Prevention.

Ehrenreich, B. (1990). The hourglass society. *New Perspectives Quarterly, 7*, 44–46.

Einat, T., & Herzog, S. (2011). A new perspective for delinquency: Culture conflict measured by seriousness perceptions. *International Journal of Offender Therapy & Comparative Criminology, 55*(7), 1072–1095.

Eitzen, D. S., & Zinn, M. B. (1992). *Social problems* (5th ed.). Boston, MA: Allyn & Bacon.

Elias, M. (n.d.). *The school to prison pipeline: Policies and practices that favor incarceration over education do us all a grave injustice.* Retrieved from www.indiana.edu/~pbisin/docs/School_to_Prison.pdf

Elliott, D. S., & Ageton, S. S. (1980). Reconciling race and class differences in self-reported and official estimates of delinquency. *American Sociological Review, 45*(1), 95–110.

Elliott, D. S., & Huizinga, D. (2006). Social class and delinquent behavior in a national youth panel: 1976–1980. *Criminology, 21*(2), 149–177.

Elliott, I. A., & Ashfield, S. (2011). The use of online technology in the modus operandi of female sex offenders. *Journal of Sexual Aggression, 17,* 1–13.

Ellis, R. A., O'Hara, M., & Sowers, K. (1999). Treatment profiles of troubled female adolescents: Implications for judicial disposition. *Juvenile and Family Court Journal, 50*(3), 25–40.

Ellis, R. A., & Sowers, K. M. (2001). *Juvenile justice practice: A cross-disciplinary approach to intervention.* Belmont, CA: Wadsworth.

Elrod, P., & Ryder, R. S. (2005). *Juvenile justice: A social, historical, and legal perspective* (2nd ed.). Sudbury, MA: Jones & Bartlett.

Emery, R. E. (1982). Interparental conflict and the children of discord and divorce. *Psychological Bulletin, 92,* 310–330.

Empey, L. T., & Stafford, M. C. (1991). *American delinquency: Its meaning and construction* (3rd ed.). Belmont, CA: Wadsworth.

Empey, L. T., Stafford, M. C., & Hay, C. H. (1999). *American delinquency: Its meaning and construction* (4th ed.). Belmont, CA: Wadsworth.

Engel, R. S., Sobol, J. J., & Worden, R. E. (2000). Further exploration of the demeanor hypothesis: The interaction effects of suspects' characteristics and demeanor on police behavior. *Justice Quarterly, 17,* 235–258.

Ennett, S., Tobler, N. S., Ringwalt, C. L., & Flewelling, R. L. (1994). How effective is drug abuse resistance education? A meta-analysis of project DARE outcome evaluations. *American Journal of Public Health, 84,* 1394–1401.

Enzmann, D., Ineke, H. M., Junger-Tas, J., Killias, M., Steketee, M., & Gruszczynska, B. (2015). *Second International Self-Reported Delinquency study, 2005–2007.* Ann Arbor, MI: Inter-university Consortium for Political and Social Research.

Ericson, N. (2001). *Public/Private ventures' evaluation of faith based programs* (OJJDP Fact Sheet No. 38). Washington, DC: Office of Juvenile Justice and Delinquency Prevention.

Erikson, K. (1962). Notes on the sociology of deviance. *Social Problems, 9,* 301–314.

Erskine, C. A, Keating, M., & Capuano, D. (2011, July 22). Courts, caring, and confidentiality. *Telegram & Gazette,* p. A10.

Ervin, J. D., & Swilaski, M. (2004). Community outreach through children's programs. *Police Chief, 71*(9), 42–45.

Esbensen, F.-A. (2004). *Evaluating G.R.E.A.T.: A school-based gang prevention program* (Research for policy). Washington, DC: National Institute of Justice.

Esbensen, F.-A., & Osgood, D. (1999). Gang resistance education and training (GREAT): Results from the national evaluation. *Journal of Research in Crime and Delinquency, 36,* 194–225.

Esbensen, F.-A., Peterson, D., Taylor, T. J., & Osgood, D. W. (2012). *Is G.R.E.A.T. effective? Does the program prevent gang joining? Results from the National Evaluation of G.R.E.A.T.* St. Louis, MO: University of Missouri–St. Louis. Retrieved from www.umsl.edu/ccj/pdfs/great/GREAT%20Wave%204%20Outcome%20Report

Espiritu, R. C., Huizinga, D., Crawford, A., & Loeber, R. (2001). Epidemiology of self-reported delinquency. In R. Loeber & D. P. Farrington (Eds.), *Child delinquents: Development, intervention, and service needs* (pp. 47–66). Thousand Oaks, CA: Sage.

Evans, D. G., & Sawdon, J. (2004, October). The development of a gang exit strategy: The Youth Ambassador's Leadership and Employment Project. *Corrections Today, 6*(66), 78–81.

Evans, W. P., Fitzgerald, C., & Weigel, D. (1999). Are rural gang members similar to their urban peers? Implications for rural communities. *Youth & Society, 30,* 267–282.

Fader, D. P., Harris, P. W., Jones, P. R., & Poulin, M. E. (2001). Factors involved in decisions on commitment to delinquency programs for first-time juvenile offenders. *Justice Quarterly, 18,* 232–342.

Fagan, A. A., Van Horn, M. L., Antaramian, S., & Hawkins, J. D. (2011). How do families matter? Age and gender differences in family influences on delinquency and drug use. *Youth Violence & Juvenile Justice, 9*(2), 150–170.

Fagan, J., & Pabon, E. (1990). Contributions of delinquency and substance use to school dropout among inner-city youths. *Youth & Society, 21,* 306–354.

Family Foundations. (2007). *Family Foundations program descriptions.* Rayville, LA: Author.

Fanton, J. (2006, May 14). Illinois a national leader in juvenile justice reforms. *Peoria Journal Star,* p. A5.

Farah, F., & Raine, A. (2011). Antisocial personality disorders. In W. J. Chambliss (Ed.), *Crime and criminal behavior: Key issues in crime and punishment* (pp. 13–28). Thousand Oaks, CA: Sage.

Farrington, D. P. (2003). Developmental and life-course criminology: Key theoretical and empirical issues—

The 2002 Sutherland address. *Criminology, 41*, 221–255.

Farrington, D. P., Jollife, D., Hawkins, J. D., Catalano, R. F., Hill, K. G., & Kosterman, R. (2003). Comparing delinquency careers in court records and self-reports. *Criminology, 41*, 933–959.

Farrington, D. P., Loeber, R., Stouthamer-Loeber, M., Van Kammen, W. B., & Schmidt, L. (1996). Self-reported delinquency and a combined delinquency scale based on boys, mothers, and teachers: Concurrent and predictive validity for African Americans and Caucasians. *Criminology, 34*, 493–517.

Farrington, D. P., & Ttofi, M. M. (2009, October). *School-based programs to reduce bullying and victimization.* Retrieved from www.ncjrs.gov/pdffiles1/nij/grants/229377.pdf

Farrington, D. P., & Welsh, B. C. (2007). *Saving children from a life of crime: Early risk factors and effective interventions.* New York, NY: Oxford University Press.

Faust, F. L., & Brantingham, P. J. (1974). *Juvenile justice philosophy.* St. Paul, MN: West.

Federal Advisory Committee on Juvenile Justice. (2010). *Annual report.* Retrieved from www.facjj.org/annualreports/00-FACJJ%20Annual%20Report-FINAL%20508.pdf

Federal Bureau of Investigation. (2015). *Crime in the United States: Table 43B.* Washington, DC: Department of Justice. Retrieved from https://ucr.fbi.gov/crime-in-the-u.s/2015/crime-in-the-u.s.-2015/tables/table-43

Federal Bureau of Investigation. (2016a). *Crime in the United States Table 43A.* Washington, DC: Department of Justice. Retrieved from https://ucr.fbi.gov/crime-in-the-u.s/2015/crime-in-the-u.s.-2015/tables/table-43

Federal Bureau of Investigation. (2016b). *Crime in the United States, 2015: Table 3.1. Current year over previous year arrest trends totals, 2014 to 2015.* Washington, DC: Department of Justice. Retrieved from https://ucr.fbi.gov/crime-in-the-u.s/2015/crime-in-the-u.s.-2015/tables/table-36

Federal Bureau of Investigation. (2016c). *Crime in the United States, 2015: Table 3.2. Five year arrest trends, totals 2011–2015.* Washington, DC: Department of Justice. Retrieved from https://ucr.fbi.gov/crime-in-the-u.s/2015/crime-in-the-u.s.-2015/tables/table-34

Federal Bureau of Investigation. (2016d). *Crime in the United States, 2015: Table 33. Ten year arrest trends by sex, 2006–2015.* Washington, DC: Department of Justice. Retrieved from https://ucr.fbi.gov/crime-in-the-u.s/2015/crime-in-the-u.s.-2015/tables/table-33

Federal Bureau of Investigation. (2016e). *Crime in the United States, 2015: Table 3.2. Ten year arrest trends by sex, totals 2011–2015.* Washington, DC: Department of Justice. Retrieved from https://ucr.fbi.gov/crime-in-the-u.s/2015/crime-in-the-u.s.-2015/tables/table-35

Federal Bureau of Investigation. (2016f). *Crime in the United States, 2015: Table 3.5. Juvenile arrests by race and ethnicity under the age of 18, 2015.* Washington, DC: Department of Justice. Retrieved from https://ucr.fbi.gov/crime-in-the-u.s/2015/crime-in-the-u.s.-2015/tables/table-61

Federal Bureau of Investigation. (2016g). *Child sex trafficking crackdown spreads to international stage in 2016.* Washington, DC: FBI National Press Office. Retrieved from www.fbi.gov/news/pressrel/press-releases/fbi-announces-results-of-operation-cross-country-x

Federal Bureau of Investigation. (n.d.). *Cyber crime.* Retrieved from www.fbi.gov/investigate/cyber.

Feld, B. C. (2006). Police interrogation of juveniles: An empirical study of policy and practice. *Journal of Criminal Law & Criminology, 97*(1), 219–316.

Fenwick, C. R. (1982). Juvenile court intake decision making: The importance of family affiliation. *Journal of Criminal Justice, 10*, 443–453.

Find Youth Info. (n.d.). *Research.* Retrieved from www.findyouthinfo.gov/research.shtml

FindLaw. (2008). *Minor crime is a major ordeal.* Retrieved from http://criminal.findlaw.com/crimes/juvenile-justice/when-minor-commits-crime.html

Finkelhor, D. (2008). *Childhood victimization: Violence, crime, and abuse in the lives of young people.* New York, NY: Oxford University Press.

Finkelhor, D., & Ormrod, R. (2001a). *Child abuse reported to the police.* Retrieved from www.ncjrs.gov/html/ojjdp/jjbul2001_5_1/contents.html

Finkelhor, D., & Ormrod, R. (2001b). Homicides of children and youth. *Juvenile Justice Bulletin.* Washington, DC: Office of Juvenile Justice and Delinquency Prevention.

Finkelhor, D., Turner, H., Ormrod, R., Hamby, S., & Kracke, K. (2009). Children's exposure to violence: A comprehensive national survey. *Juvenile Justice Bulletin.* Washington, DC: Office of Juvenile Justice and Delinquency Prevention, Office of Justice Programs.

Finkenauer, J. O. (1982). *Scared straight.* Englewood Cliffs, NJ: Prentice Hall.

Fishbein, D. H. (1990). Biological perspectives in criminology. *Criminology, 28*, 27–72.

Fitzgerald, J. D., & Cox, S. M. (2002). *Research methods and statistics in criminal justice: An introduction* (3rd ed.). Belmont, CA: Wadsworth/Thomson.

Fitzgerald, M., Stevens, A., & Hale, C. (2004). *Review of knowledge on juvenile violence: Trends, policies, and responses in Europe.* Canterbury, UK: University of Kent, European Commission.

Fitzpatrick, K. M., & Boldizar, J. P. (1993). The prevalence and consequences of exposure to violence among African-American youth. *Journal of the American Academy of Child and Adolescent Psychiatry, 3*, 424–430.

Flannery, D. J., Williams, L. L., & Vazsonyi, A. T. (1999). Who are they and what are they doing? Delinquent behavior, substance abuse, and early adolescents' after-school time. *American Journal of Orthopsychiatry, 69*, 247–253.

Fleener, F. T. (1999). Family as a factor in delinquency. *Psychological Reports, 85*(1), 80–81.

Flexon, J. L., Greenleaf, R. G., & Lurigio, A. J. (2012). The effects of self-control, gang membership, and parental attachment/identification on police contacts among Latino and African American youths. *International Journal of Offender Therapy & Comparative Criminology, 56*(2), 218–238.

Florsheim, P., Shotorbani, S., & Guest-Warnick, G. (2000). Role of the working alliance in the treatment of delinquent boys in community-based programs. *Journal of Clinical Child Psychology, 29*, 94–107.

Foley, A. (2008). The current state of gender-specific delinquency programming. *Journal of Criminal Justice, 36*(3), 262–269.

Ford, J. D., Chapman, J., Mack, M., & Pearson, G. (2006). Pathways from traumatic child victimization to delinquency: Implications for juvenile and permanency court proceedings and decisions. *Juvenile and Family Court Journal, 57*(1), 13–28.

Forgays, D. (2008). Three years of teen court offender outcomes. *Adolescence, 43*(171), 473–484.

Forum on Child and Family Statistics. (2006). *Population and family characteristics*. Retrieved from www.childstats.gov/americaschildren/index.asp

Forum on Child and Family Statistics. (2012). *America's children in brief: Key national indicators of well-being, 2012*. Retrieved from www.childstats.gov/pdf/ac2012/ac_12.pdf

Fox, J. A., & Levin, J. (1994). Firing back: The growing threat of workplace homicide. *Journal of Criminal Law, Criminology, and Police Science, 563*, 16–30.

Fox, M. (2008, July 14). *Study finds genetic link to violence, delinquency*. Retrieved from www.reuters.com/article/idUSN1444872420080714

Fox, S. (1984). *Juvenile courts in a nutshell* (2nd ed.). Saint Paul, MN: West.

Francis, A. A. (2012). The dynamics of family trouble: Middle-class parents whose children have problems. *Journal of Contemporary Ethnography, 41*(4), 371–401.

Frazier, C. E., Bishop, D. M., & Henretta, J. C. (1992). The social context of race differentials in juvenile justice dispositions. *Sociological Quarterly, 33*, 447–458.

Freng, A., & Terrance, T. J. (2013). Race and ethnicity: What are their roles in gang membership? In N. M. Ritter & T. R. Simon (Eds.), *Changing course: Preventing gang membership: Executive summary* (pp. 135–149). Washington, DC: National Institute of Justice.

Friend, T. (2000, June 27). Genetic map is hailed as new power. *USA Today*, p. 1A.

Fronius, T., Persson, H., Guckenburg, S., Hurley, N., & Petrosino, A. (2016). *Restorative justice in U.S. schools: A research review*. Retrieved from www.wested.org/wp-content/uploads/2016/11/1456766824resourcerestorativejusticeresearchreview-3.pdf

Futty, J. (2012, December 2). Dispatch special report: Child sex abuse difficult to prove. *Columbus Dispatch*. Retrieved from www.dispatch.com/content/stories/local/2012/12/02/child-sex-abuse-difficult-to-prove.html

Gagnon v. Scarpelli, 411 U.S. 778 (1973).

Gallegos v. Colorado, 370 U.S. 49 (1969).

Gandhi, A. G., Murphy-Graham, E., Anthony, P., Chrismer, S. S., & Weiss, C. H. (2007). The devil is in the details: Examining the evidence for "proven" school-based drug abuse prevention programs. *Evaluation Review, 31*, 43–74.

Gang Resistance Education and Training. (2013). *GREAT: Gang Resistance Education and Training*. Retrieved from www.great-online.org

Gardner, E., Rodriguez, N., & Zatz, M. S. (2004). Criers, liars, and manipulators: Probation officers' views of girls. *Justice Quarterly, 21*, 547–579.

Garrett, M., & Short, J. F. (1975). Social class and delinquency: Predictions and outcomes of police-juvenile encounters. *Social Problems, 22*, 368–383.

Garry, E. (1996). *Truancy: First step to a lifetime of problems*. Washington, DC: U.S. Department of Justice, Office of Juvenile Justice and Delinquency Prevention.

Gaudio, C. (2010). A call to Congress to give back the future: End the "War on Drugs" and encourage states to reconstruct the juvenile justice system. *Family Court Review, 48*(1), 212.

Gelles, R. J., & Perlman, S. (2012). *Estimated annual cost of child abuse and neglect*. Chicago IL: Prevent Child Abuse America.

Georgia Code, § 19-10-1 (2010).

Georgia Code, 15-11-47 (d) (2010).

Georgia Code, 15-11-78 (2010).

Gibson, C. L. (2012). An investigation of neighborhood disadvantage, low self-control, and violent victimization among youth. *Youth Violence & Juvenile Justice, 10*(1), 41–63.

Gladstein, J., Rusonis, E. J., & Heald, F. P. (1992). A comparison of inner-city and upper-middle-class youth's exposure to violence. *Journal of Adolescent Health, 13*, 275–280.

Glaser, D. (1960). Differential association and criminological prediction. *Social Problems, 8*, 6–14.

Glaser, D. (1978). *Crime in our changing society*. New York, NY: Holt, Rinehart & Winston.

Gleacher, A. A., Nadeem, E., Moy, A. J., Whited, A. L., Albano, A. M., Radigan, M., . . . Hoagwood, K. E. (2011). Statewide CBT training for clinicians and supervisors treating youth: The New York state evidence based treatment dissemination center. *Journal of Emotional & Behavioral Disorders, 19*(3), 182–192.

Glensor, R. W., Correia, M. E., & Peak, K. J. (Eds.). (2000). *Policing communities: Understanding crime and solving problems*. Los Angeles, CA: Roxbury.

Glueck, S., & Glueck, E. (1950). *Unraveling juvenile delinquency*. Cambridge, MA: Harvard University Press.

Goddard, H. H. (1914). *Feeblemindedness: Its causes and consequences*. New York, NY: Macmillan.

Goldberg, R. (2003). *Drugs across the spectrum* (4th ed.). Belmont, CA: Wadsworth/Thomson Learning.

Goldstein, S. L., & Tyler, R. P. (1998). Frustrations of inquiry: Child sexual abuse allegations in divorce and custody cases. *FBI Law Enforcement Bulletin, 67*(7), 1–6.

Goodkind, S., Ng, I., & Sarri, R. C. (2006). The impact of sexual abuse in the lives of young women involved or at risk of involvement with the juvenile justice system. *Violence Against Women, 12*, 456–477.

Goodrich, S. A., Anderson, S. A., & LaMotte, V. (2014). Evaluation of a program designed to promote positive police and youth interactions. *Journal of Juvenile Justice, 3*(2). Retrieved from www.journalofjuvjustice.org/JOJJ0302/article04.htm

Goring, C. (1913). *The English convict*. London, UK: Her Majesty's Stationery Office.

Gorman-Smith, D., Tolan, P. H., & Loeber, R. (1998). Relation of family problems to patterns of delinquent involvement among urban youth. *Journal of Abnormal Child Psychology, 26*, 319–333.

Gottfredson, M. R., & Hirschi, T. (1990). *A general theory of crime*. Stanford, CA: Stanford University Press.

Gough, H. G. (1948). A sociological theory of psychopathy. *American Journal of Sociology, 53*, 359–366.

Gough, H. G. (1960). Theory and measurement of socialization. *Journal of Consulting Psychology, 24*, 23–30.

Gover, A. R., Jennings, W. G., & Tewksbury, R. (2009). Adolescent male and female gang members' experiences with violent victimization, dating violence, and sexual assault. *American Journal of Criminal Justice, 34*(1/2), 103–119.

Graham v. Florida, 08-7412 (2010).

G.R.E.A.T. Program. (2016). *Central America news archive by year*. Tallahassee, FL: Institute for Intergovernmental Research.

Greenberg, D. F. (1999). The weak strength of social control theory. *Crime & Delinquency, 45*, 66–81.

Greenwood, P. W. (2008). Prevention and intervention programs for juvenile offenders. *Future of Children, 18*(2), 185–210.

Greenwood, P. W., Model, K. E., Rydell, C. P., & Chiesa, J. (1998). *Diverting children from a life of crime: Measuring costs and benefits*. Santa Monica, CA: RAND. MR-699–1-UCB/RC/IF.

Gresham, F. M., MacMillan, D. L., & Bocian, K. M. (1998). Comorbidity of hyperactivity-impulsivity-inattention and conduct problems: Risk factors in social, affective, and academic domains. *Journal of Abnormal Child Psychology, 26*, 393–406.

Griffin, B. S., & Griffin, C. T. (1978). *Juvenile delinquency in perspective*. New York, NY: Harper & Row.

Groff, E. R. (2007). Simulation for theory testing and experimentation: An example using routine activity theory and street robbery. *Journal of Quantitative Criminology, 23*(2), 75–104.

Guo, G., Roettger, M. E., & Cai, T. C. (2008, August). The integration of genetic propensities into social-control models of delinquency and violence among male youths. *American Sociological Review, 73*, 543–568.

Hagan, J., & Parker, P. (1999). Rebellion beyond the classroom: A life-course capitalization theory of the intergenerational causes of delinquency. *Theoretical Criminology, 3*(3), 259–285.

Haley v. Ohio, 332 U.S 596 (1948).

Halleck, S. (1971). *Psychiatry and the dilemmas of crime*. Berkeley, CA: University of California Press.

Halter, S. (2010). Factors that influence police conceptualizations of girls involved in prostitution in six U.S. cities: Child sexual exploitation victims or delinquents? *Child Maltreatment, 15*(2), 152–160.

Hamarman, S., & Bernet, W. (2000). Evaluating and reporting emotional abuse in children: Parent-based, action-based focus aids in clinical decision-making. *Journal of the American Academy of Child & Adolescent Psychiatry, 39*, 928–930.

Hamby, S., Finkelhor, D., Turner, H., & Ormond, R. (2011). *Children's exposure to intimate partner violence and other family violence*. Washington, DC: Office of Juvenile Justice and Delinquency Prevention. Retrieved from www.ncjrs.gov/pdffiles1/ojjdp/232272.pdf

Hamm, M. S. (1993). *American skinheads: The criminology and control of hate crime*. Westport, CT: Praeger.

Hanser, R. D. (2007a). Gang crimes: Latino gangs in America. In F. Shanty (Ed.), *Organized crime: An international encyclopedia* (pp. 120–124). Santa Barbara, CA: ABC-CLIO.

Hanser, R. D. (2007b). Global sex trade: Commercial sex, pornography & international sex tourism. In F. Shanty (Ed.), *Organized crime: From trafficking to terrorism* (pp. 194–197). Santa Barbara, CA: ABC-CLIO.

Hanser, R. D. (2007c). *Special needs offenders in the community*. Upper Saddle River, NJ: Prentice Hall.

Hanser, R. D. (2010). *Domestic human trafficking: It's here in the United States*. Invited presentation given at the Louisiana Private Investigator's Association 2010 Conference.

Hanser, R. D., & Caudill, J. (2002). Comparing juvenile justice trends in the United States and France. *Crime and Justice International, 18*(66), 7–8.

Hanser, R. D., & Gomila, M. D. (2015). *Multiculturalism and the criminal justice system*. Upper Saddle River, NJ: Pearson.

Hanser, R. D., & Mire, S. M. (2011). *Correctional counseling*. Upper Saddle River, NJ: Prentice Hall.

Hanson, R. F., Resnick, H. S., & Saunders, B. E. (1999). Factors related to the reporting of childhood rape. *Child Abuse & Neglect, 23*, 559–569.

Harcourt, B. E., & Ludwig, J. (2006). Broken windows: New evidence from New York City and a five-city social experiment. *University of Chicago Law Review, 73*, 271–320.

Harper, G. W., & Robinson, W. L. (1999). Pathways to risk among inner-city African-American adolescent females: The influence of gang membership. *American Journal of Community Psychology, 27*, 383–404.

Harris, P., Baltodano, H., Bal, A., Jolivette, K., & Malcahy, C. (2009). Reading achievement of incarcerated youth in three regions. *Journal of Correctional Education, 60*(2), 120–145.

Harris, P. W., & Jones, P. R. (1999). Differentiating delinquent youths for program planning and evaluation. *Criminal Justice & Behavior, 26*, 403–434.

Hart, T. C., & Rennison, C. (2003, March). *Reporting crime to the police: 1992–2000*. Washington, DC: U.S. Department of Justice.

Hashima, P., & Finkelhor, D. (1999). Violent victimization of youth versus adults in the National Crime Victimization Survey. *Journal of Interpersonal Violence, 14*(8), 799–820.

Hatchette, G. (1998). Why we can't wait: The juvenile court in the new millennium. *Crime & Delinquency, 44*, 83–88.

Hawaii Revised Statutes, 571-32 (h) (2010).

Hawaii Revised Statutes § 571-22 (2011).

Hawkins, J. D., & Lishner, D. M. (1987). Schooling and delinquency. In E. Johnson (Ed.), *Handbook on crime and delinquency prevention* (pp. 179–222). Westport, CT: Greenwood.

Hay, C., & Evans, M. (2006). Violent victimization and involvement in delinquency: Examining predictions from general strain theory. *Journal of Criminal Justice, 34*, 261–274.

Hayes, H. (1997). Using integrated theory to explain the movement into juvenile delinquency. *Deviant Behavior, 18*(2), 161–184.

Hayes, H. (2005). Assessing re-offending in restorative justice conferences. *Australian and New Zealand Journal of Criminology, 38*(1), 77–101.

Hayes, H., & Daly, K. (2003). Youth justice conferencing and reoffending. *Justice Quarterly, 20*(4), 725–760.

Hayes, L. (2008). *Teachers' expectations affect kids' grades, student-teacher relationships*. EduGuide. Retrieved from www.eduguide.org

Healy, W., & Bronner, A. (1936). *New light on delinquency and its treatment*. New Haven, CT: Yale University Press.

Hearn, J. (1998). *The violence of men: How men talk about and how agencies respond to men's violence to women*. London, UK: Sage.

Heck, W. P. (1999). Basic investigative protocol for child sexual abuse. *FBI Law Enforcement Bulletin, 68*(10), 19–25.

Hendricks, M. A., Sale, E. W., Evans, C. J., McKinley, L., & DeLozier Carter, S. (2010). Evaluation of a truancy court intervention in four middle schools. *Psychology in the Schools, 47*(2), 173–183.

Hernandez, A. (2011, March 28). What does officer discretion mean? *Orlando Sentinel*. Retrieved from http://articles.orlandosentinel.com/2011-03-28/news/os-law-you-officer-discretion-20110321_1_william-charles-gula-law-enforcement-officers-state-attorney

Herrera, C., Grossman, J. B., Kauh, T. J., & McMaken, J. (2011). Mentoring in schools: An impact study of Big Brothers Big Sisters school-based mentoring. *Child Development, 82*(1), 346–361.

Hester, M., Pearson, C., & Harwin, N. (2000). *Making an impact: Children and domestic violence*. Philadelphia, PA: Jessica Kingsley.

Hibbler, W. J. (1999). A message from the 14th annual National Juvenile Corrections and Detention Forum. *Corrections Today, 61*(4), 28–31.

Hieb, C. F. (1992). *Gang task force and Lakewood, CO, Police Department*. Lakewood, CO: Access.

Higgins, G. E., Piquero, N. L., & Piquero, A. R. (2011). General strain theory, peer rejection, and delinquency/crime. *Youth & Society, 43*(4), 1272–1297.

High/Scope Educational Research Foundation. (2002). *High-quality preschool program found to improve adult status*. Retrieved from www.highscope.org/Research/PerryProject/perrymain.htm

Hill, K., Lui, C., & Hawkins, J. (2001). *Early precursors of gang membership: A study of Seattle youth*. Washington, DC: Office of Juvenile Justice and Delinquency Prevention.

Hindelang, M. J., Hirschi, T., & Weis, J. G. (1981). *Measuring delinquency*. Beverly Hills, CA: Sage.

Hinduja, S., & Patchin, J. W. (2008). Cyberbullying: An exploratory analysis of factors related to offending and victimization. *Deviant Behavior, 29*, 129–156.

Hinojosa, A. (2013, January 26). Far East El Paso school beating brings call for anti-bullying aid. *El Paso Times*.

Hirschi, T. (1969). *Causes of delinquency.* Berkeley, CA: University of California Press.

Hirschi, T., & Gottfredson, M. (1993). Rethinking the juvenile justice system. *Crime & Delinquency, 39,* 262–271.

Hissong, R. (1991). Teen court—Is it an effective alternative to traditional sanctions? *Journal for Juvenile Justice and Detention Services, 6,* 14–23.

Hockenberry, S. (2013). *Juveniles in residential placement: 2010.* Washington, DC: U.S. Department of Justice, Office of Juvenile Justice and Delinquency Prevention. Retrieved from www.ojjdp.gov/pubs/241060.pdf

Hockenberry, S., Wachter, A., & Sladky, A. (2016). *Juvenile residential facility census, 2014: Selected findings.* Washington, DC: U.S. Department of Justice, Office of Juvenile Justice and Delinquency Prevention. Retrieved from www.ojjdp.gov/pubs/250123.pdf

Hollist, D. R., Hughes, L. A., & Schaible, L. M. (2009). Adolescent maltreatment, negative emotion, and delinquency: An assessment of general strain theory and family-based strain. *Journal of Criminal Justice, 37*(4), 379–387.

Holsinger, K. (2000). Feminist perspectives on female offending: Examining real girls' lives. *Women & Criminal Justice, 12*(1), 23–51.

Hong, J. S. (2009). Feasibility of the Olweus Bullying Prevention Programs in low-income schools. *Journal of School Violence, 8*(1), 81–97.

Hooton, E. (1939). *Crime and the man.* Cambridge, MA: Harvard University Press.

Howell, J. C. (1998). *Youth gangs: An overview.* Washington, DC: U.S. Department of Justice.

Howell, J. C., & Decker, S. H. (1999). *The youth gangs, drugs, and violence connection.* Washington, DC: Office of Juvenile Justice and Delinquency Prevention.

Howell, J. C., Egley, A., Tita, G. E., & Griffiths, E. (2011). *U.S. gang problem trends and seriousness, 1996–2009.* Washington, DC: Office of Juvenile Justice and Delinquency Prevention.

Hsia, H. M. (2004). *Disproportionate minority confinement 2002 update.* Washington, DC: Office of Juvenile Justice and Delinquency Prevention.

Huck, J. L., Lee, D. R., Bowen, K. N., Spraitz, J. D., & Bowers, J. H., Jr. (2012). Specifying the dynamic relationships of general strain, coping, and young adult crime. *Western Criminology Review, 13*(2), 25–45.

Huddleston, C. W., Marlowe, D. B., & Casebolt, R. (2008). *Painting the current picture: A national report card on drug courts and other problem-solving court programs in the United States.* Washington, DC: National Drug Court Institute, Bureau of Justice Assistance. Retrieved from www.ndci.org/sites/default/files/ndci/PCPII1_web%5B1%5D.pdf

Huff, C. R. (1996). The criminal behavior of gang members and nongang at-risk youth. In C. Huff (Ed.), *Gangs in America* (2nd ed., pp. 75–102). Thousand Oaks, CA: Sage.

Hughes, L. A. (2005). Studying youth gangs: Alternative methods and conclusions. *Journal of Contemporary Criminal Justice, 21,* 98–117.

Huizinga, D., Thornberry, T., Knight, K., & Lovegrove, P. (2007, September). *Disproportionate minority contact in the juvenile justice system: A study of differential minority arrest/referral to court in three cities.* Retrieved from ojjdp.ncjrs.gov/dmc

Hume, R. (2010). *Learning disabilities and the juvenile justice system.* Learning Disabilities Association of Michigan. Retrieved from www.ldaofmichigan.org/articles/ld.jj.htm

Hunter, J. A., Figueredo, A. J., & Malamuth, N. M. (2010). Developmental pathways into social and sexual deviance. *Journal of Family Violence, 25*(2), 141–148.

Hurst, Y. G. (2007). Juvenile attitudes toward the police: An examination of rural youth. *Criminal Justice Review, 32*(2), 121–141.

Hurst, Y. G., McDermott, M. J., & Thomas, D. L. (2005). The attitudes of girls toward the police: Differences by race. *Policing: An International Journal of Police Strategies and Management, 28,* 578–594.

Illinois Balanced and Restorative Justice Initiative. (n.d.). *Restorative justice practices.* Retrieved from www.ibarji.org/practices.html

Illinois Code, ch. 720—Criminal Offenses, 720 ILCS 130/neglected children offense act (2010).

Illinois Code, ch. 720—Criminal Offenses, ILCS 130 (2012).

Illinois Compiled Statutes. (1999).

Illinois Compiled Statutes. (2013). Retrieved from http://ilga.gov/legislation/ilcs/documents/070504050K5-301.htm

Illinois Compiled Statutes, ch. 325, art. 5, sec. 5/1-11 (2010).

Illinois Compiled Statutes, ch. 705, art. 1, sec. 405/1-3 (2012).

Illinois Compiled Statutes, ch. 705, art. 5, sec. 405/5-805 (3)(b) (2012).

Illinois Compiled Statutes, ch. 705, sec. 405/2-5, 3-4, 4-4, 5-401 (2011).

Illinois Compiled Statutes, ch. 705, sec. 405/2-18 (1) (2011).

Illinois Compiled Statutes, ch. 705, sec. 405/2-22 (1) (2011).

Illinois Compiled Statutes, ch. 705, sec. 405/5-22 (2011).

Illinois Compiled Statutes, ch. 705, sec. 405/5-415 (2011).

Illinois Compiled Statutes, ch. 705, sec. 405/5-301 (1) (2013).

Illinois Compiled Statutes, ch. 705, sec. 405/5-301 (2)a (2013).

Illinois Compiled Statutes, ch. 705, sec. 405/5-305 (2011).

Illinois Compiled Statutes, ch. 705, sec. 405/5-525 (2011).

Illinois Compiled Statutes, ch. 705, sec. 405/5-805 (1999).

Illinois Department of Children and Family Services. (2009). *Child protection: Mandated reporters.* Retrieved from www.state.il.us/dcfs/child/index.shtml

Illinois Juvenile Justice Commission. (2012, February 10). *Annual report to the governor and general assembly for calendar years 2007 and 2008.* Retrieved from www.dhs.state.il.us/page.aspx?item=42996

Illinois State Board of Education. (2012). *Regional safe schools program: FY 2012 data summary.* Retrieved from www.isbe.state.il.us/research/pdfs/rssp_data_summary12.pdf

Inciardi, J. A., Horowitz, R., & Pottieger, A. E. (1993). *Street kids, street drugs, street crime: An examination of drug use and serious delinquency in Miami.* Belmont, CA: Wadsworth.

Indiana Code Annotated. (1997).

Information Please Database. (n.d.). *Time line of worldwide school shootings.* Upper Saddle River, NJ: Pearson Education. Retrieved from www.infoplease.com/ipa/A0777958.html

In re Gault, 387 U.S. 1, 87 S. Ct. 1428 (1967).

In re George T., 2002 N.Y. Int. 0161 (2002).

In re Holmes, 379 Pa. 599, 109 A 2d. 523 (1954), cert. denied, 348 U.S. 973, 75 S. Ct. 535 (1955).

In re Register, 84 N.C. App. 336, 352 S. E. 2d 889 (1987) [dictum].

In re William A., 393 Md. 690, 698–699, 548 A.2d 130, 134 (1988).

In re Winship, 397 U.S. 358, 90 S. Ct. 1068 (1970).

Institute of Judicial Administration and American Bar Association. (1980a). *Standards relating to counsel for private parties.* Cambridge, MA: Ballinger. Retrieved from www.ncjrs.gov/pdffiles1/ojjdp/83582.pdf

Institute of Justice Administration and American Bar Association. (1980b). *Standards for the administration of juvenile justice.* Chicago, IL: American Bar Association.

International Association of Chiefs of Police. (2011, October 19). *Launch of IACP's Youth Focused Policing Resource Center.* Retrieved from www.theiacp.org/About/WhatsNew/tabid/459/Default.aspx?id=1631&v=1

Iowa Code Annotated, 232.47 (5) (2009).

Iowa Code Annotated, 232.50 (3) (2009).

Ireland, T. O., Smith, C. A., & Thornberry, T. P. (2002). Developmental issues in the impact of child maltreatment on later delinquency and drug use. *Criminology, 40*(2), 359–399.

Iwaniec, D. (2006). *The emotionally abused and neglected child: Identification, assessment and intervention: A practice handbook* (2nd ed.). New York, NY: Wiley.

Jackson v. Hobbs, 132 S. Ct. 548 (2011).

Jackson, D. B. (2012). The role of early pubertal development in the relationship between general strain and juvenile crime. *Youth Violence and Juvenile Justice, 10*(3), 292–310.

Jacobs, J. (1977). *Stateville: The penitentiary in mass society.* Chicago, IL: University of Chicago Press.

Jarjoura, G. R. (1996). The conditional effect of social class on the dropout-delinquency relationship. *Journal of Research in Crime and Delinquency, 33,* 232–255.

Jarjoura, G. R., Triplett, R. A., & Brinker, G. P. (2002). Growing up poor: Examining the link between persistent childhood poverty and delinquency. *Journal of Quantitative Criminology, 18,* 159–187.

Jeffery, C. R. (1978). Criminology as an interdisciplinary behavioral science. *Criminology, 16,* 149–169.

Jeffery, C. R. (1996). The genetics and crime conference revisited. *The Criminologist, 21*(2), 1–3.

Jennings, W., Gibson, C., & Lanza-Kaduce, L. (2009). Why not let kids be kids? An exploratory analysis of the relationship between alternative rationales for managing status offending and youths' self-concepts. *American Journal of Criminal Justice, 34*(3), 198–212.

Johnson, K. (2006, July 13). Police tie jump in crime to juveniles. *USA Today.* Retrieved from http://usatoday30.usatoday.com/news/nation/2006–07–12-juveniles-cover_x.htm

Johnson, R. E. (1980). Social class and delinquent behavior. *Criminology, 18,* 86–93.

Johnson, S. (1998). Girls in trouble: Do we care? The number of delinquent girls is on the rise; only a coordinated, multiagency approach can turn the tide. *Corrections Today, 60*(7), 136–138.

Joiner, C. T. (2005). An examination of racial profiling data in a large metropolitan area. *Professional Issues in Criminal Justice, 1*(2), 1–14.

Jones v. Commonwealth, 185 Va. 335, 38 S.E.2d 444 (1946).

Jones, L. M., Mitchell, K. J., & Finkelhor, D. (2012). Trends in youth Internet victimization: Findings from three youth Internet safety surveys 2000–2010. *Journal of Adolescent Health, 50,* 179–186.

Jones, M. B., & Jones, D. R. (2000). The contagious nature of antisocial behavior. *Criminology, 39,* 25–46.

Jones, R. K., & Lacey, J. H. (1999). *Evaluation of a day reporting center for repeat DWI offenders* (Report No. DOT HS 808989). Winchester, MA: Mid-America Research Institute. Retrieved from http://ntl.bts.gov/lib/25000/25900/25991/DOT-HS-808-989.pdf

Jordan, C. E., Clark, J., Pritchard, A., & Charnigo, R. (2012). Lethal and other serious assaults: Disentangling gender and context. *Crime & Delinquency, 58*(3), 425–455.

Judge approves Ferguson deal with DOJ to improve policing. (2016, April 19). *CBS News.* Retrieved from www.cbsnews.com/news/judge-approves-ferguson-deal-with-department-of-justice-to-improve-policing/

Justice Policy Institute. (2012). Juvenile Justice Policy Institute report questions effectiveness of school resource officers. *Juvenile Justice Update, 18*(4), 3–4.

Juvenile Policy Institute. (2013). *Common ground: Lessons learned from five states that reduced juvenile confinement by more than half.* Washington, DC: Author. Retrieved from www.justicepolicy .org/uploads/justicepolicy/ documents/jpicommonground.pdf

Kanof, M. (2003). *Youth illicit drug use prevention: DARE long term evaluations and federal efforts to identify effective programs.* Washington, DC: U.S. General Accounting Office.

Kaplan, C., & Merkel-Holguin, L. (2008). Another look at the national study on differential response in child welfare. *Protecting Children, 23*(1/2), 5–21.

Kaser-Boyd, N. (2002). Children who kill. In N. G. Ribner (Ed.), *Handbook of juvenile forensic psychology* (pp. 159–229). San Francisco, CA: Jossey-Bass.

Katkin, D., Hyman, D., & Kramer, J. (1976). *Juvenile delinquency and the juvenile justice system.* North Scituate, MA: Duxbury.

Kattoulas, V. (2001). *Japan's biker gangs: Young, fast, and deadly.* Retrieved from www.jingai.com/badboso .html

Kaufman, J., & Zigler, E. F. (1987). Do abused children become abusive parents? *American Journal of Orthopsychiatry, 40*, 953–959.

Kaufman, P. (2010). The long view of crime. *NIJ Journal, 265*, 26–28.

Kelley, D. H. (1977). Labeling and the consequences of wearing a delinquent label in a school setting. *Education, 97*, 371–380.

Kelling, G. (1999, October). *"Broken windows" and police discretion.* Washington, DC: National Institute of Justice Research Report. Retrieved from www.ncjrs.gov/ pdffiles1/nij/178259.pdf

Kent v. United States, 383 U.S. 541, 86 S. Ct. 1045 (1966).

Kilpatrick, D. G., Saunders, B. E., & Smith, D. W. (2003). *Youth victimization: Prevalence and implications. Research in Brief.* Washington, DC: National Institute of Justice.

Kirk, D. S. (2009). Unraveling the contextual effects on student suspension and juvenile arrest: The independent and interdependenet influences of school, neighborhood, and family social controls. *Criminology, 47*(2), 479–520.

Kitchell, G. (2013, March). Youth assessment model: Assessment, referral, and diversion. *Police Chief.* Retrieved from www.policechiefmagazine. org/magazine/index. cfm?fuseaction=display&article_ id=2890&issue_id=32013

Klein, M. W. (2005). The value of comparisons in street gang research. *Journal of Contemporary Criminal Justice, 21*, 135–151.

Klein, M., Weerman, F., & Thornberry, T. (2006). Street gang violence in Europe. *European Journal of Criminology, 3*(4), 413–437.

Klein-Saffran, J., Chapman, D. A., & Jeffers, J. L. (1993). Boot camp for prisoners. *Law Enforcement Bulletin, 62*(10), 13–16.

Klinger, D. A. (1996). More on demeanor and arrest in Dade County. *Criminology, 34*, 61–82.

Klockars, C. B. (1979). The contemporary crises of Marxist criminology. *Criminology, 16*, 477–515.

Kloess, J. A., Beech, A. R., & Harkins, L. (2014). Online child sexual exploitation: Prevalence, process, and offender characteristics. *Trauma, Violence and Abuse, 15*(2), 126–139.

Klofas, J., & Stojkovic, S. (Eds.). (1995). *Crime and justice in the year 2010.* Belmont, CA: Wadsworth.

Knudsen, D. D. (1992). *Child maltreatment: Emerging perspectives.* Dix Hills, NY: General Hall.

Kowaleski-Jones, L. (2000). Staying out of trouble: Community resources and problem behavior among high-risk adolescents. *Journal of Marriage and the Family, 62*, 449–464.

Kowalski, R., Limber, S. P., Schenck, A., Redrearn, M., Allen, J., Calloway, A., . . . Vernon, L. (2005, August). *Electronic bullying among school-aged children and youth.* Paper presented at the Annual Meeting of the American Psychological Association, Washington, DC.

Kracke, K., & Hahn, H. (2008). The nature and extent of childhood exposure to violence: What we know, why we don't know more, and why it matters. *Journal of Emotional Abuse, 8*(1/2), 29–49.

Krasner, L., & Ullman, L. P. (1965). *Research in behavior modification.* New York, NY: Holt, Rinehart & Winston.

Kreager, D. A., Rulison, K., & Moody, J. (2011). Delinquency and the structure of adolescent peer groups. *Criminology, 49*(1), 95–127.

Kretschmer, E. (1925). *Physique and character* (W. Sprott, Trans.). New York, NY: Harcourt, Brace, and World.

Krisberg, B. (2005). *Juvenile justice: Redeeming our children.* Thousand Oaks, CA: Sage.

Krisberg, B., Austin, J., & Steele, P. A. (1989). *Unlocking juvenile corrections: Evaluating the Massachusetts Department of Youth Services.* San Francisco, CA: National Council on Crime and Delinquency.

Kruttschnitt, C., & Carbone-Lopez, K. (2009, December). Customer satisfaction: Crime victims' willingness to call the police. *Ideas in American Policing, 12.* Retrieved from www.policefoundation.org/ docs/library.html

Kuanliang, A. (2010). *Thailand gang involvement.* Presentation given at Mahidol University, Bangkok, Thailand.

Kvaraceus, W. C. (1945). *Juvenile delinquency and the school.* New York, NY: World Book.

Lambert, S., & O'Halloran, E. (2008). Deductive thematic analysis of a female paedophilia website. Psychiatry. *Psychology and Law, 15*, 284–300.

Lamont, A. (2011, February). Who abuses children? *National Child Protection Clearinghouse.* Retrieved from www.aifs.gov.au/nch/pubs/sheets/rs7/rs7.pdf

Landenberger, N. A., & Lipsey, M. W. (2005). The positive effects of cognitive-behavioral programs for offenders: A meta-analysis of factors associated with effective treatment. *Journal of Experimental Criminology, 1*, 451–476.

Lander, B. (1970). An ecological analysis of Baltimore. In M. E. Wolfgang, L. Savitz, & N. Johnston (Eds.), *Sociology of crime and delinquency* (2nd ed., pp. 247–265). New York, NY: Wiley.

Lane, J., & Turner, S. (1999). Interagency collaboration in juvenile justice: Learning from experience. *Federal Probation, 63*(2), 33–39.

Langton, L., Berzofsky, M., Krebs, C., & Smiley-McDonald, H. (2012, August). *Special report: Victimizations not reported to the police, 2006–2010.* National Crime Victimization Survey. Retrieved from http://s3.documentcloud.org/documents/408260/victimizations-not-reported-to-police-2006-2010.pdf

Lanier, M., & Henry, S. (1998). *Essential criminology.* Boulder, CO: Westview.

Laub, J. H., & MacMurray, B. K. (1987). Increasing the prosecutor's role in juvenile court: Expectations and realities. *Justice System Journal, 12*, 196–209.

Leiber, M. J., Bishop, D., & Chamlin, M. B. (2011). Juvenile justice decision-making before and after the implementation of the disproportionate minority contact (DMC) mandate. *Justice Quarterly, 28*(3), 460–492.

Leiber, M. J., & Fox, K. C. (2005). Race and the impact of detention on juvenile justice decision making. *Crime & Delinquency, 51*, 470–497.

Levinson, R. B., & Chase, R. (2000). Private sector involvement in juvenile justice. *Corrections Today, 62*(2), 156–159.

Liddle, H. A., & Hogue, A. (2000). A family-based, developmental-ecological preventive intervention for high-risk adolescents. *Journal of Marital and Family Therapy, 26*, 265–279.

Lindner, C. (2004, Spring). A century of revolutionary changes in the United States court systems. *Perspectives,* 24–29.

Lipsey, M. W. (2009). The primary factors that characterize effective interventions with juvenile offenders: A meta-analytic overview. *Victims and Offenders, 4*, 124–147.

Lipsey, M. W., Wilson, D. B., & Cothern, L. (2000). *Effective intervention for serious juvenile offenders.* Washington, DC: Office of Juvenile Justice and Delinquency Prevention. Retrieved from www.ncjrs.gov/html/ojjdp/jjbul2000_04_6/contents.html

Liptak, A. (2010, May 17). Justices limit life sentences for juveniles. *New York Times.* Retrieved from www.nytimes.com/2010/05/18/us/politics/18court.html

Listenbee, R. L. (2016). *OJJDP hosts police and youth engagement roundtable.* Washington, DC: Office of Juvenile Justice and Delinquency Prevention. Retrieved from www.ojjdp.gov/newsletter/249928/sf_4.html

Listenbee, R. L., Jr., Torre, J., Boyle, G., Cooper, S. W., Deer, S., Durfee, D. T., . . . Taguba, A. (2012, December 12). *Report of the Attorney General's National Task Force on children exposed to violence.* Office of Juvenile Justice and Delinquency Prevention. Retrieved from www.justice.gov/defendingchildhood/cev-rpt-full.pdf

LoGalbo, A. P. (1998). *Is teen court a fair and effective juvenile crime diversion program?* (Unpublished manuscript). University of South Florida, New College, Tampa, FL.

Lopes, G., Krohn, M. D., Lizotte, A. J., Schmidt, N. M., Vasquez, B., & Bernburg, J. (2012). Labeling and cumulative disadvantage: The impact of formal police intervention on life chances and crime during emerging adulthood. *Crime & Delinquency, 58*(3), 456–488.

Lotz, R., & Lee, L. (1999). Sociability, school experience, and delinquency. *Youth & Society, 31*, 199–223.

Louisiana Law. (2012). *Children's code.* Retrieved from http://law.justia.com/codes/louisiana/2012/

Lowencamp, C. T., Cullen, F. T., & Pratt, T. C. (2003). Replicating Sampson and Groves's test of social disorganization theory: Revisiting a criminological classic. *Journal of Research in Crime and Delinquency, 40*, 351–373.

Ludwig, F. J. (1955). *Youth and the law: Handbook on laws affecting youth.* Brooklyn, NY: Foundation Press.

Lundman, R. J. (1993). *Prevention and control of juvenile delinquency* (2nd ed.). New York, NY: Oxford University Press.

Lundman, R. L., Sykes, R. E., & Clark, J. P. (1978). Police control of juveniles: A replication. *Journal of Research in Crime and Delinquency, 15*, 74–91.

Luxenburg, H., Limber, S. P., & Olweus, D. (2015). *Bullying in U.S. schools: 2014 status report.* Center City, MN: Hazeldon. Retrieved from www.violencepreventionworks.org/public/document/bullying_2015_statusreport.pdf

Lyerly, R. R., & Skipper, J. K. (1981). Differential rate of rural-urban delinquency. *Criminology, 19*, 385–399.

Lynam, D. R. (1998). Early identification of the fledgling psychopath: Locating the psychopathic child in the current nomenclature. *Journal of Abnormal Psychology, 107*, 566–575.

MacDonald, S. S., & Baroody-Hard, C. (1999). Communication between probation officers and judges: An innovative model. *Federal Probation, 63*(1), 42–50.

MacKenzie, D. L., & Souryal, C. C. (1991, October). Boot camp survey. *Corrections Today*, 90–96.

Maghan, J. (1999). Corrections countdown: Prisoners at the cusp of the 21st century. In P. M. Carlson & J. S. Garrett (Eds.), *Prison and jail administration: Practice and theory* (pp. 199–206). Gaithersburg, MD: Aspen.

Main, F. (2001, January 16). Gangs go global. *Chicago Sun-Times*, p. 3.

Main, F., & Spielman, F. (2000, October 5). Gang battles terrorize schools: Students locked inside after series of shootings near campuses. *Chicago Sun-Times*, p. 1.

Mallett, C. (2008). The disconnect between youths with mental health and special education disabilities and juvenile court outcomes. *Corrections Compendium, 33*(5), 1–7.

Malone, D., Romig, D., & Amstrong, T. (1998). *Juvenile probations: The balanced approach.* Reno, NV: National Council of Juvenile and Family Court Justice.

Margolin, G., & Gordis, E. B. (2000). The effects of family and community violence on children. *Annual Review of Psychology, 51*(1), 445–479.

Marshall, T. (2006, June 21). Teen interrogation not a textbook case. *St. Petersburg Times*, p. 1.

Marshall, W. L., Cripps, E., Anderson, D., & Cortoni, F. A. (1999). Self-esteem and coping strategies in child molesters. *Journal of Interpersonal Violence, 14*(9), 955–963.

Martens, W. H. J. (1999). Marcel: A case report of a violent sexual psychopath in remission. *International Journal of Offender Therapy and Comparative Criminology, 43*, 391–399.

Martin, C., Lurigio, A. J., & Olson, D. E. (2003). An examination of rearrests and reincarcerations among discharged day reporting center clients. *Federal Probation, 67*(1), 24–30. Retrieved from www.uscourts.gov/federalcourts/ProbationPretrialServices/FederalProbation Journal.aspx

Martin, G., & Peas, J. (1978). *Behavior modification: What it is and how to do it.* Englewood Cliffs, NJ: Prentice Hall.

Martin, J. R., Schulze, A. D., & Valdez, M. (1988). Taking aim at truancy. *FBI Law Enforcement Bulletin, 57*(5), 8–12.

Martin, T. H., Golder, S., Cynthia, L. C., & Sawning, S. (2013). Designing programming and interventions for women in the criminal justice system. *American Journal of Criminal Justice, 38*(1), 27–50.

Martinson, T. M. (1974). What works? Questions and answers about prison reform. *Public Interest, 35*(2), 22–54.

Massachusetts General Laws Annotated, ch. 119, sec. 55A (2016).

May, D. C. (1999). Scared kids, unattached kids, or peer pressure: Why do students carry firearms to school? *Youth & Society, 31*, 100–127.

Mays, G. L., & Winfree, L. T., Jr. (2000). *Juvenile justice.* Boston, MA: McGraw-Hill.

McAra, L., & McVie, S. (2010). Youth crime and justice: Key messages from the Edinburgh Study of Youth Transitions and Crime. *Criminology & Criminal Justice: An International Journal, 10*(2), 179–209.

McCloskey, K., & Raphael, D. (2005). Adult perpetrator gender asymmetries in child sexual assault victim selection: Results from the 2000 National Incident-Based Reporting system. *Journal of Child Sexual Abuse, 14*(4), 1–24.

McCollister, K. E., French, M. T., & Fang, H. (2010). The cost of crime to society: New crime-specific estimates for policy and program evaluation. *Drug and Alcohol Dependence, 108*(1–2), 98–109.

McCord, J., Widom, C. S., & Crowell, N. A. (2001). Preventing juvenile crime. In J. McCord, C. S. Widom, & N. A. Crowell (Eds.), *Juvenile crime, juvenile justice: Panel on juvenile crime: Prevention, treatment and control* (pp. 107–153).

Washington, DC: National Academy Press.

McGarrell, E. (2001). *Restorative justice conferences as an early response to young offenders.* Washington, DC: U.S. Department of Justice, Office of Juvenile Justice and Delinquency Prevention.

McGloin, J. M. (2005). Policy and intervention considerations of a network analysis of street gangs. *Criminology and Public Policy, 4,* 607–636.

McKay, M. D., Covell, K., & McNeil, J. (2006, October). *An Evaluation of Cape Breton regional police service's community Liaison officer program in Cape Breton-Victoria Region Schools.* Retrieved from http://cbucommons.ca/science/psychology/images/uploads/CLOPevaluation.pdf

McKeiver v. Pennsylvania, 403 U.S. 528, 91 S. Ct. (1971).

McLeod, M. (1999). *Satisfaction with youth court proceedings: A follow-up analysis of the Colonie (NY) youth court.* Paper presented at the Annual Meeting of the American Society of Criminology, Toronto, Canada.

McMahon, P. (2002, March 7). Mother convicted of Munchausen child abuse loses appeal. *Sun-Sentinel.* Retrieved from www.vachss.com/help_text/archive/kathy_bush.html

McPhee, M. (2000, November 26). Gangs waging war on street: Crips and Bloods take their deadly battle to Brooklyn. *Daily News*, p. 28.

Mears, D. P., & Butts, J. A. (2008). Using performance monitoring to improve the accountability, operations, and effectiveness of juvenile justice. *Criminal Justice Policy Review, 19*(3), 264–284.

Mednick, S. A., & Christiansen, K. O. (1977). *Biological bases of criminal behavior.* New York, NY: Gardner.

Mempa v. Rhay, 389 U.S. 128 (1967).

Mercer, R., Brooks, M., & Bryant, P. T. (2000). Global positioning satellite system: Tracking offenders in real time (Florida). *Corrections Today, 62*(4), 76–80.

Merton, R. K. (1938). Social structure and anomie. *American Sociological Review, 3,* 672–682.

Merton, R. K. (1955). *Social theory and social structure.* New York, NY: Free Press.

Michigan State Police. (2009). *MSP T.E.A.M. school liaison program.* Retrieved from www.michigan.gov/msp/0,1607,7–123–1589_1711_40754–10270—,00.html

Mihalic, S., Fagan, A., Irwin, K., Ballard, D., & Elliot, D. (2004). *Blueprints for violence prevention.* Washington, DC: U.S. Department of Justice, Office of Juvenile Justice and Delinquency Prevention.

Mihalic, S., Irwin, K., Elliot, D., Fagan, A., & Hansen, D. (2001). *Blueprints for violence prevention.* Washington, DC: U.S. Department of Justice. Retrieved from www.colorado.edu/cspv/blueprints/

Miller v. Alabama, 132 S. Ct. 2455 (2012).

Miller, H. (2010). If your friends jumped off of a bridge, would you do it too? Delinquent peers and susceptibility to peer influence. *Justice Quarterly, 27*(4), 473–491.

Miller, W. B. (1958). Lower class culture as a generating milieu of gang delinquency. *Journal of Social Issues, 14*(3), 5–19.

Miller, W. B. (1974). American youth gangs: Past and present. In A. Blumberg (Ed.), *Current perspectives on criminal behavior* (pp. 410–420). New York, NY: Knopf.

Miller, W. B. (2001, April). *The growth of gangs in the United States: 1970–1998* (OJJDP report). Washington, DC: U.S. Department of Justice.

Missouri Revised Statutes, 211.061 (2015).

Missouri Revised Statutes, 211.151 (2015).

Missouri Revised Statutes, 211.321 (2015).

Missouri Revised Statutes, 211.462 (2015).

Mitchell, K. J., Wolak, J., Finkelhor, D., & Jones, L. (2012). Investigators using the Internet to apprehend sex offenders: Findings from the Second National Juvenile Online Victimization Study. *Police Practice & Research, 13*(3), 267–281.

Mitchell, P., & Shaw, J. (2011). Factors affecting the recognition of mental health problems among adolescent offenders in custody. *Journal of Forensic Psychiatry & Psychology, 22*(3), 381–394.

Moffitt, T. E. (1993). Adolescence-limited and life-course persistent antisocial behavior: A developmental taxonomy. *Psychological Review, 100,* 674–701.

Moffitt, T. E. (2006). Life-course persistence versus adolescence-limited antisocial behavior. In D. Ciccheti & D. J. Cohen (Eds.), *Developmental psychopathology* (Vol. 3, pp. 570–598). New York, NY: Wiley.

Moffitt, T. E., & Caspi, A. (2001). Childhood predictors differentiate life-course persistent and adolescent-limited antisocial pathways among males and females. *Development and Psychopathology, 13,* 355–375.

Monk-Turner, E. (1990). The occupational achievements of community and four-year college entrants. *American Sociological Review, 55,* 719–725.

Montana Code Annotated, 41-3-425 (2011).

Montana Code Annotated, 41-5-1415 (2011).

Montana Code Annotated, 41-5-1502 (1) (2011).

Montana Code Annotated, Title 41, Minors (2011).

Montgomery v. Louisiana, 577 U.S. _____ (2016).

Moon, B., Hwang, H., & McCluskey, J. D. (2011). Causes of school bullying: Empirical test of a general theory of crime, differential association theory, and general strain theory. *Crime & Delinquency, 57*(6), 849–877.

Moore, B. M. (2001–2002). Blended sentencing for juveniles: The creation of a third criminal justice system? *Journal of Juvenile Law, 22,* 126–138.

Moraff, C. (2014, October 18). 10-year-old murder defendant shows failure of U.S. juvenile justice system. *The Daily Beast.* Retrieved from www.thedailybeast.com/articles/2014/10/18/10-year-old-murder-defendant-shows-failure-of-u-s-juvenile-justice-system.html

Morash, M. (1984). Establishment of a juvenile police record: The influence of individual and peer group characteristics. *Criminology, 22,* 97–111.

Morash, M., & Chesney-Lind, M. (1991). A reformulation and partial test of the power control theory of delinquency. *Justice Quarterly, 8,* 347–379.

Morrissey v. Brewer, 408 U.S. 471 (1972).

Mountain Education Center High School. (2017). *About MEC.* Retrieved from www.mymec.org/about/about_mec

Moyer, I. (1981). Demeanor, sex, and race in police processing. *Journal of Criminal Justice, 9,* 235–246.

Moyer, I. L. (2001). *Criminological theories: Traditional and nontraditional voices and themes.* Thousand Oaks, CA: Sage.

Muhammad, D. (2012, August 28). A roadmap to the future of juvenile justice. *New America Media, Commentary.* Retrieved from http://newamericamedia.org/2012/08/a-roadmap-to-the-future-of-juvenile-justice.php

Multijurisdictional Counterdrug Task Force Training. (2010). *Street gangs: The prison connection.* Pearl, MS: Author & St. Petersburg College.

Murray, J., Loeber, R., & Pardini, D. (2012). Parental involvement in the criminal justice system and the development of youth theft, marijuana use, and poor academic performance. *Criminology, 50*(1), 255–302.

Myers, S. M. (2004, April). *Police encounters with juvenile suspects: Explaining the use of authority and provision of support.* Executive Summary Report. Retrieved from www.ncjrs.gov/pdffiles1/nij/grants/205124.pdf

Naffine, N. (1996). *Feminism and criminology.* Philadelphia, PA: Temple University Press.

Nansel, T. R., Overpeck, M. D., Haynie, D. L., Ruan, W. J., & Scheidt, P. C. (2003). Relationships between bullying and violence among U.S. youth. *Archives of Pediatric and Adolescent Medicine, 157*(4), 348–353.

National Advisory Commission on Criminal Justice Standards and Goals. (1973). *Courts.* Washington, DC: U.S. Department of Justice.

National Center for Education Statistics. (2015). *Digest of education statistics: Table 230.70. Percentage of students ages 12–18 who reported being afraid of attack or harm, by location and selected student and school characteristics: Selected years, 1995–2013.* U.S. Department of Justice and U.S. Department of Education. Washington, DC: U.S. Government Printing Office.

National Center for Juvenile Justice. (2014). *Juvenile Offenders and Victims: 2014 National Report.* Washington, DC: Office of Juvenile Justice and Delinquency Prevention.

National Center on Education, Disability and Juvenile Justice. (2007, April 30). *Resources on prevention of delinquency.* Retrieved from www.edjj.org/focus/prevention/

National Children's Advocacy Center. (2010). *Law enforcement's initial response to child sexual abuse: Guidelines for patrol officers.* Retrieved from www.nationalcac.org/professionals/index.php?option=com_content&task=view&id=40&Itemid=60

National Conference of Commissioners on Uniform State Laws. (1968). *Uniform Juvenile Court Act.* Philadelphia, PA: Author.

National Council of Juvenile and Family Court Judges. (2005). *Improving court practice in juvenile delinquency cases.* Washington, DC: Office of Juvenile Justice and Delinquency Prevention.

National Crime Victimization Survey Resource Guide. (n.d.). Retrieved from www.icpsr.umich.edu/NACJD/NCVS

National Criminal Justice Reference Service. (2005). *Gangs: Facts and figures.* Washington, DC: U.S. Department of Justice. Retrieved from www.ncjrs.org/spotlight/gangs/facts.html

National District Attorneys Association. (2016, November 12). *National Prosecution Standards* (3rd ed). Retrieved from www.ndaa.org/pdf/NDAA%20NPS%203rd%20Ed.%20w%20Revised%20Commentary.pdf

National Gang Center. (2010). *What is a gang?* Retrieved from www.nationalgangcenter.gov/About/FAQ#q1

National Gang Center. (2012, Spring). *G.R.E.A.T initiative in Central America.* Tallahassee, FL: Author.

National Gang Center. (2013). *National Youth Gang Survey Analysis.* Retrieved from www.nationalgangcenter.gov/Survey-Analysis

National Gang Intelligence Center. (2015). *National gang report—2015.* Washington, DC: Author.

National Girls Institute. (2013). *Research brief: Translating gender-responsive theory to practice.* Retrieved from www.nationalgirlsinstitute.org/i-work-with-girls/resources-best-practices/gender-responsive-theories/

National Institute on Drug Abuse. (2013). *Facts on drugs: Prescription drugs.* Retrieved from http://teens.drugabuse.gov/drug-facts/prescription-drugs

National Institute on Drug Abuse. (2016). *Monitoring the future survey: High school and youth trends.* Bethesda, MD: NIDA. Retrieved from www.drugabuse.gov/publications/drugfacts/monitoring-future-survey-high-school-youth-trends

National Institute for Early Education Research. (2015). *State preschool yearbook.* Rutgers Graduate School of Education. Retrieved from http://nieer.org/wp-content/uploads/2016/05/Yearbook_2015_rev1.pdf

National Institute of Justice. (2010, June 4). *Evaluating G.R.E.A.T.: A school-based gang prevention program.* Washington, DC: U.S. Department of Justice.

National Juvenile Defender Center. (2016). *Defend children: A blueprint for effective juvenile defender services.* Washington, DC: National Juvenile Defender Center

National Youth Network. (2010). *Behavior modification—child behavior problems—out of control teens—behavior modification school.* Retrieved from www.nationalyouth.com/behaviormodification.html

Nederlof, E., van der Ham, A., Dingemans, P., & Oei, K. (2010, October). The relation between dimensions of personality and personality pathology and offence type and severity in juvenile delinquents. *Journal of Forensic Psychiatry & Psychology, 21*(5), 711–720.

Nelson, L., & Lind, D. (2015). The school to prison pipeline, explained. *Justice Policy Institute.* Retrieved from www.justicepolicy.org/news/8775

Neubauer, D. W., & Fradella, H. F. (2013). *America's courts and the criminal justice system.* Stamford, CT: Cengage Learning.

New Jersey Office of the Attorney General. (2005). *Attorney general guidelines for stationhouse adjustment of juvenile delinquency offenses.* Retrieved from www.nj.gov/oag/dcj/agguide/directives/directives_2005/dir-2005-4-station-guide.pdf

New Jersey Parents' Caucus. (2013). *NJPC Parents Empowerment Academy.* Retrieved from www.newjerseyparentscaucus.org/parents_acad_lp.htm

New Mexico Statutes—Section 32A-4-2—Definitions (2006).

New York Family Court Act, 342.2 (2) (2010).

New York Family Court Act, 712(a) McKinney (1999).

New York Sessions Laws. (1962).

Nichols, P. (2004). No disposable kids: A developmental look at disposability. *Reclaiming Children and Youth, 13*(1), 5–11.

North Carolina Administrative Office of the Courts. (1995). *Report on the Teen Court Programs in North Carolina.* Raleigh, NC: Author.

North Carolina Code, ch. 7B Juvenile Code, 1501 (2010).

North Dakota Century Code, 27-20-29 (2) (2007).

Novotney, L., Mertinko, E., Lange, J., & Baker, T. K. (2000). *Juvenile mentoring program: A progress report.* Washington, DC: Office of Juvenile Justice and Delinquency Prevention.

NYC mom arrested in son's death. (2006, November 16). *Journal Star* (Peoria, IL), p. A8.

Nyquist, O. (1960). *Juvenile justice: A comparative study with special reference to the Swedish Welfare Board and the California juvenile court system.* London, UK: Macmillan.

Oates, K., Jones, D., Denson, D., Sirotnak, A., Gary, N., & Krugman, R. (2000). Erroneous concerns about sexual abuse. *Child Abuse & Neglect, 24,* 149–157.

O.C.G.A. 19-10-1 (2010).

O.C.G.A. § 20-2-145 (2012).

Office of Community Oriented Police Services. (2007). *Gun violence among serious young offenders.* Washington, DC: Author.

Office of Juvenile Justice and Delinquency Prevention. (1979). *Delinquency prevention: Theories and strategies.*

Washington, DC: U.S. Government Printing Office.

Office of Juvenile Justice and Delinquency Prevention. (1980). *Juvenile justice: Before and after the onset of delinquency.* Washington, DC: U.S. Government Printing Office.

Office of Juvenile Justice and Delinquency Prevention. (1996, March). *Juvenile probation: The workhorse of the juvenile justice system.* Washington, DC: U.S. Government Printing Office.

Office of Juvenile Justice and Delinquency Prevention. (1998). *Guiding principles for promising female programming.* Retrieved from www.ojjdp.ncjrs.gov/pubs/principles/contents.html

Office of Juvenile Justice and Delinquency Prevention. (2000, September). Preventing adolescent gang involvement. *Juvenile Justice Bulletin.* Washington, DC: U.S. Department of Justice.

Office of Juvenile Justice and Delinquency Prevention. (2001, January). The decline in child sexual abuse cases. *Juvenile Justice Bulletin.* Retrieved from www.ncjrs.gov/pdffiles1/ojjdp/184741.pdf

Office of Juvenile Justice and Delinquency Prevention. (2003). *State statutes define who is under juvenile court jurisdiction* (Juveniles in Court, OJJDP National Report Series Bulletin). Washington, DC: U.S. Department of Justice.

Office of Juvenile Justice and Delinquency Prevention. (2004a). *Juveniles in corrections.* Washington, DC: Office of Justice Programs, NCJ 202885. Retrieved from www.ncjrs.gov/html/ojjdp/202885/contents.html

Office of Juvenile Justice and Delinquency Prevention. (2004b). *Model programs guide: Day treatment.* Washington, DC: Office of Justice Programs. Retrieved from www2.dsgonline.com/mpg/program_types_description.aspx?program_type=Day%20Treatment&continuum=intermediate

Office of Juvenile Justice and Delinquency Prevention. (2006). *Juvenile offenders and victims: 2006 national report.* Retrieved from www.ojjdp.ncjrs.gov/ojstatbb/nr2006/index.html

Office of Juvenile Justice and Delinquency Prevention. (2007). *Best practices to address community gang problems: OJJDP's Comprehensive Gang Model.* Washington, DC: United States Department of Justice.

Office of Juvenile Justice and Delinquency Prevention. (2008). *Highlights of the 2006 National Youth Gang Survey.* Washington, DC: U.S. Department of Justice. Retrieved from www.ncjrs.gov/pdffiles1/ojjdp/fs200805.pdf

Office of Juvenile Justice and Delinquency Prevention. (2011a). Washington, DC: U.S. Department of Justice. Retrieved from www.ojp.gov/newsroom/pressreleases/2011/JJ_PR-121611.pdf

Office of Juvenile Justice and Delinquency Prevention. (2011b, October). *OJP fact sheet: Bullying.* Retrieved from www.ojp.usdoj.gov/newsroom/factsheets/ojpfs_bullying.html

Office of Juvenile Justice and Delinquency Prevention. (2012, December 17). *OJJDP statistical briefing book.* Retrieved from www.ojjdp.gov/ojstatbb/structure_process/qa04113.asp?qaDate=2011

Office of Juvenile Justice and Delinquency Prevention. (2013, August 5). *OJJDP statistical briefing book.* Retrieved from www.ojjdp.gov/ojstatbb/structure_process/qa04205.asp?qaDate=2012

Office of Juvenile Justice and Delinquency Prevention. (2014, August 29). *OJJDP statistical briefing book.* Retrieved from www.ojjdp.gov/ojstatbb/structure_process/qa04122.asp?qaDate=2013

Office of Juvenile Justice and Delinquency Prevention. (2016, April 29). *OJJDP statistical briefing book.* Retrieved from www.ojjdp.gov/ojstatbb/structure_process/qa04101.asp?qaDate=2015

Office of Juvenile Justice and Delinquency Prevention. (2017a). *OJJDP Statistical Briefing Book*. Online. Available: http://www.ojjdp.gov/ojstatbb/structure_process/qa04111.asp?qaDate=2015. Released on March 27, 2017.

Office of Juvenile Justice and Delinquency Prevention. (2017b). *OJJDP Statistical Briefing Book*. Online. Available: http://www.ojjdp.gov/ojstatbb/structure_process/qa04113.asp?qaDate=2015. Released on March 27, 2017.

Office of Juvenile Justice and Delinquency Prevention. (2017c). *OJJDP Statistical Briefing Book*. Online. Available: http://www.ojjdp.gov/ojstatbb/structure_process/qa04110.asp?qaDate=2015. Released on March 27, 2017.

Office of Juvenile Justice and Delinquency Prevention. (2017d). *OJJDP Statistical Briefing Book*. Online. Available: http://www.ojjdp.gov/ojstatbb/structure_process/qa04112.asp?qaDate=2015. Released on March 27, 2017.

Office of Juvenile Justice and Delinquency Prevention. (n.d.). *Guide for implementing the balanced and restorative justice model*, NCJ 167887. Retrieved from www.ojjdp.ncjrs.gov/PUBS/implementing/balanced.html

Office of the Special Representative of the Secretary-General for Children and Armed Conflict. (2013). *Youth and armed conflict*. New York, NY: United Nations.

Ohio Revised Code § 2151.022 (2011).

Ohio Revised Code § 2151.04 (2011).

Ohlin, L. E. (1998). The future of juvenile justice policy and research. *Crime & Delinquency, 44*, 143–153.

OJJDP News at a Glance. (2010, January/February). *Coordinating Council charts course for the future*. Retrieved from www.ojjdp.ncjrs.gov

OJJDP News at a Glance. (2013, January/February). *OJJDP launches publication series on mental health needs and outcomes of youth in the juvenile justice system*. Retrieved from www.ojjdp.gov/newsletter/240749/sf_2.html

Onifade, E., Petersen, J., Bynum, T. S., & Davidson, W. S. (2011). Multilevel recidivism prediction. *Criminal Justice & Behavior, 38*(8), 840–853.

Onyskiw, J. E. (2003). Domestic violence and children's adjustment: A review of research. In R. A. Geffner, R. S. Igelman, & J. Zellner (Eds.), *The effects of intimate partner violence on children* (pp. 11–45). New York, NY: Haworth Maltreatment & Trauma Press.

Oregon Juvenile Code § 419C.097 (2015).

Organized Crime and Gang Section. (2013). *About violent gangs*. Washington, DC: U.S. Department of Justice.

Osborne, D., & Gaebler, T. (1992). *Reinventing government: How the entrepreneurial spirit is transforming the public sector*. Reading, MA: Addison-Wesley.

Osgood, D. W., & Chambers, J. M. (2000). Social disorganization outside the metropolis: An analysis of rural youth violence. *Criminology, 38*, 81–115.

Oshkosh, Wisconsin, Police Department. (2010). *Police school liaison officer qualifications*. Retrieved from www.waupaca.k12.wi.us/positiondescriptions/PoliceLiaison.pdf

Ostermann, M. (2009). An analysis of New Jersey's day reporting center and halfway back programs: Embracing the rehabilitative ideal through evidence-based practices. *Journal of Offender Rehabilitation, 48*(2), 139–153.

Pagani, L., Boulerice, B., & Vitaro, F. (1999). Effects of poverty on academic failure and delinquency in boys: A change and process model approach. *Journal of Child Psychology and Psychiatry and Allied Disciplines, 40*, 1209–1219.

Palmer, T., Bohnstedt, M., & Lewis, R. (1978). *The evaluation of juvenile diversion projects: Final report 1978*. California Department of the Youth Authority. Washington, DC: U.S. Department of Justice, Law Enforcement Assistance Administration.

Palumbo, M. G., & Ferguson, J. (1995). Evaluating gang resistance education and training: Is the impact the same as Drug Abuse Resistance Education (DARE)? *Evaluation Review, 19*, 597–619.

Papachristos, A. (2005, March/April). Gang world. *Foreign Policy*, 48–55.

Pardin, D. A., Raine, A., Erickson, K., & Loeber, R. (2014). Lower Amygdala volume in men is associated with childhood aggression, early psychopathic traits, and future violence. *Biological Psychiatry, 75*(1), 73–80.

Parker-Jimenez, J. (1997). An offender's experience with the criminal justice system. *Federal Probation, 61*(1), 47–52.

Parsons, A. (1998, August). Meth and cocaine: Addictive drugs alike but different. *Southeast Missourian*, pp. 1–4.

Pattillo, M. E. (1998). Sweet mothers and gangbangers: Managing crime in a black middle-class neighborhood. *Social Forces, 76*, 747–774.

Paul, R. H., Marx, B. P., & Orsillo, S. M. (1999). Acceptance-based psychotherapy in the treatment of an adjudicated exhibitionist: A case example. *Behavior Therapy, 30*, 149–162.

Paxson, C. H., & Waldfogel, J. (1999). Parental resources and child abuse and neglect. *American Economic Review, 89*, 239–244.

Peak, K. J. (1999). Gangs: Origins, status, community responses, and policy implications. In R. Muraskin & A. R. Roberts (Eds.), *Visions for change: Crime and justice in the twenty-first century* (pp. 51–63). Upper Saddle River, NJ: Prentice Hall.

Pears, K. C., & Capaldi, D. M. (2001). Intergenerational transmission of abuse: A two-generational prospective study of an at-risk sample. *Child Abuse & Neglect, 25*, 1439–1461.

Penn, B. E. (2016). *Responding to strained minority youth and police relations: Policing by TOTALS.* Houston, TX: Teen and Police Service Academy.

People ex rel. O'Connell v. Turner, Ill. 280, 286 (1870).

People v. Dominguez, 256 Cal.App. 2d 623 (1967).

Perez, C. M., & Widom, C. S. (1994). Childhood victimization and long-term intellectual and academic outcomes. *Child Abuse & Neglect, 18,* 617–633.

Perlmutter, B. F. (1987). Delinquency and learning disabilities: Evidence for compensatory behaviors and adaptation. *Journal of Youth and Adolescence, 16,* 89–95.

Perry, C. L., Komro, K. A., Veblen-Mortenson, S., Bosma, L. M., Farbakhsh, K., Munson, K. A., . . . Lytle, L. A. (2003). A randomized controlled trial of the middle and junior high school DARE and DARE Plus programs. *Archives of Pediatric and Adolescent Medicine, 157*(2), 178–184.

Peter, T. (2009). Exploring taboos: Comparing male- and female-perpetrated child sexual abuse. *Journal of Interpersonal Violence, 24*(7), 1111–1128.

Peters, S. R., & Peters, S. D. (1998). Violent adolescent females. *Corrections Today, 60*(3), 28–29.

Petition of Ferrier, 103 Ill. 367, 371 (1882).

Piliavin, I., & Briar, S. (1964). Police encounters with juveniles. *American Journal of Sociology, 70,* 206–214.

Pinnock, D. (1996). Arresting crime against children. *Child and Youth Care, 14*(3), 12.

Piquero, A. R., Gomez-Smith, Z., & Langton, L. (2004). Discerning fairness where others may not: Low self-control and unfair sanctions perceptions. *Criminology, 42,* 699–734.

Piquero, A. R., Jennings, W. G., & Farrington, D. P. (2010). On the malleability of self-control: Theoretical and policy implications

regarding a general theory of crime. *Justice Quarterly, 27*(6), 803–834.

Piscotta, A. W. (1982). Saving the children: The promise and practice of *parens patriae,* 1838–98. *Crime & Delinquency, 28*(3), 424–425.

Plass, P. S., & Carmody, D. C. (2005). Routine activities of delinquent and non-delinquent victims of violent crime. *American Journal of Criminal Justice, 29,* 235–246.

Platt, A. (1977). *The child savers* (2nd ed.). Chicago, IL: University of Chicago Press.

Polk, K. (1984). The new marginal youth. *Crime & Delinquency, 30,* 462–480.

Polk, K., & Schafer, W. B. (1972). *School and delinquency.* Englewood Cliffs, NJ: Prentice Hall.

Pollock, J. M. (1994). *Ethics in crime and justice: Dilemmas and decisions* (2nd ed.). Belmont, CA: Wadsworth.

Pollock, W., Oliver, W., & Menard, S. (2012). Measuring the problem: A national examination of disproportionate police contact in the United States. *Criminal Justice Review, 37*(2), 153–173.

Pope, C. E., & Snyder, H. N. (2003, April). Race as a factor in juvenile arrests. *Juvenile Justice Bulletin.* Retrieved from www.ncjrs.gov/pdffiles1/ojjdp/189180.pdf

Porterfield, A. L. (1946). *Youth in trouble.* Fort Worth, TX: Leo Potishman Foundation.

Portwood, S. G., Grady, M. T., & Dutton, S. E. (2000). Enhancing law enforcement identification and investigation of child maltreatment. *Child Abuse & Neglect, 24,* 195–207.

Postman, N. (1991). Quoted in D. Osborne & T. Gaebler. *Reinventing government: How the entrepreneurial spirit is transforming the public sector* (p. 19). Reading, MA: Addison-Wesley.

Poythrees, N. G., Edens, J. F., & Lilienfeld, S. O. (1998). Criterion-related validity of the Psychopathic Personality Inventory in a prison sample. *Psychological Assessment, 10,* 426–430.

President's Commission on Law Enforcement and Administration of Justice. (1967). *Task force report: Juvenile delinquency and youth crime.* Washington, DC: U.S. Government Printing Office.

Prevent Delinquency Project. (n.d.). *Prevent Delinquency Project.* Retrieved from www.preventdelinquency.org

Puzzanchera, C. H. (2003). *Delinquency cases waived to criminal court, 1990–1999* (OJJDP Fact Sheet No. 35). Washington, DC: U.S. Department of Justice, Office of Juvenile Justice and Delinquency Prevention.

Puzzanchera, C. (2009). *Juvenile arrests 2008.* Washington, DC: Office of Juvenile Justice and Delinquency Prevention. Retrieved from www.ncjrs.gov/pdffiles1/ojjdp/228479.pdf

Puzzanchera, C., Stahl, A., Finnegan, T., Snyder, H., Poole, T., & Tierney, N. (2000). *Juvenile court statistics 1997* (NCJ 180864). Washington, DC: National Center for Juvenile Justice, U.S. Department of Justice. Retrieved from www.ncjrs.gov/pdffiles1/ojjdp/180864.pdf

Pyrooz, D. (2016). *Dispelling myths about juvenile gang members in the United States.* Washington, DC: National Institutes of Health.

Quinn, K. (2012, December 17). School violence prevention: 10 things every cop should know: An SRO's perspective on school safety training. *Law Officer.* Retrieved from www.lawofficer.com/article/training/school-violence-prevention-10

Quinney, R. (1970). *The social reality of crime.* Boston, MA: Little, Brown.

Quinney, R. (1974). *Critique of legal order: Crime control in capitalist society.* Boston, MA: Little, Brown.

Quinney, R. (1975). *Criminology.* Boston, MA: Little, Brown.

Radu, M. (2005). Europe, fall 2005: Gangs in search of an ideology. *Foreign Policy Research Institute, 6*(7). Retrieved from www.fpri.org/ww/0607.200511.radu.europegangs.html

Rafter, N. (2004). Earnest Hooton and the biological tradition in American criminology. *Criminology, 42,* 735–772.

Raine, A. (2014). *The anatomy of violence: The biological roots of crime.* New York, NY: Vintage Books.

Ramsey, A. L., Rust, J., & Sobel, S. M. (2003). Evaluation of the gang resistance and training program: A school-based prevention program. *Education, 124*(2), 297–309.

Rand, M., & Catalano, S. (2007). Criminal victimization, 2006. *Bureau of Justice Statistics Bulletin.* Retrieved from www.ojp.usdoj.gov/bjs/pub/pdf/cv06.pdf

Rangel, E. (2012, December 17). Texas juvenile justice system: Sex-abuse scandal spurred positive changes. *Amarillo Globe News.* Retrieved from http://amarillo.com/news/local-news/2012-12-16/scandal-spurred-positive-changes

Raskind, M. (2010). *Research trends: Is there a link between LD and juvenile delinquency?* Great Schools. Retrieved from www.greatschools.org/LD/managing/link-between-ld-and-juvenile-delinquency.gs?content=932

Reaume, S. (2009). Improved hiring for child protective investigators. *Law & Order, 57*(2), 19–23.

Rebellon, C. J. (2002). Reconsidering the broken homes/delinquency relationship and exploring its mediating mechanism(s). *Criminology, 40,* 103–136.

Reckless, W. C. (1961). A new theory of delinquency and crime. *Federal Probation, 25,* 42–46.

Reckless, W. C. (1967). *The crime problem.* New York, NY: Appleton-Century-Crofts.

Redding, R. E. (2010, June). *Juvenile transfer laws: An effective deterrent to delinquency?* Washington, DC: Office of Juvenile Justice. Retrieved from www.ncjrs.gov/pdffiles1/ojjdp/220595.pdf

Redondo, S., Martinez-Catena, A., & Andrés-Pueyo, A. (2012). Therapeutic effects of a cognitive-behavioural treatment with juvenile offenders. *European Journal of Psychology Applied to Legal Context, 4*(2), 159–178.

Regoli, R. M., & Hewitt, J. D. (1994). *Delinquency in society: A child-centered approach.* New York, NY: McGraw-Hill.

Reichel, P. L. (2005). *Comparative criminal justice systems* (4th ed.). Upper Saddle River, NJ: Prentice Hall.

Reichel, P., & Seyfrit, C. (1984). A peer jury in juvenile court. *Crime & Delinquency, 30*(3), 423–438.

Reid, B. (2006, April 7). Teens deal out justice their way in Maryvale. *The Arizona Republic.*

Reid, S. T. (2006). *Crime and criminology* (11th ed.). New York, NY: McGraw-Hill.

Rendleman, D. R. (1974). *Parens patriae:* From chancery to the juvenile court. In F. L. Faust & P. J. Brantingham (Eds.), *Juvenile justice* (pp. 72–117). St. Paul, MN: West.

Rennison, C. M. (2003, February). Intimate partner violence, 1993–2001 (NCJ 197838). *Crime Data Brief, Bureau of Justice Statistics.* Retrieved from www.bjs.gov/content/pub/pdf/ipv01.pdf

Rennison, C. M., & Melde, C. (2009). Exploring the use of victim surveys to study gang crime: Prospects and possibilities. *Criminal Justice Review, 34,* 489–514.

Restorative Justice for Illinois. (1999). *What is restorative justice?* Des Plaines, IL: LSSI/Prison and Family Ministry.

Riggs, N. R., Greenberg, M. T., Kusché, C. A., & Pentz, M. A. (2006). The mediational role of neurocognition in the behavioral outcomes of a social-emotional prevention program in elementary school students: Effects of the PATHS curriculum. *Prevention Science, 7*(1), 91–102.

Rinehart, W. (1991). *Convicted child molesters* (Unpublished master's thesis). Western Illinois University, Macomb, IL.

Ritter, N. M., & Simon, T. R. (2013). *Changing course: Preventing gang membership.* Washington, DC: National Institute of Justice.

Ritter, N. M., Simon, T. R., & Mahendra, R. R. (2013). *Changing course: Preventing gang membership: Executive summary.* Washington DC: National Institute of Justice.

Roberts, A. R. (1989). *Juvenile justice: Policies, programs, services.* Chicago, IL: Dorsey.

Rocky Mountain High Intensity Drug Trafficking Area. (2016). *The legalization of marijuana in Colorado: The impact* (Vol. 4). Retrieved from www.rmhidta.org/html/2016%20FINAL%20Legalization%20of%20Marijuana%20in%20Colorado%20The%20Impact.pdf

Rodney, E. H., & Mupier, R. (1999). Comparing the behaviors and social environments of offending and non-offending African-American adolescents. *Journal of Offender Rehabilitation, 30*(1/2), 65–80.

Rodriguez, N. (2005). Restorative justice, communities, and delinquency: Who do we reintegrate? *Criminology and Public Policy, 4*(1), 601–629.

Rodriguez, N. (2007). Restorative justice at work: Examining the impact of restorative justice resolutions on juvenile recidivism. *Crime and Delinquency, 53*(3), 355–379.

Rodriguez, N. (2010). The cumulative effect of race and ethnicity in juvenile court outcomes and why preadjudication detention matters. *Journal of Research in Crime and Delinquency, 47*(3), 391–413.

Roman, C. G., Kane, M., Baer, D., & Turner, E. (2009). *Community organizations and crime: An examination of the social-institutional processes of neighborhoods.* Urban Institute Justice Policy Center. Retrieved from www.ncjrs.gov/pdffiles1/nij/grants/227645.pdf

Roper v. Simmons, 543 U.S. 551 (2005).

Ross, R. R., & McKay, H. B. (1978). Behavioral approaches to treatment in corrections: Requiem for a panacea. *Canadian Journal of Criminology, 20,* 279–298.

Rossler, M. T., & Terrill, W. (2012). Police responsiveness to service-related requests. *Police Quarterly, 15*(1), 3–24.

Roush, D. W. (Ed.). (1996). *Desktop guide to good juvenile detention practice. Research report.* Washington, DC: U.S. Department of Justice, Office of Justice Programs, Office of Juvenile Justice and Delinquency Prevention.

Roy, S., & Barton, S. (2006, June). Convicted drunk drivers in electronic monitoring home detention and day reporting centers: An exploratory study. *Federal Probation,* 49–55.

Ryan, E. S. (2012). Delinquent friends and reactions to strain: An examination of direct and indirect pathways. *Western Criminology Review, 13*(1), 16–36.

Ryan, J. P., Williams, A. B., & Courtney, M. E. (2013). Adolescent neglect, juvenile delinquqency, and the risk of recidivism. *Journal of Youth and Adolescence, 42*(3), 454–465.

Rydberg, J., & Terrill, W. (2010). The effect of higher education on police behavior. *Police Quarterly, 13*(1), 92–120.

Sanders, W. B. (1974). Some early beginnings of the children's court movement in England. In F. L. Faust & P. J. Brantingham (Eds.), *Juvenile justice philosophy* (pp. 46–51). St. Paul, MN: West.

Sappenfield, A. (2008, July 29). *Minimum and maximum ages for juvenile court: Delinquency jurisdiction in other states.* Wisconsin Legislative Council Staff Memorandum. Retrieved from www.legis.state.wi.us/lc/committees/study/2008/JUVE/files/memo3_juve.pdf

Satterfield, J. H. (1987). Childhood diagnostic and neurophysiological predictors of teenage arrest rates: An eight-year prospective study. In S. A. Mednick, T. E. Moffitt, & S. S. Stack (Eds.), *The causes of crime: New biological approaches* (pp. 146–167). Cambridge, UK: Cambridge University Press.

Scaramella, G. L. (2000). Methamphetamines: A blast from the past. *Crime & Justice International, 16,* 7–8.

Schafer, W. E., & Polk, K. (Eds.). (1967). Delinquency and the schools. In *Task force report: Juvenile delinquency and youth crime* (President's Commission on Law Enforcement and the Administration of Justice). Washington, DC: U.S. Government Printing Office.

Schaffner, L. (2007). Violence against girls provokes girls' violence: From private injury to public harm. *Violence Against Women, 13*(12), 1229–1248.

Schetky, D. H. (2009, September). Restorative justice: An alternative model whose time has come. *The Brown University Child and Adolescent Behavior Newsletter, 25*(9), 5–7.

Schinke, S. P., & Gilchrist, L. D. (1984). *Life counseling skills with adolescents.* Baltimore, MD: University Park Press.

Schneider, C. (2016). Foster parents indicted for murder of 2-year-old Laila Daniel. *Atlanta Journal Constitution.* Retrieved from www.ajc.com/news/local/foster-parents-indicted-for-murder-death-year-old-laila-daniel/we353XFqxOUAJsELX3Eg7I

Schreck, C. J., & Fisher, B. S. (2004). Specifying the influence of family and peers on violent victimization: Extending routine activities and lifestyles theories. *Journal of Interpersonal Violence, 19*(9), 1021–1041.

Schroeder, R. D., Osgood, A. K., & Oghia, M. J. (2010). Family transitions and juvenile delinquency. *Sociological Inquiry, 80*(4), 579–604.

Schur, E. M. (1973). *Radical non-intervention: Rethinking the delinquency problem.* Englewood Cliffs, NJ: Prentice Hall.

Schwartz, I. M., Weiner, N. A., & Enosh, G. (1998). Nine lives and then some: Why the juvenile court does not roll over and die. *Wake Forest Law Review, 33,* 533–552.

Schwartz, I. M., Weiner, N. A., & Enosh, G. (1999). Myopic justice? The juvenile court and child welfare systems. *Annals of the American Academy of Political & Social Science, 564,* 126–141.

Scott, J. W., & Vaz, E. W. (1963). A perspective on middle-class delinquency. *Canadian Journal of Economics and Political Science, 29,* 324–335.

Scudder, R. G., Blount, W. R., Heide, K. M., & Silverman, I. J. (1993). Important links between child abuse, neglect, and delinquency. *International Journal of Offender Therapy and Comparative Criminology, 37,* 310–323.

Sealock, M. D., & Simpson, S. (1998). Unraveling bias in arrest decisions: The role of juvenile offender type-scripts. *Justice Quarterly, 15,* 427–457.

Sedlak, A. J., Doueck, H. J., Lyons, P., & Wells, S. J. (2005). Child maltreatment and the justice system: Predictors of court involvement. *Research on Social Work Practice, 15,* 389–407.

Sedlak, A. J., & McPherson, K. S. (2010). *Youth's needs and services: Findings from the survey of youth in residential placement.* Washington, DC: Office of Juvenile Justice and Delinquency Prevention. Retrieved from www.ncjrs.gov/pdffiles1/ojjdp/227728.pdf

Sedlak, A. J., Mettenburg, J., Basena, M., Petta, I., McPherson, K., Greene, A., & Li, S. (2010). *Fourth National Incidence Study of Child Abuse and Neglect (NIS–4): Report to Congress.* Washington, DC: U.S. Department of Health and Human Services, Administration for Children and Families.

Semple, R., Lee, J., Rosa, D., & Miller, L. (2010). A randomized trial of mindfulness-based cognitive therapy for children: Promoting mindful attention to enhance social-emotional resiliency in children. *Journal of Child & Family Studies, 19*(2), 218–229.

Seyfrit, C. L., Reichel, P., & Stutts, B. (1987). Peer juries as a juvenile justice diversion technique. *Youth and Society, 18*(3), 302–316.

Shared Hope International. (2008). *Domestic minor sex trafficking: Baton Rouge/New Orleans, Louisiana.* Arlington, VA: Author.

Shariff, S., & Johnny, L. (2007). Cyber-libel and cyber-bullying: Can schools protect student reputations and free-expression in virtual environments? *Education Law Journal, 16*, 307–342.

Shaw, C. R., & McKay, H. D. (1942). *Juvenile delinquency and urban areas.* Chicago, IL: University of Chicago Press.

Shaw, C. R., & McKay, H. D. (1969). *Juvenile delinquency and urban areas* (Rev. ed.). Chicago, IL: University of Chicago Press.

Sheldon, W. H. (1949). *Varieties of delinquent youth: An introduction to constitutional psychiatry.* New York, NY: Harper & Row.

Shelton, T. L., Barkley, R. A., & Crosswait, C. (2000). Multimethod psychoeducational intervention for preschool children with disruptive behavior: Two-year post-treatment follow-up. *Journal of Abnormal Child Psychology, 28*, 253–266.

Sherman, L. W., Gottfredson, D., MacKenzie, D., Eck, J., Reuter, P., & Bushaway, S. (1997). *Preventing crime: What works, what doesn't, what's promising—A report to the United States Congress.* Washington, DC: U.S. Government Printing Office. Retrieved from www.ncjrs.org

Sherman, L. W., & Weisburd, D. (1995). General deterrent effects of police patrol in crime "hot spots": A randomized study. *Justice Quarterly, 12*, 625–640.

Shoenfelt, E. L., & Huddleston, M. R. (2006). The Truancy Court Diversion Program of the Kentucky Family Court System Warren Circuit Court Division III, Bowling Green, Kentucky: An evaluation of impact on attendance and academic

performance. *Family Court Review: An Interdisciplinary Journal, 44*, 673–685.

Shorkey, C. T., & Armendariz, J. (1985). Personal worth, self-esteem, anomia, hostility, and irrational thinking of abusing mothers: A multivariate approach. *Journal of Clinical Psychology, 41*, 414–421.

Short, J. F., & Nye, F. I. (1958). Extent of unrecorded juvenile delinquency: Some tentative conclusions. *Journal of Criminal Law, Criminology, and Police Science, 49*, 296–302.

Shusta, R. M., Levine, D. R., Wong, H. Z., Olson, A. T., & Harris, P. R. (2015). *Multicultural law enforcement: Strategies for peacekeeping in a diverse society* (6th ed.). Upper Saddle River, NJ: Pearson.

Sickmund, M. (2003). *Juvenile offenders and victims* (National Report Series). Washington, DC: U.S. Department of Justice, Office of Juvenile Justice and Delinquency Prevention.

Sickmund, M., & Puzzanchera, C. (Eds.). (2014, December). *Juvenile Offenders and Victims: 2014 National Report.* Pittsburgh, PA: National Center for Juvenile Justice. Retrieved from www.ojjdp.gov/ojstatbb/nr2014/downloads/NR2014.pdf

Siegel, J. A. (2011). *Disrupted childhoods: Children of women in prison.* New Brunswick, NJ: Rutgers University Press.

Siegel, J. A., & Williams, L. M. (2003). The relationship between child sexual abuse and female delinquency and crime: A prospective study. *Journal of Research in Crime and Delinquency, 40*, 71–95.

Siegel, L. J., & Senna, J. J. (1994). *Juvenile justice: Theory, practice, and law* (5th ed.). St. Paul, MN: West.

Siegel, L. J., & Welsh, B. C. (2007). *Juvenile delinquency: Theory, practice, and law* (3rd ed.). Belmont, CA: Wadsworth/Thomson Learning.

Siegel, L. J., Welsh, B. C., & Senna, J. J. (2003). *Juvenile delinquency: Theory, practice, and law* (2nd ed.).

Belmont, CA: Wadsworth/Thomson Learning.

Simons, R. L., Simons, L. G., Burt, C. H., Brody, G. H., & Cutrona, C. (2005). Collective efficacy, authoritative parenting, and delinquency: A longitudinal test of a model integrating community- and family-level process. *Criminology, 43*, 989–1030.

Simonsen, C. E. (1991). *Juvenile justice in America* (2nd ed.). New York, NY: Macmillan.

Simonsen, C. E., & Gordon, M. S. (1982). *Juvenile justice in America* (2nd ed.). New York, NY: Macmillan.

Skinner, B. F. (1953). *Science and human behavior.* New York, NY: Macmillan.

Smykla, J. O., & Willis, T. W. (1981). The incidence of learning disabilities and mental retardation in youth under the jurisdiction of the juvenile court. *Journal of Criminal Justice, 9*, 219–225.

Snyder, H. N. (2000, December). *Juvenile arrests 1999.* Washington, DC: U.S. Department of Justice.

Snyder, H. N., & Sickmund, M. (1999, November). *Juvenile offenders and victims: 1999 national report.* Washington, DC: U.S. Department of Justice.

Snyder, H. N., & Sickmund, M. (2006, March). *Juvenile offenders and victims: 2006 national report.* Washington, DC: U.S. Department of Justice. Retrieved from www.ojjdp.ncjrs.gov/ojstatbb/nr2006/index.html

Socia, K. M., & Stamatel, J. P. (2012). Neighborhood characteristics and the social control of registered sex offenders. *Crime & Delinquency, 58*(4), 565–587.

Sorrells, J. (1980). What can be done about juvenile homicide? *Crime & Delinquency, 26*, 152–161.

South Dakota Senate Bill 39. (2013). Establish a penalty for a juvenile convicted as an adult of a Class A or B felony and allow a sentence of up to life imprisonment after a sentencing hearing. Retrieved from https://legiscan.com/SD/text/SB39/2013

Spano, R., & Freilich, J. (2009). An assessment of the empirical validity and conceptualization of individual level multivariate studies of lifestyle/routine activities theory published from 1995 to 2005. *Journal of Criminal Justice, 37*(3), 305.

Spano, R., Freilich, J., & Bolland, J. (2008). Gang membership, gun carrying, and employment: Applying routine activities theory to explain violent victimization among inner city, minority youth living in extreme poverty. *Justice Quarterly, 25*(2), 381.

Speckhard, L. (2016, April 14). *Victims, not criminals: A push to stop charging children with prostitution.* Isthmus, News. Retrieved from http://isthmus.com/news/news/child-prostitution-law-enforcement/#sthash.8FsVwWLS.dpuf

Spergel, I. A., Chance, R., Ehrensaft, K., Regulus, T., Kane, C., Laseter, R., Alexander, A., & Oh, S. (1994). *Gang suppression and intervention: Community models.* Washington, DC: U.S. Department of Justice, Office of Justice Programs, Office of Juvenile Justice and Delinquency Prevention.

Stahl, A. L. (2008a). Drug offense cases in juvenile courts, 1985–2004. *OJJDP Fact Sheet.* Retrieved from www.ncjrs.gov/pdffiles1/ojjdp/fs200803.pdf

Stahl, A. L. (2008b). *Delinquency cases in juvenile courts, 2004.* Washington, DC: Office of Juvenile Justice and Delinquency Prevention.

Stanford v. Kentucky, 492 U.S. 361 (1989).

Stark, R. (1987). Deviant places: A theory of the ecology of crime. *Criminology, 25,* 893–909.

State action on cyber-bullying. (2008, February). *USA Today.* Retrieved from www.usatoday.com/news/nation/2008-02-06-cyber-bullying-list_N.htm

Stearns, M., & Garcia, M. (2001, July 29). Law challenges preacher's principles: Religious development's

founder defends the way he ministers to children. *Kansas City Star,* p. A1.

Steenbeek, W., Völker, B., Flap, H., & Oort, F. (2012). Local businesses as attractors or preventers of neighborhood disorder. *Journal of Research in Crime and Delinquency, 49*(2), 213–248.

Stein, B. D., Jaycox, L. H., Kataoka, S. H., Rhodes, H. J., & Vestal, K. D. (2003). Prevalence of child and adolescent exposure to community violence. *Clinical Child and Family Psychology Review, 6*(4), 247–264.

Stein, D. M., Deberard, S., & Homan, K. (2013). Predicting success and failure in juvenile drug treatment court: A meta-analytic review. *Journal of Substance Abuse Treatment, 44*(2), 159–168.

Stern, R. S. (1964). *Delinquent conduct and broken homes.* New Haven, CT: College and University Press.

Streib, V. L. (2000). *The juvenile death penalty today: Death sentences and executions for juvenile crimes, January 1, 1973–June 30, 2000.* Ada, OH: Northern University Clause W. Pettit College of Law.

Stroud, D. D., Martens, S. L., & Barker, J. (2000). Criminal investigations of child sexual abuse: A comparison of cases referred to the prosecutor to those not referred. *Child Abuse & Neglect, 24,* 689–700.

Stuckey, G., Roberson, C., & Wallace, H. (2004). *Procedures in the justice system* (7th ed.). Upper Saddle River, NJ: Prentice Hall.

Sudnow, D. (1965). Normal crimes: Sociological features of the penal code in a public defender office. *Social Problems, 12,* 255–276.

Sutherland, E. H. (1939). *Principles of criminology* (3rd ed.). Philadelphia, PA: J. B. Lippincott.

Sutherland, E. H., & Cressey, D. R. (1978). *Criminology* (10th ed.). New York, NY: J. B. Lippincott.

Sutherland, E. H., Cressey, D. R., & Luckenbill, D. F. (1992). *Criminology*

(11th ed.). Dix Hills, NJ: General Hall.

Sutphen, R., Kurtz, D., & Giddings, M. (1993). The influence of juveniles' race on police decision-making: An exploratory study. *Juvenile and Family Court Journal, 44*(2), 69–76.

Sykes, G. M., & Matza, D. (1957). Techniques of neutralization: A theory of delinquency. *American Sociological Review, 22,* 664–670.

Szymanski, L. A. (2005). Clear and convincing evidence as burden of proof for pre-adjudication detention. *Juvenile and Family Law Digest, 37*(1), 3963–3982.

Tapia, M. (2011). U.S. juvenile arrests: Gang membership, social class, and labeling effects. *Youth & Society, 43*(4), 1407–1432.

Tappan, P. (1949). *Juvenile delinquency.* New York, NY: McGraw-Hill.

Taylor, J., McGue, M., & Iacono, W. G. (2000). A behavioral genetic analysis of the relationship between the socialization scale and self-reported delinquency. *Journal of Personality, 69,* 29–50.

Tenbergen, G., Wittfoth, M., Frieling, H., Ponseti, J., Walter, M., Walter, H., . . . Kruger, T. H. C. (2015). The neurobiology and psychology of pedophilia: Recent advances and challenges. *Frontiers in Human Neuroscience, 9,* 344.

Tennessee Code Annotated, § 37-1-110 (2012).

Tennessee Code Annotated, § 37-1-119 (2012).

Tennessee Code Title 37-1-1-104 (2010).

Terry, R. M. (1967). The screening of juvenile offenders. *Journal of Criminal Law, Criminology, and Police Science, 58,* 173–181.

Texas Family Code Annotated, 53.07 (a) (2007).

Texas Family Code Annotated, 54.03 (c) (2007).

Texas Family Code Annotated, 54.03 (f) (2007).

Texas Family Code Annotated, 54.04 (1) (2007).

Texas Family Code Annotated, 54.08 (a) (2007).

Texas Family Code, Title 3, Juvenile Justice Code, ch. 51 (15). (2011).

Texas Family Code, Title 3—Juvenile Justice Code, ch. 51—General Provisions (2011).

Texas Family Code. Section 51.02 (2011).

Texas Family Code. Section 51.12 (2012).

Texas Youth Commission. (2004). *Family Life, delinquency, and crime: A policymaker's guide.* Retrieved from www.tyc.state.tx.us/prevention/family_life.html

Thompson v. Oklahoma, 487 U.S. 815 (1988).

Thompson, G. (2004, September 26). Shuttling between nations: Latino gangs confound the law. *New York Times*, p. 1. Retrieved from www.nytimes.com/2004/09/26/world/americas/shuttling-between-nations-latino-gangs-confound-the-law.html?_r=0

Thompson, S. (2012). Judicial gatekeeping of police-generated witness testimony. *Journal of Criminal Law & Criminology, 102*(2), 329–395.

Thornberry, T. P. (1987). Toward an interactional theory of delinquency. *Criminology, 25*, 863–891.

Thornberry, T. P., & Burch, J. H. (1997). *Gang members and delinquent behavior.* Washington, DC: Office of Juvenile Justice and Delinquency Prevention.

Thornberry, T. P., Huizinga, D., & Loeber, R. (2004). The causes and correlates studies: Findings and policy implications. *Juvenile Justice, 9*(1). Retrieved from www.ncjrs.gov/html/ojjdp/203555/jj2.html

Thornberry, T. P., Moore, M., & Christenson, R. L. (1985). The effects of dropping out of high school on subsequent criminal behavior. *Criminology, 23*, 3–18.

Thornton, W. E., Voight, L., & Doerner, W. G. (1987). *Delinquency and justice* (2nd ed.). New York, NY: Random House.

Thrasher, F. M. (1927). *The gang.* Chicago, IL: University of Chicago Press.

Tierney, J. P., Grossman, J. B., & Resch, N. L. (1995). *Making a difference: An impact study of Big Brothers Big Sisters.* Philadelphia, PA: Public/Private Ventures. Retrieved from www.ppv.org/ppv/publications/assets/111_publication.pdf

Tittle, C., Villemez, W., & Smith, D. (1978). The myth of social class and criminality. *American Sociological Review, 43*, 643–656.

Tjaden, P., & Thoennes, N. (2000, November). Full report of the prevalence, incidence, and consequences of violence against women: Findings from the National Violence Against Women Survey (Research Report, NCJ 183781). Washington, DC, and Atlanta, GA: U.S. Department of Justice, National Institute of Justice, and U.S. Department of Health and Human Services, Centers for Disease Control and Prevention.

Too poor to be defended [Editorial]. (1998, April 9). *The Economist*, pp. 21–22.

Torbet, P. M. (1996, March). Juvenile probation: The workhorse of the juvenile justice system. *Juvenile Justice Bulletin*. Washington, DC: U.S. Department of Justice.

Tower, C. C. (1993). *Understanding child abuse and neglect.* Boston, MA: Allyn & Bacon.

Towery, J. (2010, January 12). *Goodwill launches program to help youth.* Retrieved from www.pjstar.com

Tsunokai, G. T., & Kposowa, A. J. (2009). Explaining gang involvement and delinquency among Asian Americans: An empirical test of general strain theory. *Journal of Gang Research, 6*(3), 1–33.

Turk, A. (1969). *Criminality and legal order.* Chicago, IL: Rand McNally.

Turkheimer, E. (1998). Heritability and psychological explanations. *Psychological Review, 105*, 782–791.

Twentieth Century Fund Task Force on Sentencing Policy Toward Young Offenders. (1987). *Confronting youth crime: Report of the Twentieth Century Fund Task Force on Sentencing Policy Toward Young Offenders* [Background paper by F. E. Zimring]. New York, NY: Holmes & Meier.

Tzoumakis, S., Lussier, P., & Corrado, R. (2012). Female juvenile delinquency, motherhood, and the intergenerational transmission of aggression and antisocial behavior. *Behavioral Sciences & the Law, 30*(2), 211–237.

Umbreit, M., Vos, B., & Coates, R. B. (2006). Victim offender mediation: An evolving evidence-based practice. In D. Sullivan & L. Tifft (Eds.), *The handbook of restorative justice: A global perspective* (pp. 52–61). New York, NY: Routledge.

Umbreit, M., Vos, B., Coates, R. B., & Lightfoot, E. (2005). Restorative justice in the twenty-first century: A social movement full of opportunities and pitfalls. *Marquette Law Review, 89*, 251–304.

UNICEF. (2012). *Fact sheet: A summary of the rights under the Convention on the Rights of the Child.* Vienna, Austria: Author. Retrieved from www.unicef.org/crc/files/Rights_overview.pdf

United Nations. (1990a). *United Nations guidelines for the prevention of juvenile delinquency.* Vienna, Austria: Author.

United Nations. (1990b). *United Nations standard minimum rules for the administration of juvenile justice* (The Beijing rules). Vienna, Austria: Author. Retrieved from www.un.org/documents/ga/res/40/a40r033.htm

United Nations. (1990c). *United Nations convention on the rights of the child—CRC (1989).* Vienna, Austria: Author. Retrieved from www.unicef.org/crc/files/Rights_overview.pdf

United Nations. (2000). *The United Nations basic principles on the use of restorative justice programmes in criminal matters*. Vienna, Austria: Author.

United Nations. (2003). *World Youth Report 2003*. Vienna, Austria: Author.

United Nations. (2007). *Convention on the rights of the child*. Vienna, Austria: Author. Retrieved from http://untreaty.un.org/humanrightsconvs/Chapt_IV_11/Rightsofthechild.pdf

United Nations. (2012). *Fact sheet on juvenile justice*. New York, NY: United Nations.

United Nations Children's Fund. (2012). *The state of the world's children 2012: Children in an urban world*. New York, NY: UNICEF.

United Nations Office on Drugs and Crime. (2006). *Manual for the measurement of juvenile justice indicators*. Vienna, Austria: Author.

United Nations Office on Drugs and Crime. (2009). *Global report on trafficking in persons* (UNODC). Retrieved from www.unodc.org/unodc/en/human-trafficking/global-report-on-trafficking-in-persons.html

United Nations Office on Drugs and Crime. (2011). *Criteria for the design and evaluation of juvenile justice reform programmes*. New York, NY: Interagency Panel on Juvenile Justice.

United Nations Office on Drugs and Crime. (2014). *Global report on trafficking in persons*. Vienna, Austria: Author.

United Nations Office on Drugs and Crime. (2016). *Children and armed conflict*. New York, NY: Office of the Special Representative of the Secretary-General for Children and Armed Conflict.

Unnever, J. D., Cullen, F. T., & Pratt, T. C. (2003). Parental management, ADHD, and delinquency involvement: Reassessing Gottfredson and Hirschi's general theory. *Justice Quarterly, 20,* 471–500.

Unruh, D., Povenmire-Kirk, T., & Yamamoto, S. (2009). Perceived barriers and protective factors of juvenile offenders on their developmental pathway to adulthood. *Journal of Correctional Education, 60*(3), 201–224.

USAID. (2006). *Central America and Mexico gang assessment: Honduras profile*. Washington, DC: Author. Retrieved from www.usaid.gov/gt/docs/gangs_assessment.pdf

U.S. Department of Education. (2010, December 16). *Key policy letters from the education secretary and deputy secretary*. Retrieved from www2.ed.gov/policy/gen/guid/secletter/101215.html

U.S. Department of Education for Civil Rights. (2014). *Civil rights data collection data snapshot: School discipline*. Retrieved from www2.ed.gov/about/offices/list/ocr/docs/crdc-discipline-snapshot.pdf

U.S. Department of Health and Human Services. (2002). *Recruiting foster parents*. Washington, DC: Office of the Inspector General. Retrieved from http://oig.hhs.gov/oei/reports/oei-07-00-00600.pdf

U.S. Department of Health and Human Services. (2005). *Child maltreatment 2003: Reports from the states to the National Child Abuse and Neglect Data System*. Retrieved from www.acf.hhs.gov/programs/cb/pubs/cm05/summary.htm

U.S. Department of Health and Human Services. (2012). *Child maltreatment 2011*. Washington, DC: U.S. Department of Health & Human Services, Administration for Children and Families, Administration on Children, Youth and Families, Children's Bureau.

U.S. Department of Health and Human Services. (2016). *Child maltreatment 2014*. Washington, DC: Author. Retrieved from www.acf.hhs.gov/programs/cb/research-data-technology/statistics-research/child-maltreatment. Available from www.acf.hhs.gov/sites/default/files/cb/cm11.pdf#page=28

U.S. Department of Health and Human Services. (n.d.). *About faith-based and neighborhood partnerships*. Retrieved from www.hhs.gov/fbci/about/index.html

U.S. Department of Justice. (1973). *Prosecution in juvenile courts: Guidelines for the future*. Washington, DC: Author.

U.S. Department of Justice. (2006). *Attorney general Gonzales announces implementation of Project Safe Childhood*. Washington, DC: Author. Retrieved from www.justice.gov/opa/pr/2006/May/06_ag_303.html

U.S. Department of Justice. (2016). *National strategy for child exploitation prevention and interdiction*. Washington, DC: Department of Justice. Retrieved from www.justice.gov/psc/national-strategy-child-exploitation-prevention-and-interdiction

U.S. Immigration and Customs Enforcement. (2012). *Operation Predator: Targeting child exploitation and sex crimes*. Retrieved from www.ice.gov/factsheets/predator

U.S. Substance Abuse and Mental Health Services Administration. (2013, February 14). *Drug, alcohol abuse more likely among high school dropouts*. Washington, DC: Author. Retrieved from www.healthfinder.gov/News/Article.aspx?id=673547

U.S. Supreme Court. (2010). *Graham v. Florida: Syllabus*. Washington, DC: Author. Retrieved from www.supremecourt.gov/opinions/09pdf/08-7412.pdf

Utah Code Title 78A Judiciary and Judicial Administration, ch. 6 Juvenile Court Act of 1996, Section 104 Concurrent jurisdiction—District court and juvenile court (2011).

Valdez, A. (2005). *Gangs: A guide to understanding street gangs*. San Clemente, CA: LawTech.

Valdez, A. (2007). *Gangs across America: Histories and sociology.* San Clemente, CA: LawTech.

Valdez, A. (2011). *Gangs across America: Histories and sociology* (2nd ed.). San Clemente, CA: LawTech.

van Batenburg-Eddes, T., Butte, D., van de Looij-Jansen, P., Schiethart, W., Raat, H., de Waart, F., & Jansen, W. (2012). Measuring juvenile delinquency: How do self-reports compare with official police statistics? *European Journal of Criminology, 9*(1), 23–37.

Van Vleet, R. K., Hickert, A. O., & Becker, E. E. (2006, December). *Evaluation of the Salt Lake County Day Reporting Center, Utah Criminal Justice Center* (Report prepared for National Highway Traffic Safety Administration). Winchester, MA: Mid-America Research Institute. Retrieved from www.nhtsa.dot.gov/people/injury/alcohol/repeatoffenders=HS808998.pdf

Vander Ven, T. M., Cullen, F. T., Carrozza, M. A., & Wright, J. P. (2001). Home alone: The impact of maternal employment on delinquency. *Social Problems, 48,* 236–257.

VanderWaal, C. J., McBride, D. C., Terry-McElrath, Y. M., VanBuren, H. (2001). *Breaking the juvenile drug-crime cycle: A guide for practitioners and policymakers.* Washington, DC: National Institute of Justice.

Vandivere, S., Tout, K., Capizzano, J., & Zaslow, M. J. (2003). *Left unsupervised: A look at the most vulnerable children* (Child Trends Research Brief). Washington, DC: Child Trends.

Vaske, J., Boisvert, D., & Wright, J. (2012). Genetic and environmental contributions to the relationship between violent victimization and criminal behavior. *Journal of Interpersonal Violence, 27*(16), 3213–3235.

Verschuere, B., Candel, I., Reenen, L., & Korebrits, A. (2012). Validity of the modified child psychopathy scale for juvenile justice center residents. *Journal of Psychopathology & Behavioral Assessment, 34*(2), 244–252.

Viljoen, J. L., Klaver, J., & Roesch, R. (2005). Legal decisions of preadolescent and adolescent defendants: Predictors of confessions, pleas, communication with attorneys, and appeals. *Law and Human Behavior, 29,* 253–277.

Vincent, G. M., Guy, L. S., & Grisso, T. (2013). *Risk assessment in juvenile justice: A guidebook for implementation.* Chicago, IL: MacArthur Foundation. Retrieved from www.macfound.org

Vold, G. B. (1958). *Theoretical criminology.* New York, NY: Oxford University Press.

Voss, H. L. (1966). Socioeconomic status and reported delinquent behavior. *Social Problems, 13,* 314–324.

Walker, S. (1998). *Sense and nonsense about crime and drugs: A policy guide* (4th ed.). Belmont, CA: Wadsworth.

Walker, S. (2007, May). *Police accountability: Current issues and research needs.* Paper presented at the National Institute of Justice (NIJ) Policing Research Workshop: Planning for the Future, Washington, DC. Retrieved from www.ncjrs.gov/pdffiles1/nij/grants/218583.pdf

Walker, S., Spohn, C., & DeLone, M. (2004). *The color of justice: Race, ethnicity, and crime in America* (3rd ed.). Belmont, CA: Wadsworth/Thomson Learning.

Walsh, A. (2000). Behavior genetics and anomie/strain theory. *Criminology, 38,* 1075–1108.

Walsh, C., MacMillan, H., & Jamieson, E. (2002). The relationship between parental psychiatric disorder and child physical and sexual abuse: Findings from the Ontario Health Supplement. *Child Abuse & Neglect, 26*(1), 11–22.

Walters, P. M. (1993). Community-oriented policing: A blend of strategies. *FBI Law Enforcement Bulletin, 62*(11), 20–23.

Wareham, J., & Boots, D. (2012). The link between mental health problems and youth violence in adolescence: A multilevel test of DSM-oriented problems. *Criminal Justice & Behavior, 39*(8), 1003–1024.

Warr, M. (1993). Parents, peers and delinquency. *Social Forces, 72*(1), 247–264.

Watkins, A. M., & Maume, M. O. (2012). Rethinking the study of juveniles' attitudes toward the police. *Criminal Justice Studies, 25*(3), 279–300.

Watson, D. W. (2004). Juvenile offender comprehensive reentry substance abuse treatment. *Journal of Correctional Education, 55,* 211–225.

Way, I., & Urbaniak, D. (2008). Delinquent histories of adolescents adjudicated for criminal sexual conduct. *Journal of Interpersonal Violence, 23*(9), 1197–1212.

Webber, A. M. (1991, May/June). Crime and management: An interview with New York City Police Commissioner Lee P. Brown. *Harvard Business Review,* 110–126.

Wells, E., & Rankin, J. (1991). Families and delinquency: A meta-analysis of the impact of broken homes. *Social Problems, 38,* 71–93.

Wells, J. B., Minor, K. I., & Fox, J. W. (1998). *An evaluation of Kentucky's 1997–98 Teen Court Program.* Richmond, KY: Eastern Kentucky University, Center for Criminal Justice Education and Research.

Wells, K. (2006). *Methamphetamine and pregnancy.* Retrieved from www.colodec.org/decpapers/methandpregnancy.htm\

Wells, M., Mitchell, K. J., & Ji, K. (2012). Exploring the role of the Internet in juvenile prostitution cases coming to the attention of law enforcement. *Journal of Child Sexual Abuse, 21*(3), 327–342.

Werthman, C., & Piliavin, I. (1967). Gang members and the police. In D. Bordua (Ed.), *The police: Six sociological essays* (pp. 56–98). New York, NY: Wiley.

West Virginia Code Annotated, 49-5-6 (2012).

White, R. (2004). *Police and community responses to youth gangs.* Canberra, Australia: Australian Institute of Criminology.

White v. Illinois, 112 S. Ct. 736 (1992).

Whyte, W. F. (1943). *Street corner society.* Chicago, IL: University of Chicago Press.

Wice, P. B. (2005). *Public defenders and the American justice system.* Westport, CT: Praeger.

Widom, C. S., & Maxfield, M. (2001). An update on the cycle of violence. *National Institute of Justice: Research in Brief.* Washington, DC: U.S. Department of Justice, Department of Justice Programs. Retrieved from www.ncjrs.gov/pdffiles1/nij/184894.pdf

Wilkins v. Missouri, 492 U.S. 361 (1989).

Wilks, J. A. (Ed.). (1967). Ecological correlates of crime and delinquency. In *Task force report: Crime and its impact—An assessment* (President's Commission on Law Enforcement and the Administration of Justice, pp. 138–156). Washington, DC: Government Printing Office.

Williams, J. H., Ayers, C. D., & Abbott, R. D. (1999). Racial differences in risk factors for delinquency and substance abuse among adolescents. *Social Work Research, 23,* 241–256.

Williams, J. M., & Dunlop, L. C. (1999). Pubertal timing and self-reported delinquency among male adolescents. *Journal of Adolescence, 22,* 157–171.

Willis, C. L., & Welles, R. H. (1988). The police and child abuse: An analysis of police decisions to report illegal behavior. *Criminology, 26,* 695–715.

Wilson, J. J. (2000, November). *1998 national youth gang survey* (OJJDP Summary). Washington, DC: U.S. Department of Justice.

Winokur Early, K., Hand, G., Blankenship, J., & Chapman, S. F. (2010). Experimental community-based interventions for delinquent youth: An evaluation of 3 recidivism and cost effectiveness (Unpublished manuscript). Tallahassee, FL: Justice Research Center.

Winters, C. A. (1997). Learning disabilities, crime, delinquency, and special education placement. *Adolescence, 32,* 451–462.

WiredKids. (2005). *A quick guide on the escalating levels of response to a cyberbullying incident.* Retrieved from www.stopcyberbullying.org/parents/guide.html

Wisconsin Code, ch. 938.18 Jurisdiction for criminal proceedings for juveniles 14 or older; waiver hearing (2011). Retrieved from http://law.justia.com/codes/wisconsin/2011/938/938.18.html

Wolak, J., Mitchell, K., & Finkelhor, D. (2006). *Online victimization of youth: Five years later.* National Center for Missing and Exploited Children. Retrieved from www.missingkids.com/en_US/publications/NC167.pdf

Wolf, A. M., & Gutierrez, L. (2012). It's about time: Prevention and intervention services for gang-affiliated girls. *The California Cities Gang Prevention Network, Bulletin 26.* Los Angeles, CA: Institute for Youth, Education, & Families.

Wolfe, D. A. (1985). Child-abusive parents: An empirical review and analysis. *Psychological Bulletin, 97,* 462–482.

Wood, J., & Alleyne, E. (2010). Street gang theory and research: Where are we now and where do we go from here? *Aggression and Violent Behavior, 15*(2), 100–111.

Wooden, W. S., & Blazak, R. (2001). *Renegade kids, suburban outlaws: From youth culture to delinquency.* Belmont, CA: Wadsworth.

Woodward, L. J., & Fergusson, D. M. (2000). Childhood and adolescent predictors of physical assault: A prospective longitudinal study. *Criminology, 38*(1), 233.

Worthen, M. (2012). Gender differences in delinquency in early, middle, and late adolescence: An exploration of parent and friend relationships. *Deviant Behavior, 33*(4), 282–307.

Wright, J. P., & Beaver, K. M. (2005). Do parents matter in creating self-control in their children? A genetically informed test of Gottfredson and Hirschi's theory of low self-control. *Criminology, 43,* 1169–1203.

Wright, J. P., & Cullen, F. T. (2001). Parental efficacy and delinquent behavior: Do control and support matter? *Criminology, 39,* 677–705.

Yablonsky, L. (1962). *The violent gang.* New York, NY: Macmillan.

Yablonsky, L., & Haskell, M. (1988). *Juvenile delinquency* (4th ed.). New York, NY: Harper & Row.

Yang, Y., & Raine, A. (2009). Prefrontal structural and functional brain imaging findings in antisocial, violent, and psychopathic individuals: A meta analysis. *Psychiatry Research: Neuroimaging, 174*(2), 81–88.

Yates, A., & Comerci, G. (1985). Sexual abuse. In V. L. Vivian (Ed.), *Child abuse and neglect: A medical community response* (pp. 135–144). Chicago, IL: American Medical Association.

Ybarra, M. L., & Mitchell, K. J. (2004). Youth engaging in online harassment: Associations with caregiver-child relationships, Internet use, and personal characteristics. *Journal of Adolescence, 27,* 319–336.

Yogan, L. J. (2000). School tracking and student violence. *Annals of the American Academy of Political & Social Science, 567,* 108–122.

Yoshikawa, H. (1994). Prevention as cumulative protection: Effects of early family support and education on chronic delinquency and its risks. *Psychological Bulletin, 115,* 28–54.

Youth Development and Delinquency Prevention Administration, Department of Health, Education, and Welfare. (1971). *National strategy for youth development and delinquency prevention.* Washington, DC: U.S. Government Printing Office.

Yun, I., Cheong, J., & Walsh, A. (2011). Genetic and environmental influences in delinquent peer affiliation: From the peer network approach. *Youth Violence and Juvenile Justice, 9*(3), 241–258.

Zahn, M. A., Agnew, R., Fishbein, D., Miller, S., Winn, D.-M, Dakoff, G., . . . Chesney-Lind, M. (2010, April). *Causes and correlates of girls' delinquency. Girls study group: Understanding and responding to girls' delinquency.* Washington, DC: Office of Juvenile Justice and Prevention. Retrieved from www.ncjrs.gov/pdffilesl/ojjdp/226358.pdf

Zaslaw, J. G., & Balance, G. S. (1996). The socio-legal response: A new approach to juvenile justice in the '90s. *Corrections Today, 58*(1), 72.

Zehr, H. (2002). *The little book of restorative justice.* Intercourse, PA: Good Books.

Zetter, K. (2009, November 20). Prosecutors drop plans to appeal Loiri Drew case. *Wired.com.* Retrieved from www.wired.com/threatlevel/2009/11/lori-drew-appeal/

Zhang, Y., Day, G., & Cao, L. (2012). A partial test of Agnew's general theory of crime and delinquency. *Crime & Delinquency, 58*(6), 856–878.

Zimmerman, J., Rich, W. D., Keilitz, I., & Broder, P. K. (1981). Some observations on the link between learning disabilities and juvenile delinquency. *Journal of Criminal Justice, 9,* 1–17.

Index

About the Authors

Steven M. Cox earned his BS in psychology, MA in sociology, and PhD in sociology at the University of Illinois in Urbana/Champaign. Dr. Cox was a member of the Law Enforcement and Justice Administration faculty at Western Illinois University from 1975 to 2011. For 50 years he served as trainer and consultant to numerous criminal justice agencies in the United States and abroad and worked with several universities in the area of course development. In addition, Dr. Cox has authored and coauthored numerous textbooks and articles.

Jennifer M. Allen is a full-time professor and former department head of the Department of Criminal Justice at the University of North Georgia. She has worked with juveniles in detention, on probation, and with those victimized by abuse and neglect. Dr. Allen has served on advisory boards for Big Brother/Big Sister mentoring programs, Rainbow Children's Home, domestic violence/sexual assault programs, and teen courts. Dr. Allen has published in the areas of restorative justice, juvenile delinquency and justice, youth programming, police crime, and policing administration and ethics. She is also the coauthor of *Criminal Justice Administration: A Service Quality Approach.*

Robert D. Hanser is a professor of criminal justice and the coordinator of the Department of Criminal Justice at the University of Louisiana at Monroe. Dr. Hanser has an extensive background in treatment provision and administration. He sits on the 4th Judicial District's Youth Services Planning Board and also serves on regional advisory councils and community boards related to juvenile services for substance abuse and mental health treatment programming. Dr. Hanser has a PhD in marriage and family therapy and a PhD in criminal justice. He is a national certified counselor, a licensed professional counselor in the states of Louisiana and Texas, a licensed addiction counselor, and a certified anger management therapist.

John J. Conrad served as chair of the Department of Law Enforcement and Justice Administration at Western Illinois University and was very active in the department, university, and surrounding community. After teaching for more than 30 years, John retired and enjoyed spending time with his children and grandchildren. He passed away in 2014.